Lecture Notes in Computer Science

Commenced Publication in 1973
Founding and Former Series Editors:
Gerhard Goos, Juris Hartmanis, and Jan van Leeuwen

Sungdeok (Steve) Cha   Jin-Young Choi
Moonzoo Kim   Insup Lee
Mahesh Viswanathan (Eds.)

Automated Technology for Verification and Analysis

6th International Symposium, ATVA 2008
Seoul, Korea, October 20-23, 2008
Proceedings

 Springer

Volume Editors

Sungdeok (Steve) Cha
Korea University, College of Information & Communication
Anam-Dong, Seongbuk-Gu, Seoul 136-701, South Korea
E-mail: scha@korea.ac.kr

Jin-Young Choi
Korea University, Departmnet of Computer Science and Engineering
Anam-Dong, Seongbuk-Gu, Seoul 136-702, South Korea
E-mail: choi@formal.korea.ac.kr

Moonzoo Kim
KAIST, Department of Computer Science
Guseong-Dong, Yuseong-Gu, Daejon 305-701, South Korea
E-mail: moonzoo@cs.kaist.ac.kr

Insup Lee
University of Pennsylvania, School of Engineering and Applied Science
Levine Hall, Room 602, 3330 Walnut Street, Philadelphia, PA 19104-6389, USA
E-mail: lee@cis.upenn.edu

Mahesh Viswanathan
University of Illinois at Urbana-Champaign, Thomas M. Siebel Center
201 N. Goodwin Avenue, Urbana, IL 61801-2302,USA
E-mail: vmahesh@uiuc.edu

Library of Congress Control Number: Applied for

CR Subject Classification (1998): B.1.2, B.5.2, B.6, B.7.2, C.2, C.3, D.2, D.3, F.3

LNCS Sublibrary: SL 2 – Programming and Software Engineering

ISSN   0302-9743
ISBN-10   3-540-88386-X Springer Berlin Heidelberg New York
ISBN-13   978-3-540-88386-9 Springer Berlin Heidelberg New York

Springer is a part of Springer Science+Business Media

springer.com

© Springer-Verlag Berlin Heidelberg 2008
Printed in Germany

Typesetting: Camera-ready by author, data conversion by Scientific Publishing Services, Chennai, India
Printed on acid-free paper   SPIN: 12536924   06/3180   5 4 3 2 1 0

Preface

This volume contains the papers presented at the 6th International Symposium on Automated Technology for Verification and Analysis held during October 20–23 in Seoul, Korea. The primary objective of the ATVA conferences remains the same: to exchange and promote the latest advances of state-of-the-art research on theoretical and practical aspects of automated analysis, verification, and synthesis.

Among 66 research papers and 16 tool papers submitted to ATVA 2008, the Program Committee accepted 21 as regular papers, 7 as tool papers, and 5 as short papers. In all, 33 experts from 27 countries worked hard to make sure that every submission received as rigorous and fair an evaluation as possible. In addition, the program also included three excellent tutorials and keynote talks by David Dill (Stanford University), Sriram Rajamani (Microsoft Research India), and Natarajan Shankar (SRI International). The conference organizers were truly excited to have such distinguished researchers as keynote speakers.

Many worked hard and offered their valuable time so generously to make ATVA 2008 successful. First of all, the conference organizers thank all 218 researchers who worked hard to complete and submit papers to the conference. The PC members, reviewers, and Steering Committee members also deserve special recognition. Without them, a competitive and peer-reviewed international symposium simply cannot take place.

Many organizations sponsored the symposium. They include: The Korean Institute of Information Scientists and Engineers (SIGPL and Software Engineering Society), Korea University, Korea Advanced Institute of Science and Technology (KAIST), the Software Process Improvement Center and the Defense Software Research Center at KAIST. The conference organizers also thank the BK program at Korea University and the Department of Computer Science at KAIST for financial support.

We sincerely hope that the readers find the proceedings of ATVA 2008 informative and rewarding.

August 2008

Sungdeok (Steve) Cha
Jin-Young Choi
Moonzoo Kim
Insup Lee
Mahesh Viswanathan

Preface

Organization

General Chairs

Sungdeok (Steve) Cha   Korea University, Korea
Insup Lee   University of Pennsylvania, USA

Program Chairs

Moonzoo Kim   KAIST, Korea
Mahesh Viswanathan   University of Illinois at Urbana-Champaign, USA

Program Committee

Christel Baier	Technische Universität Dresden, Germany
Jonathan Billington	Univeristy of South Australia, Australia
Byeong-Mo Chang	Sookmyung Women's Univeristy, Korea
Yunja Choi	Kyungpook National University, Korea
Ching-Tsun Chou	Intel, USA
Masahiro Fujita	University of Tokyo, Japan
Susanne Graf	Verimag, France
Wolfgang Grieskamp	Microsoft Research, USA
Teruo Higashino	Osaka University, Japan
Franjo Ivancic	NEC Laboratories America, USA
Ranjit Jhala	University of California, San Diego, USA
Gihwon Kwon	Kyonggi University, Korea
Insup Lee	University of Pennsylvania, USA
Zhiming Liu	United Nations Univeristy, Macao
Shaoying Liu	Hosei University, Japan
Mila Majster-Cederbaum	University of Mannheim, Germany
Ken McMillan	Cadence, USA
In-Ho Moon	Synopsys, USA
Shin Nakajima	National Institute of Informatics, Japan
Kedar Namjoshi	Bell Labs, USA
Doron A. Peled	Univeristy of Warwick, UK and Bar Ilan Univeristy, Israel
Hiroyuki Seki	NAIST, Japan
Prasad Sistla	University of Illinois at Chicago, USA
P.S. Thiagarajan	National University of Singapore, Singapore
Yih-Kuen Tsay	National Taiwan University, Taiwan

Farn Wang	National Taiwan Univeristy, Taiwan
Bow-Yaw Wang	Academia Sinica, Taiwan
Ji Wang	National University of Defense Technology, China
Hsu-Chun Yen	National Taiwan Univeristy, Taiwan
Tomohiro Yoneda	National Institute of Informatics, Japan
Sergio Yovine	Verimag, France
Shoji Yuen	Nagoya Univeristy, Japan
Wenhui Zhang	Chinese Academy of Sciences, China

Local Arrangements Chair

Jin-Young Choi	Korea University, Korea

Steering Committee

E. Allen Emerson	University of Texas at Austin, USA
Oscar H. Ibarra	University of California, Santa Barbara, USA
Insup Lee	University of Pennsylvania, USA
Doron A. Peled	University of Warwick, UK and Bar Ilan Univeristy, Israel
Farn Wang	National Taiwan University, Taiwan
Hsu-Chun Yen	National Taiwan University, Taiwan

Referees

Abdul Mat	Jinn-Shu Chang
Amar Gupta	John Harrison
Ananda Basu	Kavita Ravi
Arvind Easwaran	Keigo Imai
Ashvin Dsouza	Li Tan
Charles Morisset	Lin Liu
Christian Lambertz	Lin-Zan Cai
Christopher Conway	Louise Avila
Eric Bodden	Masakazu Adachi
E-Y Kang	Michael Theobald
Fernando Schapachnik	Ming-Hsien Tsai
Geng-Dian Huang	Ming-Ying Chung
Gogul Balakrishnan	Moritz Martens
Guy Gallasch	Murali Talupur
HoonSang Jin	Nicolas Kicillof
Ismail Assayad	Nikhil Dinesh
Jesung Kim	Nimrod Lilith
Jim Grundy	Philippe Darondeau

Roderick Bloem
Rong-Shiun Wu
Ryo Suetsugu
Sava Krstic
Sriram Sankaranarayanan
Stavros Tripakis
Suresh Thummalapenta
Tingting Han
Truong Nghiem
Venkat Venkatakrishnan
Victor Braberman

Vijay Gehlot
Vineet Kahlon
Weikai Miao
Xiao Qu
Xiaoshan Li
Yasunori Ishihara
Yoshiaki Takata
Yoshinobu Kawabe
Yu-Fang Chen
Yukiyoshi Kameyama
Zvonimir Rakamaric

Table of Contents

Invited Talks

Model Checking

Software Verification

Decision Procedures

Linear-Time Analysis

Tool Demonstration Papers

Timed and Stochastic Systems

Theory

Short Papers

Tests, Proofs and Refinements

Sriram K. Rajamani

Microsoft Research India
sriram@microsoft.com

Counter-example driven refinement using predicate abstraction has been successfully used to find bugs and verify properties in programs [1]. We describe two recent advances in counter-example driven refinement:

- We present a counter-example driven refinement technique that combines verification and testing [4]. In our approach, we simultaneously use testing and proving, with the goal of either finding a test that demonstrates that P violates φ, or a proof that demonstrates that all executions of P satisfy φ. The most interesting aspect of the approach is that unsuccessful proof attempts are used to generate tests, and unsuccessful attempts to generate tests are used to refine proofs. Besides being theoretically elegant, the approach has practical advantages —precise alias information obtained during tests can be used to greatly aid the efficiency of constructing proofs [5].
- In the past, counter-example driven refinement schemes have worked with a particular form of abstraction called predicate abstraction [1]. We present approaches to refine any abstract interpretation automatically using counterexamples. Several challenges arise: refining using disjunctions leads to powerset domains, and the use of joins forces us to consider counterexample DAGs instead of counterexample traces. We present our solutions to these problems [3,2]. We also present experiences implementing our techniques in a tool DAGGER.

We also illustrate a dual technique that uses proof techniques to speedup runtime analysis. This arises in context of checking object invariants in object oriented programs. Checking object invariants, even at runtime, is a hard problem. This is because, the object invariant of an object o can depend on another object p and it may not hold when p is modified without o's knowledge. Therefore, whenever an object p is modified, a runtime checker will have to check the object invariant of all objects o that depend on p.

Whenever an object p is modified, a runtime checker will have to check the object invariant for all objects o such that o depends on p. Keeping track of all such dependencies at runtime can slow down a checker significantly. Interestingly, for a large class of object invariants (called object protocol invariants) we can factor out an object invariant in such a way that certain parts of the invariant can be checked statically [6]. The approach has two advantages: (1) a certain class of errors can be detected statically, and (2) the runtime overhead of checking is greatly reduced.

Cha et al. (Eds.): ATVA 2008, LNCS 5311, pp. 1–2, 2008.

Acknowledgment. We thank our collaborators Nels Beckman, Supratik Chakroborty, Tom Henzinger, Madhu Gopinathan, Bhargav Gulavani, Yamini Kannan, Aditya Nori, Rob Simmons, Sai Tetali and Aditya Thakur.

References

1. Ball, T., Rajamani, S.K.: Automatically validating temporal safety properties of interfaces. In: Dwyer, M.B. (ed.) SPIN 2001. LNCS, vol. 2057, pp. 103–122. Springer, Heidelberg (2001)
2. Gulavani, B.S., Chakroborty, S., Nori, A.V., Rajamani, S.K.: Automatically refining abstract interpretations. In: Ramakrishnan, C.R., Rehof, J. (eds.) TACAS 2008. LNCS, vol. 4963, pp. 443–458. Springer, Heidelberg (2008)
3. Gulavani, B.S., Rajamani, S.K.: Counterexample driven refinement for abstract interpretation. In: Hermanns, H., Palsberg, J. (eds.) TACAS 2006. LNCS, vol. 3920, pp. 474–488. Springer, Heidelberg (2006)
4. Gulavani, B.S., Henzinger, T.A., Kannan, Y., Nori, A.V., Rajamani, S.K.: SYNERGY: A new algorithm for property checking. In: FSE 2006: Foundations of Software Engineering, pp. 117–127. ACM Press, New York (2006)
5. Beckman, N.E., Nori, A.V., Rajamani, S.K., Simmons, R.J.: Proofs from tests. In: ISSTA 2008: International Symposium on Software Testing and Analysis, pp. 3–14. ACM Press, New York (2008)
6. Gopinathan, M., Rajamani, S.K.: Enforcing Object Protocols by Combining Static and Dynamic Analysis. In: OOPSLA 2008: ACM SIGPLAN Conference on Object Oriented Programming, Systems, Languages and Applications. ACM Press, New York (to appear, 2008)

Formal Verification and Biology

David L. Dill

Department of Computer Science
Stanford University
dill@stanford.edu

The essence of formal verification is the modeling, analysis, and, ultimately, understanding of large reactive systems. How do many parts interact to produce appropriate global behavior? How are properties guaranteed over all the possible variations of timing, non-deterministic behavior of components, and a dynamically changing environment?

Although formal verification has almost exclusively been applied to synthetic systems, I believe that these same types of questions will be of increasing interest in biology, and that similar techniques to those used in formal verification will be of value in answering them. The tutorial will discuss the rationale for modeling cellular processes as discrete transition systems and past work in modeling of biological systems using formalisms that parallel those in digital logic, along with state space search.

The conference talk will discuss two different applications of techniques from formal methods to modeling of cellular functions. The first is the use of Petri nets to model and analyze signal transduction pathways. Starting with a list of reactions in the cell, a tool was developed that can interactively answer user queries about possible cell states by solving a Petri net reachability problem in real-time, then displaying a diagram of the reactions that lead to the result.

The second application is the use of symbolic model checking to analyze the steps of the cell cycle in the bacterial cell Caulobacter Crescentus. The cell cycle even in simple organism is essentially a complex asynchronous circuit that must function reliably despite the presence of substantial noise, environmental perturbations, and variations in reaction rates due to other causes. Our findings were that, surprisingly, the cell cycle is almost completely robust to arbitrary variations in the timing of cell cycle events.

Cha et al. (Eds.): ATVA 2008, LNCS 5311, p. 3, 2008.

Trust and Automation in Verification Tools*

Natarajan Shankar

Computer Science Laboratory
SRI International
Menlo Park CA 94025 USA
shankar@csl.sri.com
http://www.csl.sri.com/~shankar/

Abstract. On the one hand, we would like verification tools to feature powerful automation, but on the other hand, we also want to be able to trust the results with a high degree of confidence. The question of trust in verification tools has been debated for a long time. One popular way of achieving trust in verification tools is through proof generation. However, proof generation could hamstring both the functionality and the efficiency of the automation that can be built into these tools. We argue that trust need not be achieved at the expense of automation, and outline a lightweight approach where the results of untrusted verifiers are checked by a trusted offline checker. The trusted checker is a verified reference kernel that contains a satisfiability solver to support the robust and efficient checking of untrusted tools.

1 Introduction

Automated verification tools are used to formalize and check properties of hardware and software systems. Verification tools need to be *sound* in the sense that any demonstrated properties do in fact hold according to the intended interpretation of the formal symbols. From the viewpoint of verification, soundness is crucial for trusting the artifact that has been verified. However, most verification tools are based on only an informal argument for soundness. Some verification tools, notably the LCF-style proof assistants [GMW79], justify their results on the basis of proof certificates. The drawback of proof certificates is that verification tools have to be instrumented to generate them, and fully expanded proofs can have sizes that are exponential in the size of the conjecture, or worse. We propose a lightweight approach to trusted verification tools based on the use of offline checkers that are themselves verified. These *verified reference kernels* need not be as efficient as the untrusted tools since they can use hints provided by the untrusted tools. We show how a large class of verification claims can be checked using a relatively small kernel checker. This kernel checker can be itself be verified to a high degree of trust.

"*Quis custodiet ipsos custodes?*" or "Who will watch the watchmen?" is a central question of both philosophical and practical significance for computing. In the case of verification, it is common to hear the question: *Who will verify the verifier?* When

---

* This research was supported NSF Grants and CCR-ITR-0325808, CNS-0823086, and CNS-0644783.

Cha et al. (Eds.): ATVA 2008, LNCS 5311, pp. 4–17, 2008.

verification tools are viewed as aids for software construction, there is no real need for the tools to be verified. If the tool is useful it will be exploited regardless of whether it has been verified. However, there are circumstances where the fidelity of the verification claims do matter. For example, in the verification of a security-critical or safety-critical system system, we need end-to-end assurance with the highest degree of certitude that is feasible. Another such example is with middleware systems where the formal properties of the middleware are used to construct assurance cases for a large class of applications.

2   Approaches to Trust in Verification Tools

Gödel's second incompleteness theorem [Smo78] eliminates the possibility of a formal system proving its own consistency, since in this case, it must be inconsistent. Thus we always need to anchor our trust by, for example, by trusting the proof rules of first-order logic and the axioms of Peano arithmetic or set theory.

Untrusted verification tools can be instrumented to generate proofs that are checked by an independent, trusted proof checker. One of the earliest proof assistants, de Bruijn's Automath, employed a typed lambda-calculus based on the Curry–Howard isomorphism between proofs and terms and formulas and types [dB70, dB80, NGdV94]. Proofs in Automath are explicitly represented as terms. Recently, Weedijk [Wie02] has recreated an Automath checker in about 5000 lines of C code. Propositional satisfiability (SAT) solvers like Zchaff [ZM03] and MiniSat (version 1.14) [ES03] generate proofs that can be checked by an independent SAT solver [Gel07]. Proof generation capabilities also exist in solvers for satisfiability modulo theories (SMT) such as CVC Lite [BB04], CVC3 [BT07] and Z3 [dMB08]. Proof logs from CVC Lite can be verified by HOL Light system discussed below [MBG06].

In the 1970s, Milner [GMW79] introduced the LCF approach where the theorems are build using an abstract datatype so that theorems can only be derived from theorems using the given inference rules. LCF auguments proof construction with tactics for defining inference patterns. With the LCF approach, it is possible to write inference procedures for simplification, rewriting, and satisfiability as long as these procedures are able to generate proof certificates. The LCF approach has been quite effective and has been adopted by a number of widely used systems such as Coq [CCF+95], HOL [GM93], HOL Light [Har96b], Isabelle [Pau94], Lego [LP92], and Nuprl [CAB+86]. The LCF approach is also adopted at a different level by PVS [ORSvH95] which builds in various decision procedures, but supports proof generation in terms of inferences steps involving these decision procedures.

Of the LCF-based systems, HOL Light is especially interesting from the point of view of trust since it employs a very small kernel written in about 400 lines of OCaml. The kernel has been proven sound using a stronger version, because of the second incompleteness theorem, of HOL Light [Har06]. More precisely, the soundness of the HOL logic without the axiom of infinity has been demonstrated using HOL with this axiom. Similarly, a HOL strengthened with an axiom that admits the construction of function spaces, is used to demonstrate the soundness of HOL with the axiom of infinity.

With the LCF approach, it takes a lot of skill and labor to write inference procedures in a form that is proof generating. The proof generation overhead is there even during experimental use. For SAT solvers, the size of the proof can be exponential in the size of the input. These proof certificates can be quite large and inefficient to check with LCF-style systems [Gel07, WA07].

Another approach is to use verification tools themselves to verify other verification tools [Sha85, Thé98, CN05, SV08] either by trusted or untrusted tools. A verified tool is likely to be far more reliable for having been carefully scrutinized in this manner. However, these verifications are quite challenging since target tools are still research prototypes that are evolving rapidly. Verifying a state-of-the-art verification tool requires a significant investment of effort which would only make sense for software that is relatively stable. The correct construction of verification tools is an interesting challenge that should be pursued in the future when the technology is more stable.

One intriguing possibility is that of using verification tools to verify their own extensions through a process known as *reflection* [BM81, Wey80, KC86]. If we start with a small and reliable core, then the extensions can be reflectively self-verified so that we can have the same degree of confidence in the overall system as the core. This has the advantage over the LCF approach that the core system can be extended using verified tactics. When these tactics are applied, the proofs do not need to be expanded. For example, Chaieb and Nipkow [CN05] recently showed that the reflected version of a verified quantifier elimination procedures ran 60 to 130 times faster than the corresponding tactic. Reflection has had only limited success [Har96a], but it is still too early to write it off.

A fourth possibility is that of using witnesses or certificates to independently confirm the results of a computation [Meh03]. Witnesses are similar to proofs but specialized to specific problem classes. For example, the witness of the infeasibility of linear arithmetic constraints is obtained from Farkas' lemma. For difference constraints, the witness is obtained from the existence of a negative cycle. Proofs can be constructed from the certificates, but it is easier to check the certificates directly. The drawback to the use of certificates is that we have to trust the individual checkers as opposed to a single proof checker. Also, many problems do not have succinct certificates.

The use of multiple verification tools is another way of checking verification claims. However, the effort of applying multiple verifiers can be quite large and there is no evidence that this approach delivers a high degree of assurance [KL86].

We propose a different approach that uses an offline, verified checker to check the results of a range of untrusted verification tools. Since the overhead of generating proofs from untrusted verification tools could limit the functionality and efficiency of these tools, our approach decouples trust from online experimental use. A Verified Reference Kernel (VeRK) is used as a trusted offline checker for the results of untrusted verifiers. This way the experimental tools can continue to evolve without significantly affecting the way in which their results are certified.

In Section 3, we present the basic background for capturing the certification of verification tools. We outline the basic architecture of a verified reference kernel in Section 4 and in Section 5, we describe a verifiable SAT solver and examine the prospects for producing a verifying reference kernel. In Section 6, we demonstrate how different untrusted verification tools can be instrumented to generate evidence that can be checked by this kernel.

3 Verification and Deduction

Verification tools span the spectrum from lightweight type checkers and static analysis tools to heavyweight interactive proof checkers. When a verification tool guarantees the absence of errors, this claim can be formally stated as a formula, and if we believe the verifier, then this formula must have a proof and must hence be a theorem. Examples of such claims include the validity of a Hoare triple, the termination proof of a program, a refinement relation between two programs, and the satisfaction relation between a transition system and a temporal property.

Verification properties can be expressed in propositional logic, modal or temporal logic, first-order logic, or higher-order logic. For modal or temporal logics, the semantics can be captured in first-order or higher-order logic. Background theories expressed in the form of axioms in first-order or higher-order logic are used for reasoning about algebra, arithmetic, set theory, graph theory, and analysis. Theories are also used to state and prove properties of computational datatypes including bit-vectors, arrays, and recursive datatypes.

Formal reasoning occurs within a trinity of language, semantics, and proof. We assume for the sake of this paper that this reasoning occurs within first-order logic. A formal *language* circumscribes the range of well-formed expressions and assertions. The *semantics* defines the intended interpretation of the expressions. The *proof system* captures sound principles for deriving valid assertions, i.e., those that hold in all possible interpretations given by the semantics.

A proof system consists of axioms and inference rules that can be used to demonstrate that a formula is provable. Proofs provide an effective calculational mechanism for deriving valid sentences, i.e., those that hold in all interpretations. A proof system is *sound* if it only proves valid sentences. A proof system can be proved sound by induction on proofs by showing that each axiom is valid and each inference rule draws valid conclusions when given valid premises. A proof system is *complete* if every valid sentence is provable, or, conversely, the negation of any unprovable sentence is satisfiable.

An inference procedure determines if a given formula is unsatisfiable or satisfiable, or indicates that the result is unknown. When an inference procedure indicates that the input formula is satisfiable, it generates an assignment of truth values to the variables. The formula can be evaluated against this assignment to check that it is indeed a satisfied by the assignment. The situation is different when the inference procedure indicates that the input formula is unsatisfiable. In this case, it is typically possible to generate a formal proof as a certificate for unsatisfiability, but even for propositional logic, there is no succinct certificate for the unsatisfiability, unless NP = co-NP.

In the next section, we outline a lightweight approach to certifying the results that uses a kernel inference engine built around a SAT solver as an offline checker.

4   The Verified Reference Kernel Approach

We propose an alternative approach based on the use of a verified inference kernel that serves as a reference for a collection of untrusted procedures. When an untrusted inference procedure fails to verify a claim, it usually generates an assignment that can be easily checked to refute the claim. However, if it finds the formula to be valid, we need to some assurance that the result is sound. In our Verified Reference Kernel (VeRK) approach, we can use an untrusted procedure U in an experimental manner to construct a verification of a claim ϕ. Once this untrusted system has proved the validity of a formula ϕ, i.e., $U(\phi) = \top$, we obtain a set of lemmas L_ϕ and a hint h_ϕ from U. This hint is used by the verified reference kernel V to show that $V(L_\phi \implies \phi, h_\phi) = \top$ and $V(\psi, h_\phi) = \top$ for each lemma ψ in L_ϕ. The hints and lemmas are provided by the untrusted checker U to assist the trusted verifier V. If the hints are inaccurate or the lemmas are not valid, then the offline verification by V will fail. We give examples of such hints and lemmas below.

One obvious question of whether the verification of V is to be trusted. In our approach, V could itself be verified using the untrusted procedure U. However, we instrument V so that it is proof generating and $V(\phi, h) = \top[\pi]$ where π is the proof of ϕ. Now, when we have the correctness of V established as $U(\phi_V) = \top$, then we generate the hint h_{ϕ_V} and verify $V(\phi_V, h_{\phi_V}) = \top[\pi]$, but in the latter case we independently verify the generated proof π with a proof checker. We are trusting this proof checker only once for the specific proof of the correctness of V. In order to trust this proof, we can use a widely trusted checker or even employ a diversity of checkers. Note that this self-verification of V does not violate Gödel's second incompleteness theorem since we are only showing that whenever $V(\phi, h)$ is $\top$, then there is a proof π of ϕ. We are not claiming that the proof system used by π is consistent.

We conjecture that a self-contained reference kernel can be built out of

1. A clausifier, including Skolemization and conversion to conjunctive normal form
2. An instantiator that checks that one formula is a substitution instance of another formula
3. Checkers for lemmas generated as clauses from the individual theories
4. A SAT solver

It is important that these components of the reference kernel be verified. The kernel components must be simple enough to be verifiable. All the components that are used need not be verifiable since in some cases, such as equality or linear arithmetic, it is feasible to generate and check the proofs of the lemmas. The efficiency of the checkers in the reference kernel need not match the efficiency of state-of-the-art tools, but they do need to be reasonably efficient so that the offline checking is not prohibitively expensive. The offline reference kernel V can use the hints and lemmas provided by the online tools to gain efficiency. For example, it has been observed that even hard propositional problems often have a small set of *strong backdoor* variables that can be used to significantly reduce the search space [WGS03].

We show that for a wide range of verification tools, the results of their verification can be reduced to checking the propositional unsatisfiability together with some lemmas. The verification of these lemmas can involve theory-based decision procedures such as those for equality, arithmetic, bit-vectors. In this way, we are harnessing the *disruptive* capabilities of modern satisfiability solvers [Rus06] to reconcile trust and efficient automation.

5   A (Verifiable) Proof Generating SAT Solver

A propositional formula can be expressed in an equivalent *conjunctive normal form* (CNF) as a conjunction (or, alternatively, as a set) of clauses, where each clause is a disjunction of atoms or their negations. A literal is an atom or its negation. The negation of a clause is a conjunction of literals that we label a *state*. A clause is a *tautology* if it contains a literal and its negation as disjuncts. Any duplicate literals in a clause are merged and the literals in a clause can be freely permuted.

We skip the details of CNF conversion. In contrast with a SAT solver for CNF formulas, it is relatively easy to show that a formula ϕ and its CNF form $CNF(\phi)$ are equisatisfiable. With a little more effort, it can be shown that $\vdash \phi \implies CNF(\phi)$ so that if the latter is unsatisfiable, then we can prove the negation of $CNF(\phi)$, and hence $\neg\phi$.

Decision procedures for satisfiability can be described as *inference systems* [SR02, Sha05] that apply satisfiability preserving transformations to an inference state until no further transformations are possible. If the final state is the manifestly unsatisfiable $\bot$, then the formula corresponding to the initial state is unsatisfiable. Otherwise, the final state is required to be satisfiable. In the latter case, the input must also be satisfiable. There must not be any infinite sequence of transformations.

Resolution can be seen as a decision procedure for unsatisfiability for propositional CNF formulas or as a proof system. As a proof system, the resolution rule proves non-tautological clauses from a set of non-tautological clauses. The resolution rule derives the clause $\kappa_1 \vee \kappa_2$ from the clauses $l \vee \kappa_1$ and $\bar{l} \vee \kappa_2$, with the proviso that these clauses are non-tautological. The clauses $l \vee \kappa_1$ and $\bar{l} \vee \kappa_2$ are said to be *compatible* if the resolvent $\kappa_1 \vee \kappa_2$ is not tautological. The empty clause represents the falsum $\bot$. When a resolution proof derives $\bot$, the input set of clauses is unsatisfiable.

As an inference system, each resolution step augments a set of clauses with a new clause obtained by resolving two clauses that are already in the set. Since the derived clause in resolution is a consequence of the premise clauses, the step preserves satisfiability. For Boolean clauses, there are a bounded number of these that can be generated by resolution, so no infinite sequences of resolution steps are possible starting from a finite set of input clauses. Finally, if no further resolution inferences are possible, and $\bot$ has not been derived, it is possible to show that the final set of clauses is satisfiable.

The inference system for propositional satisfiability based on the Davis–Putnam–Logemann–Love land (DPLL) algorithm can be given as a *proof-carrying inference system* where each formula in the state has an associated proof from the input formulas. The state of the algorithm consists of the input clauses K, the partial assignment M, and the conflict clauses C. Each clause κ in C has an associated proof π_κ from the input clauses K. The partial assignment M of truth values to variables. The assignments in M are partitioned into levels from 0 to k. The assignments are level 0 are consequences of clauses in $K \cup C$. Each of the higher levels $i + 1$ has a decision literal that is assigned

step	l	M	K	C	γ
select s	1	$; s$	K	$\emptyset$	-
select r	2	$; s; r$	K	$\emptyset$	-
propagate	2	$; s; r, \neg q[\neg q \vee \neg r]$	K	$\emptyset$	-
propagate	2	$; s; r, \neg q, p[p \vee q]$	K	$\emptyset$	-
conflict	2	$; s; r, \neg q, p$	K	$\emptyset$	$\neg p \vee q$
analyze	0	$\emptyset$	K	$q[p \vee q; \neg p \vee q]$	-
backjump	0	$q[q]$	K	$q[p \vee q; \neg p \vee q]$	-
propagate	0	$q, p[p \vee \neg q]$	K	q	-
propagate	0	$q, p, r[\neg p \vee r]$	K	q	-
conflict	0	q, p, r	K	q	$\neg q \vee \neg r$

Fig. 1. The DPLL procedure with input $\{p \vee q, \neg p \vee q, p \vee \neg q, s \vee \neg p \vee q, \neg s \vee p \vee \neg q, \neg p \vee r, \neg q \vee \neg r\}$

true at that level. The other assignments at level $i + 1$ are consequences of $K \cup C$ and the decision literals at all the levels up to and including $i + 1$.

The DPLL inference steps are

1. **Propagation:** to add a truth value at the current decision level k when there is a clause $l \vee \kappa$ in $K \cup C$ where l is unassigned and κ is falsified by M.
2. **Conflict:** If a clause κ in $K \cup C$ is falsified by M at level 0, then the original formula is unsatisfiable and a proof of the conflict can be constructed from the assignment M and the proofs of clauses in C.
3. **Backjump:** If a conflict is found at level $i + 1$, then the conflict is analyzed to yield a conflict clause κ (along with its proof π_κ) that implies a new assignment at a level i' smaller than $i + 1$. The search is continued with $\kappa[\pi_\kappa]$ added to C and with the partial assignment restricted to levels at or below i'.
4. **Decide:** The search is continued by adding a new level to M by choosing an assignment for a previously unassigned variable.

An example of the procedure is shown in Figure 1. The input clause set K is $\{p \vee q, \neg p \vee q, p \vee \neg q, s \vee \neg p \vee q, \neg s \vee p \vee \neg q, \neg p \vee r, \neg q \vee \neg r\}$. Since there are no unit (single literal) clauses, there are no implied literals at level 0. We therefore select an unassigned literal, in this case s as the decision literal at level 1. Again, there are no implied literals at level 1, and we select an unassigned literal r as the decision literal at level 2. Now, we can add the implied literals $\neg q$ from the input clause $\neg q \vee \neg r$ and p from the input clause $p \vee q$. At this point, propagation identifies a conflict where the partial assignment M falsifies the input clause $\neg p \vee q$. The conflict is analyzed by replacing $\neg p$ with q to get the unit clause q. Since the maximal level of the empty clause is 0, backjumping yields a partial assignment q at level 0 while adding the unit clause q to the conflict clause set C. Propagation then yields the implied literals p from the input clause $p \vee \neg q$ and r from the input clause $\neg p \vee r$, which leads to the falsification of the input clause $\neg q \vee \neg r$. Since this conflict occurs at level 0, we report unsatisfiability. We can then construct the proof of $\bot$ as shown in Figure 2.

With Marc Vaucher [SV08], we have recently verified the correctness of a DPLL-based SAT solver using PVS 4.2. Such proofs are still quite difficult. The verification

$$\frac{\dfrac{\overline{p \vee q} \quad \overline{\neg p \vee q}}{q} \quad \overline{\neg q \vee r}}{\dfrac{r}{\bot}} \quad \overline{\neg r}$$

Fig. 2. A proof extracted from DPLL

effort here took about three man-months. The verified solver, though quite concrete, is not executable, but it would be relatively easy to transform it to executable form. Even with this transformation, the result SAT solver would not be anywhere near as efficient as a state-of-the-art SAT solver. The VeRK approach uses the verified SAT solver as an offline checker, which does not require state-of-the-art performance, but a lot more work is needed to verify a reasonably competitive SAT solver. The SAT solver that we have verified does not generate proofs, and a modest amount of additional work will be needed to add and verify a proof generation capability. In any case, it is certainly feasible to verify a moderately efficient SAT solver that can be used as an offline checker. Our verification of a SAT solver is a preliminary step toward a verified reference kernel.

6 Checking Verification Tools with the Kernel

We now show how untrusted verification tools can be checked using a verified reference kernel that has its core, a verified SAT solver. We show for each of these that it is possible to reduce the verification to clausification, lemmas, and SAT solving.

Binary Decision Diagrams. A binary decision diagram (BDD) represents a Boolean function as an if-then-else graph with the variables as decision nodes and the truth values 0 and 1 as the leaves [Bry86]. Reduced ordered BDDs use a uniform variable ordering along all branches of the diagram and remove all redundant decision nodes. ROBDDs are canonical representation for Boolean functions. There are verified BDD libraries, but only for a limited range of operations. Now a ROBDD graph G can be converted into a sum-of-cubes form. This sum-of-cubes representation is the clausal form of the negation of $\overline{G}$. The first step is to check that if a graph G_ϕ purports to be the ROBDD representation for a Boolean formula ϕ, then we need to check that $\phi \wedge \overline{G_\phi}$ and $G_\phi \wedge \neg\phi$ are unsatisfiable. In the former case, we convert ϕ into CNF form and negate the sum-of-cubes representation $\sigma_1 \vee \ldots \vee \sigma_n$ of G_ϕ to obtain a CNF representation $\kappa_1 \wedge \ldots \wedge \kappa_2$ of the conjunction. In the latter case, we check that each instance of $\sigma_i \wedge \neg\phi$ for $1 \leq i \leq n$ is unsatisfiable. Checking equivalence between two Boolean expressions represented as ROBDDs can be certified by checking that the same BDD is a faithful representation of both expressions.

Symbolic Model Checkers. As with SAT solvers, when a model checker fails to establish a property of a model, it generates a counterexample trace that can be checked. However, when it proves the property, we do not have a witness that can be easily checked for validity. There is prior work on certifying model checkers, but here we try to reduce the certification problem to one of satisfiability solving. One of the basic operations in model checking is that of computing the reachable set of states R in a transition system with an initial state predicate I and a transition relation N. The sets I, N, and R are represented as ROBDDs which can be mapped to CNF formulas as before. Most often, all we need to confirm about the set R is that it overapproximates the set of reachable states. For this, it is enough to check that $R(s) \wedge N(s, s') \wedge \neg R(s')$ is unsatisfiable using a SAT solver. We can use R to check that the computation-tree logic (CTL) property $\mathbf{AG}P$ by checking that $R(s) \wedge \neg P(s)$ is unsatisfiable. If we want to check the CTL property $\mathbf{AF}P$, we generate a sequence of sets $S_0, \ldots, S_k$ such that $S_0 = P$ and $\neg S_i(s) \wedge N(s, s') \wedge S_{i+1}(s')$ is unsatisfiable. If $I(s) \wedge \neg S_0(s) \wedge \ldots \wedge \neg S_k(s)$ is propositionally unsatisfiable, then this confirms that AFP does hold of the transition system $\langle I, N \rangle$.

The same idea can be used to construct forms of evidence for the fixed point definitions of other temporal connectives [SS03]. The evidence in the form of the intermediate state sets can be provided by the symbolic model checker but checked using the trusted SAT solver.

Static Analyzers. Static analysis tools check programs and specifications for uninitialized variables, buffer overflows, numeric overflow and underflow, memory leaks, uncaught exceptions, worst-case execution time, termination, and type errors. In most cases, these tools generate inductive invariants that can be independently checked using SMT solvers. The results of the latter can be certified in the VeRK framework using SMT solvers (see below).

SMT Solvers. The techniques for solving propositional satisfiability can be extended to formulas that contain symbols that interpreted in specific theories [dMDS07]. A *theory* can be seen as a specific first-order axiomatization or as a class of models. For example, the theory of equality over uninterpreted function symbols admits all interpretations of these symbols. The theory of real addition interprets $+$ and $<$ over the real numbers. The theory of arrays interprets the *store* and *select* operations to satisfy the axioms $select(store(a, i, v), i) = v$ and $i \neq j \implies select(store(a, i, v), j) = select(a, j)$.

An SMT solver is an extremely complex piece of software but its results can be easily checked using a little bit more than a SAT solver. An untrusted SMT solver can be instrumented to generate theory lemmas corresponding to all the theory-specific reasoning used in deciding the unsatisfiability of a formula. For example, all the instances of the above axioms that were used in demonstrating unsatisfiable would be generated. The verification then amounts to

1. Checking that these lemma clauses are valid according to the theory.
2. Confirming the unsatisfiability of the original formula together with the lemma clauses.

Figure 3 shows the theory-based unsatisfiability of the clauses $y = z$, $x = y \vee x = z$, $x \neq y \vee x \neq z$. We can identify the lemmas from the theory of equality that are needed to demonstrate unsatisfiability. These are

1. $x \neq z \vee y \neq z \vee x = y$
2. $x \neq y \vee y \neq z \vee x = z$

Step	M	F	D	C
Propagate	$y = z$	$\{y \mapsto z\}$	$\emptyset$	$\emptyset$
Select	$y = z; x \neq y$	$\{y \mapsto z\}$	$\{x \neq y\}$	$\emptyset$
Scan	$\ldots, x \neq z$ $[x \neq z \vee y \neq z \vee x = y]$	$\{y \mapsto z\}$	$\{x \neq y, x \neq z\}$	$\emptyset$
Propagate	$\ldots$	$\{y \mapsto z\}$	$\{x \neq y\}$	
Analyze	$\ldots$	$\{y \mapsto z\}$	$\{x \neq y\}$	$\{y \neq z \vee x = y\}$
Backjump	$y = z, x = y$	$\{y \mapsto z\}$	$\{x \neq y\}$	$\{y \neq z \vee x = y\}$
Assert	$y = z, x = y$	$\{x \mapsto y, y \mapsto z\}$	$\{x \neq y\}$	$\{y \neq z \vee x = y\}$
Scan	$\ldots, x = z$ $[x = z \vee x \neq y \vee y \neq z]$	$\{x \mapsto y, y \mapsto z\}$	$\{x \neq y\}$	$\{y \neq z \vee x = y\}$
Conflict				

Fig. 3. SMT Example

It is easy to now check that the augmented set of clauses is propositionally unsatisfiable.

Since it is possible to confirm the results of an SMT solver with a SAT solver, we can use an SMT solver as an intermediary between another verification tool, like a static analyzer, and the reference kernel.

First-Order and Higher-Order Proofs. Checking the unsatisfiability of first-order logic formulas is an undecidable problem, but once the unsatisfiability has been demonstrated, the result is easily checked. For first-order logic, the Herbrand theorem states that every statement that is unsatisfiable in first-order logic has a Herbrand expansion, a disjunction of a finite number of instances of the Skolemized form of the original formula, that is propositionally unsatisfiable. The Skolemized form of a sentence is obtained by placing it in prenex normal form with the quantifiers at the outermost level. Each existentially quantified variable is then replaced by a terms of the form $f(x_1, \ldots, x_n)$ for a freshly chosen function symbol f, where $x_1, \ldots, x_n$ are the universally quantified variables governing the existential quantification. For example, the claim $\forall x. \exists y. p(x) \wedge \neg p(y)$ is unsatisfiable. The Herbrand form is just $p(x) \wedge \neg p(f(x))$. The Herbrand expansion $p(a) \wedge \neg p(f(a)) \wedge p(f(a)) \wedge p(f(f(a)))$ is propositionally unsatisfiable.

If we can instrument a prover to generate a Herbrand expansion, the unsatisfiability of the original formula can be confirmed by

1. Checking that the Herbrand expansion is indeed a valid Herbrand expansion of the original formula.
2. Checking the propositional unsatisfiability of the Herbrand expansion.

The situation is the same for first-order logic with equality. Here, finding the quantifier instantiations is hard. Even for a bounded number of copies of the formula, the search problem reduces to the probem of simultaneous rigid E-unification [DGV96, DV01], which is known to be undecidable. However, once the proof search has succeeded, Herbrand's theorem can be used to reduce the problem to that of checking that a Herbrand expansion is valid under equality [Sho67], which can easily be checked by an SMT solver. The result of the SMT solver can be checked by a SAT solver with lemmas, which in this case are instances of the equality axioms.

Similarly, for higher-order logic, the problem of checking satisfiability is undecidable, but the Herbrand expansion [Mil83] can be checked from the instances of the higher-order logic axiom schemes using an SMT solver.

Rewrite rules are a popular inference mechanism for building simplifiers and computation rules. Rewriting is a simple but useful fragment of first-order logic with equality where the inference steps are restricted to instantiation (based on matching), equality replacement, and backchaining. A fairly sophisticated rewriter has been verified by Davis [Dav07] using ACL2 [KMM00]. It is also possible to take a lighter approach to certified rewriting by recording the instances of rewrite rules that have been used. The theorem proved by means of rewriting can then be derived from these instances using an SMT solver. As before, the result of the SMT solver can be checked in conjunction with the lemmas by means of a SAT solver.

7 Conclusions

Reconciling trust and automation is a longstanding challenge in formalized reasoning. We have argued that it is possible to check the results of a range of formal verification tools using a trusted (verified) SAT solver plus a small amount of extra functionality. Our approach saves the overhead of proof generation and allows the untrusted tools to evolve without significant constraints. The main constraint is that the untrusted tools must be instrumented to generate information that is needed by the SAT solver. For example, we need quantifier instantiations, theory lemmas, and sum of cubes representations of BDDs.

The extra functionality needed beyond a SAT solver is also quite modest. For example, we need to check the conversion to conjunctive normal form. We also need to verify the theory validity of the lemmas that are given as extra clauses to the SAT solver. We need to check that the instantiation of input formulas or rewrite rules has been carried out correctly. In some of these cases, we can actually use proof generation as a way of generating certificates.

We have only made very preliminary progress in the direction of building a verified reference kernel. In particular, we have shown that it is possible to verify a simple SAT solver based on modern ideas. Once the kernel is constructed, it will be possible to instrument various untrusted tools to generate the information needed by the kernel in order to reproduce the verification results. The untrusted tools can also be instrumented to generate hints that reduce the search time for the SAT solver.

A lot can go wrong in the construction of software. The specifications can be wrong or ambiguous. The semantics of the specification and programming languages can be imprecise. The compilers, run-time systems, and hardware platforms can be faulty. Given that there are many places where an assurance case for the system can spring a leak, it seems more prudent to focus on automation than on trust. However, if we can effectively reconcile trust and automation for verification tools, then we can direct more of the resources to validating the other components of the system.

Acknowledgments. Bruno Dutertre, Sam Owre, and John Rushby offered insightful comments on earlier drafts of the paper.

References

[BB04]   Barrett, C.W., Berezin, S.: CVC lite: A new implementation of the cooperating validity checker category B. In: Alur, R., Peled, D. (eds.) CAV 2004. LNCS, vol. 3114, pp. 515–518. Springer, Heidelberg (2004)

[BM81]   Boyer, R.S., Moore, J.S.: Metafunctions: Proving them correct and using them efficiently as new proof procedures. In: Boyer, R.S., Moore, J.S. (eds.) The Correctness Problem in Computer Science. Academic Press, London (1981)

[Bry86]   Bryant, R.E.: Graph-based algorithms for Boolean function manipulation. IEEE Transactions on Computers C-35(8), 677–691 (1986)

[BT07]   Barrett, C., Tinelli, C.: CVC3. In: Damm, W., Hermanns, H. (eds.) CAV 2007. LNCS, vol. 4590, pp. 298–302. Springer, Heidelberg (2007)

[CAB⁺86]   Constable, R.L., Allen, S.F., Bromley, H.M., Cleaveland, W.R., Cremer, J.F., Harper, R.W., Howe, D.J., Knoblock, T.B., Mendler, N.P., Panangaden, P., Sasaki, J.T., Smith, S.F.: Implementing Mathematics with the Nuprl Proof Development System. Prentice Hall, Englewood Cliffs (1986), http://www.cs.cornell.edu/Info/Projects/NuPRL/

[CCF⁺95]   Cornes, C., Courant, J., Filliatre, J.C., Huet, G., Manoury, P., Paulin-Mohring, C., Munoz, C., Murthy, C., Parent, C., Saibi, A., Werner, B.: The Coq proof assistant reference manual, version 5.10. Technical report, INRIA, Rocquencourt, France (February 1995)

[CN05]   Chaieb, A., Nipkow, T.: Verifying and reflecting quantifier elimination for Presburger arithmetic. In: Sutcliffe, G., Voronkov, A. (eds.) LPAR 2005. LNCS (LNAI), vol. 3835, pp. 367–380. Springer, Heidelberg (2005)

[Dav07]   Davis, J.: The Milawa rewriter and an ACL2 proof of its soundness. In: Gamboa, R., Sawada, J., Cowles, J. (eds.) Proceedings of the Seventh International Workshop on the ACL2 Theorem Prover and its Applications (2007)

[dB70]   de Bruijn, N.G.: The mathematical language AUTOMATH, its usage and some of its extensions. In: Symposium on Automatic Demonstration. Lecture Notes in Mathematics, vol. 125, pp. 29–61. Springer, Berlin (1970)

[dB80]   de Bruijn, N.G.: A survey of the project AUTOMATH. In: Seldin, J.P., Hindley, J.R. (eds.) Essays on Combinatory Logic, Lambda Calculus and Formalism, pp. 589–606. Academic Press, New York (1980)

[DGV96]   Degtyarev, A., Gurevich, Y., Voronkov, A.: Herbrand's theorem and equational reasoning: Problems and solutions. Bulletin of the EATCS 60, 78–96 (1996)

[dMB08]   de Moura, L.M., Bjørner, N.: Z3: An efficient SMT solver. In: Ramakrishnan, C.R., Rehof, J. (eds.) TACAS 2008. LNCS, vol. 4963, pp. 337–340. Springer, Heidelberg (2008)

[dMDS07]   de Moura, L., Dutertre, B., Shankar, N.: A tutorial on satisfiability modulo theories. In: Damm, W., Hermanns, H. (eds.) CAV 2007. LNCS, vol. 4590, pp. 20–36. Springer, Heidelberg (2007)

[DV01]   Degtyarev, A., Voronkov, A.: Equality reasoning in sequent-based proof search. In: Robinson, Voronkov. (eds.) [RV01], pp. 611–706

[ES03]   Eén, N., Sörensson, N.: An extensible SAT-solver. In: Proceedings of SAT 2003 (2003)

[Gel07]   Van Gelder, A.: Verifying propositional unsatisfiability: Pitfalls to avoid. In: Marques-Silva, J., Sakallah, K.A. (eds.) SAT 2007. LNCS, vol. 4501, pp. 328–333. Springer, Heidelberg (2007)

[GM93]   Gordon, M.J.C., Melham, T.F. (eds.): Introduction to HOL: A Theorem Proving Environment for Higher-Order Logic. Cambridge University Press, Cambridge (1993), http://www.cl.cam.ac.uk/Research/HVG/HOL/

[GMW79]   Gordon, M., Milner, R., Wadsworth, C.: Edinburgh LCF: A Mechanized Logic of Computation. LNCS, vol. 78. Springer, Heidelberg (1979)

[Har96a]   Harrison, J.: Formalized mathematics. Technical Report TUCS-TR-36, Turku Centre for Computer Science, Finland, August 14 (1996)

[Har96b]   Harrison, J.: HOL Light: A tutorial introduction. In: Srivas, M., Camilleri, A. (eds.) FMCAD 1996. LNCS, vol. 1166, pp. 265–269. Springer, Heidelberg (1996), http://www.cl.cam.ac.uk/jrh13/hol-light/index.html

[Har06]   Harrison, J.: Towards self-verification of HOL Light. In: Furbach, U., Shankar, N. (eds.) IJCAR 2006. LNCS (LNAI), vol. 4130, pp. 177–191. Springer, Heidelberg (2006)

[KC86]   Knoblock, T.B., Constable, R.L.: Formalizing metareasoning in type theory. In: IEEE Symposium on Logic in Computer Science, Cambridge, MA (1986)

[KL86]   Knight, J.C., Leveson, N.G.: An empirical study of failure probabilities in multi-version software. In: Fault Tolerant Computing Symposium 16, Vienna, Austria, July 1986, pp. 165–170. IEEE Computer Society, Los Alamitos (1986)

[KMM00]   Kaufmann, M., Manolios, P., Moore, J.S.: Computer-Aided Reasoning: An Approach. Advances in Formal Methods, vol. 3. Kluwer, Dordrecht (2000)

[LP92]   Luo, Z., Pollack, R.: The LEGO proof development system: A user's manual. Technical Report ECS-LFCS-92-211, University of Edinburgh (1992)

[MBG06]   McLaughlin, S., Barrett, C., Ge, Y.: Cooperating theorem provers: A case study combining HOL-light and CVC lite. Electr. Notes Theor. Comput. Sci 144(2), 43–51 (2006)

[Meh03]   Mehlhorn, K.: The reliable algorithmic software challenge RASC. In: Jansen, K., Margraf, M., Mastrolli, M., Rolim, J.D.P. (eds.) WEA 2003. LNCS, vol. 2647, p. 222. Springer, Heidelberg (2003)

[Mil83]   Dale, A.: Miller. Proofs in Higher-order Logic. PhD thesis, Carnegie-Mellon University (August 1983)

[NGdV94]   Nederpelt, R.P., Geuvers, J.H., de Vrijer, R.C.: Selected Papers on Automath. North-Holland, Amsterdam (1994)

[ORSvH95]   Owre, S., Rushby, J., Shankar, N., von Henke, F.: Formal verification for fault-tolerant architectures: Prolegomena to the design of PVS. IEEE Transactions on Software Engineering 21(2), 107–125 (1995), http://pvs.csl.sri.com

[Pau94]   Paulson, L.C.: Isabelle: A Generic Theorem Prover. LNCS, vol. 828. Springer, Heidelberg (1994)

[Rus06]   Rushby, J.: Harnessing disruptive innovation in formal verification. In: Van Hung, D., Pandya, P. (eds.) Fourth International Conference on Software Engineering and Formal Methods (SEFM), Pune, India, September 2006, pp. 21–28. IEEE Computer Society, Los Alamitos (2006)

[RV01]   Robinson, A., Voronkov, A. (eds.): Handbook of Automated Reasoning. Elsevier Science, Amsterdam (2001)

[Sha85]   Shankar, N.: Towards mechanical metamathematics. Journal of Automated Reasoning 1(4), 407–434 (1985)

[Sha05]   Shankar, N.: Inference systems for logical algorithms. In: Ramanujam, R., Sen, S. (eds.) FSTTCS 2005. LNCS, vol. 3821, pp. 60–78. Springer, Heidelberg (2005)

[Sho67]   Shoenfield, J.R.: Mathematical Logic. Addison-Wesley, Reading (1967)

[Smo78]   Smorynski, C.: The incompleteness theorems. In: Barwise, J. (ed.) The Handbook of Mathematical Logic. Studies in Logic and the Foundations of Mathematics, vol. 90, pp. 821–865. North-Holland, Amsterdam (1978)

[SR02]   Shankar, N., Rueß, H.: Combining Shostak theories. In: Tison, S. (ed.) RTA 2002. LNCS, vol. 2378, pp. 1–18. Springer, Heidelberg (2002)

[SS03]   Shankar, N., Sorea, M.: Counterexample-driven model checking. Technical Report SRI-CSL-03-04, SRI International Computer Science Laboratory (2003)

[SV08]   Shankar, N., Vaucher, M.: The mechanical verification of a DPLL-based satisfiability solver (submitted for publication, 2008)

[Thé98]   Théry, L.: A certified version of Buchberger's algorithm. In: Kirchner, C., Kirchner, H. (eds.) CADE 1998. LNCS (LNAI), vol. 1421, pp. 349–364. Springer, Heidelberg (1998)

[WA07]   Weber, T., Amjad, H.: Efficiently checking propositional refutations in HOL theorem provers. Journal of Applied Logic (July 2007) (to appear), http://dx.doi.org/10.1016/j.jal.2007.07.003

[Wey80]   Weyhrauch, R.W.: Prolegomena to a theory of mechanized formal reasoning. Artificial Intelligence 13(1 and 2), 133–170 (1980)

[WGS03]   Williams, R., Gomes, C.P., Selman, B.: Backdoors to typical case complexity. In: Gottlob, G., Walsh, T. (eds.) IJCAI 2003, Proceedings of the Eighteenth International Joint Conference on Artificial Intelligence, Acapulco, Mexico, August 9-15, 2003, pp. 1173–1178. Morgan Kaufmann, San Francisco (2003)

[Wie02]   Wiedijk, F.: A new implementation of Automath. J. Autom. Reasoning 29(3-4), 365–387 (2002)

[ZM03]   Zhang, L., Malik, S.: Validating SAT solvers using an independent resolution-based checker: Practical implementations and other applications. In: DATE, pp. 10880–10885. IEEE Computer Society, Los Alamitos (2003)

CTL Model-Checking with Graded Quantifiers*

Alessandro Ferrante, Margherita Napoli, and Mimmo Parente

Dipartimento di Informatica ed Applicazioni "R.M. Capocelli", University of Salerno
Via Ponte don Melillo - 84084 - Fisciano (SA) - Italy
{ferrante,napoli,parente}@dia.unisa.it

Abstract. The use of the universal and existential quantifiers with the capability to express the concept of *at least k* or *all but k*, for a non-negative integer k, has been thoroughly studied in various kinds of logics. In classical logic there are *counting quantifiers*, in modal logics *graded modalities*, in description logics *number restrictions*.

Recently, the complexity issues related to the decidability of the μ-calculus, when the universal and existential quantifiers are augmented with graded modalities, have been investigated by Kupfermann, Sattler and Vardi. They have shown that this problem is ExpTime-complete.

In this paper we consider another extension of modal logic, the Computational Tree Logic CTL, augmented with graded modalities generalizing standard quantifiers and investigate the complexity issues, with respect to the model-checking problem. We consider a system model represented by a pointed Kripke structure $\mathcal{K}$ and give an algorithm to solve the model-checking problem running in time $O(|\mathcal{K}| \cdot |\varphi|)$ which is hence tight for the problem (where $|\varphi|$ is the number of temporal and boolean operators and does not include the values occurring in the graded modalities).

In this framework, the graded modalities express the ability to generate a user-defined number of counterexamples (or evidences) to a specification φ given in CTL. However these multiple counterexamples can partially overlap, that is they may share some behavior. We have hence investigated the case when all of them are completely disjoint. In this case we prove that the model-checking problem is both NP-hard and coNP-hard and give an algorithm for solving it running in polynomial space. We have thus studied a fragment of this graded-CTL logic, and have proved that the model-checking problem is solvable in polynomial time.

1   Introduction

Model-checking is the process, which is now becoming widely accepted, to check whether a given model satisfies a given logical formula [CGP99, QS82], and it can be applied to all kinds of logics. In this paper we consider model-checking of formulas expressed in a logic which extends the classical Computational Tree Logic, CTL, with graded modalities. Classical CTL can be used for reasoning

---

* Work partially supported by M.I.U.R. grant ex-60%.

about the temporal behavior of systems considering either *all the possible futures* or *at least one possible future*. Here we use *graded* extensions on the existential and universal quantifiers.

In the literature the capability to express *at least k* and *all but k*, given a non-negative integer k, has been intensively studied in various logic frameworks. In classical logics $\exists^{>k}$ and $\forall^{\leq k}$ are called *counting quantifiers*, see e.g. [GOR97, GMV99, PST00], in modal logics they are called *graded* modalities, see e.g. [Fin72, Tob01], and in description logics one speaks about *number restriction* of properties describing systems, see e.g. [HB91]. Recently the complexity issues related to the decidability of the μ-calculus when the universal and existential quantifiers are augmented with graded modalities, have been investigated in [KSV02]. They have shown that this problem is ExpTime-complete, retaining thus the same complexity as in the case of classical μ-calculus, though strictly extending it.

In this paper we introduce the *graded*-CTL, obtained by augmenting CTL with graded modalities that generalize standard path quantifiers and this logic, here too, strictly extends classical CTL. With graded-CTL formulas we can reason about more than any constant number of futures. For example, the formula $E^{>k}\mathcal{F}\neg(wait \Rightarrow A\mathcal{F}criticSection)$ expresses the fact that in several cases it is possible that a waiting process never obtains the requested resource. Note that this logic allows also to grade nested path quantifiers to express other interesting properties, such as the safety property that "a system always has at least two ways to reach a *safe state*" ($A\mathcal{G}E^{>1}\mathcal{F}safe$). Clearly formulas of this type cannot be expressed in CTL and not even in classical μ-calculus. The focus in the paper is on the complexities involved in the process of model-checking system models against specifications given in this logic. In this framework the motivation in the use of these graded modalities mainly arises from the fact that during the verification of a system design, a central feature of the technique of model-checking is the generation of counterexamples. In fact the realization process for a system passes through the "Check/Analyze/Fix" cycle: model-check the design of the system against some desired properties φ, analyze the generated counterexamples to the properties, and re-design the system, trying to fix the errors. The analysis of the counterexamples usually gives clues to that part of the system model where the specification failed. It is therefore highly desirable to have as many significative counterexamples as possible simultaneously, c.f. [CG07, CIW+01, DRS03]. Usually up-to-date model-checkers, as NuSMV and SPIN [CCGR99, Hol97], return only one counterexample of φ or, by using the so-called *onion ring* technique, may determine all the counterexamples to a given non-graded formula. Here we aim at getting more *significative* counterexamples, in the sense that by nesting the graded quantifiers we can concentrate ourselves on zones of the model for which we are more interested in. In other words with the actual model checkers we can obtain counterexamples to a formula with only the first quantifier which, in a sense, is graded, while in our scenario we can have also the inner quantifiers which are graded. On the other side, the investigation of the complexities involved in the generation and the analysis of the counterexamples is a central issue, as explained also in the survey [CV03] where the role and the structure of counterexamples is nicely investigated putting an emphasis on the complexities related to the generation problem.

Given a graded-CTL formula φ and a system model represented by a pointed Kripke structure $\mathcal{K}$, our first result is an algorithm to solve the model-checking problem in time $O(|\mathcal{K}| \cdot |\varphi|)$, the same running time of the algorithm for classical CTL. Let us remark that this complexity does not depend at all on the values representing the grading of the modalities and the size $|\varphi|$ of the formula does not depend on the representation of these values and is simply the number of the temporal and boolean operators. However the multiple counterexamples returned by this algorithm may overlap, while it can be desirable in the analysis phase to detect independent traces where the specification fails. To deal with this case, we have introduced a semantic for temporal operators to require the edge-disjointness of the paths representing the counterexamples. The same setting can be applied also, for example, to ensure that a "correct" system behavior tolerates a given number of faults of the system. We have proved that to model-check a system model against such specifications is both NP-hard and coNP-hard. The reduction has been done from the cycle-packing problem (the problem to check whether there are k disjoint cycles in a graph). This has suggested that formulas of the type $E^{>k}\mathcal{G}\varphi$ (there exist at least $k + 1$ infinite edge-disjoint paths globally satisfying φ) are hard to verify. We have then defined the still interesting fragment of the logic obtained by dropping this kind of formulas and proved that the model-checking problem can be solved in polynomial time in this case. Clearly, unless NP = coNP, the problem, in the full logic, does not belong to NP. We have then given an algorithm for it, showing that however it is in PSPACE. Finally, we have considered the scenario in which only a given number of behaviors need to be disjoint and all the remaining may overlap. In this case we have proved that the problem is *fixed parameter* tractable.

The paper is organized as follows: in Section 2 we give some preliminary definitions and introduce the model-checking problem for graded-CTL; in Section 3 we prove that the graded-CTL model-checking is solvable in polynomial time; in Section 4 we study the edge-disjoint graded-CTL model-checking. Moreover we show that the same problem restricted to a fragment of graded-CTL is solvable in polynomial time, and that we can obtain a good algorithm in practical cases by relaxing the edge-disjointness requirement; finally in Section 5 we give some conclusions and open problems.

2   Graded-CTL Logic

In this section we introduce the graded-CTL logic which extends the classical CTL logic with graded quantifiers. CTL can be used for reasoning about the temporal behavior of systems considering either "all the possible futures" or "at least one possible future". Graded extension generalizes CTL to reasoning about more than a given number of possible future behaviors.

Let us start by giving the syntax of the logic. The graded-CTL operators consist of the temporal operators $\mathcal{U}$ ("until"), $\mathcal{G}$ ("globally") and $\mathcal{X}$ ("next"), the boolean connectives $\wedge$ and $\neg$, and the graded path quantifier $E^{>k}$ ("for at least k+1 futures").

Given a set of atomic propositions AP, the syntax of the graded-CTL formulas is:

$$\varphi := p \mid \neg\varphi \mid \varphi \wedge \varphi \mid E^{>k}\mathcal{X}\varphi \mid E^{>k}\varphi\mathcal{U}\varphi \mid E^{>k}\mathcal{G}\varphi$$

where $p \in AP$ and k is a non-negative integer.

We define the semantics of graded-CTL with respect to *Kripke Structures*. As usual, a Kripke structure over a set of atomic propositions AP, is a tuple $\mathcal{K} = \langle S, s_{in}, R, L \rangle$, where S is a finite set of states, $s_{in} \in S$ is the initial state, $R \subseteq S \times S$ is a transition relation with the property that for each $s \in S$ there is $t \in S$ such that $(s, t) \in R$, and $L : S \to 2^{AP}$ is a labeling function.

A path in $\mathcal{K}$ is denoted by the sequence of states $\pi = \langle s_0, s_1, \ldots s_n \rangle$ or by $\pi = \langle s_0, s_1, \ldots \rangle$, if it is infinite. The length of a path, denoted by $|\pi|$, is the number of states in the sequence, and $\pi[i]$ denotes the state s_i, $0 \leq i < |\pi|$. Two paths π_1 and π_2 are *distinct* if there exists an index $0 \leq i < \min\{|\pi_1|, |\pi_2|\}$ such that $\pi_1[i] \neq \pi_2[i]$. Observe that from this definition if a path is the prefix of another path, then they are not distinct.

Let $\mathcal{K} = \langle S, s_{in}, R, L \rangle$ be a Kripke structure and $s \in S$ be a state of $\mathcal{K}$. The concept of satisfiability for graded-CTL formulas is established by the relation $\models$, defined as follows:

- $(\mathcal{K}, s) \models p$, $p \in AP$, iff $p \in L(s)$;
- $(\mathcal{K}, s) \models \varphi_1 \wedge \varphi_2$ iff $(\mathcal{K}, s) \models \varphi_1$ and $(\mathcal{K}, s) \models \varphi_2$;
- $(\mathcal{K}, s) \models \neg\varphi$ iff $\neg((\mathcal{K}, s) \models \varphi)$ (shortly written, $(\mathcal{K}, s) \not\models \varphi$);
- $(\mathcal{K}, s) \models E^{>k}\mathcal{X}\varphi$ iff there exist $k + 1$ different states $s_0, \ldots, s_k$ such that
    1. $(s, s_i) \in R$ and
    2. $(\mathcal{K}, s_i) \models \varphi$ for all $0 \leq i \leq k$;
- $(\mathcal{K}, s) \models E^{>k}\mathcal{G}\varphi$ iff there exist $k+1$ pairwise distinct infinite paths $\pi_0, \ldots, \pi_k$ such that for every $0 \leq j \leq k$,
    1. $\pi_j[0] = s$ and
    2. for all $h \geq 0$, $(\mathcal{K}, \pi_j[h]) \models \varphi$.
- $(\mathcal{K}, s) \models E^{>k}\varphi_1\mathcal{U}\varphi_2$ iff there exist $k+1$ pairwise distinct finite paths $\pi_0, \ldots, \pi_k$ of length $i_0, \ldots, i_k$, respectively, such that for all $0 \leq j \leq k$
    1. $\pi_j[0] = s$,
    2. $(\mathcal{K}, \pi_j[i_j - 1]) \models \varphi_2$, and
    3. for every $0 \leq h < i_j - 1$, $(\mathcal{K}, \pi_j[h]) \models \varphi_1$;

The graded-CTL formulas (as in the standard non-graded CTL) are also called *state-formulas* and a state s in $\mathcal{K}$ satisfies a state-formula φ if $(\mathcal{K}, s) \models \varphi$. On the other side, $\mathcal{X}\varphi$, $\mathcal{G}\varphi$ and $\varphi_1\mathcal{U}\varphi_2$ are called as usual *path-formulas*. In particular a path satisfying a path-formula θ is called an *evidence* of θ (note that the evidences for $\mathcal{X}$ and $\mathcal{U}$ are finite paths). Then, for the fulfillment of a formula $E^{>k}\theta$ in a state s, it is required the existence of $k + 1$ distinct evidences of θ, starting from s.

As usual, in our logic the temporal operator $\mathcal{F}$ ("eventually") can be defined in terms of the operators given above: $E^{>k}\mathcal{F}\varphi \Leftrightarrow E^{>k}$ TRUE $\mathcal{U}\ \varphi$. Moreover, it is easy to observe that CTL is a proper fragment of graded-CTL since the simple formula $E^{>1}\mathcal{X}p$ cannot be expressed in CTL, whereas any CTL formula is also a graded-CTL formula since the quantifier E is equivalent to $E^{>0}$ and for the universal quantifier A the standard relations hold, recalled here:

- $A\mathcal{X}\varphi \Longleftrightarrow \neg E\mathcal{X}\neg\varphi$;
- $A\mathcal{G}\varphi \Longleftrightarrow \neg E\mathcal{F}\neg\varphi$;
- $A\varphi_1\mathcal{U}\varphi_2 \Longleftrightarrow \neg E(\neg\varphi_2\mathcal{U}(\neg\varphi_1 \wedge \neg\varphi_2)) \wedge \neg E\mathcal{G}\neg\varphi_2$.

Finally, we also consider the graded extension of the quantifier A, $A^{\leq k}$, with the meaning that *all the paths starting from a node s, except for at most k, satisfy a given path-formula*. The quantifier $A^{\leq k}$ is the dual of $E^{>k}$ and can obviously be re-written in terms of $\neg E^{>k}$. We now formally define the model-checking problem.

Given a Kripke structure $\mathcal{K} = \langle S, s_{in}, R, L\rangle$, and a graded-CTL formula φ, the **graded-CTL model-checking** is the problem to verify whether $(\mathcal{K}, s_{in}) \models \varphi$.

In the next sections we study the complexity of the model-checking problem with respect to the size of the Kripke structure (expressed in terms of the number of edges, as by our definition $|R| \geq |S|$), and to the size of the CTL formula, where the size $|\varphi|$ of a CTL formula φ is the number of the temporal and the boolean operators occurring in it.

3   Graded-CTL Model-Checking

In this section we show that the graded-CTL model-checking problem can be solved in polynomial time and independently from the values occurring in the graded modalities, involved in the formulas. Then we discuss possible applications of our result to the generation of counterexamples.

Let us recall that an algorithm to solve the model-checking problem for a given Kripke structure $\mathcal{K}$ and a given formula φ computes the subset $\{s \in S$ s.t. $(\mathcal{K}, s) \models \varphi\}$.

Theorem 1. *Let $\mathcal{K} = \langle S, s_{in}, R, L\rangle$ be a Kripke structure and φ be a graded-CTL formula. The graded-CTL model-checking problem can be solved in time $\mathcal{O}(|R| \cdot |\varphi|)$.*

Proof. To solve the problem we give an algorithm that works on the sub-formulas ψ of φ and for each state s determines whether $(\mathcal{K}, s) \models \psi$ (and sets a boolean variable $s.\psi$ to TRUE), (see Algorithm 1). The algorithm uses a primitive function $Sub(\varphi)$ which returns all the sub-formulas of φ and moreover for a path-formula θ, if $E^{>k}\theta$ is in $Sub(\varphi)$, then $E^{>0}\theta$ is in $Sub(\varphi)$ as well. In particular we assume that such formulas are returned in non-decreasing order of complexity, with $E^{>0}\theta$ preceding $E^{>k}\theta$ in the sequence.

If a sub-formula ψ is of type $p \in AP$, $\neg\psi_1$, $\psi_1 \wedge \psi_2$, $E^{>0}\mathcal{G}\psi_1$, $E^{>0}\psi_1\mathcal{U}\psi_2$, then the algorithm (lines $3-13$) works as the classical CTL model-checking algorithm

[CGP99], and, if a sub-formula is of type $E^{>k}\mathcal{X}\psi_1$, then the algorithm checks, for each state s whether $|\{t \in S \mid (s,t) \in R \text{ and } (\mathcal{K},t) \models \psi_1\}| > k$, (lines $14-16$).

Algorithm 1. The algorithm $GradedCTL(\mathcal{K}, \varphi)$.

Input: A Kripke Structure $\mathcal{K} = \langle S, s_{in}, R, L \rangle$ and a graded-CTL formula φ.
Output: For each state s, $s.\varphi = \text{TRUE}$ if $(\mathcal{K}, s) \models \varphi$ and $s.\varphi = \text{FALSE}$ otherwise

---

1 Let $s.\psi = \text{FALSE}$ for all $s \in S$ and $\psi \in Sub(\varphi)$;
2 **forall** $\psi \in Sub(\varphi)$ **do**
3   **case** $\psi = p \in AP$: **forall** $s \in S$ s.t. $p \in L(s)$ **do** $s.\psi \leftarrow \text{TRUE}$;
4   **case** $\psi = \neg\psi_1$: **forall** $s \in S$ **do** $s.\psi \leftarrow \neg s.\psi_1$;
5   **case** $\psi = \psi_1 \wedge \psi_2$: **forall** $s \in S$ **do** $s.\psi \leftarrow (s.\psi_1 \wedge s.\psi_2)$;
6   **case** $\psi = E^{>0}\mathcal{G}\psi_1$:
7          $S' \leftarrow \{s \in S \mid s.\psi_1 = \text{TRUE}\}$; $R' \leftarrow R \cap (S' \times S')$;
8   **forall** $s \in S'$ s.t. $\exists$ *a cycle reachable from* s *in* (S', R') **do** $s.\psi \leftarrow \text{TRUE}$;
9   **end**
10   **case** $\psi = E^{>0}\psi_1\mathcal{U}\psi_2$:
11         $S' \leftarrow \{s \in S \mid s.\psi_1 = \text{TRUE or } s.\psi_2 = \text{TRUE}\}$; $R' \leftarrow R \cap (S' \times S')$;
12   **forall** $s \in S'$ s.t. $\exists t$ *with* $t.\psi_2 = \text{TRUE}$ *reachable from* s *in* (S', R') **do** $s.\psi \leftarrow \text{TRUE}$;
13   **end**
14   **case** $\psi = E^{>k}\mathcal{X}\psi_1$ *with* $k \geq 0$:
15   **forall** $s \in S$ s.t. $|\{(s,t) \in R \mid t.\psi_1 = \text{TRUE}\}| > k$ **do** $s.\psi \leftarrow \text{TRUE}$;
16   **end**
17   **case** $\psi = E^{>k}\mathcal{G}\psi_1$ *with* $k > 0$:
18         $S' \leftarrow \{s \in S \mid s.E^{>0}\mathcal{G}\psi_1 = \text{TRUE}\}$; $R' \leftarrow R \cap (S' \times S')$;
19   **forall** $s \in S'$ s.t. $\exists$ *a non-sink-cycle reachable from* s *in* (S', R') **do** $s.\psi \leftarrow \text{TRUE}$;
20   **forall** $s \in S'$ s.t. $\exists k + 1$ *distinct finite paths from* s *to sink-cycles in* (S', R') **do** $s.\psi \leftarrow \text{TRUE}$;
21   **end**
22   **case** $\psi = E^{>k}\psi_1\mathcal{U}\psi_2$ *with* $k > 0$:
23         $S' \leftarrow \{s \in S \mid s.E^{>0}\psi_1\mathcal{U}\psi_2 = \text{TRUE}\}$;
24         $R' \leftarrow (R \cap (S' \times S')) \setminus \{(s,t) \in R \mid s.\psi_1 = \text{FALSE}\}$;
25   **forall** $s \in S'$ s.t. $\exists$ *a non-sink-cycle reachable from* s *in* (S', R') **do** $s.\psi \leftarrow \text{TRUE}$;
26   **forall** $s \in S'$ s.t. $\exists k + 1$ *distinct finite paths from* s *to states where* ψ_2 *holds in* (S', R') **do** $s.\psi \leftarrow \text{TRUE}$;
27   **end**
28 **end**

Consider now a sub-formula $\psi = E^{>k}\mathcal{G}\psi_1$ with $k > 0$ (line 17). Let a *sink-cycle* be a cycle not containing *exit-nodes*, that is nodes with out-degree at least 2. The algorithm is based on the following claim, that we will prove later:

Claim 1: *Let* $G_\psi = (S_\psi, R_\psi)$ *be the graph induced by the states where* $E^{>0}\mathcal{G}\psi_1$ *holds; then, given a state* $s \in S$, $(\mathcal{K}, s) \models \psi$ *iff* $s \in S_\psi$ *and either there is a* non-sink-cycle *reachable from s, or there are $k+1$ distinct finite paths connecting s to* sink-cycles *in G_ψ.*

The algorithm looks for the states in G_ψ from which it is possible to reach a non-sink-cycle (line 19) and then looks for the states from which $k+1$ distinct finite paths start, each ending in sink-cycles (line 20).

Let us now consider a sub-formula $\psi = E^{>k}\psi_1 \mathcal{U} \psi_2$ (line 22). In this case, the algorithm is based on the following claim:

Claim 2: *Let $G_\psi = (S_\psi, R_\psi)$ be the graph induced by considering the states where $E^{>0}\psi_1 \mathcal{U} \psi_2$ holds and by deleting the edges outgoing from states where ψ_1 is not satisfied; then, given a state $s \in S$, $(\mathcal{K}, s) \models \psi$ iff $s \in G_\psi$ and either there is a non-sink-cycle reachable from s, or there are $k+1$ distinct finite paths from s to states where ψ_2 holds.*

Similarly to what has been done for the case of the operator $\mathcal{G}$, now the algorithm looks for the states in G_ψ from which it is possible to reach a non-sink-cycle (line 25), and then looks for the states from which $k+1$ distinct finite paths start, each ending in states where ψ_2 holds, (line 26). The proof of the correctness of the algorithm can be easily done by induction on the length of the formulas.

To complete the proof let us first prove Claim 1.

(if): Let $s \in S_\psi$ and $C = \langle v_0, \ldots, v_{h-1} \rangle$ be a cycle in G_ψ reachable from s via a finite path $\langle s, u_0, \ldots, u_i, v_0 \rangle$ and containing at least one exit-node, say v_j, $0 \leq j \leq h-1$ connected to a node $w_0 \in S_\psi$ such that $w_0 \neq v_{(j+1) \bmod h}$ and $(v_j, w_0) \in R_\psi$. Since $(\mathcal{K}, w_0) \models E^{>0}\mathcal{G}\psi_1$, there is an infinite path $\langle w_0, w_1, \ldots \rangle$ starting from w_0 and satisfying $\mathcal{G}\psi_1$ and there are $k+1$ pairwise distinct infinite paths π_l, $0 \leq l \leq k$, each satisfying $\mathcal{G}\psi_1$, defined as $\pi_l = \langle s, u_0, \ldots, u_i, (C)^l, v_0, \ldots, v_j, w_0, \ldots \rangle$, where $(C)^l$ denotes the fact that π_l cycles l times on C. Thus $(\mathcal{K}, s) \models \psi$. Finally, since a finite path from s to a sink-cycle in G_ψ constitutes an infinite path satisfying $\mathcal{G}\psi_1$, if there are $k+1$ distinct finite paths connecting s to sink-cycles in G_ψ then $(\mathcal{K}, s) \models \psi$.

(only if): If $(\mathcal{K}, s) \models E^{>k}\mathcal{G}\psi_1$ then obviously $(\mathcal{K}, s) \models E^{>0}\mathcal{G}\psi_1$, therefore $s \in S_\psi$. Let us consider $k+1$ distinct infinite paths $\pi_0, \ldots, \pi_k$ starting from s and satisfying $\mathcal{G}\psi_1$. Since an infinite path on a finite Kripke structure either contains a non-sink-cycle, or ends in a sink-cycle, the claim follows from the fact that each state in $\pi_0, \ldots, \pi_k$ belongs to S_ψ.

Finally let us now prove Claim 2.

(if): Let $s \in S_\psi$ and $C = \langle v_0, \ldots, v_{h-1} \rangle$ be a non-sink-cycle, reachable from s via a finite path $\langle s, u_0, \ldots, u_i, v_0 \rangle$. Let v_j, for $0 \leq j \leq h-1$, be an exit-node of C connected to a node $w_0 \in S_\psi$ such that $w_0 \neq v_{(j+1) \bmod h}$ and $(v_j, w_0) \in R_\psi$. Since $(\mathcal{K}, w_0) \models E^{>0}\psi_1 \mathcal{U} \psi_2$, then in G_ψ there is a finite path $\langle w_0, \ldots, w_r \rangle$ starting from w_0 and ending in a w_r such that $(\mathcal{K}, w_r) \models \psi_2$. Consider the $k+1$ pairwise distinct finite paths π_l, $0 \leq l \leq k$, defined as $\pi_l = \langle s, u_0, \ldots, u_i, (C)^l, v_0, \ldots, v_j, w_0, \ldots w_r \rangle$, where $(C)^l$ denotes the fact that π_l cycles l times on C. Since R_ψ does not contain edges out-going from nodes where ψ_1 is not satisfied, then $(\mathcal{K}, x) \models \psi_1$ for all x in π_l, except at most w_r, and therefore each π_l is an *evidence* of $\psi_1 \mathcal{U} \psi_2$. Thus $(\mathcal{K}, s) \models \psi$. Now, let $\pi_0, \ldots, \pi_k$ be $k + 1$ distinct finite paths connecting s to nodes where ψ_2 holds; from the definition of G_ψ, π_i is an *evidence* of $\psi_1 \mathcal{U} \psi_2$ for all $0 \leq i \leq k$, and therefore $(\mathcal{K}, s) \models \psi$, as well.

(**only if**): If $(\mathcal{K}, s) \models E^{>k} \psi_1 \mathcal{U} \psi_2$ then obviously $(\mathcal{K}, s) \models E^{>0} \psi_1 \mathcal{U} \psi_2$, therefore $s \in S_\psi$. On the other side, from the semantics of $E^{>k} \psi_1 \mathcal{U} \psi_2$, there are $k + 1$ distinct finite paths starting from s and ending in states satisfying ψ_2 and these are also paths in G_ψ, and this completes the proof of the claim.

Let us now evaluate the running-time of the algorithm. It is easy to see that to check a sub-formula of type $p \in AP$, $\neg \psi_1$, $\psi_1 \wedge \psi_2$, requires $\mathcal{O}(|S|)$ and for a sub-formula $E^{>k} \mathcal{X} \psi_1$, $E^{>0} \mathcal{G} \psi_1$, $E^{>0} \psi_1 \mathcal{U} \psi_2$ the algorithm requires time $\mathcal{O}(|R|)$. For a sub-formula $E^{>k} \mathcal{G} \psi_1$, note that the set of vertices from which it is possible to reach a non-sink-cycle can be globally calculated in time $\mathcal{O}(|R|)$ by using a Depth First Search algorithm and, as soon as a cycle is detected, checking whether the cycle contains an exit-node. Finally, also the set of vertices from which $k + 1$ paths leading to sink-cycles exist, can be globally calculated in time $\mathcal{O}(|R|)$ by using a standard DFS algorithm. The analysis for $E^{>k} \psi_1 \mathcal{U} \psi_2$ is essentially the same as that of the case $E^{>k} \mathcal{G} \psi_1$. Since the size of $Sub(\varphi)$ is $O(|\varphi|)$, then the overall complexity of the algorithm is $\mathcal{O}(|R| \cdot |\varphi|)$.   □

An example of Claim 2 is the model in Figure 1 which satisfies the formula $E^{>k} \mathcal{F}(wait1 \wedge E\mathcal{G} \neg critic1)$, for all $k \geq 0$, as contains reachable non-sink-cycles (one is depicted with bold-faced edges).

The graded-CTL model-checking can be used to obtain simultaneously more than one counterexample for a formula. For example, consider the formula $A\mathcal{F}p$ expressing a simple liveness property: in all behaviors something good eventually happens. Given a model $\mathcal{K}$, a counterexample is a path in $\mathcal{K}$ where $\neg p$ always holds. It can be useful to detect whether there are more than a fixed number k of behaviors in which the desired property fails. To get that, we can test whether $(\mathcal{K}, s_{in}) \models E^{>k} \mathcal{G} \neg p$. Analogously, we can consider a safety property expressed by $\neg E\mathcal{F}$ *error*: once fixed a number k, if $(\mathcal{K}, s_{in}) \models E^{>k} \mathcal{F}$ *error* then there are more than k wrong behaviors, each leading to an error. Note that the algorithm we introduced in Theorem 1 can be modified to return the required counterexamples.

Let us also consider the formula $A\mathcal{G}(wait \Rightarrow A\mathcal{F}critic)$ for the access control to a critical section of a system. A counterexample for this formula is an "unfair" path which is an evidence for the formula $E\mathcal{F}(wait \wedge E\mathcal{G} \neg critic)$. In this case, it is useful to detect whether the model can generate more bad behaviors. By using graded-CTL model-checking it is possible to analyze three bad situations: the first is to detect whether there are more "unfair" paths from the initial state, by verifying the formula $E^{>k_1} \mathcal{F}(wait \wedge E\mathcal{G} \neg critic)$; the second is to verify whether there is a finite path from the initial state to a state where $wait$ holds, from which more "unfair" paths stem, and this can be done by testing the formula $E\mathcal{F}(wait \wedge E^{>k_2} \mathcal{G} \neg critic)$, or, third, by using the formula $E^{>k_1} \mathcal{F}(wait \wedge E^{>k_2} \mathcal{G} \neg critic)$.

The following example shows the result of running NuSMV and SMV Cadence for a system model implementing mutual exclusion and having more than one unfair path.

Example 1. Consider the model in Figure 1 which violates the graded-CTL formula $\varphi = A^{\leq 1}\mathcal{G}(wait1 \Rightarrow A\mathcal{F}critic1)$.

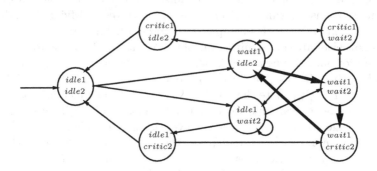

Fig. 1. A mutual exclusion system

When NuSMV (or also SMV Cadence [CCGR99, McM]) runs on this model and on the classical CTL formula corresponding to φ, then it generates as a counterexample the path:

$$\langle (idle1, idle2), (wait1, idle2), (wait1, idle2), \ldots \rangle$$

Then, if the user corrects this error by removing the self-loop on the state labeled $(wait1, idle2)$, the model-checker reports the second path

$$\langle (idle1, idle2), (wait1, idle2), (wait1, wait2), (wait1, critic2), (wait1, idle2), \ldots \rangle.$$

In practice most model-checkers implement *symbolic* algorithms which manipulates state sets represented by BDD. We have hence studied a symbolic algorithm for our setting whose complexity turns out to be $O(2^{|AP|} \cdot k \cdot |\varphi|)$, where k is the maximum value occurring in φ. The extra factor k is due to the fact that when we consider state sets represented symbolically one has to take into account also all sub-formulas of the type $E^{>i}\theta$, $0 < i < k$, for each $E^{>k}\theta$ occurring in the given formula φ. Thus we have the following theorem (whose full proof is in the extended version of the paper [FNP08]).

Theorem 2. *Let $\mathcal{K} = \langle S, s_{in}, R, L \rangle$ be a Kripke structure represented symbolically on a set of atomic propositions AP and let φ be a graded-CTL formula. The graded-CTL model-checking problem can be solved by a symbolic algorithm in time $\mathcal{O}(2^{|AP|} \cdot k \cdot |\varphi|)$, where k is the maximum value occurring in φ.*

4   Edge-Disjoint Graded-CTL Model-Checking

In this section we introduce a different semantics of graded-CTL to distinguish whether different behaviors of the system, satisfying a graded-CTL formula, are completely disjoint. This setting can be applied also to ensure that a "correct" system behavior tolerates a given number of faults of the system.

The edge-disjoint semantics of graded-CTL is given by the relation $\models_{ed}$, which differs from the previous $\models$ relation only for the formulas of the following two types $E^{>k}\mathcal{G}\psi_1$ and $E^{>k}\psi_1\mathcal{U}\psi_2$. In these two cases it is required the edge-disjointness of the *evidences*, that is of the infinite paths satisfying $\mathcal{G}\psi_1$ and of the finite paths satisfying $\psi_1\mathcal{U}\psi_2$. Let us note that the model of Figure 1 does no longer satisfy the formula $E^{>2}\mathcal{F}(wait1 \land E\mathcal{G}\neg critic1)$ now as there are only two disjoint paths that violate the formula.

The **edge-disjoint graded-CTL model-checking** is defined as the problem of determining whether $(\mathcal{K}, s_{in}) \models_{ed} \varphi$, for a Kripke structure $\mathcal{K}$ with initial state s_{in} and a graded-CTL formula φ.

We first prove that the problem is both NP-hard and CONP-hard, and we give an upper bound showing that it lies in PSPACE. Then we introduce a fragment of our logic for which the problem has a polynomial time solution. To show this, we use techniques which are standards for flow network problems, see e.g. [CLRS01]. Finally we give a polynomial time algorithm for the case in which only a given number of single actions of behaviors (edges) must be disjoint and all the others may overlap. Note that this problem is a generalization both of the graded-CTL model-checking and of the edge-disjoint graded-CTL model-checking, since it is equivalent to the former (resp. to the latter) when no actions (all the actions) have to be disjoint.

4.1   Complexity

The proof of the hardness is given by a reduction from the Cycle-Packing problem, defined as follows: given a directed graph G and an integer $n \geq 2$, check whether in G there are at least n edge-disjoint cycles. The Cycle-Packing problem is known to be NP-complete (see [CPR03]).

Theorem 3. *The edge-disjoint graded-CTL model-checking problem is both NP-hard and CONP-hard.*

Proof. We first prove that edge-disjoint model-checking problem is NP-hard for specifications in the graded-CTL fragment $FRAG$ containing only formulas $E^{>k}\mathcal{G}p$, for an atomic proposition p and $k \geq 0$.

Given a graph $G = (\mathcal{V}, \mathcal{E})$ and an instance (G, n), $n \geq 2$, of the Cycle-Packing problem, let $\mathcal{K} = \langle \mathcal{V} \cup \{\hat{s}\}, \hat{s}, R, L \rangle$ be the Kripke structure obtained from G by adding an initial state $\hat{s} \notin \mathcal{V}$, connected to all the other nodes, and by labeling each state of $\mathcal{K}$ with a single atomic proposition p. Formally, $\mathcal{K}$ is defined on the atomic propositions $AP = \{p\}$ in such a way that $R = \mathcal{E} \cup \{(\hat{s}, s)$ s.t. $s \in \mathcal{V}\}$ and $L(s) = \{p\}$ for all $s \in \mathcal{V} \cup \{\hat{s}\}$. Moreover, let us consider the graded-CTL formula $\varphi = E^{>n-1}\mathcal{G}p$. Since $\hat{s}$ is connected to each node of G and has no incoming edges, and since p holds in every node, then it follows that $(\mathcal{K}, \hat{s}) \models_{ed} \varphi$ iff G contains at least n edge-disjoint cycles. From the NP-hardness of the Cycle-Packing problem, the edge-disjoint FRAG model-checking problem is NP-hard as well. The edge-disjoint model-checking problem for specifications expressed with formulas of the type $\neg E^{>k}\mathcal{G}p$ hence turns out to be CONP-hard. Thus the theorem holds.   □

From the previous theorem, we have that the edge-disjoint graded-CTL model-checking problem is not in NP (and not in CONP as well) unless NP = CONP. However we now show an upper bound for this problem. In fact let us consider the following simple algorithm to model-check formulas $E^{>k}\theta$ with either $\theta = \mathcal{G}\psi_1$ or $\theta = \psi_1\mathcal{U}\psi_2$: the Kripke structure is visited to find paths satisfying θ and, each time a path is found, a new visit is recursively started, looking for other paths in the remaining graph, until $k+1$ edge-disjoint paths are found. This algorithm can be easily implemented by using polynomial space, as the overall size of the $k+1$ paths is bounded by $|R|$. Therefore we obtain the following theorem.

Theorem 4. *There is an algorithm to solve the edge-disjoint graded-CTL model-checking problem in space $\mathcal{O}(|R| \cdot |S| + |\varphi|)$.*

4.2   A Fragment

One question that naturally arises from Theorem 3 is whether it is possible to define interesting fragments of graded-CTL for which the edge-disjoint graded-CTL model-checking problem can be solved in polynomial-time. In particular, the proof of Theorem 3 suggests that only formulas of the type $E^{>k}\mathcal{G}\varphi$, with $k > 0$, are "hard" to verify. In this section we introduce a fragment, called graded-RCTL, of graded-CTL not containing formulas of the type $E^{>k}\mathcal{G}\varphi$, with $k > 0$ and show that for it there is a polynomial-time algorithm for the model-checking problem. Note that the fragment is an extension of CTL and that still many significant properties can be expressed within it. For example, consider the property stating that *do not exist more than k bad behaviors such that a device does not start unless a key is pressed*: such a property can be expressed in graded-RCTL with the formula $\neg E^{>k}(\neg key\ \mathcal{U}(start \wedge \neg key))$.

Theorem 5. *Let $\mathcal{K} = \langle S, s_{in}, R, L\rangle$ be a Kripke structure and φ be a graded-RCTL formula. The edge-disjoint graded-RCTL model-checking problem, for $\mathcal{K}$ and φ, can be solved in time $\mathcal{O}(|R|^2 \cdot |S| \cdot |\varphi|)$.*

Proof. Since in the graded-RCTL there are no $E^{>k}\mathcal{G}\psi_1$ formulas, we have only to show how to check sub-formulas $E^{>k}\psi_1\mathcal{U}\psi_2$ with $k > 0$. To this aim we will use ideas from flow networks of the graph theory. Let us recall that a *flow network* is a directed graph with a *source* node, a *destination* node, and with edges having a non-negative capacity representing the amount of data that can be moved through the edge. A *maximum flow* from the source to the destination is the maximum amount of data that a network can move from the source to the destination in the time unit.

The algorithm is identical to Algorithm 1 for graded-CTL, with the lines $17-27$ rewritten as follows (where $d \notin S$ is the destination node, $inDegree(s)$ returns the in-degree of a state s and $MaxFlow(S, R, c, s, d)$ returns the maximum flow from s to d on the graph (S, R) with c as the capacity function on the edges):

17 **case** $\psi = E^{>k}\psi_1 \mathcal{U}\psi_2$ *with* $k > 0$:
18 $\quad\quad S' \leftarrow \{s \in S \mid s.E^{>0}\psi_1\mathcal{U}\psi_2 = \text{TRUE}\} \cup \{d\}$;
19 $\quad\quad R' \leftarrow (R \cap (S' \times S')) \setminus \{(s,t) \mid s.\psi_1 = \text{FALSE}\} \cup \{(s,d) \mid s.\psi_2 = \text{TRUE}\}$;
20 $\quad\quad$ **forall** $e \in R'$ **do** $c(e) = inDegree(s)$ if $e = (s,d)$ and $c(e) = 1$ otherwise;
21 $\quad\quad$ **forall** $s \in S' \setminus \{d\}$ s.t. $MaxFlow(S', R', c, s, d) > k$ **do** $s.\psi \leftarrow \text{TRUE}$;
22 **end**

Our algorithm considers the graph (S', R'), subgraph of $\mathcal{K}$, of the states where the formula $E^{>0}\psi_1\mathcal{U}\psi_2$ holds (without the edges outgoing from states where ψ_1 doesn't hold), and adds a new destination node d with incoming edges from all the nodes where ψ_2 holds (the capacity of the link (s, d) is the in-degree of s, while the remaining edges have capacity 1). It is known that in graphs with all unitary edge capacities, the maximum flow is equal to the maximum number of edge-disjoint paths from the source to the destination node, see e.g. [CLRS01]. However, it is easy to see that in our network the maximum flow from a node s to d is equal to the maximum number of edge-disjoint paths from s to the set $\{t \in S' \setminus \{d\} \mid (t, d) \in R'\}$, therefore our algorithm has only to evaluate the maximum flow from each state to d.

The running-time of the algorithm on a sub-formula $E^{>k}\psi_1\mathcal{U}\psi_2$ depends on the time required to calculate the maximum flow. Note that the total capacity of the edges entering in d is at most $|R|$, therefore the maximum flow from any state to d is upper bounded by $|R|$. Since in this case, the maximum flow can be calculated in time $\mathcal{O}(|R|^2)$, see e.g. [CLRS01], the overall time complexity of the algorithm is $\mathcal{O}(|R|^2 \cdot |S| \cdot |\varphi|)$. $\square$

4.3 A Parameterized Version of the Problem

Let $\mathcal{K} = \langle S, s_{in}, R, L \rangle$ and $\hat{R}$ be a subset of R. We say that two paths π_1 and π_2 in $\mathcal{K}$ are $\hat{R}$-*edge-disjoint* if there are no edges in $\hat{R}$ belonging to both π_1 and π_2. We introduce the relation $\models_{ed}^{\hat{R}}$ which differs from the finer relation $\models_{ed}$ only for the formulas of the type $E^{>k}\mathcal{G}\psi_1$ and $E^{>k}\psi_1\mathcal{U}\psi_2$. In particular, we require the existence of $k + 1$ pairwise $\hat{R}$-edge-disjoint paths satisfying $\mathcal{G}\psi_1$ or $\psi_1\mathcal{U}\psi_2$. Then, the **subset-edge-disjoint graded-CTL model-checking** requires to verify whether $(\mathcal{K}, s_{in}) \models_{ed}^{\hat{R}} \varphi$, for a Kripke structure $\mathcal{K}$, a set $\hat{R} \subseteq R$, and a graded-CTL formula φ.

The lower bound to this problem obviously matches the lower bound of the edge-disjoint graded-CTL model-checking problem. However, in the following theorem we prove that the problem is *fixed parameter* tractable, in fact we solve it in time exponential only in the size of $\hat{R}$, obtaining thus a good algorithm for practical cases.

Theorem 6. *Let $\mathcal{K} = \langle S, s_{in}, R, L \rangle$ be a Kripke structure, $\hat{R} \subseteq R$ and φ be a graded-CTL formula. The subset-edge-disjoint graded-CTL model-checking problem can be solved in time $\mathcal{O}((4^{|\hat{R}|} \cdot |R| + 2^{|\hat{R}|^2}) \cdot |S| \cdot |\varphi|)$ and in space $\mathcal{O}(4^{|\hat{R}|} \cdot |\hat{R}| + |R| + |\varphi|)$.*

Proof. Since the difference between graded-CTL and subset-edge-disjoint graded-CTL model-checking is only in the satisfiability of formulas $E^{>k}\theta$, with the path-formula θ being either $\theta = \mathcal{G}\psi_1$ or $\theta = \psi_1\mathcal{U}\psi_2$ and $k > 0$, the algorithm to solve our problem is identical to Algorithm 1, but for the extra input value $\hat{R}$, and for the lines 17-27 replaced by these:

17 **case** $\psi = E^{>k}\theta$ with $\theta = \mathcal{G}\psi_1$ or $\theta = \psi_1\mathcal{U}\psi_2$ and $k > 0$:
18 | **forall** $s \in S$ **do**
19 | | $I \leftarrow \{i \in \{k+1-|\hat{R}|,\ldots,k+1\} \mid i \geq 0$ and $\exists\ i$ distinct paths from s satisfying θ without using edges in $\hat{R}\}$;
20 | | **if** $I \neq \emptyset$ **then**
21 | | | $\hat{k} \leftarrow k+1-\max\{i \mid i \in I\}$;
22 | | | **if** $\hat{k} = 0$ **then** $s.\psi \leftarrow$ TRUE; **continue**;
23 | | | $\mathcal{V} \leftarrow \{T \mid T$ is the set of edges of $\hat{R}$ occurring in an evidence of $\theta\}$;
24 | | | $\mathcal{E} \leftarrow \{(T,T') \in \mathcal{V}^2 \mid T \cap T' = \emptyset\}$;
25 | | | **if** $\exists$ a clique with size $\hat{k}$ in $(\mathcal{V},\mathcal{E})$ **then** $s.\psi \leftarrow$ TRUE;
26 | | **end**
27 | **end**
28 **end**

This part of the algorithm works as follows. Consider a state $s \in S$. As the number of $\hat{R}$-edge-disjoint evidences of θ which use at least one edge belonging to $\hat{R}$ is bounded by $|\hat{R}|$ itself, the number of the remaining evidences of θ (not using edges of $\hat{R}$) must be greater than $k+1-|\hat{R}|$ (otherwise $(\mathcal{K}, s) \not\models_{ed}^{\hat{R}} E^{>k}\theta$). Thus the algorithm first determines a number $\hat{k}$, lines 19-21, with the property that: $(\mathcal{K}, s) \models_{ed}^{\hat{R}} E^{>k}\theta$ if and only if there are $\hat{k}$ $\hat{R}$-edge-disjoint evidences of θ which use at least one edge belonging to $\hat{R}$. Then the graph $(\mathcal{V},\mathcal{E})$, described in lines 23 and 24, is computed, such that a vertex in $\mathcal{V}$ is a set of edges of $\hat{R}$ which occur in an evidence of θ in $\mathcal{K}$ and an edge in $\mathcal{E}$ connects two disjoint such sets. Thus, $(\mathcal{K}, s) \models_{ed}^{\hat{R}} E^{>k}\theta$ iff in the graph $(\mathcal{V},\mathcal{E})$ there is a clique of size $\hat{k}$.

Let us evaluate the running time and the space required by the algorithm. Since the set I described in line 19 is such that $|I| \leq |\hat{R}|$, the lines 19-21 can be easily computed in time $\mathcal{O}(|R| \cdot |\hat{R}|)$ by using a simple variation of Algorithm 1. Moreover, for a given subset T of $\hat{R}$, the existence of an evidence of θ which uses *all* the edges in T and possibly edges of $R \setminus \hat{R}$, can be verified in time $\mathcal{O}(|R|)$, while the set of edges outgoing from T can be computed in time $\mathcal{O}(2^{|\hat{R}|} \cdot |\hat{R}|)$; therefore the graph $(\mathcal{V},\mathcal{E})$ can be computed in time $\mathcal{O}(4^{|\hat{R}|} \cdot |R|)$. Finally, the existence of a clique of size $\hat{k} \leq |\hat{R}|$ can be verified in time $\mathcal{O}(2^{|\hat{R}|^2})$.

The algorithm needs, to model-check a formula $E^{>k}\theta$ in a state $s \in S$, space $\mathcal{O}(4^{|\hat{R}|} \cdot |\hat{R}|)$ to store the graph $(\mathcal{V},\mathcal{E})$ and space $\mathcal{O}(|R|)$ to calculate the path needed to verify whether a non-empty subset T of $\hat{R}$ is in $\mathcal{V}$. Moreover, the algorithm globally needs only $3 \cdot |S|$ truth values for the sub-formulas (two for the operands and one for the operator in each state). Therefore the space required by the algorithm is $\mathcal{O}(4^{|\hat{R}|} \cdot |\hat{R}| + |R| + |\varphi|)$. $\square$

In the extended version of the paper [FNP08] we show how to modify this algorithm to fit in polynomial space.

5 Discussion

In this paper we have introduced the graded-CTL as a more expressive extension of classical CTL. The results presented are in the model-checking setting with specifications in this logic. We have investigated the complexities involved in various scenarios, all from a theoretical perspective. One possible future direction to work on, is to verify in practice whether an existing model-checker tool could be augmented with these grading modalities, retaining the usual performances. We believe that this framework could turn out to be useful also in the verification of fault tolerant physical properties of networks.

As said in the introduction, in [KSV02] the satisfiability problem has been studied for the graded μ-calculus obtaining the same complexity as for the non-graded logic. We have investigated the problem in our setting of graded-CTL (reported in the extended version [FNP08]) and have proved that it is EXPTIME-complete, when the values in the formula are represented in unary. An open problem is hence to establish the complexity when the values are in binary.

Another theoretical aspect to investigate is also with respect to the Linear Temporal Logic LTL. Also here this *graded* framework is a strict extension of the standard logic, but, differently to what happens for graded CTL, a straightforward algorithm to solve the model-checking problem, seems here to involve the values representing the graded modalities.

Finally let us mention a drawback of our setting. As said in the introduction the generation of more than one counterexample is highly desirable, however the analyze stage (of the realization process of a system) is critical also for the size of the counterexamples and the poor human-readability of it.

References

[CCGR99]   Cimatti, A., Clarke, E.M., Giunchiglia, F., Roveri, M.: NUSMV: A new symbolic model verifier. In: Halbwachs, N., Peled, D.A. (eds.) CAV 1999. LNCS, vol. 1633, pp. 495–499. Springer, Heidelberg (1999)
[CG07]   Chechik, M., Gurfinkel, A.: A framework for counterexample generation and exploration. Int. J. Softw. Tools Technol. Transf. 9(5), 429–445 (2007)
[CGP99]   Clarke, E.M., Grumberg, O., Peled, D.: Model Checking. MIT Press, Cambridge (1999)
[CIW+01]   Copty, F., Irron, A., Weissberg, O., Kropp, N.P., Kamhi, G.: Efficient debugging in a formal verification environment. In: Margaria, T., Melham, T.F. (eds.) CHARME 2001. LNCS, vol. 2144, pp. 275–292. Springer, Heidelberg (2001)
[CLRS01]   Cormen, T.H., Leiserson, C.E., Rivest, R.L., Stein, C.: Introduction to Algorithms, 2nd edn. MIT Press, Cambridge (2001)
[CPR03]   Caprara, A., Panconesi, A., Rizzi, R.: Packing cycles in undirected graphs. Journal of Algorithms 48(1), 239–256 (2003)

[CV03]   Clarke, E.M., Veith, H.: Counterexamples revisited: Principles, algorithms, applications. In: Verification: Theory and Practice, pp. 208–224 (2003)

[DRS03]   Dong, Y., Ramakrishnan, C.R., Smolka, S.A.: Model checking and evidence exploration. In: ECBS, pp. 214–223 (2003)

[Fin72]   Fine, K.: In so many possible worlds. Notre Dame Journal of Formal Logic 13(4), 516–520 (1972)

[FNP08]   Ferrante, A., Napoli, M., Parente, M.: Graded CTL. In: Preparation (2008)

[GMV99]   Ganzinger, H., Meyer, C., Veanes, M.: The two–variable guarded fragment with transitive relations. In: LICS, pp. 24–34 (1999)

[GOR97]   Grädel, E., Otto, M., Rosen, E.: Two–variable logic with counting is decidable. In: LICS, pp. 306–317 (1997)

[HB91]   Hollunder, B., Baader, F.: Qualifying number restrictions in concept languages. In: KR, pp. 335–346 (1991)

[Hol97]   Holzmann, G.J.: The model checker SPIN. IEEE Transactions on Software Engineering 23(5), 279–295 (1997)

[KSV02]   Kupferman, O., Sattler, U., Vardi, M.Y.: The complexity of the graded μ–calculus. In: CADE-18: Proceedings of the 18th International Conference on Automated Deduction, London, UK, pp. 423–437. Springer, Heidelberg (2002)

[McM]   McMillan, K.: The Cadence smv model checker, http://www.kenmcmil.com/psdoc.html

[PST00]   Pacholski, L., Szwast, W., Tendera, L.: Complexity results for first–order two–variable logic with counting. SIAM Journal of Computing 29(4), 1083–1117 (2000)

[QS82]   Queille, J.P., Sifakis, J.: Specification and verification of concurrent systems in cesar. In: Proc. of the 5th Colloquium on Intern. Symposium on Programming, London, UK, pp. 337–351. Springer, Heidelberg (1982)

[Tob01]   Tobies, S.: PSPACE reasoning for graded modal logics. Journal Log. Comput. 11(1), 85–106 (2001)

Genetic Programming and Model Checking: Synthesizing New Mutual Exclusion Algorithms

Gal Katz and Doron Peled

Department of Computer Science
Bar Ilan University
Ramat Gan 52900, Israel

Abstract. Recently, genetic programming and model checking were combined for synthesizing algorithms that satisfy a given specification [7,6]. In particular, we demonstrated this approach by developing a tool that was able to rediscover the classical mutual exclusion algorithms [7] with two or three global bits. In this paper we extend the capabilities of the model checking-based genetic programming and the tool built to experiment with this approach. In particular, we add qualitative requirements involving locality of variables and checks, which are typical of realistic mutual exclusion algorithms. The genetic process mimics the actual development of mutual exclusion algorithms, by starting with an existing correct solution, which does not satisfy some performance requirements, and converging into a solution that satisfies these requirements. We demonstrate this by presenting some nontrivial new mutual exclusion algorithms, discovered with our tool.

1 Introduction

The development of correct code for concurrent systems can be quite challenging. Some tasks like achieving mutual exclusion, cache coherence, linearized executions or committing a database transactions, are quite intricate. Classical software engineering methods do not seem to provide the right way of approaching this kind of involved problems. Guaranteeing correctness for such programs is also not trivial. Manual proof methods, for verifying the correctness of the code against a given formal specification, were suggested in the late 60s [4,2]. The next step for achieving more reliable software was to offer an automatic verification procedure, called model checking [1,17]. Automatic synthesizing of protocols followed, although their complexity was shown to be rather high [16].

Genetic programming (GP) is an automatic program generation methodology. A population of programs is randomly created, and evolves by a biologically inspired process. The fitness of each program is usually calculated by running the program on some test cases, and evaluating its performance. Recently, Johnson [6] suggested using the model checking for providing the fitness function for synthesizing a reactive system. In his approach, the fitness is simply based on the number of properties that the generated program satisfies. In [7], we presented an approach for genetic programming based on model checking, which involves a

Cha et al. (Eds.): ATVA 2008, LNCS 5311, pp. 33–47, 2008.

deeper analysis than standard model checking. This approach assigns a weight, also called *fitness*, of 0 to 100 to each generated mutation, even if the program does not fully satisfy all the specified properties. For example, there can be bad executions of the program not satisfying some given property, but the program may still subscribe to a weaker notion of correctness, e.g., each prefix of a bad execution can be completed into a good one.

The method presented in [7] was demonstrated using a tool for the automatic generation of concurrent programs, with examples from mutual exclusion. The solutions generated by our tool were discovered quite quickly and efficiently. However, the experiments in that paper were limited to mutual exclusion based on up to three global bits. Inspired by [20], we observed that, in fact, mutual exclusion algorithms are, in practice, being developed manually in a way that is reminiscent of the genetic programming process. Namely, one combines or modifies existing algorithms that do not completely satisfy the specification, or are less efficient according to some given criterion, into a better solution. This helps in understanding the success of this approach: progressing from one version to another, while improving or optimizing various aspects of the code, rather than concentrating on finding directly a perfect solution. Thus, to some extent, genetic programming serves as a heuristic search in the domain of syntactically matching programs, based on a ranking that is provided by a model checking analysis.

In this work, we continue the work reported in [7] by performing several changes and extensions. We are still focusing on the generation of mutual exclusion algorithms, although are now aiming at finding more realistic ones, which satisfy various additional criteria than the classical ones. First, we modify the weights given to mutations generated by the genetic programming according to some qualitative properties, e.g., that processes will be able to wait only on their own variables (i.e., local-spinning, see [19]). This means that instead of always starting the genetic process with a set of randomly generated mutations, we apply the model checking-based genetic programming to solutions of the mutual exclusion that are *correct* according to the temporal specification, but score low with respect to the quality requirements.

In addition, we adopt here the use of specification formalism that is a subset of the logic $EmCTL^*$, presented in [14]. This formalism allows refining the results of model checking from the traditional yes/no and counterexample paradigm. Even if a program does not satisfy its specification formalism, we can still attach some positive score to it based on such formulas. The model checking algorithm in [14] is based on Büchi automata (an alternative algorithm, based on alternating automata can be found in [12]), and can replace the various ad-hoc algorithms presented in [7] for the different level of correctness by a uniform algorithm. Moreover, this logic allows us to easily and naturally add further levels of correctness, refining the fitness score assigned to candidate solutions during the genetic process.

Finally, we demonstrate our revised and improved tool by presenting some newly generated algorithms for mutual exclusion that, as far as we are aware, were not published before. These new solutions provide some small improvements over existing algorithms, demonstrating the ability of our method to effectively and efficiently generating code for this intricate concurrency management problem.

2 Related Work

2.1 Genetic Programming

Genetic Programming [10] (GP) is a method of automatic synthesis of computer programs by an evolutionary process. An initial population of candidate solutions is randomly generated and gradually improved by various biologically inspired operations.

The GP algorithm we use in this work progresses through the following steps: We first create an initial population of candidate solutions. Then we choose randomly a subset of μ candidates. We create new (more than μ) candidates by applying mutation (and optionally crossover, as explained below) to the above μ candidates. The fitness function for each of the new candidates is calculated, and μ individuals from the obtained set are selected proportionally to their fitness (see [5]). The selected individuals then replace the old candidates. This is repeated until a perfect candidate is found, or until the maximal permitted number of iterations is reached.

The programs are represented as trees where each instruction or expression is represented by an internal node having its parameters as its children. Strongly-typed GP [13] is used, which means that every node has a type, which also enforces the type of its offspring.

While traditional GP is heavily based on the crossover operation, i.e., the combination of two mutations of the code into one, it is currently quite controversial, especially in the case of small and sensitive programs that we investigate. Thus, crossover is not used in our work. Instead, the main operation we use is mutation. This includes randomly choosing a node (leaf or terminal) from the program tree and changing the node by one of the following operations: replacing the node subtree by a new randomly generated subtree, deleting the subtree rooted by the node, adding an immediate parent to the node, or removing the immediate parent of the node. The strong typing we apply directs each one of these changes to be accompanied by an appropriate correction of the tree structure. For example, if we add a new node above an existing one, we may need to complete some other children to this new node, according to the type of the added node.

Fitness is used by GP in order to choose which mutations have a higher probability to survive and participate in the genetic operations. The successful termination of the genetic algorithm is based on the fitness value of the most fitted individual. Traditionally, the fitness function is calculated by running the program on some typical test suite. Johnsson [6] suggested to replace the use of a test suite for fitness calculation by the more comprehensive model checking, providing fitness that is directly proportional to the number of satisfied properties. However, traditional model checking results provide a discrete ranking paradigm, whereas genetic programming is based on the ability to identify levels of success. Instead, in [7], we presented an approach for model checking that allowed identifying progress in the generated code even if some of the properties were only partially satisfied.

2.2   Model Checking

Model checking is an algorithmic approach for checking the correctness of a program or an electronic circuit against a formal specification. For the algorithms we would like to develop with our approach, we use linear specification, i.e., a specification that requires that *all* the execution satisfy some given properties, written in our selected formalism, which is Linear Temporal Logic (LTL). Other formalisms can assert about the branching structure that involves all the executions, observing the splitting points where executions start to differ from each other.

The syntax of LTL is defined over a finite set of propositions $\mathcal{P}$, with typical element $p \in \mathcal{P}$, as follows:

$$\mu ::= true \,|\, p \,|\, \mu \vee \mu \,|\, \neg \mu \,|\, X\mu \,|\, \mu \, U \, \mu \tag{1}$$

Let M be a finite structure $(S, \{s_0\}, E, \mathcal{P}, L)$ with states S, an initial state, $s_0 \in S$, edges $E \subseteq S \times S$, a set of propositions $\mathcal{P}$, and a labeling function $L : S \mapsto 2^{\mathcal{P}}$. For simplicity, we assume that each state in S has a successor. This can be forced by adding to each state without successors a self loop, marked with a special symbol ϵ. A *path* in S is a finite or infinite sequence $\langle g_0 g_1 g_2 \ldots \rangle$, where $g_0 \in S$ and for each $i \geq 0$, $g_i E g_{i+1}$. An *execution* is an infinite path, starting with $g_0 = s_0$. Sometimes executions are further restricted to satisfy various fairness assumptions.

We denote the ith state of a path π by π_i, the suffix of π from the ith state by π^i and the prefix of π up to the ith state by $\hat{\pi}^i$. The concatenation of two paths ρ and π, where the last state of ρ is the same as first state of π, is denoted by $\rho \frown \pi$. Note that $\langle \pi_0 \rangle \frown \pi = \pi$, and that $\rho \frown \langle s \rangle = \rho$, where s is necessarily the last state of ρ.

The LTL semantics is defined for a suffix of an execution π of M as follows:

$\pi \models true$.
$\pi \models p$ if $p \in L(\pi_0)$.
$\pi \models \mu_1 \vee \mu_2$ if either $\pi \models \mu_1$ or $\pi \models \mu_2$.
$\pi \models \neg\mu$ if it is not the case that $\pi \models \mu$.
$\pi \models X\mu$ if $\pi^1 \models \mu$.
$\pi \models \mu U \eta$ if there exists some i such that $\pi^i \models \eta$ and for each $0 \leq j < i$, $\pi^j \models \mu$.

We say that a structure M (or the corresponding program that is modeled as M) satisfies μ if for each execution π of μ, $\pi \models \mu$. We use the logical connections to define additional temporal operators, e.g., $\mu_1 \rightarrow \mu_2 = (\neg\mu_1) \vee \mu_2$, $\mu_1 \wedge \mu_2 = \neg((\neg\mu_1) \vee (\neg\mu_2))$, $\Diamond\mu = true U \mu$, $\Box\mu = \neg\Diamond\neg\mu$, etc.

Model checking can be conducted as follows: the negation of the checked property μ is translated into an automaton (see e.g., [3]). This is a Büchi automaton, i.e., an automaton over infinite words, which has a similar structure to an automaton over finite words. Then this automaton is intersected with the structure M. Any common execution is an execution that *does not* satisfy the checked property, hence a counterexample.

3 Model Checking-Based Genetic Programming

Our program synthesizing approach is based on genetic programming that uses analysis related to model checking for providing a scoring system (fitness) for the generated mutations. As opposed to classical model checking, we are not satisfied with a pass/failed answer. In order to direct the search towards an appropriate solution, a less discrete scoring system is required, one which allows using mutations that are not perfectly correct. Thus, the scoring system is based on the following ideas:

1. A mutation candidate may satisfy some properties but not the others. Keeping it may improve the missing properties, albeit also ruin the satisfied properties. In [20], it is shown how the classical Peterson's mutual exclusion algorithm is combined from two solutions that solve part of the specification each. This combination is similar to the result of the crossover operation in genetic programming.

   One needs to carefully select the way to weight different properties. For example, one natural approach is to make the safety properties more basic hence more dominating in the overall score than liveness.
2. Properties presented here have a universal flavor: a program satisfies a property if all of its executions satisfy it. One can relax this criterion; weaker notions of satisfactions can be considered. For example, although there are some executions that do not satisfy the given property, they can be completed into executions that satisfy it. One can define a hierarchy of satisfiability of properties by a program. In particular, programs with *no* good executions that satisfy a given property μ are ranked lowest, programs with *both* good and bad executions are ranked higher than that, while programs where *all* the executions satisfy μ are ranked even higher.
3. In addition to the correctness criteria required by the programming problem, there can be some *quality* criteria. This can involve the size of the program, and limitations on the number of access to variables (e.g., number of accesses before entering a critical section), as will be demonstrated later.

4 A Uniform Formalism for Relaxed Satisfaction of LTL Properties

In constructing the fitness function, we promote programs that are less than perfect to the next stage of the search. This means that in addition to promoting programs that satisfy part of the specification properties, we also relax the requirement that *all* the executions of the program need to satisfy the given LTL specification.

4.1 The Logic *EmCTL*

In [7] we introduced model checking algorithms that extend the usual LTL model checking approach; they were used to provide an analysis for situations where not all the executions satisfy a given property, but do not seem completely hopeless. We defined several such criteria, and provided some ad-hoc algorithms for each one of them. These algorithms were based on translating the checked property to a deterministic Streett automaton and taking the product with the checked system M. Then a slightly different analysis, one for each criterion, was applied, based on the the strongly connected components of the product and the connection between them.

We use here LTL specification μ to provide the *base* specification, where correctness means that all the executions satisfy μ. We observe that even when the system does not satisfy this correctness criterion, it may have both executions that satisfy and that do not satisfy this property. Thus, we can embed μ in an *analysis specification*, which observes the branching structure of M. The logic $EmCTL^*$ presented in [14], allows us to embed the LTL property inside a branching formula. It can distinguish the branching points where the execution splits into two branches, such that, together with the prefix so far, one satisfies μ and another satisfies $\neg\mu$.

The subset of $EmCTL^*$ that we use, and call simply $EmCTL$, has *state formulas* of the form:

$$\varphi ::= true \,|\, \varphi \vee \varphi \,|\, \neg\varphi \,|\, \exists^\mu \psi$$

with μ an LTL formula, and *path formulas* of the form

$$\psi ::= \psi \vee \psi \,|\, \neg\psi \Diamond \varphi$$

Note that these formulas do not contain any propositional variables, nor the until (U) modality.

The semantics given for an $EmCTL$ state formula is of the form $M, \rho, s \models \psi$, where ρ is a finite prefix of an execution in M, leading to (i.e., ending with) the state s. The semantics given for a path formula ψ is of the form $M, \rho, \pi \models \psi$, where ρ is again a finite prefix of an execution of M, leading up to a state from which an infinite path π of M starts (thus, $\rho \frown \pi$ is an infinite execution of M). A path subformula ψ is then evaluated in $M, \rho, \pi \models \psi$ according to the path π.

Intuitively, in the semantic definition of $M, \rho, s \models \psi$ and, similarly, in the definition of $M, \rho, \pi \models \psi$, we keep the path so far ρ, so that we can assert whether the base property holds from the beginning of the execution or not. As we progress with the temporal operators in time over some finite fragment of a path, this fragment is appended to ρ and removed from π. We can use the $\exists^\mu$ operator to assert about the existence of a path π, such that, together with the prefix ρ, forms an execution $\rho \frown \pi$ satisfying the base property μ. Similarly, we can use $\exists^{\neg\mu}$ to assert about the existence of such a path that together with the prefix ρ does not satisfy μ. The formal semantics is given as follows.

$M, \rho, s \models true$.
$M, \rho, s \models \varphi_1 \vee \varphi_2$ if either $M, \rho, s \models \varphi_1$ or $M, \rho, s \models \varphi_2$.
$M, \rho, s \models \neg\varphi$ if it is not the case that $M, \rho, s \models \varphi$.
$M, \rho, s \models \exists^{\mu}\psi$ if there exists a path π of M such that $\pi_0 = s$ and $M, \rho, \pi \models \psi$, and furthermore, $\rho \frown \pi \models \mu$ in LTL.
$M, \rho, \pi \models \psi_1 \vee \psi_2$ if either $M, \rho, \pi \models \psi_1$ or $M, \rho, \pi \models \psi_2$.
$M, \rho, \pi \models \neg\psi$ if it is not the case that $M, \rho, \pi \models \psi$.
$M, \rho, \pi \models \Diamond\varphi$ if there exists some i such that $M, \rho \frown \hat{\pi}^i, s_i \models \varphi$.

Other operators can be obtained using equivalences, e.g., $false = \neg true$, $\psi_1 \wedge \psi_2 = \neg((\neg\psi_1) \vee (\neg\psi_2))$, $\psi_1 \rightarrow \psi_2 = (\neg\psi_1) \vee \psi_2$, $\forall^{\mu}\psi = \neg\exists^{\mu}\neg\psi$, $\Box\psi = \neg\Diamond\neg\psi$.

Our choice to eliminate the propositions from the logic $EmCTL$ is based on our goal to keep the requirement on the desired program entirely in the base specification μ. The analysis specification only allows us to evaluate to what extent the program satisfies μ, providing different levels of satisfaction of μ. The elimination of the *until* operator U (which still exists in the base specification) is for simplicity, and a matter of taste: we could not find a single useful (for our purposes) analysis specification that requires U.

Examples for Relaxed LTL Satisfaction
Given an LTL property μ, we can express several EmCTL properties that are based on μ. These properties represent several levels of satisfaction of μ.

1. $\neg\exists^{\neg\mu} true$. There are no bad executions, i.e., executions that do not satisfy the property μ (hence satisfies $\neg\mu$). Equivalently, we can write $\forall^{\neg\mu} false$. This is the *perfect* (i.e., strongest) requirement from μ, and the standard interpretation for a program to satisfy the LTL specification μ (as defined above).
2. $\forall^{\neg\varphi}\Box\exists^{\varphi} true$. For each prefix of a bad execution of the program there is a completion into a good execution of the program. This means that a bad execution is a result of an infinite number of bad scheduling choices.
3. $\exists^{\neg\mu}\Diamond\neg\exists^{\mu} true$. There exists an execution such that from some point all the continuations are bad. This means that the program can reach a point where whatever choice is made, the LTL property μ will not be satisfied.
4. $\exists^{\mu} true$. There is a good execution (although there *can* also be bad ones). This is the *minimal* requirement we can write in $EmCTL$ for μ.
5. $\exists^{\mu} true \wedge \exists^{\neg\mu} true$ There is a good execution, as well as a bad one.
6. $\neg\exists^{\mu} true$. There is not a good execution.

4.2   Model Checking and Complexity

A model checking algorithm for the logic $EmCTL^*$ was given in [14]. The main principle is that one needs to translate the property μ (and $\neg\mu$, depending which appear in the formula) into a Büchi automaton. Then one needs to perform a subset construction, so that for every prefix of the execution it is known in *which states*, the (in general nondeterministic) automaton can be. This allows, depending on the path quantifier $\exists^\mu$ or $\exists^{\neg\mu}$, to check whether the current execution can satisfy, in addition to the current subformula, also the property μ or $\neg\mu$, *from the beginning of the execution*. An alternative model checking procedure, based on alternating tree automata appears in [12].

This algorithm can replace the ad-hoc algorithms that were given in [7]. These were based on translating the formula μ into a deterministic Streett automaton, and checking for several cases of strongly connected components of the intersection product with the system automaton M. In both cases, the complexity is in PSPACE in the size of a standard representation of the system M (given as a collection of processes), and EXSPACE in the size of the property μ. This makes the complexity exponentially worst than model checking in the size of μ; but it is still the same in the size of the checked system M, which is usually the dominant factor here. The lower bound for the related logic $mCTL^*$ in [12] is also the lower bound for $EmCTL$: the lower bound was shown there for a property that can be expressed in $EmCTL$ as $\forall^{\neg\mu}\Box\exists^\mu true$.

As for the emptiness of $EmCTL$ properties: one can use the translation from $EmCTL^*$ into $mCTL^*$, shown in [14], then apply the $mCTL^*$ emptiness procedure in [12], which is in 2EXPTIME.

5 New Principles for Model Checking-Based Genetic Programming

In this section we will describe the new principles that we implemented for the genetic programming using model checking. With each principle, we present a new solution to the mutual exclusion algorithm.

All of the generated algorithms should comply with the following structure:

```
Non Critical Section
Pre Protocol
Critical Section
Post Protocol
```

The goal of the evolutionary algorithm is to generate the `Pre Protocol` and `Post Protocol` parts, while the other parts are fixed. Each one of the solutions has two processes 0 and 1, where for each process, the constant me denotes the process number and the constant other denotes the other process number. Hence me+other= 1.

Table 1 describes the requirements from the generated algorithms. All of the properties are expressed in LTL, except the last one which involves a special algorithm described below. The four program parts are denoted NonCS, Pre, CS and Post respectively. The proposition **remote writing** refers to transitions on which a process modifies bits that are not assigned to it.

The fitness values for each generated algorithm are based on $EmCTL$ formulae (see section 4.1), and are depicted on table 2. In addition, a secondary measure

Table 1. Mutual Exclusion Specification

No.	Definition	Description
1	$\Box\neg(p_0$ in CS $\wedge$ p_1 in CS)	Mutual Exclusion
2,3	$\Box(p_{me}$ in Post $\rightarrow \Diamond(p_{me}$ in NonCS))	Progress
4,5	$\Box(p_{me}$ in Pre $\wedge$ $\Box(p_{other}$ in NonCS)) $\rightarrow \Diamond(p_{me}$ in CS))	No Contest
6	$\Box((p_0$ in Pre $\wedge$ p_1 in Pre) $\rightarrow \Diamond(p_0$ in CS $\vee$ p_1 in CS))	Deadlock Freedom
7,8	$\Box(p_{me}$ in Pre $\rightarrow \Diamond(p_{me}$ in CS))	Starvation Freedom
9	$\Box\neg($remote writing$)$	Single-Writer
10	Bounded number of remote operations	Local-Spinning

Table 2. *EmCTL* Properties, and Fitness Values

emCTL property	Fitness value	Description
$\neg\exists^\mu true$	0	All executions are bad
$\exists^{\neg\mu}\Diamond\neg\exists^\mu true$	1	There is a bad execution that cannot be completed into a good one
$\forall^{\neg\varphi}\Box\exists^\varphi true$	2	Every prefix of a bad execution can be completed into a good one
$\neg\exists^{\neg\mu} true$	3	All executions are good

gives fitness values to programs in inverse proportion to their size. This measure encourages the creation of shorter algorithms.

In all of the following algorithms, we start the search with an existing algorithm, such as the classical Peterson algorithm [15]:

```
Non Critical Section
A[me] = 1
turn = me
While (A[other] == 1 and turn == me);
Critical Section
A[me] = 0
```

5.1 Allowing Asymmetry

Inspired by algorithms of Kessels [8] and Tsay [20], the first step was to allow a minor asymmetry between the two processes. This is done by defining the asymmetric *not* operators *not0* and *not1*, which act only on one of the processes. Thus, for process 0, $not0(x) = \neg x$ while for process 1, $not0(x) = x$. This is reversed for $not1(x)$, which negates its bit operand x only in process 1, and is idempotent on process 0. Using these operators allows us to keep the same syntactic structure for the two-processes algorithms, while allowing them to behave in an asymmetric way.

For the first test, we used a similar configuration as in our previous paper [7], i.e., three shared bits A[0], A[1] and A[2], and allowing the constructs if, while, and assignment. The specification included properties 1-8 from table 1. The tool found two algorithms which may be considered simpler than Peterson's. The first one has only one condition on the while loop, although a more complicated atomic comparison between two bits. Note that the variable turn is in fact A[2] and is renamed here turn to accord with classical presentation of the extra global bit that does not belong to a specific process.

```
Non Critical Section
A[me] = 1
turn = me
While (A[other] != not1(turn));
Critical Section
A[me] = 0
```

When translating this algorithm to a process-dependent syntax, we get the following asymmetric algorithm:

```
Process 0                      Process 1
---------                      ---------
Non Critical Section           Non Critical Section
A[0] = 1                       A[1] = 1
turn = 0                       turn = 1
While (A[1] != turn);          While (A[0] == turn);
Critical Section               Critical Section
A[0] = 0                       A[1] = 0
```

The second algorithm discovered the idea of setting the turn bit one more time after leaving the critical section. This allows the while condition to be even simpler. Tsay [20] used a similar refinement, but his algorithm needs an additional if statement, which is not needed in our algorithm.

```
Non Critical Section
A[me] = 1
turn = not0(A[other])
While (turn != me);
Critical Section
A[me] = 0
turn = other
```

5.2   Adding New 'Qualitative' Constraints

Classical algorithms, such as Peterson's, do not take into account the additional overhead in waiting on a variable that belongs to the memory of another process, and thus do not satisfy *local-spinning* [19]. Here, we added a negative weight for such remote accesses. In fact, we can calculate the number of accesses, and by giving negative weights to such accesses, promote solutions that provide the least such number.

Calculating the Maximal Number of Non-Local Accesses. In order to calculate the number of non-local accesses, we can apply the following algorithm. First, we mark edges that correspond to transitions with access to non-local variables on the state graph M. Now, we calculate the strongly connected components of the graph, using Tarjan's classical algorithm [18]. If there is a strongly connected component that contains a marked edge and is reachable from the initial state, then the number of such accesses is unbounded, since we can generate a path that would go though the marked edge as many times as we want. Otherwise, we shrink each such strongly connected component into a single node (any path through it does not contribute any remote accesses, so it is unimportant to the analysis). The result is then a DAG (directed acyclic graph).

Now, we perform a depth first search, calculating for each node the number of maximal number of accesses from it to a leaf node (a node without successors). For a leaf node, the number of accesses is 0. For each node s that appeared in the search, we keep some value $a(s)$, which is the maximal number of accesses to a leaf node found so far. When we first reach s in the search, we set $a(s)$ to 0. When we backtrack in the DFS over an edge $s \to t$ back to s we update $a(s)$ as follows:

If $s \to t$ is marked as non-local access, then $a(s) := max(a(s), a(t) + 1)$.
Otherwise, $a(s) := max(a(s), a(t))$.

It is easy to see that during the execution the following invariant holds: upon backtracking from a node s, $a(s)$ contains the maximal number of accesses to a leaf node is maintained, until the end of the execution of the algorithm.

In order to apply the above algorithm for the case of mutual exclusion algorithm, observe that for a correct solution, the program consists of one strongly connected component. Thus, we need first to break the code and apply the above algorithm separately, first to the pre-protocol, representing the attempt to enter the critical section, and then to the post-protocol, immediately following the exit from the critical section. Then, we sum up the result of applying the algorithm to the two parts.

5.3 Applying the New Constraints

In the next attempts we tried to automatically generate more sophisticated mutual exclusion algorithms by adding new constrains. The configuration was extended into four shared bits (denoted by the two-bit vectors A and B), and two private bits (one for each process) denoted by the array T.

The first requirement was that each process can change only its 2 local bits, but can read all of the 4 shared bits (each process can also read from, and write to its private bit). The new "single-writer" constraint was specified as a safety property on the transitions, verifying that no process writes to the bits of the other process (property 9 at table 1). This yielded the following algorithm.

```
Non Critical Section
A[me] = 1
B[me] = not1(B[other])
While (A[other] == 1 and B[0] == not1(B[1]));
Critical Section
A[me] = 0
```

As can be seen, the genetic algorithm has discovered the idea of using two bits as the "turn" flag, where each process changes only its bit B[me] to set its turn, but compares both B[0] and B[1] on the while loop (and thus requires unbounded number of remote read operations). Our next goal was to avoid such unbounded remote operations by allowing busy waiting only on local bits (i.e., requiring local-spinning only). The requirement was implemented by the strongly connected components analysis described earlier. One of the results was:

```
Non Critical Section
A[other] = 1
B[0] = other
B[1] = B[0]
While (A[me] != 0 and B[me] != me);
Critical Section
A[other] = 0
```

This time, the while loop involves only local bits, but in order to set the turn, both processes have to write to the same bits (B[0] and B[1]).

At the final step, both "single-writer" and "local-spinning" were required (requirements 9 and 10 at table 1). Note that this time requirement 9 is slightly changed, so each process can modify only the bits of the other process. As a result, the following algorithm (similar to Kessels') was generated:

```
Non Critical Section
A[other] = 1
B[other] = not1(B[0])
T[me] = not1(B[other])
While (A[me] == 1 and B[me] == T[me]);
Critical Section
A[other] = 0
```

This algorithm also adds the idea of copying one of the turn bits into a private variable T[me], thus allowing the two requirements to co-exist.

One of the ideas suggested by [20] (and found by our tool, as shown above), is to add a redundant assignment of the turn flag after leaving the critical section. When trying to evolve this idea into the more advanced two-bits-turn, a problem arises. A single evolutionary step should cause the same complicated change to the two identical turn assignments at different parts of the program. While this can theoretically happen by a very rare mutation, a better solution would be to allow the reuse of the same code at multiple program places.

Biological evolution has found the idea of reuse (e.g., the symmetry in the bodies of many living organisms), and it can be adopted in genetic programming as well. While the basic tree structure we use does not allow the reuse of subroutines, it can be extended by a mechanism known as "Automatically Defined Functions" or ADFs (see [11]). In this configuration, both the main program and one or more independent functions (or macros) are evolved simultaneously, and by extending the building blocks available to the main program, it can make calls to these evolved functions.

5.4   Tests Summary

All of the tests were performed using an improved version of the tool described at [7], and were running on an Intel Xeon 2.8GHz based server. Each test started from a previously known algorithm, while adding new constraints and building blocks. For each run, The termination criterion was 1300 successive iterations without any improvement in the program's fitness. Table 3 summaries the various tests.

Table 3. Test results

Starting from	Requirements	Generated algorithms	Successful runs (%)	Avg. run dur-taion (sec)
Peterson	1-8	Standard, but asymmetric	100	133
Peterson	1-9	Single-writer	0.4	472
Peterson	1-8, 10	Local-spinning	26	651
Single-writer	1-10	Local-spinning and single-writer	34	830

6   Conclusions

We explored the ability to combine genetic programming and model checking. In particular, we focused on the generation of correct and realistic mutual exclusion algorithms.

While developing the tool and experimenting with it, we obtained several observations. The first one is that one can apply the genetic programming approach in an incremental way: first obtain some simple solutions, perhaps starting with a known one that does not satisfy some quality requirements. Then change the scoring system such that the existing solution will be ranked lower because of not satisfying some giving criteria, in an attempt to make the genetic process progress towards a better solution. Such a process is semi-manual, since one needs to constantly adapt the ranking system. One can then combine the genetic process as a tiered program evolution, combining different results of previous stages via the genetic process into a better solution.

This observation suggests that the ranking system should be open for the user with facilities to help changing the ranking, as well as the given specification. Another related feature allows combining the genetic programming results in levels, where in each level we obtain a program satisfying somewhat different goals (and where lower levels satisfy less requirements).

In the experiments we performed, we actually added verification procedures 'by need'. Thus, we modified the system to allow additional constructs, and sometimes were required to program a new algorithm for modifying the ranking system. Thus, we, as the users (apart from being the developers) of the tool, intervened in the genetic programming process and modified it according to a growing number of requirements. Although once added, these constructs become a part of the tool, it is only foreseen that new constructs will be needed and added in the future. We view this manual 'intervention' as part of the genetic programming process; rather than having a closed tool, we suggested a *methodology* for generating new, more involved and complicated, programs.

Indeed, some of the adaptations of the tool where specific for the problem of finding new mutual exclusion algorithms. For example, the algorithm in Section 5.2 makes sense for the mutual exclusion problem, and augments the model checking procedure suggested. Moreover, it is applied separately, to the pre-protocol and to the post-protocol, before summing up the results. This kind of consideration and this particular calculation of the fitness function that worked well for the mutual exclusion problem would be meaningless for some other programming problems. Nevertheless, this methodology allowed us to successfully find new solutions for the mutual exclusion problem (in this case). We believe that the 'litmus test' for the success of this approach is that, without being experts on mutual exclusion algorithms, we did discover several new interesting algorithms.

Finally, we can describe the genetic search process used here as a random heuristic search: one starts with some solution which is not optimal (or can be random), makes some small random changes around it, and use model checking as a heuristic goal function to steer the search in the right direction. This is also related to *simulated annealing* [9]; this can be described in metallurgy as generating some "heat" around initial and intermediate results to force small changes, and making some controlled "cooling" towards the required solution.

Acknowledgments

We would like to thank Yih-Kuen Tsay for suggesting the idea of looking into more complicated mutual exclusion algorithms, in particular, those satisfying local-spinning.

References

1. Emerson, E.A., Clarke, E.M.: Characterizing correctness properties of parallel programs using fixpoints. In: ICALP, pp. 169–181 (1980)
2. Floyd, R.: Assigning meaning to programs. In: American Mathematical Society symposium on Applied Mathematics, vol. 19, pp. 19–31 (1967)
3. Gerth, R., Peled, D., Vardi, M., Wolper, P.: Simple on-the-fly automatic verification of linear temporal logic. In: Protocol Specification testing and Verification, pp. 3–18 (1995)
4. Hoare, C.A.R.: An axiomatic basis for computer programming. Communication of the ACM 12, 576–583 (1969)
5. Holland, J.H.: Adaptation in Natural and Artificial Systems: An Introductory Analysis with Applications to Biology, Control and Artificial Intelligence. MIT Press, Cambridge (1992)
6. Johnson, C.G.: Genetic programming with fitness based on model checking. In: Ebner, M., O'Neill, M., Ekárt, A., Vanneschi, L., Esparcia-Alcázar, A.I. (eds.) EuroGP 2007. LNCS, vol. 4445, pp. 114–124. Springer, Heidelberg (2007)

7. Katz, G., Peled, D.: Model checking-based genetic programming with an application to mutual exclusion. In: Ramakrishnan, C.R., Rehof, J. (eds.) TACAS 2008. LNCS, vol. 4963, pp. 141–156. Springer, Heidelberg (2008)
8. Kessels, J.L.W.: Arbitration without common modifiable variables. Acta Inf. 17, 135–141 (1982)
9. Kirkpatrick Jr., S., Gelatt, D., Vecchi, M.P.: Optimization by simulated annealing. Science 220(4598), 671–680 (1983)
10. Koza, J.R.: Genetic Programming: On the Programming of Computers by Means of Natural Selection. MIT Press, Cambridge (1992)
11. Koza, J.R.: Genetic Programming II: Automatic Discovery of Reusable Programs. MIT Press, Cambridge (1994)
12. Kupferman, O., Vardi, M.: Memoryfull branching-time logic. In: Logic in Computer Science, pp. 265–274 (2006)
13. Montana, D.J.: Strongly typed genetic programming. Evolutionary Computation 3(2), 199–230 (1995)
14. Niebert, P., Peled, D., Pnueli, A.: Discriminative model checking. In: Gupta, A., Malik, S. (eds.) CAV 2008. LNCS, vol. 5123, pp. 504–516. Springer, Heidelberg (2008)
15. Peterson, F.: Economical solutions to the critical section problem in a distributed system. In: STOC: ACM Symposium on Theory of Computing (STOC) (1977)
16. Pnueli, A., Rosner, R.: On the synthesis of reactive systems. In: POPL, Austin, Texas, pp. 179–190 (1989)
17. Quielle, J.P., Sifakis, J.: Specification and verification of concurrent systems in cesar. In: 5th International Symposium on Programming, pp. 337–350 (1981)
18. Tarjan, R.E.: Depth-first search and linear graph algorithms. SIAM J. Comput. 1(2), 146–160 (1972)
19. Taubenfeld, G.: Synchronization Algorithms and Concurrent Programming. Prentice-Hall, Inc., Upper Saddle River (2006)
20. Tsay, Y.K.: Deriving a scalable algorithm for mutual exclusion. In: Kutten, S. (ed.) DISC 1998. LNCS, vol. 1499, pp. 393–407. Springer, Heidelberg (1998)

Computation Tree Regular Logic for Genetic Regulatory Networks

Radu Mateescu[1], Pedro T. Monteiro[1,2], Estelle Dumas[1], and Hidde de Jong[1]

[1] INRIA Rhône-Alpes, 655 Av. de l'Europe, F-38330 Montbonnot St Martin, France
[2] INESC-ID/IST, Rua Alves Redol 9, 1000-029 Lisboa, Portugal
{Radu.Mateescu,Pedro.Monteiro,Estelle.Dumas,Hidde.de-Jong}@inrialpes.fr

Abstract. Model checking has proven to be a useful analysis technique not only for concurrent systems, but also for the genetic regulatory networks (GRNs) that govern the functioning of living cells. The applications of model checking in systems biology have revealed that temporal logics should be able to capture both branching-time and fairness properties. At the same time, they should have a user-friendly syntax easy to employ by non-experts. In this paper, we define CTRL (Computation Tree Regular Logic), an extension of CTL with regular expressions and fairness operators that attempts to match these criteria. CTRL subsumes both CTL and LTL, and has a reduced set of temporal operators indexed by regular expressions, inspired from the modalities of PDL (Propositional Dynamic Logic). We also develop a translation of CTRL into HMLR (Hennessy-Milner Logic with Recursion), an equational variant of the modal μ-calculus. This has allowed us to obtain an on-the-fly model checker with diagnostic for CTRL by directly reusing the verification technology available in the CADP toolbox. We illustrate the application of the CTRL model checker by analyzing the GRN controlling the carbon starvation response of *Escherichia coli*.

1   Introduction

Explicit state verification has been mostly applied to the analysis of concurrent systems in engineering. Recently, however, biological regulatory networks have been recognized as special cases of concurrent systems as well, which has opened the way for the application of formal verification technology in the emerging field of systems biology (see [1,2] for reviews). The networks controlling cellular functions consist of genes, proteins, small molecules, and their mutual interactions. Most of these networks are large and complex, thus defying our capacity to understand how the dynamic behavior of the cell emerges from the structure of interactions. A large number of mathematical formalisms have been proposed to describe these networks [3], giving rise to models that can be directly or indirectly mapped to Kripke structures.

The representation of the dynamics of biological regulatory networks by means of Kripke structures enables the application of formal verification techniques to the analysis of properties of the networks, formulated as queries in temporal logic.

Cha et al. (Eds.): ATVA 2008, LNCS 5311, pp. 48–63, 2008.

Several applications of model checking exists in the bioinformatics and systems biology literature [4,5,6,7,8,9,10]. In our previous work [11,6], we have developed GNA (*Genetic Network Analyzer*), a tool for the qualitative simulation of genetic regulatory networks, and connected it to state-of-the-art model checkers like NuSmv [12] and Cadp [13].

The application to actual biological systems brought a few properties of the network dynamics to the fore that are not easily expressed in classical temporal logics. For instance, questions about multistability are important in the analysis of biological regulatory networks [14], but difficult (or impossible) to express in Ltl [15]. Ctl [16] is capable of dealing with branching time, important for multistability and other properties of non-deterministic models. However, it is not expressive enough to specify the occurrence of oscillations of indefinite length, a special kind of fairness property [6]. An obvious solution would be to consider Ctl* [17] or the propositional μ-calculus [18], both of which subsume Ctl and Ltl; however, these powerful branching-time logics are complex to understand and use by non-experts. More generally, it is not easy to express *observations* in temporal logic. Often these take the form of patterns of events corresponding to variations of system variables (protein concentrations, their derivatives, etc.) measured by experiments in the lab, which can be compared with the model predictions and thus help validate the model. Observations are conveniently and concisely formulated in terms of regular expressions, but these are not provided by standard temporal logics such as Ctl and Ltl.

In this paper, we aim at providing a temporal specification language that allows expressing properties of biological interest and strikes a suitable compromise between expressive power, user-friendliness, and complexity of model checking. Towards this objective, we propose a specification language named Ctrl (*Computation Tree Regular Logic*), which extends Ctl with regular expressions and fairness operators. Ctrl is more expressive than previous extensions of Ctl with regular expressions, such as Rctl [19] and RegCtl [20], whilst having a simpler syntax due to a different choice of primitive temporal operators, inspired from dynamic logics like Pdl [21]. Ctrl also subsumes Ctl, Ltl, and Pdl-Δ [22] allowing in particular the concise expression of bistability and oscillation properties. Although Ctrl was primarily designed for describing properties of regulatory networks in system biology, it also enables a succinct formulation of typical safety, liveness, and fairness properties useful for the verification of concurrent systems in other domains.

As regards the evaluation of Ctrl formulas on Kripke structures, we adopt as verification engine Cadp [13], a state-of-the-art verification toolbox for concurrent asynchronous systems that provides, among other functionalities, on-the-fly model checking and diagnostic generation for μ-calculus formulas on labeled transition systems (Ltss). In order to reuse this technology, we have to move from the state-based setting (Ctrl and Kripke structures) to the action-based setting (μ-calculus and Ltss). The translation from Kripke structures to Ltss is done in the standard way [16]. The translation from Ctrl to an action-based logic is carried out by considering as target language Hmlr (Hml *with recursion*) [23].

The equational representation of HMLR is closer to the boolean equation systems (BESs) used as intermediate formalism by the verification engine, namely the CÆSAR_SOLVE [24] generic library for local BES resolution.

The CTRL model checking procedure obtained in this way has a linear-time complexity w.r.t. the size of the formula and the Kripke structure for a significant part of the logic. This part notably subsumes PDL-Δ and allows the multistability and oscillation properties to be captured. The inevitability operator of CTRL and its infinitary version (inevitable looping) has an exponential worst-case complexity w.r.t. the size of its regular subformula; this complexity becomes linear, however, when the regular subformula is "deterministic" in a way similar to finite automata. In practice, the usage of CTRL and the model checker reveals that properties of biological interest can be expressed and verified efficiently. We illustrate this on the analysis of a model of the genetic regulatory network (GRN) controlling the carbon starvation response of E. coli.

The paper is organized as follows. Section 2 defines the syntax and semantics of CTRL and Section 3 presents the on-the-fly model checking procedure. Section 4 discusses the implementation of the CTRL model checker and applies it to the example of E. coli. Section 5 summarizes the results and provides directions for future work. A more extensive description of CTRL, including formal definitions and proofs, is available in [25].

2   Syntax and Semantics of CTRL

CTRL is interpreted on Kripke structures (KSs), which provide a natural formal description of concurrent systems, including biological regulatory networks. A KS is a tuple $K = \langle S, P, L, T, s_0 \rangle$, where: S is the set of states; P is a set of atomic propositions (predicates over states); $L : S \to 2^P$ is the state labeling (each state s is associated with the atomic propositions satisfied by s); $T \subseteq S \times S$ is the transition relation; and $s_0 \in S$ is the initial state. Transitions $(s_1, s_2) \in T$ are also noted $s_1 \to_T s_2$ (the subscript T is omitted if it is clear from the context). The transition relation T is assumed to be total, i.e., for each state $s_1 \in S$, there exists a transition $s_1 \to_T s_2$. A path $\pi = s_0 s_1 \ldots s_k \ldots$ is an infinite sequence of states such that $s_i \to_T s_{i+1}$ for every $i \geq 0$. The i-th state of a path π is noted π_i. The interval going from the i-th state of a path π to the j-th state of π inclusively (where $i \leq j$) is noted $\pi_{i,j}$. An interval $\pi_{0,i}$ is called prefix of π. For each state $s \in S$, $Path(s)$ denotes the set of all paths going out of s, i.e., the paths π such that $\pi_0 = s$. In the sequel, we assume the existence of a KS $K = \langle S, P, L, T, s_0 \rangle$, on which all formulas will be interpreted.

The syntax and semantics of CTRL are defined in the figure below. The logic contains state formulas φ and regular formulas ρ, which characterize properties of states and intervals, respectively. State formulas are built from atomic propositions $p \in P$ by using standard boolean operators and the EF, AF, EF^∞, AF^∞ temporal operators indexed by regular formulas ρ. Regular formulas are built from state formulas by using standard regular expression operators.

The interpretation $[\![\varphi]\!]_K$ of a state formula denotes the set of states of K that satisfy φ. The interpretation of regular formulas is defined by the satisfaction relation $\models_K$, which indicates whether an interval $\pi_{i,j}$ of a path in K satisfies a regular formula ρ (notation $\pi_{i,j} \models_K \rho$). The notation ρ^j (where $j \geq 0$) stands for the concatenation $\rho \ldots \rho$, where ρ occurs j times. The semantics of boolean operators is defined in the standard way. A state satisfies the potentiality formula $\mathsf{EF}_\rho\varphi$ iff it has an outgoing path containing a prefix satisfying ρ and leading to a state satisfying φ. A state satisfies the inevitability formula $\mathsf{AF}_\rho\varphi$ iff all of its outgoing paths contain a prefix satisfying ρ and lead to a state satisfying φ. A state satisfies the potential looping formula EF_ρ^∞ iff it has an outgoing path consisting of an infinite concatenation of intervals satisfying ρ. A state satisfies the inevitable looping formula AF_ρ^∞ iff all of its outgoing paths consist of an infinite concatenation of intervals satisfying ρ. An interval satisfies the one-step interval formula φ iff it consists of two states, the first of which satisfies φ. An interval satisfies the concatenation formula $\rho_1.\rho_2$ if it is the concatenation of two subintervals, the first one satisfying ρ_1 and the second one satisfying ρ_2. An interval satisfies the choice formula $\rho_1|\rho_2$ iff it satisfies either ρ_1, or ρ_2. An interval satisfies the iteration formula ρ^* iff it is the concatenation of (0 or more) subintervals satisfying ρ. By definition, an empty interval $\pi_{i,i}$ satisfies ρ^0 for any regular formula ρ. K satisfies φ (notation $K \models \varphi$) iff $s_0 \in [\![\varphi]\!]_K$.

SYNTAX

State formulas:

$$\varphi ::= p \mid \neg\varphi \mid \varphi_1 \vee \varphi_2 \mid \mathsf{EF}_\rho\varphi \mid \mathsf{AF}_\rho\varphi \mid \mathsf{EF}_\rho^\infty \mid \mathsf{AF}_\rho^\infty$$

Regular formulas:

$$\rho ::= \varphi \mid \rho_1.\rho_2 \mid \rho_1|\rho_2 \mid \rho^*$$

SEMANTICS

State formulas:

$$
\begin{aligned}
[\![p]\!]_K &= \{s \in S \mid p \in L(s)\} \\
[\![\neg\varphi]\!]_K &= S \setminus [\![\varphi]\!]_K \\
[\![\varphi_1 \vee \varphi_2]\!]_K &= [\![\varphi_1]\!]_K \cup [\![\varphi_2]\!]_K \\
[\![\mathsf{EF}_\rho\varphi]\!]_K &= \{s \in S \mid \exists\pi \in Path_K(s).\exists i \geq 0.\pi_{0,i} \models_K \rho \wedge \pi_i \in [\![\varphi]\!]_K\} \\
[\![\mathsf{AF}_\rho\varphi]\!]_K &= \{s \in S \mid \forall\pi \in Path_K(s).\exists i \geq 0.\pi_{0,i} \models_K \rho \wedge \pi_i \in [\![\varphi]\!]_K\} \\
[\![\mathsf{EF}_\rho^\infty]\!]_K &= \{s \in S \mid \exists\pi \in Path_K(s).\forall j \geq 0.\exists i \geq 0.\pi_{0,i} \models_K \rho^j\} \\
[\![\mathsf{AF}_\rho^\infty]\!]_K &= \{s \in S \mid \forall\pi \in Path_K(s).\forall j \geq 0.\exists i \geq 0.\pi_{0,i} \models_K \rho^j\}
\end{aligned}
$$

Regular formulas:

$$
\begin{aligned}
\pi_{i,j} \models_K \varphi &\quad \text{iff } j = i+1 \wedge \pi_i \in [\![\varphi]\!]_K \\
\pi_{i,j} \models_K \rho_1.\rho_2 &\quad \text{iff } \exists k \in [i,j].\pi_{i,k} \models_K \rho_1 \wedge \pi_{k,j} \models_K \rho_2 \\
\pi_{i,j} \models_K \rho_1|\rho_2 &\quad \text{iff } \pi_{i,j} \models_K \rho_1 \vee \pi_{i,j} \models_K \rho_2 \\
\pi_{i,j} \models_K \rho^* &\quad \text{iff } i = j \vee \exists k > 0.\pi_{i,j} \models_K \rho^k
\end{aligned}
$$

Several derived operators can be defined in order to facilitate the specification of properties. The trajectory operator $\mathsf{EG}_\rho\varphi$ and the invariance operator $\mathsf{AG}_\rho\varphi$ are the duals of $\mathsf{AF}_\rho\varphi$ and $\mathsf{EF}_\rho\varphi$, respectively. They express that for some (resp. each) path going out of a state, all of its prefixes satisfying ρ lead to states satisfying φ. The potential saturation operator $\mathsf{EG}_\rho^\dashv$ and the inevitable saturation operator $\mathsf{AG}_\rho^\dashv$ are the negations of the corresponding looping operators. They express that some (resp. each) path going out of a state may begin with at most a finite number of repetitions of intervals satisfying ρ. Fairness properties can be expressed in CTRL by means of the formula $\neg\mathsf{EF}_\rho^\infty$, which forbids the existence of unfair infinite execution sequences (see [25] for examples).

Expressiveness. CTRL is a natural extension of CTL [16] in which the until operator U is not primitive, but can be described using CTRL's EF operator as follows: $\mathsf{E}[\varphi_1 \; \mathsf{U} \; \varphi_2] = \mathsf{EF}_{\varphi_1^*}\varphi_2$. Other extensions of CTL, such as RCTL [19] and RegCTL [20], keep the U operator primitive as in the original logic. CTRL subsumes RegCTL, whose U operator indexed by a regular formula can be expressed in CTRL as follows: $\mathsf{E}[\varphi_1 \; \mathsf{U}^\rho \; \varphi_2] = \mathsf{EF}_{\rho \; \& \; \varphi_1^*}\varphi_2$, where & denotes the intersection of regular formulas (its occurrence in EF can be translated concisely in terms of the other regular operators [25]). The subsumption of RegCTL is strict because the U operator of RegCTL cannot describe an infinite concatenation of intervals satisfying a regular formula ρ, as specified by the EF_ρ^∞ operator of CTRL. In [20] it is shown that RegCTL is more expressive than RCTL [19], the extension of CTL with regular expressions underlying the SUGAR [26] specification language; consequently, RCTL is also subsumed by CTRL.

The potential looping operator EF^∞ is able to capture the acceptance condition of Büchi automata, making CTRL more expressive than LTL [15]. Assuming that p characterizes the accepting states in a Büchi automaton (represented as a Ks), the formula $\mathsf{EF}_{\mathsf{true}^* . p.\mathsf{true}}^\infty$ expresses the existence of an infinite sequence passing infinitely often through an accepting state, where the $p.\mathsf{true}$ regular subformula avoids infinite sequences consisting of a single p-state. Although EF^∞ does not allow a direct translation of the LTL operators, it may serve as an intermediate form for model checking LTL formulas; in this respect, this operator is similar to the "never claims" used for specifying properties in the early versions of the SPIN model checker [27]. Since CTL and LTL are uncomparable w.r.t. their expressive power [16], it turns out that they are strictly subsumed by CTRL. In fact, the CTRL fragment containing the boolean connectors and the temporal operators EF and EF^∞ is the state-based counterpart of PDL-Δ [22], which has been shown to be more expressive than CTL* [28].

3   On-the-Fly Model Checking

Our method for evaluating CTRL formulas on Kss on-the-fly relies on a translation from CTRL to HMLR and on the connection with an existing on-the-fly model checker for HMLR specifications on LTSs. In this section we briefly describe this translation by means of various examples of CTRL temporal operators (see [25] for formal definitions and proofs). We also illustrate the functioning of the HMLR model checker, which rephrases the verification problem as the local resolution of a boolean equation system (BES).

3.1 Translation from CTRL to HMLR

We consider as running example the following formula, stating that after every sequence matching $(p|q)^*.r$, either an r-state is eventually reached via a sequence satisfying $((p^*.q)|r^*)^*.q^*$, or p and q alternate along an infinite sequence:

$$\mathsf{AG}_{(p|q)^*.r}(\mathsf{AF}_{((p^*.q)|r^*)^*.q^*}r \vee \mathsf{EF}^{\infty}_{\mathsf{true}^*.p.\mathsf{true}^*.q})$$

This formula is neither expressible in CTL (because of the EF^{∞} subformula), nor in LTL (because of the nested $*$-operators). The translation from a CTRL formula to a HMLR specification comprises three phases:

- The CTRL formula is turned into a regular equation system (RES), which is a list of fixed point equation blocks interpreted on the KS, having propositional variables in their left-hand sides and CTRL state formulas in their right-hand sides. RESs are the state-based counterparts of PDLR (PDL *with recursion*) specifications used as intermediate formalism for model checking regular alternation-free μ-calculus formulas [29] on LTSs.
- Each equation block in the RES is subsequently refined into a modal equation system (MES) by eliminating all occurrences of regular operators contained in the regular formulas indexing the CTRL operators. This is done by applying various transformations on the RES equations, according to the kind of temporal operators present in their right-hand sides.
- Finally, the resulting MES is converted into a HMLR specification by replacing each occurrence of CTRL temporal operator (now indexed by a state formula) with a HML formula having the same interpretation on the LTS corresponding to the KS.

The CTRL formula above is translated into the following RES (μ and ν denote minimal and maximal fixed point equations, respectively):

$$\{X_1 \overset{\nu}{=} \mathsf{AG}_{(p|q)^*.r}X_2, X_2 \overset{\nu}{=} Y_1 \vee Z_1\}.\{Y_1 \overset{\mu}{=} \mathsf{AF}_{((p^*.q)|r^*)^*.q^*}r\}.\{Z_1 \overset{\nu}{=} \mathsf{EF}_{\mathsf{true}^*.p.\mathsf{true}^*.q}Z_1\}$$

We explain below how this RES is refined into a MES by applying the transformations specific to each temporal operator, and we also show how the KS and the MES are converted into an LTS and a HMLR specification, respectively.

Operators EF_ρ ***and*** AG_ρ***.*** The CTRL formula $\mathsf{AG}_\rho\varphi$ is the state-based counterpart of the PDL modality $[\rho]\varphi$, and therefore PDL-like identities hold about the distributivity of the AG_ρ operator over the regular operators contained in ρ:

$$\mathsf{AG}_{\rho_1.\rho_2}\varphi = \mathsf{AG}_{\rho_1}\mathsf{AG}_{\rho_2}\varphi \qquad \mathsf{AG}_{\rho_1|\rho_2}\varphi = \mathsf{AG}_{\rho_1}\varphi \wedge \mathsf{AG}_{\rho_2}\varphi \qquad \mathsf{AG}_{\rho_1^*}\varphi = \varphi \wedge \mathsf{AG}_{\rho_1}\mathsf{AG}_{\rho_1^*}\varphi$$

Dual identities are valid for $\mathsf{EF}_\rho\varphi$, which corresponds to the PDL modality $\langle\rho\rangle\varphi$. A repeated application of these identities to the equations of the first block of the RES above allows to eliminate all occurrences of regular operators, leading to the following MES block:

$$\{X_1 \overset{\nu}{=} X_3 \wedge X_4, X_2 \overset{\nu}{=} Y_1 \vee Z_1, X_3 \overset{\nu}{=} \mathsf{AG}_r X_2, X_4 \overset{\nu}{=} \mathsf{AG}_p X_1 \wedge \mathsf{AG}_q X_1\}$$

This transformation introduces a linear increase in size of the MES w.r.t. the RES. Note that additional equations were inserted in order to avoid nested occurrences of temporal operators; this is necessary for keeping the size of the final BES linear w.r.t. the size of the MES and of the Ks.

Operators AF_ρ ***and*** EG_ρ***.*** The AF_ρ operator does not satisfy the identities of EF_ρ, and thus the regular operators occurring in ρ cannot be eliminated simply by applying substitutions. The procedure we propose for expanding AF_ρ operators consists of the three steps below (a dual procedure holds for expanding EG_ρ operators). Without loss of generality, we assume that the RES block contains a single equation with an AF_ρ operator in its right-hand side.

(a) The equation block containing AF_ρ is first converted to *potentiality form* by replacing AF with EF and eliminating all occurrences of regular operators using the identities associated to EF. This operation does not preserve the semantics of the initial block, but we will take care to restore it at step (c). For the second block of our example RES, this yields the following MES:

$$\{ \ Y_1 \overset{\mu}{=} Y_2 \vee Y_3, \quad Y_2 \overset{\mu}{=} Y_4 \vee Y_5, \quad Y_3 \overset{\mu}{=} Y_6 \vee Y_7, \quad Y_4 \overset{\mu}{=} r, \quad Y_5 \overset{\mu}{=} \mathsf{EF}_q Y_2,$$
$$Y_6 \overset{\mu}{=} Y_8 \vee Y_9, \quad Y_7 \overset{\mu}{=} Y_1 \vee Y_{10}, \quad Y_8 \overset{\mu}{=} \mathsf{EF}_q Y_1, \quad Y_9 \overset{\mu}{=} \mathsf{EF}_p Y_6, \quad Y_{10} \overset{\mu}{=} \mathsf{EF}_r Y_7 \ \}$$

(b) The resulting MES is further transformed to *guarded* potentiality form (GPF) by eliminating all occurrences of unguarded propositional variables (not preceded by an EF operator) in the right-hand sides of equations. This is done by considering each equation $Y_i \overset{\mu}{=} \varphi_i$, by replacing with φ_i all unguarded occurrences of Y_i in other equations, and eliminating the possible self-recursive unguarded occurrences found on the way using the absorption property $Y_j \overset{\mu}{=} Y_j \vee \varphi_j \equiv Y_j \overset{\mu}{=} \varphi_j$ [25]. When brought to GPF and simplified (by deleting redundant variable occurrences using idempotency of disjunction, dropping identical equations, and renumbering variables), the MES block becomes:

$$Y_1 \overset{\mu}{=} \mathsf{EF}_p Y_3 \vee \mathsf{EF}_q Y_1 \vee \mathsf{EF}_q Y_2 \vee \mathsf{EF}_r Y_1 \vee Y_4, \quad Y_2 \overset{\mu}{=} \mathsf{EF}_q Y_2 \vee Y_4, \quad Y_3 \overset{\mu}{=} \mathsf{EF}_p Y_3 \vee \mathsf{EF}_q Y_1, \quad Y_4 \overset{\mu}{=} r$$

A MES in GPF is similar to the equation system defining the derivatives of regular expressions [30].

(c) The MES in GPF is finally *determinized* in order to retrieve the interpretation of the original RES block containing the AF operator. This is done by considering *meta-variables* (i.e., sets of propositional variables) holding at a state s and determining, for each combination of atomic propositions that may hold at s, the meta-variables that should be satisfied by the successors of s. We show below two equations obtained by determinizing the MES above ($Y_{\{1,2\}}$ stands for the meta-variable $\{Y_1, Y_2\}$, and similarly for the others):

$$Y_{\{1\}} \overset{\mu}{=} \mathsf{AF}_p Y_{\{3\}} \vee \mathsf{AF}_q Y_{\{1,2\}} \vee \mathsf{AF}_r Y_{\{1\}} \vee \mathsf{AF}_{p \wedge q} Y_{\{1,2,3\}} \vee \mathsf{AF}_{p \wedge r} Y_{\{1,3\}} \vee \mathsf{AF}_{q \wedge r} Y_{\{1,2\}} \vee$$
$$\mathsf{AF}_{p \wedge q \wedge r} Y_{\{1,2,3\}} \vee Y_{\{4\}}, \quad Y_{\{3\}} \overset{\mu}{=} \mathsf{AF}_p Y_{\{3\}} \vee \mathsf{AF}_q Y_{\{1\}} \vee \mathsf{AF}_{p \wedge q} Y_{\{1,3\}}$$

The rhs of the equations defining the meta-variables $Y_{\{1,2\}}$, $Y_{\{1,3\}}$, and $Y_{\{1,2,3\}}$ is identical to the one defining $Y_{\{1\}}$. After further simplifications (induced by the implication $\mathsf{AF}_{p\wedge q}\varphi \Rightarrow \mathsf{AF}_q\varphi$) we obtain the final MES:

$$Y_{\{1\}} \overset{\mu}{=} \mathsf{AF}_p Y_{\{3\}} \vee \mathsf{AF}_q Y_{\{1\}} \vee \mathsf{AF}_r Y_{\{1\}} \vee Y_{\{4\}}, \quad Y_{\{3\}} \overset{\mu}{=} \mathsf{AF}_p Y_{\{3\}} \vee \mathsf{AF}_q Y_{\{1\}}, \quad Y_{\{4\}} \overset{\mu}{=} r$$

The determinization step is similar to the subset construction used for determinizing finite automata [31].

The final MES produced after expanding a RES block containing an AF_p operator has in the worst-case a size exponential w.r.t. the size of ρ; however the temporal formulas encountered in practice are far from reaching this bound. In particular, when ρ is "deterministic", i.e., for each equation of the corresponding MES in GPF, the atomic propositions indexing the EF operators in the right-hand side are disjoint (e.g., p and q disjoint in the MES above), the resulting determinized MES has a size linear w.r.t. ρ.

Operators EF^∞_ρ, $\mathsf{AG}^{\dashv}_\rho$, AF^∞_ρ, ***and*** $\mathsf{EG}^{\dashv}_\rho$. The infinite iteration operators (and their saturation duals) must be translated into RESs with alternation depth 2, because they involve two mutually recursive minimal and maximal fixed points. The third RES equation block of our running example would translate as follows:

$$\{Z_0 \overset{\nu}{=} Z_1\}.\{Z_1 \overset{\mu}{=} \mathsf{EF}_{\mathsf{true}^* . p . \mathsf{true}^* . q} Z_0\}$$

However, given the very simple structure of the first equation block, we can abusively merge the two blocks into a minimal fixed point one, expand the regular subformula using the EF substitutions, and mark the Z_0 variable such that the original semantics of the equation blocks can be restored during the resolution of the underlying BES (see Sec. 3.2). The AF^∞_ρ operator is expanded in a similar manner, and the saturation operators $\mathsf{AG}^{\dashv}_\rho$ and $\mathsf{EG}^{\dashv}_\rho$ are handled dually.

Moving from the state-based to the action-based setting. In order to apply a HMLR model checker as verification back-end for CTRL, we need to interpret formulas on LTSs instead of KSs. A KS can be converted to an LTS by migrating all the atomic propositions valid at each state of the KS on the actions labeling the transitions going out from that state in the LTS [16]. This conversion is succinct (it keeps the same state set and transition relation) and can be performed on-the-fly during an incremental construction of the KS. The MES produced from a CTRL formula can be turned into a HMLR specification by replacing basic CTRL formulas with HML modalities having the same interpretation on the LTS corresponding to the KS:

$$p = \langle p \rangle \mathsf{true} \qquad \mathsf{EF}_p X = \langle p \rangle X \qquad \mathsf{AG}_p X = [p] X$$
$$\mathsf{AF}_p X = \langle p \rangle \mathsf{true} \wedge [\mathsf{true}] X \qquad \mathsf{EG}_p X = \langle p \rangle \mathsf{true} \Rightarrow \langle \mathsf{true} \rangle X$$

These replacements increase by at most a linear factor the size of the HMLR specification w.r.t. the MES.

3.2 BES Encoding and Local Resolution

The on-the-fly model checking of the HMLR specification produced from a CTRL formula on the LTS corresponding to a KS can be rephrased as the local resolution of a BES [23,32], which can be carried out using graph-based algorithms [33,34,24]. Figure 1 illustrates the evaluation of a CTRL infinite looping operator on a KS. For simplicity, we show the verification by considering directly the MES (produced as indicated in Sec. 3.1) and the KS instead of the corresponding HMLR specification and LTS.

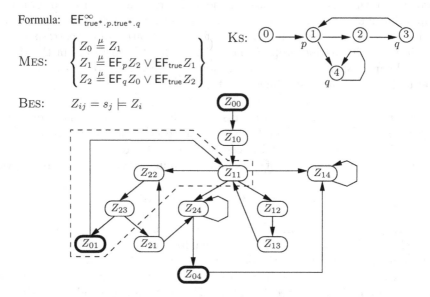

Fig. 1. Evaluation of a EF^∞ formula. The underlying BES is obtained by making a product between the MES and the KS. It is represented here by its boolean graph, which is explored on-the-fly by the $A4_{cyc}$ algorithm.

The BES encoding the model checking problem is disjunctive, and could be solved using the memory-efficient algorithm A4 proposed in [24]. If the EF^∞ formula is false, the solution of the MES is also false, since by abusively switching the sign from ν to μ we obtained an equation block with a "smaller" interpretation. If the formula is true, the KS contains a cycle going through a state satisfying the marked variable Z_0; this kind of cycle is detected in linear-time by the $A4_{cyc}$ algorithm [35], which records that all states on the cycle satisfy EF^∞, thus restoring the original meaning of the formula.

Complexity. The complexity of our CTRL model checking procedure is summarized in the table below. The EF_ρ and EF^∞_ρ operators, together with their respective duals AG_ρ and $AG^\dashv_\rho$, are evaluated in linear-time w.r.t. the size of ρ and the size of the KS. Moreover, the evaluation of these operators stores only the states (and not the transitions) of the KS, thanks to the memory-efficient algorithms A4 [24] and A4$_{cyc}$ [35] dedicated to disjunctive and conjunctive BESs. This fragment of CTRL is the state-based counterpart of PDL-Δ [22]. The linear-time evaluation of the EF$_\rho^\infty$ operator allows an efficient detection of complex cycles, such as those characterizing oscillation properties [9]. EF$_\rho^\infty$ is also useful for capturing fairness properties in concurrent systems, such as the existence of complex unfair executions in resource locking protocols [36].

The AF$_\rho$ operator and its dual EG$_\rho$ are evaluated in linear-time only when the regular subformula ρ is deterministic. In general, these operators are evaluated in exponential-time w.r.t. the size of ρ (because of the determinization step) but still in linear-time w.r.t. the KS size. In practice, the size of temporal formulas is much smaller than the size of KSS, which reduces the impact of the factor $2^{|\rho|}$ on the total cost of model checking. Finally, the AF$_\rho^\infty$ operator and its dual EG$_\rho^\dashv$ are evaluated in linear-time when ρ is deterministic (using a symmetric version of the A4$_{cyc}$ algorithm); in the general case, these operators are evaluated in doubly exponential-time w.r.t. the size of ρ and in quadratic-time w.r.t. the KS size, by applying local resolution algorithms for BESs with alternation depth 2 [34]. This complexity seems difficult to lower, since the BESs produced by translating these operators have a general shape (arbitrary nesting of disjunctions and conjunctions in the right-hand sides of equations).

CTRL	Model checking complexity	
operator	ρ deterministic	ρ nondeterministic
EF$_\rho$ AG$_\rho$	$O(\lvert\rho\rvert \cdot (\lvert S\rvert + \lvert T\rvert))$	
AF$_\rho$ EG$_\rho$	$O(\lvert\rho\rvert \cdot (\lvert S\rvert + \lvert T\rvert))$	$O(2^{\lvert\rho\rvert} \cdot (\lvert S\rvert + \lvert T\rvert))$
EF$_\rho^\infty$ AG$_\rho^\dashv$	$O(\lvert\rho\rvert \cdot (\lvert S\rvert + \lvert T\rvert))$	
AF$_\rho^\infty$ EG$_\rho^\dashv$	$O(\lvert\rho\rvert \cdot (\lvert S\rvert + \lvert T\rvert))$	$O(2^{2\lvert\rho\rvert} \cdot (\lvert S\rvert + \lvert T\rvert)^2)$

4 Implementation and Use

We implemented the model checking procedure for CTRL described in Section 3 by reusing as much as possible the on-the-fly verification technology available in the CADP toolbox [13] for concurrent asynchronous systems. This section presents the architecture of our CTRL model checker and illustrates its use for analyzing genetic regulatory networks.

4.1 An On-the-Fly Model Checker for CTRL

The tools of CADP[1] (*Construction and Analysis of Distributed Processes*) [13] operate on labeled transition systems (LTSs), which are represented either explicitly (by their list of transitions) as compact binary files encoded in the BCG (*Binary Coded Graphs*) format, or implicitly (by their successor function) as C programs compliant with the OPEN/CÆSAR interface [37]. CADP contains the on-the-fly model checker EVALUATOR [29], which evaluates regular alternation-free μ-calculus ($L\mu_1^{reg}$) formulas on implicit LTSs. The tool works by translating the verification problem in terms of the local resolution of a BES, which is

---

[1] http://www.inrialpes.fr/vasy/cadp

done using the algorithms available in the generic CÆSAR_SOLVE library [24]. EVALUATOR 3.6 uses HMLR as intermediate language: $L\mu_1^{reg}$ formulas are translated into HMLR specifications, whose evaluation on implicit LTSs is encoded as a local BES resolution. It generates examples and counterexamples illustrating the truth value of formulas, and is also equipped with macro-definition mechanisms allowing the creation of reusable libraries of derived temporal operators.

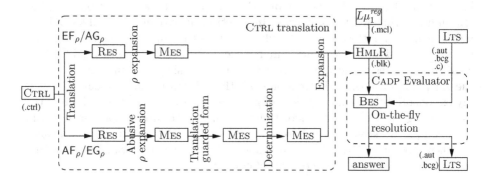

Fig. 2. CTRL translator and its connection to the EVALUATOR model checker

In order to reuse the model checking features of EVALUATOR 3.6, we had the choice of translating CTRL formulas either to $L\mu_1^{reg}$ formulas, or to HMLR specifications. We adopted the second solution because it leads to a more succinct translation and avoids the translation step from $L\mu_1^{reg}$ to HMLR present in EVALUATOR. This technical choice motivated the definition of the translation from CTRL to HMLR in the first place. The architecture of the CTRL translator (about 12,000 lines of code) is shown in Figure 2. The tool takes as input a CTRL state formula and translates it to a MES following the phases described in Section 3.1, which are different for the EF_ρ and AF_ρ operators. The MES obtained is then converted into a HMLR specification by replacing basic CTRL operators with HML modalities. The resulting HMLR specification is directly given as input to EVALUATOR 3.6, together with the LTS corresponding to the Ks. The translator from CTRL to HMLR has been completely implemented using the compiler construction technology proposed in [38].

4.2   Verification of Genetic Regulatory Networks

CTRL has been used for the analysis of so-called *genetic regulatory networks* (GRNs), which consist of genes, proteins, small molecules and their mutual interactions that together control different functions of the cell. In order to better understand how a specific dynamic behavior emerges from these interactions, and the role of each component in the network, a wide variety of mathematical formalisms are available [3].

Due to limited availability of numerical values for the kinetic parameters and the molecular concentrations, some mathematical formalisms are difficult to apply in practice. This has motivated the use of a special class of *piecewise-linear* (PL) *differential equation* models, originally introduced by [39]. Using PL models, the qualitative dynamics of the high-dimensional systems are relatively straightforward to analyze, using inequality constraints on the parameters rather than exact numerical values [40,41]. Discrete abstractions can be used to convert the continuous dynamics of the PL systems into state transition graphs (STGs) [40] that are formally equivalent to Kss. The atomic propositions describe, among other things, the concentration bounds defining a region and the trend of the variables inside regions. The generation of the STG from the PL model has been implemented in the computer tool GNA (*Genetic Network Analyzer*) [6], which is able to export the graph to standard model checkers like NuSmv [12] and Cadp [13] in order to use formal verification.

We analyse here the carbon starvation response network of *E. coli* (illustrated below), using a PL model proposed in [42], with focus on the nutrient upshift after a period of starvation, leading to exponential growth of the bacterial population. The dynamics of the system are described by 6 coupled PL differential equations, and 48 inequality constraints on the parameter values.

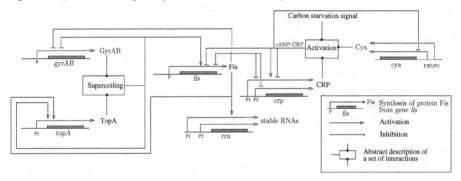

The generated graph has 743 states and contains one terminal cycle corresponding to a (damped) oscillation of some of the protein concentrations and the concentration of stable RNAs (which are transcribed from the *rrn* operons). We expressed this property using the four CTRL formulas below, where *inTermCycle* is an atomic proposition indicating that a state is part of the terminal cycle. Similarly, *dec_rrn* (*inc_rrn*) represent a decreasing (increasing) concentration of stable RNAs (ρ^+ stands for $\rho.\rho^*$).

N.	CTRL formula	Answer	Time
1.	$EF_{true^*} AF_{inTermCycle^+.(inc\_rrn^+.dec\_rrn^+)^+} true$	false	3 sec
2.	$EF_{true^*} EF^{\infty}_{inTermCycle^+.(inc\_rrn^+.dec\_rrn^+)^+}$	true	1 sec
3.	$AG_{true^*} EF^{\infty}_{inTermCycle^+.(inc\_rrn^+.dec\_rrn^+)^+}$	false	1 sec
4.	$AG_{true^*.inc\_Fis^+.dec\_Crp^+.inTermCycle} EF^{\infty}_{inTermCycle^+.(inc\_rrn^+.dec\_rrn^+)^+}$	true	2 sec

Formula 1 fails, indicating that an oscillation of stable RNAs is not inevitable once the system has reached the terminal cycle. Formula 2, obtained by replacing the AF operator with an EF$^\infty$, is valid on the graph, showing the existence of an infinite oscillation of the stable RNAs. Formula 3 is stricter, stating that all paths in the graph lead to the terminal cycle with an oscillation of stable RNAs. Formula 4 forces the model checker to consider the oscillation only on the paths satisfying the restriction that an increase of the Fis concentration is followed by a decrease of the Crp concentration before arriving at the terminal cycle.

The use of regular expressions in the CTRL formulas above clearly outlines the convenience of being able to characterize a sequence of events. Due to the presence of nested iteration operators, these properties cannot be expressed using standard temporal logics such as CTL or LTL. In addition, the EF$^\infty_\rho$ operator enables a natural formulation of infinite repetitions of sequences defined by ρ, such as those corresponding to the oscillation in the *E. coli* example.

5   Conclusion and Future Work

Applications of model checking in system biology have demonstrated its usefulness for understanding the dynamic behaviour of regulatory networks in living cells, but also pointed out certain limitations in expressiveness and user-friendliness. Our work aims at alleviating these limitations in order to promote the practical usage of model checking in the bioinformatics and systems biology communities. CTRL extends CTL with regular expressions and fairness operators, allowing a natural and concise description of typical properties of biological interest, such as the presence of multistability or oscillations. We were able to reduce the development effort and to obtain an on-the-fly model checker for CTRL by defining and implementing a translation from CTRL to HMLR, and by reusing the verification and diagnostic generation features of the EVALUATOR 3.6 model checker of the CADP toolbox.

In this paper, we have employed CTRL for the verification of dynamic properties of GRNs modeled by (but not limited to) piecewise-linear differential equations. The continuous dynamics of these models, by defining appropriate discrete abstractions, can be converted into discrete state transition graphs that are formally equivalent to KSs. The computer tool GNA is able to generate the state transition graphs and export them as LTSs to CADP. CTRL can be combined with many of the other approaches proposed for the application of formal verification tools to biological regulatory networks [4,5,6,7,8,9,10].

We plan to continue our work on several directions. First, we will extend the CÆSAR_SOLVE [24] library of CADP with resolution algorithms handling BESs of alternation depth 2 [34] in order to obtain an on-the-fly evaluation of the AF$^\infty_\rho$ operator when the regular formula ρ is nondeterministic. Second, the translation from CTRL to HMLR can be optimized by adding static analysis features on the GNA atomic propositions in order to reduce the size of the HMLR specifications produced. Third, a distributed version of the CTRL model checker can be obtained by coupling it with the distributed BES resolution algorithms proposed in [43,44]. Fourth, we will develop pattern-based tools to help nonexpert users specify queries for the analysis of biological networks [45].

Acknowledgements. This research was funded by the EC-MOAN project no. 043235 of the FP6-NEST-PATH-COM European program. Pedro T. Monteiro is also supported by the FCT program (PhD grant SFRH/BD/32965/2006).

References

1. Fisher, J., Henzinger, T.A.: Executable cell biology. Nature Biotechnology 25(11), 1239–1250 (2007)
2. Regev, A., Shapiro, E.: Cells as computation. Nature 419(6905), 343 (2002)
3. de Jong, H.: Modeling and simulation of genetic regulatory systems: A literature review. J. of Computational Biology 9(1), 67–103 (2002)
4. Antoniotti, M., Policriti, A., Ugel, N., Mishra, B.: Model building and model checking for biochemical processes. Cell Biochemistry and Biophysics 38(3), 271–286 (2003)
5. Barnat, J., Brim, L., Cerná, I., Drazan, S., Safranek, D.: Parallel model checking large-scale genetic regulatory networks with DiVinE. In: FBTC 2007. ENTCS, vol. 194 (2008)
6. Batt, G., Ropers, D., de Jong, H., Geiselmann, J., Mateescu, R., Page, M., Schneider, D.: Validation of qualitative models of genetic regulatory networks by model checking: Analysis of the nutritional stress response in *Escherichia coli*. Bioinformatics 21 (Suppl. 1), i19–i28 (2005)
7. Bernot, G., Comet, J.-P., Richard, A., Guespin, J.: Application of formal methods to biological regulatory networks: Extending Thomas' asynchronous logical approach with temporal logic. J. of Theoretical Biology 229(3), 339–348 (2004)
8. Calder, M., Vyshemirsky, V., Gilbert, D., Orton, R.: Analysis of signalling pathways using the PRISM model checker. In: CMSB 2005, pp. 79–90 (2005)
9. Chabrier-Rivier, N., Chiaverini, M., Danos, V., Fages, F., Schächter, V.: Modeling and querying biomolecular interaction networks. TCS 325(1), 25–44 (2004)
10. Fisher, J., Piterman, N., Hajnal, A., Henzinger, T.A.: Predictive modeling of signaling crosstalk during *C. elegans* vulval development. PLoS Computational Biology 3(5), e92 (2007)
11. Batt, G., Bergamini, D., de Jong, H., Gavarel, H., Mateescu, R.: Model checking genetic regulatory networks using GNA and CADP. In: Graf, S., Mounier, L. (eds.) SPIN 2004. LNCS, vol. 2989, pp. 158–163. Springer, Heidelberg (2004)
12. Cimatti, A., Clarke, E., Giunchiglia, F., Roveri, M.: NuSMV: a new symbolic model checker. STTT 2(4), 410–425 (2000)
13. Garavel, H., Lang, F., Mateescu, R., Serwe, W.: CADP 2006: A toolbox for the construction and analysis of distributed processes. In: Damm, W., Hermanns, H. (eds.) CAV 2007. LNCS, vol. 4590, pp. 158–163. Springer, Heidelberg (2007)
14. Thomas, R., Thieffry, D., Kaufman, M.: Dynamical behaviour of biological regulatory networks: I. Biological role of feedback loops and practical use of the concept of the loop-characteristic state. Bulletin of Mathematical Biology 57(2), 247–276 (1995)
15. Manna, Z., Pnueli, A.: The Temporal Logic of Reactive and Concurrent Systems. Specification, vol. I. Springer, Heidelberg (1992)
16. Clarke, E.M., Grumberg, O., Peled, D.A.: Model Checking. MIT Press, Cambridge (2000)
17. Emerson, E.A., Halpern, J.Y.: Sometimes and not never revisited: On branching versus linear time. In: POPL 1983, pp. 127–140 (January 1983)

18. Kozen, D.: Results on the propositional μ-calculus. TCS 27, 333–354 (1983)
19. Beer, I., Ben-David, S., Landver, A.: On-the-fly model checking of RCTL formulas. In: Y. Vardi, M. (ed.) CAV 1998. LNCS, vol. 1427, pp. 184–194. Springer, Heidelberg (1998)
20. Brázdil, T., Cerná, I.: Model checking of RegCTL. Computers and Artificial Intelligence 25(1) (2006)
21. Fischer, M.J., Ladner, R.E.: Propositional dynamic logic of regular programs. JCSS 18(2), 194–211 (1979)
22. Streett, R.: Propositional dynamic logic of looping and converse. Information and Control (1982)
23. Larsen, K.G.: Proof systems for Hennessy-Milner logic with recursion. In: Dauchet, M., Nivat, M. (eds.) CAAP 1988. LNCS, vol. 299, pp. 215–230. Springer, Heidelberg (1988)
24. Mateescu, R.: CÆSAR_SOLVE: A generic library for on-the-fly resolution of alternation-free boolean equation systems. STTT 8(1), 37–56 (2006)
25. Mateescu, R., Monteiro, P.T., Dumas, E., Mateescu, R.: Computation tree regular logic for genetic regulatory networks. Research Report RR-6521, INRIA (2008)
26. Beer, I., Ben-David, S., Eisner, C., Fisman, D., Gringauze, A., Rodeh, Y.: The temporal logic Sugar. In: Berry, G., Comon, H., Finkel, A. (eds.) CAV 2001. LNCS, vol. 2102, pp. 363–367. Springer, Heidelberg (2001)
27. Holzmann, G.: The SPIN Model Checker – Primer and Reference Manual. Addison-Wesley, Reading (2003)
28. Wolper, P.: A translation from full branching time temporal logic to one letter propositional dynamic logic with looping (published manuscript, 1982)
29. Mateescu, R., Sighireanu, M.: Efficient on-the-fly model-checking for regular alternation-free mu-calculus. SCP 46(3), 255–281 (2003)
30. Brzozowski, J.A.: Derivatives of regular expressions. JACM 11(4), 481–494 (1964)
31. Aho, A.V., Sethi, R., Ullman, J.D.: Compilers: Principles, Techniques and Tools. Addison-Wesley, Reading (1986)
32. Cleaveland, R., Steffen, B.: A linear-time model-checking algorithm for the alternation-free modal mu-calculus. FMSD 2(2), 121–147 (1993)
33. Andersen, H.R.: Model checking and boolean graphs. TCS 126(1), 3–30 (1994)
34. Vergauwen, B., Lewi, J.: Efficient local correctness checking for single and alternating boolean equation systems. In: Shamir, E., Abiteboul, S. (eds.) ICALP 1994. LNCS, vol. 820, pp. 304–315. Springer, Heidelberg (1994)
35. Mateescu, R., Thivolle, D.: A model checking language for concurrent value-passing systems. In: Cuellar, J., Maibaum, T.S.E. (eds.) FM 2008. LNCS, vol. 5014, pp. 148–164. Springer, Heidelberg (2008)
36. Arts, T., Earle, C.B., Derrick, J.: Development of a verified Erlang program for resource locking. STTT 5(2–3), 205–220 (2004)
37. Garavel, H.: OPEN/CÆSAR: An open software architecture for verification, simulation, and testing. In: Steffen, B. (ed.) TACAS 1998. LNCS, vol. 1384, pp. 68–84. Springer, Heidelberg (1998)
38. Garavel, H., Lang, F., Mateescu, R.: Compiler construction using LOTOS NT. In: Horspool, R.N. (ed.) CC 2002. LNCS, vol. 2304, pp. 9–13. Springer, Heidelberg (2002)
39. Glass, L., Kauffman, S.A.: The logical analysis of continuous non-linear biochemical control networks. J. of Theoretical Biology 39(1), 103–129 (1973)
40. Batt, G., de Jong, H., Page, M., Geiselmann, J.: Symbolic reachability analysis of genetic regulatory networks using discrete abstractions. Automatica 44(4), 982–989 (2008)

41. de Jong, H., Gouzé, J.-L., Hernandez, C., Page, M., Sari, T., Geiselmann, J.: Qualitative simulation of genetic regulatory networks using piecewise-linear models. Bulletin of Mathematical Biology 66(2), 301–340 (2004)
42. Ropers, D., de Jong, H., Page, M., Schneider, D., Geiselmann, J.: Qualitative simulation of the carbon starvation response in *Escherichia coli*. Biosystems 84(2), 124–152 (2006)
43. Joubert, C., Mateescu, R.: Distributed local resolution of boolean equation systems. In: PDP 2005. IEEE Computer Society, Los Alamitos (2005)
44. Joubert, C., Mateescu, R.: Distributed on-the-fly model checking and test case generation. In: Valmari, A. (ed.) SPIN 2006. LNCS, vol. 3925, pp. 126–145. Springer, Heidelberg (2006)
45. Monteiro, P.T., Ropers, D., Mateescu, R., Freitas, A.T., de Jong, H.: Temporal logic patterns for querying dynamic models of cellular interaction networks. Bioinformatics (in press, 2008)

Compositional Verification for Component-Based Systems and Application

Saddek Bensalem, Marius Bozga, Joseph Sifakis, and Thanh-Hung Nguyen

Verimag Laboratory, Université Joseph Fourier Grenoble, CNRS

Abstract. We present a compositional method for the verification of component-based systems described in a subset of the BIP language encompassing multi-party interaction without data transfer. The method is based on the use of two kinds of invariants. Component invariants which are over-approximations of components' reachability sets. Interaction invariants which are constraints on the states of components involved in interactions. Interaction invariants are obtained by computing traps of finite-state abstractions of the verified system. The method is applied for deadlock verification in the D-Finder tool. D-Finder is an interactive tool that takes as input BIP programs and applies proof strategies to eliminate potential deadlocks by computing increasingly stronger invariants. The experimental results on non-trivial examples allow either to prove deadlock-freedom or to identify very few deadlock configurations that can be analyzed by using state space exploration.

1 Introduction

Compositional verification techniques are used to cope with state explosion in concurrent systems. The idea is to aply divide-and-conquer approaches to infer global properties of complex systems from properties of their components. Separate verification of components limits state explosion. Nonetheless, components mutually interact in a system and their behavior and properties are inter-related. This is a major difficulty in designing compositional techniques. As explained in [1], compositional rules are in general of the form

$$\frac{B_1 < \Phi_1 >, \; B_2 < \Phi_2 >, \; C(\Phi_1, \Phi_2, \Phi)}{B_1 \| B_2 < \Phi >} \tag{1}$$

That is, if two components with behaviors B_1, B_2 meet individually properties Φ_1, Φ_2 respectively, and $C(\Phi_1, \Phi_2, \Phi)$ is some condition taking into account the semantics of parallel composition operation and relating the individual properties with the global property, then the system $B_1 \| B_2$ resulting from the composition of B_1 and B_2 will satisfy a global property Φ.

One approach to compositional verification is by *assume-guarantee* where properties are decomposed into two parts. One is an assumption about the global behavior of the environment of the component; the other is a property guaranteed by the component when the assumption about its environment holds. This approach

Cha et al. (Eds.): ATVA 2008, LNCS 5311, pp. 64–79, 2008.

has been extensively studied (see for example [2,3,4,5,6,7,8,9]). Many issues make the application of assume-guarantee rules diffcult. These are discussed in detail in a recent paper [10] which provides an evaluation of automated assume-guarantee techniques. The main difficulties are finding decompositions into sub-systems and choosing adequate assumptions for a particular decomposition.

We present a different approach for compositional verification of invariants based on the following rule:

$$\frac{\{B_i < \Phi_i >\}_i, \ \Psi \in II(\|_\gamma\{B_i\}_i, \{\Phi_i\}_i), \ (\bigwedge_i \Phi_i) \wedge \Psi \Rightarrow \Phi}{\|_\gamma\{B_i\}_i < \Phi >} \tag{2}$$

The rule allows to prove invariance of Φ for systems obtained by using a n-ary composition operation parameterized by a set of interactions γ. It uses global invariants which are the conjunction of individual invariants of components Φ_i and an interaction invariant Ψ. The latter expresses constraints on the global state space induced by interactions between components. It can be computed automatically from abstractions of the system to be verified. These are the composition of finite state abstractions B_i^α of the components B_i with respect to their invariants Φ_i. They can be represented as a Petri net whose transitions correspond to interactions between components. Interaction invariants correspond to traps [11] of the Petri net and are computed symbolically as solutions of a set of boolean equations.

Figure 1 illustrates the method for a system with two components, invariants Φ_1 and Φ_2 and interaction invariant Ψ. Our method differs from assume-guarantee methods in that it avoids combinatorial explosion of the decomposition and is directly applicable to systems with multiparty (not only binary) interactions. Furthermore, it needs only guarantees for components. It replaces the search for adequate assumptions for each component by the use of interaction invariants. These can be computed automatically from given component invariants (guarantees). Interaction invariants correspond to a *"cooperation test"* in

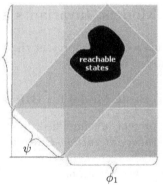

Fig. 1.

the terminology of [12] as they allow to eliminate product states which are not feasible by the semantics of parallel composition.

The paper provides a method for automated verification of component-based systems described in a subset of the BIP (Behavior-Interaction-Priority) language [13]. In BIP, a system is the composition of a set of atomic components which are automata extended with data and functions written in C. We restrict to programs where interactions are pure synchronizations. Nonetheless, the method can be easily extended for interactions involving data transfer. The main results are the following:

- We provide heuristics for computing component invariants and interaction invariants. Component invariants are over-approximations of the set of the reachable states generated by simple forward analysis. Interaction invariants are derived automatically from component invariants and their interactions. When proving invariance of a property fails, it is possible to find stronger invariants by computing stronger component invariants from which stronger interaction invariants are obtained.
- We present an implemention and application of the method in the D-Finder tool for deadlock verification. D-Finder takes as input BIP programs and progressively eliminates potential deadlocks by generating invariants. For this, it cooperates with two tools: Omega [14] for quantifier elimination and Yices [15] for checking satisfiability of predicates. It is also connected to the state space exploration tool of the BIP platform, for finer analysis when the heuristic fails to prove deadlock-freedom. We provide non trivial examples showing the capabilities of D-Finder as well as the efficiency of the method.

The paper is organized as follows. Section 2 introduces the basic definitions about BIP and invariants. The method for computing component invariants and the corresponding interaction invariants is presented in Section 3. Section 4 presents the application of the method for checking deadlock-freedom including a description of D-Finder and experimental results. Section 5 presents concluding remarks and future work.

2   Models, Invariants and Their Properties

In this section, we present the basic model for the BIP language as well as the notion of invariant.

2.1   Basic Model for BIP

We present a simplified model for component-based systems used in the *Behaviour-Interaction-Priority* (BIP) component framework developed at Verimag [13].

This framework has been implemented in a language and a toolset. The BIP language offers primitives and constructs for modelling and composing components. An atomic component consists of a set of ports used for the synchronization with other components, a set of transitions and a set of local variables. Transitions describe the behavior of the component. The BIP toolset includes an editor and a compiler for generating from BIP programs, C++ code executable on a dedicated platform.

We provide a formalization of atomic components in BIP and their composition by using interactions.

Definition 1 (Atomic Component). *An atomic component is a transition system extended with data* $B = (L, P, T, X, \{g_\tau\}_{\tau \in T}, \{f_\tau\}_{\tau \in T})$, *where:*

- (L, P, T) is a transition system, that is
  - $L = \{l_1, l_2, \ldots, l_k\}$ is a set of control locations,
  - P is a set of ports,
  - $T \subseteq L \times P \times L$ is a set of transitions,
- $X = \{x_1, \ldots, x_n\}$ is a set of variables and for each $\tau \in T$ respectively, g_τ is a guard, a predicate on X, and $f_\tau(X, X')$ is an update relation, a predicate on X (current) and X' (next) state variables.

Definition 2 (Semantics of extended transition system). *The semantics of $B = (L, P, T, X, \{g_\tau\}_{\tau \in T}, \{f_\tau\}_{\tau \in T})$, is a transition system (Q, P, T_0) such that*

- $Q = L \times \mathbf{X}$ *where $\mathbf{X}$ denotes the set of valuations of variables X.*
- T_0 *is the set including transitions $((l, \mathbf{x}), p, (l', \mathbf{x}'))$ such that $g_\tau(\mathbf{x}) \wedge f_\tau(\mathbf{x}, \mathbf{x}')$ for some $\tau = (l, p, l') \in T$. As usual, if $((l, \mathbf{x}), p, (l', \mathbf{x}')) \in T_0$ we write $(l, \mathbf{x}) \xrightarrow{p} (l', \mathbf{x}')$.*

Given a transition $\tau = (l, p, l') \in T$, l and l' are respectively, the *source* and the *target* location denoted respectively by $^\bullet\tau$ and $\tau^\bullet$.

For a location l, we use the predicate at_l which is *true* iff the system is at location l. A state predicate Φ is a boolean expression involving location predicates and predicates on X. Any state predicate can be put in the form $\bigvee_{l \in L} at\_l \wedge \varphi_l$. Notice that predicates on locations are disjoint and their disjunction is true.

We define below a parallel composition for components parameterized by a set of interactions. We consider only pure synchronizations, that is interactions do not involve data transfer between components.

Definition 3 (Interactions). *Given a set of components $B_1, B_2, \ldots, B_n$, where $B_i = (L_i, P_i, T_i, X_i, \{g_\tau\}_{\tau \in T_i}, \{f_\tau\}_{\tau \in T_i})$, an interaction a is a set of ports, subset of $\bigcup_{i=1}^n P_i$, such that $\forall i = 1, \ldots, n \ |a \cap P_i| \leq 1$.*

Definition 4 (Parallel Composition). *Given n components $B_i = (L_i, P_i, T_i, X_i, \{g_\tau\}_{\tau \in T_i}, \{f_\tau\}_{\tau \in T_i})$ and a set of interactions γ, we define $B = \gamma(B_1, \ldots, B_n)$ as the component $(L, \gamma, T, X, \{g_\tau\}_{\tau \in T}, \{f_\tau\}_{\tau \in T})$, where:*

- (L, γ, T) *is the transition system such that*
  - $L = L_1 \times L_2 \times \ldots \times L_n$ *is the set of control locations,*
  - $T \subseteq L \times \gamma \times L$ *contains transitions $\tau = ((l_1, \ldots, l_n), a, (l'_1, \ldots, l'_n))$ obtained by synchronization of sets of transitions $\{\tau_i = (l_i, p_i, l'_i) \in T_i\}_{i \in I}$ such that $\{p_i\}_{i \in I} = a \in \gamma$ and $l'_j = l_j$ if $j \notin I$, for arbitrary $I \subseteq \{1, \ldots, n\}$*
- $X = \bigcup_{i=1}^n X_i$ *and for a transition τ resulting from the synchronization of a set of transitions $\{\tau_i\}_{i \in I}$, the associated guard and function are respectively $g_\tau = \bigwedge_{i \in I} g_{\tau_i}$ and $f_\tau = \bigwedge_{i \in I} f_{\tau_i} \wedge \bigwedge_{i \notin I}(X'_i = X_i)$.*

Definition 5 (System). *A system S is a pair $\langle B, Init \rangle$ where B is a component and $Init$ is a state predicate characterizing the initial states of B.*

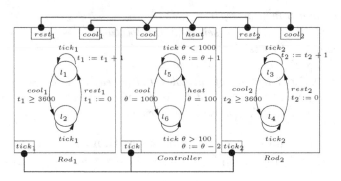

Fig. 2. Temperature Control System

Example 1 (Temperature Control System). [16] This system controls the coolant temperature in a reactor tank by moving two independent control rods. The goal is to maintain the coolant between the temperatures θ_m and θ_M. When the temperature reaches its maximum value θ_M, the tank must be refrigerated with one of the rods. The temperature rises at a rate v_r and decreases at rate v_d. A rod can be moved again only if T time units have elapsed since the end of its previous movement. If the temperature of the coolant cannot decrease because there is no available rod, a complete shutdown is required.

We provide a discretized model of the Temperature Control System in BIP, decomposed into three atomic components: a Controller and two components Rod1, Rod2 modeling the rods. We take $\theta_m = 100°$, $\theta_M = 1000°$, $T = 3600$ seconds. Furthermore, we assume that $v_r = 1°/s$ and $v_d = 2°/s$. The Controller has two control locations $\{l_5, l_6\}$, a variable θ, three ports $\{tick, cool, heat\}$ and four transitions: 2 loop transitions labeled by tick which increase or decrease the temperature as time progresses and 2 transitions triggering moves of the rods. The components Rod1 and Rod2 are identical, up to the renaming of states and ports. Each one has two control locations and four transitions: two loop transitions labeled by *tick* and two transitions synchronized with transitions of the Controller. The components are composed by using the following set of interactions, indicated by connectors in the figure: $\{tick, tick_1, tick_2\}$, $\{cool, cool_1\}$, $\{cool, cool_2\}$, $\{heat, rest_1\}$, $\{heat, rest_2\}$.

In our model, complete shutdown corresponds to a deadlock. Throughout the paper we verify deadlock-freedom of this example by taking $Init = at\_l_5 \wedge (\theta = 100) \wedge at\_l_1 \wedge (t_1 = 3600) \wedge at\_l_3 \wedge (t_2 = 3600)$.   □

2.2   Invariants and Their Properties

For a component $B = (L, P, \mathcal{T}, X, \{g_\tau\}_{\tau \in \mathcal{T}}, \{f_\tau\}_{\tau \in \mathcal{T}})$, we recall here the definition of the *post* predicate transformer allowing to compute successors of global states represented symbolically by state predicates. Given a state predicate $\Phi = \bigvee_{l \in L} at\_l \wedge \varphi_l$, we define $post(\Phi) = \bigvee_{l \in L}(\bigvee_{\tau = (l, p, l')} at\_l' \wedge post_\tau(\varphi_l))$ where $post_\tau(\varphi)(X) = \exists X'.g_\tau(X') \wedge f_\tau(X', X) \wedge \varphi(X')$. Equivalently, we have that

$post(\Phi) = \bigvee_{l \in L} at\_l \wedge (\bigvee_{\tau=(l',p,l)} post_\tau(\varphi_{l'}))$. This allows computing $post(\Phi)$ by forward propagation of the assertions associated with control locations in Φ.

We define in a similar way, the pre_τ predicate transformer for a transition τ, $pre_\tau(\varphi)(X) = \exists X'.g_\tau(X) \wedge f_\tau(X, X') \wedge \varphi(X')$.

Definition 6 (Invariants). *Given a system* $\langle B, Init \rangle$ *a state predicate* Φ *is*

- *an inductive invariant iff* $(Init \vee post(\Phi)) \Rightarrow \Phi$.
- *an invariant iff there exists an inductive invariant* Φ_0 *such that* $\Phi_0 \Rightarrow \Phi$.

Notice that invariants are over-approximations of the set of the reachable states from $Init$. We extensively use the following well-known results about invariants.

Proposition 1. *Let* Φ_1, Φ_2 *be two invariants of a component* B. *Then* $\Phi_1 \wedge \Phi_2$, $\Phi_1 \vee \Phi_2$ *are invariants of* B.

3   The Method

We consider a system $\gamma(B_1, \ldots, B_n)$ obtained by composing a set of atomic components $B_1, ..., B_n$ by using a set of interactions γ.

To prove a global invariant Φ for $\gamma(B_1, \ldots, B_n)$, we use the following rule:

$$\frac{\{B_i < \Phi_i >\}_i^n, \; \Psi \in II(\gamma(B_1, \ldots, B_n), \{\Phi_i\}_i^n), \; (\bigwedge_i^n \Phi_i) \wedge \Psi \Rightarrow \Phi}{\gamma(B_1, \ldots, B_n) < \Phi >} \qquad (3)$$

where $B_i < \Phi_i >$ means that Φ_i is an invariant of component B_i and Ψ is an interaction invariant of $\gamma(B_1, \ldots, B_n)$ computed automatically from Φ_i and $\gamma(B_1, \ldots, B_n)$.

A key issue in the application of this rule is finding component invariants Φ_i. If the components B_i are finite state, then we can take $\Phi = Reach(B_i)$, the set of reachable state of B_i, or any upper approximation of $Reach(B_i)$. If the components are infinite state, $Reach(B_i)$ can be approximated as shown in [17,18].

We provide below methods for computing component invariants used for checking deadlock-freedom (section 4). We also provide a general method for computing interaction invariants for $\gamma(B_1, \ldots, B_n)$ from a given set of component invariants Φ_i.

3.1   Computing Component Invariants

We present below a method for the lightweight computation of sequences of inductive invariants for atomic components. This method is used in the D-Finder toolset.

Proposition 2. *Given a system* $\mathcal{S} = \langle B, Init \rangle$, *the following iteration defines a sequence of increasingly stronger inductive invariants:*

$$\Phi_0 = true \quad \Phi_{i+1} = Init \vee post(\Phi_i)$$

We use different strategies for producing such invariants. We usually iterate until we find deadlock-free invariants. Their use guarantees that global deadlocks are exclusively due to synchronization.

A key issue is efficient computation of such invariants as the precise computation of *post* requires quantifier elimination. An alternative to quantifier elimination is to compute over-approximations of *post* based on syntactic analysis of the predicates. In this case, the obtained invariants may not be inductive.

We provide a brief description of a syntactic technique used for approximating $post_\tau$ for a fixed transition τ. A more detailed presentation, as well as other techniques for generating component invariants are given in [19].

Consider a transition $\tau = (l, p, l')$ of $B = (L, P, \mathcal{T}, X, \{g_\tau\}_{\tau \in \mathcal{T}}, \{f_\tau\}_{\tau \in \mathcal{T}})$. Assume that its guard is of the form $g_\tau(Y)$ and the associated update function f_τ is of the form $Z_1' = e_\tau(U) \wedge Z_2' = Z_2$ where $Y, Z_1, Z_2, U \subseteq X$ and $\{Z_1, Z_2\}$ is a partition of X.

For an arbitrary predicate φ find a decomposition $\varphi = \varphi_1(Y_1) \wedge \varphi_2(Y_2)$ such that $Y_2 \cap Z_1 = \emptyset$ i.e. which has a conjunct not affected by the update function f_τ. We apply the following rule to compute over-approximations $post_\tau^a(\varphi)$ of $post_\tau(\varphi)$

$$post_\tau^a(\varphi) = \varphi_2(Y_2) \wedge \begin{Bmatrix} g_\tau(Y) \text{ if } Z_1 \cap Y = \emptyset \\ true \text{ otherwise} \end{Bmatrix} \wedge \begin{Bmatrix} Z_1 = e_\tau(U) \text{ if } Z_1 \cap U = \emptyset \\ true \quad \text{otherwise} \end{Bmatrix}$$

Proposition 3. *If τ and φ are respectively a transition and a state predicate as above, then $post_\tau(\varphi) \Rightarrow post_\tau^a(\varphi)$.*

Example 2. For the Temperature Control System of figure 2, the predicates $\Phi_1 = (at\_l_1 \wedge t_1 \geq 0) \vee (at\_l_2 \wedge t_1 \geq 3600)$, $\Phi_2 = (at\_l_3 \wedge t_2 \geq 0) \vee (at\_l_4 \wedge t_2 \geq 3600)$ and $\Phi_3 = (at\_l_5 \wedge 100 \leq \theta \leq 1000) \vee (at\_l_6 \wedge 100 \leq \theta \leq 1000)$ are respectively invariants of the atomic components Rod1, Rod2 and Controller. □

3.2 Computing Interaction Invariants

For the sake of clarity, we first show how to compute interaction invariants for a system $\gamma(B_1, \ldots, B_n)$ without variables, that is, where the atomic components B_i are finite transition systems. Then, we show how to deal with infinite state systems.

For Finite State Systems
Definition 7. *[Forward Interaction Sets] Given a system $\gamma(B_1, \ldots, B_n)$ where $B_i = (L_i, P_i, \mathcal{T}_i)$ are transition systems, we define for a set of locations $L \subseteq \bigcup_{i=1}^n L_i$ its forward interaction set $L^\bullet = \bigcup_{l \in L} l^\bullet$ where*

$$l^\bullet = \{\{\tau_i\}_{i \in I} \mid \forall i. \tau_i \in \mathcal{T}_i \wedge \exists i.^\bullet \tau_i = l \wedge \{port(\tau_i)\}_{i \in I} \in \gamma\}$$

That is, $l^\bullet$ consists of sets of component transitions involved in some interaction of γ in which a transition τ_i issued from l can participate (see figure 3).

We define in a similar manner, for a set of location its backward interaction set $^\bullet L = \bigcup_{l \in L} {}^\bullet l$ where ${}^\bullet l = \{\{\tau_i\}_{i \in I} \mid \forall i. \tau_i \in \mathcal{T}_i \wedge \exists i. \tau_i^\bullet = l \wedge \{port(\tau_i)\}_{i \in I} \in \gamma\}$

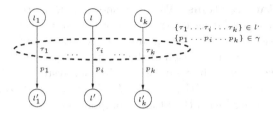

Fig. 3. Forward interaction sets

The elements of $^\bullet l$ and $l^\bullet$ can be also viewed as transitions of a Petri net, which correspond to interactions of γ. As for Petri nets, we can define the notion of trap.

Definition 8 (Traps). *Given a parallel composition* $\gamma(B_1, \ldots, B_n)$ *where* $B_i = (L_i, P_i, \mathcal{T}_i)$, *a trap is a set* L *of locations* $L \subseteq \bigcup_{i=1}^{n} L_i$ *such that* $L^\bullet \subseteq {}^\bullet L$.

The following proposition expresses a characteristic property of traps: if the initial state of $\gamma(B_1, \ldots, B_n)$ has some control location belonging to a trap then all its successor states have some control location belonging to the trap.

Proposition 4. *Given a system* $\mathcal{S} = \langle \gamma(B_1, \ldots, B_n), Init \rangle$, *if the set of locations* $L \subseteq \bigcup_{i=1}^{n} L_i$ *is a trap containing an initial state of some component then* $\bigvee_{l \in L} at\_l$ *is an invariant of* $\mathcal{S}$.

The following result given in [20] characterizes traps as solution of a system of implications.

Proposition 5. *Let* $\gamma(B_1, ..., B_n)$ *and a boolean valuation* $\mathbf{v} : \bigcup_{i=1}^{n} L_i \to \mathbb{B}$. *If* $\mathbf{v}$ *satisfies the following set of the implications, then the set*

$$\{l \in \bigcup_{i=1}^{n} L_i \mid \mathbf{v}(l) = true\}$$

is a trap, where $\mathbf{v}(l) \Rightarrow \bigwedge_{\{\tau_i\}_{i \in I} \in l^\bullet} \left(\bigvee_{l' \in \{\tau_i^\bullet\}_{i \in I}} \mathbf{v}(l') \right)$ *for* $l \in \bigcup_{i=1}^{n} L_i$

This characterization allows to compute by enumeration the minimal traps of $\gamma(B_1, ..., B_n)$. For this we use Yices [15] to successively obtain minimal solutions of the above system. As shown in [21,22] computing the set of minimal traps is a NP-complete problem and in practice the trap extraction process may not be exhaustive.

Example 3. The set of of minimal traps for the example given in figure 4 are:

$L_1 = \{\phi_{21}, \phi_{41}, \phi_{51}, \phi_{52}\}$, $L_2 = \{\phi_{11}, \phi_{12}, \phi_{21}, \phi_{31}, \phi_{32}, \phi_{41}\}$, $L_3 = \{\phi_{32}, \phi_{41}, \phi_{42}, \phi_{51}\}$, $L_4 = \{\phi_{11}, \phi_{12}, \phi_{31}, \phi_{32}, \phi_{61}, \phi_{62}\}$ and $L_5 = \{\phi_{12}, \phi_{21}, \phi_{22}, \phi_{51}\}$.

For Infinite State Systems. We have shown how to compute interaction invariants from traps relating control locations of finite state components. To compute interaction invariants for infinite state systems, we first compute composionally a finite state abstraction of the composite system. Interaction invariants are concretizations of the traps of the abstract system.

Consider a system $\mathcal{S} = \langle \gamma(B_1, \ldots, B_n), Init \rangle$ and a set of component invariants $\Phi_1 \ldots \Phi_n$ associated with the atomic components. We show below, for each component B_i and its associated invariant Φ_i, how to define a finite state abstraction α_i and to compute an abstract transition system $B_i^{\alpha_i}$.

Definition 9 (Abstraction Function). *Let Φ be an invariant of a system $\langle B, Init \rangle$ written in disjunctive form $\Phi = \bigvee_{l \in L} at\_l \wedge (\bigvee_{m \in M_l} \varphi_{lm})$ such that atomic predicates of the form $at\_l \wedge \varphi_{lm}$ are disjoint. An abstraction function α is an injective function associating with each atomic predicate $at\_l \wedge \varphi_{lm}$ a symbol $\phi = \alpha(at\_l \wedge \varphi_{lm})$ called abstract state. We denote by Φ^α the set of the abstract states.*

Definition 10 (Abstract System). *Given a system $\mathcal{S} = \langle B, Init \rangle$, an invariant Φ and an associated abstraction function α, we define the abstract system $\mathcal{S}^\alpha = \langle B^\alpha, Init^\alpha \rangle$ where*

- *$B^\alpha = (\Phi^\alpha, P, \rightsquigarrow)$ is a transition system with $\rightsquigarrow$ such that for any pair of abstract states $\phi = \alpha(at\_l \wedge \varphi)$ and $\phi' = \alpha(at\_l' \wedge \varphi')$ we have $\phi \overset{p}{\rightsquigarrow} \phi'$ iff $\exists \tau = (l, p, l') \in \mathcal{T}$ and $\varphi \wedge pre_\tau(\varphi') \neq false$,*
- *$Init^\alpha = \bigvee_{\phi \in \Phi_0^\alpha} at\_\phi$ where $\Phi_0^\alpha = \{\phi \in \Phi^\alpha \mid \alpha^{-1}(\phi) \wedge Init \neq false\}$ is the set of the initial abstract states.*

We apply the method presented in [23] and implemented in the InVeSt tool [24] in order to compute an abstract transition system B^α for a component B. The method proceeds by elimination, starting from the universal relation on abstract states. We eliminate pairs of abstract states in a conservative way. To check whether $\phi \overset{p}{\rightsquigarrow} \phi'$, where $\phi = \alpha(at\_l \wedge \varphi)$ and $\phi' = \alpha(at\_l' \wedge \varphi')$, can be eliminated, we check that for all concrete transitions $\tau = (l, p, l')$ we have $\varphi \wedge pre_\tau(\varphi') = false$.

Example 4. The table below provides the abstract states constructed from the components invariants Φ_1, Φ_2, Φ_3 of respectively Rod1, Rod2, Controller given in example 2.

$\phi_{11} = at\_l_1 \wedge t_1 = 0$	$\phi_{51} = at\_l_5 \wedge \theta = 100$	$\phi_{31} = at\_l_3 \wedge t_2 = 0$
$\phi_{12} = at\_l_1 \wedge t_1 \geq 1$	$\phi_{52} = at\_l_5 \wedge 101 \leq \theta \leq 1000$	$\phi_{32} = at\_l_3 \wedge t_2 \geq 1$
$\phi_{21} = at\_l_2 \wedge t_1 \geq 3600$	$\phi_{61} = at\_l_6 \wedge \theta = 1000$	$\phi_{41} = at\_l_4 \wedge t_2 \geq 3600$
$\phi_{22} = at\_l_2 \wedge t_1 < 3600$	$\phi_{62} = at\_l_6 \wedge 100 \leq \theta \leq 998$	$\phi_{42} = at\_l_4 \wedge t_2 < 3600$

Figure 4 presents the computed abstraction of the Temperature Control System with respect to the considered invariants.   □

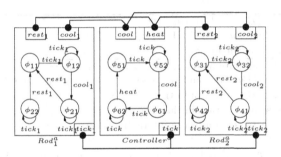

Fig. 4. Abstraction of the Temperature Control System

By combining well-known results about abstractions, we compute interaction invariants of $\langle \gamma(B_1, ..., B_n), Init \rangle$ from interaction invariants of $\langle \gamma(B_1^\alpha, ..., B_n^\alpha), Init^\alpha \rangle$.

The following proposition says that $\gamma(B_1^{\alpha_1}, ..., B_n^{\alpha_n})$ is an abstraction of $B = \gamma(B_1, ..., B_n)$

Proposition 6. *If $B_i^{\alpha_i}$ is an abstraction of B_i with respect to an invariant Φ_i and its abstraction function α_i for $i = 1, ..., n$, then $B^\alpha = \gamma(B_1^{\alpha_1}, ..., B_n^{\alpha_n})$ is an abstraction of $B = \gamma(B_1, ..., B_n)$ with respect to $\bigwedge_{i=1}^n \Phi_i$ and an abstraction function α obtained as the composition of the α_i.*

The following proposition says that invariants of the abstract system are also invariants of the concrete system.

Proposition 7. *If B^α is an abstraction of B with respect to Φ and its abstraction function α, then B^α simulates B. Moreover, if Φ^α is an invariant of $\langle B^\alpha, Init^\alpha \rangle$ then $\alpha^{-1}(\Phi^\alpha)$ is an invariant of $\langle B, Init \rangle$.*

Thus, it is possible to compute from traps which are interaction invariants of the abstract system, interaction invariants for the concrete system $B = \gamma(B_1, ..., B_n)$.

3.3 Wrap Up

We give a sketch of a semi-algorithm allowing to prove invariance of Φ by iterative application of the rule (3). The semi-algorithm takes a system $\langle \gamma(B_1, ..., B_n), Init \rangle$ and a predicate Φ. It iteratively computes invariants of the form $\mathcal{X} = \Psi \wedge (\bigwedge_{i=1}^n \Phi_i)$ where Ψ is an interaction invariant and Φ_i an invariant of component B_i. If $\mathcal{X}$ is not strong enough for proving that Φ is an invariant ($\mathcal{X} \wedge \neg\Phi = false$) then either a new iteration with stronger Φ_i is started or we stop. In this case, we cannot conclude about invariance of Φ. We can show by application of the following proposition that the iteration process gives progressively stronger invariants, in particular that for stronger component invariants we get stronger interaction invariants.

Input: $S = \langle \gamma(B_1, \ldots, B_n), Init \rangle, \Phi$
Initially: $\Phi_i = true$ for each $i = 1, \ldots, n$
Output: True or inconclusive.

---

1. For each B_i, compute a component invariant Φ_i'; $\Phi_i := \Phi_i \wedge \Phi_i'$
2. For each B_i and Φ_i compute the corresponding abstraction $B_i^{\alpha_i}$.
3. For $\gamma(B_1^{\alpha_1}, \ldots, B_n^{\alpha_n})$, compute traps $L_1, L_2, \ldots, L_m$
   containing some abstract initial state.
4. For each trap L_k, compute the interaction invariant $\Psi_k = \bigvee_{\phi \in L_k} \alpha^{-1}(\phi)$;
   $\Psi := \bigwedge_{k=1}^{m} \Psi_k$.
5. If $\neg\Phi \wedge \Psi \wedge (\bigwedge_{i=1}^{n} \Phi_i)$ = false then Φ is an invariant else goto 1 or stop.

Fig. 5. Iterative application of the rule in figure 3

Proposition 8. *Let $\langle B, Init \rangle$ be a system and Φ, Φ' two non empty invariants such that $\Phi \Rightarrow \Phi'$. If α and α' are the abstraction functions corresponding to Φ and Φ' respectively, then B^{α} simulates $B^{\alpha'}$*

For two successive component invariants Φ_i and Φ_i' for B_i, we have $\Phi_i \Rightarrow \Phi_i'$. From proposition 8 we deduce that $B_i^{\alpha_i}$ simulates $B_i^{\alpha_i'}$ where α_i and α_i' are the abstraction functions corresponding to Φ_i and Φ_i'. As the simulation relation is preserved by parallel composition, we have $\gamma(B_1^{\alpha_1}, \ldots, B_n^{\alpha_n})$ simulates $\gamma(B_1^{\alpha_1'}, \ldots, B_n^{\alpha_n'})$. We can show that for each trap L' of $\gamma(B_1^{\alpha_1'}, \ldots, B_n^{\alpha_n'})$ there exists a trap L of $\gamma(B_1^{\alpha_1}, \ldots, B_n^{\alpha_n})$ such that $L \subseteq L'$. From this we infer that for each interaction invariant of $\gamma(B_1', \ldots, B_n')$ there exists a stronger interaction invariant of $\gamma(B_1, \ldots, B_n)$.

4   Application for Checking Deadlock-Freedom

We present an application of the method for checking deadlock-freedom.

Definition 11 (Deadlock States). *We define the predicate DIS characterizing the set of the states of $\gamma(B_1, \ldots, B_n)$ from which all interactions are disabled:*

$$DIS = \bigwedge_{a \in \gamma} \neg en(a) \quad where \quad en(a) = \bigvee_{port(T') = a} \bigwedge_{\tau \in T'} en(\tau)$$

$port(T')$ for a set of transitions $T' \subseteq T$ is the set of ports labeling these transitions. That is, $en(a)$ characterizes all the states from which interaction a can be executed.

Example 5. For the Temperature Control System (see figure 2), we have:

$$DIS = (\neg(at\_l_5 \wedge \theta < 1000)) \wedge (\neg(at\_l_6 \wedge \theta = 100) \vee \neg at\_l_2)$$
$$\wedge (\neg(at\_l_6 \wedge \theta > 100)) \wedge (\neg(at\_l_5 \wedge \theta = 1000) \vee \neg(at\_l_3 \wedge t_2 \geq 3600))$$
$$\wedge (\neg(at\_l_5 \wedge \theta = 1000) \vee \neg(at\_l_1 \wedge t_1 \geq 3600)) \wedge (\neg(at\_l_6 \wedge \theta = 100) \vee \neg at\_l_4) \quad \square$$

Input: $S = \langle \gamma(B_1, \ldots, B_n), Init \rangle$
Output: S is deadlock-free or has a set of potential deadlocks.

1. Find Φ an invariant of S
2. Compute DIS for $\gamma(B_1, \ldots, B_n)$.
3. If $\Phi \wedge DIS = false$ then return "S is deadlock-free" else go to 4 or 6
4. Find Φ' an invariant of S
5. $\Phi := \Phi \wedge \Phi'$ go to 3
6. return the set of the solutions that satisfy $\Phi \wedge DIS$

Fig. 6. Heuristic for Deadlock Verification

The system $\langle \gamma(B_1, \ldots, B_n), Init \rangle$ is deadlock-free if the predicate $\neg DIS$ is an invariant of the system. To check that $\neg DIS$ is an invariant, we need a stronger invariant Φ such that $\Phi \Rightarrow \neg DIS$ or equivalently $\Phi \wedge DIS = false$.

Figure 6 presents the verification heuristic for a system $\langle \gamma(B_1, \ldots, B_n), Init \rangle$ applied by the D-Finder toolset.

Example 6. $\Phi = \Phi_1 \wedge \Phi_2 \wedge \Phi_3$ is the conjunction of the deadlock-free invariants given in example 2. The predicate $\Phi \wedge DIS$, where DIS is given in example 5, is satisfiable and it is the disjunction of the following terms:

1. $(at\_l_1 \wedge 0 \leq t_1 < 3600) \wedge (at\_l_3 \wedge 0 \leq t_2 < 3600) \wedge (at\_l_6 \wedge \theta = 100)$
2. $(at\_l_1 \wedge 0 \leq t_1 < 3600) \wedge (at\_l_4 \wedge t_2 \geq 3600) \wedge (at\_l_5 \wedge \theta = 1000)$
3. $(at\_l_1 \wedge 0 \leq t_1 < 3600) \wedge (at\_l_3 \wedge 0 \leq t_2 < 3600) \wedge (at\_l_5 \wedge \theta = 1000)$
4. $(at\_l_2 \wedge t_1 \geq 3600) \wedge (at\_l_3 \wedge 0 \leq t_2 < 3600) \wedge (at\_l_5 \wedge \theta = 1000)$
5. $(at\_l_2 \wedge t_1 \geq 3600) \wedge (at\_l_4 \wedge t_2 \geq 3600) \wedge (at\_l_5 \wedge \theta = 1000)$

Each one of the above terms represents a family of possible deadlocks. To decrease the number of potential deadlocks, we find a new invariant Φ' stronger than Φ, such that $\Phi' = \Phi \wedge \Phi_{int}$, where Φ_{int} is an invariant on the states of Rod1, Rod2 and Controller induced by the interactions:

$(\ (at\_l_2 \wedge t_1 \geq 3600) \vee (at\_l_4 \wedge t_2 \geq 3600) \vee (at\_l_5 \wedge 100 \leq \theta \leq 1000) \ )$
$\wedge (\ (at\_l_1 \wedge t_1 \geq 0) \vee (at\_l_2 \wedge t_1 \geq 3600) \vee (at\_l_3 \wedge t_2 \geq 0) \vee (at\_l_4 \wedge t_2 \geq 3600) \ )$
$\wedge (\ (at\_l_3 \wedge t_2 \geq 1) \vee (at\_l_4) \vee (at\_l_5 \wedge \theta = 100) \ )$
$\wedge (\ (at\_l_1 \wedge t_1 \geq 0) \vee (at\_l_3 \wedge t_2 \geq 0) \vee (at\_l_6 \wedge \theta = 1000) \vee (at\_l_6 \vee 100 \leq \theta \leq 998) \ )$
$\wedge (\ (at\_l_1 \wedge t_1 \geq 1) \vee (at\_l_2) \vee (at\_l_5 \wedge \theta = 100) \ )$

The predicate $\Phi' \wedge DIS$ is reduced to:

6. $(at\_l_1 \wedge 1 \leq t_1 < 3600) \wedge (at\_l_3 \wedge 1 \leq t_2 < 3600) \wedge (at\_l_5 \wedge \theta = 1000)$
7. $(at\_l_1 \wedge 1 \leq t_1 < 3600) \wedge (at\_l_4 \wedge t_2 \geq 3600) \wedge (at\_l_5 \wedge \theta = 1000)$
8. $(at\_l_2 \wedge t_1 \geq 3600) \wedge (at\_l_3 \wedge 1 \leq t_2 < 3600) \wedge (at\_l_5 \wedge \theta = 1000)$

Finally, it can be checked by using finite state reachability analysis on an abstraction of the system without variables, that only the first term represents feasible deadlocks, the two other being spurious. This term characterizes deadlock configurations leading to complete shutdown.   □

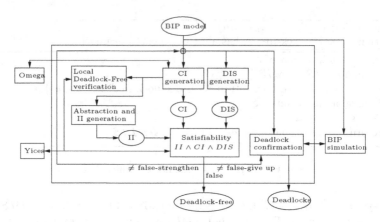

Fig. 7. D-Finder

The D-Finder Toolset. The D-Finder toolset allows deadlock verification by application of the method (figure 7). It takes as input a BIP model and computes component invariants CI by using Proposition 2. This step may require quantifier elimination by using Omega. Then, it checks for deadlock-freedom of component invariants by using Yices. From the generated component invariants, it computes an abstraction of the BIP model and the corresponding interaction invariants II. Then, it checks satisfiability of the conjunction $II \wedge CI \wedge DIS$. If the conjunction is unsatisfiable, then there is no deadlock else either it generates stronger component and interaction invariants or it tries to confirm the detected deadlocks by using reachability analysis techniques.

Experimental Results. We provide experimental results for three examples. The first example is the Temperature Control System extensively presented in the paper. The second example is Utopar, an industrial case study of the European Integrated project SPEEDS (http://www.speeds.eu.com/) about an automated transportation system. A succinct description of Utopar can be found at http://www.combest.eu/home/?link=Application2. The system is the composition of three types of components: autonomous vehicles, called U-cars, a centralized Automatic Control System and Calling Units. The latter two types have (almost exclusively) discrete behavior. U-cars are equipped with a local controller, responsible for handling the U-cars sensors and performing various routing and driving computations depending on users' requests. We analyzed a simplified version of Utopar by abstracting from data exchanged between components as well as from continuous dynamics of the cars. In this version, each U-Car is modeled by a component having 7 control locations and 6 integer variables. The Automatic Control System has 3 control locations and 2 integer variables. The Calling Units have 2 control locations and no variables. Finally, as third example, we consider Readers-Writer systems in order to evaluate how the method scales up for components without data.

The table below provides an overview of the experimental results obtained for the three examples. For the columns: n is the number of BIP components in the example, q is the total number of control locations, x_b (resp. x_i) is the total number of boolean (resp. integer) variables, D provides when possible, the estimated number of deadlock configurations in DIS, D_c (resp. D_{ci}) is the number of deadlock configurations remaining in $DIS \wedge CI$ (resp. $DIS \wedge CI \wedge II$) and t is the total time for computing invariants and checking for satisfiability of $DIS \wedge CI \wedge II$. Detailed results are available at http://www-verimag.imag.fr/~thnguyen/tool.

example	n	q	x_b	x_i	D	D_c	D_{ci}	t
Temperature Control System (2 rods)	3	6	0	3	8	5	3	3s
Temperature Control System (4 rods)	5	10	0	5	32	17	15	1m05s
Utopar System (4 U-Cars, 9 Calling Units)	14	45	4	26	-	-	0	1m42s
Utopar System (8 U-Cars, 16 Calling Units)	25	91	8	50	-	-	0	22m02s
Readers-Writer (50 readers)	52	106	0	1	$\sim 10^{15}$	$\sim 10^{15}$	0	1m15s
Readers-Writer (100 readers)	102	206	0	1	$\sim 10^{30}$	$\sim 10^{30}$	0	15m28s
Readers-Writer (130 readers)	132	266	0	1	$\sim 10^{39}$	$\sim 10^{39}$	0	29m13s

5   Conclusion

The paper presents a compositional method for invariant verification of component-based systems. In contrast to assume-guarantee methods based on assumptions, we use interaction invariants to characterize contexts of individual components. These can be computed automatically from component invariants which play the role of guarantees for individual components.

There are two key issues in the application of the method. The first is the choice of component invariants depending on the property to be proved. The second is the computation of the corresponding interaction invariants. Here there is a risk of explosion, if exhaustiveness of solutions is necessary in the analysis process.

The implementation and application of the method for proving deadlock-freedom of component-based systems is promising. We use a class of component invariants which capture well-enough guarantees for component deadlock-freedom. Their computation does not involve fixpoints and avoids state space exploration. D-Finder applies an iterative process for computing progressively stronger invariants. Best precision is achieved when component reachability sets are used as component invariants. This is feasible for finite state components. There are no restrictions on the type of data as long as we stay within theories for which there exist efficient decision procedures.

The obtained experimental results for non trivial case studies are really convincing. The method can be adapted to interactions with data transfer. Data transfer with finite domains, can be encoded by creating individual interactions for each configuration of transferred data. Otherwise, the notion of component invariant and subsequently the notion of interaction invariant can be extended to take into account transferred data. Finally, an interesting work direction is extending D-Finder to prove properties other than deadlock-fredom.

References

1. Kupferman, O., Vardi, M.Y.: Modular model checking. In: de Roever, W.-P., Langmaack, H., Pnueli, A. (eds.) COMPOS 1997. LNCS, vol. 1536, pp. 381–401. Springer, Heidelberg (1998)
2. Alur, R., Henzinger, T.: Reactive modules. In: Proceedings of the 11th Annual Symposium on LICS, pp. 207–218. IEEE Computer Society Press, Los Alamitos (1996)
3. Abadi, M., Lamport, L.: Conjoining specification. ACM Transactions on Programming Languages and Systems 17(3), 507–534 (1995)
4. Clarke, E., Long, D., McMillan, K.: Compositional model checking. In: Proceedings of the 4th Annual Symposium on LICS, pp. 353–362. IEEE Computer Society Press, Los Alamitos (1989)
5. Chandy, K., Misra, J.: Parallel program design: a foundation. Addison-Wesley Publishing Company, Reading (1988)
6. Grumberg, O., Long, D.E.: Model checking and modular verification. ACM Transactions on Programming Languages and Systems 16(3), 843–871 (1994)
7. McMillan, K.L.: A compositional rule for hardware design refinement. In: Grumberg, O. (ed.) CAV 1997. LNCS, vol. 1254, pp. 24–35. Springer, Heidelberg (1997)
8. Pnueli, A.: In transition from global to modular temporal reasoning about programs, 123–144 (1985)
9. Stark, E.W.: A proof technique for rely/guarantee properties. In: Maheshwari, S.N. (ed.) FSTTCS 1985. LNCS, vol. 206, pp. 369–391. Springer, Heidelberg (1985)
10. Cobleigh, J.M., Avrunin, G.S., Clarke, L.A.: Breaking up is hard to do: An evaluation of automated assume-guarantee reasoning. ACM Transactions on Software Engineering and Methodology 17(2) (2008)
11. Peterson, J.: Petri Net theory and the modelling of systems. Prentice-Hall, Englewood Cliffs (1981)
12. Apt, K.R., Francez, N., de Roever, W.P.: A proof system for communicating sequential processes. ACM Trans. Program. Lang. Syst. 2(3), 359–385 (1980)
13. Basu, A., Bozga, M., Sifakis, J.: Modeling heterogeneous real-time components in bip. In: SEFM, pp. 3–12 (2006)
14. Team, O.: The omega library. Version 1.1.0 (November 1996)
15. Dutertre, B., de Moura, L.: A fast linear-arithmetic solver for DPLL(T). In: Ball, T., Jones, R.B. (eds.) CAV 2006. LNCS, vol. 4144, pp. 81–94. Springer, Heidelberg (2006)
16. Alur, R., Courcoubetis, C., Halbwachs, N., Henzinger, T.A., Ho, P.H., Nicollin, X., Olivero, A., Sifakis, J., Yovine, S.: The algorithmic analysis of hybrid systems. TCS 138(1), 3–34 (1995)
17. Lakhnech, Y., Bensalem, S., Berezin, S., Owre, S.: Incremental verification by abstraction. In: Margaria, T., Yi, W. (eds.) TACAS 2001. LNCS, vol. 2031, pp. 98–112. Springer, Heidelberg (2001)
18. Bradley, A.R., Manna, Z.: Checking safety by inductive generalization of counterexamples to induction. In: FMCAD, pp. 173–180 (2007)
19. Bensalem, S., Lakhnech, Y.: Automatic generation of invariants. FMSD 15(1), 75–92 (1999)
20. Sifakis, J.: Structural properties of petri nets. In: Winkowski, J. (ed.) MFCS 1978. LNCS, vol. 64, pp. 474–483. Springer, Heidelberg (1978)
21. Yamauchi, M., Watanabe, T.: Time complexity analysis of the minimal siphon extraction problem of petri nets. IEICE Transactions on Communications/Electronics/Information and Systems (1999)

22. Tanimoto, S., Yamauchi, M., Watanabe, T.: Finding minimal siphons in general petri nets. IEICE Trans. on Fundamentals in Electronics, Communications and Computer Science E79-A(11), 1817–1824 (1996)
23. Bensalem, S., Lakhnech, Y., Owre, S.: Computing abstractions of infinite state systems automatically and compositionally. In: Y. Vardi, M. (ed.) CAV 1998. LNCS, vol. 1427, pp. 319–331. Springer, Heidelberg (1998)
24. Bensalem, S., Lakhnech, Y., Owre, S.: Invest: A tool for the verification of invariants. In: Y. Vardi, M. (ed.) CAV 1998. LNCS, vol. 1427, pp. 505–510. Springer, Heidelberg (1998)

A Direct Algorithm for Multi-valued Bounded Model Checking

Jefferson O. Andrade and Yukiyoshi Kameyama

Department of Computer Science, University of Tsukuba
joandrade@logic.cs.tsukuba.ac.jp, kameyama@acm.org

Abstract. Multi-valued Model Checking is an extension of classical, two-valued model checking with multi-valued logic. Multi-valuedness has been proved useful in expressing additional information such as incompleteness, uncertainty, and many others, but with the cost of time and space complexity. This paper addresses this problem, and proposes a new algorithm for Multi-valued Model Checking. While Chechik et al. have extended BDD-based Symbolic Model Checking algorithm to the multi-valued case, our algorithm extends Bounded Model Checking (BMC), which can generate a counterexample of minimum length efficiently (if any). A notable feature of our algorithm is that it directly generates conjunctive normal forms, and never reduces multi-valued formulas into many slices of two-valued formulas. To achieve this feature, we extend the BMC algorithm to the multi-valued case and also devise a new translation of multi-valued propositional formulas. Finally, we show experimental results and compare the performance of our algorithm with that of a reduction-based algorithm.

1 Introduction

Model Checking [7] is a way to verify (or refute) a temporal specification against a system. Multi-valued Model Checking (mvMC) [5] is an extension of the ordinary model checking with multi-valued logic [10]. Multi-valuedness can be used to express additional information on the system being verified, such as incompleteness, uncertainty, authenticity, capability, and many others, and has been proved useful in various areas of system and software verification.

The extra expressivity comes at a cost: suppose the domain of truth values is a 2^n-valued Boolean algebra. A naive approach is to decompose the multi-valued Kripke structure and specification into n components (or *slices*), each of which constitutes the i-th bit of the original one, and run an ordinary, two-valued model checker n times. Then the execution time would be n times as long as its 2-valued counterpart. In most applications of multi-valued model checking, each component of the Kripke structure is similar to each other, checking these n slices independently is obviously suboptimal to do multi-valued model checking.

To solve this problem, Chechik and others formulated the multi-valued model checking problems with Quasi-Boolean algebra as the domain of truth values

Cha et al. (Eds.): ATVA 2008, LNCS 5311, pp. 80–94, 2008.

[5,4,6,8], and proposed a symbolic model checking algorithm based on multi-valued extension of Binary Decision Diagram (BDD). If several slices of Kripke structure share the same structures, they can be shared as in the case of BDD's.

This paper takes an alternative way: we propose a multi-valued model checking algorithm based on bounded model checking (BMC) [1]. In the context of two-valued model checking, BMC is known to be useful in finding a counterexamples of minimum length (and sometimes verifying specifications) efficiently by making use of the propositional SAT solvers[1]. We consider the BMC-based approach is promising in multi-valued model checking, since, in the translation from propositional formulas to conjunctive normal forms, all common subformulas can be shared, hence the similarity among slices (components) of the multi-valued Kripke structures can be captured automatically. BMC usually finds a counterexample faster than SMC, but verification by BMC is usually slower than SMC, so these two methods are complementary.

We propose a direct algorithm, rather than a reduction-based one. The reduction-based one reduces multi-valued formulas into many bits of two-valued formulas, and uses the ordinary, two-valued model checker. A merit of this approach is that we do not have to invent a new algorithm nor a new tool. A big drawback is bad performance: if the truth domain is a finite Boolean algebra that has 2^n elements (that is, there are n slices), then we must run a two-valued model checker n times. Instead of that we propose an algorithm which keeps the multi-valued formulas as far as possible, and finally generates conjunctive normal forms directly. To achieve this feature we propose a new translation from multi-valued propositional formulas into conjunctive normal forms.

We compare the following three algorithms for multi-valued bounded model checking:

- *Naive algorithm*: we reduce the Kripke structures and the specification formula into n slices, and use the ordinary, two-valued BMC algorithm n times.
- *Reduction-based algorithm*: we generate a multi-valued propositional formula which represents a bounded model, reduce it to sliced (two-valued) propositional formulas, and finally convert them to conjunctive normal forms (CNF).
- *Direct algorithm*: we generate a multi-valued propositional formula which represents a bounded model, and translate this formula directly to CNF.

We have implemented the latter two and compared their performance, since Naive algorithm is far less efficient. The experimental results are encouraging: for CNF generation, Direct algorithm is more efficient in time and space than Reduction-based one, and for SAT solving, their execution time is comparative. Since CNF generation occupies large part of the total execution time, Direct algorithm seems to be preferable. In addition, as the size of the lattice grows, the merit of the direct algorithm becomes larger.

The contribution of this paper can be summarized as follows:

- We formulate Multi-valued Model Checking problems in the context of Bounded Model Checking.

---

[1] SAT for satisfiability.

- We develop not only a reduction-based algorithm for mvMC but also a direct translation algorithm.
- We compare the efficiency of the direct algorithm and the reduction one using our prototypical implementation, which indicates the direct translation is promising.

The rest of the article is organized as follows. Section 2 introduces multi-valued Kripke structures (mvKS) and the semantics of multi-valued LTL as well as multi-valued model checking. Section 3 introduces translations from multi-valued model checking to multi-valued propositional satisfiability. The subsequent sections 4, 5 and 6 explain the translation algorithms in detail. Section 7 explains our implementation, and gives performance measurement of experimental results. Section 8 gives conclusion and future work.

2 Basics of Multi-valued Model Checking

We introduce the basic definitions of multi-valued Model Checking (mvMC). The formalization in this section is a slightly extended version of those found in the literature [5,4,6,8], and readers are encouraged to refer to them for in-depth explanation and motivating examples on this topic.

2.1 Lattice as the Domain of Truth Values

Classical model checking works for Kripke structures and specification written as a temporal logic formula. In multi-valued model checking, both Kripke structures and temporal logic are extended to multi-valued ones where the domain of truth values forms a lattice with possibly more than two elements. In this paper we use finite Boolean algebras (with 2^n elements) as the domains of truth values. Although this is a more restrictive choice than those found in the literature (for instance, Chechik et al. studied mvMC on Quasi-Boolean algebras [5]), the focus of this paper is in the algorithmic and implementational aspects. We will discuss the extension to more general lattices briefly in Section 8.

We assume that $\mathcal{L}$ is a finite Boolean algebra with a set L of values and operations $\sqcap$ (meet), $\sqcup$ (join) and $\sim$ (negation). An order-n Boolean algebra is the one with 2^n elements for a natural number n, and its element can be represented by n bits (written, for instance, #1101). Then lattice operations join and meet can be performed in a bit-wise manner. We write $\top \overset{\text{def}}{=}$ #11...1 (top) and $\bot \overset{\text{def}}{=}$ #00...0 (bottom).

2.2 Multi-valued Kripke Structure

Classical Kripke structures are extended to multi-valued ones as follows.

Definition 1 (Multi-valued Kripke Structure). *A* Multi-Valued Kripke Structure *(mvKS) over a a lattice* $\mathcal{L} = \langle L, \sqcap, \sqcup, \sim \rangle$ *is the tuple* $\mathcal{M} = (S, \mathcal{I}, \mathcal{R}, \mathcal{AP}, \mathcal{V})$ *such that:*

- S *is a finite set of states.*
- $\mathcal{I} : S \to L$ *specifies the initial states with its "degree".*
- $\mathcal{R} : S \times S \to L$ *is the transition relation in the lattice.*
- $\mathcal{AP}$ *is a finite set of atomic propositions.*
- $\mathcal{V} : S \times \mathcal{AP} \to L$ *is the valuation function that determines the truth value of an atom at a state.*

Some authors [3] keep the transition relation defined over a two-valued lattice. Here we gave a general definition for it.

Example 1 (mvKS). *The following data determines an mvKS over order-4 Boolean algebra:*

$$S = \{s_0, s_1, s_2, s_3\}$$

$$\mathcal{I}(x) = \begin{cases} \#1100 & if \ x = s_0 \\ \#0011 & if \ x = s_3 \\ \bot & otherwise \end{cases}$$

$$\mathcal{R}(x,y) = \begin{cases} \top & if \ (x,y) \in \{(s_0,s_1),(s_1,s_2),(s_3,s_0)\} \\ \#1010 & if \ (x,y) = (s_2,s_3) \\ \#0101 & if \ (x,y) = (s_2,s_0) \\ \bot & otherwise \end{cases}$$

$$\mathcal{AP} = \{p\}$$

$$\mathcal{V}(x,p) = \begin{cases} \top & if \ x = s_3 \\ \bot & otherwise \end{cases}$$

The mvKS in Example 1 is illustrated in the left of Figure 1.

We can view an mvKS as a superposition of n classical Kripke structures, each of which corresponds to the i-th bit of the lattice. The Kripke structure corresponding to each bit is called a *slice* of the mvKS. In Figure 1, the right

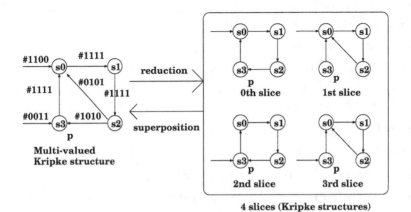

Fig. 1. Multi-Valued Kripke Structure and its Reduction

figure shows the decomposition (or reduction) of the mvKS into 4 slices. It is apparent that, in the case of order-n Boolean algebra, model checking an mvKS is equivalent to model checking of its n slices (modulo the time and space complexity).

We say an mvKS $\mathcal{M}$ is *total* if $(\bigsqcup_{s \in S} \mathcal{I}(s)) = \top$, and, for all $s \in S$, $(\bigsqcup_{s' \in S} \mathcal{R}(s, s')) = \top$. It is easy to see that an mvKS is total if and only if all its slices are total and have at least one initial state. Following Clarke et al. [7], we assume that every mvKS is total throughout the present paper.

We define a *path* as an infinite sequence of states, namely, a mapping $\pi : \mathbb{N} \to S$ where $\mathbb{N}$ is the set of natural numbers. For a path π, π^j denotes the j-th suffix (path), that is, $\pi^j(i) = \pi(i + j)$ for $i \geq 0$.

2.3   Multi-valued Linear-Time Temporal Logic

We use *Linear-time Temporal Logic* (LTL) as the specification logic with a slight extension to express multi-valuedness over a lattice $\mathcal{L}$. We call this extension mvLTL.

Definition 2 (Formulas of mvLTL). *Let $\mathcal{AP}$ be a set of atomic propositions, and $p \in \mathcal{AP}$ and $\ell \in L$ where $\mathcal{L} = \langle L, \sqcap, \sqcup, \sim \rangle$ is a finite Boolean algebra. An mvLTL formula is defined as follows:*

$$\phi, \psi ::= \ell \mid p \mid \neg\phi \mid \phi \wedge \psi \mid \phi \vee \psi$$
$$\mid \mathsf{X}\phi \mid \mathsf{F}\phi \mid \mathsf{G}\phi \mid \phi \mathsf{U} \psi \mid \phi \mathsf{R} \psi$$

Definition 3 (Semantics of mvLTL). *Let $\mathcal{M}$ be an mvKS as above, π be a path on $\mathcal{M}$, and ϕ be an mvLTL formula. We define the interpretation of ϕ with respect to π in $\mathcal{M}$, written $(\pi \models \phi)$, as an element of L as follows:*

- $(\pi \models \ell) \overset{\text{def}}{=} \ell$ *for* $\ell \in L$.
- $(\pi \models p) \overset{\text{def}}{=} \mathcal{V}(\pi(0), p)$ *for* $p \in \mathcal{AP}$.
- $(\pi \models \neg\phi) \overset{\text{def}}{=} \sim(\pi \models \phi)$.
- $(\pi \models (\phi \wedge \psi)) \overset{\text{def}}{=} (\pi \models \phi) \sqcap (\pi \models \psi)$.
- $(\pi \models (\phi \vee \psi)) \overset{\text{def}}{=} (\pi \models \phi) \sqcup (\pi \models \psi)$.
- $(\pi \models \mathsf{X}\phi) \overset{\text{def}}{=} (\pi^1 \models \phi)$.
- $(\pi \models \mathsf{F}\phi) \overset{\text{def}}{=} \bigsqcup_{i \geq 0}(\pi^i \models \phi)$.
- $(\pi \models \mathsf{G}\phi) \overset{\text{def}}{=} \bigsqcap_{i \geq 0}(\pi^i \models \phi)$.
- $(\pi \models \phi \mathsf{U} \psi) \overset{\text{def}}{=} \bigsqcup_{i \geq 0}((\pi^i \models \psi) \sqcap (\bigsqcap_{j < i}(\pi^j \models \phi)))$.
- $(\pi \models \phi \mathsf{R} \psi) \overset{\text{def}}{=} \bigsqcap_{i \geq 0}((\pi^i \models \phi) \sqcup (\bigsqcup_{j \leq i}(\pi^j \models \psi)))$.

In the interpretations of temporal operators, we take infinitary meet and join, but they always exist since we are working with finite Boolean algebras.

2.4   Multi-valued Model Checking Problem

We define the semantics of an mvLTL formula ϕ with respect to $\mathcal{M}$ by:

$$(\mathcal{M} \models \phi) \overset{\text{def}}{=} \prod_{\pi \in \mathbb{N} \to S} ((\sim\mathcal{W}(\pi)) \sqcup (\pi \models \phi))$$

where $\mathcal{W}$ is a mapping from the set of paths to L defined by:

$$\mathcal{W}(\pi) \overset{\text{def}}{=} \mathcal{I}(\pi(0)) \sqcap (\prod_{i \geq 0} \mathcal{R}(\pi(i), \pi(i+1))).$$

$\mathcal{W}(\pi)$ is the weight of the path π, which represents the degree of "being a path in $\mathcal{M}$". In particular, if the first state of the path π is not an initial state ($\mathcal{I}(\pi(0)) = \bot$), then $\mathcal{W}(\pi) = \bot$, hence such a path does not affect the value of $\mathcal{M} \models \phi$.

The *multi-valued model checking problem* is to decide if $(\mathcal{M} \models \phi) = \top$ holds or not. If it holds, ϕ is valid in $\mathcal{M}$.

A *counterexample* of ϕ with respect to $\mathcal{M}$ is a path π such that

$$(\sim\mathcal{W}(\pi)) \sqcup (\pi \models \phi) \neq \top$$

or, equivalently,

$$\mathcal{W}(\pi) \sqcap (\pi \models \neg\phi) \neq \bot.$$

It is easy to see that ϕ is valid *iff* its counterexample does not exist. In the next section, we present an algorithm to find such a counterexample, if it exists.

3   Algorithms of Multi-valued Bounded Model Checking

We aim to obtain an efficient multi-valued model checker. In the literature, the BDD-based Symbolic Model Checking (SMC) has been extended to the MDD-based one where MDD is a multi-valued extension of BDD [4]. However, as long as the authors know, there has been no attempt to exemplify the multi-valued extension of Bounded Model Checking (BMC), which is the goal of this paper.

3.1   Review of Two-Valued Bounded Model Checking

Figure 2 illustrates the process of classical Bounded Model Checking.

The process can be rephrased in words as follows.

1. Given a Kripke structure, an LTL formula ϕ, and a bound $k > 0$, it generates a propositional formula f (with state variables $x_0, x_1, \ldots, x_k$) which expresses a k-bounded model of $\neg\phi$. More precisely, $f(x_0, x_1, \ldots, x_k)$ holds if and only if $x_0, x_1, \ldots, x_k$ is either a finite path or a "lasso"-shaped looping path such that $\neg\phi$ holds along this path.
2. The formula f is converted to a conjunctive normal form (CNF) since most SAT solvers accept CNF only.

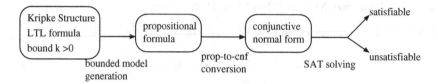

Fig. 2. Process of Bounded Model Checking

3. Finally a SAT solver decides if the CNF is satisfiable or not. If it is satisfiable, there is a counterexample of length k, and otherwise, k is incremented and the same procedure is repeated.

We have to iterate this process only finitely many times, up to the completeness threshold: if there is no counterexample until then, we can conclude that the given specification is verified [1].

3.2 Overview of Multi-valued Bounded Model Checking

We desire a BMC algorithm for the multi-valued case, but still utilizing state-of-the-art SAT solvers which works for two-valued formulas. Hence, we need to switch from the multi-valued world to the two-valued one at some point in Figure 2. There are three possibilities for this, which are illustrated by Figure 3.

Reflecting the three possibilities, we get three algorithms for Multi-valued Bounded Model Checking:

- *Naive Algorithm* is the route $1 \rightarrow 2 \rightarrow 3 \rightarrow 4$, which first reduces the mvKS and mvLTL formula to two-valued one.
- *Reduction-based Algorithm* is the route $5 \rightarrow 6 \rightarrow 3 \rightarrow 4$, which reduces the output of the mv-formula generated by bounded model generation.
- *Direct Algorithm* is the route $5 \rightarrow 7 \rightarrow 4$, which keeps the multi-valuedness as far as possible, and directly generates CNF.

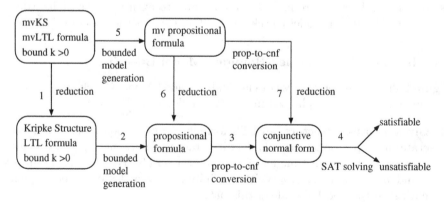

Fig. 3. Process of Multi-Valued Bounded Model Checking

Since performance of Naive Algorithm is the worst, we will investigate the latter two where we use or extend the following algorithms and tools that were developed for the two-valued case:

- For bounded model generation, we slightly extend Biere et al's algorithm [1].
- For the conversion from propositional formula to CNF, we extend the algorithm for structure-preserving conversion [12,1].
- For SAT solving, we use MiniSat solver [9].

4   Bounded Model Generation

The process of multi-valued Bounded Model Generation (Step 5 in Figure 3) is common to Reduction-based and Direct Algorithms. It generates a multi-valued propositional formula which represents a k-bounded model, namely, a counterexample for the given specification of length k.

The algorithm is an extension of the two-valued case [1] and generates a multi-valued propositional formula (mv-propositional formula), which is a propositional formula possibly with lattice elements as propositional constants.

Example 2. *As examples of mv-propositional formula, we define the formulas $\mathcal{I}'$ and $\mathcal{R}'$ which correspond to $\mathcal{I}$ and $\mathcal{R}$ in Example 1.*

$$\mathcal{I}'(x) \stackrel{\text{def}}{=} (x = s_0 \land \#\mathit{1100}) \lor (x = s_3 \land \#\mathit{0011})$$

$$\mathcal{R}'(x, y) \stackrel{\text{def}}{=} (x = s_0 \land y = s_1) \lor (x = s_1 \land y = s_2) \lor (x = s_3 \land y = s_0)$$

$$\lor (x = s_2 \land y = s_3 \land \#\mathit{1010}) \lor (x = s_2 \land y = s_0 \land \#\mathit{0101})$$

Definition 4 (Bounded Model Generation). *Let $\mathcal{M}$, ϕ, and k be an mvKS, an mvLTL formula, and a non-negative integer, resp., and $x_0, x_1, \ldots, x_k$ be variables for states. Then we construct a multi-valued propositional formula $[\![\mathcal{M}, \neg\phi]\!]_k$ with free variables $x_0, x_1, \ldots, x_k$ as follows:*

$$[\![\mathcal{M}, \neg\phi]\!]_k \stackrel{\text{def}}{=} [\![\mathcal{M}]\!]_k \land [\![\neg\phi]\!]_k, \quad \text{where}$$

$$[\![\mathcal{M}]\!]_k \stackrel{\text{def}}{=} \mathcal{I}'(x_0) \land \bigwedge_{i=0}^{k-1} \mathcal{R}'(x_i, x_{i+1})$$

$$[\![\neg\phi]\!]_k \stackrel{\text{def}}{=} \left(\neg \left(\bigvee_{l=0}^{k} \mathcal{R}'(x_l, x_k) \right) \land [\![\neg\phi]\!]_k^0 \right) \lor \bigvee_{l=0}^{k} \left(\mathcal{R}'(x_k, x_l) \land {}_l[\![\neg\phi]\!]_k^0 \right)$$

where $\mathcal{I}'$ and $\mathcal{R}'$ are the mv-propositional formulas representing $\mathcal{I}$ and $\mathcal{R}$ in $\mathcal{M}$, and the mv-formulas $[\![\neg\phi]\!]_k^0$ and ${}_l[\![\neg\phi]\!]_k^0$ are defined in Figure 4.

As in the two-valued case, the formula $[\![\mathcal{M}, \neg\phi]\!]_k$ is constructed so that it has a non-$\perp$ value if and only if $x_0, x_1, \ldots, x_k$ form either a finite path along which $\neg\phi$

$$\iota[\![\ell]\!]_k^i \overset{\text{def}}{=} \ell$$

$$\iota[\![p]\!]_k^i \overset{\text{def}}{=} \mathcal{V}'(x_i, p)$$

$$[\![\ell]\!]_k^i \overset{\text{def}}{=} \ell$$

$$\iota[\![\neg p]\!]_k^i \overset{\text{def}}{=} \neg\mathcal{V}'(x_i, p)$$

$$[\![p]\!]_k^i \overset{\text{def}}{=} \mathcal{V}'(x_i, p)$$

$$\iota[\![\phi \wedge \psi]\!]_k^i \overset{\text{def}}{=} \iota[\![\phi]\!]_k^i \wedge \iota[\![\psi]\!]_k^i$$

$$[\![\neg p]\!]_k^i \overset{\text{def}}{=} \neg\mathcal{V}'(x_i, p)$$

$$\iota[\![\phi \vee \psi]\!]_k^i \overset{\text{def}}{=} \iota[\![\phi]\!]_k^i \vee \iota[\![\psi]\!]_k^i$$

$$[\![\phi \wedge \psi]\!]_k^i \overset{\text{def}}{=} [\![\phi]\!]_k^i \wedge [\![\psi]\!]_k^i$$

$$\iota[\![\mathsf{X}\,\phi]\!]_k^i \overset{\text{def}}{=} \iota[\![\phi]\!]_k^{succ(i)}$$

$$[\![\phi \vee \psi]\!]_k^i \overset{\text{def}}{=} [\![\phi]\!]_k^i \vee [\![\psi]\!]_k^i$$

$$\iota[\![\mathsf{F}\,\phi]\!]_k^i \overset{\text{def}}{=} \bigvee_{j=\min(i,l)}^{k} \iota[\![\phi]\!]_k^j$$

$$[\![\mathsf{X}\,\phi]\!]_k^i \overset{\text{def}}{=} \begin{cases} [\![\phi]\!]_k^{i+1}, & \text{if } i < k \\ \bot, & \text{otherwise} \end{cases}$$

$$\iota[\![\mathsf{G}\,\phi]\!]_k^i \overset{\text{def}}{=} \bigwedge_{j=\min(i,l)}^{k} \iota[\![\phi]\!]_k^j$$

$$\iota[\![\phi \,\mathsf{U}\, \psi]\!]_k^i \overset{\text{def}}{=} \bigvee_{j=i}^{k}\left(\iota[\![\psi]\!]_k^j \wedge \bigwedge_{n=i}^{j-1} \iota[\![\phi]\!]_k^n\right) \vee$$

$$[\![\mathsf{F}\,\phi]\!]_k^i \overset{\text{def}}{=} \bigvee_{j=i}^{k}[\![\phi]\!]_k^j$$

$$\bigvee_{j=l}^{i-1}\left(\iota[\![\psi]\!]_k^j \wedge \bigwedge_{n=l}^{k} \iota[\![\phi]\!]_k^n \wedge \bigvee_{n=l}^{j-1}\iota[\![\phi]\!]_k^n\right)$$

$$[\![\mathsf{G}\,\phi]\!]_k^i \overset{\text{def}}{=} \bot$$

$$[\![\phi \,\mathsf{U}\, \psi]\!]_k^i \overset{\text{def}}{=} \bigvee_{j=i}^{k}([\![\psi]\!]_k^j \wedge \bigwedge_{n=i}^{j-1}[\![\phi]\!]_k^n)$$

$$\iota[\![\phi \,\mathsf{R}\, \psi]\!]_k^i \overset{\text{def}}{=} \bigwedge_{j=\min(i,l)}^{k} \iota[\![\psi]\!]_k^j \vee$$

$$[\![\phi \,\mathsf{R}\, \psi]\!]_k^i \overset{\text{def}}{=} \bigvee_{j=i}^{k}([\![\phi]\!]_k^j \wedge \bigwedge_{n=i}^{j}[\![\psi]\!]_k^n)$$

$$\bigvee_{j=i}^{k}\left(\iota[\![\phi]\!]_k^j \wedge \bigwedge_{n=i}^{j} \iota[\![\psi]\!]_k^n\right) \vee$$

(a) Translation $[\![\phi]\!]_k^i$ of an mvLTL formula ϕ without a loop.

$$\bigvee_{j=l}^{i-1}\left(\iota[\![\phi]\!]_k^j \wedge \bigwedge_{n=i}^{k} \iota[\![\psi]\!]_k^n \wedge \bigwedge_{n=l}^{j} \iota[\![\psi]\!]_k^n\right)$$

(b) Translation $\iota[\![\phi]\!]_k^i$ of an mvLTL formula ϕ for a (l, k)-loop.

Fig. 4. The inductive definition of the translation for an mvLTL formula ϕ in NNF with a bound k and $i \in \mathbb{N}$ with $i \leq k$, where $\mathcal{V}'$ is the formula representing $\mathcal{V}$

holds in the bounded semantics, or an (l, k)-loop (the next state of x_k is x_l for some $l \leq k$) along which $\neg\phi$ holds in the standard semantics. Corresponding to the two cases, the mv-formulas $[\![\neg\phi]\!]_k^0$ and $\iota[\![\neg\phi]\!]_k^0$ represent the semantics of $\neg\phi$ at the state 0. Note that, following Biere et al.[1], Figure 4 defines the translation for ϕ in NNF (Negation Normal Form) only, hence we need to convert $\neg\phi$ to NNF before applying the translation in Figure 4.

The definition above is almost the same as the two-valued one found in the literature[1] except the following points:

- The formulas $\mathcal{I}'$, $\mathcal{R}'$, and $\mathcal{V}'$ are multi-valued propositional formulas, namely, they may contain lattice elements as subformulas.
- However, the atomic formula $x = s_j$ is interpreted by either $\top$ or $\bot$, namely, it essentially remains a two-valued formula.

We say an mv-propositional formula f with free state variables $x_0, \ldots x_k$ is satisfiable if and only if f has a non-$\bot$ value for some assignment of $x_0, \ldots x_k$ to states. Then we have the following theorem.

Theorem 1 (Correctness of Bounded Model Generation). *Let $\mathcal{M}$ be an mvKS and ϕ be an mvLTL formula.*

Soundness. *If $[\![\mathcal{M}, \neg\phi]\!]_k$ is satisfiable, then there exists a counterexample of ϕ in $\mathcal{M}$ whose length is k.*

Completeness. *If ϕ is not valid in $\mathcal{M}$, then $[\![\mathcal{M}, \neg\phi]\!]_k$ is satisfiable for some k.*

Proof. For each $i < n$ (where n is the order of Boolean algebra), the i-th slice of $[\![\mathcal{M}, \neg\phi]\!]_k$ is identical to the resulting formula of two-valued Bounded Model Generation for the i-th slice of $\mathcal{M}$ and ϕ. Also the totality condition for mvKS implies totality for sliced Kripke structures. Hence the soundness and completeness for the multi-valued version of bounded model generation follows from that for the two-valued version, which was proved, for instance, in [2].

5 Reduction-Based Algorithm

Reduction-based Algorithm takes the route $5 \rightarrow 6 \rightarrow 3 \rightarrow 4$ in Figure 3, and we explain Steps 6 and 3 in this section.

Definition 5 (Reduction of mv-Propositional Formula (Step 6)). *Given a multi-valued propositional formula f, we define its i-th slice, $\mathrm{Slice}_i(f)$, as follows:*

$$\mathrm{Slice}_i(\ell) \overset{\text{def}}{=} \begin{cases} \bot & \textit{if the i-th bit of ℓ is 0} \\ \top & \textit{if the i-th bit of ℓ is 1} \end{cases}$$

For other cases, $\mathrm{Slice}_i(f)$ is defined homomorphicly, for instance, $\mathrm{Slice}_i(\phi \wedge \psi) = \mathrm{Slice}_i(\phi) \wedge \mathrm{Slice}_i(\psi)$.

For example, for $\mathcal{I}'(x)$ in Example 2, $\mathrm{Slice}_1(\mathcal{I}'(x))$ is $(x = s_0 \wedge \top) \vee (x = s_3 \wedge \bot)$, which is simplified to $(x = s_0)$. Obviously, f is satisfiable (has a non-$\bot$ value) if and only if $\mathrm{Slice}_i(f)$ is satisfiable for some i.

The result of Step 6 is n sliced propositional formulas. We then take their disjunction (since we are interested in satisfiability), and converts it to a CNF. For the Prop-to-CNF Conversion (Step 3), we use the structure-preserving conversion [12,1].

A few remarks follow.

- All common subformulas will be shared by the conversion, which is especially useful in the context of multi-valued model checking, as we assume that slices of one mvKS are similar to each other.
- However, sharing in Reduction-based Algorithm is not completely satisfactory. Since sharing occurs only among identical subformulas, a small difference in a deeply nested subformula prohibits sharing. Suppose we reduce an mv-formula $(((\texttt{\#10} \wedge a) \vee b) \wedge a) \vee b$ into two slices and convert the disjunction of these slices into CNF. Although the two slices $((a \vee b) \wedge a) \vee b$ and $(b \wedge a) \vee b$ are quite similar to each other, they do not share any subformulas except a and b. In general, if a lattice element exists in a deeply nested subformula of the given mv-formula, sharing does not take place. In such a case, Reduction-based Algorithm cannot generate a small CNF.

6   Direct Algorithm

We explain Step 7 in Figure 3, which is the key step of Direct Algorithm ($5 \to 7 \to 4$). This algorithm is motivated by occasional inefficiency of Reduction-based Algorithm as explained in the previous section. In order to generate as small CNF's as possible, we should share as many subexpressions as possible.

Our idea is simple: rather than *generating* all the sliced formulas, we introduce new propositional variables to *represent* slices, and leave the decision as to which slice should be generated to the SAT solver.

Let us give an example. Example 2 uses the order-4 Boolean algebra, so we introduce two propositional variables q_0 and q_1 to represent each slice number as a binary number. For instance, the 0th slice is $(\neg q_0 \wedge \neg q_1)$, the 1st is $(q_0 \wedge \neg q_1)$ and so on.[2] A lattice element #1100 has the bit 1 in the 0th and 1st slices, hence it is represented by $(\neg q_0 \wedge \neg q_1) \vee (q_0 \wedge \neg q_1)$, or simply $\neg q_1$. Then an mv-formula $(x = s_0) \wedge$ #1100 is represented by $(x = s_0) \wedge \neg q_1$. Then the whole formula $\mathcal{I}'(x)$ is represented by $((x = s_0) \wedge \neg q_1) \vee ((x = s_3) \wedge q_1)$. This translation increases the size of the resulting formula, compared to the original mv-formula, much less than the Reduction-based algorithm does.

Definition 6 (Representation of Lattice Values). *For an order-n Boolean algebra $\mathcal{L}$, let $h = \lceil \log_2(n) \rceil$ and $q_0, \ldots, q_{h-1}$ be propositional variables.*

- *For a natural number i such that $0 \leq i < n$, we define $Q_p(i)$ for $0 \leq p < h$ by:*

$$Q_p(i) = \begin{cases} q_p & \text{if the } p\text{-th bit of } i \text{ is } 1 \\ \neg q_p & \text{otherwise} \end{cases}$$

  and then $R(i)$ is defined as $Q_0(i) \wedge \cdots \wedge Q_{h-1}(i)$. Note that $R(i)$ is the binary representation of i in terms of $q_0, \ldots, q_{h-1}$. For instance, if $h = 5$, then $R(6)$ is $\neg q_0 \wedge q_1 \wedge q_2 \wedge \neg q_3 \wedge \neg q_4$, which is 00110 as a binary number (note that q_0 corresponds to the least significant bit).
- *For an element ℓ of $\mathcal{L}$, we define $\text{Rep}(\ell) = \bigvee_{i \in One(\ell)} R(i)$ where $One(\ell) = \{i \mid \ell\text{'s } i\text{-th bit is } 1\}$.*

Although the above representation is not quite efficient, we can make use of the Karnaugh map technique to simplify it. Note also that, we need only $\lceil \log_2(n) \rceil$ propositional variables to represent slices in the order-n Boolean algebra.

Definition 7 (Direct Algorithm (Step 7)). *Let f be a multi-valued propositional formula over the order-n Boolean algebra, and $h = \lceil \log_2(n) \rceil$.*

1. *Generate h propositional variables $q_0, \ldots, q_{h-1}$.*
2. *Replace any lattice element ℓ in f by $\text{Rep}(\ell)$.*
3. *If $n < 2^h$, let f' be $f \wedge \bigwedge_{n \leq i < 2^h} \neg R(i)$. If $n = 2^h$, let f' be f.*
4. *Apply the structure-preserving conversion [12,1] to f'.*

---

[2] Here we assume q_0 corresponds to the least significant bit.

The third step is necessary to exclude spurious slices.

The algorithm above is guaranteed to be correct. For simplicity we assume that $n = 2^h$ for some natural number h.

Theorem 2 (Correctness of Direct Algorithm). *Let f be an mv-propositional formula over the order-n Boolean algebra with $n = 2^h$. If the algorithm for Step 7 generates a CNF c with $q_0, \ldots, q_{h-1}$, then f is satisfiable (in the multi-valued sense) if and only if c is satisfiable for some truth-value assignment for $q_0, \ldots, q_{h-1}$.*

Proof. We have that f is satisfied if and only if its i-th sliced formula is satisfied for some i. Since each slice is represented by a truth-value assignment of q_j's, this is equivalent to the satisfiability of the resulting CNF for some assignment of q_j's.

7   Experimental Results

We have implemented Reduction-based and Direct Algorithms for mvMC, and compared their performance[3]. Our implementation choices are listed below.

- For Reduction-based Algorithm, we compose (fuse) Step 6 and Step 3 into a single recursive function to gain better performance. At the same time, the function simplifies the formula using $\top \wedge f \leftrightarrow f$ etc., and this choice forces us to use the bottom-up variant of the prop-to-CNF conversion.
- For Direct Algorithm, we implement the top-down algorithm in Section 6. Note that not only CNF's but also the representation of lattice elements are cached and shared, hence they are processed only once.
- For SAT solving, we use MiniSat solver version 1.14 using the DIMACS format [11] as its input.

We have implemented these algorithms in the programming language OCaml, and executed them on a machine with 1.0GB memory and Intel Celeron (2.8 GHz) processor running Linux Operating System.

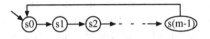

Fig. 5. Model-1

For the target of this experiment, we take a simple mvKS with m states, and the order of Boolean algebra is n. The first model, Model-1, is illustrated in Figure 5, which shows its initial state (s_0 only) and the transition relation. Transitions are essentially two-valued (with the truth values $\top$ or $\bot$ only) so we

---

[3] In fact, we have implemented many other variants, but here we list only the results of the two most efficient algorithms.

Table 1. Experimental Results for Model-1

Model-1			CNF gen.		SAT solving		CNF size			
k	n	m	red.	direct	red.	direct	one bit	red.	direct	result
14	32	16	2	0	0.0	0.0	5470	11590	6331	unsat.
15	32	16	2	0	0.0	0.0	5889	12417	6801	sat.
30	64	32	32	0	0.5	0.1	23276	72380	26569	unsat.
31	64	32	40	0	0.2	0.0	24129	74817	27521	sat.
62	128	64	683	7	5.4	0.6	95818	488938	108615	unsat.
63	128	64	715	8	1.0	0.1	97537	496897	110529	sat.

Table 2. Experimental Results for Model-2

Model-2			CNF gen.		SAT solving		CNF size			
k	n	m	red.	direct	red.	direct	one bit	red.	direct	result
10	128	64	66	1	4.4	8.2	30826	99466	33483	unsat.
12	128	64	90	2	9.7	11.1	36718	117838	39765	unsat.
14	128	64	113	2	12.5	14.0	42634	136234	46071	unsat.
16	128	64	145	2	25.4	12.2	48574	154654	52401	unsat.
18	128	64	184	2	63.7	22.9	54538	173098	58755	unsat.
20	128	64	226	2	94.4	28.6	60526	191566	65133	unsat.
22	128	64	281	3	42.8	14.0	66538	210058	71535	sat.
24	128	64	329	3	60.9	13.8	72574	228574	77961	sat.

do not write the lattice elements as their values. The valuation function only is multi-valued:

$$\mathcal{V}(s_i, p) = \#0 \cdots 010 \cdots 0$$

with the i-th bit being 1. Then $\mathsf{F}\,p$ is valid in this model if $m \geq n$, and not valid otherwise, in which case there exists a counterexample of length $k = m - 1$. The other two models, Model-2 and Model-3, are small variants of Model-1: in Model-2, $\mathcal{R}(s_i, s_j) = \top$ if and only if $i < j \leq ((i + 3) \bmod m)$, and in Model-3, $\mathcal{R}(s_i, s_j) = \top$ if and only if $i < j \leq ((i + 8) \bmod m)$. In addition, the valuation function in Model-3 is modified to: $\mathcal{V}(s_i, p) = \#0 \cdots 01 \cdots 10 \cdots 0$ with the i-th to $i + 8$-th bits being 1.

Tables 1, 2 and 3 show several experiments for these models. In the table, "red." means Reduction-based Algorithm and "direct" Direct one. The column "CNF gen." shows the execution time (in seconds) before SAT solving (Steps 6 and 3 for Reduction-based one and Step 7 for Direct one), and the column "SAT solving" shows the execution time (in seconds) for SAT solving for their output CNF's. The column "CNF size" shows the number of clauses in the generated CNF[4] where the column "one bit" shows the CNF size of one slice. The column "result" shows the result of SAT solving where "sat." means the algorithm finds a counterexample for the given bound k, the model with m states and the

---

[4] The number of propositional variables and the overall size of CNF are almost linear in the number of clauses in all cases.

Table 3. Experimental Results for Model-3

Model-3			CNF gen.		SAT solving		CNF size			
k	n	m	red.	direct	red.	direct	one bit	red.	direct	result
10	32	128	95	5	20.5	32.1	142808	138977	138320	unsat.
12	32	128	124	5	25.9	46.9	164664	169968	165423	unsat.
14	32	128	157	7	35	81.7	191032	197152	191893	unsat.
16	32	128	204	9	22.9	0.2	217424	224360	218387	sat.
18	32	128	289	13	24.1	29.8	243840	251592	244905	sat.

order-n lattice. It should be noted that our implementations show the correct answers for all cases.

We can understand the results as follows.

- Efficient implementation of mv-BMC is possible. Compared with the one-bit case, both algorithms can generate CNF's whose size is much smaller than n times of the CNF size of one-bit case. For instance, the bottom line of the first table shows that Direct Algorithm generated a CNF with 110,529 clauses which is only 13% larger than that generated by the one-bit slice (note that $n = 128$ for this experiment).
- For the comparison between Reduction-based and Direct Algorithms, the latter is better in CNF-generation: its execution time is always much faster (and the difference becomes huge when the order n becomes larger), and the size of generated CNF is smaller or roughly the same.
- The execution time of the SAT solver for the generated CNF is not easily compared between the two methods. Reduction-based one is usually better for smaller n's despite the fact that it generates a bigger CNF. However, the difference is not very big, and Direct method is sometimes better.
- Since CNF generation phase takes longer time than SAT solving, the total execution of Direct Algorithm is better than that of Reduction-based one. Since our experiments are for relatively small models, and our implementation may be suboptimal, we cannot generalize this statement at the moment. However, these results are surely encouraging.

8   Conclusion and Future Directions

We have explored the possibility to obtain an efficient Multi-valued Bounded Model Checker, and for this purpose, we have formalized Reduction-based and Direct Algorithms with correctness guarantee. We have implemented these algorithms (together with other ones) and successfully shown that Multi-Valued Bounded Model Checking is surely possible. Also, we have compared their performance: to the extent we have tested, Direct Algorithm seems to be better than Reduction-based one, but this last point should be examined further.

For future work, we need to introduce into our framework various optimizations found in the context of two-valued BMC. We have already started in investigating some of such optimizations, which are easily integrated to our algorithms. Another obvious thing to do is to extend the lattice to more general one such as Quasi-Boolean algebras, which seems not too difficult, after Chechik and others' work [5]. Experiments with larger, more realistic Kripke structures and finding good application areas are also important.

Acknowledgments. We would like to thank the anonymous referees for insightful comments. The authors were supported in part by JSPS Grant-in-Aid for Scientific Research 20650003.

References

1. Biere, A., Cimatti, A., Clarke, E., Zhu, Y.: Symbolic model checking without BDDs. In: Cleaveland, W.R. (ed.) TACAS 1999. LNCS, vol. 1579, pp. 193–207. Springer, Heidelberg (1999)
2. Biere, A., Clarke, E.M., Fujita, M., Zhu, Y.: Symbolic Model Checking Using SAT Procedures Instead of BDDs. In: Design Automation Conference, pp. 317–320 (1999)
3. Chechik, M., Devereaux, B., Easterbrook, S.: Implementing a multi-valued symbolic model checker. In: Margaria, T., Yi, W. (eds.) TACAS 2001. LNCS, vol. 2031, pp. 404–419. Springer, Heidelberg (2001)
4. Chechik, M., Devereaux, B., Easterbrook, S., Gurfinkel, A.: Multi-valued symbolic model-checking. ACM Transaction on Software Engineering and Methodology 2(4), 371–408 (2003)
5. Chechik, M., Devereaux, B., Easterbrook, S., Lai, Y.C., Petrovykh, V.: Efficient multiple-valued model-checking using lattice representations. In: Larsen, K.G., Nielsen, M. (eds.) CONCUR 2001. LNCS, vol. 2154, pp. 441–455. Springer, Heidelberg (2001)
6. Chechik, M., Gurfinkel, A., Devereaux, B., Lai, A., Easterbrook, S.: Data structures for symbolic multi-valued model-checking. Form. Methods Syst. Des. 29(3), 295–344 (2006)
7. Clarke, E.M., Grumberg, O., Peled, D.A.: Model Checking. MIT Press, Cambridge (1999)
8. Easterbrook, S., Chechik, M.: A framework for multi-valued reasoning over inconsistent viewpoints. In: International Conference on Software Engineering, pp. 411–420 (2001)
9. Een, N., Sorensen, N.: The MiniSat homepage, http://minisat.se/
10. Fitting, M.C.: Many-valued modal logics. Fundamenta Informaticae XV, 235–254 (1991)
11. Johnson, D.S., Trick, M.A. (eds.): Cliques, Coloring and Satisfiability: Second DIMACS Implementation Challenge. DIMACS Series In Discrete Mathematics and Theoretical Computer Science, vol. 26. AMS (1996)
12. Plaisted, D., Greenbaum, S.: A structure-preserving clause form translation. Journal of Symbolic Computation 2, 293–304 (1986)

Model Checking Recursive Programs with Exact Predicate Abstraction

Arie Gurfinkel[1], Ou Wei[2], and Marsha Chechik[2]

[1] Software Engineering Institute, Carnegie Mellon University
[2] Department of Computer Science, University of Toronto

Abstract. We propose an approach for analyzing non-termination and reachability properties of recursive programs using a combination of over- and under-approximating abstractions. First, we define a new concrete program semantics, *mixed*, that combines both natural and operational semantics, and use it to design an on-the-fly symbolic algorithm. Second, we combine this algorithm with abstraction by following classical fixpoint abstraction techniques. This makes our approach parametrized by different approximating semantics of predicate abstraction and enables a uniform solution for over- and under-approximating semantics. The algorithm is implemented in YASM, and we show that it can establish non-termination of non-trivial C programs completely automatically.

1 Introduction

Automated predicate abstraction is one of the key techniques for extending finite-state model-checking to software. It combines automated construction of a finite abstract model with automated analysis by model-checking and iterative abstraction refinement. Traditionally, predicate abstraction is an over-approximation of a program and thus is biased towards establishing correctness of safety properties. To exploit the bug detection ability of model-checkers and to extend the scope of abstract model-checkers to richer properties, recent research has proposed abstract analysis that combines both over- and under-approximations [9, 15, 25, 26, 4, 18, 17]. Although such a combination, which we call *exact-approximation*, has been shown to be effective in practice [17, 19], until now this line of research has focused exclusively on analyzing non-recursive programs. In this paper, we propose a novel approach to extend such over- and under-approximating analyses to *recursive* programs. Our approach has been implemented in a software model-checker YASM. We illustrate it on non-termination and reachability analysis of several C programs, including the benchmarks from BEBOP [6], VERA [1], and MOPED [14, 8], the Ack program from [10] and a buggy version of Quicksort from [14]. To our knowledge, this is the first time that *non-termination* of such C programs was established completely automatically.

As a motivation, we review an over-approximation-based approach for model-checking of non-recursive programs and its limitations. Assume we want to check whether the ERROR label is reachable in the C program EX_0 shown in Figure 1(a). This safety property is expressed in CTL as $\varphi : AG \ (pc \neq ERROR)$. An over-approximating abstraction $\alpha(EX_0)$ of EX_0 using the predicate $p : x > 0$ is shown in Figure 1(b), where '$*$' is interpreted as a non-deterministic choice. $\alpha(EX_0)$ is a finite *boolean* model

Cha et al. (Eds.): ATVA 2008, LNCS 5311, pp. 95–110, 2008.

```
        1. x=read(); y=read();              1. p = *;
        2. if(x>0){                         2. if(p){
        3.    while(x>0) {                  3.    while(p) {
        4.       x=x+1;                      4.       p = p?true:*;
(a)     5.       if(x<=0) ERROR;}    (b)    5.       if(!p) ERROR;}
        6. } else                           6. } else
        7.       while(y>0) y=y-1;          7.       while(*) p = p;
        8. END;                             8. END;
```

Fig. 1. (a) A program EX_0, and (b) its over-approximation $\alpha(EX_0)$ using predicate $p : x > 0$

which over-approximates the original program: it contains all feasible and some infeasible (or spurious) executions. For example, $\alpha(EX_0)$ has an execution which gets stuck in the while(*) loop on line 7, but EX_0 does not have the corresponding execution. Thus, if a universal temporal property, i.e., in the one expressed in ACTL, holds in $\alpha(EX_0)$, it also holds in EX_0. For example, our property φ is satisfied by $\alpha(EX_0)$, which means ERROR is unreachable in EX_0. However, when a property is falsified by $\alpha(EX_0)$, the result cannot be trusted since it may be caused by a spurious behavior. For example, consider checking whether EX_0 always terminates, i.e., whether it satisfies $\psi : AF \ (pc = END)$. ψ is falsified on our abstraction, but this result cannot be trusted due to the infeasible non-terminating execution around the while(*) loop on line 7.

The falsification (or refutation) ability of predicate abstraction can be dramatically improved by using an *under*-approximating abstraction, where each abstract behavior is simulated by some concrete one. In this case, if a bug (or an execution) is present in the abstract model, it *must* exist in the concrete program. For example, the predicate p *must* always be *true* in the while(p) loop at line 3 (assuming int is interpreted as mathematical integers). Thus, an under-approximation based on predicate p is sufficient to establish that EX_0 is non-terminating.

There has been a considerable amount of research exploring abstract analysis based on a combination of over- and under-approximating abstractions, e.g., [9, 15, 25, 26, 4, 18, 17]. Compared with an analysis based on over-approximation alone, there are two main differences:

1. Such a combination requires a non-boolean abstract model that can represent both over- and under-approximations at the same time. Examples of such models are *Modal Transition Systems* [21] (equivalently, 3-valued Kripke structures [9]) and *Mixed Transition Systems* [13] (equivalently, 4-valued Kripke structures [18]). These models use two types of transitions: *may* for over-approximation, and *must* for under-approximation.
2. It requires new model-checking algorithms for these models, such that a formula is evaluated to either *true* or *false*, which are trusted, or to *unknown*, which indicates that the abstraction is not precise enough for a conclusive analysis.

Although both theoretical and practical combinations of exact-approximation with automated CounterExample Guided Abstraction Refinement have been explored, they are all limited to analyzing non-recursive programs.

One way to extend such analysis to recursive programs is to continue to mirror the traditional approach, i.e., (a) extend push-down systems to support combined over- and under-approximations, and (b) develop analysis algorithms for this new modeling formalism. While this approach seems natural, we are not aware of any existing work along this line.

In this paper, we propose an alternative solution to this problem. Our approach does not require the development of new specialized types of push-down systems, nor new specialized analysis algorithms. The key to our approach is to separate the analysis of recursive programs from abstraction of the data domain. We accomplish this by introducing a new concrete program semantics, which we call *mixed*, and using it to derive efficient symbolic algorithms for the analysis of non-termination and reachability properties of finite recursive programs. These algorithms share many insights with techniques in related work [8, 6, 1], i.e., they are functional [24] in terms of interprocedural analysis, and apply only to *stack-independent* properties. The novelty of our approach is the formalization of the algorithms as equational systems, and the parametrization of the algorithms by data abstractions. This makes it possible to share the same analysis algorithms for over-, under-, and exact-approximations! In particular, we demonstrate that in combination with exact-approximation [17], our abstract analysis supports both verification and refutation.

The rest of this paper is organized as follows. We present preliminaries and fix our notation in Sec. 2. We present a simple programming language PL and its natural, and operational semantics in Sec. 3. In Sec. 4, we introduce mixed semantics and derive symbolic on-the-fly algorithms for analyzing recursive programs with finite data domain for reachability and non-termination. In Sec. 5, we parametrize the algorithms of Sec. 4 by abstraction for handling programs with infinite data domain. Experiments are reported in Sec. 6, and we conclude in Sec. 7. Additional illustrations are given in the Appendix.

2   Preliminaries

Valuation and Relations. A *valuation* σ on a set of typed variables V is a function that maps each variable x in V to a value $\sigma(x)$ in its domain. We assume that valuations extend to expressions in the obvious way. The domain of σ is called a *valuation type* and is denoted by $\tau(\sigma)$. For example, if $\sigma = \{x \mapsto 5, y \mapsto 10\}$ then $\tau(\sigma) = \{x, y\}$. The projection of σ on a subset $U \subseteq V$ is denoted by $\sigma|_U$.

The set of all valuations over V is denoted by $\Sigma_V \triangleq \{\sigma \mid \tau(\sigma) = V\}$. Note that $\Sigma_\emptyset$ is well-defined and consists of the unique empty valuation. A relation r on two sets of variables U and V is a subset of $\Sigma_U \times \Sigma_V$. The *relational type* of r is $U \to V$, denoted by $\tau(r)$. For example, the type of $x' = y$ is from y to x, that is, $\tau(x' = y) = \{y\} \to \{x\}$. In this paper, we use several simple relations: $true$ is the **true** relation, id is the identity relation (e.g., $id(x) \triangleq x' = x$), $decl$ is a relation for variable declaration, and $kill$ — for variable elimination. Formally, they are defined as follows, with the format *name* '$\triangleq$' *expression* '$:$' *type*:

$$true(U \to V) \triangleq \Sigma_U \times \Sigma_V : U \to V \qquad decl(V) \triangleq true(\emptyset \to V) : \emptyset \to V$$
$$kill(V) \qquad\quad \triangleq true(V \to \emptyset) : V \to \emptyset \quad id(V) \quad \triangleq \{(\sigma, \sigma') \in \Sigma_V \times \Sigma_V \mid \sigma = \sigma'\} : V \to V$$

Operations on relations are defined in Table 1, where $\vee$, $\circ$ and $\times$ are *asynchronous*, *sequential* and *parallel* composition, respectively, *assume* is a restriction of identity

Table 1. Relational operations

Operation	Assumption	Definition	Type
$r_1 \vee r_2$	$\tau(r_1) = \tau(r_2)$	$\lambda a, a' \cdot r_1(a, a') \vee r_2(a, a')$	$\tau(r_1)$
$r_1 \circ r_2$	$\tau(r_1) = U \to V$ $\wedge \tau(r_2) = V \to W$	$\lambda a, a' \cdot \vee_{a''} (r_1(a, a'') \wedge r_2(a'', a'))$	$U \to W$
$r_1 \times r_2$	$\tau(r_1) = U \to V_1$ $\wedge \tau(r_2) = U \to V_2$ $\wedge V_1 \cap V_2 = \emptyset$	$\lambda a, a' \cdot r_1(a, a'\|_{V_1}) \wedge r_2(a, a'\|_{V_2})$	$U \to (V_1 \cup V_2)$
$assume(Q)$		$\lambda a, a' \cdot Q(a) \wedge id(\tau(Q))(a, a')$	$\tau(Q) \to \tau(Q)$
$[W]r$	$\tau(r) = U \to V$	$\lambda a, a' \cdot r(a\|_U, a')$	$(U \cup W) \to V$
$(W \to Z)r$	$\tau(r) = U \to V \wedge U \subseteq W \wedge (Z \setminus V) \subseteq W$	$([W]r) \times ([W](id(Z \setminus V)))$	$W \to Z$

relation to a set Q of valuations, $[\cdot]$ is *variable introduction*, and $(\cdot \to \cdot)$ is *scope extension*. Note that $\times$ combines the outputs of two relations, and $[\cdot]$ extends the source of a relation with new variables. Together these operators allow constructing complex relations from simple ones. For example, $[\{x, y\}](x' = y) \times [\{x, y\}](y' = x)$ is the relation $(x' = y) \wedge (y' = x)$ with the type $\{x, y\} \to \{x, y\}$. Directly composing $x' = y$ and $y' = x$ without variable introduction, i.e., $(x' = y) \times (y' = x)$, is invalid because $\tau(x' = y) = \{y\} \to \{x\}$ and $\tau(y' = x) = \{x\} \to \{y\}$ have different source types. Scope extension extends a relation by combining it with the identity on new variables. For example, $(\{x, y\} \to \{x, y\})(x' = x + 1)$ is $(x' = x + 1) \wedge (y' = y)$. The assumptions for scope extension ensure that any new variable introduced in the destination of r must also be available in the source. For example, the extension $(\{x, y\} \to \{x, z\})(x' = x + 1)$ is not allowed since z is not available in the source of the relation.

For a relation r with a type $U \to V$, we define the *pre-image* of $Q \subseteq \Sigma_V$ w.r.t. r, $pre[r] : 2^{\Sigma_V} \to 2^{\Sigma_U}$, as

$$pre[r](Q) \triangleq \lambda a \cdot \vee_{a'} (r(a, a') \wedge Q(a'))$$

Reachability and Non-termination. A Kripke structure $K = \langle S, \mathcal{R} \rangle$ is a transition system, where S is a set of states and $\mathcal{R} \subseteq S \times S$ is a transition relation.

Let p be an atomic proposition, and $S_p \triangleq \{s \in S \mid s \models p\}$ be the set of states satisfying p. A *reachability* property (*EF p* in CTL) is true in a state s if there exists a path from s to a state in S_p. A *non-termination* property (*EG p* in CTL) is true in a state s if there exists an infinite path starting at s and contained in S_p.

The set RS of all states satisfying *EF p* is the least solution to equation reach, and the set NT of all states satisfying *EG p* is the greatest solution to equation non-term:

$$RS = S_p \cup pre[\mathcal{R}](RS) \quad \text{(reach)} \qquad NT = pre[\mathcal{R} \cap S_p](NT) \quad \text{(non-term)}$$

3   Programming Language and Semantics

We use a simple imperative programming language PL which allows non-determinism and recursive function calls. We assume that (a) functions have a set of call-by-value formal parameters and a set of return variables; (b) each variable has a unique name and explicit scope; (c) there are no global variables (they can be simulated by local variables); and (d) a type expression is associated with each statement and explicitly defines the pre- and post-variables of the statement.

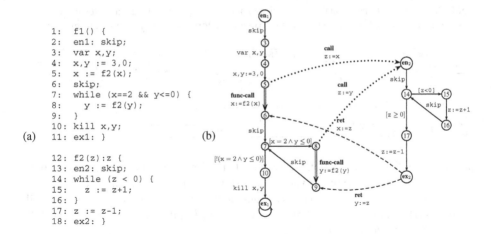

```
   1:   f1() {
   2:   en1: skip;
   3:   var x,y;
   4:   x,y := 3,0;
   5:   x  := f2(x);
   6:   skip;
   7:   while (x==2 && y<=0) {
   8:      y := f2(y);
   9:   }
  10:   kill x,y;
(a)11:   ex1: }

  12:   f2(z):z {
  13:   en2: skip;
  14:   while (z < 0) {
  15:      z := z+1;
  16:   }
  17:   z := z-1;
  18:   ex2: }
```

Fig. 2. (a) A program EX$_1$ and (b) its ICFG

Syntax. Let *var* denote variables, *func* function identifiers, *e* expressions, and *T* valuation types. The syntax of PL is defined as follows:

$$Atomic ::= \mathbf{skip} \mid var^+ := e^+ \mid \mathbf{assume}(e) \mid \mathbf{var}\ var^+ \mid \mathbf{kill}\ var^+ \mid (T \to T)Atomic$$
$$Stmt ::= Atomic \mid Stmt; Stmt \mid Stmt \parallel Stmt \mid \mathbf{if}(e)\ \mathbf{then}\ Stmt\ \mathbf{else}\ Stmt$$
$$\mid \mathbf{while}(e)\ Stmt \mid var^+ := func(var^+) \mid (T \to T)Stmt$$
$$Fdef ::= func(var^+) : var^+\ Stmt$$
$$Prog ::= Fdef^+$$

We use bold lower case letters to represent vectors, e.g., a statement $\mathbf{x} := \mathbf{e}$ means an assignment $x_1, \cdots, x_n := e_1, \cdots, e_n$. For a function f with declaration $f(p_1, \cdots, p_n) : r_1, \cdots, r_k$, $\mathbf{p}_f$ and $\mathbf{r}_f$ to denote the formal parameters and the return variables of f, respectively. $var(e)$ denotes the variables of e, and we assume that each program has a "main" function f_1, not called by other functions.

Base Semantics. Let Σ denote the set of all valuations in a PL program. With each *atomic* statement S, we associate *base semantics* that interprets the statement as a relation $[\![S]\!] \subseteq \Sigma \times \Sigma$ on valuations of program variables:

$$[\![\mathbf{skip}]\!] \triangleq id(\emptyset) \quad [\![\mathbf{var}\ \mathbf{x}]\!] \triangleq decl[\mathbf{x}] \quad [\![\mathbf{kill}\ \mathbf{x}]\!] \triangleq kill[\mathbf{x}] \quad [\![(U \to V)(S)]\!] \triangleq (U \to V)[\![S]\!]$$
$$[\![\mathbf{x} := \mathbf{e}]\!] \triangleq \{(\sigma, \sigma') \mid \tau(\sigma) = var(\mathbf{e}) \wedge \sigma' = [\mathbf{x}_i \mapsto \sigma(\mathbf{e}_i)]\}$$
$$[\![\mathbf{assume}(e)]\!] \triangleq \{(\sigma, \sigma') \mid (\sigma, \sigma') \in id(var(e)) \wedge \sigma \models e\}$$

Note that for the type cast statement $(U \to V)S$, we only consider those cases where the assumptions for the scope extension are satisfied.

Interprocedural Control Flow Graph. A PL program is represented by an *Interprocedural Control Flow Graph* (ICFG) [24]. An ICFG is a labeled graph $G = \langle Loc, Edge, \pi \rangle$, where *Loc* is a finite set of locations, $Edge \subseteq Loc \times Loc$ is a set of edges, and π labels each edge with a program statement. For example, the ICFG for the program EX$_1$ (see Fig. 2(a)) is shown in Fig. 2(b). In ICFGs, (a) each function has a unique *entry* (**en**) and *exit* (**ex**); (b) there is a self-loop at **ex** of f_1 to ensure existence of an infinite execution; (c) each function call (**func-call**) is: a **call** edge, where the values of actual

Table 2. The rules of operational and mixed semantics. U is the set of local variables in the scope of the function call; $[\![f]\!]$ is natural semantics, $\mathbf{p}_f$ are the formals, and $\mathbf{r}_f$ are the returns of f.

Statement $\pi(\langle k, l \rangle)$	Operational Semantics $r_{\langle k,l \rangle}$	Mixed Semantics $r^{\mathrm{m}}_{\langle k,l \rangle}$
func-call edge $(U \to U)$ $\mathbf{x} := f(\mathbf{a})$	$\emptyset$	$(U \to U)$ $([\![\mathbf{p}_f := \mathbf{a}]\!] \circ [\![f]\!] \circ [\![\mathbf{x} := \mathbf{r}_f]\!])$
call edge $S \equiv (U \to \mathbf{x})$ $\mathbf{x} := e$	$\Gamma_t = s \wedge (\sigma_k, \sigma_l) \in [\![S]\!]$	$[\![S]\!]$
ret edge $(U \to V)$ $\mathbf{x} := \mathbf{r}$	let $(c, \sigma_c).\Gamma_c = \Gamma_s$ in $\Gamma_t = \Gamma_c \wedge l = ret(c)$ $\wedge \; \sigma_l = \sigma_c[\{\mathbf{x}_i \mapsto \sigma_k(\mathbf{r}_i)\}]$	$\emptyset$
Intraprocedural: S	$\Gamma_t = \Gamma_s \wedge (\sigma_k, \sigma_l) \in [\![S]\!]$	$[\![S]\!]$

parameters of the callee function are assigned to the formal parameters, a function body, and a **ret** edge, where the return values are assigned to the variables of the caller.

We assume that **call** and **ret** edges are uniquely determined by each other. For a **call** edge $(k, \mathbf{en})$ and the corresponding **ret** edge $(\mathbf{ex}, l)$, k is the call location, $call(l) \triangleq k$, and l is the return location, $ret(k) \triangleq l$.

Operational Semantics of a program $P = \langle Loc, Edge, \pi \rangle$ is a transition system $K = \langle \mathcal{S}, \mathcal{R} \rangle$. Each state in $\mathcal{S}$ is a stack of activation records where each record is of the form $\langle pc, \sigma \rangle$, where $pc \in Loc$ is a program counter, corresponding to a particular control location in P, and $\sigma \in \Sigma_{V(pc)}$ is the valuation for variables in the scope of pc (denoted by $V(pc)$). For a state $s = (k, \sigma_k).\Gamma$, (k, σ_k) is the *top* element of s, $top(s)$. For a pair of states $s = (k, \sigma_k).\Gamma_s$ and $t = (l, \sigma_l).\Gamma_t$, the transition relation $\mathcal{R}$ is defined as $\mathcal{R}(s, t) \triangleq \langle k, l \rangle \in Edge \wedge r_{\langle k,l \rangle}(s, t)$, where $r_{\langle k,l \rangle}$ is a deterministic (but not necessarily total) relation on $\mathcal{S}$ at the edge $\langle k, l \rangle$, as defined in the 2nd column of Table 2. An intraprocedural statement only modifies the top activation record, and a statement on a **call** or a **ret** edge pushes a new record or pops one, respectively. The transition relations on **func-call** edges are empty, i.e., these edges are removed.

Natural Semantics [22] (a.k.a. big-step) of a block of code S is a relation $[\![S]\!] \subseteq \Sigma \times \Sigma$ between the input and output of S: i.e., $(\sigma, \sigma') \in [\![S]\!]$ iff the execution of S on σ terminates and results in σ'. Natural semantics of a program $P \equiv f_1, \cdots, f_n$ is a set of relations, one per function, i.e., $[\![P]\!] = \langle [\![f_1]\!], \cdots, [\![f_n]\!] \rangle$.

The semantic rules for PL are defined compositionally on the syntax using the function $[\![\cdot]\!]_\rho$, where ρ is an environment mapping free fixpoint variables (used for loops and functions) to relations with an appropriate type. Natural semantics for atomic statements is the same as base semantics; the other cases are:

$$[\![S_1; S_2]\!]_\rho \triangleq [\![S_1]\!]_\rho \circ [\![S_2]\!]_\rho \qquad [\![\mu X \cdot \mathcal{S}(X)]\!]_\rho \triangleq \mathrm{lfp}\left(\lambda Z \cdot [\![\mathcal{S}(X)]\!]_{\rho\{X \mapsto Z\}}\right)$$

$$[\![S_1 \parallel S_2]\!]_\rho \triangleq [\![S_1]\!]_\rho \vee [\![S_2]\!]_\rho \qquad [\![\mathbf{x} := f(\mathbf{a})]\!]_\rho \triangleq [\![\mathbf{p}_f := \mathbf{a}; X_f; \mathbf{x} := \mathbf{r}_f]\!]_\rho$$

$$[\![X]\!]_\rho \triangleq \rho(X) \qquad [\![\mathbf{while}(e) \; S]\!]_\rho \triangleq [\![\mu X_w \cdot \mathbf{if}(e) \; \mathbf{then} \; (S; X_w)]\!]_\rho$$

$$[\![\mathbf{if}(e) \; \mathbf{then} \; S_1 \; \mathbf{else} \; S_2]\!]_\rho \triangleq [\![(\mathbf{assume}(e); S_1) \parallel (\mathbf{assume}(\neg e); S_2)]\!]_\rho$$

where **lfp** denotes for least fixpoint, $\tau(\rho(X_f)) = \mathbf{p}_f \to \mathbf{r}_f$ and $\tau(\rho(X_w)) = \tau([\![S]\!]_\rho)$. A program $P \equiv f_1, \cdots, f_n$ induces the system of equations

$$\rho(X_{f_i}) = [\![S_{f_i}]\!]_\rho \quad (1 \leq i \leq n) \tag{nat}$$

Natural semantics of P is the least fixpoint solution to this system, e.g., for the program EX_1, natural semantics of f_2 is $(z > 0 \wedge z' = z - 1) \vee (z \leq 0 \wedge z' = -1)$.

Theorem 1. *Let $P \equiv f_1, \cdots, f_n$ be a program and $K = \langle \mathcal{S}, \mathcal{R} \rangle$ be its operational semantics. A pair of activation records $(\langle k, \sigma_k \rangle, \langle l, \sigma_l \rangle)$ is in $[\![f_i]\!]$ iff there exists a path $s_0, \cdots, s_m$ in K such that $s_0 = \langle k, \sigma_k \rangle . \Gamma_0$ and $s_m = \langle l, \sigma_l \rangle . \Gamma_m$, such that $\Gamma_0 = \Gamma_m$, k and l are **en** and **ex** of f_i, respectively, and for all other $s_j = \langle p, \sigma_p \rangle . \Gamma_j$ either $\Gamma_j \neq \Gamma_0$ or p is not **ex** of f_i.*

4   Reachability and Non-termination Analysis

We now turn our attention to checking reachability and non-termination of recursive programs. Reachability can be reduced to finding the least fixpoint solution to the equation reach w.r.t. a transition system of operational semantics of a program (see Sec. 2). Similarly, non-termination corresponds to finding the greatest solution to the equation non-term. However, since operational semantics explicitly exposes a potentially unbounded call stack at each state, these equations must be solved over an infinite transition system (even when all program variables range over finite domains). Thus, the exact fixpoint solution may not be computable.

However, many program properties depend only on the top of the call stack: i.e., they are *stack-independent*. Analysis of such properties can be done using *stack-free* operational semantics in which everything except for the *top* activation record is abstracted away. In this section, we apply this idea to the analysis of *EF p* (reachability) and *EG p* (non-termination) properties, where p is a proposition that depends only on the top activation record. Without loss of generality, we further assume that p only depends on program locations, i.e., it is of the form $pc = x$.

4.1   Mixed Semantics

We start by defining a stack-free operational semantics, called mixed semantics, for PL programs which removes the call stack but preserves reachability and non-termination properties w.r.t. operational semantics of Sec. 3.

Intuitively, *mixed* semantics is a combination of operational and natural semantics, in which a program is executed as follows: an atomic statement is executed as usual; a function call x := foo(y) is executed as a *non-deterministic* choice between (a) executing foo, i.e., updating the top activation record according to natural semantics of foo, and (b) entering the body of foo, *and* forgetting all but the top activation record. Upon reaching the end of the main function, the execution enters a self-loop indicating the end of the program, and blocks at all other exit locations since it does not remember the origin of the call. For example, consider mixed execution of the program EX_1 starting from line 5 with $x = 3$ and $y = 0$. At this point, the execution can either (a) move to line 6 and decrease x by one according to natural semantics of f_2, or (b) move to en2 (line 13), assign z to 3, and forget about x and y. Within f_2, the execution continues until it blocks at ex2 (line 18) with $z = 2$.

Formally, mixed semantics of a program $P = \langle Loc, Edge, \pi \rangle$ is a Kripke structure $K^m = \langle \mathcal{S}^m, \mathcal{R}^m \rangle$, where each state is a *single* activation record $\langle pc, \sigma \rangle$. For a pair of states $s = \langle k, \sigma_k \rangle$ and $t = \langle l, \sigma_l \rangle$, the transition relation is $\mathcal{R}^m(s, t) \triangleq (\langle k, l \rangle \in Edge) \wedge r^m_{\langle k, l \rangle}(\sigma_k, \sigma_l)$, where $r^m_{\langle k, l \rangle}$ is a relation on valuations, as defined in the 3rd column of Table 2. Note that r_e^m for **ret** edges is empty, which is equivalent to removing those edges from the ICFG.

Mixed semantics preserves reachability and non-termination properties w.r.t. operational semantics. If an execution of a function f reaches a state s under the latter, then either s is a location within f, or it is inside some other function that f calls (directly or indirectly). The non-deterministic treatment of function calls in the former ensures that both of these cases are covered. Similarly, if there exists an infinite execution starting inside f, then either this execution lies within f, or f calls a function that does not return the control back to f. Again, both cases are captured by mixed semantics.

Theorem 2. *Let K and K^m be operational and mixed semantics of a given program, respectively, and p be a propositional formula on control locations. Then, $(K \models EF\ p) \Leftrightarrow (K^m \models EF\ p)$ and $(K \models EG\ p) \Leftrightarrow (K^m \models EG\ p)$.*

When all variables of a given program P range over finite domains, mixed semantics of P is a finite Kripke structure. Theorem 2 implies the following analysis algorithm:

Step 1: compute natural semantics of P by solving equation nat;
Step 2: construct the structure K^m following the rules of mixed semantics;
Step 3: solve equations reach or non-term on K^m for reachability or non-termination, respectively.

While sound and complete, this algorithm is not efficient, since it relies on the (potentially unnecessary) computation of "full" natural semantics of all functions (for Step 2) and the construction of "full" mixed semantics before the analysis of the property can even begin. As a trivial example, consider checking $EF(pc = 5)$ on the program EX_1. Since reachability of line 6 is irrelevant for this analysis, there is no need to construct the transition relation corresponding to **func-call** edge $\langle 5, 6 \rangle$ and thus no need to compute natural semantics of f_2. Following this observation, in the rest of this section, we show that the three steps of the above algorithm can be combined into an *on-the-fly* algorithm that only computes the necessary parts of mixed and natural semantics.

4.2   On-the-Fly Reachability

Intuitively, the analysis of $EF\ p$ properties only needs a part of mixed semantics that is used for solving equation reach, and that, in turn, drives the computation of the necessary parts of natural semantics. To illustrate, consider checking $EF(pc = 8)$ on EX_1. Natural semantics of f_2 is $[\![f_2]\!] \equiv (z > 0 \wedge z' = z - 1) \vee (z \leq 0 \wedge z' = -1)$. After a few iterations, the reachability algorithm computes a pre-condition $Q \equiv x = 2 \wedge y \leq 0$ for reaching line 8 from line 6. To determine a pre-condition for Q w.r.t. a function call $\mathtt{x:=f2(x)}$ at line 5, it needs to compute $pre[r_{\langle 5,6 \rangle}^m](Q) = (x = 3 \wedge y \leq 0)$, where $r_{\langle 5,6 \rangle}^m \equiv (y' = y) \wedge ((x > 0 \wedge x' = x - 1) \vee (x \leq 0 \wedge x' = -1))$ is the instantiation of $[\![f_2]\!]$ to the call site. However, instead of using the "full" version of $[\![f_2]\!]$, it is sufficient to compute a pre-condition that *assumes* Q as a post-condition, i.e., to restrict r^m to $x' = 2$ (the relevant part of Q) yielding $\hat{r}^m \equiv y' = y \wedge x = 3 \wedge x' = 2$. $\hat{r}^m$ is an instantiation of $z = 3 \wedge z' = 2$ in the context of the call, obtained by (a) converting Q to a postcondition of f_2 by taking its pre-image over the **ret** edge (which eliminates y and renames x to z), and (b) restricting $[\![f_2]\!]$ to this post-condition: $[\![f_2]\!] \circ (assume(z = 2)) \equiv z = 3 \wedge z' = 2$.

We now formalize the above intuition. Recall that $V(k)$ stands for the set of variables in the scope of a location k. Let l be the return location of a function call to f_i, $Q \subseteq \Sigma_{V(l)}$ be a set of valuations at l, and the corresponding **ret** edge $\langle \mathbf{ex}_i, l \rangle$ be labeled with $\mathbf{x} := \mathbf{r}_{f_i}$. Then, function $prop(\langle \mathbf{ex}_i, l \rangle, Q) \triangleq pre [\![\mathbf{x} := \mathbf{r}_{f_i}; (\mathbf{x} \to V(l))\mathbf{var}\,(V(l) \setminus \mathbf{x})]\!] (Q)$ turns Q into a post-condition of f_i. Here, the pre-image w.r.t. **var** undeclares (or removes) all variables that are not changed by the call, and the pre-image w.r.t. **ret** edge turns the post-condition on $\mathbf{x}$ into the one on $\mathbf{r}_{f_i}$.

Let $RS : Loc \to \mathbf{2}^{\Sigma}$ map each location k to a subset of $\Sigma_{V(k)}$, and, as in Sec. 3, let ρ be the semantics environment, mapping each fixpoint variable to a relation of an appropriate type. The on-the-fly algorithm for reachability analysis is the equation system reach-otf:

$$RS(k) = \begin{cases} \Sigma_{V(k)} & \text{if } k \models p \ (k \in Loc) \\ RS(k) \cup \bigcup_{l \in succ(k)} pre[\hat{r}^{\mathrm{m}}_{\langle k,l \rangle}](RS(l)) & \text{otherwise} \end{cases} \quad \text{(reach-otf)}$$

$$\rho(X_{f_i}) = [\![S_{f_i}]\!]_{\rho} \circ assume \left(\bigcup_{l \in succ(\mathbf{ex}_i)} prop\,(\langle \mathbf{ex}_i, l \rangle, RS(l)) \right) \quad (i \in [1..n])$$

where $succ$ are the successors of a node in the ICFG, S_{f_i} is the body of f_i, and for $S \equiv \pi(\langle k, l \rangle)$, $\hat{r}^{\mathrm{m}}_{\langle k,l \rangle}$ is defined as:

$$\hat{r}^{\mathrm{m}}_{\langle k,l \rangle} = \begin{cases} (U \to U) \, ([\![\mathbf{p}_f := \mathbf{a}]\!] \circ \rho(X_{f_i}) \circ [\![\mathbf{x} := \mathbf{r}_f]\!]) & \text{if } S \equiv (U \to U) \, \mathbf{x} := f(\mathbf{a}) \\ [\![S]\!] & \text{otherwise} \end{cases}$$

This system is a combination of nat and reach, where *prop* is used to propagate the reachability information to the computation of natural semantics. Since reachability and natural semantics are both least solutions to equations reach and nat, respectively, we need the least solution to the above equation as well.

The following theorem shows that the analysis based on equation system reach-otf is sound, and computes only the necessary part of natural semantics.

Theorem 3. *Let $RS_{\downarrow}$ and $\rho_{\downarrow}$ be the least solutions to equation system reach-otf. Then,*

1. *$RS_{\downarrow}$ is the least solution to equation reach on K^{m};*
2. *$\forall i \in [1..n] \cdot \rho_{\downarrow}(X_{f_i}) \subseteq [\![f_i]\!]$;*
3. *for any ρ, if $RS_{\downarrow}$ is the least solution to the RS equations in reach-otf w.r.t. ρ, then $\forall i \in [1..n] \cdot \rho_{\downarrow}(X_{f_i}) \subseteq \rho(X_{f_i})$.*

Part 1 of Theorem 3 shows that $RS_{\downarrow}$ is the solution for the reachability analysis; part 2 – that $\rho_{\downarrow}$ is sound w.r.t. natural semantics of f_i; and part 3 – that $\rho_{\downarrow}$ only contains the information necessary for the analysis.

Since we need the least solution for both $RS(k)$ and $\rho(X_{f_i})$ equations, it can be obtained by any chaotic iteration [11] and thus is independent of the order of computation of RS and ρ. Interestingly, the algorithm derived from reach-otf is a pre-image-based variant of the post-image-based reachability algorithm of BEBOP [6], and is similar to the formalization of backward analysis with **wp** described in [3].

4.3 On-the-Fly Non-termination

The derivation of the on-the-fly algorithm for the analysis of non-termination, nt-otf, proceeds similarly, and is a combination of systems nat and non-term:

$$NT(k) = \begin{cases} \emptyset & \text{if } k \not\models p \ (k \in Loc) \\ \bigcup_{l \in succ(k)} pre[\hat{r}^m_{\langle k,l \rangle}](NT(l)) & \text{otherwise} \end{cases} \quad \text{(nt-otf)}$$

$$\rho(X_{f_i}) = [\![S_{f_i}]\!]_\rho \circ assume \left(\bigcup_{l \in succ(\mathbf{ex}_i)} prop \left(\langle \mathbf{ex}_i, l \rangle, NT(l) \right) \right) \quad (i \in [1..n])$$

where $NT : Loc \to 2^\Sigma$ maps each location k to a subset of $\Sigma_{V(k)}$, and $succ$, S_{f_i} and $\hat{r}^m$ are the same as those in reach-otf. Since non-termination requires the greatest solution to non-term, and natural semantics – the least solution to nat, in nt-otf, we need the greatest solution to $NT(k)$, and the least solution to $\rho(X_{f_i})$ equations, respectively.

The following theorem shows that the non-termination algorithm based on nt-otf is sound and computes only the necessary part of natural semantics.

Theorem 4. *Let $NT_\uparrow$ and $\rho_\downarrow$ be the greatest solution for NT and the least solution for ρ in system nt-otf, respectively. Then,*

1. *$NT_\uparrow$ is the greatest solution to the equation non-term on K^m;*
2. *$\forall i \in [1..n] \cdot \rho_\downarrow(X_{f_i}) \subseteq [\![f_i]\!]$;*
3. *for any ρ, if $NT_\uparrow$ is the greatest solution to the NT equations in nt-otf w.r.t. ρ, then $\forall i \in [1..n] \cdot \rho_\downarrow(X_{f_i}) \subseteq \rho(X_{f_i})$.*

As in Theorem 3, part 1 of Theorem 4 shows soundness of non-termination, and parts 2 and 3 – soundness and necessity of computation of natural semantics, respectively.

Unlike reachability, non-termination requires different fixpoint solutions for NT and ρ, and thus the order of computation can influence the result. For example, consider checking $EG(pc \neq \mathbf{ex}_1)$ on EX_1. Initially, lines 7, 8, and 9 are associated with all the valuations on x and y, i.e., $NT(7) = NT(8) = NT(9) = \Sigma_{\{x,y\}}$, and $\rho(f_2)$ is empty, which is not the partial semantics of f_2 restricted to $NT(9)$. If the computation of NT proceeds along the function call $y:=f2(y)$ using the initial value of $\rho(f_2)$, $NT(8)$ is assigned $\emptyset$. Eventually, $NT(7) = NT(8) = NT(9) = \emptyset$, i.e., the algorithm incorrectly concludes that any execution starting at lines 7, 8 or 9 terminates.

The correct order for computing the solution is such that the pre-image of a set Q w.r.t. a function call to f has to be delayed until the derivation of $\rho(X_f)$ w.r.t. Q is finished. Nonetheless, since this order is only restricted to **func-call** edges, the order of the computation elsewhere can be arbitrary. This can be used to avoid deriving "full" natural semantics. Going back to the previous example, one can first compute NT along all edges except for **func-call** edges, which will assign $NT(9)$ with $x = 2 \wedge y \leq 0$, and then compute natural semantics of f_2 restricted to the post-condition $z \leq 0$. Similarly, although initially $NT(6)$ is assigned $\Sigma_{\{x,y\}}$, $NT(6) = (x = 2 \wedge y \leq 0)$ after the initial computation of NT, which means that only partial natural semantics of f_2 restricted to the post-condition $z = 2$ is needed.

In this section, we have presented mixed semantics – a stack-free operational semantics of PL, and showed how it can be used to check reachability and non-termination of programs with a finite data domain. Although the use of such semantics is not new, our formalization provides a basis for a tight integration between abstraction and analysis, which is described in the next section.

5   Abstract Reachability and Non-termination Analysis

Here, we follow the framework of abstract interpretation (AI) [12] to derive an abstract version of the concrete analysis described in Sec. 4. To do so, we require two abstract domains: abstract sets A_s whose elements approximate sets in 2^Σ, and abstract relations A_r whose elements approximate relations in $2^{\Sigma \times \Sigma}$. These domains must be equipped with abstract version of all of the operations used in equations reach-otf and nt-otf. Finally, the framework of AI ensures that the solution to an abstract equation is an approximation of the solution to the corresponding concrete equation. In what follows, we identify the necessary abstract operations on A_s and A_r, and then show how to adapt predicate abstraction for our algorithm.

Abstract Domains and Operations. The domain of abstract sets A_s must be equipped with a set union $\cup$ (used in the reachability computation) and equality (to detect the fixpoint convergence). The domain of abstract relations A_r must be equipped with (a) a pre-image operator to convert abstract relations to abstract transformers over A_s, (b) asynchronous and sequential compositions of abstract relations (used in natural semantics), (c) scope extension (used to instantiate a function call using natural semantics of a function), and (d) equality (to detect the fixpoint convergence). Furthermore, we need an *assume* operator that maps an abstract set to a corresponding abstract relation; and, to apply the abstraction directly to the source code, a computable version of abstract base semantics $[\![\cdot]\!]_\alpha$ that maps each atomic statement S to an abstract relation that approximates $[\![S]\!]$ (the concrete semantics of S).

Predicate Abstraction. In the rest of this section, we show how the domain of predicate abstraction [16, 5, 18] can be extended with the necessary abstract operations to yield abstract reachability and non-termination algorithms.

Predicate abstraction provides domains for abstracting elements, sets, and relations of valuations. Let V be a set of variables, and $\mathcal{P}$ be a set of predicates over V. The *elementary* domain of predicate abstraction over $\mathcal{P}$, denoted $\Theta_\mathcal{P}$, is the set of all conjunctions of literals over $\mathcal{P}$. For example, if $\mathcal{P} = \{x > 0, x < y\}$, then $\neg(x > 0)$ and $(x > 0) \wedge \neg(x < y)$ are in $\Theta_\mathcal{P}$. An element of $\theta \in \Theta$ approximates any valuation $\sigma \in \Sigma_V$ that satisfies all literals in θ. For example, $\sigma = \langle x \mapsto 2, y \mapsto 2 \rangle$ is approximated by $x > 0$, and is also approximated by $(x > 0) \wedge \neg(x < y)$ more precisely.

The elementary domain is lifted to sets and relations in an obvious way: sets over Θ represent concrete sets, and relations over Θ – concrete relations. This extension can be either *over-* or *under-approximating*, i.e., a collection of concrete valuations corresponding to an abstract set either over-approximates or under-approximates a concrete set. The over- and under-approximating interpretations can also be combined into a single *exact*-approximation using sets and relations over Belnap logic [18].

Abstract versions of set union, set and relation equality, pre-image, and base semantics for over-approximating predicate abstraction have been defined (e.g., [5]). For example, if X and Y are two *abstract* sets, their abstract union is $X \cup_\alpha Y \triangleq \lambda z \cdot X(z) \vee Y(z)$. In [18, 17], we show that these operations also naturally extend to under-approximating and exact predicate abstractions. In the latter case, conjunctions and disjunctions, e.g., $\vee$ in the definition of $\cup_\alpha$, are interpreted in Belnap logic. We define the missing abstract relational operations $assume_\alpha$, asynchronous ($\vee_\alpha$), and se-

```
int g;                void level_i(){      void level_n(){      (b)
                        int t = 0;           int t = 0;
    void main(){        g = -1 * g;          g = -1 * g;        <stmt>:=
     level_1();         if (g<=0){           if (g<=0){            g = -1 * g;
     if (g<0){            t = t+1;             t = t+1;
(a)    ERROR: ;         } else {             } else {           (c)
     }                    level_i+1();                           <stmt>:=
     END: ;              g = -1 * g;         <stmt>                level_n();
    }                    level_i+1();                             g = -1 * g;
                       }                    }                     level_n();
                       g = -1 * g;}         g = -1 * g;}
```

Fig. 3. (a) The template for experiments. (b) <stmt> for template **T1**(n). (c) <stmt> for **T2**(n).

quential ($\circ_\alpha$) compositions similarly, using the corresponding definitions from Sec. 2, e.g., if r_1 and r_2 are abstract relations, then their abstract asynchronous composition is $r_1 \vee_\alpha r_2 \triangleq \lambda s, t \cdot r_1(s, t) \vee r_2(s, t)$, where $\vee$ is interpreted in Boolean logic for over- and under-approximating abstraction, and in Belnap logic for exact abstraction.

In concrete semantics, scope extension is used to extend a relation to additional variables. That is, if r is a relation of type $U \to V$, then $(U \to U)r$ is an extension of r to variables in $U \setminus V$. In the abstract semantics, relations are defined over predicates; thus, abstract scope extension must extend a relation to additional predicates. To do this, we assume that the elementary abstract domain Θ corresponding to U can be decomposed into two independent abstract domains: one for V and the other – for $U \setminus V$, i.e., Θ is defined using predicates that either range only over V, or only over $U \setminus V$. Then, abstract scope extension $(\cdot \to \cdot)_\alpha$, defined as in Table 1, is a sound approximation of concrete scope extension.

Theorem 5. *Abstract operations assume$_\alpha$, $\vee_\alpha$, $\circ_\alpha$, and $(\cdot \to \cdot)_\alpha$ as defined above are sound approximations of their concrete counterparts.*

In the context of our on-the-fly algorithms, the assumption on abstract scope extension means that predicates that are used to abstract valuations at a return location l of a function call $\mathbf{x} := f(\mathbf{a})$ are either defined only over $\mathbf{x}$, or only over other variables in the scope of l. For example, predicates $x = 2$ and $y \leq 0$ can be used to abstract valuations at line 6 in the program EX_1, but predicate $x > y$ cannot. This is not a severe restriction in practice since a function can always be extended to accept additional parameters and return them without modification.

To summarize, both over- and under-approximating predicate abstractions can be used to soundly abstract reachability and non-termination analysis. The choice depends on the desired algorithm. For example, over-approximation is necessary to establish un-reachability, whereas under-approximation – to establish non-termination. Since exact predicate abstraction combines them, it can be used for both verification and refutation.

6 Experiments

The technique described in this paper has been implemented in our symbolic software model checker YASM [19]. YASM is written in JAVA; it uses CVC Lite [7] to approximate program statements and CUDD [27] as a decision diagram engine. We have also

Table 3. Experimental results: overall analysis time in seconds

	T1(n)	**T2**(n)	
n	EF ($pc =$ ERROR) (reach)	EG ($pc \neq$ END) (non-terminate)	$\neg EF$ ($pc =$ ERROR) (unreach)
20	6.5	4.9	4.3
50	11.7	8.9	6.3
100	20.3	20.3	11.1
200	36.7	25.2	27.6
300	47.6	34.4	42.1
400	68.1	43.2	64.5
500	105.2	60.6	86.6

extended our proof-based refinement approach [17] to handle natural semantics of functions. In the rest of this section, we report on a preliminary evaluation of this implementation. All of the experiments have been conducted on a 2xP4Xeon-3.6GHz server and are available at http://www.cs.toronto.edu/fm/yasm/yasm-tests.zip. Our experiments demonstrate YASM's ability to analyze reachability and non-termination of recursive programs using exact-approximation. In summary:

1. We run YASM on template programs similar to those in the BEBOP and MOPED benchmarks. The experiment shows that the analysis time for *both* reachability and non-termination increases linearly w.r.t. the number of functions in a program.
2. We show that abstract analysis based on exact-approximation supports both verification and refutation.
3. We compare YASM with MOPED and VERA (BEBOP does not do non-termination), and show that YASM can prove non-termination of the original buggy Quicksort algorithm, whereas MOPED and VERA cannot.

To evaluate the reachability algorithm, we have used the template program **T1**(n) which is a variant of the one used for BEBOP in [6]. **T1**(n) is the result of replacing <stmt> in the template shown in Fig. 3(a) with the statements in Fig. 3(b). It consists of a main function and n sub-functions, where main calls level_1, and level_i calls level_i+1 twice if the global variable g is positive. Since g is not initialized, its initial value is arbitrary. Although this program has no recursion, inlining function calls increases its size exponentially, making the analysis infeasible for a sufficiently large n. We checked the reachability property EF ($pc =$ ERROR) with values of n ranging between 20 and 500, and measured the *overall* analysis time (including parsing, abstraction, model-checking, and refinement). The results are shown in the second column of Table 3. Since our technique analyzes each function separately, the analysis time increases linearly w.r.t. the number of functions (n), as expected. In all these cases, YASM was successful in proving reachability, and discovered predicates $g < 0$, $g > 0$ and $g \leq 0$. While the template **T1**(n) is similar to the one used in [6], there is a fundamental difference: BEBOP assumes an over-approximating abstract semantics of Boolean programs and cannot *conclusively verify* that the ERROR label is reachable with these predicates. YASM uses exact-approximation which results in a conclusive analysis.

We also checked the template program **T2**(n), obtained by replacing <stmt> in the template in Fig. 3(a) with statements in Fig. 3(c). Non-termination and unreachability results are presented in the third and fourth columns of Table 3, respectively. As expected, the analysis time increases linearly with the number of functions.

```
(a)  void main () {              (b)  void main () {          (c)  void main () {
       int mx, my;                      int x;                       int mleft, mright;
       ack (mx, my);                    foo(x);                      quicksort (mleft, mright);
       END:; }                          while(x!=0) {                END:;}
                                          if (x<0) {
     int ack (int x, int y) {              x = -1 * x;              void quicksort (int left, int right) {
       int r1,  n;                         x = x+2;                   int lo, hi;
       if (x > 0) {                      } else {                     if (left >= right) return;
         if (y > 0) {                      x = -1 * x;                lo = left; hi = right;
           y = y - 1;                       x = x+3;                  while (lo <= hi) {
           n = ack (x, y);                }}                            if (nondet()) {
         } else { n = 1; }           END:  ;}                            lo = lo+1;
         r1 = ack (x, n);                                             } else {
         return r1;                  void foo (int y) {                 if(lo!=left || hi!=right)
       } else {                        y = -1 * y;                        hi = hi-1;
         r1 = y + 1;                   if (y < 0) {                   }}
         return r1;                      foo (y);                   quicksort (left, hi);
       }}                            }}                             quicksort (lo, right); }
```

Fig. 4. Non-terminating programs: (a) Ack; (b) Shift; (c) Buggy Quicksort

For non-termination, we have also applied YASM to several examples inspired by [10], in particular, on programs Ack and Shift, shown in Fig. 4(a) and (b), respectively. YASM was able to automatically prove non-termination of Ack in 2.1 seconds and discovered predicates $y > 0$, $n > 0$, $x > 0$, $mx > 0$ and $my > 0$. Analysis of Shift took 1.9 seconds and yielded predicates $y < 0$, $x < 0$, $x > 3$, $x = 0$ and $x = 3$. Finally, we have compared YASM to MOPED [14] and VERA [1] on the buggy Quicksort example from [14] in Fig. 4(c), where nondet() represents non-deterministic choice. YASM has established non-termination of Quicksort in 10 seconds, finding 7 predicates. Note that both MOPED and VERA only apply to programs with finite data domain, and the analysis in [1] and [14] had to restrict the number of bits used by each variable, while YASM did not need any such restriction.

7   Conclusion and Related Work

This paper presented a model-checking technique for analysis of reachability and non-termination properties of recursive programs. The technique is based on a stack-free mixed operational semantics of programs that uses natural semantics and non-determinism to eliminate the call stack while preserving stack-independent properties. We show how to compute only the necessary part of natural semantics during the analysis, leading to on-the-fly algorithms for analysis of reachability and non-termination of programs with finite data domains. We then use the framework of abstract interpretation [12] to combine our algorithms with data abstractions, making them applicable to programs with infinite data domains as well. Although we specialize our approach to predicate abstraction, we believe that it can be extended to other abstract domains as well. We have implemented a combination of this approach with exact predicate abstraction in YASM [19] which supports both verification and refutation of properties. Our experiments indicate that YASM scales to programs with a large number of functions and is able to establish non-termination of non-trivial (although small) examples. In particular, we were able to automatically prove non-termination of Ack [10] and Quicksort [14] without any restrictions on the data domain.

In the terminology of interprocedural program analysis [24], our approach is *functional* since it uses natural semantics to handle function calls. Most other model-checking approaches for recursive programs (e.g., [23, 6, 1]) are functional as well, and only compute the necessary part of natural semantics. Our reachability algorithm can be seen as a pre-image-based variant of the RHS algorithm [23], as implemented in BEBOP [6].

Both MOPED [14] and VERA [1] can check non-termination of programs with finite data domains. Their algorithms are comparable with our non-termination algorithm. However, it is unclear how to combine their techniques with an arbitrary abstraction, whereas it is quite natural in our approach. Note that an ability to detect non-termination of over-approximating Boolean programs is of limited utility since over-approximation often introduces *spurious* non-terminating computations. Thus, non-termination of an over-approximation says nothing about non-termination of the concrete program.

Jeannet and Serwe [20] apply abstract interpretation to derive abstract analysis of recursive programs by different abstractions of the call stack. Their approach is also parameterized by an arbitrary data abstraction. However, the authors restrict their attention to reachability (i.e., invariance) properties, and do not report on an implementation.

Our interest in non-termination is motivated by the work on *termination* (e.g., [10]). We view our approach as complementary to that. As illustrated by our experiments, YASM can prove non-termination of non-trivial programs. However, its ability to prove termination is limited to cases where termination can be established by a constant ranking function. In the future, we plan to investigate how the strengths of the two approaches can be combined in a single algorithm.

In this paper, we have restricted our attention to stack-independent properties. We hope to extend our approach to a more general class of properties, e.g., the ones expressible in CARET [2]. Finally, the refinement strategies that are currently implemented in YASM were originally developed for reachability analysis only. While they were sufficient for our non-termination experiments, we believe that strategies specifically tailored to the non-termination analysis are essential for scaling the tool to large programs.

References

1. Alur, R., Chaudhuri, S., Etessami, K., Madhusudan, P.: On-the-Fly Reachability and Cycle Detection for Recursive State Machines. In: Halbwachs, N., Zuck, L.D. (eds.) TACAS 2005. LNCS, vol. 3440, pp. 61–76. Springer, Heidelberg (2005)
2. Alur, R., Etessami, K., Madhusudan, P.: A Temporal Logic of Nested Calls and Returns. In: Jensen, K., Podelski, A. (eds.) TACAS 2004. LNCS, vol. 2988, pp. 467–481. Springer, Heidelberg (2004)
3. Ball, T.: Formalizing Counterexample-driven Refinement with Weakest Preconditions. Tech. Report 134, MSR (2004)
4. Ball, T., Kupferman, O., Yorsh, G.: Abstraction for Falsification. In: Proceedings of CAV 2005. LNCS, vol. 3376, pp. 67–81. Springer, Heidelberg (2005)
5. Ball, T., Podelski, A., Rajamani, S.: Boolean and Cartesian Abstraction for Model Checking C Programs. STTT 5(1), 49–58 (2003)
6. Ball, T., Rajamani, S.: Bebop: A Symbolic Model Checker for Boolean Programs. In: Havelund, K., Penix, J., Visser, W. (eds.) SPIN 2000. LNCS, vol. 1885, pp. 113–130. Springer, Heidelberg (2000)

7. Barrett, C., Berezin, S.: CVC Lite: A New Implementation of the Cooperating Validity Checker. In: Alur, R., Peled, D.A. (eds.) CAV 2004. LNCS, vol. 3114, pp. 515–518. Springer, Heidelberg (2004)

8. Bouajjani, A., Esparza, J., Maler, O.: Reachability Analysis of Pushdown Automata: Application to Model-Checking. In: Mazurkiewicz, A., Winkowski, J. (eds.) CONCUR 1997. LNCS, vol. 1243, pp. 135–150. Springer, Heidelberg (1997)

9. Bruns, G., Godefroid, P.: Model Checking Partial State Spaces with 3-Valued Temporal Logics. In: Halbwachs, N., Peled, D.A. (eds.) CAV 1999. LNCS, vol. 1633, pp. 274–287. Springer, Heidelberg (1999)

10. Cook, B., Podelski, A., Rybalchenko, A.: Termination Proofs for System Code. In: Proceedings of PLDI 2006, pp. 415–426 (2006)

11. Cousot, P.: Asynchronous Iterative Methods for Solving a Fixed Point System of Monotone Equations in a Complete Lattice. Research report, Univ. of Grenoble (September 1977)

12. Cousot, P., Cousot, R.: Abstract Interpretation Frameworks. J. of Logic and Computation 2(4), 511–547 (1992)

13. Dams, D., Gerth, R., Grumberg, O.: Abstract Interpretation of Reactive Systems. ACM Transactions on Programming Languages and Systems 2(19), 253–291 (1997)

14. Esparza, J., Schwoon, S.: A BDD-Based Model Checker for Recursive Programs. In: Berry, G., Comon, H., Finkel, A. (eds.) CAV 2001. LNCS, vol. 2102, pp. 324–336. Springer, Heidelberg (2001)

15. Godefroid, P., Huth, M., Jagadeesan, R.: Abstraction-based Model Checking using Modal Transition Systems. In: Larsen, K.G., Nielsen, M. (eds.) CONCUR 2001. LNCS, vol. 2154. Springer, Heidelberg (2001)

16. Graf, S., Saïdi, H.: Construction of Abstract State Graphs with PVS. In: Grumberg, O. (ed.) CAV 1997. LNCS, vol. 1254, pp. 72–83. Springer, Heidelberg (1997)

17. Gurfinkel, A., Chechik, M.: Why Waste a Perfectly Good Abstraction? In: Hermanns, H., Palsberg, J. (eds.) TACAS 2006. LNCS, vol. 3920, pp. 212–226. Springer, Heidelberg (2006)

18. Gurfinkel, A., Wei, O., Chechik, M.: Systematic Construction of Abstractions for Model-Checking. In: Emerson, E.A., Namjoshi, K.S. (eds.) VMCAI 2006. LNCS, vol. 3855, pp. 381–397. Springer, Heidelberg (2005)

19. Gurfinkel, A., Wei, O., Chechik, M.: YASM: A Software Model-Checker for Verification and Refutation. In: Ball, T., Jones, R.B. (eds.) CAV 2006. LNCS, vol. 4144, pp. 170–174. Springer, Heidelberg (2006)

20. Jeannet, B., Serwe, W.: Abstracting Call-Stacks for Interprocedural Verification of Imperative Programs. In: Rattray, C., Maharaj, S., Shankland, C. (eds.) AMAST 2004. LNCS, vol. 3116. Springer, Heidelberg (2004)

21. Larsen, K., Thomsen, B.: A Modal Process Logic. In: Proceedings of LICS 1988, pp. 203–210. IEEE Computer Society Press, Los Alamitos (1988)

22. Nielson, H., Nielson, F.: Semantics with Applications: A Formal Introduction. Wiley Professional Computing, Chichester (1992)

23. Reps, T.W., Horwitz, S., Sagiv, M.: Precise Interprocedural Dataflow Analysis via Graph Reachability. In: Proceedings of POPL 1995, pp. 49–61 (1995)

24. Sharir, M., Pnueli, A.: Program Flow Analysis: Theory and Applications. In: Two Approaches to Interprocedural Data Flow Analysis, pp. 189–233. Prentice-Hall, Englewood Cliffs (1981)

25. Shoham, S., Grumberg, O.: A Game-Based Framework for CTL Counter-Examples and 3-Valued Abstraction-Refinement. In: Hunt Jr., W.A., Somenzi, F. (eds.) CAV 2003. LNCS, vol. 2725, pp. 275–287. Springer, Heidelberg (2003)

26. Shoham, S., Grumberg, O.: Monotonic Abstraction-Refinement for CTL. In: Jensen, K., Podelski, A. (eds.) TACAS 2004. LNCS, vol. 2988, pp. 546–560. Springer, Heidelberg (2004)

27. Somenzi, F.: CUDD: CU Decision Diagram Package Release (2001)

Loop Summarization
Using Abstract Transformers*

Daniel Kroening[1], Natasha Sharygina[2,5], Stefano Tonetta[3],
Aliaksei Tsitovich[2], and Christoph M. Wintersteiger[4]

[1] Oxford University, Computing Laboratory, UK
[2] University of Lugano, Switzerland
[3] Fondazione Bruno Kessler, Trento, Italy
[4] Computer Systems Institute, ETH Zurich, Switzerland
[5] School of Computer Science, Carnegie Mellon University, USA

Abstract. Existing program analysis tools that implement abstraction rely on saturating procedures to compute over-approximations of fixpoints. As an alternative, we propose a new algorithm to compute an over-approximation of the set of reachable states of a program by replacing loops in the control flow graph by their abstract transformer. Our technique is able to generate diagnostic information in case of property violations, which we call *leaping counterexamples*. We have implemented this technique and report experimental results on a set of large ANSI-C programs using abstract domains that focus on properties related to string-buffers.

1 Introduction

Abstract Interpretation [1] is a framework for the approximative analysis of discrete transition systems, and is based on fixpoint computations. It is frequently applied to verify reachability properties of software programs. Abstract interpretation is performed with respect to an *abstract domain*, which is an approximate representation of sets of concrete values. Instances are numerical abstract domains such as intervals [1] and polyhedra [2], or specialized domains as, for example, a domain specific for heap-manipulating programs. In abstract interpretation, the behavior of a program is evaluated over the abstract domain using an *abstract transformer*. This is iterated until the set of abstract states saturates, i.e., an abstract fixpoint is reached. If certain formal constraints between the abstract and concrete domains are met, this abstract fixpoint is guaranteed to be an over-approximation of the set of reachable states of the original program.

A main issue in abstract interpretation is the number of iterations required to reach the abstract fixpoint. On large benchmarks, a thousand iterations is commonly observed, even when using simplistic abstract domains. Thus, many tools implementing abstract interpretation apply *widening* in order to accelerate

---

* Supported by the Swiss National Science Foundation grant no. 200021-111687 and an award from IBM research.

Cha et al. (Eds.): ATVA 2008, LNCS 5311, pp. 111–125, 2008.

convergence. Widening, however, may yield imprecision, and thus, the abstract fixpoint may not be strong enough to prove the desired property [3].

We propose a novel technique to address this problem, which uses a *symbolic abstract transformer* [4]. A symbolic abstract transformer for a given program fragment is a relation over a pair of abstract states $\hat{s}$, $\hat{s}'$ that holds if the fragment transforms $\hat{s}$ into $\hat{s}'$. We propose to apply the transformer to perform sound *summarization*, i.e., to replace parts of the program by a smaller representative. In particular, we use the transformer to summarize loops and (recursion-free) function calls.

The symbolic abstract transformer is usually computed by checking if a given abstract transition is consistent with the semantics of a statement [4,5]. Our technique generalizes the abstract transformer computation and applies it to program fragments: given an abstract transition relation, we check if it is consistent with the program semantics. This way, we can tailor the abstraction to each program fragment. In particular, for loop-free programs, we precisely encode their semantics into symbolic formulas. For loops, we exploit the symbolic transformer of the loop body to infer invariants of the loop. This is implemented by means of a sequence of calls to a decision procedure for the program logic.

When applied starting from the inner-most loops and the leaves of the call graph, the run-time of the resulting procedure becomes linear in the number of looping constructs in the program, and thus, is often much smaller than the number of iterations required by the traditional saturation procedure. We show soundness of the procedure and discuss its precision compared to the conventional approach on a given abstract domain. In case the property fails, a diagnostic counterexample can be obtained, which we call *leaping counterexample*. This diagnostic information is often very helpful for understanding the nature of the problem, and is considered a major plus for program analysis tools. Additionally, our technique *localizes* the abstract domains: we use different abstract domains for different parts of the code. This further improves the scalability of the analysis.

We implemented the procedure in a tool called LOOPFROG and applied it to search for buffer-overflow errors in well-known UNIX programs. Our experimental results demonstrate that the procedure is more precise than any other tool we compared with. Moreover, it scales to large programs even if complex abstract domains are used. In summary, the contributions of this paper are:

- We introduce a new technique for program abstraction by using symbolic abstract transformers for summarization of loops and function calls. The technique is sound and has the advantage that the run-time is linear in the number of looping constructs.
- In contrast to most other implementations of abstract interpretation, our analysis technique produces counterexamples which can be used to diagnose the property violation. Moreover, the counterexamples can be used to refine the abstract domains.

Related work. Other work on analysis using summaries of functions is quite extensive (see a nice survey in [6]) and dates back to Cousot and Halbwachs [2], and Sharir and Pnueli [7]. In a lot of projects, function summaries are created for alias analysis or points-to analysis, or are intended for the analysis of program fragments. As a result, these algorithms are either specialized to particular problems and deal with fairly simple abstract domains or are restricted to analysis of parts of the program. An instance is the summarization of library functions in [6]. In contrast, our technique aims at computing a summary for the entire program, and is applicable to complex abstract domains. The principal novelty of our technique is that it is a general-purpose loop summarization method that (unlike many other tools) is not limited to special classes of faults.

Similarly to our technique, the Saturn tool [8] computes a summary of a function with respect to an abstract domain using a SAT-based approach to improve scalability. However, in favor of scalability, Saturn simply unwinds loops a constant number of times, and thus, bugs that require more iterations are missed. Similarly to Saturn, the Spear tool [9] summarizes the effect of larger functions, which improves the scalability of the tool dramatically. However, as in the case of Saturn, loops are unwound only once.

SAT-solvers, SAT-based decision procedures, and constraint solvers are frequently applied in program verification. Instances are the tools Alloy [10] and CBMC [11]. The SAT-based approach is also suitable for computing abstractions, as, for example, in [8,5,4] (see detailed discussion in Sec. 2.3). The technique reported in this paper also uses the flexibility of a SAT-based decision procedure for a combination of theories to compute loop summaries.

One of the benefits of our approach is its ability to generate diagnostic information for failed properties. This is usually considered a distinguishing feature of *model checking* [12], and is rarely found in tools based on abstract interpretation. Counterexamples aid the diagnosis of errors, and may also be used to filter spurious warnings.

2   Background

2.1   Notation

In this section we introduce the basic concepts of abstract interpretation [1,13]. Let U denote the universe where the values of the program variables are drawn from. The set L of *elementary commands* consists of tests L_T and assignments L_A, i.e., $L = L_T \dot\cup L_A$, where a test $q \in L_T$ is a predicate over $dom(q) \subseteq U$. An assignment $e \in L_A$ is a total map from $dom(e) \subseteq U$ to U. Given $q \in L_T$, we denote with $\bar{q}$ the predicate over $dom(q)$ such that $q(u) = \neg \bar{q}(u)$ for all $u \in dom(q)$.

A program π is formalized as the pair $\langle U, G \rangle$, where U is the universe and G is a *program graph* [13]. A program graph is a tuple $\langle V, E, v_i, v_o, C \rangle$, where

- V is a finite non-empty set of vertices called *program locations*.
- $v_i \in V$ is the initial location.
- $v_o \in V$ is the final location.
- $E \subseteq V \times V$ is a non-empty set of edges; E^* denotes the set of *paths*, i.e., the set of finite sequences of edges.
- $C : E \to L$ associates a command with each edge.

```
p=a;
while(*p!=0){
  if(*p=='/')
    *p=0;
  p++;
}
```

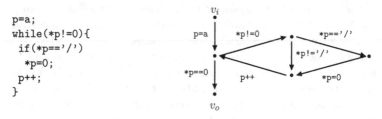

Fig. 1. The running example

We write L^* for the set of sequences of commands. Given a program π, the set $paths(\pi) \subseteq L^*$ contains the sequence $C(e_1), \ldots, C(e_n)$ for every $\langle e_1, .., e_n \rangle \in E^*$.

Example 1. We use the program fragment in Figure 1 as running example. On the left-hand side, we provide the C version. On the right-hand side, we depict its program graph.

The (concrete) semantics of a program is given by the pair $\langle A, \tau \rangle$, where

- A is the set of *assertions* of the program, where each assertion $P \in A$ is a predicate over U; $A(\Rightarrow, false, true, \vee, \wedge)$ is a complete Boolean lattice;
- $\tau : L \to (A \to A)$ is the (concrete) predicate transformer.

In forward semantic analysis, τ represents the strongest post-condition. The analysis of a program determines which assertions are true in each program location by simulating the program from the initial location to that particular program location.

2.2 Abstract Interpretation

An *abstract interpretation* is a pair $\langle \hat{A}, t \rangle$, where $\hat{A}$ is a complete lattice $\hat{A}(\sqsubseteq, \perp, \top, \sqcup, \sqcap)$, and $t : L \to (\hat{A} \to \hat{A})$ is a predicate transformer. Note that $\langle A, \tau \rangle$ is a particular abstract interpretation called the *concrete interpretation*. In the following, we assume that for every command $c \in L$, the function $t(c)$ is monotone (which is the case for all natural predicate transformers). Given a predicate transformer t, the function $\tilde{t} : L^* \to (\hat{A} \to \hat{A})$ is recursively defined as follows:

$$\tilde{t}(p)(\phi) = \begin{cases} \phi & \text{if } p \text{ is empty} \\ \tilde{t}(e)(t(q)(\phi)) & \text{if } p = q; e \text{ for some } q \in L, e \in L^*. \end{cases}$$

Example 2. We continue the running example (Fig. 1). Consider an abstract domain where abstract states are a four-tuple $\langle p_a, z_a, s_a, l_a \rangle$. The first member, p_a is the offset of the pointer p from the base address of the array a (i.e. $p - a$ in our example), the Boolean z_a holds if a contains the zero character, the Boolean s_a holds if a contains the slash character, l_a is the index of the first zero character if present. The predicate transformer t is defined as follows:
$t(p = a)(\phi) = \phi[p_a := 0]$ for any assertion ϕ;

$t(*p\,!=0)(\phi) = \phi \wedge (p_a \neq l_a)$ for any assertion ϕ;

$t(*p==0)(\phi) = \phi \wedge z_a \wedge (p_a \geq l_a)$ for any assertion ϕ;

$t(*p=='\,/')(\phi) = \phi \wedge s_a$ for any assertion ϕ;

$t(*p\,!='\,/')(\phi) = \phi$ for any assertion ϕ;

$$t(*p=0)(\phi) = \begin{cases} \bot & \text{if } \phi \Rightarrow \bot; \\ \phi[z_a := true, l_a := p_a] & \text{if } \phi \Rightarrow (p_a < l_a), \phi \neq \bot; \\ \phi[z_a := true] & \text{otherwise} \end{cases}$$

$t(p++)(\phi) = \phi[p_a := p_a + 1]$ for any assertion ϕ.

(We used $\phi[x := v]$ to denote an assertion equal to ϕ apart from the variable x that takes value v.)

Given a program π, an abstract interpretation $\langle \hat{A}, t \rangle$, and an element $\phi \in \hat{A}$, we define the *Merge Over all Paths* $MOP_\pi(t, \phi)$ as the element $\bigsqcup_{p \in paths(\pi)} \tilde{t}(p)(\phi)$.

Given two complete lattices $\hat{A}(\sqsubseteq, \bot, \top, \sqcup, \sqcap)$ and $\hat{A}'(\sqsubseteq', \bot', \top', \sqcup', \sqcap')$, the pair of functions $\langle \alpha, \gamma \rangle$, with $\alpha : \hat{A} \to \hat{A}'$ and $\gamma : \hat{A}' \to \hat{A}$ is a *Galois connection* iff α and γ are monotone and 1) for all $\phi \in \hat{A}$, $\phi \sqsubseteq \gamma(\alpha(\phi))$, and 2) for all $\phi' \in \hat{A}'$, $\alpha(\gamma(\phi')) \sqsubseteq' \phi'$.

An abstract interpretation $\langle \hat{A}, t \rangle$ is a *correct over-approximation* of the concrete interpretation $\langle A, \tau \rangle$ iff there exists a Galois connection $\langle \alpha, \gamma \rangle$ such that for all $\phi \in \hat{A}$ and $P \in A$, if $P \Rightarrow \gamma(\phi)$, then $\alpha(MOP_\pi(\tau, P)) \sqsubseteq MOP_\pi(t, \phi)$ (i.e., $MOP_\pi(\tau, P) \Rightarrow \gamma(MOP_\pi(t, \phi))$).

2.3   A SAT-Based Abstract Transformer

In order to implement abstract interpretation for a given abstract domain, an algorithmic description of the abstract predicate transformer $t(p)$ for a specific command $p \in L$ is required. Reps et al. describe an algorithm that implements the *best possible* (i.e., most precise) abstract transformer for a given finite-height abstract domain [4]. Graf and Saïdi's algorithm for constructing predicate abstractions [14] is identified as a special case.

The algorithm has two inputs: a formula $F_{\tau(q)}$, which represents a command $q \in L$ symbolically, and an assertion $\phi \in \hat{A}$. It returns the image of the predicate transformer $t(q)(\phi)$. The formula $F_{\tau(q)}$ is passed to a decision procedure, which is expected to provide a satisfying assignment to the variables. The assignment represents one concrete transition $P, P' \in A$. The transition is abstracted into a pair $\phi, \phi' \in \hat{A}$, and a blocking constraint is added to remove this satisfying assignment. The algorithm iterates until the formula becomes unsatisfiable. An instance of the algorithm for the case of predicate abstraction is the implementation of SATABS described in [5]. SATABS uses a propositional SAT-solver as decision procedure for bit-vector arithmetic. The procedure is worst-case exponential in the number of predicates, and thus, alternatives have been explored. In [15,16] a symbolic decision procedure generates a symbolic formula that represents the set of all solutions. In [17], a first-order formula is used and the computation of all solutions is carried out by a SAT modulo theories (SMT) solver. In [18], a similar technique is proposed where BDDs are used in order to efficiently deal with the Boolean component of $F_{\tau(q)}$.

3   Summarization Using Symbolic Abstract Transformers

3.1   Abstract Summarization

The idea of summarization is to replace a code fragment, e.g., a procedure of the program, by a *summary*, which is a (smaller) representation of the behavior of the fragment. Computing an exact summary of a program (fragment) is in general undecidable. We therefore settle for an over-approximation. We formalize the conditions the summary must fulfill in order to have a semantics that over-approximates the original program.

We extend the definition of a correct over-approximation (see Sec. 2) to programs. Given two programs π and π' on the same universe U, we say that π' is a *correct over-approximation* of π iff for all $P \in A(\Rightarrow, false, true, \vee, \wedge)$, $MOP_\pi(\tau, P) \Rightarrow MOP_{\pi'}(\tau, P)$.

Definition 1 (Abstract Summary). *Given a program π, and an abstract interpretation $\langle \hat{A}, t \rangle$ with a Galois connection $\langle \alpha, \gamma \rangle$ with $\langle A, \tau \rangle$, we denote the abstract summary of π by $Sum_{\langle \hat{A}, t \rangle}(\pi)$. It is defined as the program $\langle U, G \rangle$, where $G = \langle \{v_i, v_o\}, \{\langle v_i, v_o \rangle\}, v_i, v_o, C \rangle$ and $C(\langle v_i, v_o \rangle)$ is a new (concrete) command a such that $\tau(a)(P) = \gamma(MOP_\pi(t, \alpha(P)))$.*

Lemma 1. *If $\langle \hat{A}, t \rangle$ is a correct over-approximation of $\langle A, \tau \rangle$, the abstract summary $Sum_{\langle \hat{A}, t \rangle}(\pi)$ is a correct over-approximation of π.*

We now discuss algorithms for computing abstract summaries. Our summarization technique is first applied to particular fragments of the program, specifically to loop-free and single-loop programs. In Section 3.4, we use these procedures as subroutines to obtain the summarization of an arbitrary program. We formalize code fragments as *program sub-graphs*.

Definition 2. *Given two program graphs $G = \langle V, E, v_i, v_o, C \rangle$ and $G' = \langle V', E', v_i', v_o', C' \rangle$, G' is a program sub-graph of G iff $V' \subseteq V$, $E' \subseteq E$, and $C'(e) = C(e)$ for every edge $e \in E'$.*

3.2   Summarization of Loop-Free Programs

Obtaining $MOP_\pi(t, \phi)$ is as hard as assertion checking on the original program. Nevertheless, there are restricted cases where it is possible to represent $MOP_\pi(t, \phi)$ using a symbolic predicate transformer.

Let us consider a program π with a finite number of paths, in particular, a program whose program graph does not contain any cycle. A program graph $G = \langle V, E, v_i, v_o, C \rangle$ is *loop free* iff G is a directed acyclic graph.

In the case of a loop-free program π, we can compute a precise (not abstract) summary by means of a formula F_π that represents the concrete behavior of π. This formula is obtained by converting π to a static single assignment (SSA) form, whose size is linear in the size of π. The details of this step are beyond the scope of this paper; see [11].

Example 3. We continue the running example (Fig. 1). The symbolic transformer of the loop body π' is represented by:

$((*p =' \mathrel{/}' \land a' = a[*p = 0]) \lor (*p \neq' \mathrel{/}' \land a' = a)) \land (p' = p + 1)$.

Recall the abstract domain from Ex. 2. We can deduce that:

1. if $m < n$, then $MOP_{\pi'}(t, (p_a = m \land z_a \land (l_a = n) \land \neg s_a)) = (p_a = m + 1 \land z_a \land l_a = n \land \neg s_a)$
2. $MOP_{\pi'}(t, z_a) = z_a$.

This example highlights the generic nature of our technique. For instance, case 1 of the example cannot be obtained by means of predicate abstraction because it requires an infinite number of predicates. Also, the algorithm presented in [4] cannot handle this example because assuming the string length has no a-priori bound, the lattice of the abstract interpretation has infinite height.

3.3 Summarization of Single-Loop Programs

We now consider a program that consists of a single loop.

Definition 3. *A program* $\pi = \langle U, G \rangle$ *is a* single-loop program *iff* $G = \langle V, E, v_i, v_o, C \rangle$ *and there exists a program sub-graph* G' *and a test* $q \in L_T$ *such that*

- $G' = \langle V', E', v_b, v_i, C' \rangle$ *with*
  - $V' = V \setminus \{v_o\}$,
  - $E' = E \setminus \{\langle v_i, v_o \rangle, \langle v_i, v_b \rangle\}$,
  - $C'(e) = C(e)$ *for all* $e \in E'$,
  - G' *is loop free.*
- $C(\langle v_i, v_b \rangle) = q$, $C(\langle v_i, v_o \rangle) = \overline{q}$.

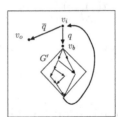

The following can be seen as the "abstract interpretation analog" of Hoare's rule for `while` loops.

Theorem 1. *Given a single-loop program* π *with guard* q *and loop body* π', *and an abstract interpretation* $\langle \hat{A}, t \rangle$, *let* ψ *be an assertion satisfying* $MOP_{\pi'}(t, t(q) (\psi)) \sqsubseteq \psi$ *and let* $\langle \hat{A}, t_\psi \rangle$ *be a new abstract interpretation s.t.*

$$MOP_\pi(t_\psi, \phi) = \begin{cases} t(\overline{q})(\psi) & \text{if } \phi \sqsubseteq \psi \\ \top & \text{elsewhere.} \end{cases}$$

If $\langle \hat{A}, t \rangle$ *is a correct over-approximation, then* $\langle \hat{A}, t_\psi \rangle$ *is a correct over-approximation as well.*

In other words, if we apply the predicate transformer of the test q and then the transformer of the loop body π' to the assertion ψ, and we obtain an assertion at least as strong as ψ, then ψ is an invariant of the loop. If a stronger assertion ϕ holds before the loop, the predicate transformer of $\bar{q}$ applied to ϕ holds afterwards.

Theorem 1 gives rise to a summarization algorithm. Given a program fragment and an abstract domain, we heuristically provide a set of formulas that encode that a (possibly infinite) set of assertions ψ are invariant (for example, $x' = x$ encodes that every ψ defined as $x = c$, with c a value in the domain U, is an invariant); we apply a decision procedure to check if the formulas are satisfiable. The construction of the summary is then straightforward: given a single-loop program π, an abstract interpretation $\langle \hat{A}, t \rangle$, and an invariant ψ for the loop body, let $\langle \hat{A}, t_\psi \rangle$ be the abstract interpretation as defined in Theorem 1. We denote the summary $Sum_{\langle \hat{A}, t_\psi \rangle}(\pi)$ by $\text{SLS}(\pi, \hat{A}, t_\psi)$ (Single-Loop Summary).

Corollary 1. *If $\langle \hat{A}, t \rangle$ is a correct over-approximation of $\langle A, \tau \rangle$, then $\text{SLS}(\pi, \hat{A}, t_\psi)$ is a correct over-approximation of π.*

Example 4. We continue the running example. Recall the abstract domain in Ex. 2. Let π' denote the loop body of the example program and let q denote the loop guard. By applying the symbolic transformer from Ex. 3, we can check that the following conditions hold:

1. $MOP_{\pi'}(t, t(q)(\phi)) \sqsubseteq \phi$ for any assertion $((p_a \le l_a) \land z_a \land \neg s_a)$.
2. $MOP_{\pi'}(t, t(q)(\phi)) \sqsubseteq \phi$ for the assertion z_a.

Thus, we summarize the loop with the following predicate transformer:

$$(z_a \to z'_a) \land (((p_a \le l_a) \land z_a \land \neg s_a) \to ((p'_a = l'_a) \land z'_a \land \neg s'_a)) .$$

3.4 Summarization for Arbitrary Programs

We now describe an algorithm for over-approximating an arbitrary program. Like traditional algorithms (e.g. [19]), the dependency tree of program fragments is traversed bottom-up, starting from the leaves. The code fragments we consider may be function calls or loops. We treat function calls as arbitrary sub-graphs (see Def. 2) of the program graph, and do not allow recursion. We support irreducible graphs using loop simulation [20].

Specifically, we define the *sub-graph dependency tree* of a program $\pi = \langle U, G \rangle$ as the tree $\langle T, > \rangle$, where

- the set of nodes of the tree are program sub-graphs of G;
- for $G_1, G_2 \in T$, $G_1 > G_2$ iff G_2 is a program sub-graph of G_1 with $G_1 \ne G_2$;
- the root of the tree is G;
- every leaf is a loop-free or single-loop sub-graph;
- every loop sub-graph is in T.

Algorithm 1 takes a program as input and computes its summary by following the structure of the sub-graph dependency tree (Line 1). Thus, the algorithm is called

```
1  SUMMARIZE(π)
    input   :  program π = ⟨U, G⟩
    output  :  over-approximation π' of π
2  begin
3      ⟨T, >⟩ :=sub-graph dependency tree of π;
4      πᵣ := π;
5      for  each G' such that G > G' do
6          ⟨U, G''⟩:=SUMMARIZE(⟨U, G'⟩);
7          πᵣ := πᵣ where G' is replaced with G'';
8          update ⟨T, >⟩;
9      if πᵣ is a single loop then
10         ⟨Â, t⟩ := choose abstract interpretation for πᵣ;
11         ψ := test invariant candidates for t on πᵣ;
12         π' := SLS(πᵣ, Â, t_ψ);
13     else
           /* πᵣ is loop-free */
14         π' := Sum_{⟨A,τ⟩}(πᵣ);
15     return π'
16 end
```

Algorithm 1: Generic program summarization

recursively on the sub-program until a leaf is found (Line 1). If it is a single loop, an abstract domain is chosen (Line 1) and the loop is summarized as described in Section 3.3 (Line 1). If it is a loop-free program, it is summarized with a symbolic transformer as described in Section 3.2 (Line 1). The old sub-program is then replaced with its summary (Line 1) and the sub-graph dependency tree is updated (Line 1). Eventually, the entire program is summarized.

Theorem 2. SUMMARIZE(π) *is a correct over-approximation of π.*

The precision of the over-approximation is controlled by the precision of the symbolic transformers. However, in general, the computation of the best abstract transformer is an expensive iterative procedure. We use the inexpensive syntactic procedure for loop-free fragments. Loss of precision only happens when summarizing loops, and greatly depends on the abstract interpretation chosen in Line 1.

Note that Algorithm 1 does not limit the selection of abstract domains to any specific type of domains, and that it does not iterate the predicate transformer on the program. Furthermore, this algorithm allows for *localization* of the summarization procedure, as a new domain may be chosen for every loop. Once the domains are chosen, it is also easy to monitor the progress of the summarization, as the number of loops and the cost of computing the symbolic transformers are known – another distinguishing feature of our algorithm.

The summarization can serve as an over-approximation of the program. It can be trivially analyzed to prove unreachability, or equivalently, to prove assertions.

3.5 Leaping Counterexamples

Let π' denote the summary of the program. The program π' is a loop-free sequence of symbolic summaries for loop-free fragments and loop summaries. A *counterexample* for an assertion in π' follows this structure: when traversing symbolic summaries for loop-free fragments, it is identical to a concrete counterexample. Upon entering a loop summary, the effect of the loop body is given as a single transition in the counterexample: we say that the counterexample *leaps* over the loop.

Example 5. Consider the summary from Ex. 4. Suppose that in the initial condition, the buffer a contains a null terminating character in position n and no $'/'$ character. If we check that, after the loop, p_a is greater than the size n, we obtain a counterexample with $p_a^0 = 0, p_a^1 = n$.

The *leaping counterexample* may only exist with respect to the abstract interpretations used to summarize the loops, i.e., they may be spurious in the concrete interpretation. Nevertheless, they provide useful diagnostic feedback to the programmer, as they show a (partial) path to the violated assertion, and contain many of the input values the program needs to read to violate the assertion. Furthermore, spurious counterexamples can be eliminated by combining our technique with counterexample-guided abstraction refinement, as we do have an abstract counterexample.

4 Experimental Evaluation

We implemented our loop summarization technique in a tool called LOOPFROG and report our experience using abstract domains tailored to the discovery of buffer overflows on a large set of ANSI-C benchmarks.[1] The loop summarization (as described in Section 3.3) relies on the symbolic execution engine of CBMC. We use bit-blasting to SAT as a decision procedure, but any SMT-BV solver is applicable as well.

We use GOTO-CC[2] to extract model files from C source code; full ANSI-C is supported. The model files essentially contain a symbol table and a control flow graph. LOOPFROG performs a field-sensitive pointer analysis, which is used to add assertions about pointers. The program is then passed to the loop summarization and, finally, the CBMC assertion checker.

The current implementation of LOOPFROG is able to automatically check user-supplied assertions of arbitrary form. In addition to these, array and dynamic object bounds checks, pointer validity, and string termination assertions are added automatically, where required. Also, abstract models for string-related functions from the ANSI-C library are provided and added if necessary.

---

[1] Note that our technique is a general-purpose loop and function call summarization method. It is not limited to special classes of faults such as buffer overflows.

[2] http://www.cprover.org/goto-cc/

4.1 An Abstract Domain for Strings

The choice of the abstract domain for the loop summarization has a significant impact on the performance of the algorithm. A carefully selected domain generates fewer invariant candidates and thus speeds up the computation of a loop summary. Besides, the abstract domain has to be sufficiently expressive to retain enough of the semantics of the original loop to show the property.

In order to evaluate the effectiveness of the summarization algorithm, we use programs that manipulate string buffers as benchmarks. We therefore implement the following string-related abstract domain, similar to the instrumentation suggested by Dor et al. [21]: for each string buffer s, a Boolean value z_s and integers l_s and b_s are tracked. The Boolean z_s holds if s contains the zero character within the buffer size b_s. If so, l_s is the index of the first zero character, otherwise, l_s has no meaning.

In our experiments, we use the following assertions for the abstract states, which we call *invariant templates*:

– Arithmetic relations between i and l_s, where i is an integer type expression, and s is a string buffer. Currently, we use $0 \leq i < l_s$.
– String termination, i.e., z_s holds.
– String length, i.e., $l_s < b_s$ holds.
– Pointer validity: p points to a specific object. Currently, we use the weaker $p \neq NULL$.

These templates are instantiated according to variables occurring in the code fragment taken into account. To lower the amount of template instantiations, the following set of simple heuristics is used:

1. Only variables of appropriate type are considered (we concentrate on string types).
2. Indices and string buffers are combined in one invariant only if they are used in the same expression, i.e., we detect instructions which contain $p[i]$ and build invariants that combine i with all string buffers pointed by p.

These templates have proven to be effective in our experiments. Other applications likely require different abstract domains. However, new domain templates may be added quite easily: they usually can be implemented with less than a hundred lines of code.

4.2 Results on Small Benchmarks

We use metrics proposed by Zitser et al. [22] to evaluate and compare the precision of our implementation. We report the *detection rate* $R(d)$ and the *false positive rate* $R(f)$. The *discrimination rate* $R(\neg f | d)$ is defined as the ratio of test cases on which an error is correctly reported, while it is, also correctly, not reported in the corresponding fixed test case. Using this measure, tools are penalized for not finding a bug, but also for not reporting a fixed program as safe.

The experiments are performed on two recently published benchmark sets. The first one, by Zitser et al. [22], contains 164 instances of buffer overflow problems, extracted from the original source code of sendmail, wu-ftpd, and bind. The test cases do not contain complete programs, but only those parts required to trigger the buffer overflow. According to Zitser et al., this was necessary because the tools in their study were all either unable to parse the test code, or the analysis used disproportionate resources before terminating with an error ([22], pg. 99). In this set, 82 tests contain a buffer overflow, and the rest represent a fix of a buffer overflow.

The results of a comparison with a wide selection of static analysis tools[3] are summarized in Table 1. Almost all of the test cases involve array bounds violations. Even though Uno, Archer and BOON were designed to detect these type of bugs, they hardly report any errors. The source code of the test cases was not annotated, but nevertheless, the annotation-based Splint tool performs reasonably well on these benchmarks. LOOPFROG is the only tool that reports all buffer overflows correctly (a detection rate of $R(d) = 1$) and with 62%, LOOPFROG also has the highest discrimination rate among all the tools. It is also worth noticing that our summarization

Table 1. Effectiveness: Detection rate $R(d)$, false positive rate $R(f)$, and discrimination rate $R(\neg f|d)$ for various static analysis tools

	$R(d)$	$R(f)$	$R(\neg f|d)$
LOOPFROG	1.00	0.38	0.62
$=, \neq, \leq$	1.00	0.44	0.56
Interval Domain	1.00	0.98	0.02
Polyspace	0.87	0.50	0.37
Splint	0.57	0.43	0.30
Boon	0.05	0.05	0
Archer	0.01	0	0
Uno	0	0	0
LOOPFROG [23]	1.00	0.26	0.74
$=, \neq, \leq$[23]	1.00	0.46	0.54

technique performs quite well, when only a few relational domains are used (the second line of Table 1). The third line in this table contains the data for a simple interval domain, not implemented in LOOPFROG, but as a traditional abstract domain; it reports almost everything as unsafe.

The second set of benchmarks was proposed by Ku et al. [23]. It contains 568 test cases, of which 261 are fixed versions of buffer overflows. This set partly overlaps with the first one, but contains source code of a greater variety of applications, including the Apache HTTP server, Samba, and the NetBSD C system library. Again, the test programs are stripped down, and are partly simplified to enable current model checkers to parse them. Our results on this set confirm the results obtained using the first set; the corresponding numbers are given in the last two lines of Table 1. On this set the advantage of selecting property-specific domains is clearly visible, as a 20% increase in the discrimination rate over the simple relational domains is witnessed. Also, the performance of LOOPFROG is much better if specialized domains are used, simply because there are fewer candidates for the invariants.

---

[3] The data for all tools but LOOPFROG, "$=$, $\neq$, $\leq$" and the Interval Domain is from [22].

The leaping counterexamples computed by our algorithm are a valuable aid in the design of new abstract domains that decrease the number of false positives. Also, we observe that both test sets include instances labelled as unsafe that LOOPFROG reports to be safe (1 in [22] and 9 in [23]). However, by manual inspection of the counterexamples for these cases, we find that our tool is correct, i.e., that the test cases are spurious.[4] For most of the test cases in the benchmark suites, the time and memory requirements of LOOPFROG are negligible. On average, a test case finishes within a minute.

4.3   Large-Scale Benchmarks

We also evaluated the performance of LOOPFROG on a set of large-scale benchmarks, that is, complete un-modified program suites. Table 2 contains a selection of the results.[5] Further experimental data, an in-depth description of LOOPFROG, the tool itself, and all our benchmark files are available on-line for experimentation by other researchers.[6] Due to the problems reported by Zitser et al., we were unable to apply other tools to the large-scale benchmarks.

These experiments clearly show that the algorithm scales reasonably well in both memory and time, depending on the program size and the number of loops contained. The time required for summarization naturally depends on the complexity of the program, but also to a large degree on the selection of (potential) invariants. As experience has shown, unwisely chosen invariant templates may generate many useless potential invariants, each requiring to be tested by the SAT-solver. This is a problem that we seek to remedy in the future, by leveraging incremental SAT-solver technology.

In general, the results regarding the program assertions shown to hold are not surprising; for many programs (e.g., texindex, ftpshut, ginstall), our selection of string-specific domains proved to be quite useful. It is also interesting to note that the results on the ftpshut program are very different on program versions 2.5.0 and 2.6.2: This program contains a number of known buffer-overflow problems in version 2.5.0, and considerable effort was spent on fixing it for the 2.6.2 release; an effort clearly reflected in our statistics. Just like in this benchmark, many of the failures reported by LOOPFROG correspond to known bugs and the leaping counterexamples we obtain allow us to analyze those faults. Merely for reference we list CVE-2001-1413 (a buffer overflow in ncompress) and CVE-2006-1168 (a buffer underflow in the same program), for which we are easily able to produce counterexamples.[7] On the other hand, some other programs (such as the ones from the freecell-solver suite) clearly require different abstract domains, suitable for other heap structures than strings. The development of suitable domains and subsequent experiments, however, are left for future research.

---

[4] We exclude those instances from our benchmarks.

[5] All data was obtained on an 8-core Intel Xeon 3.0 GHZ. We limited the runtime to 4 hours and the memory per process to 4 GB.

[6] http://www.cprover.org/loopfrog/

[7] The corresponding bug reports may be obtained from http://cve.mitre.org/

Table 2. Large-Scale Evaluation

Suite	Program	Instructions	# Loops	Time Summari-zation	Time Checking Assertions	Time Total	Peak Memory	Assertions Total	Assertions Passed	Assertions Violated
freecell-solver	aisleriot-board-2.8.12	347	26	10s	295s	305s	111MB	358	165	193
freecell-solver	gnome-board-2.8.12	208	8	0s	3s	4s	13MB	49	16	33
freecell-solver	microsoft-board-2.8.12	168	4	2s	9s	11s	32MB	45	19	26
freecell-solver	pi-ms-board-2.8.12	185	4	2s	10s	13s	33MB	53	27	26
gnupg	make-dns-cert-1.4.4	232	5	0s	0s	1s	9MB	12	5	7
gnupg	mk-tdata-1.4.4	117	1	0s	0s	0s	3MB	8	7	1
inn	encode-2.4.3	155	3	0s	2s	2s	6MB	88	66	22
inn	ninpaths-2.4.3	476	25	5s	40s	45s	49MB	96	47	49
ncompress	compress-4.2.4	806	12	45s	4060s	4106s	345MB	306	212	94
texinfo	ginstall-info-4.7	1265	46	21s	326s	347s	127MB	304	226	78
texinfo	makedoc-4.7	701	18	9s	6s	16s	28MB	55	33	22
texinfo	texindex-4.7	1341	44	415s	9336s	9757s	1021MB	604	496	108
wu-ftpd	ckconfig-2.5.0	135	0	0s	0s	0s	3MB	3	3	0
wu-ftpd	ckconfig-2.6.2	247	10	13s	43s	57s	27MB	53	10	43
wu-ftpd	ftpcount-2.5.0	379	13	10s	32s	42s	37MB	115	41	74
wu-ftpd	ftpcount-2.6.2	392	14	8s	24s	32s	39MB	118	42	76
wu-ftpd	ftprestart-2.6.2	372	23	48s	232s	280s	55MB	142	31	111
wu-ftpd	ftpshut-2.5.0	261	5	1s	9s	10s	13MB	83	29	54
wu-ftpd	ftpshut-2.6.2	503	26	27s	79s	106s	503MB	232	210	22
wu-ftpd	ftpwho-2.5.0	379	13	7s	23s	30s	37MB	115	41	74
wu-ftpd	ftpwho-2.6.2	392	14	8s	27s	35s	39MB	118	42	76
wu-ftpd	privatepw-2.6.2	353	9	4s	17s	22s	32MB	80	51	29

5   Conclusion and Future Work

We presented a novel algorithm for program verification using symbolic abstract transformers. The algorithm computes an abstraction of a program with respect to a given abstract interpretation by replacing loops and function calls in the control flow graph by their symbolic transformers. The runtime of our algorithm is linear in the number of looping constructs. It addresses the perennial problem of the high complexity of computing abstract fixpoints. The procedure over-approximates the original program, which implies soundness of our analysis. An additional benefit of the technique is its ability to generate *leaping counterexamples*, which are helpful for diagnosis of the error or for filtering spurious warnings. Experimental results show the best error-detection and error-discrimination rates comparing to a broad selection of static analysis tools. As future work, we plan to analyze the leaping counterexamples automatically in order to rule out spurious traces and to refine the abstract domain.

References

1. Cousot, P., Cousot, R.: Abstract interpretation: A unified lattice model for static analysis of programs by construction or approximation of fixpoints. In: POPL, pp. 238–252 (1977)
2. Cousot, P., Halbwachs, N.: Automatic Discovery of Linear Restraints Among Variables of a Program. In: POPL, pp. 84–96 (1978)

3. Cousot, P., Cousot, R.: Comparing the Galois connection and widening/narrowing approaches to abstract interpretation. In: Bruynooghe, M., Wirsing, M. (eds.) PLILP 1992. LNCS, vol. 631, pp. 269–295. Springer, Heidelberg (1992)
4. Reps, T.W., Sagiv, S., Yorsh, G.: Symbolic Implementation of the Best Transformer. In: Steffen, B., Levi, G. (eds.) VMCAI 2004. LNCS, vol. 2937, pp. 252–266. Springer, Heidelberg (2004)
5. Clarke, E.M., Kroening, D., Sharygina, N., Yorav, K.: Predicate abstraction of ANSI-C programs using SAT. FMSD 25, 105–127 (2004)
6. Gopan, D., Reps, T.W.: Low-level library analysis and summarization. In: Damm, W., Hermanns, H. (eds.) CAV 2007. LNCS, vol. 4590, pp. 68–81. Springer, Heidelberg (2007)
7. Sharir, M., Pnueli, A.: Two approaches to interprocedural data flow analysis. In: Program Flow Analysis: theory and applications. Prentice-Hall, Englewood Cliffs (1981)
8. Aiken, A., Bugrara, S., Dillig, I., Dillig, T., Hackett, B., Hawkins, P.: An overview of the Saturn project. In: PASTE, pp. 43–48. ACM, New York (2007)
9. Babic, D., Hu, A.J.: Calysto: scalable and precise extended static checking. In: ICSE, pp. 211–220. ACM, New York (2008)
10. Jackson, D., Vaziri, M.: Finding bugs with a constraint solver. In: ISSTA, pp. 14–25 (2000)
11. Clarke, E., Kroening, D., Lerda, F.: A tool for checking ANSI-C programs. In: Jensen, K., Podelski, A. (eds.) TACAS 2004. LNCS, vol. 2988, pp. 168–176. Springer, Heidelberg (2004)
12. Clarke, E., Grumberg, O., Peled, D.A.: Model checking. MIT Press, Cambridge (1999)
13. Cousot, P., Cousot, R.: Systematic design of program analysis frameworks. In: POPL, pp. 269–282 (1979)
14. Graf, S., Saïdi, H.: Construction of abstract state graphs with PVS. In: Grumberg, O. (ed.) CAV 1997. LNCS, vol. 1254, pp. 72–83. Springer, Heidelberg (1997)
15. Lahiri, S.K., Ball, T., Cook, B.: Predicate abstraction via symbolic decision procedures. In: Etessami, K., Rajamani, S.K. (eds.) CAV 2005. LNCS, vol. 3576, pp. 24–38. Springer, Heidelberg (2005)
16. Kroening, D., Sharygina, N.: Approximating predicate images for bit-vector logic. In: Hermanns, H., Palsberg, J. (eds.) TACAS 2006. LNCS, vol. 3920, pp. 242–256. Springer, Heidelberg (2006)
17. Lahiri, S.K., Nieuwenhuis, R., Oliveras, A.: SMT techniques for fast predicate abstraction. In: Ball, T., Jones, R.B. (eds.) CAV 2006. LNCS, vol. 4144, pp. 424–437. Springer, Heidelberg (2006)
18. Cavada, R., Cimatti, A., Franzén, A., Kalyanasundaram, K., Roveri, M., Shyamasundar, R.K.: Computing predicate abstractions by integrating BDDs and SMT solvers. In: FMCAD, pp. 69–76. IEEE, Los Alamitos (2007)
19. Tarjan, R.E.: Fast algorithms for solving path problems. J. ACM 28, 594–614 (1981)
20. Ashcroft, E., Manna, Z.: The translation of 'go to' programs to 'while' programs, pp. 49–61 (1979)
21. Dor, N., Rodeh, M., Sagiv, S.: CSSV: towards a realistic tool for statically detecting all buffer overflows in C. In: PLDI, pp. 155–167 (2003)
22. Zitser, M., Lippmann, R., Leek, T.: Testing static analysis tools using exploitable buffer overflows from open source code. In: SIGSOFT FSE, pp. 97–106 (2004)
23. Ku, K., Hart, T.E., Chechik, M., Lie, D.: A buffer overflow benchmark for software model checkers. In: ASE 2007, pp. 389–392. ACM Press, New York (2007)

Dynamic Model Checking with Property Driven Pruning to Detect Race Conditions*

Chao Wang[1], Yu Yang[2], Aarti Gupta[1], and Ganesh Gopalakrishnan[2]

[1] NEC Laboratories America, Princeton, New Jersey, USA
[2] School of Computing, University of Utah, Salt Lake City, Utah, USA

Abstract. We present a new property driven pruning algorithm in dynamic model checking to efficiently detect race conditions in multithreaded programs. The main idea is to use a lockset based analysis of observed executions to help prune the search space to be explored by the dynamic search. We assume that a stateless search algorithm is used to systematically execute the program in a depth-first search order. If our conservative lockset analysis shows that a search subspace is race-free, it can be pruned away by avoiding backtracks to certain states in the depth-first search. The new dynamic race detection algorithm is both sound and complete (as precise as the dynamic partial order reduction algorithm by Flanagan and Godefroid). The algorithm is also more efficient in practice, allowing it to scale much better to real-world multithreaded C programs.

1 Introduction

Concurrent programs are notoriously hard to debug because of their often large number of possible interleavings of thread executions. Concurrency bugs often arise in rare situations that are hard to anticipate and handle by standard testing techniques. One representative type of bugs in concurrent programs is a data race, which happens when multiple threads access a shared data variable simultaneously and at least one of the accesses is a write. Race conditions were among the flaws in the Therac-25 radiation therapy machine [12], which led to the death of three patients and injuries to several more. A race condition in the energy management system of some power facilities prevented alerts from being raised to the monitoring technicians, eventually leading to the 2003 North American Blackout.

To completely verify a multithreaded program for a given test input, one has to inspect all possible thread interleavings. For deterministic threads, the only source of nondeterminism in their execution comes from the thread scheduler of the operating system. In a typical testing environment, the user does not have full control over the scheduling of threads; running the same test multiple times does not necessarily translate into a better interleaving coverage. Static analysis has been used for detecting data races in multithreaded programs, both for a given test input [20, 16] and for all possible inputs [6, 4, 17, 11, 22]. However, a race condition reported by static analysis may be bogus (there can be many false alarms); even if it is real, there is often little information

---

* Yu Yang and Ganesh Gopalakrishnan were supported in part by NSF award CNS-0509379 and the Microsoft HPC Institutes program.

Cha et al. (Eds.): ATVA 2008, LNCS 5311, pp. 126–140, 2008.

for the user to reproduce the race. Model checking [3, 18] has the advantage of exhaustive coverage which means all possible thread interleavings will be explored. However, model checkers require building finite-state or pushdown automata models of the software [10, 1]; they often do not perform well in the presence of lock pointers and other heap allocated data structures.

Dynamic model checking as in [9, 5, 14, 23, 24] can directly check programs written in full-fledged programming languages such as C and Java. For detecting data races, these methods are sound (no bogus race) due to their concrete execution of the program itself as opposed to a model. While a bounded analysis is used in [14], the other methods [9, 5, 23, 24] are complete for terminating programs (do not miss real races) by systematically exploring the state space without explicitly storing the intermediate states. Although such dynamic software model checking is both sound and complete, the search is often inefficient due to the astronomically large number of thread interleavings and the lack of property specific pruning. Dynamic partial order reduction (DPOR) techniques [5, 23, 7] have been used in this context to remove the redundant interleavings from each equivalence class, provided that the representative interleaving has been explored. However, the pruning techniques used by these DPOR tools have been generic, rather than *property-specific*.

T_1		T_2	
	...		...
a_1	lock(f1) ;	b_1	lock(f1) ;
a_2	x++;	b_2	lock(f2) ;
a_3	unlock(f1) ;	b_3	z++;
a_4	...	b_4	c = x;
a_5	lock(f2) ;	b_5	unlock(f2) ;
a_6	y++;	b_6	unlock(f1) ;
a_7	unlock(f2) ;	b_7	...
a_8	...	b_8	lock(f1) ;
a_9	lock(f1) ;	b_9	if (c==0)
a_{10}	z++;	b_{10}	y++;
a_{11}	unlock(f1) ;	b_{11}	unlock(f1) ;

Fig. 1. Race condition on accessing variable y (assume that $x = y = 0$ initially)

Without a conservative or warranty type of analysis tailored toward the property to be checked, model checking has to enumerate all the equivalence classes of interleavings. Our observation is that, as far as race detection is concerned, many equivalence classes themselves may be redundant. Fig. 1 shows a motivating example, in which two threads use locks to protect accesses to shared variables x, y, and z. A race condition between a_6 and b_{10} may occur when b_4 is executed before a_2, by setting c to 0. Let the first execution sequence be $a_1 \ldots a_{11}b_1 \ldots b_9b_{11}$. According to the DPOR algorithm by Flanagan and Godefroid [5], since a_{10} and b_3 have a read-write conflict, we need to backtrack to a_8 and continue the search from $a_1 \ldots a_8b_1$. As a generic pruning technique, this is reasonable since the two executions are not Mazurkiewicz-trace equivalent [13]. For data race detection, however, it is futile to search any of these execution traces in which a_6 and b_{10} cannot be simultaneously reachable (which can be revealed by a conservative lockset analysis). We provide a property-specific pruning algorithm to skip such redundant interleavings and backtrack directly to a_1.

In this paper, we propose a trace-based dynamic lockset analysis to prune the search space in the context of dynamic model checking. Our main contributions are: (1) a new lockset analysis of the observed execution trace for checking whether the associated search subspace is race-free. (2) property driven pruning in a backtracking algorithm using depth-first search.

We analyze the various alternatives of the current execution trace to anticipate race conditions in the corresponding search space. Our trace-based lockset analysis relies on both information derived from the dynamic execution and information collected statically from the program; therefore, it is more precise than the purely static lockset analysis conducted *a priori* on the program [4, 6, 17, 11, 22]. Our method is also different from the *Eraser*-style dynamic lockset algorithms [20, 16], since our method decides whether the entire search subspace related to the concrete execution generated is race-free, not merely the execution itself. The crucial requirement for a method to be used in our framework for pruning of the search space is completeness—pruning must not remove real races. Therefore, neither the aforementioned dynamic lockset analysis nor the various predictive testing techniques [21, 2] based on happens-before causality (sound but incomplete) can be be used in this framework. CHESS [14] can detect races that may show up within a preemption bound; it exploits the preemption bounding for pruning, but does not exploit the lock semantics to effect reduction.

In our approach, if the search subspace is found to be race-free, we prune it away during the search by avoiding backtracks to the corresponding states. Recall that essentially the search is conducted in a DFS order. If there is a potential race, we analyze the cause in order to compute a proper backtracking point. Our backtracking algorithm shares the same insights as the DPOR algorithm [5], with the additional pruning capability provided by the trace-based lockset analysis. Note that DPOR relies solely on the *independence relation* to prune redundant interleavings (if t_1, t_2 are independent, there is no need to flip their execution order). In our algorithm, *even if t_1, t_2 are dependent*, we may skip the corresponding search space if flipping the order of t_1, t_2 does not affect the reachability of any race condition. If there is no data race at all in the program, our algorithm can obtain the desired race-freedom assurance much faster.

2   Preliminaries

2.1   Concurrent Programs

We consider a concurrent program with a finite number of threads as a state transition system. Let $Tid = \{1, \ldots, n\}$ be a set of thread indices. Threads may access local variables in their own stacks, as well as global variables in a shared heap. The operations on global variables are called *visible* operations, while those on thread local variables are called *invisible* operations. We use *Global* to denote the set of states of all global variables, *Local* to denote the set of local states of a thread. PC is the set of values of the program counter of a thread. The entire system state (S), the program counters of the threads (PCs), and the local states of threads ($Locals$) are defined as follows:

$$S \subseteq Global \times Locals \times PCs$$
$$PCs = Tid \rightarrow PC$$
$$Locals = Tid \rightarrow Local$$

A transition $t : S \rightarrow S$ advances the program from one state to a subsequent state. Following the notation of [5, 23], each transition t consists of one visible operation, followed by a finite sequence of invisible operations of the same thread up to (but excluding) the next visible operation. We use $tid(t) \in Tid$ to denote the thread index of the transition t. Let T be the set of all transitions of a program. A transition $t \in T$ is *enabled* in a state s if the next state $t(s)$ is defined. We use $s \xrightarrow{t} s'$ to denote that t is enabled in s and $s' = t(s)$. Two transitions t_1, t_2 *may be co-enabled* if there exists a state in which both t_1 and t_2 are enabled. The state transition graph is denoted $\langle S, s_0, \Gamma \rangle$, where $s_0 \in S$ is the unique initial state and $\Gamma \subseteq S \times S$ is the transition relation: $(s, s') \in \Gamma$ iff $\exists t \in T : s \xrightarrow{t} s'$. An execution sequence is a sequence of states $s_0, \ldots, s_n$ such that $\exists t_i . s_{i-1} \xrightarrow{t_i} s_i$ for all $1 \leq i \leq n$.

Two transitions are *independent* if and only if they can neither disable nor enable each other, and swapping their order of execution does not change the combined effect. Two execution trace are equivalent iff they can be transformed into each other by repeatedly swapping adjacent independent transitions. In model checking, partial order reduction (POR [8]) has been used to exploit the redundancy of executions from the same equivalence class to prune the search space; in particular, model checking has to consider only one representative from each equivalence class.

2.2 Dynamic Partial Order Reduction

Model checking of a multithreaded program can be conducted in a stateless fashion by systematically executing the program in a depth-first search order. This can be implemented by using a special *scheduler* to control the execution of visible operations of all threads; the scheduler needs to give permission to, and observe the result of every visible operation of the program. Instead of enumerating the reachable states, as in classic model checkers, it exhaustively explores all the feasible thread interleavings. Fig. 2 shows a typical stateless search algorithm. The scheduler maintains a *search stack S* of states. Each state $s \in S$ is associated with a set *s.enabled* of enabled transitions, a set *s.done* of executed transitions, and a *backtracking set*, consisting of the thread indices of some enabled transitions in s that need to be explored from s. In this context, backtracking is implemented by re-starting the program afresh under a different thread schedule [23], while ensuring that the replay is deterministic—i.e. all external behaviors (e.g., mallocs and IO) are also assumed to be replayable[1].

The procedure DPORUPDATEBACKTRACKSETS(S, t) implements the dynamic partial order reduction algorithm of [5]. It updates the backtrack set only for the last transition t_d in T such that t_d is dependent and may be co-enabled with t (line 19). The

---

[1] While malloc replayability is ensured by allocating objects in the same fashion, IO replayability is ensured by creating suitable closed environments.

1: Initially: S is empty; DPORSEARCH(S, s_0)

2: DPORSEARCH(S, s) {
3:      **if** (DETECTRACE(s)) **exit** (S);
4:      S.push(s);
5:      **for each** $t \in s.enabled$, DPORUPDATEBACKTRACKSETS(S, t);
6:      let $\tau \in Tid$ such that $\exists t \in s.enabled : tid(t) = \tau$;
7:      $s.backtrack \leftarrow \{\tau\}$;
8:      $s.done \leftarrow \varnothing$;
9:      **while** ($\exists t: tid(t) \in s.backtrack$ and $t \notin s.done$) {
10:         $s.done \leftarrow s.done \cup \{t\}$;
11:         $s.backtrack \leftarrow s.backtrack \setminus \{tid(t)\}$;
12:         let $s' \in S$ such that $s \xrightarrow{t} s'$;
13:         DPORSEARCH(S, s');
14:         S.pop(s);
15:      }
16: }
17: DPORUPDATEBACKTRACKSETS(S, t) {
18:     let $T = \{t_1, \ldots, t_n\}$ be the sequence of transitions associated with S;
19:     let t_d be the latest transition in T that is dependent and may be co-enabled with t;
20:     **if** ($t_d \neq$ null){
21:         let s_d be the state in S from which t_d is executed;
22:         let E be $\{q \in s_d.enabled \mid$ either $tid(q) = tid(t)$, or q was executed after t_d in T and a *happens-before* relation exists for $(q, t)\}$
23:         **if** ($E \neq \varnothing$)
24:             choose any q in E, add $tid(q)$ to $s_d.backtrack$;
25:         **else**
26:             $s_d.backtrack \leftarrow s_d.backtrack \cup \{tid(q) \mid q \in s_d.enabled\}$;
27:     }
28: }

Fig. 2. Stateless search with dynamic partial order reduction (c.f. [5])

set $s_d.backtrack$ is also a subset of the enabled transitions, and the set E consists of transitions q in T such that (q, t) has a *happens-before* relation (line 22). Intuitively, q happens-before t means that flipping the execution order of q and t may lead to interleavings in a different equivalence class. For a better understanding, a plain depth-first search, with no partial order reduction at all, would correspond to an alternative implementation of line 19 in which t_d is defined as the last transition in T such that $tid(t_d) \neq tid(t)$, regardless of whether t_d and t are dependent, and an alternative implementation of line 22 in which $E = \emptyset$.

Data race detection is essentially checking the simultaneous reachability of two conflicting transitions. The procedure DETECTRACE(s) used in line 3 of Fig. 2 checks in each state s whether there exist two transitions t_1, t_2 such that (1) they access the same shared variable; (2) at least one of them is a write; and (3) both transitions are enabled in s. If all three conditions hold, it reports a data race; in this case, the sequence of states $s_0, s_1, \ldots, s$ currently in the stack S serve as a counterexample. The advantage of this race detection procedure is that it does not report bogus races (of course, the race itself may be benign; detecting whether races are malicious is outside the scope of our approach, as well as most other approaches in this area). If the top-level DPORSEARCH(S, s_0) completes without finding any race, then the program is proved to be race-free under the given input. As pointed out in [5], DPOR is sound and complete for detecting data races (as well as deadlocks and assertion violations), although there is no property driven pruning employed in [5].

3 Race-Free Search Subspace

Given an execution sequence $s_0, \ldots, s_i, \ldots, s_n$ stored in the stack S and a state s_i ($0 \leq i \leq n$), we check (conservatively) whether the search space starting from s_i is race-free. This search subspace consists of all the execution traces sharing the same prefix $s_0, \ldots, s_i$. During dynamic model checking, instead of backtracking for each conflicting transition pair as in DPOR, we backtrack to state s_i only if the corresponding search subspace has potential races.

3.1 Set of Locksets

Let $T = \{t_1, \ldots, t_n\}$ be a transition sequence such that $s_0 \xrightarrow{t_1} s_1 \ldots \xrightarrow{t_n} s_n$. First, we project T to each thread as a sequence $T_\tau = \{t_{\tau_1}, \ldots, t_{\tau_k}\}$ of thread-local transitions; that is, $\forall t \in T_\tau : tid(t) = \tau$. For the example in Fig. 1, T is projected to $T_1 = \{a_1, \ldots, a_{11}\}$ and $T_2 = \{b_1, \ldots, b_9, b_{11}\}$. Next, we partition each thread-local sequence T_τ into smaller segments. In the extreme case, each segment would consist of a single transition. For each segment $seg_i \subseteq T_\tau$, we identify the global variables that may be accessed within seg_i; for each access, we also identify the corresponding *lockset*—the set of locks held by thread τ when the access happens.

Definition 1. *For each segment seg_i and global variable x, the set $lsSet_x(seg_i)$ consists of all the possible locksets that may be held when x is accessed in seg_i.*

By conservatively assuming that transitions of different threads can be interleaved arbitrarily, we check whether it is possible to encounter a race condition. Specifically, for each global variable x, and for each pair (seg_i, seg_j) of transition segments from different threads, we check whether $\exists set_1 \in lsSet_x(seg_i), set_2 \in lsSet_x(seg_j)$ such that $set_1 \cap set_2 = \emptyset$. An empty set represents a potential race condition—x is not protected by a common lock. The result of this analysis can be refined by further partitioning seg_i, seg_j into smaller fragments. To check whether the search space starting from s_i is race-free, we will conservatively assume that $t_{i+1}, \ldots, t_n$ (transitions executed after s_i in T) may interleave arbitrarily, subject only to the program orders.

Note first, that the lockset analysis is thread-local, i.e., the analysis is performed on a single thread at a time. Second, a precise computation of $lsSet_x(seg_i)$ as in Definition 1 requires the inspection of all feasible execution traces (exponentially many) in which x is accessed in seg_i; we do not perform this precise computation. For conservatively checking the race-free subspace property, it suffices to consider a set of locksets S such that any constituent lockset of S is a subset of the actually held locks. For instance, the coarsest approximation is $lsSet_x(seg_i) = \{\emptyset\}$; that is, x is not protected at all.

Under this coarsest approximation for seg_i, if another thread also accesses x in seg_j, our algorithm will report a potential race condition between seg_i and seg_j.

Consider again the example in Fig. 1, let the first execution trace be partitioned into

$$seg_1 = a_1, \ldots, a_8 \qquad seg_3 = b_1, \ldots, b_7$$
$$seg_2 = a_9, \ldots, a_{11} \qquad seg_4 = b_8, \ldots, b_{11}.$$

Since seg_2 shares only z with seg_3, and z is protected by lock $f1$, any execution trace starting from seg_1 is race-free. Therefore, we do not need to backtrack to a_8.

However, the concrete execution itself may not be able to provide enough information to carry out the above analysis. Note that, by definition, $lsSet_x(seg_i)$ must include *all the possible locksets* that may be formed in an interleaving execution of seg_i. In Fig. 1, for instance, although y is accessed in both threads (a_6 and b_{10}), the transition b_{10} does not appear in seg_4 since the else-branch was taken. However, $lsSet_y(seg_4)$ is $\{\{f1\}\}$. In general, we need a *may-set* of shared variables that are accessed in seg_i and the corresponding *must-set* of locks protecting each access. We need the information of all the alternative branches in order to compute these sets at runtime.

3.2 Handling the Other Branch

Our solution is to augment all branching statements in the form of if(c)-else, through source code instrumentation, so that the information of not-yet-executed branches (computed a priori) is readily available to our analysis during runtime. To this end, for both branches of every if-else statement, we instrument the program by inserting calls to the following routines ('rec' stands for record):

- rec-var-access-in-other-branch(x, L_{acq}, L_{rel}) for each access to x; with the set L_{acq} of locks acquired and the set of L_{rel} of locks released before the access.
- rec-lock-update-in-other-branch(L_{acq}, L_{rel}); with the set L_{acq} of locks acquired and the set L_{rel} of locks released in the other branch.

The instrumentation is illustrated by a simple example in Fig. 3. In addition to the above routines, we also add recording routines to notify the scheduler about the branch start and end. When the if-branch is executed, the scheduler knows that, in the else-branch, x is accessed and lock C is acquired before the access (line 4); it also knows that C is the only lock acquired and no lock is released throughout that branch (line 5). Similarly, when the else-branch is executed, the scheduler knows that in the if-branch, x, y are accessed and lock A is protecting x but not y. According to lines 5 and 16, lock C will be held at the branch merge point because $(L_{acq} \setminus L_{rel}) = \{C\}$. Therefore, our algorithm knows that z is protected by both B and C.

The information passed to these recording routines need to be collected a priori by a static analysis of the individual threads (in Section 5). Note that neither the set of shared variables nor any of the corresponding locksets L_{acq}, L_{rel} has to be precise. For a conservative analysis, it suffices to use an over-approximated set of shared variables, a subset $\check{L}_{acq} \subseteq L_{acq}$ of acquired locks, and superset $\hat{L}_{rel} \supseteq L_{rel}$ of released locks. By using $\check{L}_{acq}$ and $\hat{L}_{rel}$, we can compute a must-set $(\check{L}_{acq} \setminus \hat{L}_{rel})$, which is a subset of the actually held locks.

```
 1:    lock(B)
 2:    if (c) {
 3:       rec-branch-begin();                            //added
 4:       rec-var-access-in-other-branch(x,{C},{});      //added
 5:       rec-lock-update-in-other-branch({C},{});       //added
 6:       lock(A);
 7:       x++;
 8:       unlock(A);
 9:       y=5;
10:       lock(C);
11:       rec-branch-end();                              //added
12:    }else {
13:       rec-branch-begin();                            //added
14:       rec-var-access-in-other-branch(x,{A},{ });     //added
15:       rec-var-access-in-other-branch(y,{A},{A});     //added
16:       rec-lock-update-in-other-branch({A,C},{A}); //added
17:       lock(C);
18:       x++;
19:       rec-branch-end();                              //added
20:    }
21:    z++;
22:    unlock(C);
23:    unlock(B)
```

Fig. 3. Instrumenting the branching statements of each thread

3.3   Checking Race-Free Subspace

The algorithm for checking whether a search subspace is race-free is given in Fig. 4. For each transition $t \in T$ and global variable x, we maintain:

- $lsSet(t)$, the *set of locksets* held on one of the paths by t;
- $mayUse(t, x)$ if t is a branch begin, the set of locksets of x in the other branch.

In state s_i, the set ls_τ of locks held by thread τ is known. First, we use COMPUTELOCK-SETS to update $lsSet(t)$ and $mayUse(t, x)$ for all variables x accessed and transitions t executed after s_i. Potential race conditions are checked by intersecting pairwise locksets of the same variable in different threads. If any of the intersection in line 11 is empty, SUBSPACERACEFREE returns FALSE.

In Fig. 5, COMPUTELOCKSETS starts with ls_τ, which comes from the concrete execution and hence is precise. T_τ consists of the following types of transitions: (1) instrumented recording routines; (2) lock/unlock; (3) other program statements. The stack *update* is used for temporary storage. Both $lsSet(t)$ and $mayUse(t, x)$ are *sets of locksets*, of which each constituent lockset corresponds to a distinct unobserved path (a path skipped due to a false branch condition) or variable access. Note that we do not merge locksets from different branches into a single must-lockset, but maintain them as separate entities in $lsSet(t)$ and then propagate to the subsequent transitions in T_τ.

Multiple branches may be embedded in the observed sequence T_τ, as shown in Fig. 6. In the left-hand-side figure, the unobserved branch itself has two branches, each of which needs a recording routine in T_τ to record the lock updates. Inside COMPUTE-LOCKSETS, lock updates from t_{l_2} are stored temporarily in the stack *update* and finally used to compute $lsSet(t_i)$ at the merge point. In the right-hand-side figure, the observed branch (from t'_j to t'_i) contains another observed branch (from t_j to t_i). This is why a stack *update*, rather than a set, is needed. Note that t'_{l_2} is executed before t_{l_2}, but $lsSet(t'_i)$ is computed after $lsSet(t_i)$.

1: SUBSPACERACEFREE(s_i) {
2:     let $T = \{t_1, t_2, \ldots, t_m\}$ such that $s_i \xrightarrow{t_1} s_{i+1} \ldots \xrightarrow{t_m} s_{m+1}$ and $s_{m+1}.enabled = \emptyset$;
3:     **for each** ($\tau \in Tid$) {
4:         let $T_\tau = \{t_{\tau_1}, \ldots, t_{\tau_k}\}$ be a subsequence $T_\tau \subseteq T$ such that $\forall t \in T_\tau : tid(t) = \tau$;
5:         let ls_τ be the set of locks held by thread τ at s_i;
6:         COMPUTELOCKSETS(ls_τ, T_τ);
7:     }
8:     **for each** (global variable x) {
9:         let $t_1, t_2 \in T$, $tid(t_1) \neq tid(t_2)$, both may access x, and at least one is a write;
10:         let $ls_1 \in (lsSet(t_1) \cup mayUse(t_1, x))$, let $ls_2 \in (lsSet(t_2) \cup mayUse(t_2, x))$;
11:         **if** ($\exists ls_1, ls_2$ such that $ls_1 \cap ls_2 = \emptyset$) **return** FALSE;
12:     }
13:     **return** TRUE;
14: }

Fig. 4. Checking whether the search subspace from s_i is race-free at run time

1: COMPUTELOCKSETS(ls_τ, T_τ) {
2:     let $lsSet(t_0) = \{ ls_\tau \}$;
3:     let $T_\tau = \{t_1, \ldots, t_k\}$; $\forall t_i \in T_\tau, \forall x : lsSet(t_i) \leftarrow \emptyset$ and $mayUse(t_i, x) \leftarrow \emptyset$;
4:     $i \leftarrow 1$;
5:     **while** ($i \leq k$) {
6:         **if** (t_i is rec-branch-begin)
7:             $update.push(\emptyset)$;
8:         **if** (t_i is lock(f1))
9:             $lsSet(t_i) \leftarrow \{ls \cup \{f1\} \mid ls \in lsSet(t_{i-1})$;
10:         **else if** (t_i is unlock(f1))
11:             $lsSet(t_i) \leftarrow \{ls \setminus \{f1\} \mid ls \in lsSet(t_{i-1})$;
12:         **else if** (t_i is rec-var-access-in-other-branch(x, L_{acq}, L_{rel}))
13:             let t_j be the last branch begin that precedes t_i;
14:             $mayUse(t_j, x) \leftarrow mayUse(t_j, x) \cup \{ls \cup L_{acq} \setminus L_{rel} \mid ls \in lsSet(t_j)\}$;
15:         **else if** (t_i is rec-lock-update-in-other-branch(L_{acq}, L_{rel}))
16:             let t_j be the last branch begin that precedes t_i;
17:             $update.top() \leftarrow update.top() \cup \{ls \cup L_{acq} \setminus L_{rel} \mid ls \in lsSet(t_j)\}$;
18:         **else if** (t_i is rec-branch-end)
19:             $lsSet(t_i) \leftarrow update.pop() \cup lsSet(t_{i-1})$;
20:         **else**
21:             $lsSet(t_i) \leftarrow lsSet(t_{i-1})$;
22:         $i \leftarrow i + 1$;
23:     }
24: }

Fig. 5. Computing locksets that may be held by each transition in T_τ

Let $s_j \xrightarrow{t_{j+1}} s_{j+1}$ be a branch begin and $s_{i-1} \xrightarrow{t_i} s_i$ be the matching branch end. From the pseudo code in Fig. 5, it is clear that the following two theorems hold.

Theorem 1. $lsSet(t_i)$ *contains, for each unobserved path from s_j and to s_i, a must-set of locks held at s_i (if that path were to be executed).*

Theorem 2. $mayUse(t_i, x)$ *contains, for each access of* x *in an unobserved path from* s_j *to* s_i, *a must-set of locks held when accessing* x *in that path.*

Although the standard notion of locksets is used in our analysis, the combination of dynamically computed information of the observed execution and statically computed information of not-yet-executed branches differentiates us from the existing dynamic [20, 16] and static [6, 4, 17, 11, 22] lockset algorithms. It differs from the Eraser-style lockset algorithms [20, 16] in that it has to consider not only the current execution but also the not-yet-activated branches. It differs from the purely static lockset analysis [6, 4, 17, 11, 22] in that it utilizes not only the statically computed program information, but also the more precise information derived dynamically from the execution. In particular, our lockset computation starts with a precise lockset ls_τ of the concrete execution (line 5 of Fig. 4). In the presence of pointers to data and locks, a purely static analysis may be imprecise; the actual set of shared variables accessed or locks held during a concrete execution may be significantly smaller than the (conservatively computed) points-to sets of the pointers.

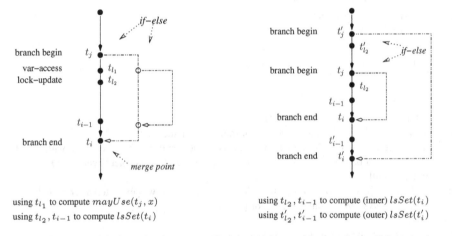

using t_{l_1} to compute $mayUse(t_j, x)$
using t_{l_2}, t_{i-1} to compute $lsSet(t_i)$

using t_{l_2}, t_{i-1} to compute (inner) $lsSet(t_i)$
using t'_{l_2}, t'_{i-1} to compute (outer) $lsSet(t'_i)$

Fig. 6. Multiple branches in an execution trace (observed and unobserved branches)

4   The Overall Algorithm

We rely on the conservative lockset analysis to prune the search space, and the concrete program execution to ensure that no bogus race is reported. The overall algorithm is given in Fig. 7. The procedure PDPSEARCH, where PDP stands for Property-Driven Pruning, takes the stack S and a state s as input. Each time PDPSEARCH is called on a new state s, lines 10-24 will be executed. DETECTRACE(s) is used to detect race conditions in s during runtime (explained in Section 2). If a race condition is found, it terminates with a counterexample in S. When an execution terminates ($s.enabled = \varnothing$ of line 3), we update the backtracking points for the entire trace. This is significantly different from the DPOR algorithm, which updates the backtracking points for each state

1: Initially: S is empty; PDPSEARCH(S, s_0)

2: PDPSEARCH(S, s) {
3:     **if** ($s.enabled = \varnothing$) {
4:         **for** ($i = 0; i < S.size(); i++$) {
5:             let s_b be the i-th element in S;
6:             **for each** ($t \in s_b.enabled$)
7:                 PDPUPDATEBACKTRACKSETS(S, t);
8:         }
9:     }
10:    **else** {
11:        **if** (DETECTRACE(s)) **exit** (S);
12:        S.push(s);
13:        let $\tau \in Tid$ such that $\exists t \in s.enabled : tid(t) = \tau$;
14:        $s.backtrack \leftarrow \{\tau\}$;
15:        $s.done \leftarrow \varnothing$;
16:        **while** ($\exists t: tid(t) \in s.backtrack$ and $t \notin s.done$) {
17:            $s.done \leftarrow s.done \cup \{t\}$;
18:            $s.backtrack \leftarrow s.backtrack \setminus \{tid(t)\}$;
19:            let $s' \in S$ such that $s \xrightarrow{t} s'$;
20:            PDPSEARCH(S, s');
21:            S.pop(s);
22:        }
23:    }
24: }

25: PDPUPDATEBACKTRACKSETS(S, t) {
26:     let $T = \{t_1, \ldots, t_n\}$ be the sequence of transitions associated with S;
27:     let t_d be the latest transition in T that (1) is dependent and may be co-enabled with t, and (2) let $s_d \in S$ be the state from which t_d is executed, **SubspaceRaceFree**(s_d) is FALSE;
28:     **if** ($t_d \neq$ null){
29:         let E be $\{q \in s_d.enabled \mid$ either $tid(q) = tid(t)$, or q was executed after t_d in T and a *happens-before* relation exists for $(q, t)\}$
30:         **if** ($E \neq \varnothing$)
31:             choose any q in E, add $tid(q)$ to $s_d.backtrack$;
32:         **else**
33:             $s_d.backtrack \leftarrow s_d.backtrack \cup \{tid(q) \mid q \in s_d.enabled\}$;
34:     }
35: }

Fig. 7. Property driven pruning based dynamic race detection algorithm

s when it is pushed into the stack S. Rather than updating the backtracking points in the pre-order of DFS as in DPOR, our algorithm waits until the information pertaining to an entire execution trace is available. In line 27, for each state t_d that is dependent and may be co-enabled with t, we check (in addition to that of DPOR) whether the search subspace from s_d is race-free. If the answer is yes, we can safely skip the backtracking points at s_d. Otherwise, we proceed in the same fashion as DPOR.

The Running Example. We show how the overall algorithm works on the example in Fig. 1. Assume that the first execution trace is

$$s_0 \xrightarrow{a_1} s_1 \xrightarrow{a_2} \ldots \xrightarrow{a_6} s_6 \ldots s_9 \xrightarrow{a_{10}} s_{10} \ldots s_{13} \xrightarrow{b_3} s_{14} \xrightarrow{b_4} s_{15} \ldots \xrightarrow{b_9} s_{20} \xrightarrow{b_{11}} s_{21} \ ,$$

produced by lines 11-20 of Fig. 7. Since $s_{21}.enabled = \emptyset$, the call PDPSEARCH$(S, s_{21})$ executes lines 3-9. For every $s_b \in S$, we update the backtrack sets; we go through the stack in the following order: $s_0, s_1, \ldots, s_{21}$.

- For $s_0, \ldots, s_{10}$, there is no need to add a backtracking point, because (per line 27) there is no t_d from a thread different from $tid(t)$.
- For s_{13}, the enabled transition b_3:z++ is dependent and may be co-enabled with $t_d = a_{10}$:z++. (We assume *lock-atomicity* by grouping variable accesses with protecting lock/unlock and regarding each block as atomic.) However, since the search subspace from s_8 is race-free, we do not add backtracking points at s_8.
- For s_{14}, the enabled transition b_4:c=x is dependent and may be co-enabled with $t_d = a_2$:x++. Since the search subspace from s_0 has a potential race condition between a_6 and b_{10}, we set $s_0.backtrack = \{2\}$ to make sure that in a future execution, thread T_2 is scheduled at state s_0.

After this, PDPSEARCH(S, s_i) keeps returning for all $i > 0$ as indicated by lines 20-21. Since $s_0.backtrack = \{2\}$, PDPSEARCH(S, s_0) executes lines 16-20. The next execution starts from $s_0 \xrightarrow{b_1} s'$.

Proof of Correctness. The correctness of the overall algorithm is summarized as follows: First, any race condition reported by PDPSEARCH is guaranteed to be real.

Second, if PDPSEARCH returns without finding any race condition, the program is guaranteed to be race-free under the given input. Finally, PDPSEARCH always returns a conclusive result (either race-free or a concrete race) for terminating programs. If a program is nonterminating, PDPSEARCH can be used for bounded analysis as in CHESS [14]—to detect bugs up to a bounded number of steps. The soundness is ensured by the fact that it is concretely executing the actual program within its target environment. The completeness (for terminating programs) can be established by the following arguments: (1) the baseline DPOR algorithm as in [5] is known to be sound and complete for detecting race conditions; and (2) our trace-based lockset analysis is conservative in checking race-free subspaces. The procedure returns 'yes' only if no race condition can be reached by any execution in the search subspace.

5 Experiments

We have implemented the proposed method on top of our implementation of the DPOR algorithm, inside Inspect [23]. We use CIL [15] for parsing, whole-program static analysis, and source code instrumentation. Our tool is capable of handling multithreaded C programs written using the Linux POSIX thread library. The source code instrumentation consists of the following steps: (1) for each shared variable access, insert a request to the scheduler asking for permission to execute; (2) for each thread library routine, add a wrapper function which sends a request to the scheduler before executing the actual library routine; (3) for each branch, add recording routines to notify about the branch begin and end, the shared variables and the lock updates in the other branch.

In order to control every visible operation, we need to identify the set of shared variables during the source code instrumentation. Shared variable identification requires a conservative static analysis of the concurrent program, e.g., pointer and may-escape analysis [19, 11]. Since this analysis [19] is an over-approximated analysis, our instrumentation is safe for intercepting all visible operations of the program. This ensures that we do not miss any bug due to missing identification of a shared variable. Similarly, when a whole program static analysis is either ineffective or not possible (due to missing source code) to identify the precise locksets, during instrumentation, we resort to subsets of acquired locks and supersets of released locks.

We have conducted experimental comparison of our new method with the baseline DPOR algorithm. The benchmarks are Linux applications written in C using the POSIX thread library; many are obtained from public domain including sourceforge.net and freshmeat.net. Among the benchmarks, fdrd2 and fdrd4 are variants of our running example. qsort is a multithreaded quick sort algorithm. pfscan is a file scanner implemented using multiple threads to search directories and files in parallel; the different threads share a dynamic queue protected by a set of mutex locks. aget implements a ftp client with the capability of concurrently downloading different segments of a large file. bzip2smp is a multithreaded version of the Linux application bzip. All benchmarks are accompanied by test cases to facilitate the concrete execution. Our experiments were conducted on a workstation with 2.8 GHz Pentium D processor and 2GB memory running Fedora 5.

Table 1 shows the experimental results. The first seven columns show the statistics of the test cases, including the name, the lines of C code, the number of threads, the number of shared variables, the number of shared variable accesses, the number of locks, and the number of data races. Columns 8-13 compare the two methods in terms

Table 1. Comparing the performance of two race detection algorithms (with 1 hour time out)

Test Program						Runtime (s)		# of Trans (k)		# of Traces		Race-free Chk		
name	loc	thrd	gvar	accs	lock	race	dpor	PDP	dpor	PDP	dpor	PDP	chks	yes	skip
fdrd2	66	2	3	3	2	1	3	1	2	0.6	89	14	88	75	75
fdrd4	66	2	3	3	2	1	11	3	10	4	233	68	232	165	165
qsort	743	2		2	2000	5	0	17	8	12	8	4	1	2	2	2
pfscan-good	918	2	21	118	4	0	179	15	71	10	2519	182	398	217	217
pfscan-bug	918	2	21	39	4	1	3	1	1	1	31	10	5	5	6
aget-0.4	1098	3	5	72	1	0	183	1	103	0.1	3432	1	6	6	9
aget-0.4	1098	4	5	78	1	0	>1h	1	-	0.1	-	1	9	9	18
aget-0.4	1098	5	5	84	1	0	>1h	1	-	0.1	-	1	12	12	30
bzip2smp	6358	4	9	18	3	0	128	3	63	2	1465	45	48	5	5
bzip2smp	6358	5	9	18	3	0	203	4	99	2	2316	45	48	5	7
bzip2smp	6358	6	9	18	3	0	287	4	135	2	3167	45	48	5	9
bzip2smp2	6358	4	9	269	3	0	291	136	63	21	1573	45	48	5	5
bzip2smp2	6358	5	9	269	3	0	487	155	85	21	2532	45	48	5	7
bzip2smp2	6358	6	9	269	3	0	672	164	116	21	3491	45	48	5	9
bzip2smp2	6358	10	9	269	3	0	1435	183	223	21	7327	45	48	5	17

of the runtime, and the number of executed transitions, and the number of completed execution traces. For DPOR, every completed trace (reported in Column 12) belongs to a distinct equivalence class of interleavings; however, many of them are pruned away by PDP since they are redundant as far as race detection is concerned. Columns 14-16 provide the following statistics of PDP: the number of race-free checks, the number of race-free check successes, and the number of skipped backtrack points.

The results show that our PDP method is significantly more efficient than DPOR in pruning the search space. For all examples, PDP took significantly less time in either finding the same data race or proving the race freedom; the number of transitions/traces that PDP has to check during the process was also significantly smaller. Although the average time for PDP to complete one execution is longer than DPOR, e.g., 4066 ms vs. 195 ms as indicated by data from the last row of Table 1 (due to the overhead of tracking branch begin/end and other auxiliary transitions), the overhead in PDP is well compensated by the skipped executions due to property driven pruning.

6   Conclusions

We have proposed a new data race detection algorithm that combines the power of dynamic model checking with property driven pruning based on a lockset analysis. Our method systematically explores concrete thread interleavings of a program, and at the same time prunes the search space with a trace-based conservative analysis. It is both sound and complete (as precise as the DPOR algorithm); at the same time, it is significantly more efficient in practice, allowing the technique to scale much better to real-world applications. For future work, we would like to extend the proposed framework to check other types of properties. Since race detection is a problem of simultaneous reachability of two transitions, the techniques developed here should be readily applicable to checking deadlocks and many other simple safety properties.

References

[1] Bouajjani, A., Esparza, J., Maler, O.: Reachability analysis of pushdown automata: Application to model-checking. In: International Conference on Concurrency Theory. LNCS, vol. 1243, pp. 135–150. Springer, Heidelberg (1997)

[2] Chen, F., Rosu, G.: Parametric and sliced causality. In: Damm, W., Hermanns, H. (eds.) CAV 2007. LNCS, vol. 4590, pp. 240–253. Springer, Heidelberg (2007)

[3] Clarke, E.M., Emerson, E.A.: Design and synthesis of synchronization skeletons using branching time temporal logic. In: Proceedings Workshop on Logics of Programs. LNCS, vol. 131, pp. 52–71. Springer, Heidelberg (1981)

[4] Engler, D., Ashcraft, K.: RacerX: effective, static detection of race conditions and deadlocks. In: ACM Symposium on Operating Systems Principles, pp. 237–252. ACM, New York (2003)

[5] Flanagan, C., Godefroid, P.: Dynamic partial-order reduction for model checking software. In: Principles of programming languages, pp. 110–121 (2005)

[6] Flanagan, C., Leino, K., Lillibridge, M., Nelson, G., Saxe, J., Stata, R.: Extended static checking for java. In: PLDI, pp. 234–245 (2002)

[7] Ganai, M., Kundu, S., Gupta, R.: Partial order reduction for scalable testing of SystemC TLM designs. In: Design Automation Conference (2008)

[8] Godefroid, P.: Partial-Order Methods for the Verification of Concurrent Systems - An Approach to the State-Explosion Problem. LNCS, vol. 1032. Springer, Heidelberg (1996)

[9] Godefroid, P.: Software model checking: The VeriSoft approach. Formal Methods in System Design 26(2), 77–101 (2005)

[10] Holzmann, G., Najm, E., Serhrouchni, A.: SPIN model checking: An introduction. STTT 2(4), 321–327 (2000)

[11] Kahlon, V., Yang, Y., Sankaranarayanan, S., Gupta, A.: Fast and accurate static data-race detection for concurrent programs. In: Damm, W., Hermanns, H. (eds.) CAV 2007. LNCS, vol. 4590, pp. 226–239. Springer, Heidelberg (2007)

[12] Leveson, N., Turner, C.: Investigation of the therac-25 accidents. IEEE Computer 26(7), 18–41 (1993)

[13] Mazurkiewicz, A.W.: Trace theory. In: Brauer, W., Reisig, W., Rozenberg, G. (eds.) APN 1986. LNCS, vol. 255, pp. 279–324. Springer, Heidelberg (1987)

[14] Musuvathi, M., Qadeer, S.: CHESS: Systematic stress testing of concurrent software. In: Puebla, G. (ed.) LOPSTR 2006. LNCS, vol. 4407, pp. 15–16. Springer, Heidelberg (2007)

[15] Necula, G., McPeak, S., Rahul, S., Weimer, W.: Cil: Intermediate language and tools for analysis and transformation of c programs. In: Horspool, R.N. (ed.) CC 2002. LNCS, vol. 2304, pp. 213–228. Springer, Heidelberg (2002)

[16] Nethercote, N., Seward, J.: Valgrind: A program supervision framework. Electr. Notes Theor. Comput. Sci. 89(2) (2003)

[17] Pratikakis, P., Foster, J., Hicks, M.: LOCKSMITH: context-sensitive correlation analysis for race detection. In: PLDI, pp. 320–331. ACM, New York (2006)

[18] Quielle, J.P., Sifakis, J.: Specification and verification of concurrent systems in CESAR. In: Proceedings of the Fifth Annual Symposium on Programming (1981)

[19] Salcianu, A., Rinard, M.: Pointer and escape analysis for multithreaded programs. In: Principles and Practices of Parallel Programming, pp. 12–23. ACM Press, New York (2001)

[20] Savage, S., Burrows, M., Nelson, G., Sobalvarro, P., Anderson, T.: Eraser: A dynamic data race detector for multithreaded programs. ACM Trans. Comput. Syst. 15(4), 391–411 (1997)

[21] Sen, K., Rosu, G., Agha, G.: Detecting errors in multithreaded programs by generalized predictive analysis of executions. In: Steffen, M., Zavattaro, G. (eds.) FMOODS 2005. LNCS, vol. 3535, pp. 211–226. Springer, Heidelberg (2005)

[22] Voung, J., Jhala, R., Lerner, S.: RELAY: static race detection on millions of lines of code. In: Foundations of Software Engineering, pp. 205–214. ACM, New York (2007)

[23] Yang, Y., Chen, X., Gopalakrishnan, G.: Inspect: A Runtime Model Checker for Multithreaded C Programs. Technical Report UUCS-08-004, University of Utah (2008)

[24] Yang, Y., Chen, X., Gopalakrishnan, G., Kirby, R.: Efficient stateful dynamic partial order reduction. In: SPIN Workshop on Model Checking Software (2008)

Automating Algebraic Specifications of Non-freely Generated Data Types

Andriy Dunets, Gerhard Schellhorn, and Wolfgang Reif

Lehrstuhl für Softwaretechnik und Programmiersprachen
Institut für Informatik, Universität Augsburg
86135 Augsburg, Germany
{dunets,schellhorn,reif}@informatik.uni-augsburg.de

Abstract. Non-freely generated data types are widely used in case studies carried out in the theorem prover KIV. The most common examples are stores, sets and arrays. We present an automatic method that generates finite counterexamples for wrong conjectures and therewith offers a valuable support for proof engineers saving their time otherwise spent on unsuccessful proof attempts. The approach is based on the finite model finding and uses Alloy Analyzer [1] to generate finite instances of theories in KIV [6]. Most definitions of functions or predicates on infinite structures do not preserve the semantics if a transition to arbitrary finite substructures is made. We propose the constraints which should be satisfied by the finite substructures, identify a class of amenable definitions and present a practical realization using Alloy. The technique is evaluated on the library of basic data types as well as on some examples from case studies in KIV.

Keywords: Algebraic specifications, abstract data types, finite models, first-order logic, theorem proving, SAT checking.

1 Introduction

The concept of abstract data types is well-established in computer science. Algebraic techniques are integrated in varieties of formal approaches in software development [10,11,20]. This work is aimed at providing automatic techniques for analysis of algebraic specifications of abstract data types. We present an integration of an automatic procedure for finding finite counterexamples or witnesses for first-order theories in the theorem prover KIV [6]. As first-order logic is undecidable we can construct either a decision procedure for decidable fragments or use an automated prover for full logic. Both approaches are useful for provable goals. Most of the time in interactive theorem proving is spent to find out why certain goals are not provable. An alternative approach however is to try to disprove conjectures and to generate counterexamples. We were inspired by the automatic analysis method for first-order *relational* logic with *transitive closure* implemented in the Alloy [1] and its successful application in the Mondex challenge by Ramananandro [24]. Alloy's algorithm handles full first-order relational logic with quantifiers and transitive closure [14].

Cha et al. (Eds.): ATVA 2008, LNCS 5311, pp. 141–155, 2008.

The reason why we are interested in the automation of the FOL part of KIV is that in almost all proof tasks carried out interactively in KIV, whether in the basic logic or in extensions for temporal logic proofs [4], ASM specifications [28], statecharts [5] or Java program proofs [30], eventually a lot of first-order proof obligations arise. These are typically discharged using *simplifier rules*. Most simplifier rules are first-order lemmas which are automatically used for rewriting and other simplifications. In large case studies the number of used rewrite rules is often several thousands, many of them imported from the KIV library of basic data types. Defining and proving such simplifier rules is therefore a regular task in interactive verification. Usually, some of these theorems are wrong at the first attempt, so a quick check that identifies unprovable ones is very helpful. Currently, to "test" an algebraic specification the proof engineer has either to perform an informal analysis or try to prove the desired property by starting an interactive proof. Most of the bugs in designs are discovered in the first step while some particularly hard to find ones - in the second. The technique presented in this work is intended to be a complementary quality improvement step which requires minimal additional user effort.

In this paper we extend the results in [15,9]. Kuncak and Jackson [15] presented a general approach of utilizing finite model finding for analysis of term algebras with language restricted to selectors only. [9] was the first step toward extending the language to arbitrary functions which however was restricted to very special class of definitions of recursive functions on freely generated data types only. We extend the application scope of the technique with non-freely generated data types. Furthermore, we define constraints which should be satisfied by the analyzed specification in order to guarantee a sound axiomatization of its operations on finite structures. The main contribution is a generic method for construction of finite instances for first-order specifications of abstract data types. We applied the method to a considerable set of examples to determine the relative size of the application domain. We showed empirically that all specifications of freely generated data types in KIV's library are amenable to the technique while the generation of instances and checking of theorems with Alloy is accomplished in a reasonable time (from several seconds to few minutes in worst case). In our experiments we used Alloy version 4.0 RC17 [1].

1.1   Outline

Section 2 introduces the background notions used throughout the work. In Section 3 using the specification of non-freely generated data type store (abstract memory model) as an example we present an approach for generation of finite models with Alloy. In Section 4 we determine the constraints necessary for a proper axiomatization of functions and predicates on finite structures. Section 5 presents results from the application to the library of basic data types in KIV. This is followed by an overview of the related work in Section 6 and conclusions in Section 7.

2   Preliminaries

2.1   Specifications of Algebraic Data Types

KIV is a tool for formal system development. It provides a strong proof support for all validation and verification tasks and is capable of handling large-scale theories by efficient proof techniques and an ergonomic user interface. The basic logic underlying the KIV system combines *Higher-Order Logic* (HOL) and *Dynamic Logic* (DL) [12], which allows to reason about partial and total correctness of imperative programs as well as expressing the program equivalence. KIV supports both functional and state-based approaches to specify systems. In this paper, we concern ourselves with the functional approach. A theory in KIV describes data types, e.g. naturals, lists, arrays or records, which afterward are used in DL programs. Theories are specified using hierarchically *structured algebraic specifications*.

Definition 1 (Language)
Let $\Sigma = (S, \mathcal{F}, \mathcal{P})$ be a signature with sorts $s \in S$ and sets $\mathcal{F}$, $\mathcal{P}$ of operations which combine the sets $\mathcal{F}_{\underline{s} \to s}$ of function symbols $f : \underline{s} \to s$ with the sets $\mathcal{P}_{\underline{s}}$ of predicate symbols $p : \underline{s}$, where $\underline{s} \in S^*$.

This definition is accompanied by some auxiliary commonly used constructs: X, X_s - sets of all variables and variables of the type s respectively, $T(\mathcal{F}_0, X_0)$ - set of terms constructed using functions from $\mathcal{F}_0$ and variables from X_0, $For(\Sigma)$ - set of formulas over Σ. Using a valuation α (assigns values to free variables) terms and formulas are evaluated over structures called *algebras*: $[\![t]\!]^{\mathcal{A},\alpha}$, $[\![\varphi]\!]^{\mathcal{A},\alpha}$.

Definition 2 (Algebra)
For Σ let $Alg(\Sigma)$ be a set of structures $\mathcal{A} = ((A_s)_{s \in S}, (f_\mathcal{A})_{f \in \mathcal{F}}, (p_\mathcal{A})_{p \in \mathcal{P}})$, where A_s denotes a nonempty domain of the sort s and $f_\mathcal{A}$, $p_\mathcal{A}$ are concrete interpretations of symbols $f \in \mathcal{F}$, $p \in \mathcal{P}$ over domains.

To specify data structures adequately, in addition to first-order axioms, axioms for induction are needed. Unfortunately, an induction scheme cannot be specified by a finite set of first-order formulas. As a replacement *generation clauses* are used. Hence, for a signature Σ the corresponding set $Gen(\Sigma)$ contains term generation clauses: "s **generated by** C_s". The set of constructors $C_s = \{c_1, \ldots, c_n\} \subseteq \mathcal{F}_{\underline{s} \to s}$ is assumed to contain at least one constructor $c_i : \underline{s} \to s$ with all its argument sorts different from s (a constant constructor). Generation clauses in $Gen(\Sigma)$ have the following semantics:

$$\mathcal{A} \models s \text{ \textbf{generated by} } C_s \Leftrightarrow$$
$$\text{for all } a \in A_s \text{ exists } \alpha, \ t \in T_s(C_s, X \backslash X_s) \ : \ a = [\![t]\!]^{\mathcal{A},\alpha}$$

The above equivalence ensures that any element in A_s is a value of some s-valued constructor term $t \in T_s(C_s, X \backslash X_s)$ using an appropriate assignment α to parameter variables $X \backslash X_s$, i.e. A_s is *term generated*.

Definition 3 (Specification)
For a signature Σ a specification $SP = (\Sigma, Ax, Gen)$ is a triple with finite sets $Ax \subseteq For(\Sigma)$ and $Gen \subseteq Gen(\Sigma)$.

Definition 4 (Model)
An algebra $\mathcal{A}$ is a model of a specification SP, $\mathcal{A} \in Mod(SP)$:

$$\mathcal{A} \models SP \quad \Leftrightarrow \quad \mathcal{A} \in Alg(\Sigma), \ \mathcal{A} \models Gen, \ \mathcal{A} \models Ax$$

A formula $\varphi \in For(\Sigma)$ is valid:

$$SP \models \varphi \quad \Leftrightarrow \quad \texttt{for all } \mathcal{A} \in Mod(SP) \ : \ \mathcal{A} \models \varphi$$

It is distinguished between free and non-free data types. Freely generated data types have the property that syntactically different terms denote different values, e.g. data type *list* which is generated by constructors *nil* and *cons* and has selectors *first* and *rest*. The corresponding models are called *term algebras* where terms have the above property.

While [9] discusses freely generated data types, in this work we are particularly interested in non-freely generated data types for which different terms can denote the same value, e.g. sets, stores, arrays (unlike for freely generated data types where syntactically different terms denote different values). For example, multiple insertions of the same element in a set have always the same result, $[\![\emptyset ++ a = \emptyset ++ a ++ a]\!]^{\mathcal{A}, \alpha}$. For a non-freely generated data type s in addition to the generation clause Gen_s the equivalence relation on s-valued terms has to be provided.

Definition 5 (Σ-congruence)
Let $\Sigma = (S, \mathcal{F}, \mathcal{P})$ and $\mathcal{A} \in Alg(\Sigma)$. Σ-congruence R is a family of equivalence relations $(R_s)_{s \in S}$ induced by S which are compatible with operations $\mathcal{F} \cup \mathcal{P}$:

1. *for all $f \in \mathcal{F}$, $f : s_1 \times \cdots \times s_n \to s$, $a_i, b_i \in \mathcal{A}_{s_i}$ holds*
   $\bigwedge_{i=1}^{n} R_{s_i}(a_i, b_i) \Rightarrow R_s(f_{\mathcal{A}}(a_1, \ldots, a_n), f_{\mathcal{A}}(b_1, \ldots, b_n))$
2. *for all $p \in \mathcal{P}$, $p : s_1 \times \cdots \times s_n$, $a_i, b_i \in \mathcal{A}_{s_i}$ holds*
   $\bigwedge_{i=1}^{n} R_{s_i}(a_i, b_i) \Rightarrow (p_{\mathcal{A}}(a_1, \ldots, a_n) \Leftrightarrow p_{\mathcal{A}}(b_1, \ldots, b_n))$

The corresponding models are *quotient algebras* $\mathcal{A}/R$.

Definition 6 (Quotient algebra)
For a Σ-congruence R on $\mathcal{A}$ is $\mathcal{A}/_R = ((Q_s)_{s \in S}, (f^\circ)_{f \in \mathcal{F}}, (p^\circ)_{p \in \mathcal{P}})$ a quotient algebra with:

1. $Q_s = \{[a] : a \in \mathcal{A}_s\}$ *where* $[a] = \{b : R_s(a, b)\}$
2. *For operations $f \in \mathcal{F}$, $p \in \mathcal{P}$ and $[a_i] \in Q_{s_i}$:*
   $f^\circ([a_1], \ldots, [a_n]) = [f_{\mathcal{A}}(a_1, \ldots, a_n)]$
   $p^\circ([a_1], \ldots, [a_n]) \Leftrightarrow [p_{\mathcal{A}}(a_1, \ldots, a_n)]$

Because R is a congruence, all operations are well defined and $\mathcal{A}/_R \in Alg(\Sigma)$. Furthermore, if $\mathcal{A}$ is a term generated algebra, then the corresponding quotient algebra $\mathcal{A}/R$ is term generated too [25]. The equivalence relation R_s (for non-free s) on terms is specified with the axiom of *extensionality*, e.g. for *sets* it states:

$$s_1 = s_2 \leftrightarrow (\forall a.\ a \in s_1 \leftrightarrow a \in s_2)$$

2.2 Multisorted Relational Logic in Alloy

The logic used by the Alloy Analyzer is a multisorted first-order relational logic with transitive closure [14]. It extends first-order logic by *relational terms* $r \in R_{\underline{s}}$ instead of just predicate symbols $p \in P_{\underline{s}}$. Thus atomic formulas have form $x_1 = x_2$ or $r(x_1, \ldots, x_n)$ where r is n-ary relational term. Relational terms are either predicate symbols or composition $r_1.r_2$ or transitive closure $^\wedge r$, where r is a binary relation. An Alloy specification SP_{Alloy} describes a finite multisorted universe $U = (D_{s_1}, \ldots, D_{s_n}, \gamma)$ with finite sets of atoms for each sort and an interpretation γ of relational symbols on domains. First-order formulas in SP_{Alloy} can be arbitrary quantified. For a specification SP_{Alloy} and a conjecture φ Alloy can be operated in two basic modes: searching for a *counterexample* $(SP_{Alloy} \wedge \neg\varphi)$ or computing a *witness* $(SP_{Alloy} \wedge \varphi)$.

We introduce a notion of a *relational specification*, where all functions are replaced by relations (predicates) that behave like corresponding functions. It is constructed from an algebraic specification $SP = (\Sigma, Ax, Gen)$ using the translation procedure τ from functional to relational form previously defined in [9] and the generation principle SUGA (selector, uniqueness, generator, acyclicity axioms for term algebras) described by Kuncak and Jackson [15].

Definition 7 (Alloy specification)
For an algebraic specification SP we define a transformation to Alloy language:

$$\tau_{\mathtt{fin}}(SP) = ((S, \tau(\mathcal{F}) \cup \mathcal{P}), \tau(Ax) \cup \mathtt{Unique}(\tau(\mathcal{F})) \cup \mathtt{SUA}(Gen))$$

where τ translates all formulas from the functional to the equivalent relational form and maps function symbols to predicates: $\tau(f) = \{F\ :\ f \in \mathcal{F}\}$ while axioms Unique require each predicate $\tau(f)$ to behave like a function:

$$\forall \underline{x}, y_1, y_2.\ F(\underline{x}, y_1) \wedge F(\underline{x}, y_2) \rightarrow y_1 = y_2$$

SUGA axioms are used to specify term generated algebras (models of free data types, e.g. lists). Dropping of the generator axiom results in SUA axioms which specify finite subterm-closed substructures of infinite term algebras (for any term all subterms are also in the finite structure). Such structures are generated for Alloy specifications $\tau_{\mathtt{fin}}(SP)$.

Definition 8 (Alloy model)
Finite algebra $\mathcal{M} = ((M_s)_{s \in S}, (p_\mathcal{M})_{p \in \mathcal{P} \cup \tau(\mathcal{F})})$ is a model of $\tau_{\mathtt{fin}}(SP)$:

$$\mathcal{M} \models \tau_{\mathtt{fin}}(SP) \Leftrightarrow \mathcal{M} \models \mathtt{SUA}(Gen),\ \mathcal{M} \models \tau(Ax),\ \mathcal{M} \models \mathtt{Unique}(\tau(\mathcal{F}))$$

In the next section we present an approach for specifying non-free data types in Alloy.

3 Example: Store

Non-freely generated data type *store* represents an abstract memory model with *addresses* and *data*. It is used in almost all bigger case studies in KIV where it specifies heaps, file systems, Java VM memory etc. In this section we present an algebraic specification of stores and the corresponding Alloy specification.

3.1 Algebraic Specification

The algebraic specification of stores is parameterized by not generated types *elem* (corresponds to addresses) and *data*, see Figure 1. Data type *store* is generated by constructors $\oslash$ (empty store) and $.\,[\,.\,,\,.\,]$ (put data in store at some address; allocate the address if necessary). The equivalence relation is specified in axiom of extensionality which uses operations $\in$ (test an address to be allocated) and $.\,[\,.\,]$ (get data at some address). The basis specification can be enriched with arbitrary operations, e.g. see enrichment with *delete* and *subset* operations. A specification of *naturals* (freely generated) is also included as it will be used later on. Altogether, we have $SP = (\Sigma, Ax, Gen)$ with

$$\Sigma = (\{store, elem, data\}, \{\oslash, .\,[\,.\,,\,.\,], .\,[\,.\,], \text{--}\}, \{\in, \subseteq\}) \cup \Sigma_{nat}$$

$$Gen = \{store \ \textbf{generated by} \ \oslash, .\,[\,.\,,\,.\,]\} \cup Gen_{nat}$$

$$Ax = \{ext, in\text{-}empty, in\text{-}put, at\text{-}same, at\text{-}other, subset, del\text{-}in, del\text{-}at\} \cup Ax_{nat}$$

3.2 Alloy Specification

For freely generated data types it would be enough to take the Alloy specification $\tau_{\tt fin}(SP)$, see Definition 7, to generate subterm-closed structures [9]. In the following, we show how to adopt translation procedure $\tau_{\tt fin}$ for non-freely generated data types.

The corresponding Alloy specification $\widehat{\tau}_{\tt fin}(SP)$ yielding finite subterm-closed structures $\mathcal{M}$ is constructed as follows:

$$\widehat{\tau}_{\tt fin}(SP) = (\widehat{\Sigma}, \widehat{Ax} \cup \text{Unique}(\tau(\mathcal{F}) \cup \{\widehat{PUT}, SIZE\}) \cup \text{SUA}(Gen) \cup \mathcal{C}^k_{store})$$

$$\widehat{\Sigma} = \widehat{\tau}_{\tt fin}(\Sigma) \cup \{\widehat{PUT}, BIGGER, SIZE\}$$

$$\widehat{Ax} = \{\Phi_{extension}, \Phi_{in}, \Phi_{at}\} \cup \{\Phi_{\widehat{PUT}}, \Phi_{SIZE}\} \cup \{\Phi_{subset}, \Phi_{del}\}[PUT/\widehat{PUT}]$$

$$\Phi_{\widehat{PUT}} \equiv \forall st, st_1 : store, \ a : elem, \ d : data. \ \widehat{PUT}(st, a, d, st_1) \leftrightarrow$$
$$IN(a, st_1) \wedge AT(st_1, a, d) \wedge$$
$$(\forall b : elem. \ \exists d_1, d_2 : data. \ a \neq b \to (IN(b, st_1) \leftrightarrow IN(b, st)) \wedge$$
$$(\exists d_1, d_2 : data. \ AT(st, b, d_1) \wedge AT(st_1, b, d_2) \to d_1 = d_2))$$

where the signature is extended with new symbols $\widehat{PUT}$, $SIZE$ and $BIGGER$. Further, all occurrences of the symbol $PUT \equiv \tau(.\,[\,.\,,\,.\,])$ in axioms Φ_{in}, Φ_{at} (relational definitions of $\in$ and $.\,[\,.\,]$) are replaced by the newly introduced symbol $\widehat{PUT}$. We have to specify $\widehat{PUT}$ to behave like the original *put* function in $\mathcal{A}$ ($.\,[\,.\,,\,.\,] : store \times elem \times data \to store$) using definition $\Phi_{\widehat{PUT}}$.

generic specification

      parameter elem, data

      target sorts store

      using nat

      constants

            $\varnothing$: store;   comment : empty

      functions

            . [. , .] : store $\times$ elem $\times$ data $\rightarrow$ store;   comment : put

            . [.] : store $\times$ elem $\rightarrow$ data;   comment : at

      predicates

            . $\in$. : elem $\times$ store;

      variables

            $st, st0, st1, st2$: store;

      induction

            store generated by $\varnothing$, . [. , .];

      axioms

            Ext : $st1 = st2 \leftrightarrow \forall a.\ (a \in st1 \leftrightarrow a \in st2) \wedge st1[a] = st2[a]$;

            In-empty : $\neg\, a \in \varnothing$;

            In-put : $a \in st[b, d] \leftrightarrow a = b \vee a \in st$;

            At-same : $(st[a, d][a]) = d$;

            At-other : $a \neq b \rightarrow (st[b, d][a]) = st[a]$;

end generic specification

enriched specification

      functions

            . -- . : store $\times$ elem $\rightarrow$ store;   comment : delete

      predicates

            . $\subseteq$. : store $\times$ store;

      axioms

            Subset : $st1 \subseteq st2 \leftrightarrow (\forall a.\ a \in st1 \rightarrow a \in st2 \wedge st1[a] = st2[a])$;

            Del-in : $a \in st\text{--}b \leftrightarrow a \neq b \wedge a \in st$;

            Del-at : $a \neq b \rightarrow (st\text{--}b)[a] = st[a]$;

end enriched specification

Fig. 1. Basis algebraic specification of the non-freely generated data type store + enrichment with two operations

The size function $\#_{store} : store \rightarrow nat$ measures the construction complexity of $store$-valued terms, e.g. $\#_{store}(\varnothing) = 0$, $\#_{store}(\varnothing[a, d]) = 1$, $a \neq b \rightarrow \#_{store}(\varnothing[a, d][b, d]) = 2$. The predicate $SIZE$ is the relational version of $\#_{store}$.

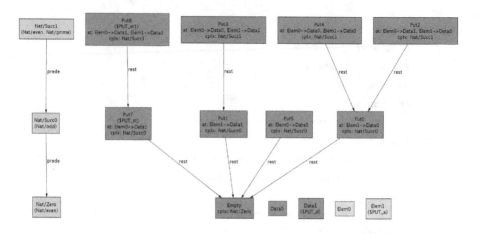

Fig. 2. Finite instance $\mathcal{M}$ for $\widehat{\tau}_{\mathtt{fin}}(SP)$ generated by Alloy

The predicate $BIGGER : store \times elem \times data$ tests whether the insertion of (a, d) into st leads to a bigger store (in terms of stored data):

$$\forall st : store, \ a : elem, \ d : data. \ BIGGER(st, a, d) \leftrightarrow a \notin st$$

Finally, we include a closedness constraint $\mathcal{C}^{k}_{store}$ which restricts only to those subterm-closed structures which contain *all* store-valued terms up to the size k. Closedness constraint $\mathcal{C}^{k}_{store}$ restricts to finite **SUA**-generated structures satisfying the following:

put-bigger : $\forall st, st_1 : store, \ a : elem, \ d : data.$

$$PUT(st, a, d, st_1) \rightarrow BIGGER(st, a, d)$$

generate : $\forall st : store, \ a : elem, \ d : data.$

$$\#_{store}(st) < k \land BIGGER(st, a, d) \rightarrow \exists st_1 : store. \ \widehat{PUT}(st, a, d, st_1)$$

bound : $\forall st : store. \ \#_{store}(st) \leq k$

The first axiom restricts the application of the constructor PUT (responsible for the generation of new *store*-atoms) only to cases where it leads to a bigger store. The axiom **generate** is responsible for filling up a model with atoms up to a certain bound k. Figure 2 is produced by Alloy and shows an instance $\mathcal{M} = (\mathcal{M}_{store}, \mathcal{M}_{elem}, \mathcal{M}_{data}, \mathcal{M}_{nat}, (p_{\mathcal{M}})_{p \in \mathcal{P}})$ which satisfies the $\mathcal{C}^{2}_{store}$ closedness constraint. The domains are composed as follows:

$$\mathcal{M}_{store} = \{\varnothing, \varnothing[a, d_1], \varnothing[a, d_2], \varnothing[b, d_1], \varnothing[b, d_2], \varnothing[a, d_1][b, d_1], \varnothing[a, d_1][b, d_2],$$
$$\varnothing[a, d_2][b, d_1], \varnothing[a, d_2][b, d_2]\}$$
$$\mathcal{M}_{elem} = \{a, b\}, \ \mathcal{M}_{data} = \{d_1, d_2\}, \ \mathcal{M}_{nat} = \{0, 1, 2\}$$

For a better clearness only essential relations allowing an identification of the values of atoms are shown. Operations at (data on the given position) and $cplx$ ($\#_{store}$) are shown as attributes of atoms.

4 Model Construction with Alloy

In this section we consider the approach from the previous section from a more general point of view and discuss the constraints which should be satisfied by the analyzed algebraic specifications to guarantee the soundness. As demonstrated in [9] for freely generated data types some definitions of functions do not preserve the semantics under the transition from an infinite structure to some finite substructure. In case of non-freely generated data types it becomes even more complicated since the generation of the carrier set depends on some definitions (axiom of *extensionality*). In this section we discuss constraints which should be satisfied by an algebraic specification SP in KIV in order the corresponding Alloy specification $\widehat{\tau}_{\mathtt{fin}}(SP)$ to yield finite structures $\mathcal{M}$ that are isomorphic to some finite substructures of the algebra $\mathcal{A}$ (model of SP). Roughly speaking, these constraints should guarantee that Alloy does not produce spurious counterexamples. We give a syntactical characterization of the constraints such that in the worst case they can be proven in the theorem prover KIV for a given specification (if not automatically discharged by some efficient heuristics). For this purpose, we enrich SP with auxiliary operations (in part even higher-order) which will be used for the reasoning about correctness, see Definition 9.

Definition 9 (Auxiliary operations)

1. $\#_s : s \to nat$ *used to measure the construction complexity of s-valued terms*
2. $\preceq: s_1 \times s_1 \ \cup \ s_1 \times s_2 \ \cup \cdots \cup \ s_k \times s_k$ *- a preorder on domains*
3. $\prec: s \times s$ *a predicate on terms in* $\mathcal{A}_s$ *(for a non-freely generated s)*
4. $\Upsilon : For(SP) \times Vars$ *identifies* $\preceq$*-compatible formulas*

The preorder $\preceq$ is used to introduce the $\preceq$-closedness of finite substructures of infinite structures which can be semantically characterized as follows (for finite structures $\mathcal{M}$ and infinite $\mathcal{A}$):

$$\forall \ d_0 \in dom(\mathcal{M}), \ d \in dom(\mathcal{A}). \quad d \preceq d_0 \to d \in dom(\mathcal{M})$$

For example, we can take the *subterm* relation for $\preceq$. The carrier set $\mathcal{A}_s/_R$ contains quotients $[t]$. We can characterize $[t]$ by their minimal representatives, i.e. terms $t_m \in [t]$ with minimal size ($\#_s$). Let $[\ ]_m : s \to s$ be a function calculating t_m. The predicate $\prec: s \times s$ is defined such that $t_1 \prec t_2 \leftrightarrow \#_{store}[t_1]_m < \#_{store}[t_2]_m$ (predicate $BIGGER$ in the example with stores). $\prec$ is used to restrict SUA axioms to generate only the terms $[t]_m$. Furthermore, we assume $\prec$ to agree with $\preceq : \prec \subseteq \preceq$.

The predicate Υ is used to define the compatibility of definitions on finite $\preceq$-closed substructures:

$$\Upsilon(\chi, \underline{x}) \equiv true, \quad for\ quantifier\text{-}free\ \chi$$

$$\Upsilon(\exists z. \ \varphi, \underline{x}) \equiv (\exists z. \ \varphi) \to (\exists z. \ \varphi \wedge (\bigvee_{u \in \underline{x}} z \preceq u) \wedge \Upsilon(\varphi, \underline{x} \cup z))$$

$$\Upsilon(\forall z. \ \varphi, \underline{x}) \equiv (\exists z. \ \neg\varphi) \to (\exists z. \ \neg\varphi \wedge (\bigvee_{u \in \underline{x}} z \preceq u) \wedge \Upsilon(\varphi, \underline{x} \cup z))$$

Now we can define a class of compatible specifications, i.e. specifications for which the transformation procedure $\hat{\mathcal{T}}_{\texttt{fin}}$ to Alloy language is sound.

Definition 10 (Compatibility)

1. *Definition[1] $\Phi \equiv \forall \underline{x}, y.\ f(\underline{x}) = y \leftrightarrow \mathcal{Q}_1 v_1 \ldots \mathcal{Q}_n v_n.\ \chi(\underline{v}, \underline{x}, y)$ of a function $f : \underline{s} \to s$ is $\preceq$-compatible iff $\Upsilon(\mathcal{Q}_1 v_1 \ldots \mathcal{Q}_n v_n.\ \chi(\underline{v}, \underline{x}, y), \underline{x} \cup \{y\})$ holds. If χ contains recursive calls to f we additionally require the recursive definition Φ to be well-founded [13] and for the associated well-founded order[2] $\preceq_r$ to satisfy $\preceq_r \subseteq \preceq$.*
2. *Extensionality axiom $\Phi_{ext} \equiv \forall x_1, x_2.\ x_1 = x_2 \leftrightarrow \mathcal{Q}_1 v_1 \ldots \mathcal{Q}_n v_n.\ \chi(\underline{v}, x_1, x_2)$ is $\preceq$-compatible iff $\Upsilon(\mathcal{Q}_1 v_1 \ldots \mathcal{Q}_n v_n.\ \chi(\underline{v}, x_1, x_2), \{x_1, x_2\})$ holds*
3. *Specification SP is $\preceq$-compatible iff all its definitions and extensionality axioms are $\preceq$-compatible.*

The following key steps in the process can not be completed automatically currently and require user creativity:

1. specification of the predicate $\prec: s \times s$ (indirectly encoded in the predicate *BIGGER* in the example with stores)
2. specification of constructor functions $\hat{c}$ for each $c \in C_s$ for a non-freely generated data type s (*PUT* and $\widehat{PUT}$ in the example in Section 3).
3. verification of $\preceq$-compatibility of SP (can be partly automated, currently for practical reasons this step is performed informally)

Although, the first two steps are the most crucial and challenging from the user point of view, they are also least labour intensive and require only a thorough understanding of $\mathcal{A}/_{\mathcal{R}}$. Furthermore, although non-free data types are used in almost every case study, typically only the standard library types (stores, sets, arrays, integers, graphs) are used, i.e. user effort is equal zero as library is already ported to Alloy. The third step can become tedious, since in the worst case proof obligations for $\preceq$-compatibility of definitions have to be discharged. The encouraging fact is, that in the considered case studies almost all definitions can be automatically proven $\preceq$-compatible using efficient heuristics. These heuristics on their part require a negligible information input from the user concerning input-output $\preceq$-relationship of a small number of basis operations.

The choice of the preorder $\preceq$ has the major impact on the size of the generated structures (performance) and on the scope of amenable definitions ($\preceq$-compatibility). The most often used alternative is the *subterm* relation which comes for free from the SUA generation principle, suffices for most practical cases and is also the most efficient choice. As demonstrated in [9] for some definitions subterm-closedness is too weak and additional constraints requiring the finite structures to be filled to a certain degree must be specified. The strongest constraint is to require s, k-completeness (C_s^k) for some data types s, see example in Section 3 where we used it.

---

[1] χ quantifier-free with free variables $\underline{v} \cup \underline{x} \cup \{y\}$.
[2] A binary relation $\prec$ on a set X is said to be well-founded *iff* every nonempty subset of X has a $\prec$-minimal element: $\forall S \subseteq X.\ S \neq \emptyset \Rightarrow \exists m \in S.\ \forall y \in S.\ y \not\prec m$.

Theorem 1 (Construction). *For a $\preceq$-compatible specification SP if a finite structure $\mathcal{M}$ is a model of $\widehat{\tau}_{\mathtt{fin}}(SP)$, then $\mathcal{M}$ is isomorphic to some finite $\preceq$-closed substructure $\mathcal{A}^0$ of $\mathcal{A}$, where $\mathcal{A} \models SP$.*

Follows from the $\preceq$-compatibility of SP and a similar theorem for freely generated term algebras by Kuncak and Jackson [15]. For the considered data types in the library the reverse direction of the implication ($\Leftarrow$) holds as well.

We refer to the previous results concerning the class of amenable theorems, which is composed of UBE (universal-bounded existential) formulas introduced in [9]. For both subtypes the reasoning on infinite structures can be reduced to reasoning on finite subterm-closed substructures, i.e. for for UBE sentences we have finite refutation. Because the considered $\preceq$-closed submodels are subterm-closed anyway (SUA generation), these results apply to them as well.

Theorem 2 (Finite refutation). *Let φ be an UBE formula in KIV, $\tau(\varphi)$ its translation to the relational form, SP the specification. Then*

$$\mathtt{exists}\ \mathcal{M}:\ \mathcal{M} \models \widehat{\tau_{\mathtt{fin}}}(SP),\ \mathcal{M} \not\models \tau(\varphi)\ \Rightarrow\ \mathtt{exists}\ \mathcal{A}:\ \mathcal{A} \models SP,\ \mathcal{A} \not\models \varphi$$

5   Results

We applied our technique to algebraic specifications of abstract data types in the theorem prover KIV. The scope of the application comprises KIV's library of the most essential freely and non-freely generated data types as well as some interesting examples from case studies carried out in KIV. For an evaluation we picked the following non-freely generated data types: stores, sets and arrays. The following algebraic specifications were considered:

- $SP_1 = (\{store, elem, data, nat\}, (\mathcal{F}, \mathcal{P}), Gen_{store} \cup Gen_{nat}, Ax)$,
- $SP_2 = (\{set, elem, nat\}, (\mathcal{F}, \mathcal{P}), \{\mathtt{set\ generated\ by}\ \emptyset, +\!\!+\} \cup Gen_{nat}, Ax)$,
- $SP_3 = (\{array, elem, nat\}, (\mathcal{F}, \mathcal{P}), Gen_{array} \cup Gen_{nat}, Ax)$.

We measure the size of the above specifications by counting defined operations (functions and predicates) and theorems. For SP_1 we get: $\#\mathcal{F} \cup \mathcal{P} = 12$, $\#ax = 16$, $\#theorems = 84$, for SP_2 : $\#\mathcal{F} \cup \mathcal{P} = 16$, $\#ax = 19$, $\#theorems = 341$, for SP_3 : $\#\mathcal{F} \cup \mathcal{P} = 12$, $\#ax = 16$, $\#theorems = 14$. We informally checked the specifications for compatible definitions and theorems amenable to the analysis. In fact all operations in all considered specifications were compatible, i.e. properly definable on finite substructures. There were some theorems not amenable to the analysis, i.e. not belonging to the *UBE* class ($\notin UBE$). In SP_1 only 3 (of 84) theorems belonged not to the *UBE* class and in SP_2 - 10 (of 341). In SP_3 all theorems were analyzable. Among those 13 *not amenable* theorems the following distribution occurs: 7 of type $\varphi \leftrightarrow \exists x.\ \psi$, 5 of type $\varphi \leftrightarrow \forall x.\ \psi$, and 1 of type $\exists x.\ \forall y.\ \psi$.

Finding a bug in the library is not possible as all theorems are proven. Still, for the evaluation purposes we performed the following two steps. First, we picked 40 proven theorems altogether having the high coverage of the intended behavior of the specification and run the tool on them to see whether they produce

Table 1. Benchmark: generating an instance (zChaff [34] SAT solver, 2.4 GHz Dual)

sorts	bounds	s,k-compl	#ops	#clauses	#vars	w-time
store,	$|S| \leq 9, |E| = 2, |D| = 2, |N| = 3$	(store,2)	12	8×10^4	3×10^4	2 s
elem,	$|S| \leq 10, |E| = 3, |D| = 3, |N| = 2$	(store,1)	12	3×10^5	1×10^5	30 s
data,	$|S| \leq 16, |E| = 1, |D| = 15, |N| = 3$	(store,2)	12	5×10^5	2×10^5	33 s
nat	$|S| \leq 16, |E| = 2, |D| = 3, |N| = 3$	(store,2)	12	3×10^5	1×10^5	> 5 min
set,	$|S| \leq 4, |E| = 2, |N| = 3$	(set,2)	16	2×10^4	1×10^4	0.3 s
elem,	$|S| \leq 7, |E| = 3, |N| = 3$	(set,2)	16	6×10^4	3×10^4	1 s
nat,	$|S| \leq 8, |E| = 3, |N| = 4$	(set,3)	16	1×10^5	5×10^4	2 s
	$|S| \leq 11, |E| = 4, |N| = 3$	(set,2)	16	2×10^5	8×10^4	30 s
	$|S| \leq 15, |E| = 4, |N| = 4$	(set,3)	16	6×10^5	2×10^5	1 min
	$|S| \leq 16, |E| = 4, |N| = 5$	(set,4)	16	8×10^5	3×10^5	14 min
array,	$|A| \leq 7, |E| = 2, |N| = 3$	(array,2)	5	5×10^4	2×10^4	2 s
elem,	$|A| \leq 14, |E| = 2, |N| = 4$	(array,2)	5	2×10^5	1×10^5	1 min
nat	$|A| \leq 17, |E| = 2, |N| = 4$	(array,3)	5	4×10^5	2×10^5	> 5 min

spurious counterexamples, which was not the case. After this kind of *empirical* correctness test we artificially introduced different kinds of anomalies which usually occur in the design process: from simple typos in a specification and/or in theorems to omitting some important cases in a definition of an operation or dropping essential preconditions in theorems. Alloy was able to detect all bugs and obviously was tremendously more efficient as compared to a human checker. It basically considers all possible finite models up to the size k leaving nothing unregarded whithin the scope. To measure the dynamics of the resources usage we performed a testing under the following changing parameters: bounds on the number of atoms in the universe (for each sort), level of s, k-completeness of the finite models and the number of the defined operations in the specification. Further, we distinguish between two kinds of analysis: generation of an instance for a given specification (*run* in Alloy notation), see Table 1, and checking a theorem for a specification (*check* in Alloy notation). For all wrong theorems it was enough to consider relatively small finite models, e.g. for stores we limited $\mathcal{M}$ to $|S| \leq 9, |E| = 2, |D| = 2, |N| = 3$ and required the *store*, 2-completeness ($\mathcal{C}^2_{store}$). Beside the number of atoms in the universe, which has a major impact on the size of the SAT instance, the arity of the relations included in the signature of Alloy's specifications significantly affects the time to generate the SAT instance (even for moderate instance sizes). For example, in an unsorted universe with only 4 atoms a simple inclusion of a 5-ary relation results in the SAT instance generation time of 3 minutes, although instance size is just 10^5 clauses and it is checked in 55 ms. Consequently, for the example with *arrays* we where not able to analyze conjectures involving function $fill : array \times elem \times nat \times nat \to array$, which is a 5-ary relation. Figure 3 shows a finite instance of SP_2 where most of 16 operations are hidden to get a clear picture of the universe. The instance $\mathcal{M}$ satisfies the highest completeness possible $\mathcal{C}^4_{set}$ (for $|E| = 4$ we get the whole power set $\mathcal{P}(E)$).

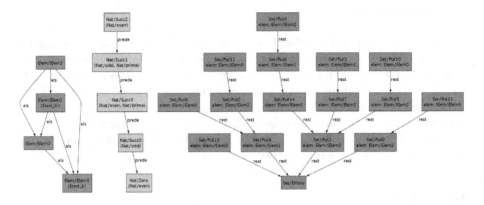

Fig. 3. Finite instance $\mathcal{M}$ for SP_2 (16 operations hidden for clarity)

6 Related Work

There exist various finite model generators: McCune's tool MACE [16] (translation to propositional logic), Kodkod [32] (used in the most recent version of Alloy), Paradox [8], SEM [35] (model search directly on a set of first-order clauses), FINDER [29], to name only a few. Combination of theorem proving and model finding techniques have been done in a number of case studies. They have in common rather symmetrical objectives: strengthen interactive proving tools by adding automatic methods on one hand and extending automatic tools with interactive formal reasoning on the other, e.g. Alloy has no support for theorem proving. Both reasoning techniques are increasingly seen as complementary activities. One approach is to use automated theorem provers based on resolution or other calculi as a *tactic* in KIV to prove first-order theorems which was investigated in [3] and in [26] with some improvements on exploiting the structure of algebraic theories. McCune's automated theorem prover Prover9 [18] (successor of Otter [17]) employs the MACE generator for search of countermodels. Reversely, the Paradox model finder has been augmented by an automated first-order theorem prover Equinox [7].

However, automated theorem provers are of limited use, since they do not support induction necessary to reason about algebraic types and recursive definitions. Weber developed a model generator [33] for higher-order logic (HOL) and integrated it in Isabelle [22]. In [19] an automation procedure for a theorem prover is described which bridges numerous differences between Isabelle with its higher-order logic and resolution provers Vampire and SPASS (restricted first-order, untyped, clause form). There exist similar approaches to integrate model checking tools in theorem provers for more efficient identification of reasons why proofs fail, e.g. Pike's [23] integration of SPIN model checker in PVS [21]. Improving quality of specifications by flaw detection plays a crucial role in practice and always remains an up-to-date issue. Earlier works by Thums et al. [31,27] and Ahrendt [2] considered an error detection in *loose* specifications of abstract data types.

7   Conclusion

We have presented a method that is aimed at refutation of unprovable first-order conjectures which in numbers arise in the interactive theorem proving practice. It is also meant to be a complementary quality improvement step in the algebraic specification development process imporving efficiency of proof engineers. A big advantage of this approach is its ability to generate finite instances (nicely visualized with Alloy) for counterexamples or witnesses. They can serve as an important source of information to designers and proof engineers, helping in getting better understanding of why their assumptions on models are wrong.

References

1. The Alloy Project, http://alloy.mit.edu
2. Ahrendt, W.: Deductive search for errors in free data type specifications using model generation. In: Voronkov, A. (ed.) CADE 2002. LNCS (LNAI), vol. 2392. Springer, Heidelberg (2002)
3. Ahrendt, W., Beckert, B., Hähnle, R., Menzel, W., Reif, W., Schellhorn, G., Schmitt, P.: Integrating Automated and Interactive Theorem Proving. In: Bibel, W., Schmitt, P. (eds.) Automated Deduction – A Basis for Applications. Kluwer Academic Publishers, Dordrecht (1998)
4. Balser, M.: Verifying Concurrent Systems with Symbolic Execution. PhD thesis, Universität Augsburg, Fakultät für Informatik (2005)
5. Balser, M., Bäumler, S., Knapp, A., Reif, W., Thums, A.: Interactive verification of UML state machines. In: Davies, J., Schulte, W., Barnett, M. (eds.) ICFEM 2004. LNCS, vol. 3308, pp. 434–448. Springer, Heidelberg (2004)
6. Balser, M., Reif, W., Schellhorn, G., Stenzel, K., Thums, A.: Formal system development with KIV. In: Maibaum, T.S.E. (ed.) FASE 2000. LNCS, vol. 1783. Springer, Heidelberg (2000)
7. Claessen, K.: Equinox, a new theorem prover for full first-order logic with equality. Dagstuhl Seminar 05431 on Deduction and Applications (October 2005)
8. Claessen, K., Srensson, N.: New techniques that improve mace-style model finding. In: Proc. of Workshop on Model Computation (MODEL) (2003)
9. Dunets, A., Schellhorn, G., Reif, W.: Bounded Relational Analysis of Free Data Types. In: Beckert, B., Hähnle, R. (eds.) TAP 2008. LNCS, vol. 4966, pp. 99–115. Springer, Heidelberg (2008)
10. Ehrig, H., Mahr, B.: Fundamentals of Algebraic Specification. Springer, Heidelberg (1985)
11. Ehrig, H., Mahr, B.: Algebraic techniques in software development: A review of progress up to the mid nineties. In: Current Trends in Theoretical Computer Science, pp. 134–152 (2001)
12. Harel, D., Kozen, D., Tiuryn, J.: Dynamic Logic. MIT Press, Cambridge (2000)
13. Harrison, J.: Inductive definitions: Automation and application. In: TPHOLs, pp. 200–213 (1995)
14. Jackson, D.: Automating first-order relational logic. In: Proceedings of the 8th ACM SIGSOFT Symposium, pp. 130–139. ACM Press, New York (2000)
15. Kuncak, V., Jackson, D.: Relational analysis of algebraic datatypes. In: Proceedings of the 13th ACM SIGSOFT Symposium (2005)

16. McCune, W.: Mace4 reference manual and guide (2003)
17. McCune, W.: Otter 3.3 reference manual (2003)
18. McCune, W.: Prover9 manual (April 2008)
19. Meng, J., Quigley, C., Paulson, L.C.: Automation for interactive proof: First proto-type. Inf. Comput. 204(10), 1575–1596 (2006)
20. Mosses, P.D.: CASL Reference Manual, The Complete Documentation of the Common Algebraic Specification Language. LNCS, vol. 2960. Springer, Heidelberg (2004)
21. Owre, S., Rushby, J.M., Shankar, N.: PVS: A Prototype Verification System. In: Kapur, D. (ed.) CADE 1992. LNCS (LNAI), vol. 607, pp. 748–752. Springer, Heidelberg (1992)
22. Paulson, L.C.: Isabelle - A Generic Theorem Prover (with a contribution by T. Nipkow). LNCS, vol. 828. Springer, Heidelberg (1994)
23. Pike, L., Miner, P., Torres-Pomales, W.: Diagnosing a failed proof in fault-tolerance: A disproving challenge problem. In: DISPROVING 2006 Participants Proceedings, pp. 24–33 (2006)
24. Ramananandro, T.: Mondex, an electronic purse: specification and refinement checks with the Alloy model-finding method. Formal Aspects of Computing 20(1), 21–39 (2008)
25. Reif, W.: Korrektheit von Spezifikationen und generischen Moduln. PhD thesis, Universität Karlsruhe, Germany (1991) (in German)
26. Reif, W., Schellhorn, G.: Theorem Proving in Large Theories. In: Bibel, W., Schmitt, P. (eds.) Automated Deduction—A Basis for Applications, vol. III, 2. Kluwer Academic Publishers, Dordrecht (1998)
27. Reif, W., Schellhorn, G., Thums, A.: Flaw detection in formal specifications. In: Goré, R.P., Leitsch, A., Nipkow, T. (eds.) IJCAR 2001. LNCS (LNAI), vol. 2083, pp. 642–657. Springer, Heidelberg (2001)
28. Schellhorn, G.: Verification of Abstract State Machines. PhD thesis, Universität Ulm, Fakultät für Informatik (1999), www.informatik.uni-augsburg.de/swt/Publications.htm
29. Slaney, J.K.: Finder: Finite domain enumerator - system description. In: CADE, pp. 798–801 (1994)
30. Stenzel, K.: A formally verified calculus for full Java Card. In: Rattray, C., Maharaj, S., Shankland, C. (eds.) AMAST 2004. LNCS, vol. 3116, pp. 491–505. Springer, Heidelberg (2004)
31. Thums, A.: Fehlersuche in Formalen Spezifikationen. Master's thesis, Universität Ulm, Germany (1998) (in German)
32. Torlak, E., Jackson, D.: Kodkod: A relational model finder. In: Grumberg, O., Huth, M. (eds.) TACAS 2007. LNCS, vol. 4424, pp. 632–647. Springer, Heidelberg (2007)
33. Weber, T.: SAT-based Finite Model Generation for Higher-Order Logic. PhD thesis, Institut für Informatik, Technische Universität München, Germany (April 2008)
34. zChaff SAT solver, http://www.princeton.edu/chaff/zchaff.html
35. Zhang, J., Zhang, H.: Sem: a system for enumerating models. In: IJCAI, pp. 298–303 (1995)

Interpolants for Linear Arithmetic in SMT

Christopher Lynch and Yuefeng Tang

Department of Mathematics and Computer Science
Clarkson University
Potsdam, NY, 13676 USA
clynch@clarkson.edu, tangy@clarkson.edu

Abstract. The linear arithmetic solver in Yices was specifically designed for SMT provers, providing fast support for operations like adding and deleting constraints. We give a procedure for developing interpolants based on the results of the Yices arithmetic solver. For inequalities over real numbers, the interpolant is computed directly from the one contradictory equation and associated bounds. For integer inequalities, a formula is computed from the contradictory equation, the bounds, and the Gomory cuts. The formula is not exactly an interpolant because it may contain local variables. But local variables only arise from Gomory cuts, so there will not be many local variables, and the formula should thereby be useful for applications like predicate abstraction. For integer equalities, we designed a new procedure. It accepts equations and congruence equations, and returns an interpolant. We have implemented our method and give experimental results.

1 Introduction

In 1957 [5] Craig presented the idea of interpolant. But, only recently interpolant are used as an important part of program verification. Interpolants are especially useful for finding inductive invariants and for predicate abstraction [1,10,11,12]. Given two sets of logical formulas A and B where $A \cup B$ is unsatisfiable, a formula P is an interpolant of (A, B) if A implies P, P contradicts B , and P only contains variables common to A and B. Informally, an interpolant gives the reason why A and B contradict, in a language common to both of them. Invariants are created iteratively, and the common variable restriction keeps the number of variables from exploding.

In this paper, we are concerned with linear arithmetic (in)equalities, either over the reals or the integers. Our method, called YAI (Yices Arithmetic Interpolants), is based on the linear arithmetic algorithm of Yices[8]. This algorithm was specially designed to work inside an SMT prover. It is able to quickly add and remove single constraints. Yices' linear arithmetic solver reduces sets of inconsistent constraints into an unsatisfiable equation. Then, our method can simply construct an interpolant from that unsatisfiable equation. Therefore, the method is not proof-based, and after detecting unsatisfiability, it can find an interpolant without much additional work.

Cha et al. (Eds.): ATVA 2008, LNCS 5311, pp. 156–170, 2008.
© Springer-Verlag Berlin Heidelberg 2008

Simplex methods are believed to be faster than Fourier Motzkin methods. Yices does not use the Simplex method, but it uses essential ideas from that method, with the idea that incremental changes must be fast. Given a set of constraints, Yices will first flatten the constraints using extension variables. What is left are equations that are pivoted and updated in a Simplex manner, and bounds on extension variables. The third component of the Yices algorithm is a set of variable assignments, which is updated as bounds are added. If the constraint set is unsatisfiable, then the algorithm will halt with an equation that conflicts with the bounds on the variables it contains. For real (in)equations, our method creates the interpolant from that equation and those bounds.

For integer (in)equations, the Yices algorithm needs to apply Gomory cuts, which introduce new variables. In this case, our formula uses the bounds, the contradicting equation, and the Gomory cut definitions to create a conditional formula which satisfies the first two conditions of the definition of interpolant. However, it is possible that the formula may contain variables that are not common to both A and B. Therefore, the formula is not exactly an interpolant. However, these offending variables are only from the Gomory cuts. So, there will not be many of them. When the purpose of requiring common variables is to keep the number of variables from exploding when the interpolant construction is iterated, we believe that these formulas are still useful in practice.

We have developed a special algorithm for interpolants over integer equations. This algorithm takes as input a set of equations and congruence equations. It is more of a Fourier Motzkin method, since new equations can be added, but in a controlled fashion. However, we still use the extensions and bounds from the Yices algorithm. This will retain the advantages of ease of adding and deleting equations. When the algorithm determines unsatisfiability, we will again have an equation which conflicts the bounds on the variables, and we will create a congruence equation from that information, which will be an interpolant.

We have implemented each of these methods. We created some random constraints and compared our implementation, YAI, with Yices. Our algorithm is the same as Yices except for integer equations, and the fact that we construct an interpolant. The time to construct the interpolant does not add significantly to the running time. However, due to clever coding techniques of the Yices programmers, YAI is slower than Yices. Our method could be incorporated into Yices without increasing its running time. For integer equations, our implementation is faster than Yices on the tested examples.

We are aware of two other implementations which create interpolants for linear arithmetic: FOCI[11] is which a proof-based method, and CLP-Prover[13] which is not proof-based. Those methods also handle uninterpreted function symbols and disjunctions. However, CLP-Prover does not handle integers, and FOCI only approximates them. Since FOCI is proof-based, it is more complicated to find an interpolant. The main difference between our implementation and those other two is that our implementation is designed to work in an SMT theorem prover which supports fast operations for adding and deleting constraints. Recently, we became aware of MATHSAT-ITP[3] and INT2[9]. For linear arithmetic over reals, both MATHSAT-ITP and YAI are based on the simplex method. MATHSAT-ITP explicitly constructs a proof of unsatisfiability and uses McMillan's method[11] to build an interpolant from the proof of unsatisfiability. But, YAI does a similar thing by directly computing an interpolant from the unsatisfiable equation with its bounds. MATHSAT-ITP converts an equality into two inequalities, which creates more constraints. However, YAI can directly handle equalities. INT2 creates interpolants for equalities over integers, but it does not use the same method as YAI. INT2 is not designed to work in SMT.

YAI cannot handle uninterpreted function symbols and disjunctions. But, YAI can easily be extended to handle those problems by using the combination methods proposed by Yorsh and Musuvathi[14] or McMillan[11]. Notice that a disequality $t \neq 0$ can be rewritten into $t > 0 \vee t < 0$.

Our paper is organized as follows. In Section 2, we introduce the preliminaries. That is followed by a brief introduction to the linear arithmetic solver of Yices. Next, we introduce YAI for linear equalities and inequalities over rational numbers. In this section, the linear arithmetic solver is the same as Yices. After that, we introduce YAI for linear equalities over integers. In this section, a new complete linear arithmetic solver is introduced, which is different from Yices. Following that, we introduce YAI for linear equalities and inequalities over integers. The linear arithmetic solver of YAI is the same as Yices. Finally, we conclude and mention future work.

2   Preliminaries

An *atom* is a single variable. A *term* is defined as a constant, an atom or cx where c is a constant and x is a variable. If c is negative, we call cx a *negative term*, otherwise cx is a *positive term*. An expression is a summation of terms. $t_1 - t_2$ is an abbreviation of $t_1 + (-t_2)$ where t_1 and t_2 are terms.

In our paper, an equation $t_1 = t_2$ is called a *standard equation* (or simply equation) where t_1 and t_2 are expressions. $t_1 \equiv_m t_2$ is a *congruence equation* where t_1 and t_2 are expressions and m is a constant. An *inequality* is of the form $t_1 \phi t_2$, where $\phi \in \{>, <, \geq, \leq\}$. A *constraint* is a standard equation, an inequality, or a congruence equation. A congruence equation $t_1 \equiv_m t_2$ is *satisfiable* if there is an assignment for the variables such that t_1 and t_2 are congruent modulo m. Any other constraint is *satisfiable* if there is an assignment for the variables which satisfies the constraint. A set of constraints is *satisfiable* if there is an assignment for the variables which satisfies all the constraints. A set of constraints is *unsatisfiable* if it is not satisfiable.

We will consider two sets of constraints A and B, and we wish to determine if $A \cup B$ is satisfiable. A variable occurring only in A or only in B is called a *local variable*. Variables occurring in both A and B are called *global variables*. If $A \cup B$ is unsatisfiable, then P is an (A, B) interpolant if A implies P, $P \cup B$ is unsatisfiable, and all variables in P are global.

3   A Linear Arithmetic Solver for DPLL(T)

Yices is an SMT solver that can efficiently check satisfiability of linear arithmetic. If the problem is satisfiable, Yices generates an assignment for each variable; else unsatisfiability is detected. Yices first converts the formula into a conjunction of equalities and bounds. The new equalities and bounds can be derived by introducing *extension* variables. For instance, given an constraint $t\phi c$ where t is an expression, c is a constant and $\phi \in \{\geq, \leq, =, >, <\}$, a new equality $s = t$ and a *bound* $s\phi c$ are generated by introducing an *extension* variable s. t is called a *definition* of s, c is a *bound value* and ϕ is a *bound operator*. This process of replacing a constraint $t\phi c$ by an extension equation $s = t$ and a bound $s\phi c$ is called *flattening*. Later on, we will need to replace the extension variables back by their definitions, so we introduce a substitution σ to do that.

Definition 1. σ *is a substitution that replaces extension variables by their definitions.*

After flattening, a set of new equalities $\sum_{i=1}^{m} s_i = t_i$ forms a constraint matrix, and a set of bounds $\sum_{i=1}^{n} s_i \phi_i c_i$ is generated too. Notice that the conversion preserves satisfiability. Here is an example. Given two linear arithmetic sets: $A = \{x - y = 0, 2y \geq 1\}$, $B = \{x \leq 0\}$.

This will be flattened into extension equations $\{s_1 = x - y,\ s_2 = 2y\}$ and bounds $\{\ s_1 = 0,\ s_2 \geq 1,\ x \leq 0\ \}$ where s_1 and s_2 are extension variables. Notice that no extension variable is introduced for the bound $x \leq 0$ because x is an atom. So, we can directly treat $x \leq 0$ as a bound. After introducing extension variables, the new set derived from A is called A_e, and the new set derived from B is called B_e. It is not hard to see that $\sigma(A_e)$ is A and $\sigma(B_e)$ is B. In this example, A_e is $\{s_1 = x - y,\ s_2 = 2y,\ s_1 = 0,\ s_2 \geq 1\ \}$, and B_e is $\{x \leq 0\}$.

The equations in the constraint matrix always maintain the following form:

$$x_i = \sum_{x_j \in \mathcal{N}} a_{ij} x_j \qquad x_i \in \mathcal{B}$$

where x_i is a *basic variable*, which only appears on the left side of the equations, x_j are *non basic variables*, which appears only on the right side of the equations, $\mathcal{B}$ is the set of basic variables, $\mathcal{N}$ is the set of non-basic variables, and a_{ij} are the coefficients. Each variable x_i has two bounds l_i(lower bound) and u_i(upper bound). If no constant bound exists, we assume the bound is $-\infty$ or $+\infty$. If $l_i = -\infty$ and $u_i = +\infty$ then x_i is a *free variable*; else if $l_i = u_i$ then x_i is a *fixed variable*. We introduce a variable assignment β that maps each variable to a constant value. Initially $\beta(x) = 0$ for all variables x. The procedure continually updates β, so that all equations and bounds will be true.

The main algorithm of this solver contains two parts. The first part containing two asserting procedures in Figure 3 [8] is to assert bounds. The second part is to resolve bound violations using the main procedure $check()$ in Figure 2[8]. Initially, for each variable x, $\beta(x) = 0$. Then, each bound will be asserted one by one. After asserting a bound, the variable assignment may be

procedure update(x_i, v)
    for each $x_j \in \mathcal{B}$, $\beta(x_j) := \beta(x_j) + a_{ji}(v - \beta(x_i))$
    $\beta(x_i) := v$

procedure pivotAndUpdate(x_i, x_j, v)
    $\theta := \frac{v - \beta(x_i)}{a_{ij}}$
    $\beta(x_i) := v$
    $\beta(x_j) := \beta(x_j) + \theta$
    for each $x_k \in \mathcal{B} \setminus x_i$, $\beta(x_k) := \beta(x_k) + a_{kj}\theta$
    pivot(x_i, x_j);

Fig. 1. Auxiliary procedures

1. **procedure** check()
2.   **loop**
3.   select the smallest basic variable x_i such that $\beta(x_i) < l_i$ or $\beta(x_i) > u_i$
4.   **if** there is no such x_i **then** return *satisfiable*
5.   **if** $\beta(x_i) < l_i$ **then**
6.   select the smallest non-basic variable x_j such that
7. $(a_{ij} > 0$ and $\beta(x_j) < u_j)$ or $(a_{ij} < 0$ and $\beta(x_j) > l_j)$
8.   **if** there is no such x_j **then return** *unsatisfiable*
9.   pivotAndUpdate(x_i, x_j, l_i)
10.   **if** $\beta(x_i) > u_i$ **then**
11.   select the smallest non-basic variable x_j such that
12. $(a_{ij} < 0$ and $\beta(x_j) < u_j)$ or $(a_{ij} > 0$ and $\beta(x_j) > l_j)$
13.   **if** there is no such x_j **then return** *unsatisfiable*
14.   pivotAndUpdate(x_i, x_j, u_i)
15.   **end loop**

Fig. 2. Check procedure

1. **procedure** AssertUpper($x_i \leq c_i$)
2.   **if** $c_i \geq u_i$ **then return** *satisfiable*
3.   **if** $c_i < l_i$ **then return** *unsatisfiable*
4. $u_i := c_i$
5.   **if** x_i is non-basic variable and $\beta(x_i) > c_i$ **then** update(x_i, c_i)
6.   **return** *ok*

1. **procedure** AssertLower($x_i \geq c_i$)
2.   **if** $c_i \leq l_i$ **then return** *satisfiable*
3.   **if** $c_i > u_i$ **then return** *unsatisfiable*
4. $l_i := c_i$
5.   **if** x_i is non-basic variable and $\beta(x_i) < c_i$ **then** update(x_i, c_i)
6.   **return** *ok*

Fig. 3. Assertion procedures

updated. Then, it is possible that the assignment of some variable could violate some asserted bound after updating the variable assignment. Thus, the procedure $check()$ will be immediately called to resolve bound violations after the assignment is updated in the asserting procedures. If a bound violation is resolved by $pivotAndUpdate(x_i, x_j, v)$ or no violation is detected, a temporary assignment satisfies all equations in the constraint matrix and the asserted bounds. So, after all bounds are asserted, if the original problem is satisfiable then a model is generated. If the algorithm determines unsatisfiability because an equation e is unsatisfiable with the bounds of its variables, then we call e an *unsat* equation. The termination of the algorithm has been proved in [8].

To handle strict inequalities over reals, Yices converts strict inequalities into non-strict inequalities by introducing a variable δ representing an infinitely small positive real number [8]. For instance, $x > 2$ is converted into $x \geq 2 + \delta$.

The linear arithmetic solver of Yices is complete to decide satisfiability for linear arithmetic over real numbers. But, it is incomplete for linear arithmetic over integers. In the next section we will introduce a method to build an interpolant when the solver of Yices detects that the problem is unsatisfiable.

4   YAI for Linear Equalities and Inequalities over Reals

In this section, our method to check satisfiability of linear arithmetic is the same as Yices. Since any disequality $t \neq 0$ can be converted into $t > 0 \vee t < 0$ [8], YAI can be easily extended to handle disequalities. As mentioned in the previous section, the solver can detect unsatisfiability in the assert and check procedures. In the assert procedures, unsatisfiability means two asserted bounds contradict each other. For instance, the bound $x \geq 5$ contradicts the bound $x \leq 0$. So, in this case the way to construct an interpolant is simple, and is presented in Figure 4. The input b_i and b_j of this procedure represents two inconsistent bounds.

1. **procedure** bound_interpolant(b_i, b_j)
2. **if**(both bounds are from A_e) **then return** $FALSE$;
3. **if**(both bounds are from B_e) **then return** $TRUE$;
4. **if**(b_i is from A_e) **then return** $\sigma(b_i)$;
5. **if**(b_j is from A_e) **then return** $\sigma(b_j)$;

Fig. 4. Bound Interpolant procedure

If the algorithm returns unsatisfiable in the checking procedure, that means that a bound violation is detected in an equation and the solver is not able to resolve the bound violation. Thus, in this case an unsat equation is detected. Notice that in an unsat equation there are no free variables because if a free variable exists then the bound violation can always be resolved by calling $pivotAndUpdate(x_i, x_j, v)$. We can rewrite the unsat equation in the form $t = 0$. Since that equation contradicts the bounds, there must exist a minimal set of bounds K such that K implies $t > 0$ or K implies $t < 0$. Let ax be a term

Table 1.

ϕ	inverse(ϕ)
$\geq$	$\leq$
$>$	$<$
$\leq$	$\geq$
$<$	$>$
$=$	$=$

in t, and let $x\phi d \in K$. If ax is a positive term, then $ax\phi a * d$ is called an *active bound*. The function *inverse* maps an operator to an operator and is defined in Table 1. If ax is a negative term, then ax $inverse(\phi)a * d$ is called an *active bound*. We say that a set of bounds has the *same direction* if all bound operators of active bounds exist only in the set $\{>, \geq, =\}$ or the set$\{<, \leq, =\}$. Since K implies $t > 0$ or K implies $t < 0$, then all active bounds in the unsat equation must have the same direction.

```
1. procedure real_interpolant(i)
2.    move the basic variable xᵢ to the right side of the equation
3.    for each variable xⱼ in the equation
4.       if the active bound of xⱼ is from Aₑ then
5.          s := s + aᵢⱼxⱼ
6.          c+ = aᵢⱼ * b_value(xⱼ)
7.          if aᵢⱼ <0 then op = inverse( b_operator(xⱼ))
8.          else op = b_operator(xⱼ)
9.          if op ≻ φ then φ =op
10. return σ(s φ c)
```

Fig. 5. Interpolant procedure over reals

Our method collects all active bounds from A_e in that equation to build an interpolant. Later on we will prove that the summation of all active bounds from A_e is an interpolant. The procedure $real\_interpolant(x_i)$ to build an interpolant over the reals is shown in Figure 5.

$real\_interpolant(i)$ will be immediately called after the linear arithmetic solver of Yices fails to find an assignment for the basic variable x_i in the unsat equation. The procedure takes as input an index i indicating the ith equation(x_i is a basic variable). We move basic variable x_i to the right hand side of the equation to express it in the form $0 = t$. The variable s, initialized to the empty string, is the sum of the left hand sides of active bounds from A_e, c, initialized to zero, is the sum of corresponding bound values and ϕ is the active bound operator. $b\_value(x_j)$ returns the active bound value of x_j, and $b\_operator(x_j)$ returns the bound operator of x_j. In the procedure an ordering is placed on operators $'>' \succ '\geq' \succ '=',$ and $'<' \succ '\leq' '='$. When adding active bounds together, the procedure selects the biggest operator among bound operators.

Example 1. Let's construct an interpolant from the example introduced in Section 3. The solver detects an unsat equation $2x = 2s_1 + s_2$ with its active bounds

$\{x \leq 0, s_1 = 0, s_2 \geq 1\}$. Running $real\_interpolant(i)$, we can derive $s = 2s_1 + s_2$, $c = 1$ and $\phi = '\geq'$ because $' \geq' \succ ' ' ='$. So, $s\phi c$ will be $2s_1 + s_2 \geq 1$. Then, the interpolant $\sigma(2s_1 + s_2 \geq 1)$ is $2x \cdot \geq 1$ because $s_1 = x - y$ and $s_2 = 2y$.

Lemma 1. $\sigma(s\phi c)$ *derived in* $real\_interpolant(i)$ *is an* (A, B)*-interpolant.*

5 YAI for Linear Equalities over Integers

Our method to check satisfiability of linear equations over integers is different from Yices. Yices employs the branch-and-bound and Gomory cut strategies to handle linear arithmetic over integers after a real assignment of variables is generated. Since in this section we only focus on integer equalities, then the Gomory cut strategy is not applicable. So, Yices only can use the branch-bound strategy. However, the branch-bound strategy is not suitable for generating interpolants because it repeatedly splits the problem into subproblems. Thus, this strategy not only increases the difficulty of constructing the interpolant, but it also makes the format of the interpolant complex involving the composition of disjunction and conjunction formulas. Therefore, we present a new linear arithmetic solver for linear equalities over integers and a simple method to construct interpolants.

Our Interpolants are standard equations or congruence equations because in some cases standard equations are not powerful to express the interpolant. For example, $A = \{2x = y\}$ and $B = \{2z = y + 1\}$. In this example, it is difficult to express the interpolant as standard equations because the interpolant could be a disjunction of infinitely many standard equations. But, if we introduce congruence equations, we can simply represent the interpolant as $y \equiv_2 0$. Another nice feature is that our method can treat congruence equations as inputs. This will be useful to find inductive invariants, when the interpolant may be an input to another call of the theorem prover.

We still use Yices' method to build the constraint matrix and bounds. In the constraint matrix we specify that all the coefficients of variables are integers. Basically, our method consists of two main procedures $reduce\_matrix()$ and $reduce\_congruence\_matrix()$. In those procedures some equations are removed from the matrices, and some equations are added into the matrices. If no equation is left After running those two procedures , then the original problem is satisfiable; else, the problem is unsatisfiable and an interpolant is constructed.

In our paper, we assume every congruence equation is simplified. The algorithm to simplify congruence equations is based on the Euclidian algorithm [4]. The definition of simplification of a congruence equation is given as follows.

Definition 2. *A congruence equation* $ax \equiv_m t$ *is simplified if* a *is a factor of* m, x *is a variable,* t *is an expression, and* a *and* m *are constants.*

The gcd test[4] is employed to check if an individual equation has an integer solution. The algorithm of the gcd test is presented in Figure 6. Notice that in the procedure, if equation i is a congruence equation, we consider the modulo as the coefficient of a free variable. Thus, $mod(i)$ returns the modulo of Equation

1. **procedure** gcd_test(i)
2.   **if**(all variables in Equation i are fixed) **then** $g = 0$
3.   **else** g = gcd of coefficients of free variables in Equation i
4.   **if** (Equation i is a congruence equation) **then** $g = gcd(g, mod(i))$
5. c is the summation of bound values of fixed variables
6.   **if** (c is not a multiple of g) **then return** *fail*
7.   **if** (all variables in Equation i are fixed) **then** remove Equation i
8.   **return** *success*

Fig. 6. gcd test procedure

i. In certain cases, it is possible that there is no free variable in equation i. In this case Equation i could be removed if c is a multiple of g. It is straightforward that removing Equation i preserves satisfiability.

1. **procedure** reduce_matrix()
2.   assert all the bounds at once
3.   **if**(bound violation exists during assert) **then return** *bound_interpolant(b_1, b_2)*
4.   **if**(Equation p fails gcd test) **then return** *integer_interpolant(p)*
5.   **while**(the matrix is not empty)
6.   select a free variable x_j from Equation i
7.   build a set M of equations containing a variable x_j
8.   **if**(for each $m \in M$ $|gcd(coef(x_j, i), coef(x_j, m))| > 1$) **then**
9.   add $\sum_{k=1}^{n} a_{ik}x_k \equiv_{a_{ij}} 0$ into the congruence matrix
11.   apply Superposition Rule to replace x_j in each equation in M by Equation i
12.   **if**(Equation p fails gcd test) **then return** *integer_interpolant(p)*
13.   apply Congruence Superposition Rule to replace x_j by Equation i
14.   **if**(Congruence Equation p fails gcd test) **then return** *integer_interpolant(p)*
15.   remove Equation i from the matrix
16. **if**(the congruence matrix is empty) **then return** *satisfiable*
17. **return** *reduce_congruence_matrix()*;

Fig. 7. Reduce_matrix procedure

Yices asserts bounds one by one. But, in our procedure *reduce_matrix()*, we assert all the bounds at once. If a bound violation occurs while asserting bounds, *bound_interpolant* (b_1, b_2) is called to construct an interpolant where b_1 and b_2 are two inconsistent bounds. Notice that the element of the set M could be a standard equation or a congruence equation. $coef(x_j, i)$ is a function that returns the coefficient of x_j in equation i. Thus, $gcd(coef(x_j, i), coef(x_j, m))$ returns the gcd of coefficients of x_j in Equation i and Equation m. To preserve satisfiability, a congruence equation $\sum_{k=1}^{n} a_{ik}x_k \equiv_{a_{ij}} 0$ may be added into the congruence matrix where $\sum_{k=1}^{n} a_{ik}x_k$ is the summation of all the terms in equation i and a_{ij} is the coefficient of x_j in equation i. Then, the procedure replaces x_j in the other equations by Equation i. In the following inference rules, we treat the left premise as Equation i and the right premise as a updated equation.

The way to replace x_j in a standard equation by Equation i is given in **Superposition Rule**.

$$\frac{ax_j = t_1 \quad bx_j = t_2}{bt_1 = at_2}$$

where x_j is a free variable, t_1 and t_2 are expressions, and a and b are integers.

The idea to replace x_j in a congruence equation by a standard equation is given in **Congruence Superposition Rule**:

$$\frac{ax_j = t_1 \quad bx_j \equiv_c t_2}{bt_1 \equiv_{ac} at_2}$$

where x_j is a free variable, t_1 and t_2 are expressions, and a, b, and c are integers.

The above two inference rules represent updates, meaning that the right premise is replaced by the conclusion in the presence of the left premise. The left premise will not be removed from the matrix until all the other equations are updated. Thus, for each iteration in the *while* loop, an equation is removed from the constraint matrix in *reduce_matrix*(). Thus, in general our method is efficient because the number of constraints in the matrix is reduced and the cost to update standard equations is dramatically decreased.

Example 2. Given $A = \{2x = y\}$ and $B = \{y = 2z + 1\}$, this is flattened into equations $\{s_1 = 2x - y, s_2 = y - 2z\}$ and bounds $\{s_1 = 0, s_2 = 1\}$. Suppose that the ordering of the selected free variables in *reduce_matrix*() is x from $s_1 = 2x - y$ and y from $s_2 = y - 2z$. For the first pass of the while loop, $y \equiv_2 s_1$ is added into the congruence matrix. For the second pass of the while loop, the congruence superposition rule is applied for $s_2 = y - 2z$ and $y \equiv_2 s_1$. The inference result is $s_2 + 2z \equiv_2 s_1$ which can be simplified to $s_2 \equiv_2 s_1$. The equation $s_2 \equiv_2 s_1$ fails gcd test because $s_1 = 0$ and $s_2 = 1$. Thus, unsatisfiability is detected.

1. **procedure** reduce_congruence_matrix()
2. **while**(the congruence matrix is not empty)
3.   select a free variable x_j from Congruence equation i
4.   build a set M of congruence equations containing x_j
5.   for an equation $m \in M$ if $|coef(x_j, m)| > 1$ **then**
6.   add congruence Equation $\sum_{k=1}^{n} a_{mk}x_k \equiv_{a_{mj}} 0$
7.   apply CC Superposition Rule replacing x_j for each pair of equations in M
8.   remove all the equations in M
9.   **if**(an equation m fails the gcd test) **then return** *integer_interpolant*(p)
10. **return** satisfiable

Fig. 8. Reduce congruence matrix procedure

Next, we will study the procedure *reduce_congruence_matrix*() which is shown in Figure 8. In the procedure, a set M is built in which each congruence equation contains x_j. For an equation $j \in M$, if the absolute value of the coefficient of x_j is greater than 1 then $\sum_{k=1}^{n} a_{mk}x_k \equiv_{a_{mj}} 0$ is added where $\sum_{k=1}^{n} a_{mk}x_k$

is a summation of all terms in Congruence Equation m and a_{mj} is the coefficient of x_j in congruence Equation m. Then **CC Superposition Rule** is applied for each pair of equations in M to replace x_j.

$$\frac{ax_j \equiv_c t_1 \quad bx_j \equiv_d t_2}{bt_1 \equiv_{gcd(b*c,a*d)} at_2}$$

After applying the CC Superposition Rule, all the equations containing x_j are removed. Next, gcd test is applied on those new generated equations. An interpolant is constructed if unsatisfiability is detected. This procedure is terminated when an interpolant is constructed or the congruence matrix is empty.

Since for each equation $a_i x \equiv_{m_i} t_i$ in M, $a_i | t_i$ (t_i is divisible by a_i) because a congruence equation may be added. Thus, in some sense our method is the successive substitution method which is a method of solving problems of simultaneous congruences by using the definition of the congruence equation. Usually, the successive substitution method is applied in cases where the conditions of the Chinese Remainder Theorem are not satisfied.

Example 3. Given $A = \{6m = 3x - y, 4n = 3x - z\}$ and $B = \{3z = y + 1\}$, this is flattened into extension equations $\{s_1 = 6m - 3x + y, s_2 = 4n - 3x + z, s_3 = 3z - y\}$ and bounds $\{s_1 = 0, s_2 = 0, s_3 = 1\}$. Suppose the ordering of the selected variables in *reduce_matrix()* is m from $s_1 = 6m - 3x + y$, n from $s_2 = 4n - 3x + z$ and z from $s_3 = 3z - y$. After running *reduce_matrix()*, all those standard equations are removed and $\{3x - y + s_1 \equiv_6 0, 3x - z + s_2 \equiv_4 0, y + s_3 \equiv_3 0\}$ is added into the congruence matrix. So, the next step is to call *reduce_congruence_matrix()*. In this procedure, let's assume that x is selected. First, $3x - y + s_1 \equiv_6 0$ and $3x - z + s_2 \equiv_4 0$ can be rewritten to $3x \equiv_6 y - s_1$ and $3x \equiv_4 z - s_2$. Second, since the coefficient of x in those two congruence equations is 3, $y \equiv_3 s_1$ and $z \equiv_3 s_2$ are generated. Third, after applying the CC Superposition Rule for $3x \equiv_6 y - s_1$ and $3x \equiv_4 z - s_2$, the inference result is $y - s_1 \equiv_2 z - s_2$. So, at this point the congruence matrix contains $y + s_3 \equiv_3 0$, $y \equiv_3 s_1$, $z \equiv_3 s_2$ and $y - s_1 \equiv_2 z - s_2$. Suppose, the next selected variable is y. Then, applying the CC Superposition Rule for $y + s_3 \equiv_3 0$ and $y \equiv_3 s_1$, we can derive $s_1 + s_3 \equiv_3 0$ which is unsatisfiable because $s_1 = 0$ and $s_3 = 1$.

So far, we have introduced a new linear arithmetic solver different from Yices for linear equations over integers. Next is to show a procedure to construct an interpolant. In *integer_interpolant(i)*, we consider that the modulo of Equation i is a coefficient of a free variable. s is a sum of the left hand sides of active bounds and c is a sum of corresponding bound values.

Example 4. In example 2, our method detects that $s_2 \equiv_2 s_1$ with $s_2 = 1$ and $s_1 = 0$ is unsatisfiable. Running *integer_interpolant(i)*, we can derive $s = s_1$, $g = 2$ and $c = 0$ because s_1 is from A_e. Since $s_1 = 2x - y$ then an interpolant $\sigma(s_1 \equiv_2 0)$ could be $y \equiv_2 0$ which is simplified from $2x - y \equiv_2 0$. Similarly, in example 3, running *integer_interpolant(i)*, we can derive an interpolant $y \equiv_3 0$.

1. **procedure** integer_interpolant(i)
2.   g = gcd of coefficients of free variables in Equation i
4.   **if** (Equation i is a congruence equation) **then** g = gcd(mod(i), g)
5.   **for** each variable x_j in the equation
6.   **if** the active bound of x_j is from A_e **then**
7. $s := s + a_{ij}x_j$
8. $c+ = a_{ij} * b\_value(x_j)$
9. $\sigma(s \equiv_g c)$
10. **return** satisfiable

Fig. 9. Interpolant over integer equations

Notice that our arithmetic solver of YAI is different from Yices. However, our solver uses the same flattening procedure as Yices does to separate constraints and bounds. Thus, our solver is also able to quickly add and delete a single constraint. To delete a constraint, we can simply delete its bound. To add a constraint, first we assert its bound. Then, we re-run $gcd\_test(i)$ on the equations, including the deleted equations which contain the corresponding extension variable for that constraint. Actually, our method saves those deleted constraints for adding and deleting operations.

In our implementation, YAI does not construct a model for a satisfiable problem because our interest is to construct interpolants. However, theoretically our method is able to construct a model. We can build a model from the reverse order of the deleted constraints using the successive substitution method [7].

Lemma 2. $\sigma(s \equiv_g c)$ derived in integer_interpolant(i) is an (A, B)-interpolant.

Lemma 3. Each pass of the while loop in reduce_matrix() preserves satisfiability.

Lemma 4. Each pass of the while loop in reduce_congruence_matrix() preserves satisfiability.

6   YAI for Linear Equalities and Inequalities over Integers

The linear arithmetic procedure of Yices tries to find an assignment for each variable and if an assignment is not an integer then branch-bound and Gomory cut strategies are employed. In this section we use the linear arithmetic solver in Yices to check satisfiability for linear arithmetic over integers. But, in our implementation only the Gomory cut strategy is employed and the reason is explained in the previous section. Notice that the linear arithmetic solver in Yices is incomplete for integer problems. So, our method to construct interpolants based on Yices is also incomplete.

Given an equation $x_i = \sum_{x_j \in \mathcal{N}} a_{ij}x_j$ where the assignment of the basic variable x_i is a rational number, then a Gomory cut [8] is generated to restrict the solution of x_i. Gomory cut implied by constraints is an inequality. A Gomory cut is a *pure cut* when the equation used to generate the cut is from A_e or B_e.

Otherwise, it is a *mixed cut*. We treat all pure Gomory cuts as constraints from A_e or B_e. For a mixed Gomory cut, a conjunction of constraints from B_e, which are used to generate the cut, will be stored with the corresponding cut.

If unsatisfiability is detected in the asserting procedure, then we can use *bound_ interpolant*(b_i, b_j) to construct the interpolant; else *cut_interpolant*(i) is called to construct the interpolant.

1. **procedure** cut_interpolant(i)
2.   move the basic variable x_i to the left side of the equation
3.   **for each** variable x_j in the equation
4.   **if** the active bound of x_j is mixed cut or from A_e **then**
5.   s $+= a_{ij}x_j$
6.   c $+= (a_{ij} * b\_value(x_j))$
7.   **if** $a_{ij} < 0$ **then** op $=$ inverse($b\_operator(x_j)$)
8.   **else** op $= b\_operator(x_j)$
9.   **if** op $\succ \phi$ **then** $\phi =$ op
10.   **if** the active bound of x_j is a mixed cut **then** b $=$ b $\wedge$ cut_info(x_j)
11. **return** σ (b $\Rightarrow$ (s ϕ c))

Fig. 10. Interpolant for linear arithmetic over integers

cut_interpolant(i) is quite similar to *real_inerpolant*(i). *cut_info*(x_j) is a set of constraints from B_e which are used to generate the cut of x_j. However, the strategy of Gomory cut is employed. So, if a mixed cut is involved in the unsatisfiability proof, then extracting information of A_e from the mixed cut is not enough because the mixed cut is derived from a combination of constraints from A_e and B_e. Thus, in the procedure we use b to collect some constraints from B_e which are used to generate corresponding cuts. We use $\Rightarrow$ as implication. Thus, we treat b as a condition to conclude $s\phi c$.

Since b is a set of some constraints from B_e, then b may contains some variables local to B_e. Thus, σ (b $\Rightarrow$ (s ϕ c)) is not an interpolant. But, it does satisfy the other two properties of (A, B)-interpolant.

Example 5. Given $A = \{5x = y + z, y \geq 0, y \leq 1\}$ and $B = \{z \geq 1, z \leq 2\}$, this can be flattened into extension equations $\{s_1 = 5x - y - z\}$ and bounds $\{s_1 = 0, y \geq 0, y \leq 1, z \geq 1, z \leq 2\}$. Running the linear arithmetic procedure in Yices, an assignment is generated but the value of x is 1/5 which be derived from $5x = y + z + s_1$ with $y \geq 0$, $z \geq 1$ and $s_1 = 0$. Then, a Gomory cut $y + z \geq 5$ is generated from that equation with its bounds. Notice that the constraint from B_e used to construct the Gomory cut is $z \geq 1$. That Gomory cut is flattened into an extension equation $s_2 = y + z$ and a bound $s_2 \geq 5$. The extension equation is added into matrix and the bound is asserted. Finally, unsatisfiability is detected in $z = -y + s_2$ with $z \leq 2$, $y \leq 1$ and $s \geq 5$. Thus, running *cut_interpolant*(i), we derive that an interpolant $\sigma(z \geq 1 \Rightarrow -y + s2 \geq 4)$ is $z \geq 1 \Rightarrow z \geq 4$ because $s_2 = y + z$. The left side of the conditional formula is the conjunction of constraints from B_e used to construct Gomory cuts and the right side of the conditional formula is the sum of constraints from A_e and Gomory cuts.

Lemma 5. $\sigma(b \Rightarrow s\phi c)$ in cut_interpoant(i) is implied by A and contradicts B.

7   Experimental Results

We implemented YAI using Microsoft Visual Studio 2008 C++ on the Windows XP operating system. All experiments are conducted on a Lenovo Think Pad T60 with the configuration of Intel 2.0GHz CPU and 2.0GB memory. YAI is available on *http://people.clarkson .edu/~tangy/*.

Since YAI for linear real inequalities and integer inequalities is based on the linear arithmetic solver in Yices and constructing interpolants does not add too much additional cost to Yices, we only compared the running time of YAI with Yices for linear integer equalities.

Most SMT benchmarks contain disjunctions and function symbols. Thus, we wrote a C program to randomly generate sample examples without containing disjunctions and function symbols. Each sample example set contains 100 examples. Let $P(e_1, e_2)$ be a pair of integers and let e_1 be the number of constraints and e_2 be the number of variables in an example. In each example of *equality_set_1*, *equality_set_2*, and *equality_set_3*, the corresponding pairs are $P(10, 5)$, $P(50, 25)$ and $P(100, 50)$. For each constraint in the example the operator is $' ='$, the number of terms is randomly selected from $[1, 10]$, the coefficient for each term is randomly selected from $[1, 100]$, the variable name is randomly generated, and a constant is randomly selected from $[1, 100]$. The results in the table are the total runtime of 100 examples. The running time of YAI for linear integer equalities mainly depends on the number of congruence equations generated from the examples because the expensive operation of YAI is to reduce congruence equations using the successive substitution method.

	Number of Examples	YAI (seconds)	Yices(seconds)
equality_set_1	100	4	5
equality_set_2	100	8	10
equality_set_3	100	6	67

Fig. 11. Comparison between YAI and Yices for linear equalities over integers

8   Conclusion and Future Work

We have shown how interpolant construction fits easily into the SMT framework in the theory of linear arithmetic. In particular, we produce an interpolant directly from the single contradictory equation. Therefore, an interpolant can be generated at no additional cost to the satisfiability procedure. We have implemented YAI and compared our results against Yices.

We have several directions to work on. First, we plan to extend our method to handle uninterpreted function symbols and disjunctions using the methods proposed by Yorsh and Musuvathi[8] and McMillan [11]. Second, We would like to compare against FOCI, CLP-prover, MATHSAT-ITP and INT2 in the size of interpolants and the efficiency of solvers. Finally, we would like to apply our method to generate invariants.

References

1. Beyer, D., Henzinger, T.A., Jhala, R., Majumdar, R.: The Software Model Checker Blast: Applications to Software Engineering. *International Journal on Software Tools for Technology Transfer (STTT)* 9(5-6), 505–525 (2007)
2. Chvatal, V.: *Linear Programming*. W. H. Freeman, New York (1983)
3. Cimatti, A., Griggio, A., Sebastiani, R.: Efficient Interpolant Generation in Satisfiability Modulo Theories. In: Ramakrishnan, C.R., Rehof, J. (eds.) TACAS 2008. LNCS, vol. 4963. Springer, Heidelberg (2008)
4. Cormen, T.H., Leiserson, C.E., Rivest, R.L., Stein, C.: *Introduction to Algorithms*, 2nd edn., pp. 856–862. MIT Press and McGraw-Hill (2001)
5. Craig, W.: Three uses of the Herbrand-Gentzen theorem in relating model theory and proof theory. *J. Symbolic Logic* 22(3), 269–285 (1957)
6. Dantzig, G.B., Curtis, B.: Fourier-Motzkin elimination and its dual. *Journal of Combinatorial Theory*, 288–297 (1973)
7. Dickson, L.E.: History of the Theory of Numbers, vol. 2. Chelsea, New York (1957)
8. Dutertre, B., de Moura, L.: Integrating Simplex with DPLL(T). CSL Technical Report SRI-CSL-06-01 (2006)
9. Jain, H., Clarke, E.M., Grumberg, O.: Efficient Craig Interpolation for Linear Diophantine (Dis)Equations and Linear Modular Equations. In: *Proc. CAV* (2008)
10. McMillan, K.L.: Interpolation and SAT-based model checking. In: Hunt Jr., W.A., Somenzi, F. (eds.) CAV 2003. LNCS, vol. 2725, pp. 1–13. Springer, Heidelberg (2003)
11. McMillan, K.L.: An interpolating theorem prover. In: Jensen, K., Podelski, A. (eds.) TACAS 2004. LNCS, vol. 2988, pp. 16–30. Springer, Heidelberg (2004)
12. McMillan, K.L.: Applications of Craig interpolants in model checking. In: Halbwachs, N., Zuck, L.D. (eds.) TACAS 2005. LNCS, vol. 3440, pp. 1–12. Springer, Heidelberg (2005)
13. Rybalchenko, A., Stokkermans, V.S.: Constraint Solving for Interpolation. In: Cook, B., Podelski, A. (eds.) VMCAI 2007. LNCS, vol. 4349, pp. 346–362. Springer, Heidelberg (2007)
14. Yorsh, G., Musuvathi, M.: A combination method for generating interpolants. In: Nieuwenhuis, R. (ed.) CADE 2005. LNCS (LNAI), vol. 3632, pp. 353–368. Springer, Heidelberg (2005)

SAT Modulo ODE:
A Direct SAT Approach to Hybrid Systems

Andreas Eggers, Martin Fränzle, and Christian Herde*

Dept. of CS, Carl von Ossietzky Universität Oldenburg, Germany
{eggers,fraenzle,herde}@informatik.uni-oldenburg.de

Abstract. In order to facilitate automated reasoning about large Boolean combinations of non-linear arithmetic constraints involving ordinary differential equations (ODEs), we provide a seamless integration of safe numeric overapproximation of initial-value problems into a SAT-modulo-theory (SMT) approach to interval-based arithmetic constraint solving. Interval-based safe numeric approximation of ODEs is used as an interval contractor being able to narrow candidate sets in phase space in both temporal directions: post-images of ODEs (i.e., sets of states reachable from a set of initial values) are narrowed based on partial information about the initial values and, vice versa, pre-images are narrowed based on partial knowledge about post-sets.

In contrast to the related CLP(F) approach of Hickey and Wittenberg [12], we do (a) support coordinate transformations mitigating the wrapping effect encountered upon iterating interval-based overapproximations of reachable state sets and (b) embed the approach into an SMT framework, thus accelerating the solving process through the algorithmic enhancements of recent SAT solving technology.

1 Introduction

Hybrid systems consist of interacting discrete and continuous components, with the continuous components often being naturally described by a combination of ordinary differential equations (ODEs), formalizing time-dependent continuous behavior, and arithmetic (in-)equations portraying autonomous jumps, invariants, and the like. Automating state-exploratory analysis of hybrid systems does thus call for effective manipulation of Boolean combinations of the above, where the large discrete state spaces encountered in real systems and the dependence of the continuous behavior on the current discrete state give rise to potentially extremely large Boolean combinations. Within this paper, we suggest a SAT modulo theory (SMT) approach for directly handling these large compositions of ODEs, arithmetic (in-)equations, and conditions on discrete states.

Our approach draws from three up to now distinct technologies, trying to combine their virtues: (1) Solving large and complex-structured Boolean combinations of arithmetic constraints by *SAT modulo theory* techniques (e.g., [10,6]).

* This work has been partially funded by the German Research Council (DFG) as part of the Transregional Collaborative Research Center "Automatic Verification and Analysis of Complex Systems" (SFB/TR 14 AVACS, www.avacs.org).

These approaches are attractive as they transfer the algorithmic enhancements that were instrumental to the enormous performance gains recently achieved in propositional SAT solving, like non-chronological backtracking and conflict-driven learning, to the mixed Boolean-arithmetic domain, as encountered in hybrid systems [2]. (2) *Interval-based safe numeric approximation of ODEs*, as suggested by, a.o., Moore, Lohner, and Stauning [14,13,16] and recently gaining renewed interest in the hybrid systems community [15]. This approach provides a technique for safely overapproximating the image under an ODE of a rectangular region in phase space and incorporates techniques based on coordinate transformations for mitigating the wrapping effect encountered upon iterating interval-based overapproximations of reachable state sets. (3) *CLP(F)* [12], offering a symbolic, constraint-based technology for reasoning about ODEs grounded in (in-)equational constraints obtained from Taylor expansions, thus being able to handle ODE parameters, error ranges in measurements, and other natural uncertainties in modeling dynamic systems. Such effects are hard to deal with, and hence often ignored, within numeric approaches to image computation.

Our design goal was to resolve the following shortcomings of the aforementioned techniques: First, the SMT framework, while being able to handle very large constraint systems involving arithmetic (in-)equations, did previously lack any native support for ODEs. Second, CLP(F) may fail to provide tight approximations of the ODE solutions due to not counterfeiting the *wrapping effect* [14] encountered in iterating interval-based, i.e. rectangular, overapproximations of state sets. Furthermore, CLP(F) lacks the sophisticated means of pruning the search space based on conflict analysis found in recent SMT solvers.[1] Third, the tighter approximations computed by interval-based safe numeric approximation of ODEs, which have successfully been used in state-exploratory verification of hybrid systems (e.g., in Hypertech [11]), lack the constraint propagation and reasoning functionality of the CLP(F) approach. Instead, their use was confined to extrapolating state sets in an a priori fixed temporal direction of exploration.

To mitigate these restrictions, we suggest a direct, seamless integration of safe approximation of ODEs into the iSAT arithmetic constraint solver [9], which is an adaptation of the SMT framework to the undecidable domain of non-linear arithmetic involving, a.o., inequations entailing transcendental functions. On the theory solver side, iSAT is based on interval constraint propagation (ICP) for arithmetic (in-)equations [3], which we extend to ODEs as follows. Interval-based safe numeric approximation of ODEs is used as an interval contractor being able to narrow candidate sets in phase space in both temporal directions: post-images of ODEs (i.e., sets of states reachable from a set of initial values) are narrowed based on partial information about the initial values and, vice versa, pre-images are narrowed based on partial knowledge about post-sets.

Structure of the paper. Section 2 states the structure of the input models we are going to address. In Sect. 3, we then start our exposition of the solver algorithms

---

[1] Due to the generality of the CLP framework, the programmer may nevertheless be able to simulate many of these pruning operators, albeit at the price of a very imperative use of CLP.

with a description of the arithmetic SAT solving technology we build upon. Thereafter, we provide a detailed exposition of its extension to ODEs (Sect. 4), an overview of the integrated algorithm (Sect. 5), and benchmark results indicating feasibility of the technique (Sect. 6).

2   Arithmetic SAT Problems Involving ODEs

Aiming at automated analysis of hybrid systems, our constraint solver addresses satisfiability of non-linear arithmetic constraints, including ODEs, over real-valued variables RV plus Boolean variables BV for encoding the control flow. The user thus may input constraint formulae built from quantifier-free (in-)equational constraints over the reals, from ODEs, and from propositional variables using arbitrary Boolean connectives. The atomic (in-)equational constraints are relations between potentially non-linear terms involving transcendental functions, like $\sin(x + \omega t) + ye^{-t} \leq z + 5$. The ODE constraints define the derivatives of the continuous variables w.r.t. time. They are given by equational constraints of the form $\frac{dx_i(t)}{dt} = f_i(\vec{x}(t))$, where the ODE-defined variables x_i constitute a vector $\vec{V}$ over a subset of RV and f_i are potentially non-linear expressions over $\vec{V}$. Additionally *flow invariants* of the form $l \leq x_i \leq u$ can be given that constrain the range of the variables in V during a continuous flow.

An input model comprises predicative encodings of the initial state set *init*, the transition relation *trans* over current-step (x) and next-step variables (x'), and the (unsafe) *target* state. ODE constraints can only occur in the transition relation where they define the relationship between two successive valuations of the variables in V by constraining the possible trajectories in between the steps.

In Fig. 1, an abstract model of a room with an indoor stove is given. Being either on or off, the stove has two discrete modes with different continuous dynamics described by ODEs. The variable ϑ_i describes the temperature in the room, ϑ_o the outside temperature (assumed to be constant but arbitrarily chosen from the interval $[-10, 20]$) and c the concentration of exhaust gases in the room. When switched off, the heater does not produce any exhaust gases and the concentration thus decreases over time. The temperature in the room changes accordingly to the difference between ϑ_o and ϑ_i. The heater is switched on only when both, the temperature and the concentration of exhaust gases in the air are below their respective thresholds. Being switched on, the room is heated up, however at the expense of a growing concentration of undesirable gases in the room's air. The heating is switched off when the temperature is comfortable again. Fig. 1 also shows the derived predicative encoding.

In order to perform bounded model checking (BMC) [4] on such model encodings, the transition relation is unwound k times and conjoined with the predicates that encode initial and target states, yielding a formula

$$\phi = init(\vec{x}^{(0)}) \wedge trans(\vec{x}^{(0)}, \vec{x}^{(1)}) \wedge \cdots \wedge trans(\vec{x}^{(k-1)}, \vec{x}^{(k)}) \wedge target(\vec{x}^{(k)}) \quad (1)$$

that is satisfiable iff a state satisfying *target* is reachable in k steps. Each variable x_i thus results in $k + 1$ instances $x_i^{(0)}, x_i^{(1)}, \ldots, x_i^{(k)}$. If ϕ is satisfied by the

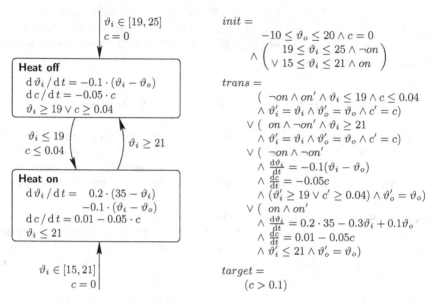

Fig. 1. Model of a room with indoor stove: hybrid system and predicative encoding

valuations of all instances for all variables occuring in ϕ, these valuations represent the evolution of the system during a particular *trace*. Like all other subexpressions of the transition system, also the ODE constraints are instantiated k times. The resulting formula ϕ thus contains ODE constraints over disjoint sets of variable instances $V^{(0)}, \ldots, V^{(k)}$, where each $V^{(i)}$ contains those instances whose ODE-defined trajectories emerge from the valuations in the i-th step.

As the ODEs that govern the hybrid-system behavior depend on the current discrete state of the system, such ODE constraints are switched on and off by propositional "triggers", such that traces need only obey the pre-/post-relation defined by those ODE constraints and the flow invariants whose triggers are forced to true by predicates formalizing the interplay between discrete state and continuous behavior.

3   Constraint Solving with the iSAT Algorithm

In this section, we first describe the internal representation of formulae handled by iSAT. Thereafter, we give an overview of the solving algorithm and provide some examples for the application of deduction rules, which are an essential part of the algorithm. Our aim is to demonstrate that deduction rules for ODEs are a natural extension of the iSAT framework.

3.1   Representation of Solver-Internal Formulae

Syntax. By the front-end of our solver, constraint formulae are rewritten into equi-satisfiable quantifier-free formulae in conjunctive normal form, with atomic propositions ranging over propositional variables and (in-)equational constraints confined to a form resembling three-address code. This rewriting is based on the standard mechanism of introducing auxiliary variables for the values of arithmetic sub-expressions and of logical sub-formulae, thereby eliminating common sub-expressions and sub-formulae through re-use of the auxiliary variables, thus reducing the search space of the solver and enhancing the reasoning power of the interval contractors used in arithmetic reasoning [3]. Thus, the *internal* syntax of constraint formulae is as follows:

$$
\begin{aligned}
formula &::= \{clause \wedge\}^* clause \\
clause &::= (\{atom \vee\}^* atom) \mid (bound \Rightarrow ode \wedge flow\_invar) \\
atom &::= bound \mid equation \\
bound &::= variable \sim rational\_constant \\
variable &::= real\_var \mid boolean\_var \\
equation &::= real\_var = real\_var \ bop \ real\_var \mid real\_var = uop \ real\_var \\
ode &::= \{\mathrm{d}\, real\_var \,/\, \mathrm{d}\,t = term \wedge\}^* \mathrm{d}\, real\_var \,/\, \mathrm{d}\,t = term \\
flow\_invar &::= \{bound \wedge\}^* bound
\end{aligned}
$$

where $\sim \in \{<, \leq, >, \geq\}$, the non-terminals bop, uop denote the binary and unary operator symbols (including arithmetic operators such as $+$ or $\sin$), and $term$ the terms over real-valued variables built using these.

Semantics. Such constraint formulae are interpreted over valuations $\sigma \in (BV \xrightarrow{total} \mathbb{B}) \times (RV \xrightarrow{total} \mathbb{R})$, where BV is the set of Boolean and RV the set of real-valued variables, being the instances of the variables that result from the BMC unwinding depicted in (1). $\mathbb{B}$ is identified with the subset $\{0,1\}$ of $\mathbb{R}$ such that bounds on a Boolean variable v correspond to literals v or $\neg v$. The definition of satisfaction is standard: a constraint formula ϕ is satisfied by a valuation iff all its clauses are satisfied. A disjunctive clause is satisfied iff at least one of its atoms is satisfied. Satisfaction of atoms is wrt. the standard interpretation of the arithmetic operators and the ordering relations over the reals. We assume all arithmetic operators to be total and therefore extend their codomain (as well as, for compositionality, their domain) with a special value $\mho \notin \mathbb{R}$ ("undefined") such that the operators manipulate values in $\mathbb{R}^\mho = \mathbb{R} \cup \{\mho\}$. The comparison operations on $\mathbb{R}$ are extended to $\mathbb{R}^\mho$ in such a way that $\mho$ is incomparable to any real number, that is, $c \not\sim \mho$ and $\mho \not\sim c$ for any $c \in \mathbb{R}$ and any relation $\sim \in \{<, \leq, =, \geq, >\}$. ODE constraints are satisfied if there exists for each BMC unwinding depth i a solution of the ODE system $\frac{d\vec{x}(t)}{dt} = \vec{f}(\vec{x}(t))$ where the activated triggers of that BMC depth i define which ODE constraints are used as components $f_1, \ldots, f_n$. Such a solution function $\vec{x}(t)$ satisfies the ODE up to a user-specified *horizon* of interest, the trajectory emerges from the current valuation of $\vec{x}$ on BMC depth i, i.e. $\vec{x}(0) = \sigma(\vec{x}^{(i)})$ holds, and there exists a $\tau_r \in [0, horizon]$ such that $\vec{x}(\tau_r) = \sigma(\vec{x}^{(i+1)})$, i.e. the trajectory eventually reaches the next value of $\vec{x}$ in the trace.

Interval-based overapproximation. Instead of real-valued valuations of variables, our constraint solving algorithm manipulates interval-valued valuations $\rho \in (BV \xrightarrow{total} \mathbb{I}_\mathbb{B}) \times (RV \xrightarrow{total} \mathbb{I}_\mathbb{R})$, where $\mathbb{I}_\mathbb{B} = 2^\mathbb{B}$ and $\mathbb{I}_\mathbb{R}$ is the set of convex subsets of $\mathbb{R}^{\mho}$.[2] Slightly abusing notation, we write $\rho(l)$ for $\rho_{\mathbb{I}_\mathbb{B}}(l)$ when $\rho = (\rho_{\mathbb{I}_\mathbb{B}}, \rho_{\mathbb{I}_\mathbb{R}})$ and $l \in BV$, and similarly $\rho(x)$ for $\rho_{\mathbb{I}_\mathbb{R}}(x)$ when $x \in RV$. In the following, we occasionally use the term *box* synonymously for interval valuation. If both ζ and η are interval valuations then ζ is called a *refinement* of η iff $\zeta(v) \subseteq \eta(v)$ for each $v \in BV \cup RV$. An interval valuation ρ is *inconsistent* with an atom $x \sim c$ iff $\rho(x) \cap \{u \mid u \sim c\} = \emptyset$ and inconsistent with an equational atom $x = y \oplus z$ iff $\rho(x) \cap \varepsilon(\rho(y) \oplus \rho(z)) = \emptyset$, where ε denotes an outward rounding enclosure of the exact evaluation of $\rho(y) \oplus \rho(z)$. Analogously for unary operators.

3.2   Solving

Starting from the cartesian product of the ranges of all variables as initial search space, the iSAT algorithm [9] operates similar to the behavior of a DPLL-based Boolean SAT solver [5] by alternating between two steps: The *decision step* involves (heuristically) selecting a variable, splitting its current interval (e.g. at its midpoint) and temporarily discarding either the lower or the upper part of the interval from the search. Each decision is followed by a sequence of *deduction steps* in which the solver applies a set of deduction rules that explore all the consequences of the previous decision. Essentially, these deduction rules narrow the search space by carving away portions that contain non-solutions only. Deduction rules are applied over and over again until no further interval narrowing is achieved or the changes become negligible. Deduction may also yield a conflict — i.e. a variable's range becomes empty — indicating the need to undo decisions and their consequences (backjumping).

3.3   Deduction

For each type of constraint occuring in the formula, at least one narrowing operator is needed: clauses (disjunctions of atoms) are handled by *unit propagation* (UP), arithmetic operators occuring in equations by narrowing operators derived from *interval constraint propagation* (ICP) [3], and ODE constraints by computing safe enclosures of their solution sets as described in Sect. 4. The following examples illustrate the role these narrowing operators play in solving.

Unit Propagation. Assume for example a clause $(a \geq 1 \vee x \leq 4 \vee y = 2)$ and interval assignments $\rho(x) = [10, 20]$, $\rho(y) = [-5, -4.7]$, and $\rho(a) = \{0, 1\}$. For each atom of this clause, the truth value can be determined in a three-valued logic: $a \geq 1$ can still become **true**, while $x \leq 4$ and $y = 2$ are inconsistent and therefore definitely **false** under ρ. In order to retain a chance for satisfiability of the formula, each clause must be satisfied and therefore also the *unit* atom $a \geq 1$, i.e. all values less than 1 can safely be pruned from $\rho(a)$.

---

[2] Note that this definition covers the open, half-open, and closed intervals over $\mathbb{R}$, including unbounded intervals, as well as the union of such intervals with $\{\mho\}$.

Interval Constraint Propagation. Consider two clauses $(x = a + b \lor c \leq 1)$ and $(a = \cos(b))$ together with bounds $\rho(x) = [-10, 10]$, $\rho(a) = [0.7, 20]$, $\rho(b) = [-1, 1.1]$, and $\rho(c) = [2, 3]$. From $\rho(c) = [2, 3]$ and $c \leq 1$ being in conflict with each other, we know that the atom $x = a + b$ has become unit as is the atom $a = \cos(b)$ in the second clause. Interval constraint propagation can now be used to find a (quasi) fixed point of the variables' ranges by propagating their bounds through these two constraints.[3] From $\rho(b) = [-1, 1.1]$ and $a = \cos(b)$ we can deduce that $\rho(a) = ([0.7, 20] \cap \cos([-1, 1.1])) = [0.7, 1]$ using the interval extension of the cosine function. Given that $a \geq 0.7$ we can further confine the range of b to the interval $[-0.8, 0.8]$ by applying the inverse of cosine on the interval of a (and subsequently rounding it outwards safely). Using these bounds in the other constraint $x = a + b$, the bounds on x can be refined to $\rho(x) = [-10, 10] \cap ([0.7, 1] + [-0.8, 0.8]) = [-10, 10] \cap [-0.1, 1.8] = [-0.1, 1.8]$.

Propagation through ODEs. Consider the ODE constraint $\frac{dc}{dt} = 0.01 - 0.05 \cdot c$ stemming from the system given in Fig. 1 as a unit atom. This ODE describes the connecting trajectories between two successive variable instances of c yielded from unwinding the BMC formula—w.l.o.g. called $c^{(0)}$ and $c^{(1)}$. Given $\rho(c^{(0)}) = [0, 0.1]$ and $\rho(c^{(1)}) = [0.15, 10]$, deduction rules for ODEs now try to narrow the boxes for $c^{(0)}$ and $c^{(1)}$. For a fixed upper bound on the time $t \leq 15$ (*temporal horizon*), no solution function of the ODE starting from $[0, 0.1]$ ever exceeds an upper bound of 0.155. This is thus a safe upper bound for $c^{(1)}$ that may be propagated without losing any possible solution. Additionally, no trajectory starting from values for $c^{(0)}$ below 0.082 can reach $\rho(c^{(1)})$ within this time horizon. It is thus also safe to propagate $c^{(0)} \geq 0.082$ as a new lower bound.

4   Contracting Pre- and Postimages of ODE Trajectories

In order to extend the concept of interval-based narrowing operators to ODEs, we first introduce the following definitions. We consider an *ODE problem*

$$\mathcal{P} := \left(\frac{d\vec{x}}{dt}(t) = \vec{f}(\vec{x}(t)), \vec{X}_{pre}, \vec{X}_{post}, \vec{X}_{flow} \right) \tag{2}$$

where $\frac{d\vec{x}}{dt}(t) = \vec{f}(\vec{x}(t))$ is an n-dimensional system of time-invariant differential equations with components $\frac{dx_i}{dt}(t) = f_i(x_1(t), \ldots, x_n(t))$, with $i \in \{1, \ldots, n\}$, and $\vec{X}_{pre}$, $\vec{X}_{post}$, and $\vec{X}_{flow}$ are the *prebox*, *postbox*, and *flowbox* respectively, which are vectors of real-valued intervals for the variables $x_1, \ldots, x_n$. The flowbox is defined by the conjunction of activated flow invariants for the BMC depth i to which $\mathcal{P}$ belongs. The prebox is given by $\vec{X}_{pre} = \rho((x_1^{(i)}, \ldots, x_n^{(i)})^T)$ and the postbox by the corresponding next values $\vec{X}_{post} = \rho((x_1^{(i+1)}, \ldots, x_n^{(i+1)})^T)$. This relationship is illustrated in Fig. 2.

Similarly to the narrowing operators from interval constraint propagation, we define narrowing operators for the ODE problem $\mathcal{P}$ that results from the active triggers on BMC depth i:

---

[3] In practice, not intervals but only the newly deduced bounds are propagated through these constraints. For the sake of illustration we will ignore this enhancement here.

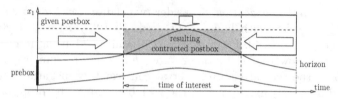

Fig. 2. Find trajectories that emerge from the prebox and eventually reach the postbox

$$\pi_{\rightarrow}^{\mathcal{P}}(\vec{X}_{post}) := \vec{X}_{post} \cap$$

$$\varepsilon\left(\left\{\vec{y} \,\middle|\, \exists \tau_r \in [0, horizon], \exists \vec{x} : [0, \tau_r] \to \mathbb{R}^n : \vec{x}(0) \in \vec{X}_{pre} \quad {}^{//\vec{x}(t)\,\text{emerges}}_{\text{from prebox}}\right.\right.$$

$$\wedge \; \forall \tau \in [0, \tau_r] : \frac{d\vec{x}}{dt}(\tau) = \vec{f}(\vec{x}(\tau)) \quad {}_{//\text{is a solution}}$$

$$\left.\left.\wedge \; \vec{y} = \vec{x}(\tau_r) \; \wedge \; \forall \tau \in [0, \tau_r] : \vec{x}(\tau) \in \vec{X}_{flow}\right\}\right) \quad {}^{//\text{eventually reaches}}_{\substack{\vec{y} \text{ without leaving}\\ \text{the flowbox}}}$$

and similarly for the inverse direction

$$\pi_{\leftarrow}^{\mathcal{P}}(\vec{X}_{pre}) := \vec{X}_{pre} \cap$$

$$\varepsilon\left(\left\{\vec{y} \,\middle|\, \exists \tau_r \in [0, horizon], \exists \vec{x} : [0, \tau_r] \to \mathbb{R}^n : \vec{x}(0) = \vec{y} \quad {}^{//\vec{x}(t)\,\text{emerges}}_{\text{from } \vec{y}}\right.\right.$$

$$\wedge \; \forall \tau \in [0, \tau_r] : \frac{d\vec{x}}{dt}(\tau) = \vec{f}(\vec{x}(\tau)) \quad {}_{//\text{is a solution}}$$

$$\left.\left.\wedge \; \vec{x}(\tau_r) \in \vec{X}_{post} \; \wedge \; \forall \tau \in [0, \tau_r] : \vec{x}(\tau) \in \vec{X}_{flow}\right\}\right) \quad {}^{//\text{reaches postbox}}_{\substack{\text{without leaving}\\ \text{flowbox}}}$$

where ε is an overapproximating interval enclosure of its argument. As all valuations that are reachable from $\vec{X}_{pre}$ are enclosed by the narrowed postbox and all starting points of trajectories that can eventually reach $\vec{X}_{post}$ are enclosed by the narrowed prebox, no solution of $\mathcal{P}$ can be lost by applying $\pi_{\rightarrow}^{\mathcal{P}}$ and $\pi_{\leftarrow}^{\mathcal{P}}$.

For the implementation of $\pi_{\rightarrow}^{\mathcal{P}}$ the goal is thus to enclose all trajectories of $\mathcal{P}$ that are (sufficiently often) differentiable solution functions $\vec{x}$, emerging from the prebox, eventually reaching the postbox, and staying in the flowbox during their evolution. These trajectories allow to define a contraction $\vec{X}'_{post} \subseteq \vec{X}_{post}$ that defines new bounds on the variables of the postbox and must contain all points that are reachable by the trajectories and are included in the given $\vec{X}_{post}$. The postbox thus defines the set of points which are interesting to the surrounding deduction. We call the points of time for which trajectories exist that have a valuation inside $\vec{X}_{post}$ (and hence also in $\vec{X}'_{post}$) the *time of interest* (ToI).

By multiplying the right hand side of the ODE, i.e. $\vec{f}(\vec{x}(t))$, with -1 and using $\vec{X}_{post}$ in place of $\vec{X}_{pre}$ and vice versa, the inverse problem

$$\mathcal{P}^{-1} := \left(\tfrac{d\vec{x}}{dt}(t) = -\vec{f}(\vec{x}(t)), \vec{X}_{post}, \vec{X}_{pre}, \vec{X}_{flow}\right)$$

is generated. $\mathcal{P}^{-1}$ then allows to also contract $\vec{X}_{pre}$ into $\vec{X}'_{pre} \subseteq \vec{X}_{pre}$ by propagating the postbox backwards through the ODE problem using the same ToI.

Enclosure mechanism. In order to enclose these trajectories, we essentially follow the approach of Lohner [13], which is based on calculating Taylor series of the unknown exact solution and enclosures of their truncation errors. It also employs coordinate transformations to fight the so-called *wrapping effect* which occurs when interval boxes are used to enclose non-rectangular or rotated solution sets.

For the unknown exact solutions $\vec{x}(t) = (x_1(t), \ldots, x_n(t))$ of a given ODE problem $\mathcal{P}$ we generate symbolic representations of the truncated Taylor series up to the user-specified order m and the corresponding Lagrange remainder term of order $m + 1$ needed to enclose all possible truncation errors:

$$x_i(t_k + h_k) = \underbrace{\sum_{j=0}^{m} \frac{h_k^j}{j!} \frac{d^j x_i}{dt^j}(t_k)}_{\text{Truncated Taylor series}} + \underbrace{\frac{h_k^{m+1}}{(m+1)!} \frac{d^{m+1} x_i}{dt^{m+1}}(t_k + \theta h_k)}_{\text{Lagrange remainder with } \theta \in]0, 1[}$$

Each enclosure step from t_k to t_{k+1} consists of two tasks: First, we generate a rough overapproximation of the trajectories ("bounding box") over $[t_k, t_{k+1}]$ along with a suitable stepsize $h_k = t_{k+1} - t_k$ for which the bounding box guarantees to enclose all trajectories. This step is based on a theorem given by Lohner [13, p. 263]. Extending the Picard-Lindelöf existence and uniqueness theorem for initial value problems, it allows to easily decide whether a given box encloses the trajectories emerging from a box $\vec{X}_k$ over $[t_k, t_k + h_k]$. We use this property in a greedy search algorithm that extends a bounding box candidate into one direction at a time and checks whether the stepsize for which this box guarantees to be a bounding box has grown. Second, we evaluate the Taylor series over the calculated box $\vec{X}_k$ at t_k and the stepsize h_k and calculate interval bounds for the Lagrange remainder over the bounding box using outward rounding for interval calculations as described in Sect. 2.

We call the vector of truncated Taylor series $\vec{TT}(\vec{X}_k, h_k) =$

$$\begin{pmatrix} \sum_{j=0}^{m} \frac{h_k^j}{j!} \frac{d^{j-1} f_1}{dt^{j-1}}(\vec{X}_k) \\ \vdots \\ \sum_{j=0}^{m} \frac{h_k^j}{j!} \frac{d^{j-1} f_n}{dt^{j-1}}(\vec{X}_k) \end{pmatrix} \supseteq \begin{pmatrix} \sum_{j=0}^{m} \frac{h_k^j}{j!} \frac{d^{j-1} f_1}{dt^{j-1}}(\vec{x}(t_k)) \\ \vdots \\ \sum_{j=0}^{m} \frac{h_k^j}{j!} \frac{d^{j-1} f_n}{dt^{j-1}}(\vec{x}(t_k)) \end{pmatrix} = \begin{pmatrix} \sum_{j=0}^{m} \frac{h_k^j}{j!} \frac{d^j x_1}{dt^j}(t_k) \\ \vdots \\ \sum_{j=0}^{m} \frac{h_k^j}{j!} \frac{d^j x_n}{dt^j}(t_k) \end{pmatrix}$$

with $\vec{X}_k \supseteq \vec{x}(t_k)$ being an overapproximating enclosure of the exact solution set at t_k. The first enclosure at $t_0 = 0$ is given by the prebox: $\vec{X}_0 = \vec{X}_{pre} = \vec{x}(t_0)$. Similarly we call the vector of error enclosure terms $\vec{EE}(\vec{BB}_k, h_k) =$

$$\begin{pmatrix} \frac{h_k^{m+1}}{(m+1)!} \frac{d^m f_1}{dt^m}(\vec{BB}_k) \\ \vdots \\ \frac{h_k^{m+1}}{(m+1)!} \frac{d^m f_n}{dt^m}(\vec{BB}_k) \end{pmatrix} \supseteq \begin{pmatrix} \frac{h_k^{m+1}}{(m+1)!} \frac{d^{m+1} x_1}{dt^{m+1}}(t_k + \theta h_k) \\ \vdots \\ \frac{h_k^{m+1}}{(m+1)!} \frac{d^{m+1} x_n}{dt^{m+1}}(t_k + \theta h_k) \end{pmatrix}$$

where $\vec{BB}_k \supseteq \vec{x}([t_k, t_k + h_k])$ is a bounding box over $[t_k, t_k + h_k]$.

Calculating the interval overapproximation of the symbolically given truncated Taylor term and adding the safely enclosed error remainder yields a box that encloses all trajectories at the next point of time $t_{k+1} = t_k + h_k$:

$$\vec{X}_{k+1}^{\text{naive}} \supseteq \vec{TT}(\vec{X}_k, h_k) + \vec{EE}(\vec{BB}_k, h_k) \tag{3}$$

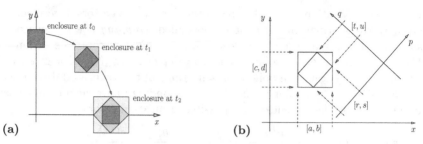

Fig. 3. (a) wrapping effect, (b) coordinate transformation (origin shifted for clarity)

This "naive" enclosure can be iterated up to the given horizon. Evaluating this expression over the interval $[0, h_k]$ of time

$$\vec{X}^{\text{naive}}_{[k,k+1]} \supseteq \vec{TT}(\vec{X}_k, [0, h_k]) + \vec{EE}(\vec{BB}_k, [0, h_k])$$

instead of at the endpoint h_k only, as in (3), yields an enclosure for the timespan of the k-th step. By intersecting the local enclosures and bounding boxes with the given flowbox (not shown here), trajectories that are not interesting any longer because they leave the flowbox can be pruned away. Generating the union

$$\vec{X}^{\text{naive}}_{post} = \bigcup_{k \in \{0,\dots,q-1\}} \vec{X}^{\text{naive}}_{[k,k+1]}, \quad \text{with } t_q \geq horizon$$

of these enclosures, one actually receives a correct enclosure of all possible trajectories emerging from $\vec{X}_{pre}$ over the entire timespan $[t_0, t_q]$.

The quality of this enclosure, however, strongly depends on the influence of the so-called *wrapping effect* which may cause exponential growth of the width of the enclosure over time even when the exact trajectories themselves do not diverge at all. Moore [14] uses the example of a harmonic oscillator to illustrate this effect: $\frac{dx}{dt} = y \wedge \frac{dy}{dt} = -x$. At any point of time, all trajectories emerging from a given initial rectangular box can again be enclosed by a rotated rectangular box. Iterating the naive enclosure algorithm sketched above, each step would, however, "wrap in" additional points by using boxes that are parallel to the coordinate axes. As the algorithm cannot differentiate between points belonging to the exact solution set and points thus wrapped in, all trajectories emerging from this box need to be enclosed, resulting in excessive growth of the enclosure.

The standard approach to mitigate this problem is given already by Moore as well: In order to keep the enclosure tight, the coordinate system is adapted such that it minimizes the wrapping effect, i.e. the coordinate system with respect to which the enclosure boxes are given is rotated and even sheared along with the solution set and thereby allows to enclose the solutions much more tightly. This is illustrated in Fig. 3. Precautions need to be taken in order to avoid that the involved transformation matrices become singular (cf. [13]). The enclosure mechanism described above is therefore extended by determining suitable coordinate systems and performing coordinate transformations, for which we leave out the details here due to space constraints.

As seen above, this method can generate almost optimal enclosures for solution sets that are affine images of the prebox. Lohner points out that we cannot expect this method to work for nonlinear ODEs as good as it works in the case of linear ODEs [13], whose solution sets are always given by affine transformations. Though the method has no fundamental restriction to linear ODEs, coordinate transformations of the described flavor are in general only effective in the case of linear ODEs. The coarseness of the enclosures of nonlinear ODEs thus strongly depends on whether the ODE itself causes a contraction of the solution sets that is stronger than the expansion caused by the wrapping effect.

5   Integration into the iSAT Algorithm

Being a sound narrowing operator for ODE constraints, the above enclosure mechanism can together with unit propagation and interval constraint propagation [3] form the backbone of a constraint solver directly handling the constraint problems defined in Sect. 2. The overall algorithm is an extension of the iSAT arithmetic constraint solver [9] obtained through adding the enclosure-based narrowing operator for ODE constraints. Searching for a satisfying valuation, iSAT starts from the initial interval assignment $\rho(v_i) = [\min \mathrm{dom}(v_i), \max \mathrm{dom}(v_i)]$ for each $v_i \in RV \cup BV$. Its *implication queue*, which is the central data structure mediating the constraint propagation process by holding a list of implied bounds on the individual variables which have their consequences still to be explored, initially contains the respective bounds $v_i \geq \min \mathrm{dom}(v_i)$ and $v_i \leq \max \mathrm{dom}(v_i)$. Furthermore, for each clause in the formula we initialize two — if possible, distinct — "watches" to not yet inconsistent wrt. ρ atoms in the clause. The algorithm then iterates the following steps:

1. If the implication queue is non-empty then retrieve a bound $x \sim c$ from the queue and visit all watched atoms containing x. Visiting watched atoms, the algorithm performs the following actions:

   (a) If the visited atom is not the only watched atom in the clause (i.e., there are two distinct watches) and is not inconsistent under ρ then the algorithm proceeds to the next watched atom.

   (b) If it is not the only watched one but is inconsistent under ρ then we try to replace it by instead watching a still not inconsistent one in the same clause, if possible distinct from the other watched atom. If this replacement strategy succeeds (i.e., there are still two distinct watched atoms in the clause), proceed to the next watched atom, else to step 1c.

   (c) If the replacement strategy failed or if there already was only one watched atom in this clause, this single watched atom is checked for inconsistency with ρ. If inconsistent, a conflict has been detected and the algorithm proceeds to step 4, else to step 1d.

   (d) *Interval constraint propagation* is pursued wrt. the watched atom. I.e., if the watched atom is a bound $x \sim c$, the interval valuation ρ is narrowed accordingly and the bound $x \sim c$ pushed to the implication queue. If the watched literal is an equation $x = \oplus y$ or $x = y \oplus z$, the corresponding contractors (including those originating from the possible reshufflings of the equation) are applied over and over to ρ until no further interval narrowing is achieved.[4] and the resulting new, i.e. narrowed, bounds are pushed onto the implication queue. Thereafter, proceed to the next watched atom, unless the narrowed interval valuation has become empty.

2. Whenever the implication queue obtained by ICP runs empty, we try to advance by *ODE constraint propagation*. In contrast to arithmetic constraints, the method described above to perform enclosures of ODE trajectories requires a definitionally closed ODE problem featuring a defining ODE for each variable occurring freely in itself. As definitions may be distributed over more than one ODE constraint, it is necessary to collect the activated ODE constraints prior to executing the enclosure algorithm. During this first step, the active ODE constraints are grouped by their BMC unwinding depths and common variables, i.e. all activated ODE constraints on BMC depth i are collected and this set is then clustered into the smallest definitionally closed subsets. This yields a family $(\mathcal{P}_{i,j})$ of definitionally closed ODE problems, where each definitionally closed problem $\mathcal{P}_{i,j}$ is an (in general, proper) subset of the ODE constraints active at step i of the BMC problem.

Enclosures are then calculated for the ODE problems $\mathcal{P}_{i,j}$, in a round-robin fashion. Thereby, new bounds on the postbox deduced by forward propagation through an ODE problem $\mathcal{P}_{i,j}$ can subsequently be used to also tighten the prebox by propagation through its inverse $\mathcal{P}_{i,j}^{-1}$ and vice versa. When the deduced bounds cease to become tighter, they are spilled out to the implication queue and thus returned to the other constraint propagation mechanisms, proceeding at step 1. Only if neither arithmetic nor ODE deductions were effective, a decision step is performed.

3. *Decision:* The interval assignment is split by selecting a variable v for which ρ assigns a non-point interval, pushing a bound for v tighter than the bounds assigned by ρ, e.g. a bisecting bound, to the implication queue, applying it to ρ, and proceeding at step 1. We do *not* store the converse of that bound as a possible backtracking point, since an appropriate assertion will in case of conflict be generated by the conflict analysis scheme explained in step 4.

4. *Conflict analysis and backjump:* In order to be able to tell reasons for conflicts (i.e., empty interval valuations) encountered, our solver maintains an implication graph akin to that known from propositional SAT solving: all asserted bounds are recorded in a stack-like data structure which is unwound upon backtracking when the bounds are retracted. Within the stack, each bound not originating from a split, i.e. each bound a originating from a contraction, comes equipped with pointers to its antecedents. The antecedent of a bound a is an equation e, a set of ODE constraints $p_1, \ldots, p_n$ constituting a definitionally closed ODE problem, or some clause c containing the variable v plus a set of bounds for the other free variables of e (of $p_1, \ldots, p_n$ or of c, resp.) which triggered the contraction a.

---

[4] In practice, one stops as soon as the changes become negligible.

By following the antecedents of a conflicting assignment, a reason for the conflict can be obtained: reasons correspond to cuts in the antecedent graph and can be "learned" for pruning the future search space by adding a *conflict clause* containing the disjunction of the negations of the bounds in the reason. We use the unique implication point technique to derive a conflict clause which is general in that it contains few bounds and which is asserting upon *backjumping* (thereby adjusting implication queue and watches) to the decision level where it would have become unit had it existed then already.

The algorithm terminates and reports that a solution has been found if the maximum diameter of the interval valuations $\max_{v \in RV \cup BV} \{\sup \rho(v) - \inf \rho(v)\}$ is smaller than a given, very small threshold (note that the solution thus found actually constitutes a — due to the small threshold, relatively tight — overapproximation of the constraints).

6   First Experimental Results

In order to test the presented ideas, we have implemented the method described in the previous section by straightforward integration into iSAT. This integration is prototypical, lacking any optimizations like reuse of inferences along the isomorphic copies of the transition relation in a BMC problem [8]. Given the extremely high computational cost of computing an interval enclosure of an ODE, such mechanisms for copying inferences across isomorphic sub-formulae rather than recomputing them should provide large speedups. Without such optimizations, performance figures like runtime and memory consumption are not indicative of the actual performance of the algorithm. This implementation can, however, serve as a proof of concept that a tight integration of interval-based ODE-enclosures as yet another interval narrowing operator in ICP provides a viable alternative to conventional schemes of hybrid system analysis, where computation of ODE images and transition images are strictly separate phases.

Heater example. For the heater depicted in Fig. 1, our tool was able to find an error trace at an outside temperature of approximately $-7°C$ at which the indoor temperature ϑ_i stabilizes just below $21°C$, leading to continuous heat supply and, consequently, build-up of a critical concentration of exhaust fumes.

Bouncing ball. The bouncing ball is a simple, classical example of a hybrid system, suitable as a test for the handover between the different interval narrowing mechanisms. In free fall, height h and speed v of the ball are governed by $\frac{dh}{dt} = v$ and $\frac{ds}{dt} = -g$ where g is the gravitational constant. Whenever the ball hits the ground at $h = 0$, it bounces by discontinuous change of the sign of v. Searching for a ground impact at a time $t \geq 8$ starting from a limited start height, solving required 664 hand-overs between equation-based and ODE-based interval narrowing, entailing the computation of 1754 ODE enclosures which delivered 55

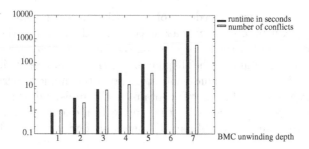

Fig. 4. Runtime and number of conflicts for the moving heaters benchmark

tightened intervals and 5 conflicts[5], the latter being memorized through conflict-driven learning and thus eliminating multiple candidate traces.

Moving heaters. The current limitations of our implementation become visible in the "room heating benchmark" proposed in [7]. For the scenario (two heaters in three rooms, fixed initial temperature, reach a temperature below threshold), we can check up to seven unwindings of the transition relation but fail to check the resulting formulae for larger unwinding depths due to quickly increasing runtimes. For all unwinding depths, over 97% of the runtime was spent on enclosing ODEs. Figure 4 shows the runtime and the number of conflicts that occured during ICP and ODE deduction. Since backjumping after encountering a conflict always involves undoing decisions and deductions, especially also deductions obtained from ODE enclosures, this data strongly indicates that a more sophisticated scheme for storing the results from ODE deductions (e.g. by adding them as clauses that are preserved during backjumps) could have a significant impact on runtimes.

7   Conclusion

Within this paper, we have presented a seamless integration of safe numeric integration of ODEs into SAT-modulo-theory (SMT) solving. From the practical point of view, such an integration extends the scope of SMT algorithms from mixed arithmetic-Boolean problems involving relations defined by arithmetic inequations to problems additionally comprising relations defined by initial value problems of ODEs. It therefore permits the direct application of SMT to hybrid systems without the need for a preprocessing step replacing ODEs with pre-post-relations defined by (in-)equations. Technically, it involves the embedding of interval-based safe numeric approximation of ODE images and ODE preimages as a further rule for theory propagation in SMT solving.

First experiments show the feasibility of such an integration, yet do also indicate that the computational cost of the individual ODE-related deductions is

---

[5] I.e. proofs that the gap between the set of endpoints of one and startpoints of another partial trace cannot be bridged by any continuous trajectory.

extremely high. In the future we will thus try to drastically reduce their frequency by adding further ODE-related pruning operators and through proven methods for reuse of deductions within isomorphic subformulae [8] in order to attain performance competitive with existing tools optimized for the domain.

References

1. Alur, R., Pappas, G.J. (eds.): HSCC 2004. LNCS, vol. 2993. Springer, Heidelberg (2004)
2. Audemard, G., Bozzano, M., Cimatti, A., Sebastiani, R.: Verifying industrial hybrid systems with MathSAT. ENTCS 89(4) (2004)
3. Benhamou, F., Granvilliers, L.: Continuous and interval constraints. In: Rossi, F., van Beek, P., Walsh, T. (eds.) Handbook of Constraint Programming, Foundations of Artificial Intelligence, ch. 16, pp. 571–603. Elsevier, Amsterdam (2006)
4. Biere, A., Cimatti, A., Zhu, Y.: Symbolic model checking without BDDs. In: Cleaveland, W.R. (ed.) TACAS 1999. LNCS, vol. 1579. Springer, Heidelberg (1999)
5. Davis, M., Logemann, G., Loveland, D.: A machine program for theorem proving. Communications of the ACM 5, 394–397 (1962)
6. Dutertre, B., de Moura, L.: A Fast Linear-Arithmetic Solver for DPLL(T). In: Ball, T., Jones, R.B. (eds.) CAV 2006. LNCS, vol. 4144, pp. 81–94. Springer, Heidelberg (2006)
7. Fehnker, A., Ivančić, F.: Benchmarks for hybrid systems verification. In: Alur, Pappas (eds.) in [1] pp. 326–341
8. Fränzle, M., Herde, C.: HySAT: An efficient proof engine for bounded model checking of hybrid systems. Formal Methods in Syst. Design 30(3), 179–198 (2007)
9. Fränzle, M., Herde, C., Ratschan, S., Schubert, T., Teige, T.: Efficient solving of large non-linear arithmetic constraint systems with complex boolean structure. JSAT Special Issue on Constraint Programming and SAT 1, 209–236 (2007)
10. Ganzinger, H., Hagen, G., Nieuwenhuis, R., Oliveras, A., Tinelli, C.: DPLL(t): Fast decision procedures. In: Alur, R., Peled, D.A. (eds.) CAV 2004. LNCS, vol. 3114. Springer, Heidelberg (2004)
11. Henzinger, T.A., Horowitz, B., Majumdar, R., Wong-Toi, H.: Beyond HYTECH: Hybrid systems analysis using interval numerical methods. In: Lynch, N.A., Krogh, B.H. (eds.) HSCC 2000. LNCS, vol. 1790, pp. 130–144. Springer, Heidelberg (2000)
12. Hickey, T., Wittenberg, D.: Rigorous modeling of hybrid systems using interval arithmetic constraints. In: Alur, Pappas (eds.) in [1], pp. 402–416
13. Lohner, R.J.: Enclosing the solutions of ordinary initial and boundary value problems. In: Computerarithmetic: Scientific Computation and Programming Languages, pp. 255–286. Teubner, Stuttgart (1987)
14. Moore, R.E.: Automatic local coordinate transformation to reduce the growth of error bounds in interval computation of solutions of ordinary differential equations. In: Ball, L.B. (ed.) Error in Digital Computation, vol. II, pp. 103–140. Wiley, New York (1965)
15. Ramdani, N., Meslem, N., Candau, Y.: Rechability of unvertain nonlinear systems using a nonlinear hybridization. In: Egerstedt, M., Mishra, B. (eds.) HSCC 2008. LNCS, vol. 4981, pp. 415–428. Springer, Heidelberg (2008)
16. Stauning, O.: Automatic Validation of Numerical Solutions. PhD thesis, Danmarks Tekniske Universitet, Kgs.Lyngby, Denmark (1997)

SMELS: Satisfiability Modulo Equality with Lazy Superposition

Christopher Lynch[1] and Duc-Khanh Tran[2]

[1] Clarkson University, USA
[2] Max-Planck-Insitut für Informatik, Germany

Abstract. We give a method for extending efficient SMT solvers to handle quantifiers, using Superposition inference rules. In our method, the input formula is converted into CNF as in traditional first order logic theorem provers. The ground clauses are given to the SMT solver, which runs a DPLL method to build partial models. The partial model is passed to a Congruence Closure procedure, as is normally done in SMT. Congruence Closure calculates all reduced (dis)equations in the partial model and passes them to a Superposition procedure, along with a justification. The Superposition procedure then performs an inference rule, which we call Justified Superposition, between the (dis)equations and the nonground clauses, plus usual Superposition rules with the nonground clauses. Any resulting ground clauses are provided to the DPLL engine. We prove the completeness of this method, using a nontrivial modification of Bachmair and Ganzinger's model generation technique. We believe this combination uses the best of both worlds, an SMT process to handle ground clauses efficiently, and a Superposition procedure which uses orderings to handle the nonground clauses.

1 Introduction

Deciding the satisfiability of a formula with respect to a background theory is crucial for verification. There exist specialized reasoning methods for many background theories of interest, such as lists, arrays, records, integer-offsets, and linear arithmetic, etc., which go under the name of Satisfiability Modulo Theories (SMT) solvers, but they used to be limited to the particular class of first order formulae without quantifiers. Finding good heuristics for lifting SMT techniques from ground to quantified formulas is a current topic of research. For instance [5,8,1] use heuristics based on the instantiation method of the theorem prover Simplify [11]. However those heuristics are incomplete, i.e. they may fail to prove unsatisfiability of formulas. Another problem is that instantiation-based heuristics cannot say anything about satisfiable formulas. This is because they instantiate universally quantified variables, and it is never known when it is safe to stop instantiating. On the other hand, there exist mature Automated Theorem Provers (ATPs), Spass [17], Vampire [15], E [16] to name a few, implementing Resolution/Superposition calculi (see e.g., [3,14]) which are complete for first order logic with or without equality. A key property of the aforementioned

Cha et al. (Eds.): ATVA 2008, LNCS 5311, pp. 186–200, 2008.

ATP's is that an ordering is placed on the literals which yields a drastic reduction in the search space. On several classes of problems, it causes termination and therefore the inference procedure becomes a decision procedure. However, Resolution ATPs are believed to not be as fast as SAT solvers on ground propositional problems having complex boolean structures. The same thing is true for Superposition ATPs versus SMT solvers on ground equational problems. Recently, the topic of instantiation-based ATP's has become popular. See [6] for some examples. These ATP's take better advantage of the boolean structure, but they do not take advantage of orderings.

In this paper we are concerned with the problem of lifting SMT solvers (with equality as a background theory) from ground to quantified formulas in an efficient and complete way. We propose a novel method, that we call Satisfiability Modulo Equality with Lazy Superposition (SMELS), which combines the best of both worlds ATPs and SMT: completeness for quantified problems; and efficiency for ground problems. An ordering is used for the quantified part of the problem and a SMT solver is used for the ground part. We show how to do this without losing completeness. As far as we know, this is the first complete combination of a SAT solver with orderings. It is designed for a set of clauses that is mostly ground, with a small nonground part representing a theory. If the clauses are mostly nonground, traditional methods would probably work better.

In SMELS, the input formula is first converted into CNF as in traditional first order logic theorem provers. The set of clauses is partitioned into two subsets: a set of ground clauses and a set of nonground clauses. Then we run a DPLL solver to build a partial model, i.e. a set of ground literals, along with justifications of elements in the model. The Congruence Closure algorithm is used to reduce the partial model and to calculate justifications of elements in the reduced partial model. The reduced partial model is next checked for consistency together with the nonground clauses using a Superposition procedure. The main issue is that the literals in the reduced partial model are not consequences of the input formula, and hence any formula derived by the Superposition procedure may not be a consequence of the input formula. To cope with this problem, we design a rule called Justified Superposition, involving a literal from the reduced partial model and a nonground clause, taking into account the justification of the literal. The newly derived clause is a consequence of the input formula, and thereby we ensure soundness of SMELS. We also perform usual Superposition inferences among nonground clauses. Any ground clauses resulting from the Superposition procedure are provided to the DPLL solver. No Superposition inferences among ground clauses are performed because they are treated by DPLL and the Congruence Closure algorithm.

Figure 1 summarizes how SMELS works. In Figure 1, DPLL and Congruence Closure are handled by a standard SMT tool. The SMELS inference system described in this paper shows the nonground inference rules. We assume that DPLL and Congruence Closure have done their job, and the SMELS inference system gives the necessary Superposition rules for completeness. Therefore, it

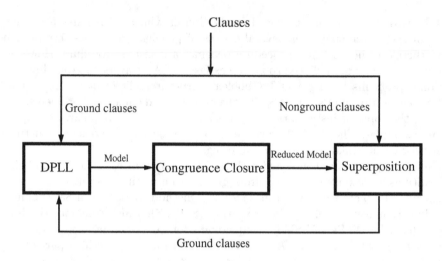

Fig. 1. SMELS architecture

will not be necessary to refer to DPLL and Congruence Closure in this paper, except to explain how SMT tools work.

We prove completeness of SMELS, using a nontrivial modification of Bachmair and Ganzinger's model generation technique. Completeness of SMELS ensures that one of the following will happen when applying our calculus: (i) the original set of clauses is satisfiable, and after a finite number of steps the process will halt, giving a ground model modulo the nonground background theory; or (ii) the original set of clauses is satisfiable, and in the limit, there is a set of clauses for which we can build a model; or (iii) the original set of clauses is unsatisfiable, and after a finite number of steps the process will halt with an unsatisfiable set of ground clauses. Possibilities (i) and (iii) are the most interesting compared to instantiation-based heuristics.

The paper is structured as follows. Section 2 introduces some background notions. Section 3 presents a complete inference system, called SLR, for first order logic. Section 4 presents SMELS, which is a complete calculus for first order logic with equality. In Section 5, we outline the completeness proof of SMELS. We do not prove the completeness of SLR as it is a special case of SMELS. In Section 6 we give an example to illustrate the ideas. Section 7 discusses closely related works. Section 8 concludes and mentions future works. Detailed proofs can be found in the appendix.

2   Preliminaries

We assume the usual rewriting definitions, as defined in [10]. Atoms are represented by symbols A, B, literals by L. An atom is also called a positive literal, and the negation of an atom is a negative literal. Equations will be written as $s = t$, disequations as $s \neq t$. The formula $s \bowtie t$ is either $s = t$ or $s \neq t$. Given a set of ground literals M, then M^+ (resp. M^-) represents the positive (resp. negative) literals in M. A clause is s disjunction of literals, thought of as a multiset. If L is A (resp. $\neg A$) then $\neg L$ is $\neg A$ (resp. A).

Given a set of clauses S, let $g(S)$ (resp. $v(S)$) be the set of ground (resp. nonground) clauses in S. Define $Gr(S)$ as the set of all ground instances of S. For a clause C, let $g(C)$ (resp. $v(C)$) be the multiset of ground (resp. nonground) literals in C. Let $GL(S)$ be the set of all ground literals in S.

We will be working on ground instances of clauses, called *closures* [4]. If L is a literal and θ is a ground substitution, we write $L \cdot \theta$ to indicate the θ instance of L. A closure represents a ground instance, but makes it clear which is the original literal and which is the grounding substitution. The literal L is the *skeleton* of the closure, and θ is the *substitution*. A clause can be considered as a multiset of closures, where the meaning of the closure $L \cdot \theta$ is just $L\theta$. When it is convenient, we will treat the closure $L \cdot \theta$ as the instantiated literal $L\theta$.

We define a quasiordering $\preceq_g$ on closures, so that for literals K and L and substitutions σ and θ, $K \cdot \sigma \preceq_g L \cdot \theta$ if 1) K and L are both ground, or 2) K and L are both nonground, or 3) K is ground and L is nonground. Define the ordering $\preceq_r$ to be a reduction ordering on terms, extended to equations by considering them as multisets of terms, then extended to disequations in such a way that a disequation $s \neq t$ is larger than an equation $s = u$ if $s \succ_r t$ and $s \succ_r u$. The ordering $\preceq_r$ is extended to closures so that $K \cdot \sigma \preceq_r L \cdot \theta$ if $K\sigma \preceq_r L\theta$. This is the way a reduction ordering is normally extended to literals in theorem proving. Next we define an ordering $\preceq_i$, called an *instance ordering*, defined on closures of literals to be the lexicographic combination of $\preceq_g$ and $\preceq_r$. So, to compare two closures in the instance ordering, first check if one skeleton is ground and the other is nonground, otherwise apply the substitution and compare using the reduction ordering. The instance ordering is extended to clauses by considering them as multisets of literals.

An interpretation M is defined as a set of ground equations. For an interpretation M and an equation $s = t$, we write $M \models s = t$ if $s = t$ is a logical consequence of M. We write $M \models s \neq t$ if $M \not\models s = t$. Given an interpretation M and a ground clause C, $M \models C$ if and only if $M \models L$ for some L in C. Given a set of ground clauses S, an interpretation M is a *model of S* if $M \models C$ for all C in S. If T is a set of literals, we say that T is *satisfiable* if T has a model.

For a reduction ordering $\preceq_r$ an interpretation M and a literal L, let $M^L = \{L' \in M \mid L' \preceq_r L\}$. We write $M \models_{\preceq_r} L$ if $M^L \models L$. An equation $s = t$ has a rewrite proof using E if s and t have the same normal forms with respect to E, and we will write $E \vdash s = t$. For an interpretation M and an equation $s = t$, we write $M \vdash s = t$ if there is a set of equations $E \subseteq M$ such that $E \vdash s = t$.

For a clause C, $M \models_{\preceq_r} C$ (resp. $M \vdash C$) if $M \models_{\preceq_r} L$ (resp. $M \vdash L$) for some $L \in C$. For a set of ground clauses S, we write $M \models_{\preceq_r} S$ (resp. $M \vdash S$) if $M \models_{\preceq_r} C$ (resp. $M \vdash C$) for all $C \in S$. A set of literals T is *consistent with respect to* $\models_{\preceq_r}$ if there is no disequation $s \neq t \in T$ such that $T \models_{\preceq_r} s = t$, similarly T is *consistent with respect to* $\vdash$ if there is no disequation $s \neq t \in T$ such that $T \vdash s = t$. For a reduction ordering $\preceq_r$, a given interpretation M

and an equation $s = t$, $M \models s = t$ and $M \vdash s = t$ and $M \models_{\preceq_r} s = t$ are not equivalent. However, if M is confluent then $\models$, $\models_{\preceq_r}$ and $\vdash$ coincide.

For example, consider $M = \{a = b, a = c\}$. If $\preceq_r$ is an ordering such that $b \preceq_r a$ and $c \preceq_r a$, then $M \models b = c$ but $M \not\models_{\preceq_r} b = c$ and $M \not\vdash b = c$. But if $\preceq_r$ is defined such that $a \preceq_r b$ and $a \preceq_r c$, then $M \models b = c$, $M \models_{\preceq_r} b = c$, and $M \vdash b = c$.

3   Resolution Inference System

We give a Resolution inference system for first order logic, which is a special case of the Superposition inference system given later. We give this inference system to illustrate some ideas in a simpler setting, and to relate our work to some previous work.

We represent a *truth assignment GM* as the set of ground literals made true by GM. GM is a *satisfying truth assignment* for a set of ground clauses S if GM makes all clauses in S true. Given a set of clauses S, assume a SAT procedure has been run on $g(S)$ to produce a satisfying truth assignment GM of $g(S)$. SAT procedures also construct justification functions from which lemmas are constructed. Justification functions are formally defined as follows.

Definition 1. *Given a set of ground clauses and literals S, we define $cons(S)$ as the set of literals implied by S. Let G be a set of ground clauses. Let M be a truth assignment satisfying G. A function $j : cons(M) \to \mathcal{P}(M)$ is called an (M, G)-justification function if $L \in cons(G \cup j(L))$ for all L in $cons(M)$.*

If $j(L) = \{L\}$, then L is said to be self-justified. *If all literals in $cons(M)$ are self-justified, then j is a* self-justification function.

Given a set of ground clauses G and a truth assignment M there is always a self-justification function, since M is always a consequence of M.

Example 1. Let $G = \{p, \neg p \vee q, r \vee \neg s, \neg q \vee s \vee \neg t\}$. Then $M = \{p, q, \neg s, \neg t\}$ is a satisfying truth assignment of G. Let j_1 be the function such that $j_1(p) = \emptyset$, $j_1(q) = \emptyset$, $j_1(\neg s) = \{\neg s\}$, and $j_1(\neg t) = \{\neg s\}$. Then j_1 is a justification function. But there are many justification functions. For example, let j_2 be identical to j_1 except that $j_2(\neg t) = \{p, \neg s\}$. Then j_2 is also a justification function. There is also the self-justification function j_3 such that $j_3(L) = \{L\}$ for all L in M.

Let us briefly explain the relevance of justification functions. As mentioned previously, our aim is to check consistency of the truth assignment GM along with the set of nonground clauses $v(S)$. However, the literals in GM may not be consequences of S, and anything derived from GM and $v(S)$ using Resolution inferences may not be a consequence of S. Our solution to this problem is to consider the justifications of the literals in GM, that is for a given literal $L \in GM$, $\neg j(L) \vee L$ is a consequence of the input set of clauses S.

We need the following notion for the presentation of our Resolution inference system.

Definition 2. *Given a clause C containing literal L and a substitution σ, we say that L is σ-var-maximal in C if $L \in v(C)$ and there is no literal $L' \in C$ such that $L' \cdot \sigma \succ_i L \cdot \sigma$.*

For completeness of our Resolution inference system, we need the following assumption.

Assumption 1. *Each satisfying truth assignment GM of $g(S)$ has been extended to the atoms of $GL(S)$ in any way such that it is defined on all literals of $GL(S)$.*

The $(GM, g(S))$-justification function j must be extended along with the extension of the model.

A simple way to extend the justification function is to make all the additional literals self-justified.

We call our Resolution inference system SLR, Satisfiability with Lazy Resolution. It consists of the inference rules in Figure 2. The Nonground Resolution and Factoring inference rules differ from the usual Ordered Resolution and Factoring inference rules in two ways:

1. They are only allowed on nonground clauses.
2. They are not performed on the maximal literals of the premises, but instead on the maximal nonground literals of the premises.

The Justified Resolution rule involves one nonground premise C with maximal nonground literal L. It produces a new clause D, where a ground instance of L is replaced by its justification. This is similar to the process in SAT procedures where a lemma is created. The Justified Resolution inference rule could be viewed as a Resolution inference between C and a new clause $C' = L\sigma \vee \neg j(L\sigma)$. However, C' does not need to be explicitly created. By definition of justification function, C' is implied by $g(S)$. Note that the Justified Resolution rule may still apply if all clauses are nonground but contain ground literals, because those the truth assignment is extended to give a truth value to all ground literals.

In the case where the literal L is self-justified, we call the inference *Self-justified Resolution*. This corresponds to an inference with $L\sigma \vee \neg L\sigma$, a tautology. The inference then effectively just applies σ to its premise. This is a proper instantiation, because L must be nonground since it is in $v(C)$. Therefore, SLR with a self-justification function can be viewed as a combination of an Instantiation-based inference system such as InstGen[12] with Ordered Resolution, the first such combination we are aware of.

In the inference rules, we have not considered selection functions. Our completeness results can be adapted to deal with selection rules, but we chose to present just the ordered case to make the presentation as simple as possible.

4   Superposition Inference System

Now we extend our inference system to first order logic with equality.

Nonground Resolution	$\dfrac{\Gamma \vee A \quad \Delta \vee \neg B}{(\Gamma \vee \Delta)\sigma}$	if $\sigma = mgu(A, B)$, $A\sigma \in max(v(\Gamma \vee A)\sigma)$, and $\neg B\sigma \in max(v(\Delta \vee \neg B)\sigma)$
Factoring	$\dfrac{\Gamma \vee A \vee B}{(\Gamma \vee A)\sigma}$	if $\sigma = mgu(A, B)$ and $A\sigma \in max(v(\Gamma \vee A \vee B)\sigma)$
Justified Resolution	$\dfrac{\Gamma \vee \neg L}{\Gamma\sigma \vee \neg j(L\sigma)}$	if $L\sigma \in GM$, and $\neg L\sigma \in max(v(\Gamma \vee \neg L)\sigma))$

where all premises are from $v(S)$, GM is a satisfying truth assignment of $g(S)$ which is defined on $GL(S)$, and j is a $(GM, g(S))$ justification function.

Fig. 2. Inference Rules of SLR

Definition 3. *A set M of ground equations and disequations is called* reduced *if M never contains a literal of the form $L[s]$ along with another literal of the form $s = t$, where $s \succ_r t$.*

A set M of ground equations and disequations is called left-reduced *if there does not exist $u[s] \bowtie v$ and $s = t$ in M with $u[s] \succ_r v$ and $s \succ_r t$.*

If M is left-reduced then M^+ is a convergent rewrite system. A Congruence Closure algorithm can replace a set of literals with a logically equivalent reduced set of literals. The Congruence Closure algorithm may add new constants by flattening, which we call *extension constants*. Extension constants are generally assumed to be smaller than all other symbols.

Again, we assume a set of clauses S, a satisfying truth assignment GM extended so that it is defined on all atoms of $GL(S)$, and a $(GM, g(S))$ justification function, as in Assumption 1. The only difference between here and the nonequality case is that we now assume in addition the following.

Assumption 2. *GM is reduced.*

We will see in Section 5 that the reducedness of GM is necessary for the completeness of SMELS. Of course, if GM is not reduced, the Congruence Closure algorithm can be used to reduce it.

The inference rules for SMELS, Superposition Modulo Equality with Lazy Superposition, are given in Figure 3. The ideas are all the same as in the nonequality case. The inference rules are like the usual Superposition rules on nonground clauses, except that the ordering only involves the nonground literals. The Justified Superposition rules can be viewed as a Superposition between a nonground clause and an implicit ground clause. We think this will be efficient, because no inferences between ground clauses are necessary, and orderings are used to prevent many cases of nontermination.

Let S be a set of clauses. Let GM be a reduced satisfying truth assignment of $g(S)$, extended so that it is defined on $GL(S)$. Let j be a $(GM, g(S))$ justification function. A SMELS inference system is parameterized by GM and j. So we will refer to SMELS(GM, j) to indicate what the parameters are. An actual implementation of this inference system will consist of a fair application of the inference rules. When an inference rule adds a new ground clause, that clause will be added to $g(S)$, and a new satisfying truth assignment GM may be created. Therefore, the parameters of SMELS may change as inferences are performed.

Nonground Superposition	$\dfrac{\Gamma \vee u[s'] \bowtie v \quad \Delta \vee s = t}{(\Gamma \vee \Delta \vee u[t] \bowtie v)\sigma}$	$(i), (ii), (iii), (iv)$
Eq. Resolution	$\dfrac{\Gamma \vee s \neq s'}{\Gamma \sigma}$	(v)
Eq. Factoring	$\dfrac{\Gamma \vee s = t \vee s' = t'}{(\Gamma \vee t \neq t' \vee s = t')\sigma}$	$(iii), (iv), (vi)$
Justified Superposition Into	$\dfrac{\Gamma \vee u[s'] \bowtie v}{(\Gamma \vee \neg j(s = t) \vee u[t] \bowtie v)\sigma}$	$(i), (ii), (iii)$
Justified Superposition From	$\dfrac{\Delta \vee s = t}{(\Delta \vee \neg j(u[s'] \bowtie v) \vee u[t] \bowtie v)\sigma}$	$(i), (iii), (iv)$

where all premises are from $v(S)$, GM is a reduced satisfying truth assignment of $g(S)$ which is defined on $GL(S)$, j is a $(GM, g(S))$ justification function, s' is not a variable in Nonground Superposition and Superposition Into, $\sigma = mgu(s, s')$, $s = t \in GM$ in Justified Superposition Into, $u[s'] \bowtie v \in GM$ in Justified Superposition From, and

(i) $u[s']\sigma \not\preceq_r v\sigma$, *(ii)* $u[s'] \bowtie v$ is σ-var- maximal in its clause, *(iii)* $s\sigma \not\preceq_r t\sigma$, *(iv)* $s = t$ is σ-var-maximal in its clause, *(v)* $s \neq s'$ is σ-var-maximal in its clause, *(vi)* $t\sigma \not\preceq_r t'\sigma$ and $s'\sigma \not\preceq_r t'\sigma$.

Fig. 3. Inference Rules of *SMELS*

A closure C is *redundant* in a set of closures S if the following hold:

1. there is a subset E of S, where E is a set of equations; and
2. all members of E are smaller than C with respect to both orderings $\preceq_i$ and $\preceq_r$; and
3. there is a closure D such that either D is in S or D is a tautology; and
4. D is smaller than C with respect to both orderings $\preceq_i$ and $\preceq_r$; and
5. for every literal L in D, there is a literal L' in C such that L and L' are equivalent modulo E and L' is larger or equal to L with respect to both orderings $\preceq_i$ and $\preceq_r$.

Our definition of redundant closures obeys the usual properties of redundancy. In particular, if C is redundant in S, and S' is the result of removing a redundant clause from S, then C is still redundant in S'. Also, usual redundancy elimination techniques such as simplification, tautology deletion and some cases of subsumption fit well into our redundancy notion.

An inference is said to be redundant in S if its premises are redundant in S or its conclusion is redundant in S. We say that S is *saturated with respect to SMELS* if all SMELS(GM, j) inferences are redundant in S, for some satisfying truth assignment GM and justification function j.

We define a *SMELS derivation* as a sequence of triples of the form

$$(S_0, G_0, j_o), (S_1, G_1, j_1), \cdots$$

where each S_i is a set of clauses, each G_i is a truth assignment defined over $GL(S_i)$ such that $G_i \models g(S_i)$, and each j_i is a $(G_i, g(S_i))$ justification function. Furthermore, one of the following is true of each S_{i+1}

1. S_{i+1} is a conservative extension of S_i, or
2. S_{i+1} is formed by removing a redundant clause from S_i, or
3. S_{i+1} is formed by removing a ground clause C that is implied by $g(S_i) \setminus \{C\}$.

The conditions on S_{i+1} are more general than the conditions in the standard definition of theorem proving derivation. We allow conservative extensions to allow for the fact that the SMT procedure may add new symbols. We also allow for any ground clause to be removed if it is implied by other ground clauses, although strictly speaking theorem provers generally only remove redundant clauses. For example, given the equation $g(f(a)) = b$, an SMT procedure may create a new constant c, and add equations $f(a) = c$ and $g(c) = b$. This creates a conservative extension of the original set of clauses. Then the procedure may delete $g(f(a)) = b$ which is implied by the new clauses.

We have assumed the existence of one satisfying truth assignment of the set of ground clauses whenever this set is satisfiable. This is trivial if the derivation is finite. The main problem is the case where the derivation is infinite, and ground clauses are added infinitely. We need to ensure that there are some truth values for the ground literals that occur infinitely often in the same triple, so that we can assume the existence of a single satisfying truth assignment. This motivates the following definitions of persistence and fairness for infinite derivations.

Given a SMELS derivation $(S_0, G_0, j_o), (S_1, G_1, j_1), \cdots$, we say that a clause C is *persistent* if $C \in \bigcup_{i \geq 0} \bigcap_{j \geq i} S_j$. This is the usual definition of persistent clauses. If L is a ground literal, and M is a set of ground literals, we say that the pair (L, M) is *persistent* if $\bigcup \{(S_i, G_i, j_i) \mid L \in G_i, j_i(L) = M\}$ is infinite. This means that the ground literal occurs infinitely often in the derivation with the same justification.

A Nonground Superposition, Equality Resolution, or Equality Factoring inference is *persistent* in a SMELS derivation if its premises are persistent. A Justified Superposition Into derivation is *persistent* if its premise is persistent, and the pair $(s = t, j(s = t))$ is persistent. A Justified Superposition From derivation is *persistent* if its premise is persistent, and the pair $(u \bowtie v, j(u \bowtie v))$ is persistent.

A SMELS derivation is *fair* if all persistent inferences are redundant and there exists an enumeration of all literals $L_1, L_2, \cdots$ and an n such that for all $m \geq n$, $L_i \in j_m(L_j)$ implies that $i < j$. In this definition, we call n a *justification stabilizer* of the derivation. This last condition ensures that we will not continually add new literals and use those literals to justify previous literals, which may create a non-well-founded chain that could destroy completeness.

Given a fair SMELS derivation $(S_0, G_0, j_0), (S_1, G_1, j_1), \cdots$, let T_0 be the sequence $G_n, G_{n+1}, \cdots$, where n is a justification stabilizer of the derivation. Therefore, T_0 is just the subsequence of the derivation where we can be assured that literals are justified by smaller ones. We define a sequence of sequences inductively, based on the enumeration $A_1, A_2, \cdots$ of the positive literals. We need to define what T_i is, in terms of T_{i-1} and A_i from the enumeration of positive literals. The idea is to make T_i be a subsequence of T_{i-1} such that either A_i or $\neg A_i$ occurs in all ground truth assignments, and has the same justification each time.

We define T_i as follows:

1. If there exists an M such that (A_i, M) is persistent in the sequence T_{i-1}, then T_i is the subsequence of all triples (S, G, j) in T_{i-1} such that $A_i \in G$ and $j(A_i) = M$. In this case, define $Gprod_i = \{A_i\}$, and define $jprod_i = M$

2. Else if there exists an M such that $(\neg A_i, M)$ is persistent in the sequence T_{i-1}, then T_i is the subsequence of all triples (S, G, j) in T_{i-1} such that $\neg A_i \in G$ and $j(\neg A_i) = M$. In this case, define $Gprod_i = \{\neg A_i\}$, and define $jprod_i = M$.

3. Else T_i is the subsequence of all triples (S, G, j) in T_{i-1} such that $A_i \notin G$ and $\neg A_i \notin G$. In this case, define $Gprod_i = \emptyset$.

By definition, each T_i must be infinite. Let $GM = \bigcup Gprod_i$, and let $just$ be the justification function so that for all $L \in GM$ with $Gprod_i = \{L\}$, we have $just(L) = jprod_i$. Let S be the set of all persisting clauses in the derivation. Then every SMELS$(GM, just)$ inference with a premise in S is redundant.

5   Completeness

We will show that if S is saturated with respect to SMELS and does not contain the empty clause then there is a model M of S with $GM^+ \subseteq M$. This shows that if the inference rules are applied fairly, then one of the following three things will happen.

1. The original set of clauses is satisfiable, and after a finite number of steps the process will halt with a set of clauses S and a satisfying truth assignment GM of $g(S)$ such that $GM^+ \cup v(S) \models S$.

2. The original set of clauses is satisfiable, and in the limit, there is a set of clauses S and a satisfying truth assignment GM of $g(S)$ such that $GM^+ \cup v(S) \models S$.

3. The original set of clauses is unsatisfiable, and after a finite number of steps the process will halt with a set of clauses S such that $g(S)$ is unsatisfiable.

The first item is the most interesting. Instantiation methods based on Simplify do not have this property, because they instantiate universally quantified variables, and it is never known when it is safe to stop instantiating. Of course, our inference system is only useful if the first item will happen frequently, and we suspect that it will, because of the orderings. In this case, we can think of $v(S)$ as representing a theory, and then GM is actually a satisfying truth assignment of S modulo the theory $v(S)$. This is useful, because the entire model M cannot always be represented with a finite number of ground clauses. In the case of the second item above, we consider the limit of the saturation process. In this case, the satisfying truth assignment GM referred to is a limit of the satisfying truth assignments constructed during the saturation process, which was defined in the previous section.

For the completeness proof, we build a model as in Bachmair and Ganzinger's model construction process. However, our model is more complicated because of the satisfying truth assignment GM. We construct a model of $v(S)$, which must be consistent (wrt. $\models_{\preceq_r}$) with GM. The proof of completeness will work as follows. Let $Gr(v(S))$ represent all the ground closures of closures in $v(S)$. As usual, we will create an interpretation M. But M will be created in such a way that $M \models_{\preceq_r} S$. Then we will prove that this implies that $M \models S$. Informally, the model is constructed inductively on the clauses of $Gr(v(S))$, using the ordering $\preceq_i$. The idea of using $\preceq_i$ is that the inference system takes place over nonground clauses, but the completeness proof works over ground instances of those clauses. In order for the ground inference to be able to be lifted, we need to remember whether the clause it was an instance of was ground or not.

Definition 4. *Let S be a set of nonground clauses. For a given ground closure $C \cdot \sigma$ of the form $(\Gamma \vee s = t) \cdot \sigma$ in $Gr(S)$, define $I_{C\sigma} = \{(s = t)\sigma\}$ if and only of all the following hold:*

1. $(s = t) \cdot \sigma$ *is maximal in $C \cdot \sigma$ wrt. $\preceq_i$,*
2. $M_{\prec_i C\sigma} \not\models_{\preceq_r} C\dot\sigma$,
3. *there is no $u \neq v \in GM^-$ such that $M_{\prec_i C\sigma} \cup (s = t)\sigma \models_{\preceq_r} u = v$,*
4. $(s = t)\sigma$ *is left irreducible by $M_{\prec_i C\sigma}$, and*
5. Γ *does not contain an equation $s = u$ such that $M_{\prec_i C\sigma} \models_{\preceq_r} (s = t)\sigma$ implies*
   $M_{\prec_i C\sigma} \models_{\preceq_r} (s = u)\sigma,$

where $M_{\prec_i C\sigma} = \bigcup_{D\theta \prec_i C\sigma \wedge D\theta \in Gr(S)} I_{D\theta} \cup GM^+$. We say that $C\dot\sigma$ produces $(s = t)\sigma$ when $I_{C\sigma} = \{(s = t)\sigma\}$; and $C\sigma$ is called a productive clause.

Definition 5. *Define $M_{C\sigma} = M_{\prec_C C\sigma} \cup I_{C\sigma}$.*
   Define $M_\infty = \bigcup_{C\sigma \in Gr(S)} M_{C\sigma}$.

Let us compare this definition with the usual definition in Bachmair and Ganzinger's model construction process. The first difference from the usual completeness proof is that we build a model using $\models_{\preceq_r}$ instead of $\models$. Recall that in SMELS we begin with a model of the ground clauses, and we extend this to a model of all the nonground clauses. Therefore the model construction is only defined over the nonground clauses. The second difference of our model construction compared with the usual definition is that we begin our construction using GM^+ instead of the empty set as is normally done. The third difference in our method is that whenever we want to add an equation to the model, we can only add it if the model is consistent with GM^-. As a consequence, the completeness proof in our case is more difficult than usual. One of the main issues is to show the confluence of the model constructed. In the usual model construction it is trivial, as a result of the fact that only reduced equations are added to the model. Here, it is not so simple. It is true that we only add reduced literals to the model. So literals added during the model construction process can be assumed be reduced on the left hand side. Equations in GM^+ are reduced by GM^+ by definition. However, it is possible that we may add an equation during the model construction process that reduces the left hand side of an equation from GM^+. Therefore, the model we are constructing may not be fully reduced.

But by saturation, we can show that in the end the model will be confluent. As in the usual completeness proof, the confluence of the model constructed is the key to proving completeness of SMELS.

Theorem 1 (Refutation Completeness). *Let S be saturated with respect to SMELS. Then S is satisfiable if and only if it does not contain the empty clause.*

6   Example

Let S_0 contain the following clauses:

$$p(a, b) = p_1$$
$$p(c, d) = p_2$$
$$p(e, f) = p_3$$
$$p_1 = p_2 \lor p_1 = p_3$$
$$a \neq c$$
$$a \neq e$$
$$p(x_1, y_1) \neq p(x_2, y_2) \lor x_1 = x_2$$

By running a DPLL procedure on $g(S_0)$, we obtain a model M_0. Suppose that the DPLL engine finds a model M_0, then a Congruence Closure algorithm reduces the model M_0 to the model G_0, as in the table below.

$g(S_0)$	M_0	G_0	Justification of G_0
$p(a, b) = p_1$	$p(a, b) = p_1$	$p(a, b) = p_2$	$\{p_1 = p_2\}$
$p(c, d) = p_2$	$p(c, d) = p_2$	$p(c, d) = p_2$	$\emptyset$
$p(e, f) = p_3$	$p(e, f) = p_3$	$p(e, f) = p_3$	$\emptyset$
$p_1 = p_2 \lor p_1 = p_3$	$p_1 = p_2$	$p_1 = p_2$	$\{p_1 = p_2\}$
$a \neq c$	$a \neq c$	$a \neq c$	$\emptyset$
$a \neq e$	$a \neq e$	$a \neq e$	$\emptyset$

Now the Superposition procedure is applied on $G_0 \cup v(S_0)$. For instance, we have the following *Justified Superposition Into* inference

$$\frac{p(x_1, y_1) \neq p(x_2, y_2) \lor x_1 = x_2}{p_1 \neq p_2 \lor p_2 \neq p(x_2, y_2) \lor a = x_2}$$

where the equation $p(a, b) = p_2$ in the G_0 is used, and its justification is $p_1 = p_2$.

After an exhaustive application of inference rules and redundancy deletion, we obtain a new set of clauses, noted S_1. The new clauses resulting from the Superposition procedure are those in the $S_1 \setminus S_0$ column of the following table.

G_0	$v(S_0)$	$S_1 \setminus S_0$
$p(a,b) = p_2$	$p(x_1,y_1) \neq p(x_2,y_2) \vee x_1 = x_2$	$p_1 \neq p_2 \vee p_2 \neq p(x_2,y_2) \vee a = x_2$
$p(c,d) = p_2$		$p_2 \neq p(x_2,y_2) \vee c = x_2$
$p(e,f) = p_3$		$p_3 \neq p(x_2,y_2) \vee e = x_2$
$p_1 = p_2$		$p_1 \neq p_2 \vee a = c$
$a \neq c$		$p_1 \neq p_2 \vee p_2 \neq p_3 \vee a = e$
$a \neq e$		

Again, by running a DPLL procedure and a Congruence Closure algorithm on $g(S_1)$, we obtain the following:

$g(S_1)$	M_1	G_1	Justification of G_1
$p(a,b) = p_1$	$p(a,b) = p_1$	$p(a,b) = p_3$	$\emptyset$
$p(c,d) = p_2$	$p(c,d) = p_2$	$p(c,d) = p_2$	$\emptyset$
$p(e,f) = p_3$	$p(e,f) = p_3$	$p(e,f) = p_3$	$\emptyset$
$p_1 = p_2 \vee p_1 = p_3$	$p_1 = p_3$	$p_1 = p_3$	$\emptyset$
$a \neq c$	$a \neq c$	$a \neq c$	$\emptyset$
$a \neq e$	$a \neq e$	$a \neq e$	$\emptyset$
$p_1 \neq p_2 \vee a = c$	$p_1 \neq p_2$	$p_3 \neq p_2$	$\emptyset$
$p_1 \neq p_2 \vee p_2 \neq p_3 \vee a = e$			

The Superposition procedure is again applied on $G_1 \cup v(S_1)$. The new set of clauses obtained is noted S_2. The new clauses resulting from the Superposition procedure are in the $S_2 \setminus S_1$ column of the following table.

G_1	$v(S_1)$	$S_2 \setminus S_1$
$p(a,b) = p_3$	$p(x_1,y_1) \neq p(x_2,y_2) \vee x_1 = x_2$	$p_3 \neq p(x_2,y_2) \vee a = x_2$
$p(c,d) = p_2$	$p_1 \neq p_2 \vee p_2 \neq p(x_2,y_2) \vee a = x_2$	$a = e$
$p(e,f) = p_3$	$p_2 \neq p(x_2,y_2) \vee c = x_2$	
$p_1 = p_3$	$p_3 \neq p(x_2,y_2) \vee e = x_2$	
$a \neq c$		
$a \neq e$		
$p_3 \neq p_2$		

Then DPLL outputs unsatisfiable running on the new set of clauses $g(S_2)$ because it contains both $a = e$ and $a \neq e$.

7   Related Works

There are various techniques and tools adressing the satisfiability problems for first order formulae. SMT solvers such as [5,8,1], are quite effective and efficient on certain classes of problems. SMELS has, at least in principle, several advantages compared to SMT solvers. On quantified problems, it is complete, in contrast with SMT solvers, which use incomplete heuristics to handle quantifiers. On satisfiable quantified problems, SMELS may have an edge over SMT, because on many examples, the ordering will cause SMELS to terminate with the result satisfiable while SMT solvers diverge or are forced to halt with the result unknown.

Instantiation theorem proving based on [12] also uses an SMT solver at the bottom to handle ground clauses resulting from instantiations. However the calculus given in [12] does not use ordering to limit search space. Instead, the authors propose semantic selection of clauses to be used for instantiations. On satisfiable quantified problems, SMELS may have an edge over the method in [12] because it may terminate while the method in [12] will diverge. Of course, SMELS is interesting on these problems only if it often halts. We suspect that it will often happen because SMELS uses powerful orderings to limit the search space and prevent many nonterminating cases. The Model Evolution calculus [7] provides another theorem proving method based on model finding. It is a lifted version of the DPLL method to first order logic. It is not easy to compare Resolution/Superposition theorem proving with Instatiation theorem proving based on Model Evolution calculus. For some problems Reslution/Superposition methods are better, and for some others instantiation methods based on Model Evolution calculus are better. On satisfiable quantified problems, we suspect that methods like [7] perform better as they are designed to be model finders.

Resolution/Superposition theorem provers like Spass [17] and Vampire [15] use splitting to improve efficiency. Vampire uses explicit propositional symbols to keep track splitting while splitting in Spass relies on labels to keep track the split levels. Since SMELS does not perform any ground inferences in the Superposition procedure but delegates them to an efficient SMT solver instead, we believe that it can be better than existing Resolution/Superposition theorem provers on large problems containing mostly ground clauses. If the clauses are mostly nonground, traditional methods would probably work better.

The theorem prover haRVey [9] combines a Boolean solver (SAT or BDD) with the equation themorem prover E [16]. The integration is loose, compared to SMELS, because resulting non-unit ground clauses are handled by E, and not by the SMT solver like in SMELS.

8   Conclusion

We have presented SMELS, which is a novel complete method for solving satisfiability in first order logic with equality. We believe that SMELS inherits the best of the two worlds SMT and ATPs: a DPLL(T) procedure to handle efficiently ground equational clauses; and a complete Superposition procedure to efficiently handle nonground equational clauses using powerful orderings. We plan to implement SMELS and to compare it with existing SMT and ATP methods. An interesting line of future work is to study how SMELS can be used to derive decision procedures for finitely presented theories, along the line of [2]. Finally, we plan to study how to integrate a solver for linear arithmetic into SMELS. Although we know that there exists no complete calculus for the first order theory of linear arithmetic and uninterpreted symbols [13], it is interesting to identify subclasses of formulae which enjoy completeness.

References

1. The Yices SMT Solver, http://yices.csl.sri.com/tool-paper.pdf
2. Armando, A., Ranise, S., Rusinowitch, M.: A Rewriting Approach to Satisfiability Procedures. Journal of Information and Computation 183(2), 140–164 (2003)
3. Bachmair, L., Ganzinger, H.: Resolution theorem proving. In: Robinson, A., Voronkov, A. (eds.) Handbook of Automated Reasoning, ch.2, vol. 1, pp. 19–100. North Holland, Amsterdam (2001)
4. Bachmair, L., Ganzinger, H., Lynch, C., Snyder, W.: Basic paramodulation and superposition. In: Kapur, D. (ed.) CADE 1992. LNCS, vol. 607, pp. 462–476. Springer, Heidelberg (1992)
5. Barrett, C., Tinelli, C.: CVC3. In: Damm, W., Hermanns, H. (eds.) CAV 2007. LNCS, vol. 4590, pp. 298–302. Springer, Heidelberg (2007)
6. Baumgartner, P.: Logical engineering with instance-based methods. In: Pfenning, F. (ed.) CADE 2007. LNCS (LNAI), vol. 4603, pp. 404–409. Springer, Heidelberg (2007)
7. Baumgartner, P., Tinelli, C.: The model evolution calculus as a first-order DPLL method. Artificial Intelligence 172, 591–632 (2008)
8. de Moura, L., Bjorner, N.: Z3: An Efficient SMT Solver. In: Ramakrishnan, C.R., Rehof, J. (eds.) TACAS 2008. LNCS, vol. 4963, pp. 337–340. Springer, Heidelberg (2008)
9. Déharbe, D., Ranise, S.: Light-Weight Theorem Proving for Debugging and Verifying Units of Code. In: Press, I.C.S. (ed.) Proc. of the Int. Conf. on Software Engineering and Formal Methods (SEFM 2003) (2003)
10. Dershowitz, N., Jouannaud, J.-P.: Rewrite Systems, Handbook of Theoretical Computer Science, ch. 6, vol. B, pp. 244–320 (1990)
11. Detlefs, D., Nelson, G., Saxe, J.B.: Simplify: A Theorem Prover for Program Checking. Technical Report HPL-2003-148, HP Laboratories (2003)
12. Ganzinger, H., Korovin, K.: New directions in instantiation-based theorem proving. In: Proc. 18th IEEE Symposium on Logic in Computer Science (LICS 2003), pp. 55–64. IEEE Computer Society Press, Los Alamitos (2003)
13. Korovin, K., Voronkov, A.: Integrating linear arithmetic into superposition calculus. In: Duparc, J., Henzinger, T.A. (eds.) CSL 2007. LNCS, vol. 4646, pp. 223–237. Springer, Heidelberg (2007)
14. Nieuwenhuis, R., Rubio, A.: Paramodulation-based theorem proving. In: Robinson, A., Voronkov, A. (eds.) Hand. of Automated Reasoning. Elsevier and MIT Press (2001)
15. Riazanov, A., Voronkov, A.: The design and implementation of VAMPIRE. AI Commun. 15(2), 91–110 (2002)
16. Schulz, S.: E – A Brainiac Theorem Prover. Journal of AI Communications 15(2/3), 111–126 (2002)
17. Weidenbach, C.: Spass version 0.49. Journal of Automated Reasoning 14(2), 247–252 (1997)

Controllable Test Cases for the Distributed Test Architecture[*]

Robert M. Hierons[1], Mercedes G. Merayo[1,2], and Manuel Núñez[2]

[1] Department of Information Systems and Computing, Brunel University
Uxbridge, Middlesex, UB8 3PH United Kingdom
`rob.hierons@brunel.ac.uk, mgmerayo@fdi.ucm.es`
[2] Departamento de Sistemas Informáticos y Computación
Universidad Complutense de Madrid, Madrid, Spain
`mn@sip.ucm.es`

Abstract. In the distributed test architecture, a system with multiple ports is tested using a tester at each port/interface, these testers cannot communicate with one another and there is no global clock. Recent work has defined an implementation relation for testing against an input-output transition system in the distributed test architecture. However, this framework placed no restrictions on the test cases and, in particular, allowed them to produce some kind of nondeterminism. In addition, it did not consider the test generation problem. This paper explores the class of controllable test cases for the distributed test architecture, defining a new implementation relation and a test generation algorithm.

1 Introduction

If the system under test (SUT) has physically distributed interfaces/ports then it is normal to place a tester at each port. If testing is black-box, there is no global clock, and the testers cannot directly communicate with each other then we are testing in the distributed test architecture, which has been standardised by the ISO [1]. The use of the distributed test architecture reduces test effectiveness (see, for example, [2,3,4,5]).

The area of testing against a state-based model has received much attention [6,7,8,9]. The main advantage of using a formal approach is that many testing processes can be automated (see [10] for a discussion on the advantages of formal testing and [11] for a survey). However, most previous work on testing in the distributed test architecture has considered deterministic finite state machine (DFSM). The IOTS formalism is more general: in a DFSM input and output alternate and DFSMs have a finite state structure and are deterministic. The last restriction is particularly problematic since distributed systems are often nondeterministic. While the implementation relation **ioco** [9], that is usually used in testing from an IOTS, has been adapted in a number of ways (see, for example,

---

[*] Research partially supported by the Spanish MEC project WEST/FAST (TIN2006-15578-C02-01) and the Marie Curie project MRTN-CT-2003-505121/TAROT.

Cha et al. (Eds.): ATVA 2008, LNCS 5311, pp. 201–215, 2008.

[12,13,14,15,16,17,18,19]), only recently has the problem of testing from an IOTS in the distributed test architecture been investigated [20].This work introduced an implementation relation **dioco** but this assumes that any deterministic test case can be applied including test cases that are not *controllable*. Controllable test cases are such that there does not exist a situation where a local tester has observed a trace after which either it should apply an input or wait for output, depending on what has happened at the other port. The problem is that in such situations local testers do not know when they have to apply their input.

This paper defines what it means for a test case to be controllable and shows that we can decide in polynomial time whether a test case has this property. We define a new implementation relation for controllable testing in the distributed test architecture. Finally, we give an algorithm for generating these test cases. This paper therefore extends the work of [20] by considering controllable testing. In addition, it is the first paper to give a test generation algorithm for testing against an IOTS in the distributed test architecture.

2   Preliminaries

This section defines input-output transition systems and associated notation and outlines the distributed test architecture.

2.1   Input Output Transition Systems

We use *input-output transition systems* to describe systems. These are labelled transition systems in which we distinguish between inputs and outputs [9].

Definition 1. *An* input-output transition system *s (IOTS) is defined by (Q, I, O, T, q_{in}) in which Q is a countable set of states, $q_{in} \in Q$ is the initial state, I is a countable set of inputs, O is a countable set of outputs, and $T \subseteq Q \times (I \cup O \cup \{\tau\}) \times Q$, is the transition relation, where τ represents an internal (unobservable) action. A transition (q, a, q') means that from state q it is possible to move to state q' with action $a \in I \cup O \cup \{\tau\}$. We let $\mathcal{IOTS}(I, O)$ denote the set of IOTSs with input set I and output set O.*

State $q \in Q$ is quiescent *if from q it is not possible to produce output without first receiving input. We can extend T to T_δ by adding (q, δ, q) for each quiescent state q. We let $\mathcal{A}ct = I \cup O \cup \{\delta\}$ denote the set of observable actions and so $\tau \notin \mathcal{A}ct$. Process s is* input-enabled *if for all $q \in Q$ and $?i \in I$ there exists $q' \in Q$ such that $(q, ?i, q') \in T$. s is* output-divergent *if it can reach a state in which there is an infinite path that contains outputs and internal actions only.*

Given action a and process s, $a.s$ denotes the process that performs a and then becomes s. Given a countable set S of processes, $\sum S$ denotes the process that can nondeterministically choose to be any one of the processes in S. We will sometimes use the binary operator $+$ to denote the election between processes.

Processes and states are effectively the same since we can identify a process with its initial state and we can define a process corresponding to a state q of s by making q the initial state. Thus, we use states and process and their notation interchangeably.

We use the normal notation in which we precede the name of an input by ? and the name of an output by !. We assume that all processes are input-enabled and are not output-divergent. The intuition behind the first restriction is that systems should be able to respond to any signal received from the environment. Regarding the second restriction, in the distributed testing architecture quiescent states can be used to combine the traces observed at each port and reach a verdict. If a process is output-divergent then it can go through an infinite sequence of non-quiescent states, so that local traces cannot be combined.

Traces are sequences of visible actions, possibly including quiescence, and are often called *suspension traces*. Since they are the only type of trace we consider, we call them *traces*. The following is standard notation in the context of **ioco**.

Definition 2. *Let* $s = (Q, I, O, T, q_{in})$ *be an IOTS.*

1. *If* $(q, a, q') \in T_\delta$, *for* $a \in \mathcal{Act} \cup \{\tau\}$, *then we write* $q \xrightarrow{a} q'$.
2. *We write* $q \xRightarrow{a} q'$, *for* $a \in \mathcal{Act}$, *if there exist* $q_0, \ldots, q_m$ *and* $k \geq 0$ *such that* $q = q_0$, $q' = q_m$, $q_0 \xrightarrow{\tau} q_1, \ldots, q_{k-1} \xrightarrow{\tau} q_k$, $q_k \xrightarrow{a} q_{k+1}$, $q_{k+1} \xrightarrow{\tau} q_{k+2}, \ldots, q_{m-1} \xrightarrow{\tau} q_m$.
3. *We write* $q \xRightarrow{\epsilon} q'$ *if there exist* $q_1, \ldots, q_k$, *for* $k \geq 1$, *such that* $q = q_1$, $q' = q_k$, $q_1 \xrightarrow{\tau} q_2, \ldots, q_{k-1} \xrightarrow{\tau} q_k$.
4. *We write* $q \xRightarrow{\sigma} q'$ *for* $\sigma = a_1 \ldots a_m \in \mathcal{Act}^*$ *if there exist* $q_0, \ldots, q_m$, $q = q_0$, $q' = q_m$ *such that for all* $0 \leq i < m$ *we have that* $q_i \xRightarrow{a_{i+1}} q_{i+1}$.
5. *We write* $s \xRightarrow{\sigma}$ *if there exists* q' *such that* $q_{in} \xRightarrow{\sigma} q'$ *and we say that* σ *is a trace of* s. *We let* $\mathcal{Tr}(s)$ *denote the set of traces of* s.

Let $q \in Q$ *and* $\sigma \in \mathcal{Act}^*$ *be a trace. We consider*

1. q **after** $\sigma = \{q' \in Q | q \xRightarrow{\sigma} q'\}$
2. $out(q) = \{!o \in O | q \xRightarrow{!o}\}$
3. *Given a set* $Q' \subseteq Q$, *we consider that* Q' **after** $\sigma = \cup_{q \in Q'} q$ **after** σ *and* $out(Q') = \cup_{q \in Q'} out(q)$.

Process s *is* deterministic *if for all* $\sigma \in \mathcal{Act}^*$, $|out(q_{in} \text{ after } \sigma)| \leq 1$.

In testing from a single-port IOTS it is usual to use **ioco** [9,21].

Definition 3. *Given* $s, i \in \mathcal{IOTS}(I, O)$ *we write* i **ioco** s *if for every trace* $\sigma \in \mathcal{Tr}(s)$ *we have that* $out(i \text{ after } \sigma) \subseteq out(s \text{ after } \sigma)$.

2.2   Multi-port Input-Output Transition Systems

The two standard (ISO) test architectures are shown in Figure 1. In the local test architecture a global tester interacts with all of the ports of the SUT. In the distributed test architecture there is a local tester at each port [1]. For the sake of simplicity, in this paper we will sometimes assume that there are only two ports which we call U and L. However, all the results can be easily extended to $n > 2$ ports. We use the term IOTS where there are multiple ports and when there is only one port we use the term single-port IOTS.

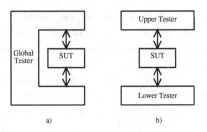

Fig. 1. The local and distributed test architectures

For an IOTS (Q, I, O, T, q_{in}) with port set $\mathcal{P} = \{U, L\}$ we partition I into sets I_U and I_L of inputs that can be received at U and L respectively. Similarly, O can be partitioned into sets O_U and O_L that can be produced at U and L respectively[1]. Inputs and outputs will often be labelled in a manner that makes their port clear. For example, $?i_U$ is an input at U and $!o_L$ is an output at L. A *global tester* observes both ports and so observes a trace in $\mathcal{Act}^*$, called a *global trace*. These traces can be transformed into two *local traces*.

Definition 4. *Let $\sigma \in \mathcal{Act}^*$ and $p \in \mathcal{P}$. We let $\pi_p(\sigma)$ denote the projection of σ onto p; this is called a* local trace. *The function π_p can be defined by the following rules.*

1. $\pi_p(\epsilon) = \epsilon$.
2. *If $z \in (I_p \cup O_p \cup \{\delta\})$ then $\pi_p(z\sigma) = z\pi_p(\sigma)$.*
3. *If $z \in I_q \cup O_q$, for $q \neq p$, then $\pi_p(z\sigma) = \pi_p(\sigma)$.*

Given global traces $\sigma, \sigma' \in \mathcal{Act}^*$ we write $\sigma \sim \sigma'$ if σ and σ' cannot be distinguished in the distributed test architecture. Thus, $\sigma \sim \sigma'$ if and only if $\pi_U(\sigma) = \pi_U(\sigma')$ and $\pi_L(\sigma) = \pi_L(\sigma')$.

The **dioco** implementation relation has been devised for testing in the distributed test architecture using a function *in* that returns the input potion of a trace [20].

Definition 5. *Let $s, i \in \mathcal{IOTS}(I, O)$. We write i **dioco** s if for every trace σ such that $i \overset{\sigma}{\Longrightarrow} i'$ for some i' that is in a quiescent state, if there is a trace $\sigma_1 \in \mathcal{Tr}(s)$ such that $in(\sigma_1) \sim in(\sigma)$ then there exists a trace $\sigma' \in \mathcal{Tr}(s)$ such that $s \overset{\sigma'}{\Longrightarrow}$ and $\sigma' \sim \sigma$.*

Only traces reaching quiescent states are considered in **dioco** since these allow us to put together the local traces; a non-quiescent state can receive additional output at a port and this situation is uncontrollable [20]. Since in this paper all processes are input-enabled we can simplify the previous definition.

---

[1] An alternative, used in [20], is to allow outputs to be tuples of values but the formalism used in this paper has the advantage of simplifying the notation and analysis.

Proposition 1. *Given* $s, i \in \mathcal{IOTS}(I, O)$, *if* s *and* i *are input-enabled then we have that* i **dioco** s *if and only if for every trace* σ *such that* $i \overset{\sigma}{\Longrightarrow} i'$ *for some* i' *that is in a quiescent state, there exists a trace* σ' *such that* $s \overset{\sigma'}{\Longrightarrow}$ *and* $\sigma' \sim \sigma$.

3 Test Cases for the Distributed Test Architecture

A test case is a process with a finite number of states that interacts with the SUT. A test case may correspond to a test objective: It may be intended to examine some part of the behaviour of the SUT. When designing test cases it is thus simpler to consider *global test cases*, that is, test cases that can interact with all of the ports of the system. However, in the distributed test architecture we do not have a global tester that can apply a global test case: Instead we place a *local tester* at each port. The local tester at port p only observes the behaviour at p and can only send input to the SUT at p.

A global test case is an IOTS that has the same input and output sets as the specification process s. A *local test case* is a tuple containing a test case for each of the available ports and has the input and outputs sets corresponding to its port. If $s \in \mathcal{IOTS}(I, O)$ then every global test case for s is a process from $\mathcal{IOTS}(I, O \cup \{\delta\})$. In our setting, with two ports, a local test case for s is a pair (t_U, t_L) such that $t_p \in \mathcal{IOTS}(I_p, O_p \cup \{\delta\})$ $(p \in \{U, L\})$. Test cases, either global or local, synchronize on values with either specifications or SUTs and do not contain internal actions. As usual, (global or local) test cases cannot block output from the SUT: If the SUT produces an output then the test case should be able to record this situation. Thus, for every state t' of a test case t and output $!o \in O$ we have that $t' \overset{!o}{\longrightarrow}$. $\bot$ is the global test case that cannot send input to the SUT and thus whose traces are all elements of $(O \cup \{\delta\})^*$. We let $\bot_p$ denote the corresponding local tester for port p, whose set of traces is $(O_p \cup \{\delta\})^*$.

Definition 6. *Let* $s \in \mathcal{IOTS}(I, O)$ *be an IOTS with port set* $\mathcal{P} = \{U, L\}$. *A local test case is a tuple* (t_U, t_L) *of local testers in which for all* $p \in \mathcal{P}$ *we have that* t_p *is a test case in* $\mathcal{IOTS}(I_p, O_p \cup \{\delta\})$. *In addition, if* $t_p \overset{\sigma}{\Longrightarrow} t'_p$ *for some* σ *then* $t'_p \overset{!o_p}{\Longrightarrow}$ *for all* $!o_p \in O_p \cup \{\delta\}$.

The following function, defined in [20], takes a global test case and returns local testers.

Definition 7. *Given global test case* t *and port* p, $local_p(t)$ *denotes the local tester at* p *defined by the following rules.*

1. *If* t *is the null process* $\bot$ *then* $local_p(t)$ *is* $\bot_p$.
2. *If* $a \in I_p \cup O_p \cup \{\delta\}$ *then* $local_p(a.t) = a.local_p(t)$.
3. *If* $a \in I_q \cup O_q$, $q \neq p$, *then* $local_p(a.t) = local_p(t)$.
4. $local_p(t_1 + \cdots + t_k) = local_p(t_1) + \cdots + local_p(t_k)$.

Next we introduce a notion of parallel composition between a system and a (global or local) test case.

Definition 8. *Let $s \in \mathcal{IOTS}(I, O)$, t be a global test case for s and $t' = (t_U, t_L)$ be a local test case for s. We introduce the following notation.*

1. *$s \| t$ denotes the application of t to s. The system $s \| t$ belongs to $\mathcal{IOTS}(I, O)$ and is formed by s and t synchronizing on all visible actions. Internal actions can be autonomously performed by s.*
2. *$s \| t'$ denotes the application of t' to s, often represented by $s \| t_U \| t_L$. $s \| t'$ belongs to $\mathcal{IOTS}(I, O)$ and it is formed from s and t' by s and t_U synchronizing on actions in $I_U \cup O_U$ and by s and t_L synchronizing on actions in $I_L \cup O_L$. s, t_U, and t_L synchronize on δ. Internal actions can be autonomously performed by s.*
3. *Since $s \| t$ and $s \| t'$ are systems, the notation introduced in Definition 2 can be applied to them.*
4. *We let $\mathcal{T}r(s, t)$ (resp. $\mathcal{T}r(s, t')$) denote the set of traces that can result from $s \| t$ (resp. $s \| t'$) and their prefixes.*

The following notation is used in order to reason about the application of test cases to systems.

Definition 9. *Let $s, i \in \mathcal{IOTS}(I, O)$ and t be a test case.*

1. *A trace σ is a test run for i with t if $i \| t \overset{\sigma\delta}{\Longrightarrow}$ (and so at the end of this test run the SUT is quiescent).*
2. *Implementation i **passes** test run σ with t for s if there exists $\sigma' \in \mathcal{T}r(s)$ such that $\sigma' \sim \sigma$. Otherwise i **fails** σ with t for s.*
3. *Implementation i **passes** test case t for s if i **passes** every possible test run of i with t for s and otherwise i **fails** t.*

A local test case t is said to be *deterministic* for a specification s if the interaction between s and t cannot reach a situation in which both local testers are capable of sending input [20] since in such a situation, the order in which these inputs are received by the SUT cannot be known.

Definition 10. *Let $s \in \mathcal{IOTS}(I, O)$. We say that the local test case (t_U, t_L) is deterministic for s if there do not exist traces σ_1 and σ_2, with $\sigma_2 \sim \sigma_1$, and $a_1, a_2 \in I$, with $a_1 \neq a_2$, such that $s \| t_U \| t_L \overset{\sigma_1 a_1}{\Longrightarrow}$ and $s \| t_U \| t_L \overset{\sigma_2 a_2}{\Longrightarrow}$.*

The local testers being deterministic does not guarantee that the local test case is deterministic. For example, deterministic local testers t_U and t_L could both start by sending input to the SUT.

Now let us consider a specification s such that $\mathcal{T}r(s)$ is the set of prefixes of $?i_U!o_L!o_U?i_L$ plus the traces obtained by completing this to make it input-enabled. We could have a local test case (t_U, t_L) in which t_U sends $?i_U$ and expects to observe $!o_U$ and t_L sends $?i_L$ after observing $!o_L$. Then (t_U, t_L) is deterministic for s but t_L does not know when to send $?i_L$ and this is a form of nondeterminism. We obtain the same problem with the corresponding global test case if we wish to apply it in the distributed test architecture. The following, which adapts a definition from [22] for nondeterministic finite state machines, is a necessary and sufficient condition under which we avoid this form of nondeterminism.

Definition 11. *A (local or global) test case t is* controllable *for IOTS s if there does not exist port $p \in \mathcal{P}$, $\sigma_1, \sigma_2 \in Tr(s,t)$ and $?i_p \in I_p$ with $\sigma_1 ?i_p \in Tr(s,t)$, $\sigma_2 ?i_p \notin Tr(s,t)$ and $\pi_p(\sigma_1) = \pi_p(\sigma_2)$.*

If a test case is controllable then, as long as no failures occur in testing, each input is supplied by a local tester at the point specified in the test case.

Proposition 2. *Let us suppose that we are testing $i \in \mathcal{IOTS}(I,O)$ with a test case t that is controllable for specification $s \in \mathcal{IOTS}(I,O)$. If an input $?i$ is supplied after $\sigma \in Tr(s,t)$ then $\sigma ?i \in Tr(t)$.*

Proof. Proof by contradiction: assume that $?i$ is supplied after the trace $\sigma \in Tr(s,t)$, where $\sigma ?i \notin Tr(t)$. Since $?i$ is supplied after σ at a port $p \in \mathcal{P}$ there exists a trace $\sigma' ?i \in Tr(s,t)$ such that $\pi_p(\sigma) = \pi_p(\sigma')$. Thus, there exists $\sigma, \sigma' \in Tr(s,t)$, port $p \in \mathcal{P}$ and input $?i \in I_p$ that should be sent after σ' but not after σ and $\pi_p(\sigma) = \pi_p(\sigma')$. This contradicts t being controllable for s as required.   □

If a test case t is controllable for s and a global trace $\sigma \in Tr(s,t)$ has been produced then each local tester knows what to do next (apply an input or wait for output). It is natural to now ask whether we can always implement a controllable global test cases using a controllable local test case.

Proposition 3. *If t is a global test case for $s \in \mathcal{IOTS}(I,O)$ and $t_p = local_p(t)$ for $p \in \{U, L\}$ then:*

1. *$Tr(s,t) \subseteq Tr(s,(t_U,t_L))$*
2. *$Tr(s,(t_U,t_L)) \subseteq Tr(s,t)$ if and only if t is controllable.*

Proof. It is straightforward to prove that for all $\sigma \in Tr(t)$ and $p \in \mathcal{P}$ there exists $\sigma_p \in Tr(local_p(t))$ such that $\sigma_p = \pi_p(\sigma)$. The first part of the result follows from the fact that $Tr(s,t) = Tr(s) \cap Tr(t)$ and $Tr(s,(t_U,t_L)) = Tr(s) \cap Tr((t_U,t_L))$, where $Tr((t_U,t_L))$ is the set of traces formed from interleavings of traces in $Tr(t_U)$ and $Tr(t_L)$ and so $Tr(t) \subseteq Tr((t_U,t_L))$.

Now assume that t is controllable and we prove that for all $\sigma \in Tr(s,(t_U,t_L))$ we have that $\sigma \in Tr(s,t)$, using proof by induction on the length of σ. Clearly the result holds for the base case $\sigma = \epsilon$. Thus, let us assume that the result holds for all traces of length less than $k > 0$ and σ has length k. Thus, $\sigma = a\sigma'$ for some $a \in \mathcal{A}ct$.

If $a = \delta$ then $t_U \xrightarrow{a} t'_U$, $t_L \xrightarrow{a} t'_L$, and $t \xrightarrow{a} t'$ for some t'_U, t'_L, t' and the result follows by observing that $t'_U = local_U(t')$, $t'_L = local_L(t')$, and t' is controllable for the process s' such that $s \xRightarrow{a} s'$ and thus by applying the inductive hypothesis to σ'.

Let us assume that $a \in I \cup O$. Without loss of generality, a occurs at U and so $a \in I_U \cup O_U$. Thus, there exists t'_U such that $t_U \xrightarrow{a} t'_U$. Since $t_U = local_U(t)$ it must be possible to have event a at U in t before any other event at U and so there must exist some minimal $\sigma_L \in (I_L \cup O_L)^*$ such that $\sigma_L a \in Tr(t)$. But $\pi_U(\sigma_L) = \pi_U(\epsilon)$ and so, since t is controllable for s, by the minimality of σ_L we must have that $\sigma_L = \epsilon$. Thus, there exists t' such that $t \xrightarrow{a} t'$. The result now follows observing that $t'_U = local_U(t')$, $t_L = local_L(t')$, t' is controllable for the process s' such that $s \xRightarrow{a} s'$ and by applying the inductive hypothesis to σ'.

Next we prove the left to right implication: We assume that $Tr(s, (t_U, t_L)) \subseteq Tr(s, t)$ and will prove that t is controllable for s. The proof is by contradiction. We assume that t is not controllable for s and so there exist $\sigma_1, \sigma_2 \in Tr(s, t)$ and port $p \in \mathcal{P}$ such that $\pi_p(\sigma_1) = \pi_p(\sigma_2)$ and there exists $?i_p \in I_p$ such that $\sigma_1?i_p \in Tr(s, t)$ and $\sigma_2?i_p \notin Tr(s, t)$. But clearly, since $\sigma_1?i_p \in Tr(s, t)$, we have that $\pi_p(\sigma_1)?i_p \in Tr(t_p)$ and so, since $\pi_p(\sigma_1) = \pi_p(\sigma_2)$ we have that $\pi_p(\sigma_2)?i_p \in Tr(t_p)$. Further, for $q \in \mathcal{P}$, $q \neq p$, we have that $\pi_q(\sigma_2) \in Tr(t_q)$ and so $\sigma_2?i_p \in Tr((t_U, t_L))$. Finally, since $\sigma_2 \in Tr(s, t)$ and s is input enabled we have that $\sigma_2?i_p \in Tr(s)$. Thus, we conclude that $\sigma_2?i_p \in Tr(s, (t_U, t_L))$ as required. $\square$

The controllability of a test case t for s is defined in terms of the traces that can be produced by $t \| s$. Thus, if two test cases define the same sets of traces when applied to s then either both are controllable or neither is controllable. The proof of the following is immediate from Proposition 3 and Definition 11.

Proposition 4. *Let t be a global test case for $s \in \mathcal{IOTS}(I, O)$ and $t' = (local_U(t), local_L(t))$. Then t' is controllable for s if and only if t is controllable for s.*

Proposition 5. *Let t be a global test case and $t_p = local_p(t)$, $p \in \mathcal{P}$. If t is controllable for s then (t_U, t_L) is deterministic for s. However, it is possible for t to be deterministic for s but for t not to be controllable for s.*

Proof. We have seen that a test case can be deterministic for s and not controllable for s. We therefore assume that t is controllable for s and use proof by contradiction and so assume that (t_U, t_L) is not deterministic for s. By Proposition 3, $Tr(s, t) = Tr(s, (t_U, t_L))$. Since (t_U, t_L) is not deterministic for s there exist $\sigma_1, \sigma_2 \in Tr(s, t)$ with $\sigma_1 \sim \sigma_2$ and inputs $?i_U \in I_U$ and $?i_L \in I_L$ such that $\sigma_1?i_U, \sigma_2?i_L \in Tr(s, t)$. Since global test cases are deterministic, in t it is possible to input $?i_U$ after σ_1 but not after σ_2, both of these are in $Tr(s, t)$ and $\pi_U(\sigma_1) = \pi_U(\sigma_2)$. Thus, t is not controllable as required. $\square$

4   Deciding Whether a Test Case Is Controllable

It is clear that it is desirable to apply controllable test cases since this allows each local tester to know when to apply an input. In this section we show that it is possible to determine whether a local test case is controllable in low order polynomial time. This result will be used in Section 5 in a test generation algorithm that returns controllable test cases.

The work reported in [23,24] investigated Message Sequence Charts (MSCs) and whether a set of MSCs implies other MSCs[2]. This is achieved by considering the language defined by a set of MSCs. A trace can be seen as an MSC and in this section we use a definition and a complexity result from [23].

Let us consider an MSC with message alphabet Σ. If message $a \in \Sigma$ is sent from process p to process q then the sending of a is represented by event $send(p, q, a)$ and the receiving of a is represented by event $receive(p, q, a)$. $\hat{\Sigma}$ denotes the set of send and receive events, $\hat{\Sigma}^S$ denotes the set of send events and $\hat{\Sigma}^R$ denotes the set of receive events. An MSC with processes $P_1, \ldots, P_k$ and alphabet Σ can be defined by the following:

1. A set E of events, partitioned into a set S of send events and a set R of receive events.
2. A mapping occ such that each event in E is mapped to the process on which it occurs.
3. A bijective function f between send and receive events.
4. A mapping $label$ from events to elements of $\hat{\Sigma}$. Naturally, for $e \in E$ we must have that $label(e) \in \hat{\Sigma}^S$ if and only if $e \in S$.
5. For each process P_i a total ordering $\leq_i$ on the events that occur at P_i such that the transitive closure of the relation

$$\bigcup_i \leq_i \cup \{(s, r) | s \in S, r \in R, r = f(s)\}$$

is a partial order on E. We include $\{(s, r) | s \in S, r \in R, r = f(s)\}$ since a message cannot be received before it is sent.

An MSC defines a partial order on E and a language with alphabet $\hat{\Sigma}$ that preserves this partial order: The set of words that are linearizations of the MSC. A word is *well-formed* if for every receive event there is a corresponding earlier send event. [23] looks at projections of words onto the processes of an MSC. In our case, each local tester is a process and the SUT is also a process. Given word w and process p, $w|_p$ is the sequence of events in w at p. We will use the following closure condition [23].

Definition 12. *A language L over $\hat{\Sigma}$ satisfies closure condition CC3 if and only if for every well-formed word w we have that if for each process p there is a word $v^p \in pre(L)$ such that $w|_p = v^p|_p$, then w is in $pre(L)$.*

A (global or local) test case defines a set of traces and each trace defines an MSC. Results in [23] concern asynchronous communications but they apply when communications and synchronous [24] by restricting the language defined by a set of MSCs to only include words that are consistent with synchronous communications. Given a (global or local) test case t and specification s, $L(s, t)$ will denote the language of words that are defined by the MSCs corresponding to traces in $Tr(s, t)$ where communications are synchronous and so every send is immediately followed by the corresponding receive. We now prove that test case t is controllable for s if and only if the corresponding language satisfies CC3.

---

[2] They restrict attention to basic MSCs, which we call MSCs.

Proposition 6. *Given $s \in \mathcal{IOTS}(I, O)$, test case t is controllable for s if and only if the language $L = L(s, t)$ satisfies closure condition CC3.*

Proof. First, assume that t is not controllable for s and we will prove that L does not satisfy CC3. Since t is not controllable for s there exist a port $p \in \mathcal{P}$, traces $\sigma_1, \sigma_2 \in \mathcal{T}r(s, t)$, and input $?i_p$ at p such that $\pi_p(\sigma_1) = \pi_p(\sigma_2)$, $\sigma_1 ?i_p \in \mathcal{T}r(t)$ but $\sigma_2 ?i_p \notin \mathcal{T}r(t)$.

Let us consider $w \in \hat{\Sigma}$ that corresponds to σ_2 followed by $send(p, SUT, ?i_p)$. For every $q \in \mathcal{P} \cup \{SUT\}$ such that $q \neq p$ we have that $w|_q$ is a projection of the string from $pre(L)$ corresponding to σ_2 and so there is some $v^q \in pre(L)$ such that $w|_q = v^q|_q$. Since $\pi_p(\sigma_1) = \pi_p(\sigma_2)$ we know that there is some $v^p \in pre(L)$ such that $w|_p = v^p|_p$. Thus, since $w \notin L$, L does not satisfy CC3 as required.

Now assume that L does not satisfy CC3 and we will prove that t is not controllable for s. Since L does not satisfy CC3 there is a well-formed word $w \notin pre(L)$ such that for all $p \in \mathcal{P} \cup \{SUT\}$ there is some $v^p \in pre(L)$ such that $w|_p = v^p|_p$. Let w be a shortest such word and $w = w'e$ for some event e. Clearly w' is well-formed and for all $p \in \mathcal{P} \cup \{SUT\}$ there is some $v^p \in pre(L)$ such that $w'|_p = v^p|_p$. By the minimality of w, $w' \in pre(L)$.

If e is a receive event then there is a corresponding send event e' that is an event for some process in w. Thus, since $w' \in pre(L)$ and communications are synchronous we must have that $w'e \in pre(L)$, providing a contradiction, and so e must be a send event. Now let us suppose that e is the sending of a message from process SUT. Then since $w'e|_{SUT} = v^{SUT}|_{SUT}$ for some $v^{SUT} \in pre(L)$, after $w'|_{SUT}$ the SUT must be able to send e and so $w = w'e \in pre(L)$, providing a contradiction. Thus e is the sending of an input $?i_p$ from the local tester at some port p to the SUT.

Let σ_2 denote the sequence from $\mathcal{T}r(s, t)$ that corresponds to w': There must be some such word since w' is well-formed and can be followed by a send event and communications are synchronous. There is a shortest $v^p \in pre(L)$ such that $w'e|_p = v^p|_p$. Let $v_1^p \in pre(L)$ be equal to the sequence v^p with the event e removed. Let σ_1 denote the sequence from $\mathcal{T}r(s, t)$ that corresponds to v_1^p. It is possible to follow σ_1 by the sending of $?i_p$ in $\mathcal{T}r(s, t)$ but it is not possible to follow σ_2 by the sending of $?i_p$ in $\mathcal{T}r(s, t)$ and $\pi_p(\sigma_1) = \pi_p(\sigma_2)$. Thus, t is not controllable for s as required. $\qquad\square$

Given k MSCs with n processes, if r is the total number of events in the MSCs then it is possible to decide whether the language defined by the MSCs satisfies CC3 in time of $O(k^2 n + rn)$ [23]. Thus, this result holds if $\mathcal{T}r(s, t)$ contains k traces and in our case $n = 3$. In addition, if l is an upper bound on the lengths of traces in $\mathcal{T}r(s, t)$ then there are at most $r = 2lk$ events. Thus, the worst time complexity is of $O(k^2 + lk)$.

5 An Implementation Relation for Controllable Testing

We obtain a new implementation relation if we restrict testing to the use of controllable test cases.

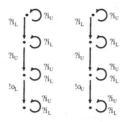

Fig. 2. Processes s_1 and i_1

Definition 13. *Given $s, i \in \mathcal{IOTS}(I, O)$ we write i **c-dioco** s if for every controllable local test case (t_U, t_L) we have that i **passes** (t_U, t_L) for s.*

We now investigate how **c-dioco** relates to **dioco** and **ioco**; **dioco** is strictly weaker than **ioco** if all processes are input enabled [20].

Proposition 7. *If i **dioco** s then i **c-dioco** s. Further, there exists processes i_1 and s_1 such that i_1 **c-dioco** s_1 but we do not have that i_1 **dioco** s_1.*

Proof. The first part follows from **c-dioco** restricting consideration to controllable local test cases. Consider the processes s_1 and i_1 shown in Figure 2, which are incomparable under **dioco**. The only controllable local test cases involve input at no more than one port and for each such test case neither process can produce output. We therefore have that i_1 **c-dioco** s_1 as required. $\square$

We now define an algorithm that returns a *complete* test suite. We talk of *completeness in the limit*, requiring that for all non-conforming SUT the algorithm will eventually produce a controllable local test case that will be failed by the SUT. Completeness is usually split into two results. A test suite is *sound* if conforming implementations pass all the tests in the suite. It is *exhaustive* if non-conforming implementations fail some of the tests. Our algorithm, given in Figure 3, is an adaption of an algorithm to derive test cases from timed FSMs [19]. This algorithm is *non-deterministic* since in each recursive step it can proceed in different ways. Each election generates a different controllable local test case. By applying the algorithm in all the possible ways we generate a test suite from a specification s that we call *tests(s)*.

The algorithm keeps track of states of the local testers by storing tuples (Q', s^U, s^L) that indicate that the specification could be in any of the states in Q'. We construct test cases by iteratively applying one of six possibilities. The first two return a minimal local tester and are the base cases. The third and fourth consider the possibility of adding an input. First, it is necessary to check that the addition of this input will produce a controllable local tester. If this is the case, we add a transition labelled by this input to the corresponding local tester, updating the set of auxiliary tuples and considering all possible outputs at the corresponding port. If the output is expected by the specification then we can continue testing after receiving the output; otherwise, we should reach a state

Input: Specification $s = (Q, I, O, T, q_{in})$.
Output: Controllable local test case (t_U, t_L); $t_p = (Q_p, I_p, O_p, T_p, q_{in}^p)$ for $p \in \{U, L\}$.

{Initialization}
$S_{aux} := \{(q_{in} \text{ after } \epsilon, q_{in}^U, q_{in}^L)\}$; $Q_U := \{q_{in}^U\}$; $Q_L := \{q_{in}^L\}$; $T_U, T_L := \emptyset$;
while $S_{aux} \neq \emptyset$ do

- Choose $(Q', s^U, s^L) \in S_{aux}$;
- Choose one of the following six possibilities:
    1. {s^U will be $\perp_U$ if it has not been defined yet}
        (a) if $s^U \neq \perp_U$ then $s^U := \perp_U$;
        (b) If $s^L = \perp_L$ then $S_{aux} := S_{aux} - \{(Q', s^U, s^L)\}$;
        {Remove the tuple if both local testers are $\perp$}
    2. {s^L will be $\perp_L$ if it has not been defined yet}
        {Similar to the previous case, substituting U by L}
    3. {Add an input at port U if the result is controllable}
        (a) Let $?i_U \in I_U$ be such that $(\hat{t}_U, t_L)$ is controllable for s, where $\hat{t}_U$ is formed
            from t_U after making the following changes:
                i. $\hat{t}_U := (\hat{Q}_U, I_U, O_U, \hat{T}_U, \hat{q}_{in}^U)$, where $\hat{Q}_U := Q_U$; $\hat{T}_U := T_U$;
                ii. $\hat{s}^U$ and $\hat{q}_{in}^U$ are the copies of s^U and q_{in}^U in $\hat{Q}_U$;
                iii. Consider a fresh state $\hat{q}' \notin \hat{Q}_U$; $\hat{Q}_U := \hat{Q}_U \cup \{\hat{q}'\}$; $\hat{q}' := \perp_U$;
                iv. For all $a \in O_U \cup \{\delta\} \cup \{?i_U\}$ do $\hat{T}_U := \hat{T}_U \cup \{(\hat{s}^U, a, \hat{q}')\}$;
                v. For all $\hat{s} \in \hat{Q}_U \setminus \{\hat{s}^U\}$ such that $\exists Q'', \hat{s}' : (Q'', \hat{s}, \hat{s}') \in S_{aux}$ do $\hat{s} := \perp_U$;
                vi. For all $\hat{s}$ such that $\exists Q'', \hat{s}' : (Q'', \hat{s}', \hat{s}) \in S_{aux}$ do $\hat{s} := \perp_L$
        (b) $S_{aux} := S_{aux} - \{(Q', s^U, s^L)\}$;
        (c) Consider a fresh state $q' \notin Q_U$; $Q_U := Q_U \cup \{q'\}$;
        (d) $T_U := T_U \cup \{(s^U, ?i_U, q')\}$; $S_{aux} := S_{aux} \cup \{(Q' \text{ after } ?i_U, q', s^L)\}$;
        (e) For all $!o_U \in O_U$ such that $!o_U \notin out(Q')$ do
            {These are unexpected outputs: Construct $\perp_U$ after them}
                i. Consider a fresh state $q' \notin Q_U$; $Q_U := Q_U \cup \{q'\}$; $q' := \perp_U$;
                ii. $T_U := T_U \cup \{(s^U, !o_U, q')\}$
        (f) For all $!o_U \in O_U$ such that $!o_U \in out(Q')$ do
            {These are expected outputs: Testing can continue after them}
                i. Consider a fresh state $q' \notin Q_U$; $Q_U := Q_U \cup \{q'\}$;
                ii. $T_U := T_U \cup \{(s^U, !o_U, q')\}$; $S_{aux} := S_{aux} \cup \{(Q' \text{ after } !o_U, q', s^L)\}$
    4. {Add an input at port L if the result is controllable}
        {Similar to the previous case, substituting U by L}
    5. {Wait for an output at port U}
        (a) $S_{aux} := S_{aux} - \{(Q', s^U, s^L)\}$;
        (b) For all $o \in O_U \cup \{\delta\}$ such that $o \notin out(Q')$ do
            {These are unexpected outputs: Construct $\perp_U$ after them}
                i. Consider a fresh state $q' \notin Q_U$; $Q_U := Q_U \cup \{q'\}$; $q' := \perp_U$;
                ii. $T_U := T_U \cup \{(s^U, o, q')\}$;
        (c) For all $o \in O_U \cup \{\delta\}$ such that $o \in out(Q')$ do
            {These are expected outputs: Testing can continue after them}
                i. Consider a fresh state $q' \notin Q_U$ and let $Q_U := Q_U \cup \{q'\}$;
                ii. $T_U := T_U \cup \{(s^U, o, q')\}$; $S_{aux} := S_{aux} \cup \{(Q' \text{ after } o, q', s^L)\}$
    6. {Wait for an output at port L}
        {Similar to the previous case, substituting U by L}

Fig. 3. Controllable test cases generation algorithm

where we do not provide further input. The fifth and sixth consider the case where a local tester patiently waits to receive an output; we also have to consider the possibility of receiving no output represented by δ.

Now we show the completeness of $tests(s)$. First, using Definition 13, it is obvious that i **c-dioco** s implies that for every local test case $t \in tests(s)$ we have i **passes** t for s. The other implication is shown in the following result.

Proposition 8. *Let $s, i \in \mathcal{IOTS}(I, O)$. If for every local test case $t \in tests(s)$ we have i passes t for s then we also have i c-dioco s.*

Proof. We use proof by contradiction: Assume that i **c-dioco** s does not hold and we have to prove that i fails a controllable test case belonging to $tests(s)$.

Since i **c-dioco** s does not hold, there exists a controllable test case t_1 such that i **fails** t_1 for s. If t_1 belongs to $tests(s)$ then we conclude the proof. Otherwise, i must fail a test run with t_1. Consider a minimal length sequence $\sigma = a_1 a_2 \ldots a_n \in \mathcal{Act}^*$ such that i **fails** σ for t_1. Due to the minimality of σ, for every proper prefix σ_1 of σ such that i can be quiescent after σ_1, there exists $\sigma_1' \in \mathcal{Tr}(s)$ such that $\sigma_1' \sim \sigma_1$. The following algorithm defines a controllable local test case (t_U, t_L), $t_p = (Q_p, I_p, O_p, T_p, q_{in}^p)$ for $p \in \{U, L\}$, that belongs to $tests(s)$ and is failed by i.

$S_{aux} := \{(q_{in} \text{ after } \epsilon, q_{in}^U, q_{in}^L)\}$; $Q_U := \{q_{in}^U\}$; $Q_L := \{q_{in}^L\}$; $T_U, T_L := \emptyset$;
$aux := (q_{in} \text{ after } \epsilon, q_{in}^U, q_{in}^L)$; {We have $aux := (Q_{aux}, s_{aux}^U, s_{aux}^L)$}
for $j := 1$ to n do
    Consider aux {aux belongs to S_{aux}};
    if $a_j \in I_U$ then Apply case 3 of Algorithm; $aux := (Q_{aux} \text{ after } a_j, q', s_{aux}^L)$;
    if $a_j \in I_L$ then Apply case 4 of Algorithm; $aux := (Q_{aux} \text{ after } a_j, s_{aux}^U, q')$;
    if $a_j \in O_U$ then Apply case 5 of Algorithm; $aux := (Q_{aux} \text{ after } a_j, q', s_{aux}^L)$;
    if $a_j \in O_L$ then Apply case 6 of Algorithm; $aux := (Q_{aux} \text{ after } a_j, s_{aux}^U, q')$;
{Now we apply the base cases}
for all non-initialized s_U such that $\exists Q', s_L : (Q', s_U, s_L) \in S_{aux}$ do $s_U := \perp_U$;
for all non-initialized s_L such that $\exists Q', s_U : (Q', s_U, s_L) \in S_{aux}$ do $s_L := \perp_L$

It is clear that this local test case belongs to $tests(s)$, the last two steps corresponding to the application of the base cases. Moreover, $i \| t_U \| t_L \overset{\sigma}{\Longrightarrow}$ since, by construction, σ is a trace of (t_U, t_L). Thus, since there does not exist $\sigma' \in \mathcal{Tr}(s)$ such that $\sigma' \sim \sigma$, we obtain i **fails** (t_U, t_L), concluding i **passes** (t_U, t_L) for s does not hold. □

From Proposition 8 we immediately obtain the desired result.

Corollary 1. *Let $s, i \in \mathcal{IOTS}(I, O)$. We have i c-dioco s if and only if for every local test case $(t_U, t_L) \in tests(s)$ we have that i passes (t_U, t_L) for s.*

6 Conclusions

If we are testing a state based system with physically distributed interfaces/ports then we place a tester at each port. If these testers cannot communicate with one another and there is no global clock then we are testing in the distributed test architecture. While testing in the distributed test architecture has received much attention, most previous work considered the problem of testing against a deterministic finite state machine. Only recently has the problem of testing from an input-output transition system (IOTS) been investigated.

This paper considered what it means for a test case to be controllable in the distributed test architecture, showing that it is not sufficient for a test case to be deterministic. A new implementation relation, **c-dioco**, was defined: This corresponds to controllable testing from an IOTS in the distributed test architecture.

We have shown that it is possible to decide in low order polynomial time whether a test case is controllable. This allowed us to define a test generation algorithm. The algorithm is guaranteed to return controllable test cases and, in addition, any controllable test case can be returned by the algorithm. Thus, in the limit the test generation algorithm is complete.

There are several possible areas of future work. The test generation algorithm does not aim to return test cases that, for example, achieve a given test objective. It would therefore be interesting to combine this with approaches that direct test generation. It would also be interesting to investigate formalisms in which a transition can be triggered by the SUT receiving input at several ports [25].

References

1. ISO/IEC JTC 1, J.T.C.: International Standard ISO/IEC 9646-1. Information Technology - Open Systems Interconnection - Conformance testing methodology and framework - Part 1: General concepts. ISO/IEC (1994)
2. Sarikaya, B., v. Bochmann, G.: Synchronization and specification issues in protocol testing. IEEE Transactions on Communications 32, 389–395 (1984)
3. Luo, G., Dssouli, R., v. Bochmann, G.: Generating synchronizable test sequences based on finite state machine with distributed ports. In: 6th IFIP Workshop on Protocol Test Systems, IWPTS 1993, pp. 139–153. North-Holland, Amsterdam (1993)
4. Tai, K.C., Young, Y.C.: Synchronizable test sequences of finite state machines. Computer Networks and ISDN Systems 30(12), 1111–1134 (1998)
5. Rafiq, O., Cacciari, L.: Coordination algorithm for distributed testing. The Journal of Supercomputing 24(2), 203–211 (2003)
6. Lee, D., Yannakakis, M.: Principles and methods of testing finite state machines: A survey. Proceedings of the IEEE 84(8), 1090–1123 (1996)
7. Brinksma, E., Tretmans, J.: Testing transition systems: An annotated bibliography. In: Cassez, F., Jard, C., Rozoy, B., Dermot, M. (eds.) MOVEP 2000. LNCS, vol. 2067, pp. 187–195. Springer, Heidelberg (2001)
8. Petrenko, A., Yevtushenko, N.: Testing from partial deterministic FSM specifications. IEEE Transactions on Computers 54(9), 1154–1165 (2005)
9. Tretmans, J.: Test generation with inputs, outputs and repetitive quiescence. Software – Concepts and Tools 17(3), 103–120 (1996)
10. Utting, M., Legeard, B.: Practical Model-Based Testing: A Tools Approach. Morgan-Kaufmann, San Francisco (2007)

11. Hierons, R., Bogdanov, K., Bowen, J., Cleaveland, R., Derrick, J., Dick, J., Gheorghe, M., Harman, M., Kapoor, K., Krause, P., Luettgen, G., Simons, A., Vilkomir, S., Woodward, M., Zedan, H.: Using formal methods to support testing. ACM Computing Surveys (in press, 2008)
12. Brinksma, E., Heerink, L., Tretmans, J.: Factorized test generation for multi-input/output transition systems. In: 11th IFIP Workshop on Testing of Communicating Systems, IWTCS 1998, pp. 67–82. Kluwer Academic Publishers, Dordrecht (1998)
13. Núñez, M., Rodríguez, I.: Towards testing stochastic timed systems. In: König, H., Heiner, M., Wolisz, A. (eds.) FORTE 2003. LNCS, vol. 2767, pp. 335–350. Springer, Heidelberg (2003)
14. Brandán Briones, L., Brinksma, E.: A test generation framework for quiescent real-time systems. In: Grabowski, J., Nielsen, B. (eds.) FATES 2004. LNCS, vol. 3395, pp. 64–78. Springer, Heidelberg (2005)
15. Krichen, M., Tripakis, S.: Black-box conformance testing for real-time systems. In: Graf, S., Mounier, L. (eds.) SPIN 2004. LNCS, vol. 2989, pp. 109–126. Springer, Heidelberg (2004)
16. Bijl, M.v., Rensink, A., Tretmans, J.: Action refinement in conformance testing. In: Khendek, F., Dssouli, R. (eds.) TestCom 2005. LNCS, vol. 3502, pp. 81–96. Springer, Heidelberg (2005)
17. López, N., Núñez, M., Rodríguez, I.: Specification, testing and implementation relations for symbolic-probabilistic systems. Theoretical Computer Science 353(1–3), 228–248 (2006)
18. Frantzen, L., Tretmans, J., Willemse, T.: A symbolic framework for model-based testing. In: Havelund, K., Núñez, M., Roşu, G., Wolff, B. (eds.) FATES 2006 and RV 2006. LNCS, vol. 4262, pp. 40–54. Springer, Heidelberg (2006)
19. Merayo, M., Núñez, M., Rodríguez, I.: Formal testing from timed finite state machines. Computer Networks 52(2), 432–460 (2008)
20. Hierons, R., Merayo, M., Núñez, M.: Implementation relations for the distributed test architecture. In: Suzuki, K., Higashino, T., Hasegawa, T., Ulrich, A. (eds.) TestCom/FATES 2008. LNCS, vol. 5047, pp. 200–215. Springer, Heidelberg (2008)
21. Tretmans, J.: Testing concurrent systems: A formal approach. In: Baeten, J.C.M., Mauw, S. (eds.) CONCUR 1999. LNCS, vol. 1664, pp. 46–65. Springer, Heidelberg (1999)
22. Hierons, R.: Controllable testing from nondeterministic finite state machines with multiple ports (submitted, 2008)
23. Alur, R., Etessami, K., Yannakakis, M.: Inference of message sequence charts. IEEE Transactions on Software Engineering 29(7), 623–633 (2003)
24. Alur, R., Etessami, K., Yannakakis, M.: Inference of message sequence charts. Technical report, University of Edinburgh (2003),
http://homepages.inf.ed.ac.uk/kousha/msc_inference_j_v.ps
25. Haar, S., Jard, C., Jourdan, G.V.: Testing input/output partial order automata. In: Petrenko, A., Veanes, M., Tretmans, J., Grieskamp, W. (eds.) TestCom/FATES 2007. LNCS, vol. 4581, pp. 171–185. Springer, Heidelberg (2007)

Goanna: Syntactic Software Model Checking

Ralf Huuck, Ansgar Fehnker, Sean Seefried, and Jörg Brauer

National ICT Australia Ltd. (NICTA)*
Locked Bag 6016
University of New South Wales
Sydney NSW 1466, Australia

Abstract. Goanna is an industrial-strength static analysis tool used in academia and industry alike to find bugs in C/C++ programs. Unlike existing approaches Goanna uses the off-the-shelf NuSMV model checker as its core analysis engine on a syntactic flow-sensitive program abstraction. The CTL-based model checking approach enables a high degree of flexibility in writing checks, scales to large number of checks, and can scale to large code bases. Moreover, the tool incorporates techniques from constraint solving, classical data flow analysis and a CEGAR inspired counterexample based path reduction. In this paper we describe Goanna's core technology, its features and the relevant techniques, as well as our experiences of using Goanna on large code bases such as the Firefox web browser.

1 Introduction

Model checking and static analysis are automated techniques promising to ensure (limited) correctness of software and to find certain classes of bugs automatically. One of the drawbacks of software model checkers [1,2,3] is that they typically operate on a low level semantic abstraction making them suitable for small code bases, but less so for larger software and, when soundness is paramount, are not applicable to industrial C/C++ code containing pointer arithmetic, unions, templates and alike. On the other hand, static analysis tools [4] have been concentrating on a shallower but more scalable and applicable analysis of large code bases. Typically, soundness is sacrificed for performance and practicality [5].

There are, however, many advantages in using a model checker. Specifications can often be given elegantly in temporal logic, there are many built-in optimizations in state-of-the-art tools, and especially CTL model checkers have been shown to be rather insensitive to the number of different checks performed on the same model.

In this work we present Goanna, a tool for static program analysis that makes use of the advances of modern model checkers and combines it with constraint

* National ICT Australia is funded by the Australian Governments Department of Communications, Information Technology and the Arts and the Australian Research Council through Backing Australias Ability and the ICT Research Centre of Excellence programs.

Cha et al. (Eds.): ATVA 2008, LNCS 5311, pp. 216–221, 2008.

solving and counterexample based abstraction refinement (CEGAR) techniques [6,1]. Goanna uses standard symbolic CTL model checking as implemented in the NuSMV [7] tool on a high-level program abstraction. This abstraction includes the control flow graph (CFG) of a program and labels (atomic propositions) consisting of syntactic occurrences of interest. On this level of abstraction model checking is fast, scalable to large code fragments and scalable to many such checks in the same model. Given that there are typically only a few bugs in every thousand lines of code [8] the abstraction is also appropriate for a first approximation. In a second step, more advanced features are used such a constraint solving and CEGAR-inspired path reduction to exclude false alarms. On top we incorporated alias analysis and summary-based interprocedural analysis to gain additional depth while remaining scalable.

In Section 2 we briefly explain the underlying technology, followed by a list of additional features in Section 3. A summary of our experiences from analyzing industrial code can be found in Section 4.

2   Core Technology

Goanna is built on an automata based static analysis framework as described in [9], which is related to [10,11,12]. The basic idea of this approach is to map a C/C++ program to its CFG, and to label this CFG with occurrences of syntactic constructs of interest automatically. The CFG together with the labels can be seen as a transition systems with atomic propositions, which can easily be mapped to the input language of a model checker, in our case NuSMV, or directly translated into a Kripke structure for model checking.

A simple example of this approach is shown in Fig. 1. Consider the contrived program foo which is allocating some memory, copying it a number of times to a, and freeing the memory in the last loop iteration.

One example of a property to check is that after freeing some resource it will not be used, i.e., otherwise indicating some memory corruption. In our approach we syntactically identify program locations that allocate, use, and free resource p. This is done automatically by pattern matching for the pre-defined relevant constructs on the program's abstract syntax tree. Next, we automatically label the program's CFG with this information as shown on the right hand side of Fig. 1 and encode the check itself as follows in CTL:

$$AG \ (malloc_p \Rightarrow AG \ (free_p \Rightarrow \neg EF \ used_p)),$$

which means that whenever there is free after malloc for a resource p, there is no path such that p is used later on. Neglecting any further semantic information will lead to a false alarm in the current example since p is only freed once in the last loop iteration and there is no access to it later. However, the abstraction in Fig. 1 does not reflect this. We will come back to this issue in Section 3.2.

One of the advantages of the proposed approach is that, e.g., a stronger variant of the above check can easily be obtained by switching from EF to AF, i.e., warning

```
1   void foo() {
2      int x, *a;
3      int *p=malloc(sizeof(int));
4      for(x = 10; x > 0; x--) {
5         a = *p;
6         if(x == 1)
7            free(p);
8      }
9   }
```

Fig. 1. Example program and labeled CFG for use-after-free check

only when something goes wrong on all paths. As such, CTL model checking is an easy and powerful approach to defining different properties with different strength quickly.

3   Features

The aforementioned static analysis approach allows for describing properties in a simple straightforward fashion. In this section we present a number of more advanced features integrated in Goanna. In particular, we describe new techniques to increase the precision of the analysis and the type of bugs that can be found by the tool.

3.1   Constraint Analysis

The model-checking based static analysis approach described in Section 2 is well suited for checking control-flow dependent properties such as certain types of memory leaks, uninitialized variables, potential null-pointer dereferences or alike. However, one of the major concerns for software correctness as well as software security are buffer overruns such as accesses to arrays beyond their bounds.

Typically, these problems have been addressed by abstract interpretation solutions [13]. In Goanna we added an interval constraint solving approach that uses the approach first developed by [14]. These techniques guarantee a precise least solution for interval analysis including operations such as additions, subtraction and multiplication without any widening in the presence of (simple) loops. Goanna uses interval analysis to infer for every integer variable in every program statement its potential range and uses it to, e.g., check for buffer over- and underruns.

3.2   False Path Reduction

Not every bug is a real one, i.e., the initial coarse syntactic abstraction might lead to a number of false positives. For instance in the example in Figure 1 the memory will only be accessed as long as the memory is not freed. A straightforward flow-sensitive analysis will not catch this fact.

In Goanna we make use of the aforementioned interval constraint solving approach to rule out some of those spurious alarms automatically [15]. For a given counterexample path Goanna subjects it to the interval analysis as described in the previous Section 3.1. This means, for every variable every possible value will be approximated along the counterexample path. E.g., in the program of Figure 1 the counterexamples loops trough the program after condition x==1 becomes true. However, when $x = 1$, the loop counter will be set to $x = 0$ in the next iteration, invalidating the loop condition of $x > 0$ and preventing the loop body to be re-entered. An interval constraint analysis over the counterexample path will come to the same conclusion by discovering that here is no possible satisfying valuation for x.

Goanna will learn this fact and create an observer automaton as described in [15]. This observer rules out a minimum set of conflicts, i.e., those conditions responsible for a false path. Observers are put in parallel composition to the existing coarse grained model to obtain a more precise model showing fewer false positives. While the parallel composition adds some overhead to the overall computation time, it is only added in a few cases were spurious alarms are found, ensuring an overall efficient analysis.

Similar to CEGAR the above process is iterated until no more bugs are found or no more counterexample paths can be eliminated. Note that since the interval analysis is an approximation itself, it is not guaranteed that all false positives can be removed.

3.3   Interprocedural Analysis

The aforementioned analysis techniques are mostly applicable for intraprocedural analysis, i.e., analyzing one function at a time. While this is sufficient for returning good results on standard software, it neglects, e.g., null pointers being passed on through several functions and then finally dereferenced without being properly checked. Therefore, we developed a summary-based interprocedural analysis. This analysis includes two features: The computation of alias information by inferring points-to sets [16] and computing a summary based on the lattice of the property under investigation. In the case of passing null pointer information, the summary records for every passed pointer if it points to Null, to something not Null or to an unknown value.

Given the call graph of the whole program Goanna computes the fixed point on the summary information, rerunning the local analysis when needed. Even in the presence of recursion this procedure typically terminates within two to three iterations involving a limited set of functions.

3.4   Additional Features

We briefly summarize a number of additional features built into Goanna, which are mostly on a usability level.

Integration. Goanna can be run from the command line as well as be tightly integrated in the Eclipse IDE. In the latter case, all the warnings are displayed in the IDE, settings and properties can be set in the IDE and for every bug a counterexample trace created by the model checker can be displayed. As a consequence, Goanna can be used during software development for every compilation.

Incremental analysis. To minimize the analysis overhead Goanna creates hashes of every function and object. If those functions and objects are not changed between compilations there will be no re-analysis. Of course, hashes are insensitive to additional comments, line breaks and minor code rearrangements.

User defined checks. Goanna comes with a simple language including CTL-style patterns, which enables the user to define his own checks. The language builds on pre-defined labels for constructs of interest. This language does not enable full flexibility, but it is safe to use and covers most scenarios. A full abstract language is in preparation.

4   Experiences

We have been evaluating Goanna on numerous open source projects as well as on industrial code. The largest code base has been the Firefox web browser, which has 2.5 million lines of code after preprocessing. Run-time is roughly 3 to 4 times slower than compilation itself for intraprocedural analysis. Interprocedural analysis can double the run-time, but it is worth to mention, that most of the time is spent in the alias analysis that is not yet efficiently implemented.

In a typical analysis run over 90% of files are analyzed in less than 2 seconds. Roughly 40% of the analysis time is spent for model checking, 30% for interval analysis and 30% for pattern matching, parsing and other computations. Adding more checks gives modest penalties, i.e., a threefold increase in the number of checks doubles the analysis time. Interval analysis is fast as long as the number of constraints is below a few hundred, i.e., resulting in a maximal overhead of one second.

In very rare cases, due to C/C++ macros or C++ templates a function might contain several hundreds of variables and very long code fragments. In these cases the overall analysis might take considerable time. However, in our experience from analyzing the source code of Firefox a time out of 2 minutes was only exceeded once out of roughly $250,000$ functions for the complete analysis.

The overall defect density is between 0.3 to 2 bugs per 1000 lines of code, depending on the code base and type of checks enabled. This is comparable with other commercial static code checkers [4].

References

1. Clarke, E., Kroening, D., Sharygina, N., Yorav, K.: SATABS: SAT-based Predicate Abstraction for ANSI-C. In: Halbwachs, N., Zuck, L.D. (eds.) TACAS 2005. LNCS, vol. 3440, pp. 570–574. Springer, Heidelberg (2005)
2. Clarke, E., Kroening, D., Lerda, F.: A Tool for Checking ANSI-C Programs. In: Jensen, K., Podelski, A. (eds.) TACAS 2004. LNCS, vol. 2988, pp. 168–176. Springer, Heidelberg (2004)

3. Henzinger, T.A., Jhala, R., Majumdar, R., McMillan, K.L.: Abstractions from proofs. In: POPL, pp. 232–244 (2004)
4. Emanuelsson, P., Nilsson, U.: A comparative study of industrial static analysis tools. Electronic notes in theoretical computer science (2008)
5. Engler, D., Chelf, B., Chou, A., Hallem, S.: Checking system rules using system-specific, programmer-written compiler extensions. In: Proc. Symposium on Operating Systems Design and Implementation, San Diego, CA (October 2000)
6. Henzinger, T., Jhala, R., Majumdar, R., SUTRE, G.: Software verification with BLAST. In: Ball, T., Rajamani, S.K. (eds.) SPIN 2003. LNCS, vol. 2648, pp. 235–239. Springer, Heidelberg (2003)
7. Cimatti, A., Clarke, E., Giunchiglia, E., Giunchiglia, F., Pistore, M., Roveri, M., Sebastiani, R., Tacchella, A.: NuSMV Version 2: An OpenSource Tool for Symbolic Model Checking. In: Brinksma, E., Larsen, K.G. (eds.) CAV 2002. LNCS, vol. 2404. Springer, Heidelberg (2002)
8. scan.coverity.com: Open source report. Technical report, Coverity Inc (2008)
9. Fehnker, A., Huuck, R., Jayet, P., Lussenburg, M., Rauch, F.: Model checking software at compile time. In: Proc. TASE 2007. IEEE Computer Society Press, Los Alamitos (2007)
10. Holzmann, G.: Static source code checking for user-defined properties. In: Proc. IDPT 2002, Pasadena, CA, USA (June 2002)
11. Dams, D., Namjoshi, K.: Orion: High-precision methods for static error analysis of C and C++ programs. Bell Labs Tech. Mem. ITD-04-45263Z, Lucent Technologies (2004)
12. Schmidt, D.A., Steffen, B.: Program analysis as model checking of abstract interpretations. In: Levi, G. (ed.) SAS 1998. LNCS, vol. 1503, pp. 351–380. Springer, Heidelberg (1998)
13. Cousot, P., Cousot, R.: Systematic design of program analysis frameworks. In: Conference Record of the Sixth Annual ACM SIGPLAN-SIGACT Symposium on Principles of Programming Languages, San Antonio, Texas, pp. 269–282. ACM Press, New York (1979)
14. Gawlitza, T., Seidl, H.: Precise fixpoint computation through strategy iteration. In: De Nicola, R. (ed.) ESOP 2007. LNCS, vol. 4421, pp. 300–315. Springer, Heidelberg (2007)
15. Fehnker, A., Huuck, R., Seefried, S.: Counterexample guided path reduction for static program analysis. In: Correctness, Concurrency, and Compositionality. Volume number to be assigned of Festschrift Series, LNCS. Springer, Heidelberg (2008)
16. Andersen, L.: Program Analysis and Specialization for the C Programming Language. PhD thesis, DIKU, Unversity of Copenhagen (1994)

A Dynamic Assertion-Based Verification Platform for Validation of UML Designs

Ansuman Banerjee[1], Sayak Ray[1], Pallab Dasgupta[1], Partha Pratim Chakrabarti[1],
S. Ramesh[2], and P. Vignesh V. Ganesan[2]

[1] Indian Institute of Technology Kharagpur
[2] General Motors India Science Labs

Abstract. For quite some time, the Unified Modeling Language (UML) [5] has been adopted by designers of safety critical control systems such as automotive and aviation control. This has led to an increased emphasis on setting up a validation flow over UML that can be used to guarantee the correctness of UML models. In this paper, we present a dynamic property verification (DPV) framework for validation of UML designs. The verification engine is built on top of Rhapsody [3], a popular UML simulator, using the concept of dynamic property monitoring over simulation runs. In view of the growing popularity of model-based development, we believe that the verification methodology presented in this paper is of immediate practical value to the UML-based design community.

1 Introduction

In recent years, the safety-critical software development community is increasingly moving towards a *model-based* development process, in which the largely textual way of requirement capturing is replaced by executable specification models at different levels of abstraction. For the past few decades, the Unified Modeling Language (UML) [5] has been one of the preferred choices in the software community for the design of a wide variety of applications at a higher level of abstraction, ranging from automotive control to medical instrumentation. This has led to an increased emphasis on setting up a validation flow over UML that can be used to guarantee the correctness of UML models.

In the last few decades, formal property verification has established itself as an effective validation methodology, both in the hardware and software verification community for its ability of automatic and exhaustive reasoning. Verification practitioners have also been able to uncover flaws in the specifications of complex protocols and intricate bugs in live designs. Unfortunately, the exponential increase in complexity and the increasingly distributed nature of functions as used in application software renders formal verification infeasible for intricate software systems because of its inherent capacity bottleneck in handling large systems. In the last decade, the more popular validation methodology (at least in the hardware domain) has been dynamic property verification (DPV). DPV is a semi-formal approach where the formal properties are checked over simulation runs. DPV is highly scalable and can support a richer specification language as compared to languages supported by formal verification tools.

Cha et al. (Eds.): ATVA 2008, LNCS 5311, pp. 222–227, 2008.

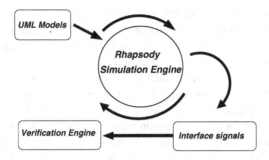

Fig. 1. The DPV platform over Rhapsody

The main contribution of this paper is in developing an integrated platform for validating behavioral requirements over UML Statecharts using DPV. The salient features of our contribution are (a) Action-LTL, an extension of Linear Temporal Logic (LTL) [2] to facilitate the expression of properties arising in the context of software systems, (b) A verification engine for dynamic assertion monitoring over Rhapsody simulation runs, and (c) An integrated interface for facilitating DPV for checking Action-LTL requirements on the UML model under test in Rhapsody. The main novelty of this work lies in the way this framework has been built to facilitate dynamic property verification in the UML context in Rhapsody. Figure 1 shows the overall architecture.

A number of different approaches for the verification of UML Statecharts have been developed by researchers. [1] presents a survey of these approaches. The main principle behind many of these approaches is to translate the Statecharts into some format which is amenable to formal verification tools, and on the other hand, use the power of temporal logic for specifying behavioral requirements. A model checker is then invoked to establish the truth or falsify the specification on the model. The main novelty of our work is in developing a DPV solution for validating behavioral requirements over UML Statecharts. With the growing popularity of model-based development, we believe that this work will have value for the model-based design community.

2   Tool Architecture

In this section, we describe the overall architecture of our verification platform, along with details of its main components. To emphasize the challenges overcome in the process, we discuss the issues in building a DPV tool for UML and our approach in handling these. The requirements of a DPV platform are as follows:

1. A modeling language for the system under test and a simulator for that language
2. An assertion specification language
3. A verification engine running on top of the simulator

2.1   Modeling Language and Simulator

In this work, we used UML as the model development language, and Rhapsody [3] as the UML simulator. For this, we needed to understand the simulation semantics of

Rhapsody, the way it handles concurrency and communication. The main idea behind our framework is to evaluate assertion requirements on the basis of responses produced by the model under test during simulation inside Rhapsody. The behavior of a system described in Rhapsody is a set of possible runs. A run consists of a series of detailed snapshots of the system's situation. Such a snapshot is called a *status*. The first in the sequence is the initial status, and each subsequent one is obtained from its predecessor by executing a *step* triggered by the dispatch of an event. In Rhapsody, events form the central component for communication among Statecharts for different concurrent modules of a system. A status contains information about the present condition of all the objects in the system, data values, events and history information for states. The concept of status and step are of utmost importance since properties in Action-LTL are expressed over data values at status points and events at steps.

2.2   Action-LTL: Assertion Specification Language

To describe correctness properties, one needs to describe properties over data attributes and events as well. Property specification languages that have been widely used in the verification community are pre-dominantly either state-based or event-based. However, for our purpose, we need to specify both *state* information and events (communication among components). For example, the Local Interconnect Network (LIN) [4] protocol specification has the following requirement: *In slave node, detection of break/synch frame shall abort the transfer in progress and processing of the new frame shall commence.* As this shows, both states (for describing a transfer in progress) and events (break/synch event) are required to capture the desired behavior.

To address the above issue, we extended Linear Temporal Logic (LTL) with some interesting features, specifically, the ability to express requirements over events, ability to express arithmetic and relational queries over data attributes, the concept of local variables and the concept of parameterized events. Our logic is called Action-LTL and is used within our DPV framework for specifying assertions. We call the logic Action-LTL to distinguish it from the standard LTL used in the hardware verification community. However, it may be noted that this is *not* a new logic altogether. While the temporal features remain as earlier, the only major difference is in the definition of events that allow us to capture state-event requirements of protocols and a support for verification of properties involving the actual parameter values of parameterized events. The additional novelty of Action-LTL lies in its semantics, which had to be defined in accordance to the simulation semantics of Rhapsody, and was therefore, non-trivial. The following example illustrates the way Action-LTL properties are expressed and interpreted with respect to Rhapsody simulation runs.

Example 1. Consider the system in Figure 2 consisting of objects M1 and M2. x is a data member of M1, y is a data member of M2. ev1 is an external event which is at the top of the event queue at the start of simulation. ev2 (a) is an event with payload, while ev3 and ev4 are normal events. State A is the initial state of M1 and State P is the initial state of M2. Hence, the initial status of the system consists of (M1.A, M2.P). Consider the following execution of the system: M1 receives event *ev*1 from the user. The transition from state A to state B is fired. This transition involves sending event

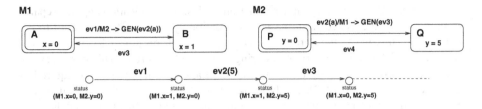

Fig. 2. A Sample System

$ev2(a)$ to object M2 (by placing a new event $ev2$ in the event queue with a value for parameter a), as specified by the action M2 $\rightarrow$ GEN($ev2$ (a)) [1]. Once the transition to state B of M1 is completed, the status variable shows (M1.B, M2.P). In the next step, event $ev2$ is removed from the event queue, and is dispatched to object M2 with a value for a, causing it to take the transition from state P to Q. A sample snapshot of the Rhapsody execution trace of the system (consisting of status and steps) is shown in Figure 2. To demonstrate the power of Action-LTL, we present some correctness requirements on this system and the corresponding Action-LTL encodings.

- $M1.x = 0$: The property formally expresses the requirement that M1 has x=0 in the initial status. In this case, $M1.x = 0$ evaluates to true if the data attribute x has the value 0. This property is true in our example model.
- $G\,(M2.ev2(a) \Rightarrow X\,(M2.y = a))$: This expresses the requirement that always when event ev2 (a) is dispatched to M2, the value of $M2.y$ equals the value of a in the next cycle. This evaluates to true vacuously in the first simulation step since ev2 is absent. It becomes true in the subsequent step considering the Rhapsody execution trace shown in Figure 2 (ev2 is instantiated with 5).
- $F\,((M1.x = 0) \wedge (M2.y = 6))$: This expresses the requirement that in some future status, the value of the data attributes x and y are 0 and 6 respectively.   □

2.3 The Verification Engine

The main idea of DPV is based on examining the responses of the system under test during simulation. Therefore, one of the primary requirements was to define a *interface* for accessing model variables. The system under verification must allow some external hooks to access the model attributes and events visible to the verification engine. In addition, the granularity of model attribute sampling is also important, due to the absence of a universal clock (as in the hardware domain) and values of data attributes and events sampled at different points may result in different validation results. To address this issue, we had to understand the simulation semantics of Rhapsody and make necessary modifications. The model parameters are sampled by the assertion engine.

The verification engine plays the most crucial role in the DPV process. Its main task is to sample the model attribute values from the interface at the end of every simulation cycle and evaluate the assertions on the basis of the sampled values. If any assertion evaluates to true or false, it reports the corresponding status to the user. For assertions

---

[1] GEN is a Rhapsody macro used for event generation.

whose success/failure span multiple simulation cycles, the verification engine prepares the property to be checked from the next simulation cycle and returns control to the simulator. In this work, the verification engine was built on top of Rhapsody, using the concept of dynamic property monitoring over simulation runs. This posed several challenges, starting from creation to integration of assertion monitors, and required us to engineer the internals of Rhapsody In our methodology, Action-LTL specifications are compiled into an assertion monitor and integrated with the Rhapsody models of the system under test. The assertion monitor is built as a Rhapsody object with embedded C routines for dynamic verification. The assertion monitor is then cosimulated with the model of the design-under-test and assertion violations/satisfactions are shown as events on the generated sequence diagram to facilitate debug.

Action-LTL properties are interpreted in a similar manner as in case of simulation-based dynamic property verification. The status (satisfaction/violation) of a property can only be concluded if we can reach a decisive report within the number of cycles for which simulation is carried out. For example, violation of liveness properties and satisfaction of safety properties cannot be concluded. The task of dynamically monitoring the truth of a given Action-LTL property along a simulation run is intuitively simple. If we are required to check a property, φ, from a given time step, t, we rewrite the property into a set of propositions over the signals (data and events) at time t and a set of properties over the run starting from time $t + 1$. The rewriting rules are standard [2]. The assertion monitor reads the variable values from the active status at time t and substitutes these on the rewritten properties and derives a new property that must hold on the run starting from $t + 1$. Consider Example 2.

Example 2. Consider the property:

$$\psi = \text{M1.p U (M2.q U M3.r)}$$

at time t, where p, q, r are all Boolean data attributes. We rewrite ψ as:

$$\psi = (\text{M3.r} \vee (\text{M2.q} \wedge \text{X (M2.q U M3.r)})) \vee (\text{M1.p} \wedge \text{X (M1.p U (M2.q U M3.r))})$$

If the simulation at time t gives $p = 0, q = 1, r = 0$, then by substituting these values, the assertion monitor obtains the property X (M2.q U M3.r). At $t + 1$, it needs to check M2.q U M3.r. The same methodology is repeated on M2.q U M3.r at time $t + 1$. □

2.4   The Integrated Framework

Assertions in Action-LTL are written over the model attributes, specifically, the data members and events. Hence, to determine satisfaction/refutation of an assertion at a simulation step due to the model behavior, it is necessary to be able to sample values of the model attributes. In addition, the assertion monitor must be able to sense all the events dispatched in the model. Whenever an event is dispatched in the model, the verifier should be informed about the event, its parameters, if any, and its target. With inception of every event, the assertion monitor must check if the model configuration satisfies/refutes the desired specification. The assertion monitor must remember the context of verification; it must remember what has to be checked after dispatch of each event to certify correctness of the model at that point of time. We overloaded GEN,

Table 1. Results of DPV

Module	No. of Properties	Project building time	Sim. Time (without DPV)	Sim. time (with DPV)
LIN	25	54 mins	12.9 mins	15.4 mins
CMS	11	28.7 mins	7 mins	10.2 mins

to make the assertion monitor aware of any event transaction in the model. Whenever an event is dispatched in the original model, a copy of the event is instantaneously delivered to the assertion monitor. The assertion monitor has been implemented as a Rhapsody object with an embedded C routine. At every simulation step, on an event dispatch, the assertion monitor samples the data attribute values and checks for satisfaction/refutations. To read the values of the data attributes of each object at each simulation step, the assertion monitor object is integrated at the appropriate class hierarchy.

3 Results

We deployed the DPV framework for the verification of two benchmarks, (a) an industrial implementation of the Local Interconnect Network (LIN) [4] protocol, and (b) an implementation of an access control mechanism in a web-based conference management system (CMS). The properties were extracted from the specification document.

The dynamic ABV platform was tested on an industrial Rhapsody based LIN implementation and an in-house implementation of CMS. Table 1 shows the results obtained by our tool on a Pentium-4 with 1 GB RAM. Column 2 shows the number of properties. Column 3 shows the time required by Rhapsody in building the project. Column 4 shows the time required by the simulation platform to simulate the model without the assertion checking feature. Column 5 shows the respective times required when the assertion monitor is inserted inside the simulation platform for verifying properties. Results show that not much simulation overhead is incurred due to assertion checking.

References

1. Bhaduri, P., Ramesh, S.: Model Checking of Statechart Models: Survey and Recent Directions (2004)
2. Dasgupta, P.: A Roadmap for Formal Property Verification. Springer, Heidelberg (2006)
3. Harel, D., Kugler, H.: The Rhapsody semantics of Statecharts (or, On the Executable Core of the UML). In: Ehrig, H., Damm, W., Desel, J., Große-Rhode, M., Reif, W., Schnieder, E., Westkämper, E. (eds.) INT 2004. LNCS, vol. 3147, pp. 325–354. Springer, Heidelberg (2004)
4. http://www.lin-subbus.org/
5. Object Management Group, Unified Modeling Language Specification, Version 1.4, Draft, OMG(2001), http://cgi.omg.org/cgibin/docad/018214

CheckSpec: A Tool for Consistency and Coverage Analysis of Assertion Specifications

Ansuman Banerjee[1], Kausik Datta[1], and Pallab Dasgupta[2]

[1] Interra Systems India Pvt. Ltd.
[2] Indian Institute of Technology Kharagpur

Abstract. As more and more chip design companies attempt to integrate *formal property verification* (FPV) and *assertion-based verification* (ABV) into their pre-silicon validation flows, the main challenge that they face is in the task of expressing the design intent correctly and accurately in terms of formal properties. Incomplete specifications allow bugs to escape detection, while inconsistent specifications lead to the loss of validation effort, since the error lies in the specification itself. In this paper, we present CheckSpec, a tool for automatically checking the consistency and completeness of assertion specifications written in System Verilog Assertions (SVA). CheckSpec comprises of two main engines, namely (a) *Certify*: that certifies a given assertion suite to be free from inconsistencies and (b) *Quantify*: that quantifies the completeness of a given assertion suite. On one hand, CheckSpec will help verification teams to avoid significant waste of validation effort arising out of inconsistent specifications. On the other hand, this will provide a first-cut estimate of the comprehensiveness of an assertion specification suite. The adoption of CheckSpec in the mainstream validation flow can significantly increase the productivity of assertion verification technologies.

1 Introduction

In recent times, most leading chip design companies are seriously attempting to induct assertion-based verification techniques in the pre-silicon validation flows. The advantages of specifying the key features of the design intent in terms of formal properties are increasingly being acknowledged and accepted by validation engineers and design managers. Property suites for standard interfaces, such as PCI Express, ARM AMBA, and USB are in considerable demand. System Verilog Assertions (SVA) [3] and PSL [3] are being extensively used for expressing formal properties.

One of the main tasks in all forms of assertion-based verification is to write a set of assertions that express the design specification. The most important issues that must be addressed while developing an assertion suite are:

1. *Are my properties correct?* If not then the property may fail on a valid design, and the validation engineer will have to debug both the specification and the implementation in order to isolate the problem.
2. *Have I written enough properties?* If the answer to this question is negative, then we have a more serious problem. All the properties may pass on an invalid design because the erroneous behavior was not covered by the incomplete set of properties.

Cha et al. (Eds.): ATVA 2008, LNCS 5311, pp. 228–233, 2008.

Typically, formal property suites are derived manually from informal design specifications. This formalization often requires direct interaction between the validation engineers and the architects of the design/protocol. The task of designing an assertion IP is non-trivial, and inconsistencies are common, even for a designer who is well versed with the semantics of assertion specification languages. Beyond a point, human debugging of the specification becomes infeasible because many properties may together create a conflict. This is aggravated by the fact that popular assertion specification languages (e.g. SVA, PSL) have very powerful constructs that not only widen the expressive power of the language, but also allow the verification engineer to write very complex properties that are completely unreadable (and un-debuggable). The second issue mentioned above comes under the ambit of *verification coverage* [3], which has been a subject of considerable research [3].

In this paper, we present *CheckSpec*, a tool that facilitates consistency and completeness analysis of a given assertion suite designed in System Verilog Assertions (SVA). Our implementation of the consistency and coverage analysis features is based on known methods. These methods have been developed over Linear Temporal Logic (LTL) [3] that forms the backbone of most of the assertion specification languages today. The main novelty of our work is in adapting these methods in the SVA perspective, thereby increasing the value of CheckSpec. With assertion suites becoming more and more popular for interface protocol specification, we believe that our tool will have significant value to the verification community.

CheckSpec comprises of two main engines:

- **Certify:** This is used for consistency analysis of SVA assertions. In particular, this takes into account two types of assertion inconsistencies, namely (a) satisfiability violations and (b) implementability or realizability violations. The methods underlying the tool are standard [3]. Certify has several building blocks. The main components of this engine developed by us are as follows:
    - **A satisfiability checker for SVA** for checking satisfiability of SVA specifications. This supports facilities for both bounded and unbounded satisfiability checking using a symbolic approach.
    - **A realizability checker for SVA** for realizability or implementability analysis of SVA specifications.
- **Quantify:** This is used for coverage estimate of an assertion suite. This is independent of any implementation and can be obtained directly from the properties.

Fig 1 shows the architecture of our tool. The tool accepts the assertions in SVA with the information of the interface signals (direction, width etc). On the given set of assertions, we first perform the consistency check using Certify. If we have any violation, the specification needs to be refined. Once the specification passes the satisfiability check, it is subjected to realizability analysis. For this, we have used Lily [4], a realizability checker for LTL and PSL. Lily implements the most state-of-the-art algorithms for realizability. The certified assertions in SVA are translated to PSL using an in-house SVA to PSL translator and Lily is used for realizability checking. Lily has support for a limited subset of PSL and hence, our translator also supports the supported subset. Once the Certify loop is closed, we perform the completeness analysis on the given set of assertions. This step uses the realizability checker of Certify to deduce the coverage.

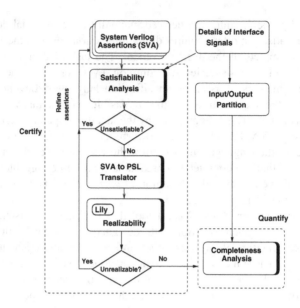

Fig. 1. The Architecture of CheckSpec

The notions of satisfiability and realizability of temporal assertions have been well studied in the verification community for LTL [3]. The main novelty of CheckSpec is in adopting these problems in the SVA context. Our work on completeness analysis is based on the idea proposed in [2] over LTL. Our contribution has been to extend this to SVA and provide a prototype implementation for analyzing SVA assertion suites. The fundamental idea used in [2] is to use a single stuck-at fault model as the reference, and verify the realizability of the specification in the presence of the fault to determine coverage gaps. If the given specification becomes unrealizable in the presence of a fault then it should lead to a refutation if any design exhibits that fault. Otherwise it is inert to the fault and the fault is not covered.

2   CheckSpec: Major Building Blocks

Certify: The satisfiability checking Engine: Given a set of SVA properties, Certify can perform a satisfiability check on these properties in two modes, namely (a) bounded mode and (b) unbounded automaton-based mode. The two modes have been added as a feature to make the tool more flexible. The user can switch between the two modes depending on the number and complexity of the assertions under consideration. The satisfiability checking is done using a BDD-based representation of the assertions using an in-house BDD package. The overall flow of the satisfiability engine is shown in Figure 2. In the first stage, we use our in-house System Verilog Assertion parser to parse the SVA specification and create an object model to hold the property expression. Once this is done, we traverse this object model to build the BDD-based representation of the property expression and analyze for satisfiability.

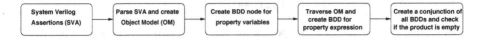

Fig. 2. Work-Flow of the satisfiability checking engine

Bounded Satisfiability Engine: The idea behind this is to reduce SVA satisfiability to an instance of Boolean satisfiability. In this mode, apart from the SVA specifications, the user is required to give as input the depth k (number of clock cycles) for which he wishes to examine the satisfiability of the assertions. This depth is utilized to create a k-bounded Boolean unfolding of each SVA property. The unfolded properties are represented using BDDs. The idea behind Boolean unfolding of properties is standard [3] and widely used in the Bounded Model Checking (BMC) community. Example 1 illustrates this.

Example 1. Consider the following SVA properties.

```
property P1                    property P2
@(posedge clk) a |-> ##1 b;    @(posedge clk) ##1 (a && !b);
endproperty                    endproperty
```

To illustrate the idea, we create a Boolean unfolding of P1 and P2 with k=2.

P1: $(a^1$ |-> $b^2) \wedge (a^2$ |-> $b^3)$;P2: $(a^2$ && !$b^2) \wedge (a^3$ && !$b^3)$;

where x^t represents the value of x in clock cycle t. The unfolded formulae are individually represented using BDDs. The conjunction of P1 and P2 gives an empty BDD. Hence, we can conclude that they are unsatisfiable. It is interesting to note that the bounded satisfiability analysis depends on the depth upto which the analysis is done. If k=1, the unsatisfiability would not be revealed.

Unbounded Satisfiability Mode: Given a SVA property $\mathcal{P}$, this approach builds the corresponding (*tableau*) [3]. The transformation is a straightforward adaptation of the corresponding rules for LTL [3]. Inside Certify, we create a BDD-based symbolic representation of the automaton and check for its emptiness as per standard methods [3].

Certify: The Realizability Engine: Popular temporal logics such as SVA/PSL do not syntactically distinguish between inputs and outputs, thereby allowing the designer to freely mix the input and output signals in the properties. This leads to realizability problems, since a property that is consistent when interpreted over a closed system can be inconsistent when interpreted over all open systems. A closed system property over a set of variables is *satisfiable* if there exists an assignment of values to the variables in each time step such that the property is satisfied. On the other hand, the semantics of realizability of a property is defined with respect to a open system and its environment. A property is *realizable* if the module is able to set the values of the output variables in a way that the property is satisfied for *all* possible behaviors of the environment. For example, suppose we have the following requirement for an arbiter: *Whenever the high priority req, hreq, arrives, the grant line, hgnt, is given for one cycle with highest priority.* Suppose we interpret the requirement as – *whenever hreq arrives, assert hgnt in the next cycle and lower it after one cycle.* We will then code this property as:

```
PO: hreq |-> ##1 hgnt ##1 !hgnt ;
```

This property is unrealizable. Suppose hreq arrives in two consecutive cycles, t and $t + 1$. We will have a conflict at time $t + 2$, because the request at t will require hgnt to be lowered at $t + 2$, and the request at $t + 1$ will require hgnt to be asserted at $t + 2$.

The realizability engine of Certify is a wrapper around Lily that can be used for checking realizability of SVA specifications. The flow of this has been explained in Figure 1. Below, we describe its major components.

SVA to PSL translator: Given a SVA specification, we translate it to its semantically equivalent PSL. The transformation rules are one-to-one and intuitively simple for most of the SVA constructs. For some SVA features like first_match, we had to generate additional SystemVerilog code to transform it to its semantic equivalent. We do not present the details of the transformation rules here. For this translator, we utilized our in-house SVA parser to parse the SVA specification suite and create the object model (OM). The translation is done by a traversal of this OM and decompiling it.

Realizability Checking Engine: This is a wrapper module that invokes the SVA to PSL translator on a given SVA specification suite to generate the equivalent PSL and passes it to Lily for realizability checking. Lily is a linear logic synthesizer, which can check for realizability of a a formal specification. Lily takes a set of properties and a partition of the used signals into input and output signals and reports if the given set of properties is realizable. Lily has support for LTL and a limited subset of PSL.

Quantify – Specification Coverage with respect to a fault model: Quantify implements the completeness analysis methods discussed in [2]. The core idea behind this approach is as follows: If a given specification becomes unrealizable in the presence of a fault on an interface signal, it should lead to a refutation if any design exhibits that fault. Otherwise it is inert to the fault and the fault is not covered. [2] uses a single stuck-at fault model as the reference. The high-level stuck-at fault model is quite effective in practice for finding input and output signals whose behaviors have not been appropriately expressed in the assertion specification.

Quantify reads as input the interface signal list (name, width, direction) and the SVA specification suite to be analyzed for completeness. The properties are first translated to PSL and then the analysis engine is invoked. The analysis engine is written using Perl.

3   Results

We tested the algorithms on 2 of our in-house assertion IPs, namely, the ARM AMBA AHB [1] protocol suite and the OCP [5] protocol suite. CheckSpec found some anomalies where properties turned out to be unsatisfiable. Some properties turned out to be unrealizable when interpreted over individual modules due to improper decomposition of the system level assertions into the module level ones. Certify pointed out interesting inconsistencies in the assertion suite. Quantify was used to deduce the coverage of the properties with respect to single stuck-at faults on the signals.

Table 1. Results for ARM AMBA AHB and OCP

Ckt	#i/p	#o/p	#Ass.	# B. Sat.	# U. Sat.	Tr.	#Ass.	# Rlz.	% Op.	% Ip.	Tm
AHB Master	11	9	22	20.2	43.16	3.2	15	2043.16	85	83	2067.1
AHB Slave	13	4	9	18.33	28.3	4.7	8	192.3	72	95	1768.3
AHB Arbiter	14	3	5	18.5	21	3	5	19.6	75	75	1578.3
OCP Master	26	25	63	78.6	211.5	99.1	35	NT	NT	NT	NT
OCP Slave	24	22	34	58.5	95.3	68.1	25	2219.6	78	87	2578.3

Table 1 shows the runtimes on on a 2.4 Ghz Pentium-IV with 1 GB RAM. Column 1 indicates the interface type (master / slave / arbiter), while Columns 2 and 3 show the number of input and output signals in these interfaces respectively. Column 4 shows the number of assertions. Columns 5 and 6 show the satisfiability checking time (in seconds) using the bounded satisfiability mode and the unbounded mode respectively. We used k=10 (chosen arbitrarily) as the analysis depth for the bounded satisfiability mode. Column 7 shows the time required to translate the SVA assertions to equivalent PSL. Column 8 shows the number of assertions that could be used for realizability and coverage analysis (limited support of Lily) while Column 9 shows the checking time. Columns 10 and 11 respectively show the coverage obtained for the output and input signals while Column 12 shows the time required for completeness analysis. All times are in seconds. For the OCP Master, Lily could not handle the large number of assertions, hence the analysis did not terminate (indicated as NT in Table 1).

References

1. ARM AMBA Specification Rev 2.0, http://www.arm.com
2. Das, S., et al.: Formal Methods for Analyzing the Completeness of an Assertion Suite against a High-Level Fault model. In: VLSI Design (2005)
3. Dasgupta, P.: A Roadmap for Formal Property Verification. Springer, Heidelberg (2006)
4. Lily, http://www.ist.tugraz.at/staff/jobstmann/lily/
5. Open Core Protocol, http://www.ocpip.org

DiVinE Multi-Core – A Parallel LTL Model-Checker*

Jiri Barnat, Lubos Brim, and Petr Ročkai**

Faculty of Informatics, Masaryk University
Brno, Czech Republic
{barnat,brim,xrockai}@fi.muni.cz

Abstract. We present a tool for parallel shared-memory enumerative LTL model-checking and reachability analysis. The tool is based on distributed-memory algorithms reimplemented specifically for multi-core and multi-cpu environments using shared memory. We show how the parallel algorithms allow the tool to exploit the power of contemporary hardware, which is based on increasing number of CPU cores in a single system, as opposed to increasing speed of a single CPU core.

1 Introduction

DiVinE Multi-Core has evolved from DiVinE Tool [2], sharing its input language and state space generator. As DiVinE Tool, it is an enumerative LTL model checker based on parallel fair cycle detection. The full source code can be obtained from [6] and compiled on a number of computer architectures.

The groundwork of tool design and algorithm choice has been laid down in [1]. We have crafted a tool from the ground up with shared-memory parallelism in mind. Due to natural choices of algorithms and memory organisation (the latter explored in more detail in [3]), the tool implementation closely resembles a distributed-memory one and may lend itself to extension to clusters of multi-core machines.

The primary motivation behind DiVinE Multi-Core has always been performance. Until recently, improvements in hardware architecture have been providing verification tools with performance increases mostly for free – without any need for implementational or algorithmic changes in the tools. However, this trend appears to be diminishing in favour of increasing parallelism in the system – which is nowadays much cheaper and easier to implement than it is to build computers with even faster sequential operation.

However, this architectural shift means that it is no longer possible to benefit from hardware progress, without introducing algorithmic changes to our tools. This is what DiVinE Multi-Core is striving for – providing algorithms able to exploit such parallel architectures and offering an implementation that can

---

* This work has been partially supported by the Grant Agency of Czech Republic grant No. 201/06/1338 and the Academy of Sciences grant No. 1ET408050503.
** This work has been partially supported by Red Hat, Inc.

Cha et al. (Eds.): ATVA 2008, LNCS 5311, pp. 234–239, 2008.

be deployed in practical situations. The main challenging aspect of the design of a parallel application is to achieve practical scalability – a decrease in runtime with an increase in the number of involved CPU cores.

Other researchers have recognized this trend and multi-core algorithms have been added to at least to previously purely serial model checker SPIN [7]. Unfortunately, only a dual-core algorithm has been devised for full LTL model checking, limiting the multi-core capabilities to reachability analysis.

2   DiVinE-MC Algortihm

DiVinE Multi-Core is based on automata-theoretic approach to LTL model checking [9]. The input language allows for specification of processes in terms of extended finite automata and the verified system is then obtained as an asynchronous parallel composition of these processes. This system is in turn synchronously composed with a property process (negative claim automaton) obtained from the verified LTL formula through a Büchi automaton construction.

The resulting finite product automaton is then checked for presence of accepting cycles (fair cycles), indicating nonemptiness of its accepted language – which in turn indicates invalidity of the verified LTL property.

The algorithm employed for accepting cycle detection is OWCTY [5] augmented with a heuristic for on-the-fly cycle detection inspired by the MAP algorithm [4]. It is not the purpose of this tool paper to go into details of the algorithm, so for in-depth description, we refer the reader to the two cited papers.

The main idea behind the OWCTY algorithm is to use topological sort for cycle detection – an algorithm that does not depend on DFS postorder and can be thus parallelized reasonably well. Detection of cycles in this way is linear, but since we do accepting cycle detection, provisions for removing non-accepting cycles need to be added. This makes the algorithm quadratic in the worst case for general LTL properties, although for a significant subset of formulae (those that translate to weak Büchi automata) the algorithm runs in linear time in the size of the product automaton.

The MAP algorithm uses maximal accepting predecessors to identify accepting cycles in the product automaton. The main idea is based on the fact that each accepting vertex lying on an accepting cycle is its own predecessor. Instead of expensively computing and storing all accepting predecessors for each accepting vertex (which would be sufficient to conclude the presence of an accepting cycle), the algorithm computes only a single representative accepting predecessor for each vertex – the maximal one in a suitable ordering. Clearly, if an accepting vertex is its own maximal accepting predecessor then it lies on an accepting cycle. This condition is used as the heuristic mentioned above. Note that the opposite direction does not hold in general. It can happen that the maximal accepting predecessor for an accepting vertex on a cycle does not lie on the cycle and the original MAP algorithm employs additional techniques to handle such a case.

```
process P_$1 {
byte j=0, k=0;
state NCS, CS, wait, q2, q3;
init NCS;
trans
 NCS -> wait { effect j = 1, active = $1, waiting[$1] = 1; },
 wait -> q2 { guard j < N;
                effect pos[$1] = j, active = $1; },
 q2 -> q3 { effect step[j-1] = $1, k = 0, active = $1; },
 q3 -> q3 { guard (k == $1 || pos[k]< j) && k < N;
                effect k = k+1, active = $1; },
 q3 -> wait { guard step[j-1] != $1 || k == N;
                effect j = j+1, active = $1; },
 wait -> CS { guard j == N;
                effect in_critical = in_critical+1,
                       active = $1, waiting[$1] = 0; },
 CS -> NCS { effect pos[$1] = 0, in_critical = in_critical-1,
                       active = $1; };
}
```

Fig. 1. An example of model specification: A single process participating in peterson mutual exclusion protocol (the $1 placeholder signifies the id of the process)

```
#define a_0 (active == 0)
#define a_1 (active == 1)

#define w_0 (waiting[0] == 1)
#define w_1 (waiting[1] == 1)

#define c_0 (P_0.CS)
#define c_1 (P_1.CS)

#property G(F(c_0)) && G(F(c_1))
#property ((GF(a_0 && w_0)) -> GF(c_0)) && ((GF(a_1 && w_1)) -> GF(c_1))
```

Fig. 2. Atomic propositions and LTL properties for the model in a .ltl file

If the heuristic fails, the OWCTY run will still detect accepting cycles if present. The heuristic does not interfere in any way when there are no accepting cycles – OWCTY will detect that condition by itself. The cost of the heuristic is a very slight increase in per-state memory usage, and a small runtime penalty in the first phase of the first iteration of OWCTY. Overall, it does not increase the time complexity compared to OWCTY and in a number of cases it detects property violation without generating the entire state space, which makes the combined algorithm on-the-fly.

However, even though the algorithm is not asymptotically optimal, in practice it is hardly a problem when it comes to performance – the bottlenecks can be found elsewhere.

```
$ divine-mc owcty mutex_peterson.naive.dve
  initialize...                 |S| = 81219
------------- iteration 0 -------------
  reachability...               |S| = 81219
  elimination & reset...        |S| = 59736
------------- iteration 1 -------------
  reachability...               |S| = 59736
  elimination & reset...        |S| = 59736
=====================================
        Accepting cycle FOUND
=====================================
  generating counterexample...      done
```

Fig. 3. Invocation of the tool for LTL model checking

3   Using the Tool

First and foremost, the model needs to be specified in the DVE modelling language and the property needs to be specified either as an LTL formula or as a Büchi automaton. We will present usage of the tool on a simple example of a mutual exclusion protocol. Source code of DVE specification of a single process of such a model can be found in Figure 1. The first LTL property we will use is $\mathbf{GF}c_0 \wedge \mathbf{GF}c_1$, which is a naïve formulation of the idea that the two processes are infinitely often in the critical section. An improved version of the formula that enforces fairness will be $(\mathbf{GF}(a_0 \wedge w_0) \rightarrow \mathbf{GF}c_0) \wedge (\mathbf{GF}(a_1 \wedge w_1) \rightarrow \mathbf{GF}c_1)$. The propositions a and w mean that the given process is active (when a holds) and that it is waiting (when w holds). First of these formulae is invalid (and the tool produces a counterexample), whereas the second one will be shown to hold for the model presented.

An example invocation of the tool for the model with 3 processes (and the formulae extended to 3 processes straightforwardly) can be seen in Figure 3. The counterexample could be browsed by running divine-mc.simulator on the produced mutex_peterson.naive.trail. The simulator is currently fairly rudimentary, but it still serves the purpose. When the same verifier command is used on the second formula, no counterexample is generated and the tool declares that an acceeping cycle has not been found, which means that the LTL property holds.

It can be seen that the input file to the verifier is a single DVE file that already contains a property process. Such a file could be written by hand (when the property has been specified as a Büchi automaton) or produced by divine-mc.combine, which takes a set of LTL formulae as input (in an .ltl file containing definitions of atomic propositions and the formulae – an example of such file containing the 2 discussed properties can be seen in Figure 2). The divine-mc.combine script will produce a single DVE file for each property, which can then be used as an input for the verifier.

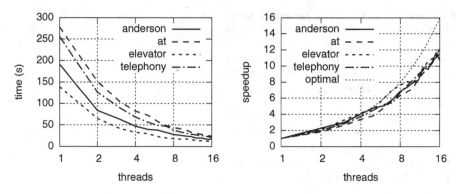

Fig. 4. Timing and speedup of reachability analysis

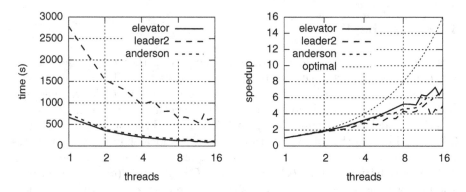

Fig. 5. Timing and speedup of LTL model checking, the algorithm used is OWCTY

4   Implementation

DIVINE MULTI-CORE is implemented on top of the POSIX Threads standard. Similarly to the distributed-memory approach, the state space is partitioned into parts, each thread being responsible for states of one of the parts. A thread maintains its own hashtable, explores successors of states of its part of the state space, and communicates with other threads by means of lock-free shared-memory message passing.

5   Experiments

The figures presented come from a 16-way AMD Opteron 885 (8 CPU units with 2 cores each) machine, with 64G of RAM, compiled with gcc 4.2.2 in 64-bit mode, using -O2. The models have been taken from a DVE model database [8]. Their descriptions and the verified properties can be found in the database: *anderson* is `anderson.6.dve` and `anderson.6.prop4.dve`, *elevator* is `elevator2.3.dve` and `elevator2.3.prop4.dve`, *at* is `at.5.dve`, *leader2* is `leader_election.5.prop2.dve` and finally *telephony* is `telephony.7.dve`. The property-less models have been used in reachability timing, whereas those containing LTL property (suffixed `propN.dve`) have been used for OWCTY timing. More experimental data can be found on the tool webpage [6].

6 Future Work

To improve the usefulness of the tool we plan to implement a graphical interface for counterexample browsing, which would be much more intuitive than the current fairly rudimentary simulator available.

Moreover, we intend to further optimize the state space generator, which currently seems to be the main bottleneck of the tool – therefore the tool would benefit greatly from an improved interpreter.

Another future goal is to adapt and implement some of the known distributed memory partial order reduction techniques.

References

1. Barnat, J., Brim, L., Ročkai, P.: Scalable multi-core ltl model-checking. In: Bošnački, D., Edelkamp, S. (eds.) SPIN 2007. LNCS, vol. 4595, pp. 187–203. Springer, Heidelberg (2007)
2. Barnat, J., Brim, L., Černá, I., Moravec, P., Ročkai, P., Šimeček, P.: DiVinE – A Tool for Distributed Verification (Tool Paper). In: Ball, T., Jones, R.B. (eds.) CAV 2006. LNCS, vol. 4144, pp. 278–281. Springer, Heidelberg (2006)
3. Barnat, J., Ročkai, P.: Shared Hash Tables in Parallel Model Checking. In: Participant proceedings of the Sixth International Workshop on Parallel and Distributed Methods in verifiCation (PDMC 2007), pp. 81–95. CTIT, University of Twente (2007)
4. Brim, L., Černá, I., Moravec, P., Šimša, J.: Accepting Predecessors are Better than Back Edges in Distributed LTL Model-Checking. In: Hu, A.J., Martin, A.K. (eds.) FMCAD 2004. LNCS, vol. 3312, pp. 352–366. Springer, Heidelberg (2004)
5. Černá, I., Pelánek, R.: Distributed explicit fair cycle detection (set based approach). In: Ball, T., Rajamani, S.K. (eds.) SPIN 2003. LNCS, vol. 2648, pp. 49–73. Springer, Heidelberg (2003)
6. DiVinE – Distributed Verification Environment, Masaryk University Brno, `http://anna.fi.muni.cz/divine-mc/`
7. Holzmann, G.J., Bosnacki, D.: The design of a multicore extension of the spin model checker. IEEE Transactions on Software Engineering 33(10), 659–674 (2007)
8. Pelánek, R.: BEEM: BEnchmarks for Explicit Model checkers (February 2007), `http://anna.fi.muni.cz/models/index.html`
9. Vardi, M.Y., Wolper, P.: An automata-theoretic approach to automatic program verification. In: Proc. IEEE Symposium on Logic in Computer Science, pp. 322–331. IEEE Computer Society Press, Los Alamitos (1986)

ALASKA

Antichains for Logic, Automata and Symbolic Kripke Structures Analysis[*]

Martin De Wulf[1], Laurent Doyen[2], Nicolas Maquet[1,**], and Jean-Francois Raskin[1]

[1] Université Libre de Bruxelles (ULB), Belgium
[2] École Polytechnique Fédérale de Lausanne (EPFL), Switzerland

1 Introduction

ALASKA is a verification tool that implements new algorithms based on antichains [5, 7, 6] to efficiently solve the emptiness problem for both alternating finite automata (AFW) and alternating Büchi automata (ABW). Using the well-known translation from LTL to alternating automata, the tool can decide the satisfiability and validity problems for LTL over finite or infinite words. Moreover, ALASKA can solve the model-checking problem for ABW, LTL, AFW and finite-word LTL over symbolic (BDD-encoded) Kripke structures.

While several tools (notably NUSMV [2], and SPIN [17]) have addressed the satisfiability and model-checking problems for LTL [16], ALASKA uses new algorithms that are often more efficient, especially when LTL formulas are large. Moreover, to the best of our knowledge, ALASKA is the first publicly available tool to provide a direct interface to efficient algorithms to decide the emptiness of ABW and AFW.

Given the promising experimental results obtained recently [6], we have decided to polish our prototype and make it available to the research community. Our goal with ALASKA is not to compete with industrial-level tools such as SPIN or NUSMV but rather provide an open and clearly-documented library of antichain-based verification algorithms.

2 Classical and New Algorithms

A *linear-time specification* over a set of propositions P is a set of infinite words over $\Sigma = 2^P$. Linear-time specifications can be expressed using LTL formulas or ABW. An LTL formula φ over P defines the set of words $[\![\varphi]\!] = \{w \in \Sigma^\omega \mid w \models \varphi\}$ that satisfy φ. The *satisfiability problem* for LTL asks, given an LTL formula φ, if $[\![\varphi]\!]$ is empty. The *model-checking problem* for LTL asks, given an effective representation of an omega-regular language $\mathcal{L} \subseteq \Sigma^\omega$ (*e.g.*, the set of all computations of a reactive system) and a LTL formula φ, if $\mathcal{L} \subseteq [\![\varphi]\!]$. The language $L_b(A)$ of an ABW A is the set of words over which it has an accepting run [15]. The *emptiness problem* for

---

[*] This research was supported by the Belgian FNRS grant 2.4530.02 of the FRFC project "Centre Fédéré en Vérification" and by the project "MoVES", an Interuniversity Attraction Poles Programme of the Belgian Federal Government.

[**] This author is supported by an FNRS-FRIA grant.

Cha et al. (Eds.): ATVA 2008, LNCS 5311, pp. 240–245, 2008.

ABW asks, given an ABW A, if $L_b(A) = \varnothing$. The *model-checking problem* for ABW asks, given an omega-regular language $\mathcal{L}$ and an ABW A, if $\mathcal{L} \subseteq L_b(A)$. Note that since ABW are closed under complementation and intersection in polynomial time, the model-checking problem $\mathcal{L} \subseteq L_b(A)$ reduces in polynomial time to the emptiness problem $\mathcal{L} \cap \overline{L_b(A)} = \varnothing$. All these problems are PSPACE-COMPLETE.

Due to lack of space, the following focuses mainly on the LTL satisfiability and ABW emptiness problems. Extensions to model-checking and to the finite-word case are rather straightforward.

Classical approaches. The link between LTL and omega-regular languages is at the heart of the so-called *automata-theoretic approach* to LTL [23]. Given an LTL formula φ, one constructs a nondeterministic Büchi automaton (NBW) A_φ whose language corresponds exactly to the models of φ, *i.e.* $L_b(A_\varphi) = [\![\varphi]\!]$. This reduces the satisfiability and model-checking problems for LTL to automata-theoretic questions. This elegant framework has triggered a large body of works (*e.g.* [22,3,21,4,13,19,10,9,11,18,1,12,20]) that have been implemented in explicit-state model-checking tools such as SPIN [17] and in symbolic-state model-checking tools such as SMV and NUSMV [2]. The translation from LTL to NBW is central to the automata-theoretic approach to model-checking. This construction is however *worst-case exponential*. An explicit translation is required for explicit state model-checking, while in the symbolic approaches [3] the NBW is symbolically encoded using boolean constraints. In [16], Rozier and Vardi have extensively compared several symbolic and explicit tools for satisfiability checking of LTL. According to their experiments, the symbolic approach scales better.

The classical approach to solve ABW emptiness (and therefore LTL satisfiability) is to transform the ABW into an equivalent NBW. The first construction is due to Miyano and Hayashi [14], and many other constructions or variants have been proposed [4, 10, 9, 1]. Again, these constructions can be implemented either explicitly or symbolically.

The antichain approach. Given an LTL formula, ALASKA constructs an ABW over the symbolic alphabet $\Sigma = 2^P$ that recognizes the models of the formula. This translation is very fast, as the number of states of the ABW is linear in the size of the formula. This construction is well-known and is an intermediate step in several translators from LTL to explicit NBW [21].

Once the ABW has been constructed, our tool *implicitly* uses the Miyano-Hayashi construction (MH for short) to obtain an equivalent NBW (which is not explicitly computed). This NBW is then explored efficiently in an on-the-fly fashion. ALASKA exploits a *simulation relation* to prune the search towards the most promising states (*i.e.*, minimal for the simulation relation) during the exploration. The crucial point is the that this simulation relation exists by construction for all NBW defined by the Miyano Hayashi construction, and does not need to be computed.

The tools which use explicit translation from LTL to NBW typically spend much effort in minimizing the constructed NBW. The rationale of this approach is that while the size of the NBW is worst-case exponential, it should often be possible to minimize it sufficiently in practice. In contrast, ALASKA systematically explores an NBW which is of exponential size *in all cases* (MH), but does the exploration efficiently by exploiting the special structure of the MH state-space (the simulation relation).

To compute the emptiness of the MH NBW, ALASKA begins by computing the set of reachable accepting states $\mathcal{R}_\alpha \equiv \mathrm{Post}^*(\iota^{\mathsf{MH}}) \cap \alpha^{\mathsf{MH}}$, where ι^{MH} and α^{MH} are respectively the initial and accepting states of MH. It then computes the following fixpoint formula[1]: $\mathcal{F} \equiv \nu X \cdot \mathrm{Post}^*(\mathrm{Post}(X) \cap \mathcal{R}_\alpha)$. Analogously to the Emerson-Lei backward fixpoint formula [8], $\mathcal{F}$ contains exactly those states that are reachable from an accepting state which (1) is reachable from the initial states, and (2) can reach itself by a non-trivial loop. The set $\mathcal{F}$ is thus empty if and only if the NBW is empty.

The computation of the fixpoint $\mathcal{F}$ is done efficiently by ALASKA as follows. The simulation relation that exists by construction on MH is such that ι^{MH} and α^{MH} are both *upward closed sets* for this relation. Also, the Post operation preserves closedness[2] (and so do $\cup$ and $\cap$), which means that *all* the sets of states that appear in the computation of $\mathcal{F}$ are closed sets. ALASKA achieves its performance because the Post operation of a set of states that is closed for a simulation relation is *easier* than for an arbitrary set of states. Indeed, upward closed sets can be canonically represented by a (generally small) number of *minimal* states that are incomparable for the simulation relation (which we call an *antichain*), and all operations can be done on those elements only. ALASKA exploits the fact that antichains are often small in practice by computing the Post operation in the following *semi-symbolic* manner. Given a set of states X symbolically encoded using a BDD, ALASKA computes $\mathrm{Post}(X)$ by first enumerating the antichain elements of X (which we note $\lfloor X \rfloor$) and computing the set $X' = \bigcup_{s \in \lfloor X \rfloor} \mathrm{Post}(\{s\})$. By the simulation relation, we know that $X' = \mathrm{Post}(X)$. Because the input and output of this algorithm are symbolic (X and X' are BDD) but an explicit representation is used internally ($\lfloor X \rfloor$ is an explicit list of states), we call this algorithm semi-symbolic.

Interested readers will find all the details of the algorithms and proofs in [6], along with experimental results comparing the relative performance of an early version of ALASKA and NUSMV for LTL satisfiability and model-checking. More information is available at http://www.antichains.be

3   Implementation

Programming Language

ALASKA is written in Python, except for the BDD package which is written in C. We use the CUDD BDD library, with its PYCUDD Python binding. There is some performance overhead in using Python, but we chose it for enhanced readability and to make the code easy to change. We believe this is especially important in the context of academic research, as we expect other research teams to experiment with the tool, tweak the existing algorithms and add their own.

User Interface

ALASKA is made of two components: a *library* (alaskalib) and an *executable script* (alaska). The executable script is a simple command-line interface (See Fig. 1) to the algorithms provided with the library. The user interface currently provides access to the following features: finite and infinite-word LTL satisfiability, validity and equivalence

---

[1] This section details the *forward* algorithm; a *backward* algorithm is also implemented.

[2] There are some details involved, see [6].

checking, AFW and ABW emptiness, and model-checking of specifications expressed with finite or infinite-word LTL, AFW or ABW. Human-readable counter-example generation is available for all the aforementioned features. ALASKA can parse LTL formulas in the SPIN or NUSMV syntax and has a custom syntax for alternating automata (see Fig. 1 for an example). ALASKA uses the NUSMV input syntax for symbolic Kripke structures.

```
(
    automaton_type = "sABW"
  , locations = [0,1,2]
  , propositions = ["a","b"]
  , initial_constraint = "0 | 1"
  , accepting_locations = [2]
  , transition_function = {
        0 : "(a & 0 & 1) | ~a | (a & b & 2)"
      , 1 : "b"
      , 2 : "b & 2"
    }
)
```

```
nmaquet@linuxmachine: ~
nmaquet@linuxmachine:~$ alaska ls -c '(a & X(!b)) U (a & X(b))'
initial part :
[ a, !b ] [ a, b ]
omega loop :
[ !a, b ]
formula is SATISFIABLE
nmaquet@linuxmachine:~$ []
```

Fig. 1. On the top: example of an ABW encoded in the ALASKA syntax. On the bottom: example of a command-line invocation of ALASKA for LTL satisfiability with counter-example generation.

Library Architecture

As a research tool, we believe that the most important contribution of the ALASKA project is the availability of its source code. As such, we give an overview of its core library components. The ALASKA library is divided into *data* packages[3], *state-space* packages and *solver* packages. The data packages contain the data-structures with the associated parsers, pretty-printers and translation modules (e.g., LTL to ABW). The state-space packages provide intuitive abstractions of on-the-fly-explorable *implicit*

data packages	state-space packages	solver packages
automata	afasubset	afaemptiness
bdd	miyanohayashi	abwemptiness
boolean	kripkemiyanohayashi	ltlsatisfiability
ltl		ltlmodelchecking
nusmv		

Fig. 2. Package structure of ALASKA

---

[3] A Python *package* is a directory containing *.py files called *modules*.

state-spaces. Finally, the solver packages contain the high-level fixpoint algorithms. Each problem (ABW emptiness, AFA emptiness, LTL satisfiability, etc.) resides in its own module which provides several algorithmic variants (backward, forward, hybrid, etc.). Each solver uses a state-space package to evaluate a fixpoint formula and return the answer, along with a witness or counter-example if appropriate.

The original aspects of ALASKA reside in the state-space packages. They implement the antichain-based techniques which make ALASKA different from existing tools. There are currently three available state-space packages: afasubset represents the NFA state-space obtained from an AFA by a powerset construction, miyanohayashi represents the NBW state-space obtained from an ABW by the Miyano-Hayashi construction, and kripkemiyanohayashi represents the product state-space of a symbolic Kripke structure and a Miyano-Hayashi NBW. Each state-space package provides functions for converting between the BDD-encoding of sets of states and the antichain encoding, computing upward/downward closures, converting sets of states and traces to human-readable output, etc. They also each implement the Pre and Post operations in both fully-symbolic (using only BDD) and semi-symbolic (with antichains) variants.

package name	input structure	explorable state-space
afasubset	AFA	NFA
miyanohayashi	ABW	NBW
kripkemiyanohayashi	Kripke, ABW	Kripke $\otimes$ NBW

Fig. 3. Available sate-space packages

Possible Extensions

The ALASKA library can be used to implement various automata-based algorithms. One possibility of extension would be to mix backward with forward analysis into one algorithm. Also, as sometimes antichains do blowup in size, it might be interesting to have heuristics to detect such blowups in advance and proceed fully-symbolically in that case. For many such purposes, the ALASKA library could be a good starting point.

4   Tool Download, Examples, and Benchmarks

ALASKA is available for download at http://www.antichains.be. The tool is available for Linux, Macintosh and Windows (by using Cygwin[4]). For convenience, the tool can also be tested through a web interface, for which a number of examples and benchmarks are provided.

References

1. Bloem, R., Cimatti, A., Pill, I., Roveri, M., Semprini, S.: Symbolic implementation of alternating automata. In: Ibarra, O.H., Yen, H.-C. (eds.) CIAA 2006. LNCS, vol. 4094, pp. 208–218. Springer, Heidelberg (2006)
2. Cimatti, A., Clarke, E., Giunchiglia, F., Roveri, M.: Nusmv: A new symbolic model checker. STTT 2(4), 410–425 (2000)

---

[4] Cygwin is an open-source Linux-like environment for Windows. See http://www.cygwin.com

3. Clarke, E., Grumberg, O., Hamaguchi, K.: Another look at LTL model checking. In: CAV 1994. LNCS, vol. 818, pp. 415–427. Springer, Heidelberg (1994)
4. Daniele, M., Giunchiglia, F., Vardi, M.Y.: Improved automata generation for linear temporal logic. In: Halbwachs, N., Peled, D.A. (eds.) CAV 1999. LNCS, vol. 1633, pp. 249–260. Springer, Heidelberg (1999)
5. De Wulf, M., Doyen, L., Henzinger, T.A., Raskin, J.-F.: Antichains: A new algorithm for checking universality of finite automata. In: Ball, T., Jones, R.B. (eds.) CAV 2006. LNCS, vol. 4144, pp. 17–30. Springer, Heidelberg (2006)
6. De Wulf, M., Doyen, L., Maquet, N., Raskin, J.-F.: Antichains: Alternative algorithms for LTL satisfiability and model-checking. In: Ramakrishnan, C.R., Rehof, J. (eds.) TACAS 2008. LNCS, vol. 4963, pp. 63–77. Springer, Heidelberg (2008)
7. Doyen, L., Raskin, J.-F.: Improved algorithms for the automata-based approach to model-checking. In: Grumberg, O., Huth, M. (eds.) TACAS 2007. LNCS, vol. 4424, pp. 451–465. Springer, Heidelberg (2007)
8. Emerson, E.A., Lei, C.-L.: Efficient model checking in fragments of the propositional μ-calculus. In: LICS, pp. 267–278 (1986)
9. Fritz, C.: Constructing Büchi automata from LTL using simulation relations for alternating Büchi automata. In: Ibarra, O.H., Dang, Z. (eds.) CIAA 2003. LNCS, vol. 2759, pp. 35–48. Springer, Heidelberg (2003)
10. Gastin, P., Oddoux, D.: Fast LTL to Büchi automata translation. In: Berry, G., Comon, H., Finkel, A. (eds.) CAV 2001. LNCS, vol. 2102, pp. 53–65. Springer, Heidelberg (2001)
11. Hammer, M., Knapp, A., Merz, S.: Truly on-the-fly LTL model checking. In: Halbwachs, N., Zuck, L.D. (eds.) TACAS 2005. LNCS, vol. 3440, pp. 191–205. Springer, Heidelberg (2005)
12. Heljanko, K., Junttila, T.A., Keinänen, M., Lange, M., Latvala, T.: Bounded model checking for weak alternating büchi automata. In: Ball, T., Jones, R.B. (eds.) CAV 2006. LNCS, vol. 4144, pp. 95–108. Springer, Heidelberg (2006)
13. Löding, C., Thomas, W.: Alternating automata and logics over infinite words. In: IFIP TCS, pp. 521–535 (2000)
14. Miyano, S., Hayashi, T.: Alternating finite automata on omega-words. In: CAAP, pp. 195–210 (1984)
15. Muller, D., Saoudi, A., Schnupp, P.: Alternating automata. The weak monadic theory of the tree, and its complexity. In: Knott, L. (ed.) ICALP 1986. LNCS, vol. 226, pp. 275–283. Springer, Heidelberg (1986)
16. Rozier, K., Vardi, M.Y.: LTL satisfiability checking. In: Bošnački, D., Edelkamp, S. (eds.) SPIN 2007. LNCS, vol. 4595, pp. 149–167. Springer, Heidelberg (2007)
17. Ruys, T., Holzmann, G.: Advanced Spin tutorial. In: Graf, S., Mounier, L. (eds.) SPIN 2004. LNCS, vol. 2989, pp. 304–305. Springer, Heidelberg (2004)
18. Sebastiani, R., Tonetta, S., Vardi, M.Y.: Symbolic systems, explicit properties: On hybrid approaches for LTL symbolic model checking. In: Etessami, K., Rajamani, S.K. (eds.) CAV 2005. LNCS, vol. 3576, pp. 350–363. Springer, Heidelberg (2005)
19. Somenzi, F., Bloem, R.: Efficient Büchi automata from LTL formulae. In: Emerson, E.A., Sistla, A.P. (eds.) CAV 2000. LNCS, vol. 1855, pp. 248–263. Springer, Heidelberg (2000)
20. Tsay, Y.-K., Chen, Y.-F., Tsai, M.-H., Chan, W.-C., Luo, C.-J.: Goal extended: Towards a research tool for omega automata and temporal logic. In: Ramakrishnan, C.R., Rehof, J. (eds.) TACAS 2008. LNCS, vol. 4963, pp. 346–350. Springer, Heidelberg (2008)
21. Vardi, M.Y.: An automata-theoretic approach to linear temporal logic. In: 8th Banff Higher Order Workshop. LNCS, vol. 1043, pp. 238–266. Springer, Heidelberg (1995)
22. Vardi, M.Y., Wolper, P.: An automata-theoretic approach to automatic program verification. In: LICS, pp. 332–344. IEEE Computer Society Press, Los Alamitos (1986)
23. Vardi, M.Y., Wolper, P.: Reasoning about infinite computations. Information and Computation 115(1), 1–37 (1994)

NetQi: A Model Checker for Anticipation Game

Elie Bursztein

LSV, ENS Cachan, CNRS, INRIA
eb@lsv.ens-cachan.fr

Abstract. NetQi is a freely available model-checker designed to analyze network incidents such as intrusion. This tool is an implementation of the anticipation game framework, a variant of timed game tailored for network analysis. The main purpose of NetQi is to find, given a network initial state and a set of rules, the best strategy that fulfills player objectives by model-checking the anticipation game and comparing the outcome of each play that fulfills strategy constraints. For instance, it can be used to find the best patching strategy. NetQihas been successfully used to analyze service failure due to hardware, network intrusion, worms and multiple-site intrusion defense cooperation.

1 Introduction

Using model-checking for intrusion analysis is an active area of research [7,8,6]. Models and tools have been developed to analyze how an intruder can combine vulnerabilities as step-stones to compromise a network. However, Anticipation Game (AG) [4,3] is currently the only game framework for network security. Netqi [2] is the complete implementation of AG. With Uppaal Tiga [1], NetQi is the only model-checker for timed ATL (Alternating-time Temporal Logic).

Anticipation games are an evolution of attack graphs based on game theory. More specifically they are timed games based on a TATL variant designed for network security analysis purpose. An AG is a kripke structure where each node represents a network state and the transition between the nodes models the players (administrator and intruder) actions on the network. Therefore an AG models the evolution of the network as the result of players actions on it. Typically it is used to analyze how the network will be impacted by various attacks and how administrator actions can counter them. Using Anticipation game instead of attack graph offers the following advantages.

First it allows to model the concurrent interaction of the intruder and the administrator with the network. For example it is possible to model that the intruder is trying to exploit a vulnerability while the administrator is trying to patching.

Secondly the use of timed rules allows to model the temporal dimension of the attack. It captures that each interaction with the network requires a different time. For instance developing and launching an exploit is somewhat slower than downloading and launching a public available one. Modeling the time also allows to model the so called *"element of surprise"* [5], which occurs when one player takes the other by surprise because he is faster. For example when the administrator is patching a service she can be taken by surprise by the intruder if he is able to exploit the vulnerability before the patch is complete.

Cha et al. (Eds.): ATVA 2008, LNCS 5311, pp. 246–251, 2008.

Finally since anticipation game has been designed for network security analysis, it takes into account network topological information such as dependency between network services. This allow to model attack *collateral effects*. For example that when a DNS server is unavailable by collateral effect the web service is merely available because the DNS resolution failed.

The reminder of this paper is organized as follows. Sect. 2, details how the anticipation game framework and NetQi differs from previous tools and work on TATL and what makes NetQi effective for network security analysis. In Sect. 3 discusses how NetQi is implemented and presents some of its main optimizations. Sect. 4 presents an example of the game analyzed by NetQi. In Sect. 5 we conclude and give future directions.

2 The Framework

The AG framework differs from standard timed games in several points. The two most prominent features are the use of a dual layer structure and the use of a compact model description. In AG, the lower layer is used to model network information. It is composed of two parts, a graph used to model network service dependency that is fixed over time and a set of states that is meant to evolve over the time. States, which are Boolean values, are used to describe nodes information such as which are compromised, and which are vulnerable. States value are changed by player action effect. The upper layer is a standard timed game structure used to model the evolution of the network layer due to player action. Legal actions for each player are described by sets of timed rules. Each rule is of the form:

$$\Gamma_x : \mathbf{Pre}\ F \xrightarrow{\Delta,\ \mathrm{p,\ a,\ c}} P$$

where F is the set of *preconditions* that needs to be satisfied in order to use the rule. Δ is the amount of time needed to execute the rule, p is the player that uses the rule, a is the rule label (string), c is the rule cost. P is the rule *post-condition* that states rule effects and Γ_x is the rule location. Locations are used to restrict rules to a specific set of network nodes. A example of rules set is given in Section 4. Describing the model only with the network initial state and a set of rules relieve the security analyst from the tedious and error prone burden of explicitly describing each network states and transitions. While working on large network, explicitly describing each network state is almost impossible because such game have millions of states. Therefore in AG the model-checking algorithm uses the set of rules to infers automatically every transitions and network states reachable from the network initial state. As a result, it is possible to express very large and complex model in a very compact form which is handy while working on large network and complex attack. Additionally modeling players action by rules allows to capture security expert reasoning in an intuitive manner as it allows to write things like: if a service is vulnerable then an intruder can compromise it, and if a service is compromised then an administrator can isolate it by using a firewall.

Beside anticipation games specificity, the main differences between Uppaal Tiga and NetQi are the game representation and the analysis goal. While Uppaal Tiga requires an expended model, NetQi uses a concise model described above. The other difference is that Uppal Tiga verifies TATL property whereas NetQi searches for strategy that matches player objectives. The use of player objectives is required to select between all the play that fulfills the TATL property, the one that will be the most efficient. For example an administrator wants to find a play that allows to patch her network efficiently but she probably wants the one that allows her to patch it efficiently for the minimal cost. Being able to provide the most effective solution in term of time and cost is a central issue in network security. Many natural questions that arise in network security require such answer for instance : which attack will cause the most damage ? what is the patching strategy that will minimize my loss ? Specifying analysis goal as strategy objective is possible because each rule has a cost and a possible reward. The rule reward is based on the value of the targeted network node. The use of time, cost and reward allows to take into account the financial and temporal dimension of the attack in the analysis. Theses objectives are described in the game file by a strategy objective tuple. This tuple is:

$$S : (name, player, objectives, objectives\ order, constraints, location)$$

where $name$ is the strategy name, $player$ specifies for which player this strategy is, $objectives$ are strategy objectives based on player and opponent cost and reward, $objectives\ order$ is used to indicate which objectives are the more important, $constraints$ is a set of LTL constraints used to determine if a play should be considered as a potential strategy, and finally $location$ specifies which group of service the strategy has to consider. There are five possible objectives : player cost and reward, opponent cost and reward and strategy time. A typical set of objectives is player cost minimization and opponent cost maximization. This is equivalent to search for the less costly strategy against opponent best play because in network security there is a direct correlation between the cost of the attack and its efficiency. For finding a new vulnerability (0 day exploit) is more expensive than reusing a public one. On the other hand the 0 day exploit is more efficient because there is no patch or intrusion detection rule to catch it. Constraints can be used to express that a strategy is valid if and only if no host was compromised during the play or that at the end of the strategy at least one host is compromised for instance. Note that NetQi is able to model-check TATL property as well. Model-checking a property is used for instance to prove that given an initial network state and a given set of rules, whatever the intruder do, he cannot compromise a given set of services.

3   The Implementation

NetQi is composed of two parts: the game engine written in C for speed, and the frontend gui written in java for portability. NetQi can be run on Linux, OSX and Windows. NetQi takes as input a game file (see figure 2) that describes the network information, the strategy objectives, and player rules. It returns the strategy found either on the standard output or in a XML file. The Gui is used to build and display the game file and analyze the output file. It draws a visual representation of the lower layer graph and the strategy timeline.

NetQi uses a search in depth strategy based on rules time and node value. This search strategy is driven by the idea that since the fastest rule wins in timed game, if the player is not able to reach his strategy objective with his fastest rules, it is unlikely that he will reach them with slower rules. NetQi does not suffer from memory explosion because it is used to find memoryless strategy. One of the most effective optimization used in NetQi at runtime, is the use of early cut, which apply when the strategy constraints use a standard LTL □ operator. This operator is used to have a constraint that holds during the entire play. In this case, the strategy constraints are evaluated dynamically at each step on the play. If a step violates the strategy constraint, NetQi cuts the play and immediately backtracks, because this play will never be an acceptable strategy. As shown in figure 1, this optimization can reduce greatly the number of plays and states considered during the analysis. The standard defense strategy uses the □ operator to ensure that no host is ever compromised.

Early cut	plays	states	time (s)
No	6 113 459	18 444 859	515
Yes	124 047	366 829	9

Fig. 1. Early cut impact on performance

Before the execution of the analysis, NetQi perform a static analysis of the game file to determine if some optimization can be made. For example the static analysis involves removing the set of rules that will never be executed because there pre-conditions are in conflict with strategy constraints. For example, if the strategy constraints requires that not a single service is ever compromise then all the rules that requires in their pre-conditions that one service is already compromised are removed.

4   Example

An hello world example of game file is presented in figure 2, the resulting strategy found by NetQi is depicted in figure 3. The game file is composed of five sections. The first section is the general options section, in the example only the number of lower-layer node to consider is specified but other options exist such as timeout. The second section contains the set of states used and their initial values. In the example two sets are used: The $Vuln$ set is used to model that the node 1 is vulnerable and the set $Compr$ is used to model that no node is compromised at the beginning. The third section is the rule section. In the example 3 rules are used. The first one states in its precondition that if a node is vulnerable ($Vuln$), then in 3 units of time for a cost of 200$ the intruder (I) can compromise ($Compr$) it (rule effect). The two other rules state that the administrator can patch a vulnerable ($Vuln$) service. They differ by their costs and execution time. The fast rule requires less time, 1 instead of 6, but for a greater cost: 5000$ instead of 500$. The fourth section is the dependency graph description. Here only the node 1 value is specified (42) but other type of information can be specified here such as dependency between nodes and node location. Finally the last section is the strategy objectives. The administrator (A) example strategy called Defense aims at minimizing player cost and ensuring by constraints that in the selected play no node is ever compromised. The play considered as the best strategy, visible on the right of the figure, is as expected the one that uses the fast patch rule. Note that the intruder is taken by surprise by the administrator and its compromise rule fails.

```
nodes=1
<sets>
Vuln:1
Compr:false
</sets>
<rules>
I:3:Compromise:Vuln=>Compr=200
A:6:Patch slow:Vuln=>!Vuln=500
A:1:Patch fast:Vuln=>!Vuln=5000
</rules>
<graph>
1=42
</graph>
strategy(Defense,A,MIN(Cost),Cost,|!Compr)
```

Fig. 2. The Game file

Time	Player	Action	Rule	Target	Reward	Cost
0	Intruder	choose	Compromise	1	-	-
0	Admin	choose	Patch fast	1	-	-
1	Admin	**execute**	Patch fast	1	42	5000
3	Intruder	fail	Compromise	1	0	200

Fig. 3. The resulting strategy

5 Conclusion

NetQi has been run successfully on complex network attack scenario. For example to find a multiple-site defense strategy, that involves 5 sites with 10 services each and 11 action rules analysis, the run-time on a Linux core2 2.9 GHz is less than 5 minutes. We expect that with a suitable service collapsing abstraction, NetQi will scale to much larger network. NetQi is very stable and therefore can be run on very large example without crash or memory leak. So far, the biggest successful analysis was a game with 1 148 893 596 distinct states. This analysis took 527 minutes which is an average of 36290 states per seconds. In addition because NetQi game files are easy to write even for a non game theory specialist, we hope it will be of use and interest to security experts. For futher information on NetQi, including downloads, examples, and documentation, see http://www.netqi.org

References

1. Behrmann, G., Cougnard, A., David, A., Fleury, E., Larsen, K.G., Lime, D.: Uppaal-tiga: Time for playing games! In: Damm, W., Hermanns, H. (eds.) CAV 2007. LNCS, vol. 4590, pp. 121–125. Springer, Heidelberg (2007)
2. Bursztein, E.: Netqi, http://www.netqi.org
3. Bursztein, E.: Network administrator and intruder strategies. Technical Report LSV-08-02, LSV, ENS Cachan (January 2008)
4. Bursztein, E., Goubault-Larrecq, J.: A logical framework for evaluating network resilience against faults and attacks. In: 12th annual Asian Computing Science Conference (ASIAN), December 2007, pp. 212–227. Springer, Heidelberg (2007)
5. de Alfaro, L., Faella, M., Henzinger, T., Majumdar, R., Stoelinga, M.: The element of surprise in timed games. In: Amadio, R., Lugiez, D. (eds.) CONCUR 2003. LNCS, vol. 2761, pp. 144–158. Springer, Heidelberg (2003)
6. Ramakrishan, C., Sekar, R.: Model-based analysis of configuration vulnerabilities. Journal of Computer Security 1, 198–209 (2002)
7. Ritchey, R.W., Ammann, P.: Using model checking to analyze network vulnerabilities. In: SP 2000: Proceedings of the 2000 IEEE Symposium on Security and Privacy, Washington, DC, USA, pp. 156–165. IEEE Computer Society Press, Los Alamitos (2000)
8. Sheyner, O., Haines, J., Jha, S., Lippmann, R., Wing, J.M.: Automated generation and analysis of attack graphs. In: SP 2002: Proceedings of the 2002 IEEE Symposium on Security and Privacy, Washington, DC, USA, pp. 273–284. IEEE Computer Society Press, Los Alamitos (2002)

Component-Based Design and Analysis of Embedded Systems with UPPAAL PORT

John Håkansson[1], Jan Carlson[2], Aurelien Monot[3], Paul Pettersson[2], and Davor Slutej[2]

[1] Department of Information Technology, Uppsala University, Sweden
johnh@it.uu.se
[2] Mälardalen Real-Time Research Centre, Västerås, Sweden*
jan.carlson@mdh.se, paul.pettersson@mdh.se, davor@slutej.com
[3] Ecole des Mines, Nancy, France
aurelien.monot@mines-nancy.org

Abstract. UPPAAL PORT is a new tool for component-based design and analysis of embedded systems. It operates on the hierarchically structured continuous time component modeling language SaveCCM and provides efficient model-checking by using partial-order reduction techniques that exploits the structure and the component behavior of the model. UPPAAL PORT is implemented as an extension of the verification engine in the UPPAAL tool. The tool can be used as back-end in to the Eclipse based SaveCCM integrated development environment, which supports user friendly editing, simulation, and verification of models.

1 Introduction

UPPAAL PORT[1] is a new extension of the UPPAAL tool. It supports simulation and model-checking of the component modelling language SaveCCM [1,6], which has been designed primarily for development of embedded systems in the area of vehicular systems. In SaveCCM, an embedded system is modelled as interconnected components with explicitly defined input and output ports for data and control. A component can be an encapsulation of a system of interconnected components, which externally behaves as a component, or a primitive component. In the latter case the functional and timing behaviour of a component is described as a timed automaton [2].

UPPAAL PORT accepts the hierarchical SaveCCM modelling language, represented in XML format, and provides analysis by model-checking *without* conversion or flattening to the model of network of timed automata normally used in the UPPAAL tool. The hierarchical structure of the model, and the particular "read-execute-write" component semantics adopted in SaveCCM is exploited in the tool to improve the efficiency of the model-checking analysis, which is further improved by a partial order reduction technique [10].

To provide user friendliness, UPPAAL PORT can serve as back-end in the SaveCCM integrated development environment (SAVE-IDE) based on Eclipse, see Fig. 1. We have

---

* This work was partially supported by the Swedish Foundation for Strategic Research via the strategic research centre PROGRESS.

[1] UPPAAL PORT is available from the web page www.uppaal.org/port

Cha et al. (Eds.): ATVA 2008, LNCS 5311, pp. 252–257, 2008.

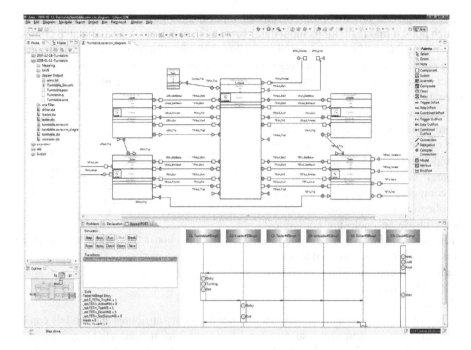

Fig. 1. SAVE-IDE architectural editor (upper view) and UPPAAL PORT simulator (lower view)

developed several plug-ins to integrate the two tools: an editor for timed automata descriptions of the functional and timing behaviour of components, support for mapping internal timed automata variables to external ports, a simulator that can be used to validate the behaviour of a SaveCCM system, and support for verifying reachability and liveness properties formalised in a subset of Timed CTL.

Related work includes for example the BIP component framework [9], where a system is constructed in three layers: behaviour, interaction, and priorities. Partial order techniques for timed automata are described for example in [11,7,5]. See also [10] for additional related work.

2   Real-Time Component Specification

The modelling language employed in UPPAAL PORT is SaveCCM — a component modelling language for embedded systems [1,6]. In SaveCCM, systems are built from interconnected components with well-defined interfaces consisting of input- and output ports. The communication style is based on the pipes-and-filters paradigm, but with an explicit separation of data transfer and control flow. The former is captured by connections between *data ports* where data of a given type can be written and read, and the latter by *trigger ports* that control the activation of components. Fig. 2 shows an example of the graphical SaveCCM notation. Triangles and boxes denote trigger ports and data ports, respectively.

A component remains passive until all input trigger ports have been activated, at which point it first reads all its input data ports and then performs the associated computations over this input and an internal state. After this, the component writes to its output data ports, activates the output trigger ports, and returns to the passive state again. This strict "read-execute-write" semantics ensures that once a component is triggered, the execution is functionally independent of any concurrent activity.

Components are composed into more complex structures by connecting output ports to input ports of other components. In addition to this "horizontal" composition, components can be composed hierarchically by placing a collection of interconnected components inside an enclosing component. From the outside, such a composite component is indistinguishable from a primitive component where the behaviour is given by a single model or piece of code.

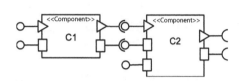

Fig. 2. Composition of two SaveCCM components

To support analysis and synthesis, a number of quality attributes and models can be associated with a component, such as execution time information, reliability estimates, safety models, etc. For UPPAAL PORT, it is required that each component is associated with a behavioural model consisting of a timed automaton and a mapping between component data ports and automata variables.

3   Model-Checking Real-Time Components

To support the dependability requirements of embedded real-time systems, SaveCCM is designed for predictability in terms of functionality, timeliness, and resource usage. In particular, the independence introduced by the "read-execute-write" semantics can be exploited for analysis purposes using partial order reduction techniques (PORT).

When model-checking, PORTs explore only a subset of the state space. The idea is to define equivalence between traces based on reordering of independent actions, and to explore a representative trace for each equivalence class. This approach has been successful for untimed systems, but for timed automata (TA) the implicit synchronization of global time restricts independence of actions [3,11].

In [10] we have described a PORT for SaveCCM which we have implemented in the UPPAAL PORT tool. As in [3,12] we use local time semantics to increase independence. The structure of a SaveCCM system is used to partition local time-scales, to determine independence of activities, and to construct the Ample-set.

Fig. 3 shows the tool architecture of UPPAAL PORT. The SAVE-IDE integrates an editor for SaveCCM systems in the Eclipse framework, as well as a TA editor to model the timing and behaviour of components. UPPAAL PORT adds support for simulation and verification, using a client-server architecture. When a new SaveCCM system is loaded into the server, the XML parser builds internal representations of UPPAAL TA

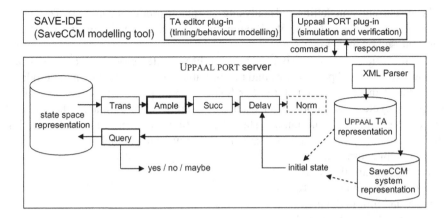

Fig. 3. Overview of the UPPAAL PORT tool architecture

and the SaveCCM system. By separating the UPPAAL TA representation when a new SaveCCM system is parsed we can reuse much of the source code from the UPPAAL model-checker.

The verification setup is shown in Fig. 3 as pipeline stages connected to the state space representation, as described in [8]. Unexplored states are put into the transition filter (Trans), which computes the enabled transitions. Each transition is forwarded with a copy of the state to the successor filter (Succ), which computes the resulting state after the transition. These two filters of the UPPAAL verifier are extended to implement the SaveCCM semantics. An additional filter (Ample) selects a sufficiently large subset of enabled transitions to be explored in order to model-check the property. This filter implements the PORT described in [10].

The zone representation is replaced with local time zones that are implemented as a data structure similar to Difference Bound Matrices (DBMs), as described for example in [3]. When a component writes data to other components, the local time-scales of participating components are synchronized by the successor filter. In combination with a modified filter (Delay) this implements local time semantics. The purpose of the normalisation filter (Norm) is to ensure that the state space is finite. This remains to be updated in order to handle the 'difference constraints' introduced by using local time.

The transition, successor, and delay filters are used also during simulation to compute possible transitions from the current state of the simulator, and to compute a new state for the simulation when the user selects to make a transition.

4   Case Studies

UPPAAL PORT has so far been applied to some benchmark examples, and two larger case studies. In [1], we present how an early version of UPPAAL PORT is applied to analyse a SaveCCM model of an adaptive cruise controller. A small benchmark of the partial order reduction technique implemented in the tool is described in [10], showing significant improvement over the standard global time semantics of, e.g., UPPAAL.

We are currently modelling and analysing a turntable production unit [4]. The system has been modelled and the specified requirements (similar to those given in [4]) have been analysed by model-checking.

The turntable system consists of a rotating disc (turntable) with four product slots and four tools in fixed positions around the turntable; the tools operate on the products, as illustrated in Fig. 4. Each slot either holds a single product in some state of the production cycle or is empty. After each 90° rotation of the turntable, the tools are allowed to operate - the turntable is stationary until all tools have finished operating. All slots can hold products and tools are allowed to work in parallel.

The architecture of the system is encapsulated by five SaveCCM components (a turntable and four tools) modelled using SaveCCM timed automata, which are passive and activated by trigger ports. Each component TA wraps C-style code that defines the actual behaviour of the component. This C-style code is directly interpreted by UP-PAAL PORT and is suitable as basis for expansion into a production system (the code used in the model for verification has no timeout-detection and error-handling).

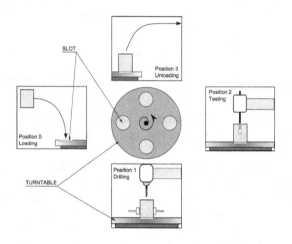

Fig. 4. Turntable system overview

The control system communicates with the environment by means of external ports that are defined at the root application level. When the code is generated for the target platform these ports are connected to the sensors and actuators. For simulation and verification purposes however, the external ports are mapped to global variables in the environment model. The environment model is constructed using the UPPAAL tool and utilizes UPPAAL timed automata, which, contrasting the SaveCCM TAs, are active.

Properties of safety and liveness are expressed as statements in the UPPAAL requirement specification language. To support more complex queries (involving a sequence of states), a test automaton is constructed in UPPAAL as a part of the environment model. The test automaton is connected to relevant ports in the SaveCCM model, to eliminate the need for test flags and other verification specific (as opposed to functional) additions to the control system model.

Model-checking the properties requires around 16MB at peak and an average of around 3 seconds per verified property (on an Intel T2600 2.16 GHz processor). The verification tool only needs to explore a maximum of 38,166 states to verify properties such as deadlock freedom.

5   Conclusion

In this paper, we have briefly described the new tool UPPAAL PORT that extends the verification engine of UPPAAL with partial order verification techniques for the real-time component language SaveCCM. Our initial experiments with the new verifier have been very encouraging and we are now in progress with evaluating UPPAAL PORT (together with the SaveCCM component modeling language and Save IDE) in a larger case study. As future work, UPPAAL PORT will be expended to support a richer component modeling language with components that may be active, have multiple service interfaces, or use other forms of communication.

References

1. Åkerholm, M., Carlson, J., Fredriksson, J., Hansson, H., Håkansson, J., Möller, A., Pettersson, P., Tivoli, M.: The SAVE approach to component-based development of vehicular systems. Journal of Systems and Software 80(5), 655–667 (2007)
2. Alur, R., Dill, D.L.: A theory of timed automata. Theoretical Computer Science 126(2), 183–235 (1994)
3. Bengtsson, J., Jonsson, B., Lilius, J., Yi, W.: Partial order reductions for timed systems. In: Sangiorgi, D., de Simone, R. (eds.) CONCUR 1998. LNCS, vol. 1466, pp. 485–500. Springer, Heidelberg (1998)
4. Bortnik, E., Trčka, N., Wijs, A.J., Luttik, S.P., van de Mortel-Fronczak, J.M., Baeten, J.C.M., Fokkink, W.J., Rooda, J.E.: Analyzing a χ model of a turntable system using Spin, CADP and Uppaal. Journal of Logic and Algebraic Programming 65(2), 51–104 (2005)
5. Bouyer, P., Haddad, S., Reynier, P.-A.: Timed unfoldings for networks of timed automata. In: Graf, S., Zhang, W. (eds.) ATVA 2006. LNCS, vol. 4218, pp. 292–306. Springer, Heidelberg (2006)
6. Carlson, J., Håkansson, J., Pettersson, P.: SaveCCM: An analysable component model for real-time systems. In: Proc. of the 2nd Workshop on Formal Aspects of Components Software (FACS 2005). Electronic Notes in Theoretical Computer Science. Elsevier, Amsterdam (2005)
7. Cassez, F., Chatain, T., Jard, C.: Symbolic unfoldings for networks of timed automata. In: Graf, S., Zhang, W. (eds.) ATVA 2006. LNCS, vol. 4218, pp. 307–321. Springer, Heidelberg (2006)
8. David, A., Behrmann, G., Larsen, K.G., Yi, W.: A tool architecture for the next generation of UPPAAL. In: Aichernig, B.K., Maibaum, T.S.E. (eds.) Formal Methods at the Crossroads. From Panacea to Foundational Support. LNCS, vol. 2757, pp. 352–366. Springer, Heidelberg (2003)
9. Gössler, G., Sifakis, J.: Composition for component-based modelling. Science of Computer Programming 55(1-3), 161–183 (2005)
10. Håkansson, J., Pettersson, P.: Partial order reduction for verification of real-time components. In: Proc. of 1st International Workshop on Formal Modeling and Analysis of Timed Systems. LNCS. Springer, Heidelberg (2007)
11. Lugiez, D., Niebert, P., Zennou, S.: A partial order semantics approach to the clock explosion problem of timed automata. Theoretical Computer Science 345(1), 27–59 (2005)
12. Minea, M.: Partial order reduction for model checking of timed automata. In: Baeten, J.C.M., Mauw, S. (eds.) CONCUR 1999. LNCS, vol. 1664, pp. 431–446. Springer, Heidelberg (1999)

Time-Progress Evaluation for Dense-Time Automata with Concave Path Conditions*

Farn Wang

Dept. of Electrical Engineering
Graduate Institute of Electronic Engineering
National Taiwan University
farn@cc.ee.ntu.edu.tw
http://cc.ee.ntu.edu.tw/~farn
http://sourceforge.net/projects/redlib

Abstract. The evaluation of successor or predecessor state spaces through time progress is a central component in the model-checking algorithm of dense-time automata. The definition of the time progress operator takes into consideration of the path condition of time progress and usually results in high complexity in the evaluation. Previous algorithms in this aspect usually assume that the original location invariance conditions of an automaton are convex in the dense-time state space. Based on this assumption, efficient algorithms for convex path conditions can be designed for reachability analysis. However, it is not clear whether the path conditions are still convex in the general setting of TCTL model-checking. In this work, we discuss the concept of time-convexity that allows us to relax the restrictions on the application of time-progress evaluation algorithm for convex path conditions. Then we give examples in TCTL model-checking that engenders time-concave path conditions even when the original automaton location invariance conditions are time-convex. Then we present two techniques that allow us to apply the evaluation algorithms for time-convex path conditions to time-concave path conditions. Finally, we report our experiment with the techniques. For some benchmarks, our techniques may enhance the performance of model-checking by an order of magnitude.

Keywords: Timed automaton, time progress, model-checking, TCTL, convex, concave.

1 Introduction

In the last two decades, we have witnessed significant progress in both theory and applications of the model-checking technology of dense-time systems [1,4,11,8]. One popular framework in this regard is called *TCTL model-checking* [1] which assumes a given dense-time system description as a *timed automaton (TA)* [3] and

---

* The work is partially supported by NSC, Taiwan, ROC under grants NSC 95-2221-E-002-067 and NSC 95-2221-E-002-072.

Cha et al. (Eds.): ATVA 2008, LNCS 5311, pp. 258–273, 2008.

a given specification formula in *Timed Computation Tree Logic* (*TCTL*) [1] and checks whether the TA satisfies the TCTL formula. The TCTL model-checking technology could be an attractive choice to the industry as long as the performance of the related verification algorithms could handle industrial projects. However, at this moment, many algorithms used in TCTL model-checking still suffer from low performance. To achieve the promise of TCTL model-checking, the performance of related algorithms has to be enhanced.

One important algorithm in TCTL model-checking is the time-progress evaluation algorithm. For simplicity, we focus on the backward time-progress operation. However, the ideas discussed in this work should also apply to the forward counterpart. Usually we are given a *path condition* ϕ and a *destination condition* ψ and want to compute the condition, $\texttt{Tbck}(\phi, \psi)$ in symbols, of *those states that can go to a state satisfying ψ through a time progression along which all states satisfying ϕ*. For convenience, given $t \in \mathbb{R}^{\geq 0}$, we let $\phi + t$ be the condition for states that satsify ϕ after the progression of t time units [1]. Then $\texttt{Tbck}(\phi, \psi)$ can be formulated as follows [7].

$$
\begin{aligned}
\texttt{Tbck}(\phi, \psi) &\stackrel{\text{def}}{=} \exists t \in \mathbb{R}^{\geq 0} \left(\psi + t \wedge \forall t' \in \mathbb{R}^{\geq 0} \left(t' \leq t \rightarrow \phi + t' \right) \right) \\
&\equiv \exists t \in \mathbb{R}^{\geq 0} \left(\psi + t \wedge \neg \exists t' \in \mathbb{R}^{\geq 0} \left(t' \leq t \wedge \neg \phi + t' \right) \right)
\end{aligned} \tag{T}
$$

The outer quantification on t specifies the "*through a time progression*" part. The inner quantification specifies that every state along the finite computation also satisfies ϕ. As can be seen, $\texttt{Tbck}(\phi, \psi)$ incurs two existential quantifications (or Fourier-Motzkin elimination [6]), two complementations, and two conjunctions. Since the time-progress algorithm is fundamental to TCTL model-checking, such an involved formulation usually results in significant performance degradation.

One way to enhance the evaluation efficiency of $\texttt{Tbck}()$ is to make an assumption of the TAs. An observation is that if the path condition ϕ characterizes a *convex*[1] state space, then $\texttt{Tbck}(\phi, \psi)$ can be rewritten as follows.

$$
\texttt{Tbck}'(\phi, \psi) \stackrel{\text{def}}{=} \exists t \in \mathbb{R}^{\geq 0} \left(\psi + t \wedge \phi \wedge \phi + t \right) \tag{T'}
$$

The reason is that for two states ν and ν', that respectively represent the starting state and the destination state of a time progression, we know that the following two conditions are true.

- Both ν and ν' are in the convex space characterized by ϕ.
- All states that happen during this time progress actually form a straight line segment between ν and ν'.

According to the definition of convexity, then all states in this straight line segment (and time progression) must also be in the space characterized by ϕ. As can be seen from $\texttt{Tbck}'()$, one existential quantification and two complementations can be avoided with this assumption. It will be interesting to see to what extent in TCTL model-checking [1,10], we can use $\texttt{Tbck}'()$ in place of $\texttt{Tbck}()$. According

---

[1] A space is *convex* if for any two points in the space, any point in the straight line segment between the two points is also in the space. A space that is not convex is *concave*.

to our knowledge, there is no related work in this regard. In this work, we have the following contributions.

- We propose the idea of *time-convexity* to relax the applicability of Tbck'() to concave path conditions.[2]
- We show that if the location invariance conditions of a TA are all time-convex, then all path conditions used in the reachability analysis are also time-convex.
- We show that there are examples in TCTL model-checking [1] that entail the computation of time progress through *time-concave* path conditions even when all the location invariance conditions of the TA are time-convex.
- We present two techniques that allow us to apply Tbck'() for the time progress evaluation through time-concave path conditions. For several benchmarks, the techniques have significantly enhanced the performance of our TCTL model-checker.

We have the following presentation plan. Section 2 reviews the background theory. Section 3 explains the concept of time-convexity. Section 4 investigates the possibilities of time-concave and time-convex path conditions in reachability analysis and model-checking. Sections 5 and 6 respectively present a technique for efficient time progress evaluation with time-concave path conditions. Section 7 reports our implementation and experiment. Section 8 is the conclusion.

2   TCTL Model-Checking Problem

2.1   Timed Automata

Let $\mathbb{N}$ be the set of non-negative integers, $\mathbb{Z}$ the set of all integers, and $\mathbb{R}^{\geq 0}$ the set of non-negative reals. Also 'iff' means "if and only if." Given a set Q of atomic propositions and a set X of clocks, a *location predicate* is a Boolean combination of atoms of the forms q and $x \sim c$, where $q \in Q$, $x \in X$, '$\sim$' is one of $\leq, <, =, >, \geq$, and $c \in \mathbb{N}$. The set of all location predicates of Q and X is denoted as $\mathcal{L}(Q, X)$.

Definition 1. Timed automaton (TA) A *TA* is a tuple $\langle Q, X, I, H, E, \sigma, \delta, \tau, \pi \rangle$ with the following restrictions. Q is a finite set of control locations. X is a finite set of clocks. $I \in \mathcal{L}(Q, X)$ is the initial condition. $H \in \mathcal{L}(Q, X)$ is the location invariance condition. $E \subseteq Q \times Q$ is a finite set of transition rules. $\sigma : E \mapsto Q$ and $\delta : E \mapsto Q$ respectively specify the source and the destination locations of each transition. $\tau : E \mapsto \mathcal{L}(\emptyset, X)$ defines the triggering condition of each rule execution. For each $e \in E$, $\pi(e) \subseteq X$ specifies the set of clocks to reset during the transition.   ∎

For convenience, given a TA $A = \langle Q, X, I, H, E, \sigma, \delta, \tau, \pi \rangle$, we use $Q_A, X_A, I_A,$ $H_A, E_A, \sigma_A, \delta_A, \tau_A,$ and π_A to denote $Q, X, I, H, E, \sigma, \delta, \tau,$ and π respectively.

---

[2] For convenience, we say a condition is convex iff the state space that it characterizes is convex. A non-convex condition is concave.

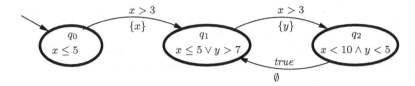

Fig. 1. An example TA

Example 1. We have the transition diagrams of an example TA A in figure 1. The ovals represent control locations q_0, q_1, and q_2. Location q_0 is the initial one. In each control location, we label the name and the constraint at that location. Thus the initial condition is $I_A \equiv q_0 \wedge x \leq 5$ and the location invariance condition is $H_A \equiv (q_0 \wedge x \leq 5) \vee (q_1 \wedge (x \leq 5 \vee y > 7)) \vee (q_2 \wedge x < 10 \wedge y < 5)$. The arcs represent transitions between locations. On each arc, we label the triggering condition and the clock reset set. ∎

A *valuation* of a set Y *(domain)* is a mapping from Y to a *codomain*.

Definition 2. States of a TA A *clock valuation* of a TA A is a total valuation from X_A to $\mathbb{R}^{\geq 0}$. A *state* of A is a pair (q, ν) such that $q \in Q_A$ and ν is a clock valuation. Let V_A denote the set of states of A. ∎

For any clock valuation ν of a TA A and $t \in \mathbb{R}^{\geq 0}$, $\nu + t$ is a valuation identical to ν except that for every $x \in X_A$, $(\nu + t)(x) = \nu(x) + t$. Given a set $X' \subseteq X_A$, we let $\nu X'$ be a valuation that is identical to ν except that all variables in X' are mapped to zero.

A state (q, ν) *satisfies* a location predicate η, in symbols $(q, \nu) \models \eta$, if η is evaluated true when q is interpreted true, all other location names are interpreted false, and all clock variables are interpreted according to ν. Given two states $(q, \nu), (q', \nu')$ and a transition e of a TA A, we say A *transits with* e from (q, ν) to (q', ν'), in symbols $(q, \nu) \overset{e}{\longrightarrow} (q', \nu')$, if $\sigma_A(e) = q$, $\delta_A(e) = q'$, $(q, \nu) \models \tau_A(e) \wedge H_A$, $\nu \pi_A(e) = \nu'$, and $(q', \nu') \models H_A$.

Definition 3. Runs Given a TA A, a *run* of A is an infinite sequence of state-time pairs $((q_0, \nu_0), t_0)((q_1, \nu_1), t_1) \ldots ((q_k, \nu_k), t_k) \ldots \ldots$ with the following three restrictions. (1) $t_0 t_1 \ldots t_k \ldots \ldots$ is a monotonically, non-decreasing, and divergent real-number sequence. That is, $\forall k \geq 0 (t_{k+1} \geq t_k)$ and $\forall c \in \mathbb{N} \exists k > 1 (t_k > c)$. (2) For all $k \geq 0$, for all $t \in [0, t_{k+1} - t_k]$, $(q_k, \nu_k + t) \models H_A$. (3) For all $k \geq 0$, either $(q_k, \nu_k + t_{k+1} - t_k) = (q_{k+1}, \nu_{k+1})$ or there is an $e \in E_A$ such that $(q_k, \nu_k + t_{k+1} - t_k) \overset{e}{\longrightarrow} (q_{k+1}, \nu_{k+1})$. The run is *initial* if $(q_0, \nu_0) \models I_A$. ∎

2.2 Timed Computation Tree Logic (TCTL)

Given a set Q of atomic propositions, a set X of clocks, and a $b \in \mathbb{N}$, a *zone predicate* within bound b is a Boolean combination of atoms of the forms q and $x - y \sim c$, where $q \in Q$, $x, y \in X \cup \{0\}$, '$\sim$'$\in \{<, \leq, =, \neq, \geq, >\}$, and $c \in \mathbb{Z} \cap [-b, b]$. The set of all zone predicates of Q and X within bound b is denoted as $\mathcal{Z}_b(Q, X)$. The satisfaction of zone predicates by a state is defined similarly as that of location predicates.

TCTL is a language for the specification of timing behaviors with branching structure [1]. A TCTL formula ϕ is of the following syntax.

$$\phi ::= \eta \mid \phi_1 \vee \phi_2 \mid \neg\phi_1 \mid \exists\Box_{\sim c}\phi_1 \mid \exists\phi_1\mathcal{U}_{\sim c}\phi_2$$

Here η is a zone predicate in $\mathcal{Z}_\infty(Q, X)^3$, $\sim \in \{<, \leq, =, \neq, \geq, >\}$, and c is a non-negative integer constant. For modal formulas $\exists\Box_{\sim c}\phi_1$ and $\exists\phi_1\mathcal{U}_{\sim c}\phi_2$, ϕ_1 is called the *path condition* while ϕ_2 is called the *destination condition*. Standard shorthands like *true*, *false*, $\phi_1 \wedge \phi_2$, $\phi_1 \rightarrow \phi_2$, $\exists\Diamond_{\sim c}\phi_1$, $\forall\Box_{\sim c}\phi_1$, $\forall\Diamond_{\sim c}\phi_1$, and $\forall\phi_1\mathcal{U}_{\sim c}\phi_2$ are also adopted.

Note that, unlike the original definition of TCTL [1], we allow inequalities in $\mathcal{Z}_\infty(Q, X)$ to appear in TCTL formulas. The reason is that in the evaluation of nested modal formulas, the evaluation of inner modal formulas may yield predicates in $\mathcal{Z}_\infty(Q, X)$ anyway. Thus, in the general context of TCTL model-checking, it makes no difference to have zone predicates in TCTL formulas.

Given a state (q, ν) of a TA A and a TCTL formula ϕ, we use the notation $A, (q, \nu) \models \phi$ to mean that state (q, ν) *satisfies* ϕ in A. The definition of satisfaction of zone (location) predicates and Boolean formulas are straightforward. Those of satisfaction of the modal formulas are as follows.

- $A, (q, \nu) \models \exists\Box_{\sim c}\phi_1$ iff there is a run from (q, ν) such that for all states (q', ν') that is t time units from (q, ν) in the run with $t \sim c$, $A, (q', \nu') \models \phi_1$.
- $A, (q, \nu) \models \exists\phi_1\mathcal{U}_{\sim c}\phi_2$ iff there is a run from (q, ν) such that
  - there is a state (q', ν') that is t time units from (q, ν) in the run with $t \sim c$ and $A, (q', \nu') \models \phi_2$; and
  - for all states (q'', ν'') before (q', ν') in the run, $A, (q'', \nu'') \models \phi_1$.

The TCTL *model-checking problem* asks if all initial states of a TA satisfy a TCTL formula in the TA. Given a TA A and a TCTL formula ϕ, we use $[\![\phi]\!]_A$ to denote the state space characterized by ϕ in A. It is easy to see that for any state (q, ν), $(q, \nu) \in [\![\phi]\!]_A$ iff $A, (q, \nu) \models \phi$.

For convenience, given a condition η for a set of destination state and a transition e, we let $\texttt{Xbck}_e(\eta)$ be the condition for states that can directly go to states in η through transition e. Formally speaking, $(q, \nu) \models \texttt{Xbck}_e(\eta)$ iff there exists a $(q', \nu') \models \eta$ and $(q, \nu) \xrightarrow{e} (q', \nu')$. According to [7,10], the formulation for the evaluation of a formula like $\exists\Box_{\sim c}\phi_1$ can be represented as follows.

$$\exists z \left(z = 0 \wedge \mathbf{gfp}Z \left(\bigvee_{e \in E_A} \texttt{Tbck}\left(z \sim c \rightarrow (\phi_1 \wedge H_A), \texttt{Xbck}_e(Z) \right) \right) \right) \qquad (\exists\Box)$$

Here $\mathbf{gfp}$ is the greatest fixpoint operator. The evaluation of the greatest fixpoint operator works by iteratively eliminating states from Z until we find that there is no more elimination possible. z is an auxiliary clock variable not used in ϕ_1, I_A, H_A, and the transitions of A. As can be seen, formula $z \sim c \rightarrow (\phi_1 \wedge H_A)$ appears in formula (T) as a path condition.

Also, the formulation for the evaluation of a formula like $\exists\phi_1\mathcal{U}_{\sim c}\phi_2$ can be represented as follows.

---

³ We abuse the notation $[-\infty, \infty]$ for $(-\infty, \infty)$.

$$\exists z \left(z = 0 \wedge \mathbf{lfp} Z. \left((\phi_2 \wedge z \sim c \wedge H_A) \vee \bigvee_{e \in E} \mathrm{Tbck}(\phi_1 \wedge H_A, \mathrm{Xbck}_e(Z)) \right) \right) \quad (\exists \mathcal{U})$$

Here **lfp** is the least fixpoint operator. It characterizes the space of those states that can reach states satisfying ϕ_2 through a run segment along which all states satisfy ϕ_1. The evaluation of the least fixpoint operator works by iteratively adding states to Z until we find that there is no more addition possible. z is an auxiliary clock variable not used in ϕ_1, ϕ_2, I_A, H_A, and the transitions of A. As can be seen, formula $\phi_1 \wedge H_A$ appears in formula (T) as a path condition.

3 Zones, Convexity, and Time-Convexity

Given a TA A and a TCTL formula ϕ, we let C_A^ϕ be the biggest timing constant used in A and ϕ. A *clock zone* of A and ϕ is a set of clock valuations characterizable with a conjunctive[4] zone-predicate in $\mathcal{Z}_{C_A^\phi}(\emptyset, X_A)$. A clock zone is a convex space of clock valuations. Without loss of generality, we assume that the given characterization zone predicate for a clock zone is always *tight*. That is, for every inequality $x - y \sim c$ in the characterization zone predicate, we cannot change the value of c without changing the members of the corresponding clock zone. Such a tight zone predicate for a clock zone can be obtained with an all-pair shortest-path algorithm with cubic time complexity [5].

A *zone* of A and ϕ is a set of states in V_A characterizable with a conjunctive zone-predicate like $q \wedge \eta$ with a $q \in Q_A$ and $\eta \in \mathcal{Z}_{C_A^\phi}(\emptyset, X_A)$. The states in a zone share the same control location. According to [7], the state spaces of A that we need to manipulate in model-checking for ϕ are finite unions of zones. Such a union can be characterized with zone predicates in $\mathcal{Z}_{C_A^\phi}(Q_A, X_A \cup \{z\})$ where z is an auxiliary clock variable not used in A [7,10]. Many model-checkers for TAs are based on symbolic manipulation algorithms of *zone predicates* represented in various forms [4,8,11].

For convenience, we may also represent a zone as a pair like (q, η) with $q \in Q_A$ and $\eta \in \mathcal{Z}_{C_A^\phi}(\emptyset, X_A \cup \{z\})$. A set S of zones is *convex* if for each $q \in Q_A$, $\bigcup_{(q,\eta) \in S} [\![\eta]\!]_A$ is convex. If S is not convex, it is *concave*. The reachable state space of a TA is usually concave. Most state-spaces that we need to manipulate in TCTL model-checking are likely concave. For convenience, we say a formula ϕ is convex iff $[\![\phi]\!]_A$ is convex. If ϕ is not convex, then it is concave.

Example 2. The initial condition I_A of the TA in example 1 is convex while the location invariance condition H_A is concave. Specifically, the following subformula $\dot{H} \equiv q_1 \wedge (x \le 5 \vee y > 7)$ is concave. For example, we may have two states (q_1, ν_1) and (q_1, ν_2) with $\nu_1(x) = \nu_1(y) = 4$ and $\nu_2(x) = \nu_2(y) = 8$. It is clear that $(q_1, \nu_1) \in [\![\dot{H}]\!]_A$ and $(q_1, \nu_2) \in [\![\dot{H}]\!]_A$. However, the middle point, say $(q_1, \nu_{3/2})$, between (q_1, ν_1) and (q_1, ν_2) with $\nu_{3/2}(x) = \nu_{3/2}(y) = 6$ is not in $[\![\dot{H}]\!]_A$.

Concavity may also happen with difference constraints between two clocks. For example, the following zone predicate $\ddot{H} \equiv q_1 \wedge (x - y < 3 \vee x - y > 7)$ is also concave. For example, we may have two states (q_1, ν_3) and (q_1, ν_4) with $\nu_3(x) = 9$, $\nu_3(y) = 1$, $\nu_4(x) = 1$, and $\nu_4(y) = 9$. It is clear that (q_1, ν_3) and

---

[4] A conjunctive predicate does not have negation and disjunction in it.

(q_1, ν_4) are both in $[\![\ddot{H}]\!]_A$. However the middle point, say $(q_1, \nu_{7/2})$, between (q_1, ν_1) and (q_1, ν_2) with $\nu_{7/2}(x) = \nu_{7/2}(y) = 5$ is not in $[\![\ddot{H}]\!]_A$. ∎

It is known that procedure $\mathtt{Tbck'}()$ for time progress evaluation can be applied to convex path conditions.

Example 3. In example 1, $\mathtt{Tbck'}()$ is not applicable to H_A which is concave. For example, $\mathtt{Tbck}(H_A, q_1 \wedge x = 10 \wedge y = 10)$ is $q_1 \wedge x > 7 \wedge y > 7 \wedge x \leq 10 \wedge y \leq 10 \wedge x - y = 0$. However, $\mathtt{Tbck'}(H_A, q_1 \wedge x = 10 \wedge y = 10)$ is $q_1 \wedge x \geq 0 \wedge y \geq 0 \wedge x \leq 10 \wedge y \leq 10 \wedge x - y = 0$ which is incorrect. ∎

Here we relax the restriction of the applicability of $\mathtt{Tbck'}()$ with the following concept.

Definition 4. Time-convexity A union U of clock zones is *time-convex* iff for any $\nu \in U$ and $t \in \mathbb{R}^{\geq 0}$ with $\nu + t \in U$, then for any $t' \in [0, t]$, $\nu + t' \in U$. Otherwise, it is called *time-concave*. A set S of zones is time-convex if for each $q \in Q_A$, $\bigcup_{(q,\eta) \in S} [\![\eta]\!]_A$ is time-convex; it is time-concave else. ∎

Example 4. In examples 1 and 2, I_A is time-convex while H_A is time-concave. Moreover, zone predicate $\ddot{H} \equiv q_1 \wedge (x - y < 3 \vee x - y > 7)$ is concave. But we have the following derivation for any state (q, ν) and real $t \in \mathbb{R}^{\geq 0}$.

$$(q_1, \nu) \models q_1 \wedge (x - y < 3 \vee x - y > 7)$$
$$\equiv (q_1, \nu + t) \models q_1 \wedge (x + t - y - t < 3 \vee x + t - y - t > 7)$$
$$\equiv (q_1, \nu + t) \models q_1 \wedge (x - y < 3 \vee x - y > 7)$$

Thus it is clear that $q_1 \wedge (x - y < 3 \vee x - y > 7)$ is time-convex. ∎

Lemma 1. *Given a TA A, a time-convex path zone predicate ϕ, and a destination zone predicate ψ, $[\![\mathtt{Tbck}(\phi, \psi)]\!]_A = [\![\mathtt{Tbck'}(\phi, \psi)]\!]_A$.*

Proof: We can prove this lemma in two directions. First, we want to prove that $\mathtt{Tbck}(\phi, \psi) \subseteq \mathtt{Tbck'}(\phi, \psi)$. Given a state $(q, \nu) \models \mathtt{Tbck}(\phi, \psi)$, we have the following derivation.

$$(q, \nu) \models \mathtt{Tbck}(\phi, \psi)$$
$$\equiv (q, \nu) \models \exists t \in \mathbb{R}^{\geq 0} \left(\psi + t \wedge \forall t' \in \mathbb{R}^{\geq 0} (t' \leq t \rightarrow \phi + t') \right)$$
$$\Rightarrow (q, \nu) \models \exists t \in \mathbb{R}^{\geq 0} \left(\begin{array}{c} \psi + t \wedge \phi \wedge \phi + t \\ \wedge \forall t' \in \mathbb{R}^{\geq 0} (t' \leq t \rightarrow \phi + t') \end{array} \right), \text{ instantiating } t' \text{ with } t$$
$$\Rightarrow (q, \nu) \models \exists t \in \mathbb{R}^{\geq 0} (\psi + t \wedge \phi \wedge \phi + t), \text{ restriction relaxation.}$$
$$\equiv (q, \nu) \models \mathtt{Tbck'}(\phi, \psi), \text{ defnition}$$

Now we prove $\mathtt{Tbck'}(\phi, \psi) \subseteq \mathtt{Tbck}(\phi, \psi)$ with the following derivation.

$$(q, \nu) \models \mathtt{Tbck'}(\phi, \psi)$$
$$\equiv (q, \nu) \models \exists t \in \mathbb{R}^{\geq 0} (\psi + t \wedge \phi \wedge \phi + t)$$
$$\Rightarrow (q, \nu) \models \exists t \in \mathbb{R}^{\geq 0} \left(\begin{array}{c} \psi + t \wedge \phi \wedge \phi + t \\ \wedge \forall t' \in \mathbb{R}^{\geq 0} (t' \leq t \rightarrow \phi + t') \end{array} \right), \text{ since } \phi \text{ is time-convex}$$
$$\equiv (q, \nu) \models \exists t \in \mathbb{R}^{\geq 0} (\psi + t \wedge \forall t' \in \mathbb{R}^{\geq 0} (t' \leq t \rightarrow \phi + t')), \text{ since } t \leq t \wedge 0 \leq t$$
$$\equiv (q, \nu) \models \mathtt{Tbck}(\phi, \psi), \text{ defnition}$$

With the proof for the two directions, we know the lemma is correct. ∎

Lemma 1 implies that we can also apply the more efficient $\mathtt{Tbck'}()$ to concave but time-convex path conditions.

Example 5. In example 2, $\mathtt{Tbck'}()$ was not thought to be applicable to path zone predicate $\ddot{H}$ either. But now, $\mathtt{Tbck}(\ddot{H}, q_1 \wedge x = 8 \wedge y = 8)$ and $\mathtt{Tbck'}(\ddot{H}, q_1 \wedge x = 8 \wedge y = 8)$ both evaluate to $q_1 \wedge x \geq 0 \wedge y \geq 0 \wedge x \leq 8 \wedge y \leq 8 \wedge x - y = 0$. ∎

4   Time-Concavity and Convexity in Verification Problems

In this section, we show two things for TCTL model-checking. First, time-convexity of the location invariance condition H_A is good enough to guarantee the time-convexity of all path conditions used in the reachability analysis of A. Second, time-convexity of H_A is not good enough to guarantee the time-convexity of all path conditions in the TCTL model-checking of A.

4.1   For Reachability Analysis

The most used verification framework is *reachability analysis*. In this framework, we are given a TA A and a safety predicate η and want to check whether there is an initial run of A along which some state satisfies $\neg\eta$. The system is *safe* iff A satisfies $\forall\Box\eta \equiv \neg\exists true\,\mathcal{U}\neg\eta$. According to formula $(\exists\mathcal{U})$ in page 263, we find that all the path conditions used in the time progress evaluation is exactly the H_A of a TA A. Thus we have the following lemma.

Lemma 2. *For reachability analysis of a TA A, if H_A is time-convex, then* $\mathtt{Tbck'}()$ *can be used in place of* $\mathtt{Tbck}()$ *in formula ($\exists\mathcal{U}$) without affecting the result of analysis.* ∎

4.2   For TCTL Model-Checking

We have identified some generic cases in examples 6 through 10 that can cause time-concave path conditions in model-checking.

Example 6. **Disjunction in the path conditions in modal formulas.** We may have a formula: $\exists(q_1 \wedge (x \leq 5 \vee y > 7))\mathcal{U}q_2$. Given a TA A with a time-convex H_A, according to formula ($\exists\mathcal{U}$) in page 263, the path condition is $q_1 \wedge (x \leq 5 \vee y > 7) \wedge H_A$. As can be checked, the path condition is time-concave when $[\![q_1 \wedge x \leq 5 \wedge H_A]\!]_A \neq \emptyset$, $[\![q_1 \wedge y > 7 \wedge H_A]\!]_A \neq \emptyset$, and $[\![q_1 \wedge x > 5 \wedge y \leq 7 \wedge H_A]\!]_A \neq \emptyset$.
    For another example, according to formulation ($\exists\Box$) in page 262, formula $\exists\Box(q_1 \wedge (x \leq 5 \vee y > 7))$ also incurs time-concavity in path condition. ∎

Example 7. **Complementation in the path conditions in modal formulas.** We have a formula: $\forall\Diamond(q_1 \rightarrow (x > 5 \wedge y \leq 7))$ which can be rewritten as $\neg\exists\Box(q_1 \wedge (x \leq 5 \vee y > 7))$. According to formulation ($\exists\Box$) in page 262, the path

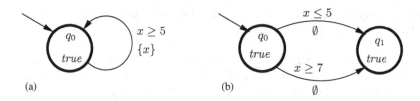

Fig. 2. Another example TA

condition $q_1 \wedge (x \leq 5 \vee y > 7) \wedge H_A$ is time-concave when $[\![q_1 \wedge x \leq 5 \wedge H_A]\!]_A \neq \emptyset$, $[\![q_1 \wedge y > 7 \wedge H_A]\!]_A \neq \emptyset$, and $[\![q_1 \wedge x > 5 \wedge y \leq 7 \wedge H_A]\!]_A \neq \emptyset$.   ∎

Note that in TCTL model-checking, we usually need to calculate the complement of time-convex state spaces and end up with time-concave state spaces.

Example 8. **Timing constraints with $\exists\square$-formulas.** According to formula ($\exists\square$) in page 262, formula: $\exists\square_{<7}x \leq 5$ incurs a path condition $z \leq 7 \rightarrow x \leq 5 \equiv z > 7 \vee x \leq 5$. Then following the argument in examples 2 and 4, it is easy to see that this path condition is also time-concave.   ∎

The following two examples show that path condition concavity may also happen due to the structures of TAs.

Example 9. **Time-concavities due to TA structures.** We may have the example TA A in figure 2(a) and want to check $A, (q_0, \nu) \models \exists\square\exists x > 3\mathcal{U}x \leq 0$ with $\nu(x) = 0$. Note that the location invariance condition is time-convex. $(q_0, \nu) \in [\![\exists x > 3\mathcal{U}x \leq 0]\!]_A$ since $x \leq 0$ is immediately fulfilled at ν. Also $(q_0, \nu + 4) \in [\![\exists x > 3\mathcal{U}x \leq 0]\!]_A$ with the firing of the transition at $\nu + 5$. But it is clear that $(q_0, \nu + 1) \notin [\![\exists x > 3\mathcal{U}x \leq 0]\!]_A$.   ∎

According to the original definition of TCTL [1], only propositions may appear as atoms. Thus we may argue that the above-mentioned formulas in examples 6 to 9 may not happen in the original TCTL definition. The following example is interesting in this regard.

Example 10. **Nested $\exists\mathcal{U}$-formulas with modal timing constraints.** Now we may want to check the TA in figure 2(b) for a formula $\exists\square\exists q_0\mathcal{U}_{<1}q_1$ at a state (q_0, ν) with $\nu(x) = 5$. Then $(q_0, \nu) \in [\![\exists q_0\mathcal{U}_{<1}q_1]\!]_A$ and $(q_0, \nu+2) \in [\![\exists q_0\mathcal{U}_{<1}q_1]\!]_A$. However, it is clear that $(q_0, \nu + 1) \notin [\![\exists q_0\mathcal{U}_{<1}q_1]\!]_A$.   ∎

5   Algorithm with Cascading Convexities

We have experimented with several techniques for performance enhancement of time progress evaluation for time-concave path conditions. We present one such technique that we have found useful. The technique breaks a time-concave zone predicate into time-convex ones and then applies Tbck'() on each time-convex ones for the evaluation of time progress.

Given a zone predicate ϕ that describes a time-concave state space, we want to characterizes those states in $[\![\phi]\!]_A$ that can first go through a state outside $[\![\phi]\!]_A$ through time progression and then again end up at a state in $[\![\phi]\!]_A$. To calculate the time progress operation to such states in $[\![\phi]\!]_A$, we cannot use $\mathtt{Tbck}'()$ in place of $\mathtt{Tbck}()$ since such states are evidence for the time-concavity of ϕ. Formally speaking, such states can be characterized as follows.

$$TConcave(\phi) \overset{\text{def}}{=} \phi \wedge \exists t \in \mathbb{R}^{\geq 0} \left(\phi + t \wedge \exists t' \in \mathbb{R}^{\geq 0}(t' < t \wedge (\neg\phi) + t') \right)$$

We have the following lemma that establishes some properties of the characterizaton useful for our performance-enhancing techniques.

Lemma 3. *Given a zone predicate ϕ for a TA A, $[\![\phi]\!]_A - [\![\text{TConcave}(\phi)]\!]_A$ is time-convex.*

Proof: This is straightforward from the definition of $TConcave(\phi)$. ∎

Given two state spaces S and S', we say S is *time-connected* to S' if there is a state $(q, \nu) \in S$ and a $t \in \mathbb{R}^{\geq 0}$ such that $(q, \nu + t) \in S'$ and for every $t' \in [0, t]$, $(q, \nu + t') \in S \cup S'$. If S is not *time-connected* to S', then it is *time-disconnected* to S'. The concept of time-connectivity is important for the correctness of piecewise evaluation of time progress.

Lemma 4. *Suppose we are given two zone predicates ϕ and ϕ' such that $[\![\phi]\!]_A$ is not time-connected to $[\![\phi']\!]_A$ and vice versa. Then for every zone predicate ψ, $[\![\mathtt{Tbck}(\phi, \psi)]\!]_A \cup [\![\mathtt{Tbck}(\phi', \psi)]\!]_A = [\![\mathtt{Tbck}(\phi \vee \phi', \psi)]\!]_A$.*
Proof: It is easy to see that $[\![\mathtt{Tbck}(\phi, \psi)]\!]_A \cup [\![\mathtt{Tbck}(\phi', \psi)]\!]_A \subseteq [\![\mathtt{Tbck}(\phi \vee \phi', \psi)]\!]_A$. On the other hand, $[\![\mathtt{Tbck}(\phi, \psi)]\!]_A \cup [\![\mathtt{Tbck}(\phi', \psi)]\!]_A \supseteq [\![\mathtt{Tbck}(\phi \vee \phi', \psi)]\!]_A$ is false if either of the following two cases are true.

- There is a state $(q, \nu) \in [\![\phi]\!]_A$ and a $t \in \mathbb{R}^{\geq 0}$ such that $(q, \nu + t) \in [\![\phi']\!]_A$ and for every $t' \in [0, t]$, $(q, \nu + t') \in [\![\phi]\!]_A \cup [\![\phi']\!]_A$. But this exactly violates the assumption that $[\![\phi]\!]_A$ is not time-connected to $[\![\phi']\!]_A$.
- There is a state $(q, \nu) \in [\![\phi']\!]_A$ and a $t \in \mathbb{R}^{\geq 0}$ such that $(q, \nu + t) \in [\![\phi]\!]_A$ and for every $t' \in [0, t]$, $(q, \nu + t') \in [\![\phi]\!]_A \cup [\![\phi']\!]_A$. This is symmetric to the first case and violates the assumption that $[\![\phi']\!]_A$ is not time-connected to $[\![\phi]\!]_A$.

Since both of these cases are false, we know the lemma is proven. ∎

Lemma 5. *Given a TA A and a zone predicate ϕ, $[\![\phi]\!]_A - [\![\text{TConcave}(\phi)]\!]_A$ is not time-connected to $[\![\text{TConcave}(\phi)]\!]_A$ and vice versa.*

Proof: We first assume that $[\![\phi]\!]_A - [\![TConcave(\phi)]\!]_A$ is time-connected to $[\![TConcave(\phi)]\!]_A$. This implies that there is a state $(q, \nu) \in [\![\phi]\!]_A - [\![TConcave(\phi)]\!]_A$ and a $t \in \mathbb{R}^{\geq 0}$ such that $(q, \nu + t) \in [\![TConcave(\phi)]\!]_A$ and for each $t' \in [0, t]$, $(q, \nu + t') \in [\![\phi]\!]_A$. According to the definition of $TConcave(\phi)$, there is a $t'' \in \mathbb{R}^{\geq 0}$ such that $(q, \nu + t + t'') \in [\![\phi]\!]_A$ while there is a $\bar{t}$ such that $t < \bar{t} < t + t''$ and $(q, \nu + \bar{t}) \notin [\![\phi]\!]_A$. This contradicts our assumption that $(q, \nu) \in [\![\phi]\!]_A - [\![TConcave(\phi)]\!]_A$.

We then assume that $[\![TConcave(\phi)]\!]_A$ is time-connected to $[\![\phi]\!]_A - [\![TConcave(\phi)]\!]_A$. This implies that there is a state $(q, \nu) \in [\![TConcave(\phi)]\!]_A$ and a $t \in \mathbb{R}^{\geq 0}$

such that $(q, \nu + t) \in [\![\phi]\!]_A - [\![TConcave(\phi)]\!]_A$ and for each $t' \in [0, t]$, $(q, \nu + t') \in [\![\phi]\!]_A$. According to the definition of $TConcave(\phi)$, there is a $t'' \in \mathbb{R}^{\geq 0}$ such that $(q, \nu + t'') \in [\![\phi]\!]_A$ while there is a $\bar{t}$ such that $0 < \bar{t} < t''$ and $(q, \nu + \bar{t}) \notin [\![\phi]\!]_A$. With the assumption on t, we know that $0 \leq t < \bar{t} < t''$. This implies that $(q, (\nu + t) + \bar{t} - t) \notin [\![\phi]\!]_A$ and $(q, (\nu + t) + t'' - t) \in [\![\phi]\!]_A$. This contradicts the assumption that $(q, \nu + t) \in [\![\phi]\!]_A - [\![TConcave(\phi)]\!]_A$.   ∎

Based on lemmas 3, 4, and 5, we present the following procedure that breaks a zone predicate ϕ into a finite set of zone predicates such that for each two state predicates ϕ_1, ϕ_2 in the set, $[\![\phi_1]\!]_A$ is not time-connected to $[\![\phi_2]\!]_A$.

CascadingConvexities(ϕ) /* ϕ is a zone predicate for a TA A. */ {
  Let $\Phi := \emptyset$.
  While $[\![\phi]\!]_A \neq \emptyset$, { $\eta := TConcave(\phi)$; $\Phi := \Phi \cup \{\phi \wedge \neg \eta\}$; $\phi := \eta$. }
  return Φ.
}

Note that this procedure terminates since the number of zone sets is finite. Thus we repeatedly remove some zones from $[\![\phi]\!]_A$ and eventually reduce it to $\emptyset$. According to lemma 3, we know that every zone predicate in CascadingConvexities(ϕ) characterizes a time-convex state space. Moreover, with lemma 3, 4, and 5, we can establish the following lemma for a new formulation of backward time progress evaluation.

Lemma 6. *For every two zone predicates ϕ and ψ, $[\![\text{Tbck}(\phi, \psi)]\!]_A = \bigcup_{\eta \in \text{CascadingConvexities}(\phi)} \text{Tbck}'(\eta, \psi)$.*   ∎

6   Algorithm with Approximate Time-Concavity Checking

As can be seen in section 5, procedure $TConcave()$ can be executed many times in procdeure CascadingConvexities() and incur great computation cost. We want to investigate if it may pay off to use an alternative technique that avoids the evaluation of procedure $TConcave()$. Given a path zone predicate ϕ and a destination zone predicate ψ, this alternative technique works in the following two steps.

---

(1) Partition ϕ into two zone predicates ϕ_1 and ϕ_2 such that $[\![\phi_1]\!]_A \cap [\![\phi_1]\!]_A = \emptyset$, $[\![\phi_1]\!]_A \cup [\![\phi_1]\!]_A = [\![\phi]\!]_A$, $[\![\phi_1]\!]_A$ is time-convex, and $[\![\phi_1]\!]_A$ and $[\![\phi_2]\!]_A$ are time-disconnected to each other.

(2) Then we return $\text{Tbck}'(\phi_1, \psi) \vee \text{Tbck}(\phi_2, \psi)$ as the result of time progress evaluation.

The performance of the technique relies on the efficiency in carrying out step (1). We have the following lemma that helps us carrying out step (1). First, we need some notations for the convenience of discussion. Given a zone predicate ϕ, we assume that we can construct a set $ZoneSet(\phi)$ with zone elements of the form (q, η) such that $[\![\phi]\!]_A = [\![\bigvee_{(q,\eta) \in ZoneSet(\phi)} q \wedge \eta]\!]_A$. Depending on the implementation of ϕ, there are various ways to do this. If ϕ is implemented with DBMs [5], then ϕ should already have been represented as $ZoneSet(\phi)$ with η represented as a DBM for each $(q, \eta) \in ZoneSet(\phi)$. If ϕ is implemented as a CRD (Clock-Restriction Diagram) [8], then each $(q, \eta) \in ZoneSet(\phi)$ corresponds to a path in the CRD.

Given a $q \in Q$, we let $ZoneSet_q(\phi) = \{(q, \eta) \mid (q, \eta) \in ZoneSet(\phi)\}$. Also, given a set Φ of zone predicates and two clocks $x, y \in X_A \cup \{0\}$, we let $UB_{x-y}(\Phi)$ be the minimum upper-bound for expression $x - y$ in all states $(q, \nu) \in [\![\bigvee_{(q,\eta) \in \Phi} q \wedge \eta]\!]_A$. That is, $UB_{x-y}(\Phi) = \min\{u \mid (q, \nu) \in [\![\bigvee_{(q,\eta) \in \Phi} q \wedge \eta]\!]_A, \nu(x) - \nu(y) \leq u\}$.[5] If $UB_{x-y}(\Phi)$ does not exist, then we denote $UB_{x-y}(\Phi) = \infty$.

Moreover, we define a predicate $ConcavityNecessary_\phi()$ of two zone representations that share the same control location. Specifically, given two such zone representations (q, η) and (q, η'), $ConcavityNecessary_\phi((q, \eta), (q, \eta'))$ is true if and only if there are two clocks $x, y \in X_A \cup \{z\}$ such that

- $UB_{x-0}(\{(q, \eta)\}) < UB_{x-0}(ZoneSet_q(\phi))$;
- $UB_{0-y}(\{(q, \eta')\}) < UB_{0-y}(ZoneSet_q(\phi))$; and
- for all $z, w \in X_A \cup \{z\}$, $UB_{z-w}(\{(q, \eta)\}) + UB_{w-z}(\{(q, \eta')\}) \geq 0$.

Lemma 7. *Given a zone predicate ϕ, if ϕ is time-concave, then there are (q, η), $(q, \eta') \in$ ZoneSet(ϕ) satisfying ConcavityNecessary$_\phi((q, \eta), (q, \eta'))$.*

Proof: We assume there is a state (q, ν) and two reals $t' < t \in \mathbb{R}^{\geq 0}$ such that $(q, \nu), (q, \nu + t) \in [\![\phi]\!]_A$ while $(q, \nu + t') \notin [\![\phi]\!]_A$. Assume that there are $(q, \eta_1), (q, \eta_2) \in ZoneSet(\phi)$ such that $(q, \nu) \in [\![q \wedge \eta_1]\!]_A$ and $(q, \nu + t) \in [\![q \wedge \eta_2]\!]_A$. Note that for all clocks $z, w \in X_A$, $\nu(z) - \nu(w) = (\nu + t)(z) - (\nu + t)(w) = (\nu + t')(z) - (\nu + t')(w)$. This implies that there is a clock $x \in X_A$ such that $UB_{x-0}(\{(q, \eta_1)\}) < (\nu + t')(x) < (\nu + t)(x) \leq UB_{x-0}(\{(q, \eta_2)\}) \leq UB_{x-0}(ZoneSet_q(\phi))$. This implies that $UB_{x-0}(\{(q, \eta_1)\}) < UB_{x-0}(ZoneSet_q(\phi))$. This means that the first bullet is correct. Similarly, the second bullet is correct.

Note that for all clocks $z, w \in X_A$, $\nu(z) - \nu(w) = (\nu + t)(z) - (\nu + t)(w)$ which implies that $0 = \nu(z) - \nu(w) + (\nu + t)(w) - (\nu + t)(z)$. According to the definition of $UB_{z-w}()$ and $UB_{w-z}()$, we know that $\nu(z) - \nu(w) \leq UB_{z-w}(\{(q, \eta_1)\})$ and $(\nu + t)(w) - (\nu(z) + t) \leq UB_{w-z}(\{(q, \eta_2)\})$. Thus the third bullet is also proven for (q, η_1) and (q, η_2).

By letting η and η' be η_1 and η_2 respectively, the lemma is proven. ∎

Based on lemma 7, for step (1) in the above, we let

$$\phi_2 = \bigvee_{(q,\eta),(q,\eta') \in ZoneSet(\phi), ConcavityNecessary_\phi((q,\eta),(q,\eta'))} (q \wedge \eta)$$

and $\phi_1 = \phi \wedge \neg\phi_2$. We have the following lemma that shows this is indeed what we can use in step (1).

Lemma 8. *With the ϕ_1 and ϕ_2 defined in the last paragraph, for any ψ, $[\![\mathbf{Tbck}(\phi, \psi)]\!]_A = [\![\mathbf{Tbck'}(\phi_1, \psi) \vee \mathbf{Tbck}(\phi_2, \psi)]\!]_A$.*

---

[5] For convenience, we let $\nu(0) = 0$.

Proof: The lemma is true if ϕ_1 is time-convex and ϕ_1, ϕ_2 are time-disconnected to each other. If ϕ_1 is time-concave, then according to lemma 7, there are $(q, \eta), (q, \eta') \in ZoneSet(\phi_1)$ such that $ConcavityNecessary_\phi((q, \eta), (q, \eta'))$ is true. Then no states in $[\![(q \wedge \eta) \vee (q \wedge \eta')]\!]_A$ should be in $[\![\phi_1]\!]_A$. This is a contradiction.

If ϕ_1 is time-connected to ϕ_2, then there are $(q, \eta) \in ZoneSet(\phi_1)$ and (q, η'), $(q, \eta'') \in ZoneSet(\phi_2)$ such that $[\![q \wedge \eta]\!]_A$ is time-connected to $[\![q \wedge \eta']\!]_A$ and $ConcavityNecessary_\phi((q, \eta'), (q, \eta''))$ is true. This implies $ConcavityNecessary_\phi$ $((q, \eta), (q, \eta''))$ which is also a contradiction.

With an argument similar to the one in the last paragraph, we can also prove that ϕ_2 is not time-connected to ϕ_1. Thus the lemma is proven. ∎

Finally, the technique has been realized with a symbolic manipulation algorithm for zone predicates represented with CRD.

7   Implementation and Experiments

We have implemented our ideas in sections 5 and 6 in **RED** 7.0, a model-checker for TAs and a parametric safety analyzer for LHAs (linear hybrid automata) [2] based on CRD and HRD (Hybrid-Restriction Diagram) technology [8, 9]. We used the following two parameterized benchmarks from the literature.

1. *Fischer's timed mutual exclusion algorithm* [8]: The algorithm relies on a global lock and a local clock per process to control access to the critical section. Three timing constants used are 10, 19, and 30. The first formula that we check is the following.

$$\forall \square \neg (\exists(\texttt{critical}_1) \mathcal{U}((\neg\texttt{critical}_1) \wedge \exists\lozenge_{<19}\texttt{critical}_1)) \qquad (C)$$

   This formula intends to say that if process one leaves the critical section, then it cannot enter the critical section again in 19 time units. However, since the $\exists\mathcal{U}$-formula can be satisfied at a state that directly fulfills $(\neg\texttt{critical}_1) \wedge \exists\lozenge_{<19}\texttt{critical}_1$, the formula is not satisfied.

   The second formula is the following.

$$\forall \square \left(\begin{array}{l} \texttt{critical}_1 \rightarrow \\ \exists\lozenge\exists\texttt{idle}_1\mathcal{U}\exists\texttt{ready}_1\mathcal{U}_{<10}\exists\texttt{waiting}_1\mathcal{U}_{>19}\exists\texttt{critical}_1\mathcal{U}\texttt{idle}_1 \end{array} \right) \qquad (D)$$

   It says that if process 1 is in the critical section, then it can go through an expected mode sequence with timing restrictions back to the idle mode. The third formula is the following.

$$\forall \square (\texttt{ready}_1 \rightarrow \forall\lozenge_{<10}(\texttt{waiting}_1 \wedge \forall\square(\texttt{critical}_1 \rightarrow \forall\lozenge_{<30}\texttt{idle}_1))) \qquad (E)$$

   The formula says that if process 1 is in the ready mode, it enters the waiting mode in 10 time units and from that point on, if it enters the critical section, it returns to the idle mode in 30 time units. Note that the formula is not satisfied with Zeno computations[6]. So we have to use option '-Z' for quantification for non-Zeno computations.

---

[6] A Zeno computation runs forever without time converging to a finite value.

Table 1. Performance data of scalability w.r.t. various strategies

benchmarks	TCTL spec's	m	Tbck() time	mem	*Cascading* time	mem	*ATCC* time	mem	answer
Fischer's mutual exclusion (m processes)	(C)	3	0.024s	186k	0.004s	186k	0.012s	3.1M	
		4	0.42s	32M	0.044s	413k	0.044s	13M	violated
		5	8.38s	162M	1.80s	69M	1.83s	71M	
	(D)	3	0.008s	186k	0.008s	186k	0.012s	2.7M	
		4	0.060s	413k	0.044s	413k	0.036s	9.9M	satisfied
		5	4.18s	116M	0.588s	34M	0.536s	40M	
	(E)	3	0.036s	186k	0.032s	186k	0.032s	6.5M	satisfied
		4	1.06s	59M	0.048s	413k	0.128s	25k	with
		5	26.9s	344M	5.36s	113M	4.25s	116M	non-Zenoness
CSMA/CD (1 bus+m senders)	(F)	2	0.024s	168k	0.048s	168k	0.028s	2.5M	
		3	0.072s	333k	0.068s	333k	0.116s	20M	satisfied
		4	5.49s	100M	4.38s	90M	4.72s	109M	
	(G)	2	0.028s	168k	0.028s	168k	0.020s	1.2M	violated
		3	0.104s	333k	0.092s	333k	0.088s	4.1M	
		2	0.096s	168k	0.068s	168k	0.096s	166k	violated with
		3	108s	662M	93.2s	584M	96.7s	605M	non-Zenoess
	(H)	2	0.040s	168k	0.032s	168k	0.076s	1.6M	violated
		3	0.100s	333k	0.084s	333k	0.100s	5.6M	
		2	0.13s	168k	0.092s	168k	0.152s	24M	satisfied with
		3	266s	1199M	214s	1036M	222s	1082M	non-Zenoess

data collected on a Pentium 4 1.7GHz with 2G memory running LINUX;
s: seconds; k: kilobytes of memory in diagram data-structure;
M: megabytes of memory in diagram data-structure

2. *CSMA/CD* [11]: This is the Ethernet bus arbitration protocol with collision-and-retry. The timing constants used are 26, 52, and 808. The first property that we want to check is the following.

$$\forall\Box((\texttt{transm}_1 \wedge x_1 = 52) \rightarrow \forall\Box_{<756}\neg\texttt{transm}_2) \qquad (F)$$

It says that if sender 1 is in the transmission mode for 52 time units, then in all computations, sender 2 cannot be in the transmission mode for at least 756 time units.

The second formula is as follows.

$$\forall\Box\neg(\exists\texttt{transm}_1\mathcal{U}(\texttt{transm}_2 \wedge \exists\Box_{<26}\neg\texttt{retry}_1)) \qquad (G)$$

It intends to say that it is not possible that sender 1 remains in the transmission mode until sender 2 also does so and sender 1 does not enter the retry mode in 26 time units. This formula is not satisfied since the $\exists\mathcal{U}$-formula can be satisfied immediately with a state that directly fulfills $\texttt{transm}_2 \wedge \exists\Box_{<26}\neg\texttt{retry}_1$. From that state on, there is a computation along which sender 2 stays in the transmission mode for 808 time units.

The final formula is the following.

$$\forall\Box(\texttt{bus\_collision} \rightarrow \forall(\forall\Diamond_{<52}(\texttt{wait}_1 \vee \texttt{retry}_1))\mathcal{U}_{<52}\texttt{bus\_idle}) \qquad (H)$$

Note that the formula is not satisfied with Zeno computations. So we have to use option '-Z' for quantification for non-Zeno computations.

We have collected data respectively with three tool configurations.

- Tbck() represents the one that uses Tbck() for all time progress evaluation.
- *Cascading* represents the one with the technique in section 5.
- *ATCC* represents the one with the technique in section 6.

The performance data is reported in table 1. The CPU time used, the total memory consumption for the data-structures in state-space representations, and the answers of model-checking are reported. As can be seen, our technique in section 5 always performs better than Tbck(). For some benchmark, the performance enhancement is one order of magnitude. This shows that our techniques could be useful in applying TCTL model-checking technology to industrial projects.

The technique in section 6 did not perform as well as we expected. Further investigation revealed that special arrangement for garbage CRD nodes might have slowed down the hash table operations and blown up the memory consumption. In our present implementation, garbage collection cannot be invoked inside the procedures for the technique. In the future, we may gain more performance with an implementation of a more powerful garbage collector.

8   Concluding Remarks

In this work, we discuss how to improve the performance of an important component algorithm, the time progress evaluation algorithm, for the model-checking of TAs. Techniques in section 6 may worth further investiagtion for better precision in the approximation and more efficient algorithms.

References

1. Alur, R., Courcoubetis, C., Dill, D.L.: Model Checking for Real-Time Systems. In: IEEE LICS (1990)
2. Alur, R., Courcoubetis, C., Henzinger, T.A., Ho, P.-H.: Hybrid Automata: an Algorithmic Approach to the Specification and Verification of Hybrid Systems. In: Grossman, R.L., Nerode, A., Ravn, A.P., Rischel, H. (eds.) HS 1991 and HS 1992. LNCS, vol. 736, pp. 209–229. Springer, Heidelberg (1993)
3. Alur, R., Dill, D.L.: A Theory of Timed Automata. Theoretical Computer Science 126, 183–235 (1994)
4. Bengtsson, J., Larsen, K., Larsson, F., Pettersson, P., Yi, W.: UPPAAL - a Tool Suite for Automatic Verification of Real-Time Systems. In: Hybrid Control System Symposium. LNCS. Springer, Heidelberg (1996)
5. Dill, D.L.: Timing Assumptions and Verification of Finite-state Concurrent Systems. In: Sifakis, J. (ed.) CAV 1989. LNCS, vol. 407. Springer, Heidelberg (1990)
6. Fourier, J.B.: (reported in:) Analyse des travaux de l'Académie Royale des Sciences pendant l'année 1824, Partie Mathématique (1827)
7. Henzinger, T.A., Nicollin, X., Sifakis, J., Yovine, S.: Symbolic Model Checking for Real-Time Systems. IEEE LICS (1992)

8. Wang, F.: Efficient Verification of Timed Automata with BDD-like Data-Structures, STTT (Software Tools for Technology Transfer). vol. 6(1) (June 2004) In: Zuck, L.D., Attie, P.C., Cortesi, A., Mukhopadhyay, S. (eds.) VMCAI 2003. LNCS, vol. 2575, pp. 189–205. Springer, Heidelberg (2002)
9. Wang, F.: Symbolic Parametric Safety Analysis of Linear Hybrid Systems with BDD-like Data-Structures. IEEE Transactions on Software Engineering 31(1), 38–51 (2005); A preliminary version. In: Alur, R., Peled, D.A. (eds.) CAV 2004. LNCS, vol. 3114, pp. 38–51. Springer, Heidelberg (2004)
10. Wang, F., Huang, G.-D., Yu, F.: TCTL Inevitability Analysis of Dense-Time Systems: From Theory to Engineering. IEEE Transactions on Software Engineering 32(7) (2006)
11. Yovine, S.: Kronos: A Verification Tool for Real-Time Systems. International Journal of Software Tools for Technology Transfer 1(1/2) (October 1997)

Decidable Compositions of O-Minimal Automata[*]

Alberto Casagrande[1,2,3], Pietro Corvaja[2], Carla Piazza[2,**], and Bud Mishra[4,5]

[1] Istituto di Genomica Applicata, Via J. Linussio, 51, 33100 Udine, Italy
[2] DIMI, Università di Udine, Via delle Scienze, 206, 33100 Udine, Italy
carla.piazza@dimi.uniud.it
[3] DISA, Università di Udine, Via delle Scienze, 208, 33100 Udine, Italy
[4] Courant Institute of Mathematical Science, NYU, New York, U.S.A.
[5] NYU School of Medicine, 550 First Avenue, New York, 10016 U.S.A.

Abstract. We identify a new class of decidable hybrid automata: namely, parallel compositions of semi-algebraic o-minimal automata. The class we consider is fundamental to hierarchical modeling in many exemplar systems, both natural and engineered. Unfortunately, parallel composition, which is an atomic operator in such constructions, does not preserve the decidability of reachability. Luckily, this paper is able to show that when one focuses on the composition of semi-algebraic o-minimal automata, it is possible to translate the decidability problem into a satisfiability problem over formulæ involving both real and integer variables. While in the general case such formulæ would be undecidable, the particular format of the formulæ obtained in our translation allows combining decidability results stemming from both algebraic number theory and first-order logic over $(\mathbb{R}, 0, 1, +, *, <)$ to yield a novel decidability algorithm. From a more general perspective, this paper exposes many new open questions about decidable combinations of real/integer logics.

Introduction

We wish to suggest a novel algebraic framework for the purpose of studying composition of hybrid automata. In this framework, we exploit various algebraic techniques (both semi-algebraic geometric and algebraic-number theoretic) to provide effective procedures to solve reachability problems for at least one important class, namely, semi-algebraic o-minimal hybrid automata. We believe that these techniques are applicable more generally and will motivate further applications to other classes and subclasses of hybrid-automata. Our techniques show how to model state-space evolution (as quantified semi-algebraic formulae) separately from the temporal synchronization (modeled as a system of linear algebraic Diophantine equations and inequalities) and yet, seek a combined solution to represent simultaneous arrival at a point in the product state-space by each individual component automaton. In order to obtain this decidability result, we needed to innovate in at least three different areas: to be precise, (1) theory of automata: how to effectively reduce an automata theoretic problem to an algebraic problem by

---

[*] This work is partially supported by PRIN "BISCA" 2006011235, FIRB "LIBI" RBLA039M7M, two NSF ITR grants, and one NSF EMT grant.
[**] Corresponding author.

modeling and by seeking solutions for algebraic systems described via algebraic geometric and number theoretic formulations—thus, circumscribing difficulties faced by the usual finite-quotient-techniques; (2) algorithmic algebra: how to solve a system of equations and inequalities involving semi-algebraic geometric formulae combined with linear algebraic-Diophantine relations—a rather non-trivial problem that had remained unsolved till now, except for the special system arising in case of composition of just two automata (see [1]); and (3) recursive function theory: how to better recognize the boundary separating decidability from undecidability in the context of automata, and along the way, expand the body of techniques applicable to such questions. To the best of our knowledge, this paper is the first to explicitly connect discrete-continuous hybridness of these automata to their algebraic analog of mixed real-integer formulations and also first in proposing how to solve them algorithmically.

The paper is organized as follows: Section 1 and 2 introduce hybrid automata and their parallel composition, respectively; in Section 3, we prove the decidability of linear Diophantine systems with semi-algebraic coefficients and, in Section 4, we show how one can reduce to it the reachability problem for hybrid automata obtained by parallel composition of semi-algebraic o-minimal automata; Section 5 hints some simple applications of the proposed techniques; in Section 6, we discuss some possible extentions and Section 7 summarizes the results presented in the paper and draws some comparisons with related literature. *All the missing proofs can be found in [2].*

1   Motivations and Notations

Since their introduction (see, e.g., [3]), hybrid automata have initiated a new tradition, promising powerful tools for modeling and reasoning about complex engineered or natural systems: e.g., embedded and real time systems, or computational biology, where the resulting analyses are providing many new insights. Unfortunately, in their flexibility in capturing dynamics, resides also their limitations: many different undecidability and complexity results have been proven over general hybrid automata [4] and cast doubt on their suitability as a general tool that can be algorithmized and efficiently implemented. However, if these representations are further restricted, as in the powerful family of o-minimal systems [5], one could hope to still enjoy fidelity of representation that far surpasses that of both discrete models and differential equations, and yet avoid undecidability. In particular, reachability has been shown decidable over semialgebraic o-minimal automata [5].

In order to build a theoretical framework that can also use these hybrid representations in a natural manner, one must shift one's attention to the description of large and complex hybrid systems that can be described in a compositional manner, built out of many elementary modules at many different levels of hierarchy. Since the basic fundamental step in a compositional construction is through a parallel composition, an essential desideratum of this new theoretical framework is that the reachability property of the product hybrid automaton be decidable, provided that the component hybrid automata belong to a suitably restricted decidable family of automata, e.g., one in the class of o-minimal automata. In general, the product operation does not assure a closure of decidability property for reachability condition. Nonetheless, in [1], we establish decidability of the reachability condition considering the parallel composition of two semi-algebraic o-minimal automata. Even if such hybrid automata could be used to model interesting systems (e.g., in system biology), the limitation on the number of composable automata poses many restrictions on the applicability of the suggested techniques. To address these shortcomings, in this paper, we have generalized the decidability result for the reachability problem over parallel composition of semi-algebraic o-minimal automata by allowing the composition of an arbitrary number of automata and we extend the applicability of the proposed framework to more complex systems.

1.1 Basic Notions

A *directed graph* is a pair $\langle \mathcal{V}, \mathcal{E} \rangle$ where $\mathcal{V}$ is a finite set of *vertices* and $\mathcal{E}$ is a finite set of *edges*. The functions $\text{Source} : \mathcal{E} \longrightarrow \mathcal{V}$ and $\text{Dest} : \mathcal{E} \longrightarrow \mathcal{V}$ characterize the vertex exited by an edge and the vertex entered by an edge, respectively. In particular, we say that $\text{Source}(e) = v$ and $\text{Dest}(e) = v'$ are the *source* and the *destination* of e, respectively. In this paper, when we refer to graphs, we always intend directed graphs. A *path* ph *from* $v \in \mathcal{V}$ *to* $v' \in \mathcal{V}$ in $G = \langle \mathcal{V}, \mathcal{E} \rangle$ is either the vertex v, if $v = v'$, or a sequence of edges $"e_1, \ldots, e_n"$ such that, for all $i \in [1, n-1]$, $\text{Source}(e_{i+1}) = \text{Dest}(e_i)$, $\text{Source}(e_1) = v$, and $\text{Dest}(e_n) = v'$. A path $p = "e_1, \ldots, e_n"$ is a *cycle* if $e_1 = e_n$ and $n > 1$. Moreover, if $e_i \neq e_j$ for all $i, j \in [1, n-1]$ with $i \neq j$, then we say that p is a *simple cycle*. The standard definition of cycle requires that the first node coincides with the last one, while in our definition we impose that the first and the last edges are identical. Similarly, the standard definition of simple cycle requires that in the cycle the internal nodes are not repeated, while in our definition we require that the internal edges are not repeated. The two definitions are obviously not equivalent, however, a graph has only a finite number of simple cycles under both definitions. Later on we write $|p|$ to denote the length of the path p, i.e., the number of its edges.

Next, we introduce some notations and conventions that we will need to define hybrid automata. Capital letters X, X', X_m, and X_m', where $m \in \mathbb{N}$, denote variables ranging over $\mathbb{R}$. Analogously, Z denotes the vector of variables $\langle X_1, \ldots, X_d \rangle$ and Z' denotes the vector $\langle X_1', \ldots, X_d' \rangle$. The temporal variables T, T', $T_0, \ldots, T_n$ model time and range over $\mathbb{R}_{\geq 0}$. We use the small letters $p, q, r, s, \ldots$ to denote d-dimensional vectors of real numbers. Occasionally, we may use the notation $\varphi[X_1, \ldots, X_m]$ to stress the fact that the set of free variables of the first-order formula φ is included in the set of variables $\{X_1, \ldots, X_m\}$. By extension, if $\{Z_1, \ldots, Z_n\}$ is a set of variable vectors, $\varphi[Z_1, \ldots, Z_n]$ indicates that the free variables of φ are included in the set of components of $Z_1, \ldots, Z_n$. Moreover, given a formula $\varphi[Z_1, \ldots, Z_i, \ldots, Z_n]$ and a vector p of the same dimension as the variable vector Z_i, the formula obtained by component-wise substitution of Z_i with p is denoted by $\varphi[Z_1, \ldots, Z_{i-1}, p, Z_{i+1}, \ldots, Z_n]$. When in φ the only free variables are the components of Z_i, after the substitution we can determine the truth value of $\varphi[p]$.

We are now ready to define hybrid automata. For each node of a graph we have an invariant condition and a dynamic law. The dynamic law may depend on the initial conditions, i.e., on the values of the continuous variables at the beginning of the evolution in the state. The jumps from one discrete state to another are regulated by the activation and reset conditions.

Definition 1 (Hybrid Automata - Syntax). *A hybrid automaton $H = (Z, Z', \mathcal{V}, \mathcal{E}, Inv, \mathcal{F}, Act, Res)$ of dimension d consists of the following components:*

1. *$Z = \langle X_1, \ldots, X_d \rangle$ and $Z' = \langle X_1', \ldots, X_d' \rangle$ are two vectors of variables ranging over the reals $\mathbb{R}$;*
2. *$\langle \mathcal{V}, \mathcal{E} \rangle$ is a graph. Each element of $\mathcal{V}$ will be dubbed* location.
3. *Each vertex $v \in \mathcal{V}$ is labeled by the formula $Inv(v)[Z]$;*
4. *$\mathcal{F}$ is a function assigning to each vertex $v \in \mathcal{V}$ a continuous vector field over $\mathbb{R}^d$; we will use $f_v : \mathbb{R}^d \times \mathbb{R}_{\geq 0} \longrightarrow \mathbb{R}^d$ to indicate the solution of the vector field $\mathcal{F}(v)$ and $Dyn(v)[Z, Z', T] \stackrel{def}{=} Z' = f_v(Z, T)$;*
5. *Each edge $e \in \mathcal{E}$ is labeled by the two formulæ $Act(e)[Z]$ and $Res(e)[Z, Z']$;*

Note that, without loss of generality, we may consider only hybrid automata whose formulæ are satisfiable. In fact, if this is not the case, we can transform the automaton and eliminate the unsatisfiable formulæ. For instance, if there is an edge e such that $Res(e)[Z, Z']$ is unsatisfiable, we can simply delete the edge from the automaton. We use $d(H)$ to denote the dimension of the automaton H.

Definition 2 (Hybrid Automata - Semantics). *A state ℓ of H is a pair $\langle v, r \rangle$, where $v \in \mathcal{V}$ is a location and $r = \langle r_1, \ldots, r_d \rangle \in \mathbb{R}^{d(H)}$ is an assignment of values for the variables of Z. A state $\langle v, r \rangle$ is said to be* admissible *if $Inv(v)[r]$ is true.*

The continuous reachability transition relation $\xrightarrow{t}_C$, *where $t \geq 0$ is the transition elapsed time, between admissible states is defined as follows:*

$$\langle v, r \rangle \xrightarrow{t}_C \langle v, s \rangle \iff \begin{array}{l} \textit{It holds that } r = f_v(r, 0) \textit{ and it holds that } s = f_v(r, t) \textit{ (see 1),} \\ \textit{and for each } t' \in [0, t] \textit{ the formula } Inv(v)[f_v(r, t')] \textit{ is true.} \end{array}$$

The discrete reachability transition relation $\rightarrow_D$ *between admissible states is defined as follows:*

$$\langle v, r \rangle \xrightarrow{e}_D \langle u, s \rangle \iff \begin{array}{l} \textit{it holds that } e \in \mathcal{E}, \textsf{Source}(e) = v, \textsf{Dest}(e) = u, \textit{ and} \\ \textit{both } Act(e)[r] \textit{ and } Res(e)[r, s] \textit{ are true.} \end{array}$$

We write $\ell \rightarrow_C \ell'$ and $\ell \rightarrow_D \ell'$ meaning respectively that there exists a $t \in \mathbb{R}_{\geq 0}$ such that $\ell \xrightarrow{t}_C \ell'$ and that there exists an $e \in \mathcal{E}$ such that $\ell \xrightarrow{e}_D \ell'$. Moreover, we use the notation $\ell \rightarrow \ell'$ to denote that either $\ell \rightarrow_C \ell'$ or $\ell \rightarrow_D \ell'$.

Building upon a combination of both continuous and discrete transitions, we can formulate a notion of *trace* as well as a resulting notion of *reachability*. A trace is a sequence of continuous and discrete transitions. A point s is reachable from a point r if there is a trace starting from r and ending in s.

Definition 3 (Hybrid Automata - Reachability). *Let I be either $\mathbb{N}$ or an initial finite interval of $\mathbb{N}$. A trace of H is a sequence of admissible states $\ell_0, \ell_1, \ldots, \ell_i, \ldots$, with $i \in I$, such that $\ell_{i-1} \rightarrow \ell_i$ holds for each $i \in I$ greater than zero; such a trace is also denoted by $(\ell_i)_{i \in I}$.*

The automaton H reaches a point $s \in \mathbb{R}^d$ (in time t) from a point $r \in \mathbb{R}^d$ if there exists a trace $tr = \ell_0, \ldots, \ell_n$ of H such that $\ell_0 = \langle v, r \rangle$ and $\ell_n = \langle u, s \rangle$, for some $v, u \in \mathcal{V}$ (and t is the sum of the continuous transitions elapsed times). In such a case, we also say that s is reachable *from r in H.*

Given a hybrid automaton H and trace, tr, of H, a *corresponding path* of tr is a path ph obtained by considering the discrete transitions occurring in tr. In this case, we also say that ph *corresponds* to tr. Notice that if tr is a trace, then there is a set of corresponding paths of tr and such a set is finite and hence, computable.

We are interested in the reachability problem for hybrid automata, namely, given an automaton H, an initial set $I \subseteq \mathbb{R}^d$, and a final set $F \subseteq \mathbb{R}^d$ we wish to decide whether there exists a point in I from which a point in F is reachable.

An interesting class of hybrid automata is the class of *o-minimal automata* [5,6]. The formulæ $Dyn(v)$, $Inv(v)$, $Act(e)$, and $Res(e)$ of such automata are defined in a o-minimal theory for each $v \in \mathcal{V}$ and $e \in \mathcal{E}$. Moreover, their resets are constant, i.e., they do not depend on the point from which the edge is crossed. In the case of o-minimal automata defined by a decidable theory, reachability and temporal logic properties can be decided through bisimulation [5]. O-minimal automata always possess a finite bisimulation quotient whose computation is effective when the o-minimal theory is decidable. An o-minimal and decidable theory is the first-order theory of $(\mathbb{R}, 0, 1, +, *, <)$ [7], also known as the theory of semi-algebraic sets.

Definition 4 (Semi-Algebraic O-Minimal Automata). *An* o-minimal automaton *is a hybrid automaton such that* $Dyn(v)$, $Inv(v)$, $Act(e)$, *and* $Res(e)$ *are formulæ of an o-minimal theory [8] and the truth value of* $Res(e)[Z, Z']$ *does not depend on* Z, *for any* $v \in \mathcal{V}$ *and* $e \in \mathcal{E}$. *A* semi-algebraic o-minimal automaton *is an o-minimal automaton such that* $Dyn(v)$, $Inv(v)$, $Act(e)$, *and* $Res(e)$ *are semi-algebraic formulæ.*

The decidability of reachability problem for such class follows directly from [5,7] and the problem itself has been reduced to the satisfiability of a finite disjunction of formulæ of the form $Reach(H)(ph)[Z, Z', T]$ in [9]. In particular, if H is a semi-algebraic o-minimal automaton, then $q \in \mathbb{R}^{d(H)}$ is reachable from $p \in \mathbb{R}^{d(H)}$ in H through a trace whose corresponding path is ph in time t if and only if the formula $Reach(H)(ph)[p, q, t]$ holds.

2   Parallel Composition of Hybrid Automata

Given two or more hybrid automata with distinct variables we are interested in analyzing the reachability problem when we let them run independently.

Definition 5 (Parallel Composition). *Let* $H_a = (Z_a, Z_a', \mathcal{V}_a, \mathcal{E}_a, Inv_a, \mathcal{F}_a, Act_a, Res_a)$ *and* $H_b = (Z_b, Z_b', \mathcal{V}_b, \mathcal{E}_b, Inv_b, \mathcal{F}_b, Act_b, Res_b)$ *be two hybrid automata over distinct variables. The* parallel composition *of* H_a *and* H_b *is the hybrid automaton* $H_a \otimes H_b = (Z, Z', \mathcal{V}, \mathcal{E}, Inv, \mathcal{F}, Act, Res)$, *where:*

- Z (Z') *is the vector obtained by concatenating* Z_a *and* Z_b (Z_a' *and* Z_b', *respectively);*
- $\mathcal{V} = \mathcal{V}_a \times \mathcal{V}_b$;
- $\mathcal{E} = (\mathcal{E}_a \times \mathcal{E}_b) \cup (\mathcal{E}_a \times \mathcal{V}_b) \cup (\mathcal{V}_a \times \mathcal{E}_b)$ *and* $\theta(\langle e_a, e_b \rangle) \stackrel{def}{=} \langle \theta(e_a), \theta(e_b) \rangle$, $\theta(\langle v_a, e_b \rangle) \stackrel{def}{=} \langle v_a, \theta(e_b) \rangle$, *and* $\theta(\langle e_a, v_b \rangle) \stackrel{def}{=} \langle \theta(e_a), v_b \rangle$ *for all* $\theta \in \{$Source, Dest$\}$;
- $Inv(\langle v_a, v_b \rangle)[Z] \stackrel{def}{=} Inv_a(v_a)[Z_a] \wedge Inv_b(v_b)[Z_b]$;

- $Dyn(\langle v_a, v_b \rangle)[Z, Z', T] \stackrel{def}{=} Dyn_a(v_a)[Z_a, Z_a', T] \wedge Dyn_b(v_b)[Z_b, Z_b', T];$
- $Act(\langle e_a, e_b \rangle)[Z] \stackrel{def}{=} Act_a(e_a)[Z_a] \wedge Act_b(e_b)[Z_b],\ Act(\langle e_a, v_b \rangle)[Z] \stackrel{def}{=} Act_a(e_a)[Z_a],$ and
  $Act(\langle v_a, e_b \rangle)[Z] \stackrel{def}{=} Act_b(e_b)[Z_b];$
- $Res(\langle e_a, e_b \rangle)[Z, Z'] \stackrel{def}{=} Res_a(e_a)[Z_a, Z_a'] \wedge Res_b(e_b)[Z_b, Z_b'],\ Res(\langle e_a, v_b \rangle)[Z, Z'] \stackrel{def}{=}$
  $Res_a(e_a)[Z_a, Z_a'] \wedge Z_b' = Z_b,$ and $Res(\langle v_a, e_b \rangle)[Z, Z'] \stackrel{def}{=} Z_a' = Z_a \wedge Res_b(e_b)[Z_b, Z_b'];$

where $v_a \in V_a,\ e_a \in \mathcal{E}_a\ v_b \in V_a,$ and $e_b \in \mathcal{E}_b.$

Our notion of parallel composition is equivalent to those in [10,11] in the case of disjoint set of events. The discrete graph underlying a parallel composition $H_a \otimes H_b$ can be a multigraph, i.e., there can be more than one edge connecting two nodes. In particular, this could happen if in either H_a or H_b there are self-loop edges. Hence, we should introduce labels to distinguish different edges connecting the same pair of nodes. For the sake of simplicity, we avoid this additional labeling in the rest of the paper, when no ambiguity may result.

Example 1. Let us consider the o-minimal automata $H_a = (\langle X_a \rangle, \langle X_a' \rangle, V_a, \mathcal{E}_a, Dyn_a, Inv_a, Act_a, Res_a)$ and $H_b = (\langle X_b \rangle, \langle X_b' \rangle, V_b, \mathcal{E}_b, Dyn_b, Inv_b, Act_b, Res_b),$ where $V_i = \{v_i\}$ and $\mathcal{E}_i = \{e_i\},$ for any $i \in \{a, b\},$ and

$H_a: Dyn_a(v_a) \stackrel{def}{=} \dot{X}_a = -1$ $H_b: Dyn_b(v_b) \stackrel{def}{=} \dot{X}_b = -1$

$\quad Inv_a(v_a) \stackrel{def}{=} 0 \le X_a \wedge X_a \le 1$ $\quad Inv_b(v_b) \stackrel{def}{=} 0 \le X_b \wedge (X_b)^2 \le 2$

$\quad Act_a(e_a) \stackrel{def}{=} X_a = 0$ $\quad Act_b(e_b) \stackrel{def}{=} X_b = 0$

$\quad Res_a(e_a) \stackrel{def}{=} X_a' = 1$ $\quad Res_b(e_b) \stackrel{def}{=} (X_b')^2 = 2.$

The automaton $H_a \otimes H_b$ is depicted in Figure 1. $H_a \otimes H_b$ is not o-minimal since it has also identity resets. Moreover, it is possible that a variable is never reset along a cycle of $H_a \otimes H_b$, e.g., X_b is never reset in the cycle $"\langle e_a, v_b \rangle, \langle e_a, v_b \rangle"$.

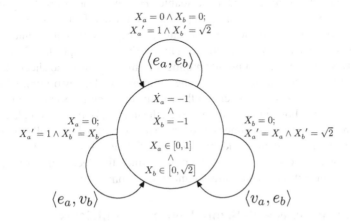

Fig. 1. The hybrid automaton $H_a \otimes H_b$ of Example 1

It is easy to prove that $(H_1 \otimes H_2) \otimes H_3$ reaches q from p in time t through a trace tr if and only if $H_1 \otimes (H_2 \otimes H_3)$ reaches q from p in time t through tr. Hence, we denote by $H_1 \otimes \ldots \otimes H_m$ and $\bigotimes_{i=1}^{m} H_i$ the composition of n automata.

As far as reachability is concerned, we first point out that we will study the reachability problem over $\bigotimes_{i=1}^{m} H_i$ considering only sets of points of the form $I = \prod_{i=1}^{m} I_i$ and $F = \prod_{i=1}^{m} F_i$, where $I_i, F_i \subseteq \mathbb{R}^{d(H_i)}$. To some extent, this simplification will allow us to work on each H_i independently. In the general case, our results can be used to both under-estimate and over-estimate reachability. Unfortunately, even with this assumption, one may not always be able to ascertain the closure of reachability condition under composition; namely, starting from a set I_1 it may be possible to reach a set F_1 in the automaton H_1 and similarly, starting from a set I_2 it may be possible to reach a set F_2 in H_2, and yet starting from $I_1 \times I_2$ in $H_1 \otimes H_2$ it may not be possible to reach $F_1 \times F_2$. For instance, this happens if F_1 is reachable only at time $t = 1$, while F_2 is reachable only at time $t = 2$. Moreover, the decidability of reachability is not always preserved under parallel composition i.e., it is possible that reachability is decidable over m classes $C_1, \ldots, C_m$ of hybrid automata, but not over the product class $\bigotimes_{i=1}^{m} C_i = \{\bigotimes_{i=1}^{m} H_i \mid \forall i \in [1, m] \, H_i \in C_i\}$ (see [11]).

O-minimal hybrid automata have always a finite bisimulation quotient. In [1], we proved that the parallel composition of two o-minimal automata can have an infinite simulation quotient. Hence, the standard quotienting techniques cannot be applied to decide reachability on product automata.

However, it holds that the automaton $\bigotimes_{i=1}^{m} H_i$ reaches the set $\prod_{i=1}^{m} F_i$ from $\prod_{i=1}^{m} I_i$ in time t if and only if H_i reaches F_i from I_i in time t for each $i \in [1, m]$. Hence, in order to study reachability over $\bigotimes_{i=1}^{m} H_i$, it would be necessary to better understand the nature of timed reachability over each H_i for $i \in [1, m]$.

Definition 6 (Timed-Reachability). *Let H be a hybrid automaton. Given $t \geq 0$, $I, F \subseteq \mathbb{R}^{d(H)}$ the (H, t, I, F)-timed-reachability problem consists in deciding whether there exist two points $i \in I$ and $f \in F$ such that H reaches f from i in time t.*

Timed-reachability is in general undecidable. However, the decidability of timed-reachability is preserved by parallel composition and, when I and F are semi-algebraic sets, timed-reachability is decidable over semi-algebraic o-minimal automata (see [2]). Unfortunately, decidability of timed-reachability does not imply the decidability of reachability, since there are an infinite number of time instants to be checked.

Intuitively, to decide reachability over the composition of many o-minimal automata, we need to check that we can cycle on their loops elapsing the same amount of time. This check involves both integer variables (i.e., the number of times a simple cycle is repeated) and real ones (i.e., the time elapsed on a simple cycle). In the following sections, we first prove a result about decidability of a particular class of Diophantine systems with semi-algebraic coefficients and, then, we reduce the decidability of reachability for parallel composition of an arbitrary number of automata to it.

3   Linear Systems with Semi-algebraic Coefficients

A *semi-algebraic* set over $\mathbb{R}_{\geq 0}$ is a finite union of intervals and points such that: each interval is characterized by algebraic numbers greater or equal to 0; each point is an algebraic number greater or equal to 0. Semi-algebraic sets are exactly those character-izable through first-order formulæ over $(\mathbb{R}, 0, 1, +, *, <)$.

We consider systems of the following form

$$
\begin{cases}
\sum_{i=1}^{n_1} A_i * \alpha_i + \alpha = \sum_{i=1}^{n_2} B_i * \beta_i + \beta \\
\sum_{i=1}^{h_1} A_i * \alpha_i + \alpha = \sum_{i=1}^{h_3} C_i * \gamma_i + \gamma \\
\cdots \\
\sum_{i=1}^{n_1} A_i * \alpha_i + \alpha = \sum_{i=1}^{n_w} W_i * \omega_i + \omega
\end{cases}
\tag{1}
$$

where capital letters denote variables ranging over $\mathbb{N}_{>0}$, while Greek letters denote real coefficients. In particular, each coefficient can either be a non negative algebraic number or range over a non negative interval characterized by algebraic numbers. Notice that, since the coefficients can range over intervals, this can also be seen as a system of equations and disequations in which some variables range in $\mathbb{N}_{>0}$, while other range in $\mathbb{R}_{\geq 0}$. Intuitively, we can look at it as both a generalization of a linear system of Diophantine disequations and an existential first-order formula involving both integer and real variables. We are interested in the question of satisfiability of such systems.

We distinguish thee cases for the expressions involved in our systems: (a) $\sum_{i=1}^{n_d} D_i * \delta_i + \delta$ is *punctual* if all the involved coefficients are algebraic numbers; (b) $\sum_{i=1}^{n_d} D_i * \delta_i + \delta$ is *quasi-punctual* if all δ_i's are algebraic numbers, while δ ranges over an interval; (c) $\sum_{i=1}^{n_d} D_i * \delta_i + \delta$ is *non-punctual* if at least one of the δ_i's ranges over an interval. An equation is *punctual* if both its left and right hand sides are punctual. It is *quasi-punctual* if at least one of the involved expressions is quasi-punctual, while the other one is either punctual or quasi-punctual. It is *non-punctual* if it involves at least a non-punctual expression.

The algorithm we propose for deciding the satisfiability of System (1) first finds the solutions of the punctual equations. Then these are refined considering the quasi-punctual equations. And in the last step the non-punctual ones come into play. In particular, systems involving only punctual equations can be proved equivalent to linear systems of Diophantine equations, which are decidable [12]. We can deal with the quasi-punctual equations exploiting properties of the additive subgroups of $\mathbb{R}^q$ and other results from Diophantine approximations [13,14]: closed subgroups of $\mathbb{R}^q$ are decomposable in a discrete component and a dense one; the discrete component requires a "finite" number of checks; the dense one is "easy" to deal with. On the one hand, if the punctual together with the quasi-punctual equations admit a finite number of solutions, then we can test them on the non-punctual ones. On the other hand, if the punctual and quasi-punctual equations have an infinite set of solutions, then we can always satisfy also the non-punctual equations. All the details can be found in [2].

Since semi-algebraic sets are composed of a finite number of intervals and points, the techniques presented above not only lead us to the decidability of systems of the form (1) when each coefficient ranges over an interval, but also do so when they range over non negative semi-algebraic sets.

Theorem 1. *Let S be a system of the form (1), where capital letters denote variables ranging over $\mathbb{N}_{>0}$, while Greek letters denote real coefficients ranging over some given semi-algebraic sets included in $\mathbb{R}_{\geq 0}$. The satisfiability of S is decidable.*

4 Reachability over Parallel Composition

Now let $H = \bigotimes_{i=1}^{m} H_i$ be the parallel composition of m semi-algebraic o-minimal automata. We are interested in the reachability problem over H, i.e., we want to check whether the set $F = \prod_{i=1}^{m} F_i$ is reachable from $I = \prod_{i=1}^{m} I_i$. The considerations presented in Section 2 lead us to the following characterization.

Lemma 1. *Let $H_1, \ldots, H_m$ be m o-minimal hybrid automata. Moreover, for all $i \in [1, m]$, let $I_i, F_i \subseteq \mathbb{R}^{d(H_i)}$ be sets of points characterized by the first-order formulæ $\mathcal{I}_i[Z_i]$ and $\mathcal{F}_i[Z_i]$, respectively. It holds that $\bigotimes_{i=1}^{m} H_i$ can reach $\prod_{i=1}^{m} F_i$ from $\prod_{i=1}^{m} I_i$ if and only if, for all $i \in [1, m]$, there is a path ph_i in H_i such that the following formula holds[1].*

$$\exists T \geq 0 \exists Z_1, \ldots, Z_m \exists Z_1', \ldots, Z_m' \bigwedge_{i=1}^{m} \left(\mathcal{I}_i[Z_i] \wedge Reach(H_i)(ph_i)[Z_i, Z_i', T] \wedge \mathcal{F}_i[Z_i'] \right)$$

Unfortunately, the model suggested by above lemma does not immediately provide any decidability result, since we have to consider also an infinite number of cyclic paths. In fact, it may be the case that in order to synchronize all the automata, it is necessary to spend some time over their cycles.

To construct a decidable characterization for reachability over parallel compositions, we exploit the existence of a canonical path decomposition: namely, given a semi-algebraic o-minimal hybrid automaton, from any cyclic path of the automaton, we can extract both an acyclic part, by removing all the cycles occurring in it, and a set of simple cycles. The global time necessary to cover the path is then equal to the sum of the time necessary to cover the acyclic part plus multiples of the times we can spend over the simple cycles. What is important is that in the case of o-minimal automata the time we can spend over a cycle does not depend on the starting and ending point. We define the operation which allows us to add a simple cycle to a path.

Definition 7 (Path Augmentability). *Let ph, ph' be two paths. We say that ph' is augmentable to ph if ph' is a simple cycle starting and ending with the edge e and ph is a path involving the edge e. If ph' is augmentable to ph we denote by $ph \oplus ph'$ the path obtained by inserting ph' in ph over the first occurrence of their common edge e, i.e., if $ph' = "e, ph_1', e"$ and $ph = "e_1, \ldots, e_{i-1}, e, e_{i+1} \ldots, e_n"$ where we explicitly identify the first occurrence of e, then $ph \oplus ph' = "e_1, \ldots, e_{i-1}, e, ph_1', e, e_{i+1} \ldots, e_n"$*

Let PH' be a set of (simple cyclic) paths we say that PH' is augmentable to a path ph if either $\mathsf{PH}' = \emptyset$ or there exists an ordering $ph_1, \ldots, ph_l$ of the elements of PH' such that for each $i \in [1, l]$ either ph_i is augmentable to ph or there exists $j < i$ such that ph_i is augmentable to ph_j.

Notice that if ph' is augmentable to ph, then it is augmentable to $ph \oplus ph'$ also. Moreover, if ph is a cyclic path, then there exist $ph_1, \ldots, ph_n$, simple cyclic and acyclic, such that $ph = ph_1 \oplus \ldots \oplus ph_n$.

---

[1] The formula $Reach(H)(ph)[Z, Z', T]$ has been defined in [15].

Let H be an o-minimal hybrid automaton and let $ph = "e_1, \ldots, e_m"$ be a path of H. We define the following formula

$$\widetilde{Reach}(H)(ph)[Z, Z', T] \stackrel{\text{def}}{=} \exists \overline{Z}, \overline{Z}' \left(\overline{Reach}(H)(e_1)[Z, \overline{Z}] \wedge \overline{Reach}(H)(e_m)[\overline{Z}', Z'] \wedge \right.$$
$$\left. Reach(H)("e_2, \ldots, e_{m-1}")[\overline{Z}, \overline{Z}', T] \right)$$

where $\overline{Reach}(H)(e)[Z, Z'] \stackrel{\text{def}}{=} (Act(e)[Z] \wedge Res(e)[Z, Z'])$. It is easy to see that the above formula characterizes all the traces, corresponding to ph, which start and end with a discrete transition. Because of the constant reset condition imposed on o-minimal automata, if both the formulæ $\widetilde{Reach}(H)(ph)[a, b, t]$ and $\widetilde{Reach}(H)(ph)[c, d, t']$ hold, then $\widetilde{Reach}(H)(ph)[a, b, t']$ holds also.

It follows that, if H is an o-minimal automaton, then we can use the formula $\widetilde{Reach}(H)(ph)[Z, Z', T]$ to define the set of time instants $Time(ph)$ in which ph can be covered, i.e., $Time(ph) \stackrel{\text{def}}{=} \{t \mid \exists Z, Z' \widetilde{Reach}(H)(ph)[Z, Z', t] \text{ holds}\}$. Notice that, since H is o-minimal by hypothesis, for each path ph of H the set $Time(ph)$ is o-minimal. It is easy to see that if a path ph' is augmentable to a path ph and t is the time needed to evolve through ph then the automaton can elapse a time $t + t'$, where $t' \in Time(ph')$, to evolve through $ph \oplus ph'$.

By using observations such as these, we can deduce the following lemma, which characterizes the existence of a trace with elapsed time t, without having to examine an infinite number of formulæ.

Lemma 2. *Let H be an o-minimal hybrid automaton, let $r, s \in \mathbb{R}^{d(H)}$ and let $t \in \mathbb{R}_{\geq 0}$. There exists a path ph such that $Reach(H)(ph)[r, s, t]$ holds if and only if there exist a path ph_0 and a set of paths PH such that: (1) ph_0 is acyclic; (2) $\mathsf{PH} = \{ph_1, \ldots ph_l\}$ is augmentable to ph_0; (3) we can choose α, a vector $\langle A_1, \ldots, A_n \rangle \in \mathbb{N}_{>0}^n$ and a vector $\langle \alpha_1, \ldots, \alpha_n \rangle \in \mathbb{R}_{\geq 0}^n$, with $\{\alpha_{k_j}, \ldots, \alpha_{(k_{(j+1)}-1)}\} \in Time(ph_j)$ and $1 = k_1 < \ldots < k_{l+1} = n + 1$, such that $Reach(H)(ph_0)[r, s, \alpha]$ holds and $t = \alpha + \sum_{i=1}^{n} A_i * \alpha_i$.*

This result suggests a class of verification techniques for timed-reachability on o-minimal automata, but avoids testing an infinite set of formulæ. Moreover, exploiting such result, we can propose the following characterization.

Theorem 2. *Let $H_1, \ldots, H_m$ be o-minimal automata and $I_j, F_j \subseteq \mathbb{R}^{d(H_j)}$ be characterized by the first-order semi-algebraic formulæ $I_j[Z_j], F_j[Z_j]$ for all $j \in [1, m]$. The automaton $\bigotimes_{i=1}^{m} H_i$ reaches $\prod_{i=1}^{m} F_i$ from $\prod_{i=1}^{m} I_i$ if and only if, for each $h \in \{1, \ldots, m\}$, there exist an acyclic path ph_h, a set of paths $\mathsf{PH}_h = \{ph_{h,1}, \ldots, ph_{h,m_h}\}$, augmentable to ph_h, a vector $\langle A_{h,1}, \ldots, A_{h,m_h} \rangle \in \mathbb{N}_{>0}^{m_h}$, and a vector $\langle \alpha_{h,1}, \ldots, \alpha_{h,m_h} \rangle \in \mathbb{R}_{\geq 0}^{m_h}$ such that $\{\alpha_{k_{h,j}}, \ldots, \alpha_{(k_{h,j+1}-1)}\} \in Time(ph_{h,j})$, with $1 = k_{h,1} < \ldots < k_{h,m_h+1} = m_h + 1$, and there is $\alpha_h \in \mathbb{R}_{\geq 0}$, satisfying both $\exists Z_h, Z_h'(Reach(H_h)(ph_h)[Z_h, Z_h', \alpha_h] \wedge I_h[Z_h] \wedge F_h[Z_h'])$ and the system*

$$\begin{cases} \sum_{i=1}^{n_1} A_{1,i} * \alpha_{1,i} + \alpha_1 = \sum_{i=1}^{n_2} A_{2,i} * \alpha_{2,i} + \alpha_2 \\ \sum_{i=1}^{n_1} A_{1,i} * \alpha_{1,i} + \alpha_1 = \sum_{i=1}^{n_3} A_{3,i} * \alpha_{3,i} + \alpha_3 \\ \ldots \\ \sum_{i=1}^{n_1} A_{1,i} * \alpha_{1,i} + \alpha_1 = \sum_{i=1}^{n_m} A_{m,i} * \alpha_{m,i} + \alpha_m \end{cases} \quad (2)$$

The number of both acyclic and simple cyclic paths of a hybrid automaton can be bounded from above. Moreover, given a semi-algebraic set $S \subseteq \mathbb{R}$, we can compute the number of its connected components. Since, by Theorem 1, we can decide systems such as the one shown above (Eq. 2), we get the following result.

Corollary 1. *Let* $H_1, \ldots, H_m$ *be semi-algebraic o-minimal hybrid automata. For all* $j \in [1, m]$, *let* $I_j, F_j \subseteq \mathbb{R}^{d(H_j)}$ *be sets of points characterized by first-order semi-algebraic formulæ. Whether* $\bigotimes_{j=1}^{m} H_j$ *reaches* $\prod_{j=1}^{m} F_j$ *from* $\prod_{j=1}^{m} I_j$ *is decidable.*

In this direct formulation of the positive result stating the decidability of reachability problem, we have simply focused on the existence of a decision procedure and not its time or space complexity. Furthermore, the infiniteness of simulation quotient gives a hint of its inherent "hardness". However, since the problem is central to any program that focuses on a modular and hierarchical representation of hybrid automata, further work will need to be devoted to the complexity issues. From what we wrote in Section 3, we can deduce an algorithm which, in some (but frequent) cases, decides the reachability problem over parallel composition of o-minimal hybrid automata with a small overhead with respect to the time needed to decide the reachability problem over its components.

Corollary 2. *Let* $H_1, \ldots, H_m$ *be semi-algebraic o-minimal hybrid automata. For all* $j \in [1, m]$, *let* $I_j, F_j \subseteq \mathbb{R}^{d(H_j)}$ *be sets of points characterized by first-order semi-algebraic formulæ. If, for all* $j \in [1, m]$, *there exists an acyclic path* ph'_j, *a cyclic path* ph''_j, *and a proper interval* $O_j \subseteq \mathbb{R}_{\geq 0}$ *such that* ph''_j *is augmentable to* ph'_j, $O_j \subseteq Time(ph''_j)$, *and* H_j *reaches* F_j *from* I_j *through* ph'_j, *then* $\bigotimes_{j=1}^{m} H_j$ *reaches* $\prod_{j=1}^{m} F_j$ *from* $\prod_{j=1}^{m} I_j$.

Hence, if the hypothesis in the above corollary holds, the reachability problem is compositional and can be decided by testing each component separately. In this case on each component we can apply either the bisimulation based algorithm proposed in [5] or the semi-algebraic geometry based one proposed in [9].

5   Applications in System Biology

As a first example assume that we are monitoring a patient who is under therapy with two drugs, X and Y. X and Y have non-commensurate degradation curves and, hence, they cannot be always injected at the same time. Let $X' = f_x(X, T)$ and $Y' = f_y(Y, T)$ be degradation curves of X and Y. We can imagine that the levels of X and Y have to stay in the ranges $[x_m, x_M]$ and $[y_m, y_M]$, respectively. When the machine monitoring the patient found that X is in the critical range $[x_m, x_l]$ (near the lowest admissible value) it injects X. Similarly, when Y enters in the critical range $[y_m, y_l]$ it is injected. We can model this situation with the hybrid automata depicted in Figure 2. Since there are some interactions between X and Y, we can imagine that, if X is in the interval $[x_a, x_b]$ and at the same time Y is in the interval $[y_a, y_b]$, the patient can have some problems. Let us assume that at time $t = 0$ the drug levels are x_0 and y_0, respectively. We have to check if in the product of these automata the region $[x_a, x_b] \times [y_a, y_b]$ is reachable from the initial point $\langle x_0, y_0 \rangle$. This check can be performed automatically. If the answer is positive, then critical ranges have to be refined.

Fig. 2. The hybrid automata depicting a clinical application of parallel composition

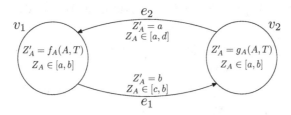

Fig. 3. The hybrid automaton representing the expression level of gene A

Our second example concerns the analysis of metabolic pathways. Imagine we are studying two genes A and B involved in the same pathway. We have some time evolution traces for the expression levels of both A and B. Analyzing the traces of A we observe that we can represent its behavior with the automaton depicted in Figure 3. Similarly, we can draw an analogous automaton for B. We can now exploit these automata to study whether there exists a strong interaction between A and B. For instance if A is a repressor for B and vice-versa, then in the product of the two automata from a region near the maximum value of A and the minimum of B it should be possible to reach a region near the minimum of A and the maximum of B and vice-versa.

In [16] we proposed a method to translate sets of gene profiles data coming from Real-Time PCR experiments into semi-algebraic hybrid automata. In particular, we proposed clustering techniques which allow to reduce the dimensions of the involved automata. The automata we used in [16] are not o-minimal, since some edges can involve reset conditions of the form $\bigvee_{i=1}^{r}(Z = a_i \wedge Z' = b_i)$. However, since the disjunctions range over finite sets, it is immediate to translate them into o-minimal semi-algebraic automata with multiple edges. Hence, the reasoning proposed above on genes A and B can be applied and generalized in that context, in order to infer relationships between genes. The combination of the techniques proposed in [16] with the results of this paper suggests us to build one hybrid automaton for each cluster of genes and then to use their parallel composition for the analysis of the relationships between different clusters. The fact of building one hybrid automaton for each cluster ensures us to get substantial reductions on the automaton dimensions, as proved in [16]. The results presented in this paper allow us to combine and compare the behaviors of different clusters represented by separate automata.

6   Synchronizing Automata and Exchanging Information

As noticed above, parallel composition provides a powerful and theoretically clean way of modeling complex systems by combining simple component models. However, since the original hybrid automata should not share variables by definition, components cannot "communicate" in models built by parallel composition, i.e., they evolve in isolated environments without interacting. Still, the results of Section 4 can be used to prove the decidability of reachability problem over a different kind of composition operator, similar to that proposed in [10,11], which allows both interactions and synchronizations between components during system evolution. For the sake of example, let us consider the two semi-algebraic o-minimal hybrid automata $H_1 = (Z_1, Z_1', \mathcal{V}_1, \mathcal{E}_1, Inv_1, \mathcal{F}_1, Act_1, Res_1)$ and $H_2 = (Z_2, Z_2', \mathcal{V}_2, \mathcal{E}_2, Inv_2, \mathcal{F}_2, Act_2, Res_2)$ depicted in Figure 4, where:

H_1: $Z_1 = \langle X_1, X_2, X_3 \rangle$
  $Dyn_1(v_1) \stackrel{\text{def}}{=} X_1' = X_1 + T \wedge X_3' = X_3$
  $Dyn_1(v_1') \stackrel{\text{def}}{=} X_1' = 0 \wedge X_3' = X_3 + T$
  $Res_1(e_1) \stackrel{\text{def}}{=} X_1' = 0 \wedge X_3' = 0$
  $Res_1(e_1') \stackrel{\text{def}}{=} X_1' = 0 \wedge X_3' = 0 \wedge X_2' = 0$
  $Inv_1(v_1) \stackrel{\text{def}}{=} X_1 \leq 1, Inv_1(v_1') \stackrel{\text{def}}{=} X_1 = 0$
  $Act_1(e_1) \stackrel{\text{def}}{=} X_1 = 1, Act_1(e_1') \stackrel{\text{def}}{=} X_1 + X_2 > 2$

H_2: $Z_2 = \langle X_2 \rangle$
  $Dyn_2(v_2) \stackrel{\text{def}}{=} X_2' = X_2 + T$

  $Res_2(e_2) \stackrel{\text{def}}{=} X_2' = 0$

  $Inv_2(v_2) \stackrel{\text{def}}{=} X_2 \leq \sqrt{2}$
  $Act_2(e_2) \stackrel{\text{def}}{=} X_2 = \sqrt{2}$

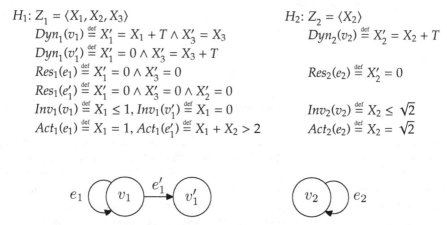

Fig. 4. The discrete projection of H_1 and H_2

Since H_1 and H_2 share the variable X_2, we cannot model their synchronous evolution by using parallel composition. However, one may notice that all the formulæ involving X_2 in H_1 are related with e_1'. Let H_1' be the automaton obtained by removing e_1' from H_1. It is easy to see that the concurrent evolution of H_1 and H_2 is representable by the hybrid automaton H_* obtained by providing $H_1' \otimes H_2$ of a further edge $\bar{e}$, from $\langle v_1, v_2 \rangle$ to $\langle v_1', v_2 \rangle$, whose activation and reset formulæ are $Act_1(e_1')$ and $Res_1(e_1')$, respectively.

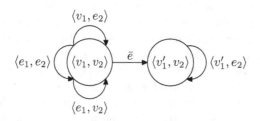

Fig. 5. The discrete projection of H_*

It follows that F is reachable from I in H_* if and only if either F is reachable from I or $Act_1(e_1')$ is reachable from I and F is reachable from $Res_1(e_1')$ in $H_1' \otimes H_2$. Hence, we can exploit the results presented in this paper to decide reachability property on H_*. Notice that a similar approach can be used also when shared variables appear in either dynamics or invariants. We leave both formal definition and applicability analysis of synchronous composition for future work.

7 Conclusions

This paper extends our earlier work [1] showing that the reachability problem for parallel composition of semi-algebraic o-minimal hybrid automata is decidable. To achieve such a result, it exploited Tarski's decidability result on semi-algebraic theory, density results over ℝ, algorithms for the membership problems over algebraic fields, and algorithms for solving systems of linear Diophantine systems. Further, by showing that this class of automata does not admit a finite simulation quotient (see [1,2]), we have proved impossibility of obtaining such a result through standard finite quotient techniques.

Time-complexity issues limit the practical applicability of our result. Nevertheless, it presents some intriguing theoretical features. Note first that, to prove the decidability of parallel composition, we took advantage of the decidability of a rather simple mixed real/integer problem. Such mixed approaches, in some sense, reflect the continuous-discrete behavior described by hybrid systems.

Our decidability results may be surprising, in the context of Miller's undecidability results [11], but can be explained as follows. While we require constant resets on automata components, Miller admitted both constant and identity resets. Hence, he could test the value of a variable through an activation and do not change it by applying an identity reset. This is a fundamental gadget in the construction of the two-counter Minsky machine encoding needed to prove the undecidability result (see Figure 3 in [11]), but it is inapplicable in our case.

Finally, the technique of this paper emphasizes the hardest cases to decide and suggests a class of automata for which the reachability problem of parallel composition can be reduced to reachability problems on each component.

References

1. Casagrande, A., Corvaja, P., Piazza, C., Mishra, B.: Composing semi-algebraic o-minimal automata. In: Bemporad, A., Bicchi, A., Buttazzo, G. (eds.) HSCC 2007. LNCS, vol. 4416, pp. 668–671. Springer, Heidelberg (2007)
2. Casagrande, A., Corvaja, P., Piazza, C., Mishra, B.: Parallel composition of semi-algebraic o-minimal automata (January 2008),
   http://www.dimi.uniud.it/piazza/PAPERS/parallel.pdf
3. Alur, R., Henzinger, T.A., Ho, P.H.: Automatic Symbolic Verification of Embedded Systems. In: IEEE Real-Time Systems Symposium 1993, pp. 2–11. IEEE Press, Los Alamitos (1993)
4. Henzinger, T.A., Kopke, P.W., Puri, A., Varaiya, P.: What's decidable about hybrid automata? In: Proc. of Symp. on Theory of Computing (STOCS 1995), pp. 373–382 (1995)
5. Lafferriere, G., Pappas, G.J., Sastry, S.: O-minimal Hybrid Systems. Mathematics of Control, Signals, and Systems 13, 1–21 (2000)
6. Brihaye, T., Michaux, C., Rivière, C., Troestler, C.: On O-Minimal Hybrid Systems. In: Alur, R., Pappas, G.J. (eds.) HSCC 2004. LNCS, vol. 2993, pp. 219–233. Springer, Heidelberg (2004)

7. Tarski, A.: A Decision Method for Elementary Algebra and Geometry. Univ. California Press (1951)
8. van den Dries, L.: Tame Topology and O-minimal Structures. London Mathematical Society Lecture Note Series, vol. 248. Cambridge University Press, Cambridge (1998)
9. Casagrande, A., Piazza, C., Mishra, B.: Semi-Algebraic Constant Reset Hybrid Automata - SACoRe. In: Proc. of the 44rd Conference on Decision and Control (CDC 2005), pp. 678–683. IEEE Press, Los Alamitos (2005)
10. Henzinger, T.A.: The Theory of Hybrid Automata. In: Proc. of IEEE Symposium on Logic in Computer Science (LICS 1996), pp. 278–292. IEEE Press, Los Alamitos (1996)
11. Miller, J.S.: Decidability and Complexity Results for Timed Automata and Semi-linear Hybrid Automata. In: Lynch, N.A., Krogh, B.H. (eds.) HSCC 2000. LNCS, vol. 1790, pp. 296–309. Springer, Heidelberg (2000)
12. Pottier, L.: Minimal solutions of linear diophantine systems: Bounds and algorithms. In: Book, R.V. (ed.) RTA 1991. LNCS, vol. 488, pp. 162–173. Springer, Heidelberg (1991)
13. Bourbaki, N.: Elements of Mathematics. General topology II. Springer, Heidelberg (1989)
14. Cohen, H.: A Course in Computational Algebraic Number Theory. Graduate Texts in Mathematics, vol. 138. Springer, Heidelberg (1993)
15. Casagrande, A., Corvaja, P., Piazza, C., Mishra, B.: Synchronized product of semi-algebraic o-minimal hybrid automata. Technical report, University of Udine (October 2006), http://fsv.dimi.uniud.it/papers/syncro.pdf
16. Casagrande, A., Casey, K., Falchi, R., Piazza, C., Ruperti, B., Vizzotto, G., Mishra, B.: Translating Time-Course Gene Expression Profiles into Semi-algebraic Hybrid Automata Via Dimensionality Reduction. In: Anai, H., Horimoto, K., Kutsia, T. (eds.) AB 2007. LNCS, vol. 4545, pp. 51–65. Springer, Heidelberg (2007)

On the Applicability of Stochastic Petri Nets for Analysis of Multiserver Retrial Systems with Different Vacation Policies

Nawel Gharbi

Department of Computer Science,
University of Sciences and Technology USTHB,
Algiers 16111, Algeria
ngharbi@wissal.dz

Abstract. This paper deals with retrial systems where servers are subject to random vacations. So far, these systems were analyzed only by queueing theory and almost works assumed that the service station consists of one server and the customers source is infinite. In this paper, we give a detailed qualitative and performance analysis of finite-source multiserver retrial systems with multiple and single vacations of servers or all station, using Generalized Stochastic Petri nets. We show how this high level stochastic model allows us to cope with the complexity of such systems involving the simultaneous presence of retrials and vacations, and how stationary performance indices can be expressed as a function of Petri net elements.

Keywords: Multiserver retrial systems, Finite-source, Vacation policies, Generalized Stochastic Petri nets, Modeling and Performance measures.

1 Introduction

Retrial systems (or systems with repeated calls) have gained a particular attention in the last two decades from practicians and theoreticians searchers [4,9,26]. That is mainly explained by the advances in telecommunication and computer networks areas. These systems are characterized by the following feature: a customer finding all servers busy or unavailable upon arrival, is obliged to leave the service area, but after some random time, he repeats his demand. Between trials, the customer is said to be in *orbit*. For a comprehensive review of the fundamental methods and results, the interested reader is referred to the surveys papers by Artalejo [4,11] and the monograph by Falin and Templeton [10].

In this paper, we consider multiserver retrial systems in which each server sometimes takes a vacation i.e. becomes unavailable to the primary and repeated calls for a random period of time. These vacation periods are usually introduced in order to exploit the idle time of the servers for other secondary jobs as: servicing customers of another system, inspection tasks and preventive maintenance actions which are mainly doing to prevent the risk of failure, to preserve the sanity of the system, to provide a high reliability and to improve the quality

Cha et al. (Eds.): ATVA 2008, LNCS 5311, pp. 289–302, 2008.

of service. Similarly, the servers breakdowns which may occur randomly, independently of the system status, and also the repair periods may be regarded as server vacations.

A wide class of policies for governing the vacation mechanism, have been discussed in the literature, namely the multiple vacation policy [6,22] and the single vacation policy [19,25,27]. On the other hand, some works have considered the vacation of a server independently of other servers [5,20] and other studies have considered synchronous vacations of some servers [22,27,28] or all the station servers (station vacation) [6]. However, all these works on multiserver vacation queueing models [23], do not take into account the repeated calls of blocked customers.

In retrial systems with vacations, customers who arrive while all servers are busy or on vacation, have to join the orbit to repeat their call after a random period. Thus, there is a natural interest in the study of this class of models, which has been used in concrete applications as digital cellular mobile networks [16], local area networks with nonpersistent CSMA/CD protocols [17], with star topology [14] and so on. However, almost works combining retrial and vacation phenomenon, assume that the service station consists of one single server [1,3,7,14,15,16,17,24] and the customers source is infinite [1,3,7,15,24]. On the other hand, in all the works cited above, the retrial systems with vacations are analyzed only by the queueing theory.

The Generalized Stochastic Petri nets (GSPNs) [2] are an important graphical and mathematical model appropriate for describing and analyzing stochastic systems that exhibit concurrency and synchronization. It allows to verify the qualitative properties and to obtain performance indices either with analytic means or by numerical algorithms. On the other hand, using GSPNs allows us to incorporate features that may be difficult to model directly by Markov chains.

In the past decade, this formalism has received much attention from researchers in the performance and reliability arena, and have been extensively used for analytical modeling in the context of independability, performance and performability of computer, telecommunication, manufacturing and aerospace systems.

In this paper, we give a detailed qualitative and performance analysis of finite-source retrial systems with multiple servers subject to vacations, using the GSPNs. We show how this high level stochastic model allows us to cope with the complexity of such systems involving the simultaneous presence of retrials and vacations, and how several performance indices can be expressed as a function of Petri net elements, for the different vacation policies.

The modeling and the analysis of single server systems with vacations (without retrials) using the GSPN model, was initially introduced by Trivedi in [21]. It was then applied for retrial systems (without vacations) by Gharbi in [12]. The present paper aims to combine both retrials and vacations in the same system.

The paper is organized as follows: First, we describe the systems under study. In section 3, we present the GSPN models describing multiserver retrial systems with station and server vacations mechanisms and under multiple and single vacation policy. Qualitative analysis and performance indices are given in section 4. Next, several numerical examples are presented with some comments and discussions. Finally, we give a conclusion.

2 Description of Retrial Systems with Different Vacation Policies

In the analysis of retrial systems with vacations, it is usually assumed that the customers source is infinite. However, in many practical situations, it is very important to take into account the fact that the rate of generation of new primary calls decreases as the number of customers in the system increases. Examples of this behavior arise from the performance analysis of hybrid fiber-coax [13], cellular mobile networks [18] and local area networks with collision avoidance circuits and CSMA/CD protocols [14]. This can be done with the help of finite-source retrial models where each customer generates its own flow of primary demands.

In this paper, we consider retrial systems with finite source (population), that is, we assume that a finite number K of potential customers generate the so called quasi-random input of primary calls with rate λ. Each customer can be in three states: generating a primary call (free), sending repeated calls (in orbit) or under service by one of the servers.

If a customer is free at time t, it can generate a primary request for service in any interval $(t, t + dt)$ with probability $(K - n)\lambda dt + o(dt)$ as $dt \to 0$, where n is the number of customers in the system. Each customer requires to be served by one and only one server.

The service station consists of c $(c \geq 1)$ homogeneous and parallel servers. Each server can be idle, busy or on vacation. If one of the servers is idle at the moment of the arrival of a call, then the service starts. The requests are assigned to the free servers randomly and without any priority order. The service times are independent, identic and exponentially distributed with rate μ. After service, the customer becomes free, so it can generate a new primary call, and the server becomes idle.

We consider the two vacation mechanisms: *server vacation* and *station vacation*. For the first one, which is encountered even more often in practice, each server is an independent working unit, and it can take its own vacation independently of other servers states. In the model with station vacation mechanism, all the servers take vacations simultaneously. That is, whenever the system is empty, all the station leaves the system for a vacation, and returns when the vacation is completed. So, station vacation is group vacation for all servers. This occurs in practice, for example, when a system consists of several interconnected machines that are inseparable, or when all the machines are run by a single operator. In such situations, the whole station has to be treated as a single entity for vacation. Hence, if the system (or the operator who runs the system) is used for a secondary task when it becomes empty (or available), all the servers (the operator) will then be utilized to perform a secondary task. During this amount of time, the servers are unavailable to serve any primary or repeated call and this is equivalent to taking a station vacation.

The *exhaustive service discipline* is considered here. That is, each free server (or all station) can take a vacation only if the system is empty at either a service completion or at the end of a vacation, and only at these epochs. On the other hand, upon completing a vacation, the server returns to the idle state and starts to serve customers, if any, till the system becomes empty. Otherwise, if the server (or the station) at the moment of returning from vacation, finds the system empty, it takes one of the two actions:

- Under the *multiple vacation policy*, the server (station) shall leave immediately for another vacation and continues in this manner until he finds at least one customer (not being served) in the system upon returning from a vacation.
- Under the *single vacation policy*, the server (station) should wait until serving one call at least before commencing another vacation.

The vacation times of all servers (or station) are assumed to be independent and exponentially distributed with rate θ.

At the moment of the arrival of a call, if all the servers are busy or on vacation, the customer joins the orbit to repeat his demand after an exponential time with parameter ν.

As usual, we assume that the interarrival periods, service times, vacation times and retrial times are mutually independent.

3   GSPN Models of Multiserver Retrial Systems with Vacations

In this section, we present our approach for modeling finite-source multiserver retrial systems with station and server vacations, under multiple and single vacation policies using the generalized stochastic Petri nets model.

A GSPN is a directed graph that consists of places (drawn as circles), timed transitions (drawn as rectangles) which describe the execution of time consuming activities and immediate transitions (drawn as thin bars) that model actions whose duration is negligible, with respect to the time scale of the problem. This class of transitions has priority over timed transitions and fire in zero time once they are enabled.

Formally, a GSPN is an eight-tuple $(P, T, W^-, W^+, W^h, \pi, M_0, \theta)$ where :

- $P = \{P_1, P_2, ..., P_n\}$ is the set of places;
- $T = \{t_1, t_2, ..., t_m\}$ is the set of timed and immediate transitions;
- $W^-, W^+, W^h : P * T \rightarrow IN$ are the input, output and inhibitor functions respectively;
- $\pi : T \rightarrow IN$ is the priority function;
- $M_0 : P \rightarrow IN$ is the initial marking which describes the initial state of the system;
- $\theta : T \rightarrow IR^+$ is a function that associates rates of negative exponential distribution to timed transitions and weights to immediate transitions.

3.1   Retrial Systems with Multiple Vacations of Servers

This model is used for describing many practical problems where servers take individual vacations. This means, whenever a server completes servicing and there are no more requests in the system, it takes a vacation independently of other servers states. On the other hand, multiple vacations policy means that at the end of a vacation period, if the orbit is empty and there is no primary or repeated arrival, the server takes immediately another vacation. The process continues until the server upon returning finds any customer in the system.

Fig. 1 shows the GSPN model describing the above system.

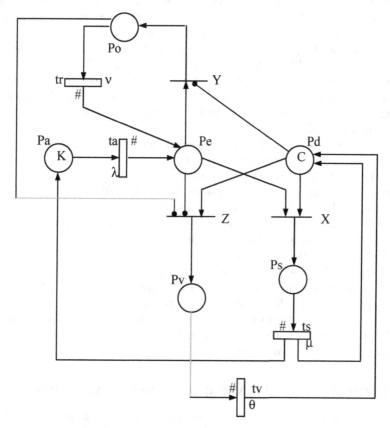

Fig. 1. GSPN model of retrial systems with multiple vacations of servers

- The place P_a contains the free customers;
- The place P_e contains the primary or repeated (returning) calls ready for service;
- The place P_d contains the free (available) servers;
- The place P_o represents the orbit;
- The place P_s contains customers in service (or busy servers);
- The place P_v contains the servers that are on vacation.

The initial marking of the net is:
$M_0 = \{M(P_a), M(P_e), M(P_d), M(P_o), M(P_s), M(P_v)\} = \{K, 0, c, 0, 0, 0\}$, which represents the fact that all customers are initially free, the c servers are available, no server is on vacation and the orbit is empty. Hence, at time $t = 0$, all servers take a vacation simultaneously. So, this initial state is vanishing and equivalent to the tangible state $(K, 0, 0, 0, 0, c)$.

- The firing of transition t_a indicates the arrival of a primary request generated by a free customer. It has an *infinite servers semantics*, which is represented by the symbol # placed next to transition. This means that the firing rate of t_a is marking dependent and equals $\lambda.ED(t_a, m)$ where $ED(t_a, m)$ is the enabling degree of the transition t_a in the marking m. Hence, all potential customers are able to generate requests for service.
- At the arrival of a primary or repeated request to the place P_e, if P_d contains at least one available server, the immediate transition X fires and one token is deposited in P_s, which represents the beginning of the service. Otherwise, if all servers are busy or on vacation (ie. no token in P_d), the immediate transition Y fires and a token will be deposited in the place P_o. So, the customer joins the orbit.
- When the transition t_r fires, the customer in orbit tries again for service, so the system receives a repeated request.
- The firing of the immediate transition Z represents the event that an idle server is commencing a vacation since there is no call left to be served. This represents the exhaustive service discipline.
- The firing of transition t_v represents the end of the vacation time. Hence, the server is returned to the available state.
- When the timed transition t_s fires, the customer under service returns to the idle state and the server becomes ready to serve another customer.
- The service semantics of the timed transitions t_s and t_v are *infinite servers semantics*, because the c servers are parallel. So, several servers can be in service or on vacation at the same time. Similarly, the transition t_r is marking dependent because the customers in orbit are independent and can generate repeated calls simultaneously.

3.2   Retrial Systems with Multiple Vacations of the Station

In this model, as soon as the system is empty of requests, all the servers become idle, and consequently the station takes a vacation. As one may expect, this situation appears to be more complicated that the previous one. In fact, it is more simple, because all servers take a vacation simultaneously and return to the system at the same time also. Hence, the GSPN modeling this system with multiple vacations of the station, is the same model as the one given in Fig. 1, in which the multiplicity of the arc connecting the place P_d to transition Z and transition t_v to place P_d equals c (rather than 1), because the c servers of the station take a vacation together. So, if the place P_d contains c idle servers, the orbit (P_o) is empty and there is no arrival to the place P_e, the immediate transition Z fires, which represents the beginning of the station vacation time. At the end of this period (after a mean delay equals $1/\theta$), c tokens corresponding to the c servers of the station will be deposited in P_d. On the other hand, the symbol # placed next to transition t_v should be omitted, because only one token can ever be in place P_v.

3.3   Retrial Systems with Single Vacations of Servers

This model corresponds to systems where each server is an independent working unit. The single vacation policy means that at the end of a vacation period, even if the system is empty, the server is obliged to wait until serving one call at least, before commencing another vacation.

Fig. 2 shows the GSPN model describing the above system.

In the previous models with multiple vacations, the place P_d contains all the free servers. Hence, at the end of a service or vacation period, the server returns to the idle state represented by the place P_d. However, in the model with single vacations given in Fig. 2, at a service completion, the server joins the place P_d

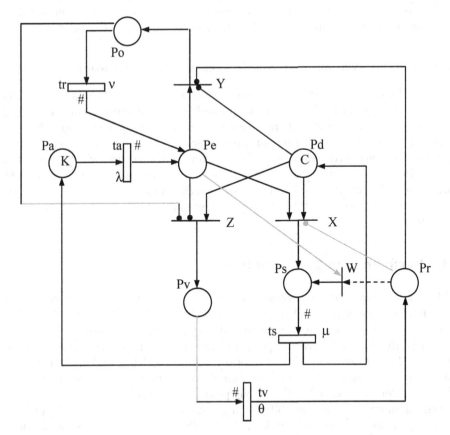

Fig. 2. GSPN model of retrial systems with single vacations of servers

which contains the servers having served at least one call since the last vacation period. So, they can serve other calls if any (firing of transition X). Otherwise, they can take a vacation after the firing of the immediate transition Z. However, at the end of a vacation period, the server joins the place P_r which represents the servers having just finished a vacation. Hence, the servers of P_r are obliged to serve at least one call after the firing of the immediate transition W to join the place P_d, where they can commence another single vacation.

Initially, all customers are free, the orbit is empty and the c servers are available to serve the calls or to take a vacation.

At the arrival of a primary or repeated request to the place P_e, several alternatives are possible:

- If the place P_r of servers just returning from vacation, contains at least one server, the immediate transition W fires and the service of the arriving call starts.
- If the place P_r is empty and the place P_d contains at least one free server, the immediate transition X fires and the service period starts.
- If the two places P_d and P_r are empty which represents the fact that all the servers are busy or on vacation, the immediate transition Y fires and a token will be deposited in the place P_o. So, the customer joins the orbit.

3.4   Retrial Systems with Single Vacations of the Station

The GSPN modeling systems with single vacations of the station is the same as the model given in Fig. 2, in which the multiplicity of the arc connecting the place P_d to transition Z and transition t_v to place P_r equals c (rather than 1), because the c servers of the station take a vacation together. At the end of this period, c tokens corresponding to the c servers of the station will be deposited in P_r. Hence, the station can't take another vacation until each server serves at least one call. On the other hand, as the place P_v contains one token at the most, the symbol # describing the infinite server semantics of transition t_v should be omitted.

4   Performance Evaluation

The aim of this study is twofold. Firstly, we have to verify the correctness of our models (bounded and live nets) and their ergodicity. Next, we derive the formulas of the most important steady-state performance indices.

To verify the qualitative properties of the models under study, we used the GreatSPN package [8] which is a software tool for modeling and analysis of parallel systems, based on the Petri net formalism. It provides a friendly framework to experiment with GSPNs. The strong points of this package are: the use friendliness (in particular the availability of a graphical interface for model definition), portability, modularity and particularly the efficiency of the analysis algorithms which allow its use on complex systems.

Compared with other tools, the peculiarity of GreatSPN is the attempt of providing a more complete modeling and analysis environment, in which a variety of efficient qualitative and quantitative analysis algorithms, for the steady-state as well as transient performance evaluation are available. On the other hand, this tool allows one to gain insight into the memory and CPU time requirements of the solutions algorithms, because most of the algorithms currently implemented in GreatSPN represent the state-of-the-art in terms of efficient utilization of CPU and memory.

GreatSPN is composed of many separate programs that cooperate in the construction and analysis of GSPN models by sharing files. Using network file system capabilities, different analysis modules can be run on different machines in a distributed computing environment.

4.1   Qualitative Analysis

The primordial qualitative property we have to verify is the *boundness* of the proposed models. This property ensures that each place of the net is bounded. The verification of this property is based on semi-flows computation and study, which is in the GreatSPN implementation. We found that all places of each model are covered by a semi-flow, so the nets are bounded. Hence, their state spaces are finite. This is an important preliminary step, because it is hopeless to try to compute the model state space for further analysis, if we know that the model is unbounded.

The second important qualitative property is the *liveness*. A transition t is live if from any reachable marking, there is a reachable marking enabling t. Thus, t is live implies that the activity modeled by this transition can always take place from any state. In the proposed models, all transitions are live.

Finally, another interesting qualitative property we had to check is the presence of *home states*. In fact, in the four models the initial marking is a home state.

4.2   Stochastic Analysis

The proposed GSPN models are bounded and the initial marking is a home state. Thus, the underlying continuous time Markov chains are ergodic.

The solution of each CTMC at steady-state is the probability distribution vector π. This is computed as the solution of the linear system of equations $\pi.Q = 0$ and $\sum_i \pi_i = 1$, where Q is the infinitesimal generator matrix.

The numerical computation of the steady-state probability vector is implemented in the GreatSPN by a variation of the Gauss-Seidel iterative solution.

Having the steady-state probability distribution π, several performance measures of multiserver retrial systems with vacations can be derived as follows.

In these formulas, $M_i(P)$ denotes the number of tokens in the place P in the marking M_i, RS is the set of all accessible markings (Reachability Set) and $E(t)$ is the set of markings where the transition t is enabled.

- **The mean number of customers in orbit (n_o):**
  This correspond to the mean number of tokens in the place P_o.

$$n_o = \sum_{i:M_i \in RS} M_i(P_o).\pi_i \qquad (1)$$

- **The mean number of busy servers (n_s):**
  This corresponds to the mean number of tokens in the place P_s which is also the mean number of customers under service.

$$n_s = \sum_{i:M_i \in RS} M_i(P_s).\pi_i \qquad (2)$$

- **The mean number of customers in the system (n):**

$$n = n_s + n_o \qquad (3)$$

- **The mean number of servers on vacation (n_v):**
  This represents the mean number of tokens in the place P_v.

$$n_v = \begin{cases} \sum_{i:M_i \in RS} M_i(P_v).\pi_i & \text{in servers vacations} \\ \sum_{i:M_i \in RS} M_i(P_v).c.\pi_i & \text{in station vacations} \end{cases} \qquad (4)$$

- **The mean number of idle servers (n_f):**

$$n_f = c-(n_s+n_v) = \begin{cases} \sum_{i:M_i \in RS} M_i(P_d).\pi_i & \text{in multiple vacations} \\ \sum_{i:M_i \in RS} [M_i(P_d) + M_i(P_r)].\pi_i & \text{in single vacations} \end{cases} \qquad (5)$$

- **The mean rate of generation of primary calls $(\bar{\lambda})$:**
  This represents the throughput of the transition t_a.

$$\bar{\lambda} = \sum_{i:M_i \in E(t_a)} M_i(P_a).\lambda.\pi_i \qquad (6)$$

- **The mean rate of generation of repeated calls $(\bar{\nu})$:**
  This represents the retrial frequency of customers in orbit. It corresponds to the throughput of the transition t_r.

$$\bar{\nu} = \sum_{i:M_i \in E(t_r)} M_i(P_o).\nu.\pi_i \qquad (7)$$

- **The mean rate of service $(\bar{\mu})$:**
  This represents the throughput of the transition t_s.

$$\bar{\mu} = \sum_{i:M_i \in E(t_s)} M_i(P_s).\mu.\pi_i \qquad (8)$$

- **The mean rate of vacation** $(\bar{\tau})$:
  This represents the throughput of the transition t_v.

$$\bar{\tau} = \sum_{i:M_i \in E(t_v)} M_i(P_v).\theta.\pi_i \tag{9}$$

- **The blocking probability of a primary call** (B_p):

$$B_p = \begin{cases} \dfrac{\sum_{i:M_i \in RS} \sum_{j=1}^{K} j.\lambda.Prob[M_i(P_a)=j\,and\,M_i(P_d)=0]}{\lambda} & \text{in multiple vacations} \\[2ex] \dfrac{\sum_{i:M_i \in RS} \sum_{j=1}^{K} j.\lambda.Prob[M_i(P_a)=j\,and\,M_i(P_d)=0\,and\,M_i(P_r)=0]}{\lambda} & \text{in single vacations} \end{cases} \tag{10}$$

- **The blocking probability of a repeated call** (B_r):

$$B_r = \begin{cases} \dfrac{\sum_{i:M_i \in A} \sum_{j=1}^{K} j.\nu.Prob[M_i(P_o)=j\,and\,M_i(P_d)=0]}{\overline{\nu}} & \text{in multiple vacations} \\[2ex] \dfrac{\sum_{i:M_i \in A} \sum_{j=1}^{K} j.\nu.Prob[M_i(P_o)=j\,and\,M_i(P_d)=0\,and\,M_i(P_r)=0]}{\overline{\nu}} & \text{in single vacations} \end{cases} \tag{11}$$

- **The blocking probability** (B):
  This represents the probability that a call either primary or repeated, finds no idle server.

$$B = B_p + B_r \tag{12}$$

- **The admission probability** (A): This represents the probability that a primary or a repeated call finds at least one idle server.

$$A = 1 - B \tag{13}$$

- **Utilization of s servers** (U_s): $(1 \leq s \leq c)$
  This corresponds to the probability that s servers **at least** are busy:

$$U_s = \sum_{i:M_i(P_s) \geq s} \pi_i \tag{14}$$

- **Vacation of s servers** (V_s): $(1 \leq s \leq c)$
  This corresponds to the probability that s servers **at least** are on vacation:

$$V_s = \begin{cases} \sum_{i:M_i(P_v) \geq s} \pi_i & \text{in servers vacations} \\ \sum_{i:c.M_i(P_v) \geq s} \pi_i & \text{in station vacations} \end{cases} \tag{15}$$

- **Availability of s servers** (A_s): $(1 \leq s \leq c)$
  This represents the probability that s servers **at least** are idle.

$$A_s = 1 - (U_s + V_s) \tag{16}$$

- The mean waiting time ($\overline{W}$):
  The mean waiting time $\overline{W}$ of the customers in the steady state, can be easily obtained with the help of Little's formula:

$$\overline{W} = n_o/\overline{\lambda} \qquad (17)$$

- The mean response time ($\overline{R}$):

$$\overline{R} = (n_o + n_s)/\overline{\lambda} \qquad (18)$$

5   Validation of Results

In this section, we consider some numerical results to validate the proposed models and also to show the influence of system parameters and vacation policies on the performance measures of multiserver retrial systems. The numerical results were established using the GreatSPN tool.

In Table 1, some experimental results are collected when the servers vacation rate and the station vacation rate are very large. The results were validated by the Pascal program given in the book of Falin and Templeton [10] for the analysis of multiserver retrial queues without vacations. As it was expected, we can see from this table, that for high vacation rate, the corresponding performance measures for models with server vacation policy and station vacation policy are very close to each other and to the case without vacation.

The parameter $\rho = N\lambda/\mu$, is defined as the largest offered load in the system. Table 2 shows the variation of the mean response time with ρ, for the single and multiple vacation policies, when the service station consists of one server and the retrial rate is very high. From this table, we can see that the numerical results are very close to those obtained by Trivedi [21] for single server queueing systems with vacations and without retrials, since the retrial rate is very large.

Table 1. Validation of results in multiserver retrial case without vacations

	Model without vacation [10]	Model with servers vacation	Model with station vacation
Number of servers	4	4	4
Size of source	20	20	20
Primary call generation rate	0.1	0.1	0.1
Service rate	1	1	1
Retrial rate	1.2	1.2	1.2
Vacation rate	-	1e+25	1e+25
Mean number of busy servers	1.800 748	1.800 768	1.800 758
Mean number of customers of repeated calls	0.191 771	0.191 788	0.191 786
Mean rate of generation of primary calls	1.800 748	1.800 744	1.800 746
Mean waiting time	1.106 495	1.106 518	1.106 510

Table 2. Mean response time with $N = 50$, $\mu = 1$, $\theta = 0.5$, $c = 1$

ρ	Models without retrials [21]		Models with $\nu = 1e + 25$	
	Multiple vacations	Single vacations	Multiple vacations	Single vacations
0.1	3.107	1.494	3.106 810	1.493 581
0.3	3.391	2.370	3.390 962	2.370 404
0.5	3.834	3.172	3.833 990	3.172 221
0.7	4.592	4.152	4.592 591	4.152 760
0.9	6.000	5.718	6.000 657	5.719 090

6 Conclusion

In this paper, we proposed a technique that allows modeling and analyzing finite-source multiserver retrial systems with different vacation policies using GSPNs. The novelty of the investigation is essentially the combination of multiplicity of servers with the simultaneous presence of repeated calls and vacations, which make the system rather complicated.

The flexibility of GSPNs modeling approach allowed us a simple construction of detailed and compact models for these systems. Moreover, it made it possible to verify many qualitative properties of interest by inspection of the reachability graph. From a performance point of view, the proposed approach offers a rich means of expressing interesting performance indices as a function of the Petri net elements.

Finally, many retrial and vacation systems problems and their solutions can be simplified using the stochastic Petri nets modeling approach with all the methods and tools developed within this framework.

References

1. Aissani, A.: An $M^x/G/1$ retrial queue with exhaustive vacations. Journal of Statistics and Management Systems 3, 269–286 (2000)
2. Ajmone Marsan, M., Balbo, G., Conte, G., Donatelli, S., Franceschinis, G.: Modelling with Generalized Stochastic Petri Nets. John Wiley and Sons, New York (1995)
3. Artalejo, J.R.: Analysis of an M/G/1 queue with constant repeated attempts and server vacations. Computers and Operations Research 24, 493–504 (1997)
4. Artalejo, J.R., Falin, G.I.: Standard and retrial queueing systems: A comparative analysis. Revista Matematica Complutense XV, pp. 101–129 (2002)
5. Artalejo, J.R., López-Herrero, M.J.: On the M/M/m queue with removable servers, Stochastic Point Processes. In: Srinivasan, S.K., Vijayakumar, A. (eds.), pp. 124–144. Narosa Publishing House (2003)
6. Chao, X., Zhao, Y.Q.: Analysis of multi-sever queues with station and server vacations. European Journal of Operational Research 110, 392–406 (1998)
7. Choudhury, G.: A two phase batch arrival retrial queueing system with Bernoulli vacation schedule. Applied Mathematics and Computation 188, 1455–1466 (2007)

8. Chiola, G., Franceschinis, C., Gaeta, R., Ribaudo, M.: GreatSPN 1.7: Graphical Editor and Analyzer for Timed and Stochastic Petri Nets. Performance Evaluation 24, 47–68 (1995)
9. Falin, G.I.: A survey on retrial queues. Queueing Systems 7, 127–168 (1990)
10. Falin, G.I., Templeton, J.G.C.: Retrial Queues. Chapman and Hall, London (1997)
11. Falin, G.I., Artalejo, J.R.: A finite source retrial queue. European Journal of Operational Research 108, 409–424 (1998)
12. Gharbi, N., Ioualalen, M.: GSPN Analysis of retrial systems with servers breakdowns and repairs. Applied Mathematics and Computation 174, 1151–1168 (2006)
13. Houck, D.J., Lai, W.S.: Traffic modeling and analysis of hybrid fiber-coax systems. Computer Networks and ISDN systems 30, pp. 821–834 (1998)
14. Janssens, G.K.: The quasi-random input queueing system with repeated attempts as a model for collision-avoidance star local area network. IEEE Transactions on Communications 45, 360–364 (1997)
15. Krishna Kumar, B., Arivudainambi, D.: The M/G/1 retrial queue with Bernoulli schedules and general retrial times. Computers and Mathematics with Applications 43, 15–30 (2002)
16. Kwon, S.J.: Performance analysis of CDPD Sleep mode for power conservation in mobile end systems. IEICE Trans. Commun. E84 (2001)
17. Li, H., Yang, T.: A single server retrial queue with server vacations and a finite number of input sources. European Journal of Operational Research 85, 149–160 (1995)
18. Roszik, J., Sztrik, J., Kim, C.: Retrial queues in the performance modeling of cellular mobile networks using MOSEL. International Journal of Simulation: Systems, Science and Technology 1-2, 38–47 (2005)
19. Sikdar, K., Gupta, U.C.: Analytic and Numerical Aspects of Batch Service Queues with Single Vacation. Computers and Operations Research 32, 943–966 (2005)
20. Tian, N., Zhang, Z.G.: Quantifying the performance effects of idle time utilization in multiserver systems. Naval Research Logistics 54, 189–199 (2006)
21. Trivedi, K.S., Ibe, O.C.: Stochastic Petri net analysis of finite-population vacation queueing systems. Queueing Systems 8, 111–128 (1991)
22. Tian, N., Xu, X.: M/M/c queue with synchronous multiple vacation of partial servers. Oper. Resear. Trans. 5, 85–94 (2001)
23. Tian, N., Zhang, Z.G.: Vacation Queueing Models: Theory and Applications. International Series in Operations Research & Management Science 93 (2006)
24. Wenhui, Z.: Analysis of a single-server retrial queue with FCFS orbit and Bernoulli vacation. Applied Mathematics and Computation 161, 353–364 (2005)
25. Xu, X., Zhang, Z.G.: Analysis of multi-server queue with a single vacation (e,d)-policy. Performance Evaluation 63, 825–838 (2006)
26. Yang, T., Templeton, J.G.C.: A survey on retrial queues. Queueing Systems 2, 201–233 (1987)
27. Zhang, Z.G., Tian, N.: Analysis of queueing systems with synchronous single vacation for some servers. Queueing Systems: Theory and Applications 45, 161–175 (2003)
28. Zhang, Z.G., Tian, N.: Analysis of queueing systems with synchronous vacations of partial servers. Performance Evaluation 52, 269–282 (2003)

Model Based Importance Analysis
for Minimal Cut Sets*

Eckard Böde[1], Thomas Peikenkamp[1], Jan Rakow[2],
and Samuel Wischmeyer[2]

[1] OFFIS e.V., Oldenburg, Germany
[2] Carl von Ossietzky University, Oldenburg, Germany

Abstract. We show how fault injection together with recent advances
in stochastic model checking can be combined to form a crucial ingredi-
ent for improving quantitative safety analysis. Based on standard design
notations (Statecharts) annotated with fault occurrence distributions we
compute to what extent certain fault configurations contribute to the
probability of reaching a safety-critical state.

1 Introduction

Today's transportation systems become ever more complex and rely to a large
extent on embedded systems. Typically such systems come equipped with sophisticated redundancy and monitoring concepts to achieve a high degree of
fault-tolerance. Fault injection, that is the injection of particular failure behaviour into the nominal behaviour of a formal system model, has been proven to be
a suitable method to investigate the effectiveness of these fault-tolerance recipes.
Based on such an extended system model the ISAAC project [1] developed methods and tools to automatically compute fault trees [2] and extract *Minimal Cut
Sets (MCSs)*. Intuitively, a MCS describes a minimal combination (i. e. no sub
set of an MCS is still an MCS) of faults that can cause a safety critical situation to occur. In [3] the application of these tools to an actual system from
the avionics domain and their integration into the established safety process are
presented.

However, in practice such *qualitative* analyses are not sufficient and *quantitative* safety assessment, taking concrete fault occurrence rates (e. g. taken from
technical specification) into account, becomes imperative. The key problem for
assessing the quantitative impact of safety-critical fault configurations is to factor in the actually possible fault ordering as well as the transient nature of faults
that are both deeply integrated in the system and far from being evident. Expensive manual analyses of the concrete system dynamics and fault interplay
have to be performed in order to set up accurate stochastic models. But, since

---

* This work is supported by the German Research Council (DFG) as part of the
Transregional Collaborative Research Center "Automatic Verification and Analysis
of Complex Systems" (SFB/TR 14 AVACS). See `www.avacs.org` for more information.

Cha et al. (Eds.): ATVA 2008, LNCS 5311, pp. 303–317, 2008.

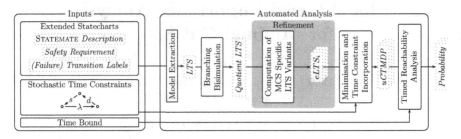

Fig. 1. Timed reachability analysis for STATEMATE - extended tool chain

those analyses are quite time consuming and can usually only be performed by experts, simplified, naive methods are often employed to approximate results. Making use of recent advances in stochastic model checking, in [4,5] a (plug-in) extension of the industrial design tool STATEMATE [6] is presented enabling the automated evaluation of timed reachability properties of the form:

"The probability to enter a safety critical system state within a mission time of 100 hours is at most 10^{-6}."

This paper presents a valuable extension of the work presented in [4,5]. Based on a STATEMATE model extended by fault injection and annotated with fault occurrence distributions the probability of reaching a safety critical state is analysed, taking into account *all* faults. Our extension makes it possible to determine the contribution of particular MCSs to the over-all probability and thus to identify those components, whose failing contributes most to reach a safety critical system state. These components should be replaced or improved first in order to improve the over-all system safety, for example if the requirements for certification cannot be met. The benefits of our model-based approach are as follows: The quantitative analysis is automated and can be performed directly on the formal system model. Thus, no extra efforts are required and, as only the actually possible failure sequences are taken into account, more accurate probability measures are derived compared to naive approaches.

We achieve this by encoding path information into the state space of a labelled transition system (LTS). The principal set-up of the tool chain presented in [4,5] and extended by this processing step is depicted in Fig. 1. We will refer to this figure later. A brief overview of the tool chain is given in the next paragraph.

Tool Chain Overview. The over-all approach presented in [4,5] is compositional: *Stochastic Time Constraints*, used to delay firing of particular (failure) transitions, are introduced to the non-stochastic system model in a *Minimisation and Time Constraint Incorporation* step, after the model has been minimised drastically by building the *Branching Bisimulation* quotient. In particular, unique *(Failure) Transition Labels* are used in the *Extended Statechart* formalism to expose relevant transitions by labels in a corresponding LTS. The same labels are used to enrich absorbing continuous Markov chains (CTMCs) with "synchronisation potential" yielding a *Stochastic Time Constraint* [7]. This way, for example, time to failure distributions can be integrated into the system model LTS. Using phase-type approximation [8] the incorporation of arbitrary stochastic delay distributions is possible [4,5]. The stochastic process algebra of Interactive Markov Chains (IMCs) [9] is the key enabler that makes it possible to handle the orthogonal combination of LTSs and CTMCs. The path encoding, we present in this paper, allows for the *Computation of MCS Specific LTS Variants*, retaining the contribution of the faults in a particular minimal cut set, while disregarding contributions of other faults. Note that the time constraint CTMCs are made uniform. This uniformity is preserved during the different processing steps finally yielding a uniform continuous time Markov decision process (CTMDP) [10]. Further note that the *Timed Reachability Analysis* copes with model inherent non-determinism (often used to represent under-specification or to specify an unpredictable environment) by computing the *worst-case probability* to reach a safety critical state within a given *Time Bound* among the existing choices.

Structure. In Sect. 2 we describe the modelling approach, how faults are specified and furthermore introduce an example model that we will extend in Sect. 4 to highlight benefits of our approach. Section 3 shows the construction of cut set specific LTS variants. Concluding remarks are given in Sect. 5.

Related Work. Fault trees (FTs) are used to represent the dependencies of failures and other system events. Based on a FT stochastic models can be developed to establish a quantitative analysis. Dynamic fault-trees (DFT), described in the latest revision of the Fault Tree Handbook [2], are an extension of traditional fault-trees and can be used to describe fault-tolerant systems and also relate the FT to Markov models. The main differences to conventional FTs are the introduction of the new, dynamic gate types *Priority-And (PAND)*, Functional Dependency (FDEP) and *Spare*. With these new gates it becomes possible to express also *sequences of events*. For example only if all sub-events to a *PAND* gate occur in the same order in which they are connected will the gate be activated. The *Spare* gate enables describing several standby configurations where in the case of a fault in one basic component the function will be taken over by another spare component. A spare gate allows sharing of these replacement components between the different branches of the FT and will only propagate the fault if no more spares are available that means all inputs to the spare gate have failed. With these additional gates fault-trees become more expressive and can be used to model systems that could previously not be described adequately. However there are also drawbacks most notably the increased complexity of the formalism for analysis as well as for the construction of the fault-tree although there are some approaches (cf. [11]) that strive to overcome this issue. But another problem of classical fault-tree analysis is still present with this extended approach. Generating a DFT is usually a non-automated approach that requires lots of manual steps and expert knowledge. This is an expensive step in terms of money as well as in terms of time required to build the fault-tree. Keeping the fault-tree in sync with an evolving system design requires even more effort.

2   Extended Statecharts

In this section, following the lines of [5], we introduce *extended Statecharts* as the user-visible formalism to specify behavioural models. We show how an extended Statechart is translated into an LTS and thereby present a concise definition of the formalism. The focus is set on the relevant core needed to clearly expose the syntactical and semantic extensions to the conventional STATEMATE formalism. We present a simple example to illustrate the translation and furthermore the tool chain's principles.

As indicated in Fig. 1, extended Statecharts rest upon two constituents, namely (i) a STATEMATE description of the system under study and (ii) a set of (failure) transition labels. These ingredients determine the semantics of extended Statecharts. Additionally (iii) a safety requirement is used to characterise a subset of system states to be safety critical. For example we identify all the states where *"sensor has failed without being detected"* holds as safety critical. These are the states we are interested in the timed reachability analysis, reaching one of them is also considered as top level event (TLE).

While conventional Statecharts [12] support non-determinism, but no stochastic time aspects, extended Statecharts allow one to refer to particular Statechart transitions by a distinguished set of labels A that are later used as reference anchors to synchronise with appropriately labelled stochastic time constraints. This enables the modelling of stochastic, non-deterministic systems.

Example 1. The extended Statechart of Fig. 2 describes a simple train odometer controller component. It comprises three orthogonal components. The *Monitor* component detects faults in the *Wheelsensor* component, so that, in case of a sensor fault, a brake manoeuvre can be initiated. A third component *Observer* is not part of the system but a means to identify safety critical states.

Depending on the value of a non-deterministic input variable SPEED_FAST, the *Wheelsensor* can reach the node WF representing "sensor failed". As soon as the state WF is entered, the *Monitor* component will detect this and fire the (thin) edge pointing to node BRAKE. Note that initiating this "emergency brake" is only

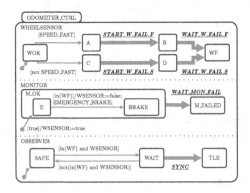

Fig. 2. An extended Statechart: a simple train odometer controller

possible, if the *Monitor* is still working (i. e. in node E). In particular after firing the (bold) edge pointing to node M_FAILED node E will be left and the *Monitor* is no longer sensitive to the guard in(WF) and thus can neither signal the *Wheelsensor* status to other train components (WSENSOR:=false) nor initiate a break manoeuvre (EMERGENCY_BRAKE). The over-all compositional modelling approach allows us to delay the occurrence of the WAIT_MON_FAIL edge using for instance a simple exponential distribution determined by a rate λ. Likewise, the firing of edge WAIT_W_FAIL_F can be delayed w. r. t. START_W_FAIL_F by rate μ. Thus, we can describe arbitrary failure behaviour of a component as part of the Statechart model and control the occurrence of the injected failure behaviour by means of stochastic delays. In addition, it is possible to incorporate delays to describe aspects of the nominal (i. e. non failure related) behaviour.

Statecharts have an intuitive graphical syntax. We vary the corresponding textual syntax as follows.

Definition 1 (Extended Statecharts). *An* extended Statechart *$SC = (N, A, V, G, S, E, m, r, d, c)$ is a 10-tuple, with*

- N *is a finite set of nodes,*
- A *a finite set of action labels,*
- V *a finite set of variables with a (possibly empty) subset I of input variables,*
- G *a finite set of boolean expressions on V,*
- S *a finite set of variable assignment statements,*
- $E \subset N \times A \cup \{\tau\} \times G \times 2^S \times N$ *is a finite set of edges,*
- $m : N \rightarrow \{Basic, Or, And\}$ *is a type function, identifying nodes as Basic nodes, Or nodes, or And nodes.*
- $r \in N$, $m(r) = Or$ *is the root node of SC,*
- $d : \{n : n \in N \wedge m(n) = Or\} \longrightarrow N$ *assigns a default node to each node of type Or,*
- $c : N \rightarrow 2^N$ *a child relation introducing hierarchy on N.*

Example 2. The nodes WAIT and WHEELSENSOR are of type *Basic* and *Or*, respectively. *And* node ODOMETER_CTRL is the only child of the root node r. The hierarchy determined by c is shown by nesting of states. Here $d(\text{Monitor}) = E$. The underlined identifiers in the Statechart define the set A (e. g. {SYNC, WAIT_MON_FAIL} $\subset A$). Edge $e_{01} = (\text{E}, \tau, \text{in(WF)}, \{\text{WSENSOR:=false; EMERGENCY\_BRAKE;}\}, \text{BRAKE})$ is a τ-labelled Statechart edge which we draw as a thin line by convention, while edges $e_{02} = (\text{M\_OK, WAIT\_MON\_FAIL, true}, \{\}, \text{M\_FAILED})$ and $e_{03} = (\text{WAIT, SYNC, true}, \{\}, \text{TLE})$ are labelled by elements of A and hence drawn bold. We implicitly define the guard g of such bold edges to be always true.

For the sake of brevity, the above definition omits some well-formedness conditions (cf. [12]) that are unchanged with respect to STATEMATE Statecharts. The substantial extension to conventional Statecharts is the labelling of edges by elements of $A \cup \{\tau\}$. We use the label τ for system internal behaviour, that is for ordinary Statechart edges. Labels in A will be used for synchronisation with "start" and "delay-expired" events of stochastic time-constraints. We emphasise that the behaviour of an extended Statechart is essentially in line with that of conventional STATEMATE Statecharts, except that extended Statecharts allow for a more refined control over which edges are allowed to be fired in orthogonal components within one step. We introduce the following usual notions to determine this semantics. The *scope* $sc(e)$ of an edge $e \in E$ is the most nested *Or* state that contains the edges nodes. We use $de(n)$ to denote the depth of node $n \in N$ in the node hierarchy c and define $de(SC) = max(\{de(n) : n \in N\})$. The *priority* of an edge e is given by its scope distance from the root r. We define the priority relation $e \leq_p e'$, s.t. $e \leq_p e'$ iff $de(SC) - de(sc(e)) \leq de(SC) - de(sc(e'))$. Two edges $e, e' \in E$ are orthogonal, denoted $e \bot e'$, iff either $e = e'$ or their scopes are different children of some *And* node or their descendants. In the example Statechart, it holds $e_{01} \bot e_{03}$ and $e_{01} \not\bot e_{02}$, for example.

Definition 2 (Configurations). *Let $\mathcal{D}$ be the data domain of the variables V. A configuration of an extended Statechart SC is a pair $\mathfrak{c} = (M, \sigma) \in \mathfrak{C} \subset 2^N \times \Sigma$, where Σ is the set of all variable valuations $\sigma : V \backslash I \to \mathcal{D}$ and M is a set satisfying*
1. $r \in M$
2. $n \in M$, $m(n) = Or$ implies $\exists! n' \in c(n) : n' \in M$
3. $n \in M$, $m(n) = And$ implies $\forall n' \in c(n) : n' \in M$

Such a node set M is called a valid node configuration. *We denote $\mathfrak{c}_0$ for the unique initial configuration of Statechart SC, given by an initial valuation of the variables σ_0 and the node configuration determined by d. The set of all configurations of SC is denoted by $\mathfrak{C}$.*

With $dc(M \subset N)$ we refer to the *default completion*, as the smallest superset of node set M, so that $dc(M)$ is a valid node configuration. In particular $dc(M)$ comprises the default node $d(n)$, for all those *Or* nodes $n \in dc(M)$, that are not already represented by a child node in M. The scope completion $scc(e)$ of edge e is the maximal set of child nodes derived by recursive application of c to the edges scope node $sc(e)$.

Intuitively, configurations comprise all current *Basic* nodes and their parent nodes (given by inverse of c) and a valuation of the variables V. The state space of the system LTS is defined over such configurations. We will now define the transition relation between configurations and thus define how labels in A affect the semantics of the edges they label. An extended Statechart can be considered as a labelled transition system using the following transition relation.

Definition 3 (Transition Relation). *For extended Statechart SC the transition relation $\longrightarrow \subseteq \mathfrak{C} \times A \stackrel{.}{\cup} \tau \times \mathfrak{C}$ is composed of two types of transitions:*
Internal Step. $\mathfrak{c} = (M, \sigma) \stackrel{\tau}{\longrightarrow} \mathfrak{c}' = (M', \sigma')$, *iff there exists a maximal set of edges $\mathcal{E} = \{e_i : e_{1 \leq i \leq k} = (n_i, a_i, g_i, s_i, n_i') \in E\}$ so that*

1. $\mathcal{E} \subseteq \mathcal{E}_{en} = \{e = (n, a, g, s, n') \in E : n \in M \text{ and } g \text{ evaluates to true in } \sigma\}$.
2. $\forall e_i \in \mathcal{E} : a_i = \tau$ and $\forall e_i, e_j \in \mathcal{E} : e_i \bot e_j$.
3. $\forall e \in \mathcal{E}_{en} \setminus \mathcal{E} \, \exists e' \in \mathcal{E}$, s.t. $e \not\bot e'$ and $e \leq_p e'$.

and σ' is obtained from σ by applying the statement sets $s_{1 \leq i \leq k}$ in some permutation on σ and $M' = dc((M \setminus \bigcup_{i=1}^{k} scc(e_i)) \cup \{n_i'\}_{1 \leq i \leq k})$.
External Step. $\mathfrak{c} = (M, \sigma) \stackrel{a}{\longrightarrow} \mathfrak{c}' = (M', \sigma')$, *iff*

1. $\nexists e = (n, \tau, g, s, n') \in E : n \in M$ and g evaluates to true in σ.
2. $\exists e = (n, a, g, s, n') \in E : a \in A$ and $n \in M$

and σ' is obtained from σ by applying the statement set s on σ and $M' = dc((M \setminus scc(e)) \cup \{n'_i\}_{1 \leq i \leq n})$.

In a nutshell, the *Internal Step* rule defines conventional Statechart configuration transitions that comprise firing of a maximal set of τ-labelled (thin) edges in orthogonal components and thus implements truly concurrent executions. Instead the *External Step* rule restricts the (bold) labelled edges to be fired in mutual isolation and only if no τ-labelled edge can be taken. Since bold edges relate to time-relevant events, this mutual isolation allows us to recover particular configuration transitions, relative to other transitions. The semantics also gives (non time consuming) internal steps precedence over external steps. This idea of timeless computation is typical for the super-step semantics of STATE-MATE Statecharts [12]. We allow hiding of action labels (i. e. replace particular labels in A by τ). This allows us to maintain the effect of external steps without keeping their labels. For example we can hide the label sync in the example Statechart. However, within this paper, we will keep the sync label for simplicity. Given an extended Statechart and a set N_{cr} of safety-critical nodes (as specified by a *Safety Requirement*, cf. Fig. 1) we derive an LTS as follows.

Definition 4 (LTS Extraction). *Given a set of safety critical nodes $N_{cr} \subset N$ of extended Statechart $SC = (N, A, V, G, S, E, m, r, d, c)$, with initial configuration c_0, SC can be considered as an LTS $M = (S^M, Act^M, C^M, T^M, s_0^M)$ by setting*

- $S^M = \mathfrak{C} \mathbin{\dot{\cup}} \{c_{init}\}$, *the set of all valid configurations in SC plus a unique pre-initial state c_{init}.*
- $Act^M = A \mathbin{\dot{\cup}} \{\tau\} \mathbin{\dot{\cup}} \{INIT\}$, *the set of labels occurring in the Statechart steps plus a unique label INIT.*
- $C^M = \{c = (M_c, \sigma_c) \in S^M : M_c \cap N_{cr} \neq \emptyset\}$, *the set of safety critical states.*
- $T^M = \{(c_{init}, INIT, c_0)\} \cup \{(c, a, c') : c \xrightarrow{a} c'\} \subseteq S^M \times Act^M \times S^M$, *the set of transitions possible between the Statechart configurations plus an additional transition $c_{init} \xrightarrow{INIT} c_0$, introduced to represent the system start.*
- $s_0^M = c_{init}$, *a pre-initial configuration of Statechart SC.*

Note that here we use nodes, such as the node TLE in the example, to identify safety critical states of SC and thus also the set C^M of critical LTS states. Instead of this explicit automata based encoding other specification mechanisms such as temporal logic expressions could also be used.

Example 3. The left part of Fig. 3 shows the LTS that has been constructed from the extended Statechart in Fig. 2 with $N_{cr} = \{TLE\}$ (defining the top-level event to be an undetected sensor fault). The dashed boxes indicate which states are considered equivalent under branching bisimulation yielding the depicted quotient LTS. We use shortcuts to refer to the labelling in the extended Statechart (e. g. SF stands for START_W_FAIL_F). In Fig. 3 the state c_{01} is the only safety critical state. If the Wheelsensor fails (leaving state c_{02} by edge WS or state c_{03} by edge WF)

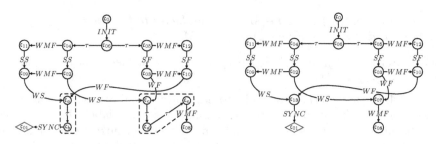

Fig. 3. LTS and quotient LTS for the odometer Statechart

the system goes to a configuration where no safety-critical states can be reached anymore (the Monitor detected the sensor fault). If the monitor fault occurs before the Wheelsensor fails (e. g. leaving state c_{04} or state c_{03} by edge WMF), then the system will finally enter state c_{01}. There are two pairs of (failure) sequences that lead to the safety critical state: (i) INIT,τ,WMF,SS,WS,SYNC;INIT,τ,SS,WMF,WS,SYNC and (ii) INIT,τ,WMF,SF,WF,SYNC; INIT,τ,SF,WMF,WF,SYNC. In each of this sequences WMF precedes the label WS or WF, respectively. The pairs result from the different failure scenarios in the *Wheelsensor* component.

Thus, to actually assess the *quantitative* impact of the faults on the top-level event, we have to distinguish the *paths* where these faults occur. Section 3 shows how we can incorporate the necessary path information into the state space of the investigated system. We complete the specification of the example by providing the time constraints for the extended Statechart of Fig. 2. We furthermore provide the uCTMDP derived for this model.

Example 4. The left part of Fig. 4 shows the time constraint IMCs (cf. Fig. 1) that are incorporated into the LTS of Fig. 3. Each of the three time constraints is derived by a simple absorbing CTMC (drawn grey). These CTMCs are then equipped with a new initial state and labelled edges for synchronisation with the system model LTS. Note that the derived IMCs are made uniform. This uniformity is preserved all along the tool chain. Given these time constraint IMCs and the LTS of Fig. 3 the tool chain presented in [5] computes the uCTMDP depicted in the right part of Fig. 4. Here state s_5 is the critical state as indicated by the self-loop labelled *tle*. State s_3 is a sink state that results from those paths in the LTS that do not finally yield a safety critical system state. In our example, the Monitor introduces such a sink by a *safe* shutdown. Non-determinism is present

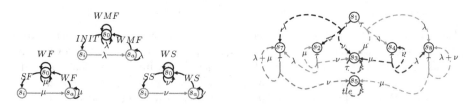

Fig. 4. Time constraints and uCTMDP for the odometer

in the states where more than one τ labelled edge emanates. The forking (dashed drawn) edges represent *races*. For the sake of brevity, we introduce rate $\kappa = \lambda + \nu + \mu$.

3   LTS Transformation

In this section, we show how we encode the context of faults into the state space of an LTS. The basic idea of our approach to establish model based importance analysis for minimal cut sets is as follows. First, given an LTS $M = (S^M, Act^M, T^M, C^M, s_0^M)$, we compute an *enhanced* variant $L = (S^L, Act^M, T^L, C^L, s_0^L)$, by coding label sets describing the path history (starting in the initial state of M) to each particular state in M into the state space of L. Note, that for optimisation purposes we follow [4,5] and use the equivalent quotient LTS, derived by symbolic branching bisimulation minimisation to compute the enhanced variant LTS.

A path $s_0 \xrightarrow{b} s_1 \xrightarrow{\tau} s_2 \xrightarrow{a} s_3 \xrightarrow{\tau} s_4 \xrightarrow{a} s_5$ in M, for example, would yield a new state, described by the pair $(s_5, \{a, b\})$ representing the fact that state s_5 is reachable in M by a path that comprises at least single occurrences of the labels b and a. That is, we do neither code the concrete number of labels nor occurrences of τ transitions into the state space of L, keeping the overall number of states, $O(|S^M| \cdot 2^{|Act^M|})$ in the worst case, in L manageable in size. We formalise this notion of *path history* in the following definition.

Definition 5 (Path History). *Let $M = (S^M, Act^M, T^M, C^M, s_0^M)$ be an LTS. Path. A possibly infinite sequence of transitions*

$$\pi = \left(\pi_i = (s_i, a_i, s_i')\right)_{i \in \mathbb{N}} = \pi_0, \pi_1, ... \in (S^M \times Act^M \times S^M)^* \cup (S^M \times Act^M \times S^M)^\omega$$

is called a path *in M, iff $\forall(s_i, a_i, s_i')\forall(s_j, a_j, s_j')$*

$$\left((s_i, a_i, s_i') \in T^M \wedge (s_j, a_j, s_j') \in T^M \wedge j = i + 1 \rightarrow s_j = s_i'\right).$$

We denote π_0 to refer to the first transition in π and π_i for the i-th transition. $src(\pi)$ denotes the source state of π_0, $last(\pi)$ the target state of the last transition in a finite path π.

Path History. *For a given label set $D \subseteq Act^M$ and state $s_0 \in S^M$, we define $\Pi_M^D(s_0) = \{\pi : src(\pi) = s_0 \wedge (\forall a \in D \; \exists s_i, s_i' \in S^M : \pi_i = (s_i, a, s_i')) \wedge \pi \text{ is a path in } M \}$ as the set of D-history paths in M.*

The set $\Pi_M^D(s_0)$ of *D-history* paths, describes all paths in M, starting in s_0, that comprise at least one occurrence of the labels in D. Given an LTS $M = (S^M, Act^M, T^M, C^M, s_0^M)$, we compute the *enhanced* variant LTS $L = (S^L, Act^M, T^L, C^L, s_0^L)$ as follows.

Definition 6 (eLTS). *Let $M = (S^M, Act^M, T^M, C^M, s_0^M)$ be an LTS. We call the LTS $L = (S^L \subseteq S^M \times 2^{Act^M}, Act^M, T^L, C^L, (s_0^M, \{\}))$ enhanced M, iff*

1. $((s, D), a, (s', D \cup \{a\})) \in T^L \Leftrightarrow a \neq \tau \wedge (s, a, s') \in T^M \wedge \left(\exists \pi \in \Pi_M^D(s_0) : last(\pi) = s \vee s = s_0 \wedge D = \{\}\right) \wedge s \notin C^M$

2. $((s, D), a, (s', D)) \in T^L \Leftrightarrow a = \tau$ and $(s, a, s') \in T^M \wedge \left(\exists \pi \in \Pi^D_M(s_0) : last(\pi) = s \vee s = s_0 \wedge D = \{\}\right) \wedge s \notin C^M$

3. $C^L = \left\{(s, D) : s \in C^M \wedge \exists \pi \in \Pi^D_M(s_0) : last(\pi) = s\right\}$

While computing L, we preserve the semantics of M w. r. t. the timed reachability analysis, that is, we neither remove nor add paths starting in the initial state of M to the first occurrence of its critical states. In particular, the LTS M and its enhanced variant are obviously strong (and thus also branching) bisimilar [13,14] by construction. The equivalence classes on L are induced by the state-pairs state component, yielding the coarsest branching bisimulation equivalent M (that we originally computed using the symbolic branching bisimulation [15] as described in [4,5][1]). The property of the enhanced LTS to be in a strong bisimilarity relation to the original LTS is sufficient to justify their substitutability for the subsequent analysis (cf. [9], p.73, theorem 4.3.1 and [17]).

Example 5. For our running example, we derive the enhanced LTS of Fig. 5 from the LTS depicted in Fig. 3. This representation comprises the same sequences as the original LTS but allows for a more detailed analysis: The two critical states $(c_{01}, \cdot)$ correspond to the different failure scenarios described in example 3. Thus, now these states may be distinguished by the failure sequences that caused them.

In a second step, we establish differentiated timed reachability analysis for L. We only have to shrink the set of critical states C^L to particular subsets dependent on a given minimal cut set $mcs_i \in MCS$, where $MCS = \{mcs_1, \ldots, mcs_n\} \subseteq 2^{Act^M}$ denotes the set of all MCSs. In the enhanced variant LTS L for each state $s_{cr} = (s^{cr}, D^{cr}) \in C^L$ label set D^{cr} encodes the concrete failure (label) set that caused the particular safety critical state s_{cr}. As we are interested in the contribution of all failure scenarios (i. e. paths) that require at least the occurrence of the faults in the minimal cut set mcs_i, we analyse cut set specific LTS variants. For an enhanced LTS L we analyse the LTS $L_{mcs_i} = \left(S^L, Act^M, T^L, C_{mcs_i}, (s_0, \{\})\right)$, where $C_{mcs_i} = \{(s, D) : (s, D) \in C^L \wedge mcs_i \subseteq D\}$. Note that our prototypical implementation of the described LTS transformation is able to extract the set of minimal cut sets MCS by analysing all label sets D^{cr}. Fig. 6 summarises the intuition of the transformation step. Given an LTS (a), the enhanced variant (b) is computed by unfolding the paths in (a). This LTS encodes the paths of the original LTS in a differentiated manner. Here, each of the critical states is related to one particular minimal cut set. The analysis of the two cut set specific variants (c) and (d) using the tool chain back-end (cf. Fig. 1) entails the disregard of minimal cut set $\{a, c\}$ for (c) and $\{a, b\}$ for (d), respectively. One benefit of our model based approach is that only those failure sequences that indeed cause a safety critical state are considered. For example the multiple occurrence of fault c. In contrast the *naive* approach, frequently used in practice, to determine the cut set specific measures would be to multiply the single failure probabilities. For cut set $\{a, c\}$, given

---

[1] As detailed in [4,5] we consider safety-critical states and non safety-critical states non-bisimilar *by definition*. A more detailed discussion of the related issue of state vs. transition labelling in IMCs can be found in [16].

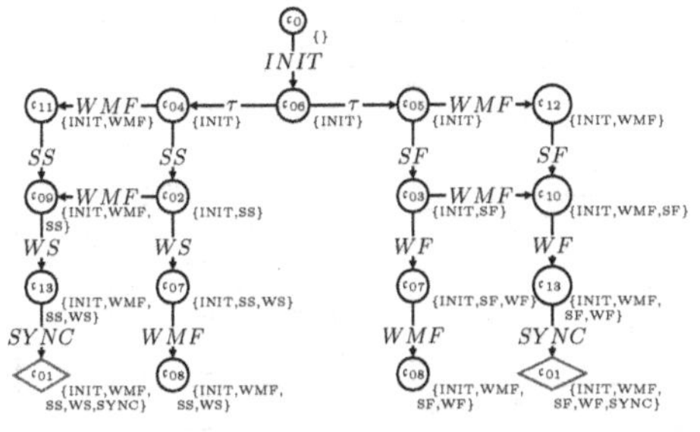

Fig. 5. Unfold LTS for the odometer

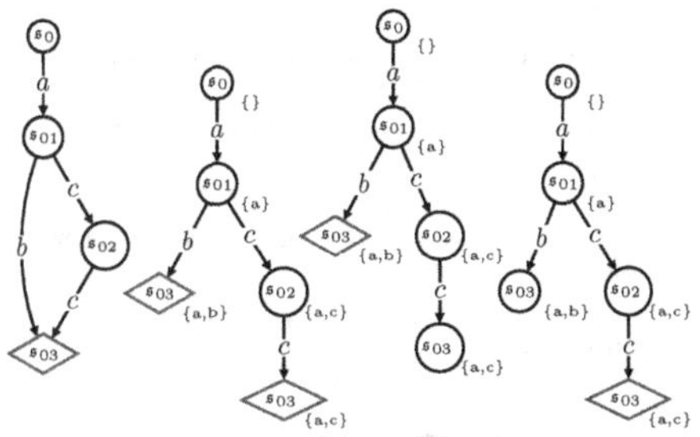

Fig. 6. Overview: (a) LTS (b) eLTS (c) $LTS_{mcs\{a,b\}}$ (d) $LTS_{mcs\{a,c\}}$

the constant failure rates λ_a, λ_c this approach yields a less accurate probability measure: $Q(t)_{\{a,c\}} = (1 - e^{-\lambda_a t}) \cdot (1 - e^{-\lambda_c t})$. We consider all faults (stochastic) independent and assume that *common mode analysis* has been carried out in order to validate this assumption.

4   Case Study

In this section, we enrich the train odometer example of Sect. 2 and furthermore present numbers for a more complex model, to show the general feasibility and scalability of our approach[2].

4.1   A Train Odometer Controller

The odometer system under study consists of two independent sensors used to measure speed and position of a train. A *Wheelsensor* is mounted to an unpowered wheel of the train to count the number of revolutions. A *Radarsensor* determines the current speed by evaluating the Doppler shift of the reflected radar signal. We consider transient faults for both sensors. For example water on or beside the track could interfere with the detection of the reflected signal and thus cause a transient fault in the measurement of the *Radarsensor*. Similarly, skidding of the wheel affects the *Wheelsensor*. Due to the sensor redundancy the system is robust against faults of a single sensor. However it has to be detectable to other components in the train, when one of the sensors provides invalid data. For this purpose a *Monitor* continuously checks the status of both sensors. We will focus on this monitoring aspect of the system. Figure 7 shows the corresponding Statechart model. The *Radarsensor* starts in the initial state ROK and, when a fault occurs, enters state RF. The transient nature of the fault is implemented by the transition back to the state ROK. The *Wheelsensor* behaves like the *Radarsensor* with the exception that the rate for the fault depends on the current, non-deterministically selected, speed of the train. Whenever either

---

[2] The experiments were carried out on a PC with P4 3GHz processor and 1GB RAM.

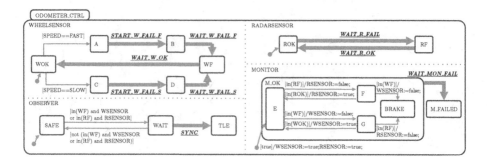

Fig. 7. A train odometer controller

the *Wheelsensor* or the *Radarsensor* fail and enter the wf or rf state respectively this is detected by the *Monitor* and the corresponding status variable (wsensor or rsensor) is set to *false*. This information can be used by other train components that have to disregard temporary erroneous sensor data. Due to the robustness against single faults and since both sensor faults are transient the system even can recover completely from such a situation. If both sensors fail the system is shut down by the *Monitor* (i. e. a brake manoeuvre is initiated), but also in this case the system is safe. Only if the *Monitor* fails first, any subsequent faults in the sensors will no longer be detected. Since now the train may be guided by invalid speed and position information such situations are safety critical. We therefore define the entering of node tle of the *Observer* component as the safety critical state. Consequently, three minimal cut sets (mcs_a, mcs_b, mcs_c) exist in this model. Table 1 shows all labelled transitions and their mapping to the particular cut sets. Note, that we do not list implicit labels, such as the system-start transition (init) used for instance to delay the *Monitor* fault. Based on the listed rates, the lower part of the tables compare the concrete probabilities, we computed for the model using the stochastic model checker MRMC[3] [18],

Table 1. Rates and minimal cut set probabilities

Label	mcs_a	mcs_b	mcs_c	rate	mcs_a	mcs_b	mcs_c	rate
WAIT_MON_FAIL	yes	yes	yes	0.001	yes	yes	yes	0.01
WAIT_R_FAIL	yes	no	no	0.015	yes	no	no	0.04
START_W_FAIL_F	no	yes	no	-	no	yes	no	-
WAIT_W_FAIL_F	no	yes	no	0.025	no	yes	no	0.003
START_W_FAIL_S	no	no	yes	-	no	no	yes	-
WAIT_W_FAIL_S	no	no	yes	0.01	no	no	yes	0.3
WAIT_W_OK	no	no	no	240	no	no	no	0.001
WAIT_R_OK	no	no	no	360	no	no	no	0.002
time bound (h)	method	$P(t)$	$P(t)$	$P(t)$	-	$P(t)$	$P(t)$	$P(t)$	-
10	mrmc	0.0007122	0.0011479	0.0005027	-	0.0149402	0.0014070	0.0318196	-
	naive	0.0013860	0.0022010	0.0009469	-	0.0313732	0.0028125	0.0904247	-
100	mrmc	0.0479257	0.0605680	0.0397182	-	0.2343468	0.0724729	0.1887776	-
	naive	0.0739289	0.0873512	0.0601542	-	0.6205429	0.1638341	0.6321206	-
1000	mrmc	0.5973047	0.6078448	0.5677622	-	0.7310061	0.5490308	0.2095549	-
	naive	0.6321204	0.6321206	0.6320919	-	0.9999546	0.9501698	0.9999546	-

---

[3] That in particular supports uCTMDP analysis [17].

with those derived following the naive approach (cf. Sect. 3). It can be observed that our model based approach yields probabilities well below those of the naive approach. Moreover the numbers of the right table show that even the *ranking* of the MCSs induced by the probabilities can *diverge*. While the naive approach indicates 1. mcs_c, 2. mcs_a, 3. mcs_b, the model based approach yields 1. mcs_a, 2. mcs_b, 3. mcs_c for sufficiently large time bounds. Intuitively, in this example, the high failure rates make it probable that the monitor signals the sensor to be inoperable before failing itself and thus prevents a safety critical situation. Thus, here, the naive approach that does not take the concrete system dynamics into account, even yields a misleading importance measure.

4.2   Performance Remarks

The upcoming *European Train Control System (ETCS)*, is designed to replace the multitude of incompatible safety systems used by European Railways and enable safe fast transnational railway service. Based on a fault tree description taken from the ETCS specification [19], we developed an ETCS Level 2 train model that we use to show the inherent worst case complexity of the path encoding to be negligible in practice. Table 2 depicts the numbers of the intermediate models (cf. Fig. 1). Note that the LTS extraction and the branching bisimulation are implemented using efficient representations of the state space using binary decision diagrams. The remaining steps rely on explicit representations of the state space and make use of the CADP [20] tool box. We found that (i) the efficient symbolic branching bisimulation on the *LTS* yields enormous reductions of the state space in the *quotient LTS* and thus is a crucial preprocessing step to our unfolding step. Moreover (ii) the *stochastic* branching bisimulation [21,17] that interleaves the (one-by-one) incorporation steps of the stochastic time constraints balances the introduced complexity (cf. column *eLTS*) of the unwinding: the finally computed stochastic models are of similar size to the model generated for the original LTS (cf. uCTMDP-LTS and uCTMDP-$eLTS_{mcs_{1-4}}$).

Table 2. ETCS Level 2 Train Model - comparison of LTSs and uCTMDP state spaces

	LTS	quotient LTS	uCTMDP-LTS	eLTS	uCTMDP-$eLTS_{mcs_1}$	uCTMDP-$eLTS_{mcs_2}$	uCTMDP-$eLTS_{mcs_3}$	uCTMDP-$eLTS_{mcs_4}$
states	8266964	142789	3230	1071250	10023	3911	3919	1654
transitions	18313109	727609	15680	5538073	48066	22347	19137	8348
time (sec.)	12222.1	4714.24	173.15	5617.79	1013.48	674.42	635.77	628.52

5   Conclusion

In this paper we presented an automated model-based approach to determine the quantitative contribution of safety critical fault configurations (MCSs) to the over-all probability of reaching a safety critical state.

Therefore we extended the tool chain presented in [4,5] by an encoding of path information into the state space of an LTS that enables to distinguish (and relate) all relevant paths leading to a safety critical state to a MCS. This also allows for the extraction of the MCSs itself, but this is secondary. We gave a detailed explanation of the LTS encoding as well as of how the LTS is derived from an extended Statechart [5]. The over-all approach was successfully applied to a case-study taken from the train-control domain. In particular, we observed that the sophisticated combination of the symbolic branching and stochastic branching minimisation steps balances the encodings inherent complexity.

On the application side the benefits are obvious. The derived MCS importance measures enable the system developer to direct their work on those parts of the systems where improvements will yield most impact. Due to the preservation of the actual sequences of faults, the derived measures are more accurate than conventional naive or manual safety assessment techniques that may even yield misleading results. And – thanks to the automation – they can be derived without any extra effort directly from the design model. Furthermore, by incorporating stochastic non failure behaviour (e. g. repair rates of transient faults) into the modelling and cut set analyses, again the accuracy can be improved, that is, a less pessimistic assessment is derived.

All in all the (extended) tool chain seems to be a crucial step towards a better integration of system development and quantitative safety analysis. Future work will therefore strive for further integration of conventional safety assessment tasks and refinements such as the inclusion of common mode failures.

Acknowledgements. We would like to thank our co-authors of [4,5] for the tight cooperation resulting in those works making this work possible at all.

References

1. Åkerlund, O., et al.: ISAAC, a framework for integrated safety analyses of functional, geometrical and human aspects. ERTS (2006)
2. Vesely, W.E., Dugan, J., Fragola, J., Minarick III, J., Railsback, J.: Fault Tree Handbook with Aerospace Applications. National Aeronatics and Space Administration (August 2002)
3. Peikenkamp, T., Cavallo, A., Valacca, L., Böde, E., Pretzer, M., Hahn, E.M.: Towards a unified model-based safety assessment. In: Górski, J. (ed.) SAFECOMP 2006. LNCS, vol. 4166, pp. 275–288. Springer, Heidelberg (2006)
4. Böde, E., Herbstritt, M., Hermanns, H., Johr, S., Peikenkamp, T., Pulungan, R., Wimmer, R., Becker, B.: Compositional performability evaluation for statemate. In: 3rd International Conference on the Quantitative Evaluation of Systems, QEST 2006, Riverside (USA), pp. 167–178. IEEE Computer Society Press, Los Alamitos (2006)
5. Böde, E., Herbstritt, M., Hermanns, H., Johr, S., Peikenkamp, T., Pulungan, R., Rakow, J., Wimmer, R., Becker, B.: Compositional performability evaluation for statemate. In: Quantitative Evaluation of Computer Systems - Special issue of IEEE Transactions on Software Engineering (to appear, 2008)
6. Harel, D., Politi, M.: Modelling Reactive Systems with Statecharts: The STATE-MATE Approach. McGraw-Hill, New York (1998)

7. Hermanns, H., Katoen, J.P.: Automated compositional markov chain generation for a plain-old telephone system. Science of Computer Programming 36(1), 97–127 (2000)
8. Pulungan, R., Hermanns, H.: Orthogonal distance fitting for phase-type distributions. Reports of SFB/TR 14 AVACS 10, SFB/TR 14 AVACS (November 2006) ISSN: 1860-9821, http://www.avacs.org
9. Hermanns, H.: Interactive Markov Chains – The Quest for Quantified Quality. LNCS, vol. 2428. Springer, Heidelberg (2002)
10. Hermanns, H., Johr, S.: Uniformity by construction in the analysis of nondeterministic stochastic systems. In: International Conference on Dependable Systems and Networks, DSN 2007 (2007)
11. Boudali, H., Crouzen, P., Stoelinga, M.: Dynamic fault tree analysis using input/output interactive markov chains. In: DSN 2007: Proceedings of the 37th Annual IEEE/IFIP International Conference on Dependable Systems and Networks, Washington, DC, USA, pp. 708–717. IEEE Computer Society Press, Los Alamitos (2007)
12. Harel, D., Naamad, A.: The STATEMATE semantics of statecharts. ACM Transactions on Software Engineering and Methodology 5(4), 293–333 (1996)
13. Milner, R.: A Calculus of Communicating Systems. LNCS, vol. 92. Springer, Heidelberg (1980)
14. Glabbeek, R., Weijland, W.P.: Branching time and abstraction in bisimulation semantics. Journal of the ACM 43(3), 555–600 (1996)
15. Wimmer, R., Herbstritt, M., Hermanns, H., Strampp, K., Becker, B.: Sigref – a symbolic bisimulation tool box. In: Graf, S., Zhang, W. (eds.) ATVA 2006. LNCS, vol. 4218, pp. 477–492. Springer, Heidelberg (2006)
16. Hermanns, H., Johr, S.: May we reach it? or must we? in what time? with what probability? In: Proceedings 14th GI/ITG Conference on Measuring, Modelling and Evaluation of Computer and Communication Systems (MMB 2008), Dortmund, Germany, March 31 - April 2, 2008, VDE Verlag (to appear, 2008)
17. Johr, S.: Model Checking Compositional Markov Systems. PhD thesis, Universität des Saarlandes, Saarbrücken (2007)
18. Katoen, J.P., Khattri, M., Zapreev, I.S.: A markov reward model checker. In: Second International Conference on the Quantitative Evaluaiton of Systems (QEST 2005), Torino, Italy, 19-22 September 2005, pp. 243–244. IEEE Computer Society Press, Los Alamitos (2005)
19. ERTMS User Group, UNISIG: ETCS Application Level 2 - Safety Analysis - Part 1 - Functional Fault Tree. Technical report, ALCATEL,ALSTOM,ANSALDO SIGNAL,BOMBARDIER,INVENSYS RAIL,SIEMENS
20. Garavel, H., Lang, F., Mateescu, R.: An overview of CADP 2001. European Assoc. for Software Science and Technology (EASST) Newsletter 4, 13–24 (2002)
21. BCG_MIN: Project Website (March 2006), http://www.inrialpes.fr/vasy/cadp/man/bcg_min.html

Approximate Invariant Property Checking Using Term-Height Reduction for a Subset of First-Order Logic

Hiroaki Shimizu, Kiyoharu Hamaguchi, and Toshinobu Kashiwabara

Graduate School of Information Science & Technology, Osaka University,
Machikaneyama 1-3, Toyonaka, Osaka, 560-8531, Japan
{hama,kashi}@ist.osaka-u.ac.jp

Abstract. In order to verify larger and more complicated systems with model checking, it is necessary to apply some abstraction techniques. Using a subset of first-order logic, called EUF, is one of them. The EUF model checking problem is, however, generally undecidable. In this paper, we introduce a technique called term-height reduction, to guarantee the termination of state enumeration in EUF model checking. This technique generates an over-approximate set of states including all the reachable states. By checking a designated invariant property, we can guarantee whether the invariant property always holds for the design, when verification succeeds. We apply our algorithm to a simple C program and a DSP design and show the experimental results.

Keywords: Quantifier-free first order logic, state exploration, term-height reduction, model checking.

1 Introduction

Model checking, which has been widely put to practical use, has still difficulties in handling large and complicated designs. To tackle this problem, abstraction techniques needs to be applied. In this paper, for the purpose, we adopt abstraction by a quantifier-free first-order logic with equality and uninterpreted functions (EUF) [2,3].

Model checking using EUF is, however, known to be generally undecidable[4]. In fact, straightforward state exploration for transition functions defined with EUF terms does not terminate, because the number of terms which possibly occur in state variables can be infinite. Bounded model checking[11], which handles transitions up to a given number of cycles, is an approach for this problem, and some bounded model checkers have been developed such as UCLID[15], EUREKA[7] or SAL[6] which utilize SAT solvers for EUF and its extension, e.g. with memories, or SMT solvers.

In this paper, we consider *unbounded* invariant property checking. For this problem, we introduce a technique called *term-height reduction* to restrict the number of terms occurring in state variables. When the height of some term

Cha et al. (Eds.): ATVA 2008, LNCS 5311, pp. 318–331, 2008.

which occurs in a state variable exceeds a given limit, its innermost sub-term is replaced by a new variable so that its height is lower than or equal to the limit. Intuitively, this manipulation discards least recently performed operation to the corresponding term.

This height reduction technique, together with the state reduction technique similar to that in [5], generates an over-approximate set of states including all the reachable states, and guarantees termination of state enumeration to check if a designated invariant always holds for the design. The degree of approximation is controlled by the term-height parameter. Although our algorithm is based on explicit state enumeration, in the experiments we performed, it effectively curtails state explosion.

We applied our technique to a simple C program for Bisection Method and a DSP design, that is, ADPCM encoder. Since both of the systems has an indeterminate number of executions in their parts, state enumeration does not terminate if we apply a naive procedure. Furthermore, both of them contain arithmetic operations such as multiplication or division, formal verification without an abstraction technique, or that at Boolean level, is significantly difficult. Our verification algorithm was able to verify them successfully.

The remainder of this paper is organized as follows. We describe related works first, and give the definition of EUF, its state machine, and invariant checking problem. Next, we present the procedure of state traversal with EUF, followed by the detail of our algorithm. We also show the experimental results for some examples. For brevity, we generally omit the proofs for the theorems in this paper.

2   Related Works

Unbounded model checking using EUF or its extension has been studied in some literature[4,5,8]. In [5], Isles et al. show a state enumeration procedure for transition systems using EUF terms extended with memories. They use some state reduction techniques shown in [4], which utilize replaceability of sub-terms that comprise two states. In [8], Corella et al. show a procedure using Multiway Decision Graphs, which can represent characteristic functions for state sets. They also use state reduction techniques similar to [5]. In both of these works, termination is not guaranteed.

In [9], Bryant et al. show a criterion for convergence test, which checks if newly added states are all included in the previously enumerated state set. This criterion is formulated as a quantified second-order formula, for which they show a semi-decidable procedure. This criterion gives a precise definition of convergence, but they have also reported that their approach leads to high computational complexity.

In this paper, we use state reduction techniques similar to [5]. Together with term-height reduction, this provides a decidable procedure for computing an over-approximate state set.

3　EUF and State Machine

We abstract designs by a subset of the first-order logic, called EUF. In this section, we define the syntax and the semantics of EUF and its state machine, and then, invariant checking problem.

3.1　EUF Syntax

EUF is a subset of first-order logic. It does not have universal or existential quantifiers, but has the equal sign as a special predicate. It is composed of *terms* and *formulas*, and the syntax is shown in Fig.1. ITE term represents *if-then-else*. The arities of function symbols and predicate symbols are finite.

> term := variable | function-symbol(term, ... , term) |
> ITE(formula, term, term)
> formula := *true* | *false* | Boolean-variable |
> (term=term) | predicate-symbol(term, ..., term) |
> formula ∨ formula | formula ∧ formula | ¬ formula

Fig. 1. The syntax of EUF

Let t be a term which does not contain ITE terms, then t has nested structure of function symbols. The term-height of t, denoted by $term\text{-}height(t)$, is defined as follows:

$$term\text{-}height(t) =$$
$$\begin{cases} MAX(term\text{-}height(t_1), \ldots, term\text{-}height(t_n)) + 1, & \text{if } t = f(t_1, \ldots, t_n). \\ 0, & \text{if } t \text{ is a variable}. \end{cases}$$

where MAX is the function which returns maximum value from its arguments and f is a function symbol. For example, let c1 and c2 be terms, f and g be function symbols, then the term-heights of terms c1, f(c1) and g(g(c1,f(c2)), f(c1)) are 0, 1 and 3, respectively.

In this paper, an equation, a predicate and a Boolean variable are called *atomic formulas*. An atomic formula and negation of an atomic formula are *literals*. A *product term* is a literal or conjunction of more than one literals. A *disjunction normal form*(DNF) is a product term or disjunction of more than one product terms.

Here we assume, in the following operations, all of the ITE terms have been removed. This can be done by recursively replacing $t = \text{ITE}(\alpha, t_1, t_2)$ with $(\alpha \land t = t_1) \lor (\neg\alpha \land t = t_2)$.

3.2　EUF Semantics

For a nonempty domain $\mathcal{D}$ and an interpretation σ, the truth of a formula is defined. The interpretation σ maps a function symbol and predicate symbol of arity k to a function $\mathcal{D}^k \rightarrow \mathcal{D}$ and $\mathcal{D}^k \rightarrow \{true, false\}$, respectively. Also, σ assigns each variable to an element in $\mathcal{D}$. Boolean variables are assigned to $\{true, false\}$.

Valuation of a term t and a formula α, denoted by $\sigma(t)$ and $\sigma(\alpha)$ respectively, are defined as follows. Note that f is a function symbol and p is a predicate symbol. 1) For a term $t = f(t_1, t_2, \ldots, t_n)$, $\sigma(t) = \sigma(f)(\sigma(t_1), \sigma(t_2), \ldots, \sigma(t_n))$. 2) For a term $t = ITE(\alpha, t_1, t_2)$, $\sigma(t) = \sigma(t_1)$ if $\sigma(\alpha) = true$, otherwise $\sigma(t) = \sigma(t_2)$. 3) For a formula $\alpha = p(t_1, t_2, \ldots, t_n)$, $\sigma(\alpha) = \sigma(p)(\sigma(t_1), \sigma(t_2), \ldots, \sigma(t_n))$. 4) For a formula $\alpha = (t_1 = t_2)$, $\sigma(\alpha) = true$ if and only if $\sigma(t_1) = \sigma(t_2)$. 5) For a formula $\alpha = \neg\alpha_1$, $\sigma(\alpha) = \neg\sigma(\alpha_1)$. 6) For a formula $\alpha = \alpha_1 \circ \alpha_2$, where $\circ$ is $\vee$ or $\wedge$, $\sigma(\alpha) = \sigma(\alpha_1) \circ \sigma(\alpha_2)$.

A formula α is *valid* if and only if $\sigma(\alpha) = true$ for any interpretation σ and any domain $\mathcal{D}$.

For simplicity, we introduce a new special constant $TRUE$, and treat $p(t_1, \ldots, t_n)$ and $\neg p(t_1, \ldots, t_n)$ as $p(t_1, \ldots, t_n) = TRUE$ and $\neg(p(t_1, \ldots, t_n) = TRUE)$, respectively. Then each literal can be treated as an equation, a Boolean variable or negative forms of them.

3.3   EUF State Machine

An EUF state machine is defined by a set of transition functions. To describe transition functions, we assume four types of variables as follows: 1) Boolean state variables: $b_1, \ldots, b_m$, 2) term state variables: $t_1, \ldots, t_n$, 3) Boolean variables: $a_1, \ldots, a_p$, 4) (EUF) variables: $c_1, \ldots, c_q$.

We introduce next state variables $b'_1, \ldots, b'_m$ and $t'_1, \ldots, t'_n$ corresponding to $b_1, \ldots, b_m$ and $t_1, \ldots, t_n$ respectively. Then, transition functions are described by $b'_i := F_i$ ($1 \leq i \leq m$) and $t'_j := T_j$ ($1 \leq j \leq n$), where F_i is a propositional logic formula whose variables are Boolean state variables and Boolean variables, and T_j is a term which includes all types of variables. Transition functions can have some variables, which are term variables or boolean variables, as inputs, that is, each of these input variables at each step is treated as distinct, and an interpretation for such a variable at step i can be different from that at step j ($i \neq j$).

We call the following formula *transition relation*:

$$\bigwedge_{1 \leq i \leq m} (b'_i = F_i) \wedge \bigwedge_{1 \leq j \leq n} (t'_j = T_j) \tag{1}$$

The behavior of an EUF state machine depends on an initial state and a sequence of interpretations for each step. At an initial state, each Boolean variable is assigned to *true* or *false*, and each variable is assigned to an element in $\mathcal{D}$. We define an *interpretation sequence* as $\tilde{\sigma} = (\sigma^0, \sigma^1 \ldots)$, where σ^i is an interpretation at i step. Note that the length of an interpretation sequence is infinite. Any interpretation sequence is required to satisfy the following conditions.

- The interpretation of variables, Boolean variables, function symbols and predicate symbols are the same at every step. In other words, for each variable c_j, each Boolean variable a_j, each function symbol f_j and each predicate symbol p_j, $\sigma^0(c_j) = \sigma^i(c_j)$, $\sigma^0(a_j) = \sigma^i(a_j)$, $\sigma^0(f_j) = \sigma^i(f_j)$ and $\sigma^0(p_j) = \sigma^i(p_j)$ for all i.

- For transition functions $b'_j := F_j$ and $t'_j := T_j$, $\sigma^{i+1}(b_j) = \sigma^i(F_j)$, $\sigma^{i+1}(t_j) = \sigma^i(T_j)$ for all i.
- For an initial state in which each (term) state variable t_j is assigned to variable c_j, $\sigma^0(t_j) = \sigma^0(c_j)$.

We call a interpretation sequence which satisfies the above conditions a *normal interpretation sequence*. In this paper, we assume that interpretation sequences are normal.

3.4   Invariant Checking Problem Using EUF

The inputs of our problem are an EUF state machine M, which models a design we want to verify, and a property P, which is composed from Boolean state variables, term state variables, Boolean variables and (EUF) variables. The invariant checking problem is to check whether M always satisfies P.

Since the contents of the boolean or term state variables used in P depends on each state, so does the formula to be checked at each state. The details are given in Section 4.2

4   State Traversal and Invariant Checking

Invariant checking is performed by enumerating all the reachable states from the initial states and by checking whether the designated property holds for all of them. In this section, we show a state traversal method for an EUF state machine.

4.1   State Traversal

Each state is composed of the following two elements:

- State vector $\vec{v} = (\vec{b}, \vec{t})$
- Condition set $C \subseteq T \times T \times Rel$

where T is the set of all terms which do not contain ITE terms, and $Rel = \{=, \neq\}$. We suppose $\vec{b} = (b_1, \ldots, b_m)$ and $\vec{t} = (t_1, \ldots, t_n)$, where for $1 \leq i \leq m$, b_i is *true* or *false*, and for $1 \leq j \leq n$, t_j is a term. C is the set of all conditions which must be satisfied in order to reach the state.

According to the transition relation, we enumerate all the reachable states by obtaining a state reachable from initial states one by one. Firstly, we perform a preprocess for the transition relation to convert the relation into DNF (disjunctive normal form).

The next state $s' = (\vec{v}', C')$ is constructed from the current state $s = (\vec{v}, C)$ according to the following rule. First, all the current state variables occurring in the transition relation are replaced with the corresponding values or terms in $\overrightarrow{v}$. Then, we can get the formula $\alpha \triangleq \alpha_1 \vee \alpha_2 \vee \ldots \vee \alpha_p$, where each $\alpha_i (1 \leq i \leq p)$ is a product term whose variables are next state variables b'_k $(1 \leq k \leq m)$ and t'_l $(1 \leq l \leq n)$, Boolean variables and variables. Note that any current state variable is not contained in α_i.

For each $\alpha_i \triangleq \beta_1 \wedge \beta_2 \wedge \ldots \wedge \beta_q$, where β_j $(1 \leq j \leq q)$ are literals, the next state s' is generated as follows. The contents of $\overrightarrow{v}'$ and C' are initialized with the ones of $\overrightarrow{v}$ and C, respectively. Next, according to each β_j, the appropriate process shown in the below is performed.

- If β_j is an equation $b'_k = b$, where b'_k is a next Boolean state variable and b is a propositional formula, the Boolean state variable b_k at the next state is assigned to the valuation of b.
- If β_j is an equation $t'_l = t$, where t'_l is a next term state variable and t is a term, the term state variable t_l at the next state is assigned to t.
- If β_j is an equation $t_1 = t_2$ or its negation $\neg(t_1 = t_2)$, where t_1 and t_2 are terms which do not contain any next state variable, the new condition $(t_1, t_2, =)$ or $(t_1, t_2, \neq)$ is added to C', respectively.
- If β_j is an Boolean variable or its negation, the Boolean variable is assigned to *true* or *false* so that β_j is true.

Finally, all conditions containing variables which do not occur in $\overrightarrow{t}'$ are deleted from C'.

State s' is reachable from state s in one step if s' can be composed from s by applying the above rule once. For an EUF state machine M and an initial state s^0, $(s^0, s^1, \ldots)$ is a *state transition sequence* if s^{i+1} is reachable from state s^i in one step for any $i \geq 0$.

4.2   Invariant Checking

A property P, which is restricted to an invariant in this paper, is an EUF formula containing Boolean state variables, term state variables, Boolean variables and variables.

For a state transition sequence $s = (s^0, s^1, \ldots)$, the formula whose state variables are all replaced with corresponding contents of $\overrightarrow{v}^i$, where state $s^i = (\overrightarrow{v}^i, C^i)$, is denoted by P_{v^i}. The property P holds at state s^i if the formula P^i defined below is valid.

$$P^i \triangleq \bigwedge_{(t_1, t_2, R_e) \in C^i} t_1 R_e t_2 \rightarrow P_{v^i} \tag{2}$$

5   Over-Approximation for Reachable States

In this section, we propose an over-approximate algorithm using term-height reduction. We introduce the maximum value of term-height $maxh$ and restrict the heights of terms occurring in the state variables. The algorithm guarantees that a property P always holds if P holds for the approximated state set, otherwise the verification result is inconclusive.

5.1   Overview of Algorithm

The overview of our algorithm is shown in Fig.2. R is the set which contains all the visited states. First, we initialize R with initial states. After that, each state reachable from R in one step is visited and added to R. When the terms whose heights are larger than $maxh$ occur in a state vector $\vec{v}$ or a condition set C, we perform term-height reduction to restrict the heights of terms. Furthermore, for a state $s \in R$, if the inclusion relation between states $s \geq s'$ holds, then we consider s includes s'. Thus s' is not added to R, and all the states reachable from s' are not visited.

We detail term-height reduction and inclusion relation in the remainder of this section.

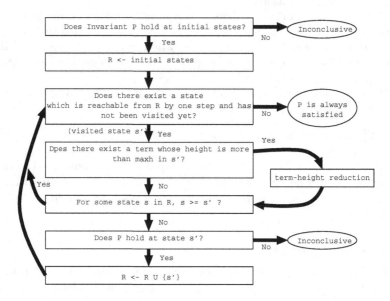

Fig. 2. Overview of Algorithm

5.2   Term-Height Reduction

When the terms whose heights are larger than $maxh$ occur in a state vector $\vec{v}$ or a condition set C, we reduce their term-heights by replacing the subterms with new variables, so that the term-heights are all restricted to less than or equal to $maxh$.

Definition 1. *For a term t whose height is larger than 0, the reduced subterms of t, denoted RT_t, are defined as those satisfying all the following conditions:*

1. *For any $t_r \in RT_t$, term-height$(t_r) = 1$.*
2. *Let t' be the term obtained from t by replacing all the subterms of t in RT_t with new variables. Then, term-height$(t) = $ term-height$(t') + 1$.*
3. *If some term is deleted from RT_t, condition 2. does not hold.*

Term-height reduction for a term t is an manipulation replacing each subterm of t in RT_t with a new variable. For example, the reduced subterm of the term g(g(c1,f(c2)), f(c1)) is f(c2). By applying term-height reduction for this term, we get the term g(g(c1,c3),f(c1)), where c3 is a new variable. Also, the reduced subterms of g(g(c1,c3),f(c1)) are { g(c1,c3), f(c1) }. We apply term-height reduction to this term and get the term g(c4,c5), where c4 and c5 are new variables. By applying term-height reduction for a term, we can decrease the term-height by just one. Note that for any term t whose height is larger than 0, the reduced subterms of t exist uniquely. Also, our algorithm replaces the same subterm with the same variable.

We keep the record of the mapping from a subterm to a new variable until the algorithm terminates. When term state variables are updated by new terms in state traversal, this mapping is applied to all the subterms included. Note that the record of the mapping can get larger in the progress of state traversal, but this does not affect termination of the procedure, because the termination condition does not depend on this record of mapping.

Theorem 1. *For any EUF formula F, F is valid if the formula obtained by applying term-height reduction for a term in F is valid.*

Using term-height reduction, the procedure which constructs the next state $s' = (\overrightarrow{v}', C')$ of the current state $\overrightarrow{v} = (\overrightarrow{b}, \overrightarrow{t})$ is as follows.

1. s' is initialized with s.
2. According to transition relation, $\overrightarrow{v}'$ and C' are updated (See Section 4.1).
3. If $\overrightarrow{v}'$ or C' contains terms whose heights are larger than $maxh$, their heights are reduced repeatedly until becoming less than or equal to $maxh$.
4. The conditions containing any variable which does not occur in $\overrightarrow{t}'$ are all deleted.

5.3   State Merging Based on Inclusion Relation

For a state $s = (\overrightarrow{v}, C)$, where $\overrightarrow{v} = (\overrightarrow{b}, \overrightarrow{t})$ and $\overrightarrow{t} = (t_1, \ldots, t_n)$, let V_t be the set of variables occurring in $\overrightarrow{t}$, D be a set of variables $\{d_1, d_2, \ldots, d_{|V_t|}\}$, where $V_t \cap D = \phi$, and map_t^D be a bijective function from V_t to D. We denote by $map_t^D[t_i]$ the term obtained from a term t_i in which each variable $c \in V_t$ is replaced with $map_t^D(c)$. Furthermore, we denote by $map_t^D[\overrightarrow{t}]$ the vector of terms obtained from $\overrightarrow{t}$ in which each term t_i is replaced with $map_t^D[t_i]$. Also, we denote by $map_t^D[C]$ the condition set obtained from C in which each condition (t_1, t_2, R_e) is replaced with $(map_t^D[t_1], map_t^D[t_2], R_e)$.

Definition 2. *For two states $s = (\overrightarrow{v}, C)$ and $s' = (\overrightarrow{v}', C')$, where $\overrightarrow{v} = (\overrightarrow{b}, \overrightarrow{t})$, $\overrightarrow{v}' = (\overrightarrow{b}', \overrightarrow{t}')$, we say "s includes s'", denoted by $s \geq s'$, if the following conditions are all satisfied.*

1. $\overrightarrow{b} = \overrightarrow{b}'$
2. $|V_t| = |V_{t'}|$
3. *For a set of variables D, there exist two functions map_t^D and $map_{t'}^D$ such that:*

- $map_t^D[\overrightarrow{t}] = map_{t'}^D[\overrightarrow{t}']$ and
- $\models \bigwedge\limits_{(t_1',t_2',R_e')\in map_{t'}^D[C']} (t_1' R_e' t_2') \longrightarrow \bigwedge\limits_{(t_1,t_2,R_e)\in map_t^D[C]} (t_1 R_e t_2)$

The third condition in Definition 2 means that when we compare $\overrightarrow{t}$ with $\overrightarrow{t}'$, or C with C', we focus on the forms of terms and disregard the names of variables. Note that the operation to be performed to check the third condition is similar to *unification* in logic programming, but more restricted. Our algorithm does not regard $g(f(x),z))$ and $g(y,w)$ as "equivalent" under any mapping map_t^D, because map_t^D maps only variables in the terms to other variables. On the other hand, unification allows these two terms to be unified by replacing y with $f(x)$ and z with w.

In our implementation, the terms in $\overrightarrow{t}$ are compared with those in $\overrightarrow{t}'$ from the top of the lists, one by one. If renaming of the variables can make the two terms syntactically equivalent, then the two mappings map_t^D and $map_{t'}^D$ are updated. Otherwise, checking the conditions of Definition 2 is aborted. If construction of map_t^D and $map_{t'}^D$ is successful, the implication of C by C' is checked under the mappings, which can be done by using an SMT solver.

In a state traversal, for a state r and its next state s', if $s \geq s'$ for some state s we have already visited, then we move from r to s instead of s', and do not visit s' and its successors. We say that "s' is merged into s." s is said to be a merging state of s'.

The state transition graph which is obtained by applying the term-height reduction and the state merging technique is called the *abstract state transition graph*. The following is the key property for our state enumeration algorithm.

Theorem 2. *For any state transition graph, the size of the abstract state transition graph is finite.*

(*Sketch of Proof*). Suppose that term-height is restricted to a finite value. Then, the number of term forms occurring in a state vector is finite because a function and a predicate have the finite number of arguments. Also, the number of elements in a condition set is finite because the conditions containing any variable which does not occur in the state variables are all deleted. Thus, disregarding the name of variables, there exists only the finite number of components for a state. Since state merging resolves the difference among variable names, the size of the abstract state transition graph is finite.   Q.E.D.

Theorem 3. *For any state transition graph G and its abstract state transition graph G_a, a property P holds at any state in G if P holds at any state in G_a.*

5.4   Example

We show state traversal for an EUF code in the following:

```
0:   while (t1!=t2){
          t1 := f(t1,t2);
     }
1:   t2 := g(t2);
```

The transition function for this code is as follows:

$b1' := ITE(b1 = 0, ITE(t1 = t2, 1, 0), 1)$
$t1' := ITE(b1 = 0, ITE(t1 = t2, t1, f(t1, t2)), t1)$
$t2' := ITE(b1 = 1, ITE(t1 = t2, g(t2), t2), t2)$

State enumeration for this example does not terminate without term-height reduction. Here, we introduced a Boolean state variable $b1$ to hold a current execution point.

Fig.3 shows state traversal for this transition function under $maxh = 1$. We initialize the state variables $t1$, $t2$ and $b1$ with $c1$, $c2$ and *false* respectively. When the transition from s to s' occurs, the height of $t1$ gets larger than $maxh$ and term-height reduction is performed. Then, $s \geq s'$ holds under the domain $D = \{d1, d2\}$ and functions $map_t^D = \{c1 \rightarrow d1, c2 \rightarrow d2\}$, $map_{t'}^D = \{c3 \rightarrow d1, c2 \rightarrow d2\}$. Therefore, s' is merged into s and we can obtain the abstract state transition graph with four states.

6   Experimental Results

We implemented our algorithm in the C++ language and performed some experiments with Intel Celeron 1.46GHz of 2GB Memory under Windows XP. We used Yices [16] as an EUF SAT solver. The SAT solver was used to check Equation (2) and the third condition of Definition 2.

We applied our technique to designs of a simple C program for Bisection Method and an ADPCM encoder.

The run-times we show in this section do not include construction of a DNF of the transition relation from transition functions. In the following examples, we gave the transition relations in DNF as inputs.

6.1   Bisection Method

Bisection method is an algorithm for solving an equation. We show its pseudo code in Fig. 4. The number of executions of the while body depends on input value diff, and thus is indeterminate.

We verify equivalence of returned values between BISECT1 which executes the code sequentially, and BISECT2 which is obtained by modifying BISECT1 to execute the loop body in one step. Both of the obtained EUF state machines were executed concurrently.

The experimental result is shown in Table 1, where *# of new vars.* means the total number of new variables introduced by term-height reduction and *# of states* means the number of states in the obtained abstract state transition graph.

6.2   ADPCM Encoder

An ADPCM (Adaptive Differential Pulse Code Modulation) encoder transforms sound data to digital data. The high-level description of an ADPCM encoder [17]

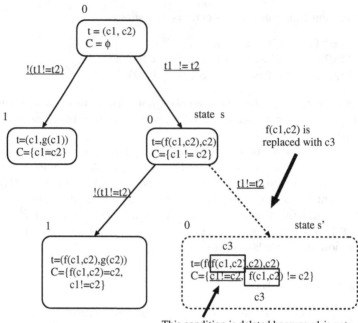

Fig. 3. State Traversal Example ($maxh = 1$)

```
float bisect(float left, float right, // left < right
        float diff, float (*f)(float)) // diff >= 0 is an allowed error
{
    float mid, fleft, fright, fmid;

    fleft = f(left);
    fright = f(right);
    if (fleft == 0) return left;
    if (fright == 0) return right;
    if (samesign(fleft, fright)) {
        exit;
    }
    while (true) {
        mid = (left + right) / 2;
        if (mid - left <= diff) break;
        if (right - mid <= diff) break;
        fmid = f(mid);
        if (fmid == 0) return mid;
        if (samesign(fmid, fleft)) {
            left = mid;
            fleft = fmid;
        } else {
            right = mid;
            fright = fmid;
        }
    }
    return mid;
}
```

Fig. 4. Pseudo Code for Bisection Method

Table 1. Experimental Result: Bisection Method

maxh	# of new vars.	# of states	time(sec)
1	6	113	13.7
2	5	113	13.8
3	6	117	16.0
4	7	127	18.5
5	8	205	45.8
6	13	283	59.0
7	14	448	148.7
8	27	595	188.4
9	28	964	516.2

Table 2. Experimental Result: ADPCM Encoders

maxh	# of new vars.	# of states	time(sec)
0	47	266	50.0
1	30	1016	234.9
2	21	1974	588.4
3	16	2956	1275.4

is written in the C language and has about 70 lines. This description also contains multiplication and division. Furthermore, since it has a loop structure whose number of iteration depends on an input parameter, state enumeration for it does not terminate if our technique is not used. The loop structure contains 9 if-branches.

We verify equivalence of output values between ADPCM1 which executes the high-level description sequentially, and ADPCM2 which is obtained by modifying ADPCM1 to execute the loop body in less steps. Table 2 shows the experimental result.

6.3 Observation

In both of the above examples, term-heights at state variables continue to get larger infinitely as state traversal proceeds. For larger $maxh$, state merging is delayed at later steps, and as a result, both of the number of states and the run-time increase. This suggests that we should increase $maxh$ from a smaller value.

On the other hand, verification for the design which does not contain feedback structures, such as filter designs, is expected to terminate without term-height reduction, because the term-height of any term state variable does not exceed some constant. In this case, term-height reduction would not be necessary, and can even degrade the performance. For determining $maxh$, it would be necessary to analyze the high-level structure of the designs.

7   Conclusion

In this paper, we proposed term-height reduction to terminate state enumeration for an EUF state machine. Together with the state merging technique, our algorithm can show equivalences of modified C programs as well as two DSP designs, which the existent methods cannot verify.

Our technique, however, can naturally fail to check invariants, if the invariant depends on the property of operators. For example, although both $c1 + c2 = c2 + c1$ and $c + c = c \times 2$ always hold, their abstractions in EUF, $f(c1, c2) = f(c2, c1)$ and $f(c, c) = g(c, 2)$, are not valid. To compensate for this, we will study some approach using the other logic together with EUF, or some other method such as [10] to consider the property of functions when we check satisfiability for EUF formulas.

As other future works, we would like to develop a scheme which can handle the cases in which the designated property does not hold. For this purpose, we would need to combine the other logic such as Boolean logic or linear arithmetic, together with EUF. Also, it would be necessary to extend the algorithm to deal with arrays or memories of arbitrary length, or to check more general temporal properties which are not invariants.

In our approach, a limit on term-height influences the degree of over-approximation. Since the term-height reduction implies discarding the least recent operations done to state variables, larger height means less of approximation. Finding an appropriate limit depends on the properties to be checked and also affects the performance. In this paper, this is not considered much, because small heights are sufficient for the examples we handled. In order to automate this process in general, we could increase the limit from some small value, while checking generated counter-examples are surely spurious by, for example, boolean SAT. This also remains as a future work.

Acknowledgment

We would like to thank anonymous reviewers for their helpful comments. This study was supported in part by funds from the Grant-in-Aid for Scientific Research (C) under Grant No. 19500043, from Japan Society for the Promotion of Science (JSPS).

References

1. Clarke, E.M., Grumberg, O., Peled, D.A.: Model Checking. MIT Press, Cambridge (1999)
2. Burch, J.R., Dill, D.L.: Automated verification of pipelined microprocessor control. In: Dill, D.L. (ed.) CAV 1994. LNCS, vol. 818, pp. 68–80. Springer, Heidelberg (1994)
3. Hamaguchi, K., Urushihara, H., Kashiwabara, T.: Symbolic Checking of Signal-Transition Consistency for Verifying High-Level Designs. In: Hunt Jr., W.A., Johnson, S.D. (eds.) FMCAD 2000. LNCS, vol. 1954, pp. 455–469. Springer, Heidelberg (2000)
4. Hojati, R., Isles, A., Kirkpatrick, D., Brayton, R.K.: Verification using uninterpreted functions and finite instantiations. In: Srivas, M., Camilleri, A. (eds.) FMCAD 1996. LNCS, vol. 1166, pp. 218–232. Springer, Heidelberg (1996)

5. Isles, A.J., Hojati, R., Brayton, R.K.: Computing Reachable Control States of Systems Modeled with Uninterpreted Functions and Infinite Memory. In: 10th International Conference on Computer Aided Verification, pp. 256–267 (1998)
6. SAL, http://sal.csl.sri.com/
7. Armando, A., Benerecetti, M., Carotenuto, D., Mantovani, J., Spica, P.: The Eureka Tool for Software Model Checking. In: 22nd IEEE/ACM ASE Conference (2007)
8. Corella, F., Zhou, Z., Song, X., Langevin, M., Cerny, E.: Multiway Decision Graphs for Automated Hardware Verification. Formal Methods in System Design, vol. 10(1), pp. 7–46 (1997)
9. Bryant, R.E., Lahiri, S.K., Seshia, S.A.: Convergence Testing in Term-Level Bounded Model Checking. In: Geist, D., Tronci, E. (eds.) CHARME 2003. LNCS, vol. 2860, pp. 348–362. Springer, Heidelberg (2003)
10. Kozawa, H., Hamaguchi, K., Kashiwabara, T.: Satisfiability Checking for Logic with Equality and Uninterpreted Functions under Equivalence Constraints. In: IEICE Trans. on Fundamentals of Electronics, Communications and Computer Sciences, pp. 2778–2789 (2007)
11. Biere, A., Cimatti, A., Clarke, E.M., Zhu, Y.: Symbolic Model Checking without BDDs. In: Cleaveland, W.R. (ed.) TACAS 1999. LNCS, vol. 1579, pp. 193–207. Springer, Heidelberg (1999)
12. McMillan, K.L.: Symbolic Model Checking. Kluwer Academic Publishers, Dordrecht (1993)
13. Holzmann, G.J.: The model checker SPIN. IEEE Trans. Softw. Eng. 23(5), 279–295 (1997)
14. Clarke, E.M., Kroening, D., Lerda, F.: A Tool for Checking ANSI-C Programs. In: Proceedings of Tools and Algorithms for the Analysis and Construction of Systems, pp. 168–176 (2004)
15. Bryant, R.E., German, S., Velev, M.N.: Modeling and Verifying Systems using a Logic of Counter Arithmetic with Lambda Expressions and Uninterpreted Functions. In: Brinksma, E., Larsen, K.G. (eds.) CAV 2002. LNCS, vol. 2404, pp. 78–92. Springer, Heidelberg (2002)
16. Yices: An SMT Solver, http://yices.csl.sri.com/
17. OPENCORES.ORG, http://www.opencores.org/

Tree Pattern Rewriting Systems[*]

Blaise Genest[3], Anca Muscholl[1], Olivier Serre[2], and Marc Zeitoun[1]

[1]LaBRI, Bordeaux
[2]LIAFA, Paris 7 & CNRS
[3]IRISA, Rennes 1 & CNRS

Abstract. Classical verification often uses abstraction when dealing with data. On the other hand, dynamic XML-based applications have become pervasive, for instance with the ever growing importance of web services. We define here *Tree Pattern Rewriting Systems* (TPRS) as an abstract model of dynamic XML-based documents. TPRS systems generate infinite transition systems, where states are unranked and unordered trees (hence possibly modeling XML documents). Their guarded transition rules are described by means of tree patterns. Our main result is that given a TPRS system $(T, \mathcal{R})$, a tree pattern P and some integer k such that any reachable document from T has depth at most k, it is *decidable* (albeit of non elementary complexity) whether some tree matching P is reachable from T.

1 Introduction

Classical verification techniques often use abstraction when dealing with data. On the other hand, dynamic *data-intensive* applications have become pervasive, for instance with the ever growing importance of web services. The format of the data exchanged by web services is based on XML, which is nowadays the standard for semistructured data. XML documents can be seen as unranked trees, *i.e.* trees in which every node can have an arbitrary (but finite) number of children, not depending on its labels. Very often, the order of siblings in the document is of no importance. In this case, trees are in addition unordered. There is a rich body of results concerning the analysis of fixed XML documents (with or without data), see e.g [13,11] for surveys on this topic.

The analysis of the *dynamics* of XML documents accessed and updated in a multi-peer environment has been considered only very recently [2,3]. Dynamically evolving XML documents are of course crucial, for instance when doing static analysis of XML-based web services. A general framework, Active XML (*AXML* for short), has been defined in [2] to unify data (XML) and control (services), by allowing data to be given implicitly in form of service calls.

In this paper we propose an abstract model for dynamically evolving documents, based on guarded rewriting rules on unranked, unordered tree. We show that basic properties, such as reachability of tree patterns and termination, are decidable for a natural subclass of our rewriting systems.

---

[*] Work supported by ANR DocFlow, ANR DOTS and CREATE ACTIVEDOC.

Cha et al. (Eds.): ATVA 2008, LNCS 5311, pp. 332–346, 2008.

A standard technique to analyze unranked trees is to encode them as binary trees [13]. However, this encoding does not preserve the depth of the tree, neither locality, nor path properties. For these reasons, we define guarded tree rewriting systems directly on unranked trees. The rewriting rules are based on tree patterns, that occur in two distinct contexts. First, tree patterns are used for describing how the structure of the tree changes through the rules: subtrees can be moved or deleted, and new nodes can be added. Thus, documents evolve in a *non monotonous* way. Second, rules are guarded, and the guard condition is tested via a *Tree Pattern Query* (TPQ). The role of the TPQ is actually twofold: it is used in the pre-condition of the rule, and the query results can enhance the information of the new tree. We call such systems *Tree Pattern Rewriting System, TPRS* for short. For an easier comparison with other works, we include an example of a Mail-Order System in our presentation, close to the one used in [3].

The main tool we use to show decidability of various properties of TPRS are well-structured systems [1,8]. Such systems cover several interesting classes of infinite-state systems, such as Petri nets and lossy channel systems. Our TPRS are of course not well-structured, in general. We impose two restrictions in order to obtain well-structured systems. First, guards must be used positively: equivalently, a rule cannot be disabled because of the existence of some tree pattern. Second, we need a uniform bound on the depth of the trees obtained by rewriting. Indeed, we show that if the depth is not uniformly bounded, then TPRS can encode Turing machines. Notice that the depth restriction is very realistic in the XML setting, since such documents are usually large, but shallow. We show that TPRS that satisfy both conditions yield well-structured transition systems, and we show how to apply forward and backward analysis of well-structured systems for obtaining the decidability of pattern reachability as well as termination. On the negative side, we show that exact reachability, confluence and the finite state property are undecidable for such TPRS. One can notice that the reachability of a given tree pattern is more likely to be useful in practice than exact reachability, that supposes the complete knowledge about the target document. In the decidable cases, we also show that the complexity is at least non elementary.

Related work. We review here other approaches where it is possible to decide behavioral properties of active documents.

The systems called *positive AXML* in [2] are *monotonous*: a document is modified by adding subtrees at nodes labeled by service calls, deletions are not possible. In particular, trees can only grow, which is not the case for the TPRS defined here. For instance, for the mail order example this means that a product cannot be deleted from the cart. Moreover, there is no deterministic description of the semantics of a service: a service call can create any tree, granted that it satisfies some DTD. Such a system is always confluent, and one can decide whether, after some finite number of steps, the system will stabilize [2].

Guard AXML [3] is very similar to our model, service calls being based on tree pattern queries. The focus of [3] is to analyze the action of non recursive services over documents satisfying a given schema, and with potentially unbounded data (trees are labeled by symbols from an infinite alphabet and tree patterns use data constraints). Compared with our framework, [3] uses more powerful guards, namely Boolean combinations of tree patterns guards. However, the price to pay is that decidability results in [3] require a uniform bound on the length of the rewriting chains. In contrast, our TPRS model active documents with possibly recursive service calls.

A seemingly related area are term rewriting systems modulo associativity and commutativity [10]. However, these rewriting systems act on *ranked trees*, so applying results from this area on unranked trees requires to work on some ranked encoding of the tree. Also, it is not clear how to simulate e.g. TPRS rules that move all but some specific subtrees of a given node by term rewriting rules. Tree rewriting on unranked (ordered) trees has been considered in [12]. The difference to our setting is that the rewriting is *ground*, i.e., rules can only be applied at the deepest levels of the tree, which makes reachability decidable.

2   Tree Pattern Rewriting

The tree rewriting model presented in this section is inspired by the Active XML (AXML) system developed at INRIA [4]. Active XML extends the framework of XML to describe semi-structured data by a dynamic component, describing data implicitly via service (function) calls. The evaluation of such calls is based on queries, resulting in extra data that can be added to the document tree. The abstract model is that of XML, *i.e.*, unranked, unordered, labeled trees, together with a specification of the semantics for each service.

Trees considered in this paper are labeled by tags from a finite set $\mathcal{T}$. We will distinguish a subset $\mathcal{T}_{var} \subseteq \mathcal{T}$ of so-called *tag variables*. In addition, we use the special symbol $ to mark nodes where service calls insert new data. Trees are in the following unranked and unordered, with nodes labeled by $\mathcal{T} \cup \mathcal{T}_\$$, where $\mathcal{T}_\$ = \mathcal{T} \times \{\$\}$. We will not distinguish function/service nodes, since we consider here an abstract model for AXML documents, that is based on tree rewriting. We also do not consider multiple peers actually: their joint behavior can be described as the evolution of a unique document tree.

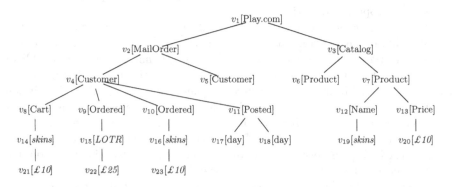

Fig. 1. Tree document representing a catalog of products and customers history

A *tree* $(V, \text{parent}, \textit{root}, \lambda)$ consists of a set of nodes V with a distinguished node called *root*, a mapping $\text{parent} : V \setminus \{\textit{root}\} \rightarrow V$ associating a node with its parent, and a mapping $\lambda : V \rightarrow \mathcal{T} \cup \mathcal{T}_\$ $ labeling each node by a tag. Moreover, for each node $v \in V$, there is some $k \geq 0$ such that $\text{parent}^k(v) = \textit{root}$. Such a tree is called a *document* if its labeling satisfies $\lambda(V) \subseteq \mathcal{T} \setminus \mathcal{T}_{var}$, that is, no node label uses a tag variable or the $\$$ sign. A *forest* is a finite multiset of trees.

Consider for instance the tree in Fig. 1. Informally, it represents a simplified version of the Play.com database, containing several products and information about customers. Bracketed strings denote node labels. The subtrees of nodes v_5 and v_6 are not represented in the figure. The document shows two customers, one of which is currently shopping on the website with one product in her cart. This customer has 3 outstanding orders, one of which was posted 2 days ago (the counter *days* is encoded in unary in the tree - under node v_{11} for this customer). One can represent a tree in a term-like way. For example, to denote the empty catalog with no customer, we write $v_1[\text{Play.com}](v_2[\text{MailOrder}], v_3[\text{Catalog}])$, or if node names are irrelevant, $[\text{Play.com}]([\text{MailOrder}], [\text{Catalog}])$. Since trees are unordered, a tree can have several such representations.

The atomic operations in our model are from a set $\mathcal{R}$ of guarded tree rewriting rules, as described below. On an abstract level we view a service s as described for instance by a regular expression $R(s)$ over the set of rewriting rules $\mathcal{R}$. For example, the following expression describes an order service on Play.com:

$(\text{add-product} + \text{delete-product})^*\text{checkout}.$

The tree resulting in the invocation of service s corresponds to the application of some sequence of rewriting rules in $R(s)$. The atomic rewriting rules will use queries based on tree patterns (the descendant relation can be used together with the child relation), as described next. The symbol $\uplus$ used below stands for the disjoint union.

Definition 1 (Tree-Pattern). *A tree pattern (TP for short) is a tuple $P = (V, \text{parent}, \text{ancestor}, \textit{root}, \lambda)$, where $(V, \text{parent} \uplus \text{ancestor}, \textit{root}, \lambda)$ is a tree.*

A tree pattern represents a set of trees that have a similar shape. As for trees, a TP can be described in a term-like way, ancestor-edges being represented by the symbol $-$ (such edges are represented by a double line in the figures). For instance, the tree pattern LQBill shown in Fig. 2 can be written as $w_1(-w_2(w_3(w_4)))$, with $\lambda(w_1) = \text{Play.com}, \lambda(w_2) = \text{Ordered}, \lambda(w_3) = X, \lambda(w_4) = Y$ (here X and Y are tag variables: $X, Y \in \mathcal{T}_{var}$). This pattern represents trees with root "Play.com", having a node "Ordered", having itself a grandchild.

Definition 2 (Matching). *A tree $T = (V, \text{parent}, \lambda, \textit{root})$ matches a TP $P = (V', \text{parent}', \text{ancestor}', \lambda', \textit{root}')$ if there exist two mappings $f : V' \rightarrow V$ and $t : \mathcal{T}_{var} \rightarrow \mathcal{T} \setminus \mathcal{T}_{var}$ such that:*

- *$f(\textit{root}') = \textit{root}$,*
- *For all $v \in V'$, $\lambda(f(v)) = \lambda'(v)$ if $\lambda'(v) \notin \mathcal{T}_{var}$, and else $\lambda(f(v)) = t(\lambda'(v))$,*
- *For all $v \in V'$ the following holds*
  - *If $\text{parent}'(v)$ is defined, then $f(\text{parent}'(v)) = \text{parent}(f(v))$;*
  - *If $\text{ancestor}'(v)$ is defined, then $f(\text{ancestor}'(v))$ is an ancestor of $f(v)$ in T.*

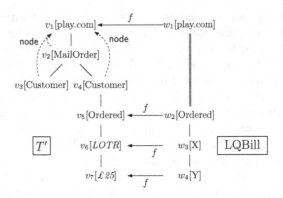

Fig. 2. A tree T' matching the TP LQBill

Mappings (f, t) as above are called a matching between T and P. Furthermore, if f is injective, then (f, t) is called an injective matching.

Fig. 2 shows an example of an injective matching between a tree T' and the TP LQBill. The only possible matching is $f(w_1) = v_1, f(w_2) = v_5, f(w_3) = v_6, f(w_4) = v_7$ and $t(X) = LOTR$, $t(Y) = £25$. With a matching $f : V' \to V$ we associate the mapping node : $V \setminus f(V') \to f(V')$, with node$(v)$ being the lowest ancestor of v belonging to $f(V')$. For instance, for the mapping f matching T to LQBill, we have node$(v_2) =$ node$(v_3) =$ node$(v_4) = v_1$.

Similarly to [2] we use in our model tree-pattern queries (TPQ for short, also called *positive queries* in [2]). Such queries have the form $Q \rightsquigarrow P$, with Q a TP and P a tree, and the variables used in Q are also used in P. The TP Q selects tags in the tree. The result of a query query $= Q \rightsquigarrow P$ on T is the forest query(T) of all instantiations of P by matchings between T and Q. That is, for each matching (f, t) between T and Q we obtain an instance of P in which each $\mathcal{T}_{var}$-label X has been replaced by the tag $t(X)$. For instance, let RQBill be the tree Product (Name(X),Price(Y)). Then the result of the TPQ (LQBill $\rightsquigarrow$ RQBill) on the tree in Fig. 1 is the forest depicted in Fig. 3.

We now define a generic kind of (guarded) rewriting rules, as a model for active documents. Our rules are based on tree patterns, that occur in two distinct contexts. First, tree patterns are used for describing how the structure of the document tree changes through the rule - some subtrees might be deleted, new

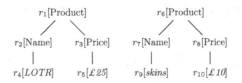

Fig. 3. Result forest of the TPQ *LQBill $\rightsquigarrow$ RQBill* on document T

nodes can be added. Second, rules are guarded, and the guard condition is tested via a TPQ. The role of the query is actually twofold: it is used in the pre-condition of the rule, and its result can enhance the information of the new tree.

Definition 3 (TP rules). *A TP rule is a tuple* (left, query, guard, right), *such that:*

- *left is a TP* $(V_l, parent_l, ancestor_l, \lambda_l, root_l)$ *over* $\mathcal{T}$,
- *right is a TP* $(V_r, parent_r, ancestor_r, \lambda_r, root_r)$ *over* $\mathcal{T} \cup \mathcal{T}_\$$,
- *query is a TPQ,*
- *guard is a set of forests.*

We require the following additional properties:

1. *all tag variables used in* right *appear also in* left, *and*
2. $ancestor_r(x) = y$ *iff* $x, y \in V_l \cap V_r$ *and* $ancestor_l(x) = y$.

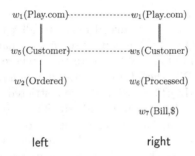

left   right

Fig. 4. Tree patterns left and right of a rule

The additional conditions on right ensure that the right-hand side of a TP rule determines the form of the resulting tree, as it is explained below. For instance, Bill = (left, (LQBill $\rightsquigarrow$ RQBill), guard, right) is a TP rule, with left, right defined as in Fig. 4. Informally, the rule says that the system will process a bill for the current order, and will tag the order as processed. The guard guard will be usually specified as a finite set of trees. In this case, the guard is fulfilled if the result of the query covers one of the tree of guard (see Section 4 on decidability).

We first describe the semantics of a rule using the rule Bill as an example on the tree in Fig. 1. First, we compute an *injective* mapping f which maps the nodes w_1, w_5, w_2 of left with the nodes v_1, v_4, v_{10} of T, respectively. We produce a new tree by rearranging and relabeling the nodes of T in the image of f, that is v_1, v_4, v_{10}. Some nodes can be deleted and others created. The resulting tree is shown in Fig. 5. We keep all nodes of T which are matched by nodes of left also present in right (v_1 and v_4), as well as their descendants by node^{-1}. That is, we keep all nodes labeled by v_i in Fig. 5. In particular, a node matched in left which does not appear in right is deleted (as v_{10}, matched to w_2), as well as its node^{-1} descendants (v_{16} and v_{23}). The TP right makes it possible to create new nodes,

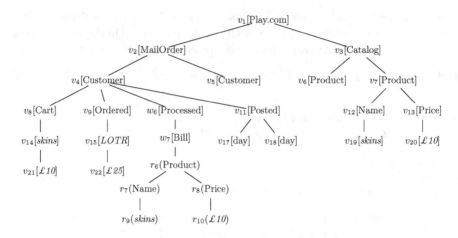

Fig. 5. The tree document T' resulting of the application of the rule Bill

present in right but not in left, as w_6, w_7. In addition, the TPQ query of the rule is used to attach a copy of the returned forest to all \$-marked nodes of right. Furthermore, if the TPQ $Q \rightsquigarrow P$ uses in Q some node name m common to left, then the results of the TPQ are restricted to those where m matches $f(m)$. For instance, in the TP rule Bill, the TP LQBill uses names w_1, w_2 common to left, so the results of the TPQ (LQBill $\rightsquigarrow$ RQBill) are restricted to the particular order chosen by the matching f between T and left. The result is thus the subtree rooted at node r_6 in Fig. 3, but not the subtree rooted at r_1, since it would require $f(w_2) = v_9$, while $f(w_2) = v_{10}$. This restriction is desirable, since we want to issue a bill only for the products of this particular order. Here, w_7 is \$-marked, and the result forest is defined by nodes $r_6, \cdots r_{10}$.

More formally, let query $= Q \rightsquigarrow P$ be a TPQ and let (f, t) be an injective matching between T and left. Moreover, let V_l be the nodes of left and V_Q those of Q. Let $S_1, \ldots, S_k$ be the trees composing the resulting forest query(T), and let $g_1, \ldots, g_k$ be the respective associated matchings (that is, $g_i : V_Q \rightarrow V$ and S_i is the instantiation of P by g_i). Then we define query$_f(T)$ as the forest $S_{i_1}, \ldots, S_{i_l}$ of those trees S_j such that g_j agrees with f over $V_l \cap V_Q$. That is, query$_f(T)$ is the subset of query(T) that is *consistent* with the matching f. We now turn to the formal semantics of rules.

Definition 4 (Semantics of rules). *Let $T = (V, \mathsf{parent}, \lambda, \mathsf{root})$ be a tree and $R = (\mathsf{left}, \mathsf{query} = Q \rightsquigarrow P, \mathsf{guard}, \mathsf{right})$ be a rule. Let $\mathsf{left} = (V_l, \mathsf{parent}_l, \mathsf{ancestor}_l, \lambda_l, \mathsf{root}_l)$ and $\mathsf{right} = (V_r, \mathsf{parent}_r, \mathsf{ancestor}_r, \lambda_r, \mathsf{root}_r)$.*

We say that R is enabled if there exists an injective matching (f, t) from left into T, such that query$_f(T) \in$ guard. The result of the application of R via (f, t) is the tree $T' = (V', \mathsf{parent}', \lambda', \mathsf{root}')$ defined as follows:

- *$V' = V_1 \uplus V_2 \uplus V_3 \uplus V_4$ with*
  1. *$V_1 = f(V_l \cap V_r)$,*   % in the example on Fig. 5, $V_1 = \{v_1, v_4\}$.
  2. *$V_2 = \mathsf{node}^{-1}(V_1)$,*   % in the example on Fig. 5, $V_2 = \{v_i \mid i \notin \{1, 4\}\}$.

3. $V_3 = f(V_r \setminus V_l)$,   % in the example on Fig. 5, $V_3 = \{w_6, w_7\}$.

4. V_4 consists of distinct copies of the nodes of the forest query$_f(T)$, one for each node marked by \$ in **right**.
   % in the example on Fig. 5, $V_4 = \{r_i \mid i \in \{6, \ldots, 10\}\}$.

- Setting $f(u) = u$ for all $u \in V_3$, we extend $f : V_r \cup V_l \to V_1 \uplus V_3$.
- $root' = f(root_r)$.
- Let $u \in V_1$ and let $\bar{u} = f^{-1}(u)$ be the associated node in $V_l \cap V_r$. If $\lambda_r(\bar{u}) \notin \mathcal{T}_{var}$ then $\lambda'(u) = \lambda_r(\bar{u})$, else $\lambda'(u) = t(\lambda_r(\bar{u}))$. For all $u \neq root'$, if parent$_r(\bar{u})$ is defined, then parent$'(u) = f(\text{parent}_r(\bar{u}))$ else parent$'(u) = \text{parent}(u)$.
- For all $u \in V_2$, parent$'(u) = \text{parent}(u)$ and $\lambda'(u) = \lambda(u)$.
- For all $u \in V_3 \setminus \{root_r\}$, parent$'(u) = f(\text{parent}_r(u))$ and $\lambda'(u) = \lambda_r(u)$.
- To each node $u \in V'$ marked by \$, we add a copy of the forest query$_f(T)$ as children of u, and we unmark the node u.

Note that if $x \in V_2$, then its parent is in $V_1 \cup V_2$. The same stands if ancestor$_r(x)$ is defined. Note also that we indeed obtain a tree: for instance, if $u \in V_1$ and parent$_r(\bar{u})$ is not defined, then parent(u) is defined. This is because $v = $ ancestor$_r(\bar{u})$ is then defined, so by Def. 3, $v = $ ancestor$_l(\bar{u})$ in **left**, so that $u = f(\bar{u})$ cannot be the root of T.

We write $T \xrightarrow{R} T'$ if T' can be obtained from T by applying the rule R. More generally, given a set of rules $\mathcal{R}$ we write $T \to T'$ if there is some rule $R \in \mathcal{R}$ with $T \xrightarrow{R} T'$, and $T \xrightarrow{*} T'$ for the reflexive-transitive closure of the previous relation. Notice that the tree T' matches **right**, through the matching $f' : V_r \to V'$ defined by $f'(v) = f(v)$ if $v \in V_r \cap V_l$, and $f'(v) = v$ if $v \in V_r \setminus V_l$.

Example (Play.com rules). To show how easily rules can be defined, we describe now some rules of the Play.com system. When the rule does not use a query or a guard, we only describe the **left** and **right** components.

- The rule New-Customer adds a new customer and its cart.
  - left $= w_1[\text{Play.com}](w_2[\text{MailOrder}])$.
  - right $= w_1[\text{Play.com}](w_2[\text{MailOrder}](w_3[\text{Customer}](w_4[\text{Cart}])))$.
- Every new day, if a posted parcel has not yet been received yet, then the *day* counter is incremented.
  - left $= w_1[\text{Play.com}](-w_2[\text{Posted}])$.
  - right $= w_1[\text{Play.com}](-w_2[\text{Posted}](w_3[\text{day}]))$.
- If after 21 days a posted parcel is still not received, the customer can require a payback. We use the guard to ensure this time limit. Notice that the query is $Q \leadsto P$, where Q uses the same w_2 as in **left**, that is the number of days will be counted only for this particular parcel.
  - left $= w_1[\text{Play.com}](-w_2[\text{Posted}])$.
  - $Q = w_1[\text{Play.com}](-w_2[\text{Posted}](w_3[day]))$.
  - $P = w_4[day]$.
  - guard: a forest containing at least 21 trees (and possibly more nodes) whose root is labeled *day*.
  - right $= w_1[\text{Play.com}]$.

3 Static Analysis of TPRS

We assume from now on that an active document is given by a *tree pattern rewriting systems (TPRS)* $(T, \mathcal{R})$, consisting of a set $\mathcal{R}$ of TP rules and a T-labeled tree T. That is, we assume that each service corresponds to a rule. Our results are easily seen to hold in the more general setting where services are regular expressions over $\mathcal{R}$.

A tree T with node set V is *subsumed* by a tree T' with node set V', noted $T \preceq T'$, if there is an injective mapping from V to V' that preserves the labeling, the root, and the parent relation. A forest F is *subsumed* by a forest F', written $F \preceq F'$, if F is mapped injectively into F' such that each tree in F is subsumed by its image in F'. Similarly, a TP P with node set V is *subsumed* by a TP P' with node set V', if there is an injective mapping from V to V' that preserves the labeling, the root, the parent and the ancestor relations.

With a TPRS $(T, \mathcal{R})$ we can associate the (infinite-state) transition system $\langle S(T, \mathcal{R}), \rightarrow \rangle$ with $S(T, \mathcal{R}) = \{T' \mid T \xrightarrow{*} T'\}$. We are interested in checking the following properties:

- Termination: Are all derivation chains $T \rightarrow T_1 \rightarrow T_2 \rightarrow \cdots$ of $(T, \mathcal{R})$ finite?
- Finite-state property: Is the set $S(T, \mathcal{R})$ of reachable trees finite?
- Reachability: Given $(T, \mathcal{R})$ and a tree T', is T' reachable in $(T, \mathcal{R})$?
- Confluence (joinability): For any pair of trees $T_1, T_2 \in S(T, \mathcal{R})$, does there exist some T' such that $T_1 \xrightarrow{*} T'$ and $T_2 \xrightarrow{*} T'$?
- Pattern reachability (coverability): Given $(T, \mathcal{R})$ and a tree pattern P, does $T \xrightarrow{*} T'$ hold for some T' matching P?
- Weak confluence: For any pair of trees $T_1, T_2 \in S(T, \mathcal{R})$, does there exist $T_1' \preceq T_2'$ such that $T_1 \xrightarrow{*} T_1'$ and $T_2 \xrightarrow{*} T_2'$?

Pattern reachability is a key property. For example, we might ask whether an already cancelled order could still be delivered, which would mean a problem in the system. For this, it suffices to tag cancelled orders with a special symbol #, and check for the pattern $w_1[\text{Play.com}](-w_2[\text{delivered}](w_3[\#]))$. This is the same kind of properties which are checked in [3]. As expected, any of the nontrivial questions above is undecidable in the general case, see Theorem 1 below.

We are thus looking for relevant restrictions yielding decidability of at least some of these problems. In the next section we consider a subclass of TPRS, which is a special instance of the so-called *well-structured* systems. We say that $(T, \mathcal{R})$ is *positive* if all guards occurring in the rules from $\mathcal{R}$ are upward-closed. This means that for every guard G, and all forests F, F' with $F \preceq F'$, $F \in G$ implies $F' \in G$, too. In particular, if a rule R in a positive system is enabled for a tree T, then R is enabled for any tree T' that subsumes T. The reason is that for any TPQ query, we have that for every tree T_1' in query(T'), there is some tree T_1 in query(T) such that T_1 is subsumed by T_1'. Notice that positive TPRS allow deletion of nodes, so they are more powerful than the positive AXML systems considered in [2].

The next theorem shows that upward-closed guards alone do not suffice for obtaining decidability of termination:

Theorem 1. *Any two-counter machine M can be simulated by a positive TPRS $(T, \mathcal{R})$ in such a way that M terminates iff $(T, \mathcal{R})$ terminates.*

Theorem 1 shows that any non trivial property is undecidable for positive TPRS without further restrictions. However, notice that the proof of the above result needs trees of unbounded depth. A realistic restriction in the XML setting is to consider only trees of bounded depth: XML documents are usually large, but shallow. A TPRS $(T, \mathcal{R})$ is called *depth-bounded*, if there exists some fixed integer K such that every tree T' with $T \xrightarrow{*} T'$ has depth at most K. Of course, Theorem 1 implies that it is undecidable to know whether a TPRS is depth-bounded. However, in many real-life examples this property is easily seen to hold (see *e.g.* the Play.com example, which has depth at most 8).

4   Decidability for Positive and Depth-Bounded TPRS

For positive and depth-bounded TPRS, we can apply well-known techniques from the verification of infinite-state systems that are *well-structured*. Well-structured transition systems were considered independently in [1,8] and they cover many interesting models, such as Petri nets or lossy channel systems. We recall first some basics of well-structured systems.

Definition 5. *A well-quasi-ordering (wqo) on a set X is a quasi-ordering (that is, a reflexive and transitive binary relation) $\preceq$, such that in every infinite sequence $(x_n)_{n \geq 0} \subseteq X$, there exist some indices $i < j$ with $x_i \preceq x_j$.*

In general, the "subsumed" relation $\preceq$ on the set X of $\mathcal{T}$-labeled trees is not a wqo.[1] However, using Higman's lemma (see, *e.g.*, [6, Chap. 12]), one can show that $\preceq$ is a wqo on the set of trees of depth at most K (for any fixed K):

Proposition 1. *Fix $K \in \mathbb{N}$, and let X_K denote the set of unordered $\mathcal{T}$-labeled trees of depth at most K. The "subsumed" relation $\preceq \subseteq X_K \times X_K$ is a wqo.*

By the previous statement, a positive and depth-bounded TPRS $(T, \mathcal{R})$ yields a well-structured transition system $\langle S(T, \mathcal{R}), \rightarrow \rangle$ as defined in [8] (see also[2] [1]). This follows from the transition relation $\rightarrow$ being *upward compatible*: whenever $T \xrightarrow{R} T'$ and $T \preceq T_1$, there exists T_1' with $T_1 \xrightarrow{R} T_1'$ and $T' \preceq T_1'$.

For the next theorem we need first some notation. Given a set X and a preorder $\preceq$, we denote by $\uparrow X$ the upward closure $\{T' \mid T \preceq T'$ for some $T \in X\}$ of X. By $\min(X)$ we denote the set of minimal elements[3] of X. Finally, by

---

[1] Indeed consider the sequence of trees $(T_n)_{n \geq 0}$ where for each $n \geq 0$, T_n is the tree formed by a single branch of length $n + 1$ whose internal nodes are labeled by a and the unique leaf is labeled by b.

[2] As shown in the proof of Theorem 2, $\langle S(T, \mathcal{R}), \rightarrow \rangle$ is also well-structured as defined in [1], which requires in addition that the set of predecessors of upward-closed sets is effectively computable.

[3] For a wqo $(X, \preceq)$ and $Y \subseteq X$, the set $\min(Y)/\sim$ is finite, where $\sim = \preceq \cap \preceq^{-1}$. For the subsumed relation $\preceq$, note that $\sim$ is the identity.

Pred(X) we denote the set of immediate predecessors of elements of X. Note that whenever the transition relation $\rightarrow$ is upward compatible and X upward-closed, the set Pred(X) is upward-closed, too.

Since the subsumed relation $\preceq$ is a wqo, the $\preceq$ relation on forests is a wqo as well. Thus, each guard G in a positive, depth-bounded TPRS $(T, \mathcal{R})$ can be described by the (finite) set of forests min(G). Define the size $|G|$ of G as the maximal size of a forest in min(G).

Theorem 2. *Termination and pattern reachability are both decidable for positive and depth-bounded TPRS.*

Proof. First, termination is decidable for well-structured systems such that 1) $\preceq$ is decidable, 2) $\rightarrow$ is computable and 3) upward compatible, see [8, Thm. 4.6].

For pattern reachability, it is easy to see that the set of trees of depth bounded by some K and matching a TP P is upward-closed, and that the set of its minimal elements is effectively computable. We can thus use [1], which shows decidability of the reachability of $\uparrow T$ under the assumption that the set min(Pred($\uparrow T$)) is computable. This makes it possible to use the obvious backward exploration algorithm. So let us fix a tree T and a bound K of the system $(T_0, \mathcal{R})$. We claim that min(Pred($\uparrow T$)) is indeed computable. Fix a rule $R = (\mathsf{left}, \mathsf{query}, \mathsf{guard}, \mathsf{right})$.

Let $\mathcal{S}_R(T)$ be the finite set of all trees T' with $T' \xrightarrow{R} T$, and of size at most $|T| + |\mathsf{left}| + K|\mathsf{query}||\mathsf{guard}|$. We show that min(Pred($\uparrow T$)) $= \min \bigcup_{R \in \mathcal{R}} \mathcal{S}_R(T)$. Since the right member of this equality is clearly computable, this will prove the claim. The inclusion from right to left is obvious. Let then $T_1 \in$ min(Pred($\uparrow T$)). Thus, there exist some rule R and some injective matching (f, t) with $T_1 \xrightarrow{R} T$ via (f, t). Let also $F \in \min(\mathsf{guard})$ be a forest with $F \preceq F'$, where F' is the result of query on T_1 (consistent with the matching f).

Let V_l be the nodes of left and V_r be those of right. The nodes of T_1 can then be partitioned into 4 sets: $V_1 = f(V_l \cap V_r)$, $V_2 = \mathsf{node}^{-1}(V_1)$, $V_1' = f(V_l \setminus V_r)$, $V_2' = \mathsf{node}^{-1}(V_1')$. By Def. 4, T shares with T_1 the nodes of both V_1 and V_2, hence $|T_1| \leq |T| + |V_1'| + |V_2'|$. Now, $|V_1'| \leq |\mathsf{left}|$. We now explain that V_2' has at most $|\mathsf{query}||\mathsf{guard}|$ leaves, hence $|V_2'| \leq K|\mathsf{query}||\mathsf{guard}|$ which shows that $T_1 \in \mathcal{S}_R(T)$. Otherwise one can delete a leaf from V_2' and get a tree $T_1' \preceq T_1$ with $T_1' \xrightarrow{R} T$ (via (f, t)), and still $F \preceq F''$, where F'' denotes the result of query on T_1'. This contradicts the minimality of T_1. $\square$

On the negative side, depth-bounded well-structured systems can simulate reset Petri nets (i.e., nets with an additional transition that empties a place), hence we can deduce the following from known results:

Theorem 3. *Exact reachability, confluence, weak confluence and the finite-state property are undecidable for positive and depth-bounded TPRS.*

On the positive side, we can show that the finite-state property is decidable for positive, depth-bounded TPRS, that are *strict*, i.e., such that for any rule (left, query, guard, right), we require $V_l \subseteq V_r$. One cannot encode reset Petri nets with such systems because deletion is no longer possible (actually one can only relabel an existing node and create new nodes). Strict systems enjoy the additional property that whenever $T \xrightarrow{R} T'$ and $T \prec T_1$, there exists T_1' with $T_1 \xrightarrow{R} T_1'$ and $T' \prec T_1'$ (notice that for non strict systems, we can only guarantee that $T' \preceq T_1'$). The results from [8] yield the following theorem.

Theorem 4. *The finite-state property and reachability are decidable for TPRS that are positive, depth-bounded, and strict.*

Note that the finite-state property is not very interesting in itself, but if it holds, then the other problems become decidable as we are dealing with a finite-state system. In particular, in order to test for confluence, it suffices to test that $(S(T, \mathcal{R}), \to)$ has a unique maximal strongly connected component.

Observe that reachability is decidable for positive, depth-bounded and strict TPRS simply because $T \to T'$ implies $|T| \leq |T'|$, so that reachability of a tree T_1 reduces to its reachability in the finite state system $(\{T' \mid |T'| \leq |T_1|\}, \to)$.

The table below sums up the results we obtained so far. It presents (un)decidability results concerning the various classes of positive TPRS we considered (depth-bounded and strict). The negative results about strict TPRS come from Theorem 1 (results on strict TPRS are obtained using slight variations of our proofs). Term., FS, Reach., P-reach, Confl. and W-confl. stand respectively for termination, finite state property, reachability, pattern reachability, confluence and weak confluence.

Model	Term.	FS	Reach.	P-reach.	Confl.	W-confl.
Strict	U	U	U	U	U	U
Depth-Bounded	D	U	U	D	U	U
Depth-Bounded & Strict	D	D	D	D	U	U

5   Lower Bounds and Extensions

Decidability results are obtained with non-constructive proofs coming from Higman's Lemma. This ensures termination of the algorithms, but without yielding complexity bounds. It is thus relevant to obtain lower bounds for these results.

Theorem 5. *The following problems have at least non-elementary complexity:*

– *Input: A TP P, a TPRS system $(S, \mathcal{R})$ and an integer k such that the depth of $(S, \mathcal{R})$ is bounded by k.*
– *Problem1: Is the pattern P reachable in $(S, \mathcal{R})$?*
– *Problem2: Does $(S, \mathcal{R})$ terminate, that is, does it have an infinite path?*

Proof. Let $\mathrm{tower}(0, n) = n$ and $\mathrm{tower}(k + 1, n) = 2^{\mathrm{tower}(k,n)}$. Fix some integer k, and let M be an $n \mapsto \mathrm{tower}(k, n)$-space bounded deterministic Turing machine and x be an input of M. Denote by $\log^* n$ the smallest integer m such that $n \leq \mathrm{tower}(m, 2)$ and let $K = k + \log^* |x|$, so that the computation of M on x uses at most $\mathrm{tower}(k, |x|) \leq \mathrm{tower}(K, 2)$ tape cells. We build a $(K + 1)$-depth bounded TPRS of size $O(|M| + |x|)$ simulating M on x.

Informally, we encode each configuration of M by a tree. Each cell is encoded by a subtree of the root, labeled at its own root by the cell content, with the forest below it encoding the position of the cell. Since such a position is smaller than tower$(K, 2)$, it can itself be encoded recursively by a forest of depth at most K (such a recursive encoding of large integers, by words, has already been used in [15]). For instance, one can encode integers from 0 to $15 = \text{tower}(\mathbf{2}, 2) - 1$ at depth $\mathbf{2}$. The forest of Fig. 6 encodes 13 (**1101** in binary). To recover its position, each bit of the base 2 representation has under itself a forest of depth 1 encoding its position (recursively with the same encoding scheme). For instance, the leftmost **1** is at position 00, which is encoded by the forest $\{[0]([0]), [0]([1])\}$.

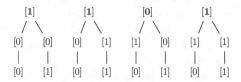

Fig. 6. A level 2 counter encoding 13

Let $N = \text{tower}(K, 2) - 1$. We encode the configuration C of M with tape content $a_0 \cdots a_N$, current state q and scanned position m, by the forest $F_C = [M](\bar{a}_0(F_0^K) \cdots \bar{a}_N(F_N^K))$ of depth $K+1$, with $\bar{a}_m = [a_m, q]$ and $\bar{a}_i = [a_i]$ for $i \neq m$, and where F_i^K is the forest of depth K encoding the number $i \leq N$. The head position is thus doubly tagged: by the letter, and by the state. Such a node with a double tag $[\alpha, \beta]$ is said *marked by* β, or a β-*node*.

In order to navigate through the cells, we use for each level $\ell \leq K$ an additional placeholder node, child of the root, named c_ℓ for holding a level ℓ counter below it. The idea is that the counter attached below c_K will be able to count up to N, and hence can pinpoint a tape position. The other counters c_ℓ are needed in the inductive process. During the computation, additional markers will be used either as pebbles, or to guide the control. Figure 7 shows a typical tree reached during the computation. The rules of the TPRS are set up so that it performs successively the following actions:

1. It creates the forest F_{C_0} corresponding to the initial configuration C_0, and attaches it under the root, leaving c_K labeled by $[c_K, \mathsf{run}]$ and for $\ell < K$, c_ℓ labeled by $[c_\ell, \mathsf{ready}]$.
2. It simulates repeatedly transitions of M, stopping if the final state is reached.

We only show how to encode transitions. The generation of the initial configuration, starting from $[M]([c_0, \mathsf{ready}], \ldots, [c_{K-1}, \mathsf{ready}], [c_K, \mathsf{create\text{-}init\text{-}config}])$, is done using similar routines. We use a finite set of rules without query/guard part. Although the TPRS will be nondeterministic, appropriate tags shall ensure that rules applicable at some step have all the same *left* member. When the TPRS discovers that a nondeterministic guess was wrong, it blocks. Therefore, if M halts on x, then the TPRS always terminate. If M does not halt on x, then the corresponding run of the TPRS where all guesses are correct does not either. This ensures termination iff M halts on x.

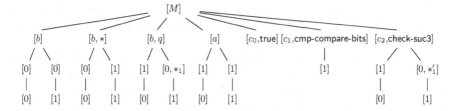

Fig. 7. The tree coding the tape $bbqba$ of the Turing machine M

To simulate a transition, the TPRS first performs the changes in the configuration, nondeterministically guessing the new head position. To check whether the head has been properly placed, it $*$-marks the original head position. The node c_K is marked by tags from a set $\{\mathsf{run}, \mathsf{check\text{-}suc}, \mathsf{check\text{-}pred}, \ldots\}$ to encode the current stage of the simulation. For instance, the simulation of a transition $p \xrightarrow{a/b/\rightarrow} q$ starts the application of one of the rules:

- left $= r[M](x[a,p],\, y[d],\quad z[c_K, \mathsf{run}]),$
- right $= r[M](x[b,*],\, y[d,q],\, z[c_K, \mathsf{check\text{-}suc}]),$ for all d in the tape alphabet.

To complete the simulation of the transition, the TPRS checks whether the position written below the node pinpointed by q is a successor of that below the node pinpointed by $*$. If yes, it deletes the mark $*$, and labels c_K back to $[c_K, \mathsf{run}]$. If not, the head position was incorrectly guessed and the system blocks.

The verification that the nodes marked $*$ and q occur successively has itself several steps. First, we copy under c_K the level K counter located below the $*$-node. Then we increment that copy. Finally we compare the result to the counter below the q-node. We use auxiliary markers $*_\ell$, $*'_\ell$ for each level ℓ, attached to nodes below an ℓ counter: $*_\ell$ in the part of the tree representing the configuration, and $*'_\ell$ under some c_i, $i > \ell$. We define inductively rules to achieve the following tasks for each level $\ell \leq K$:

- copy(ℓ) copies below the $*'_\ell$-marked node the level ℓ counter found below c_ℓ.
- increment(ℓ) increments the level ℓ counter below c_ℓ.
- compare(ℓ) compares level ℓ counters below c_ℓ and below the $*_\ell$-marked node.
- test-max(ℓ) tests if the level ℓ counter below c_ℓ has its maximal value.
- zero(ℓ) generates under c_ℓ the level ℓ counter F_0^ℓ.

Each task of level ℓ is implemented by a sequence of tasks of level $(\ell - 1)$, using some fresh tags to correctly organize the order of these level $(\ell - 1)$ tasks. See [9] for rules and proof details.   □

The bounded depth restriction needed for our decidability results can be relaxed if we forbid the use of the direct parent-child edges in tree patterns. This leads to the following preorder on unranked, unordered $\mathcal{T}$-labeled trees, which is a well quasi-ordering by Kruskal's theorem (see [6, Chap. 12]). For two trees T, T' with sets of nodes V, V' respectively, we write $T \lessdot T'$, if there is an injective mapping from V to V' that preserves the labeling, the root, and the ancestor relation. So compared to the relation $\preceq$ used previously, we do not require that the parent relation is preserved.

Clearly, we need to restrict the TPRS rules in order to obtain well-structured systems. Namely we require that all TP occurring in query and left use only ancestor edges (right can still use parent edges, but the parent relation cannot be tested for). We call such TPRS *undirected*. Using similar proofs as in Sect. 4, we get the same decidability results. For the lower bound we obtain a stronger result, by encoding reachability for lossy channel systems (LCS). These are finite-state machines communicating over FIFO channels that can loose arbitrary many messages. Reachability for LCS has non primitive recursive complexity [14], already for LCSs made up of two finite-state machines and two channels [5].

Theorem 6. *Termination and pattern reachability have at least non primitive recursive complexity for undirected TPRS.*

References

1. Abdulla, P.A., Cerans, K., Jonsson, B., Tsay, Y.-K.: General decidability theorems for infinite-state systems. In: LICS 1996, pp. 313–321. IEEE Comp. Soc, Los Alamitos (1996)
2. Abiteboul, S., Benjelloun, O., Milo, T.: Positive Active XML. In: PODS 2004, pp. 35–45. ACM, New York (2004)
3. Abiteboul, S., Segoufin, L., Vianu, V.: Analysis of Active XML Services. In: PODS 2008. ACM Press, New York (to appear, 2008)
4. Active XML, http://www.activexml.net/
5. Chambart, P., Schnoebelen, P.: The Ordinal Recursive Complexity of Lossy Channel Systems. In: LICS 2008, pp. 205–216. IEEE Comp. Soc., Los Alamitos (2008)
6. R. Diestel. *Graph theory* (2005), http://www.math.uni-hamburg.de/home/diestel
7. Dufourd, C., Finkel, A., Schnoebelen, P.: Reset Nets between Decidability and Undecidability. In: Larsen, K.G., Skyum, S., Winskel, G. (eds.) ICALP 1998. LNCS, vol. 1443, pp. 103–115. Springer, Heidelberg (1998)
8. Finkel, A., Schnoebelen, P.: Well-structured transition systems everywhere. Theor. Comput. Sci. 256(1-2), 63–92 (2001)
9. Genest, B., Muscholl, A., Serre, O., Zeitoun, M.: Tree Pattern Rewrite Systems. Internal report, http://www.crans.org/~genest/GMSZ08.pdf
10. Dershowitz, N., Plaisted, D.: In: Robinson, A., Voronkov, A. (eds.) Handbook of Automated Reasoning, ch. 9, vol. 1. Elsevier, Amsterdam (2001)
11. Libkin, L.: Logics over unranked trees: an overview. Logical Methods in Computer Science 2(3) (2006)
12. Löding, C., Spelten, A.: Transition Graphs of Rewriting Systems over Unranked Trees. In: Kučera, L., Kučera, A. (eds.) MFCS 2007. LNCS, vol. 4708, pp. 67–77. Springer, Heidelberg (2007)
13. Neven, F.: Automata, Logic, and XML. In: Bradfield, J.C. (ed.) CSL 2002 and EACSL 2002. LNCS, vol. 2471, pp. 2–26. Springer, Heidelberg (2002)
14. Schnoebelen, P.: Verifying Lossy Channel Systems has Nonprimitive Recursive Complexity. Inf. Process. Lett. 83(5), 251–261 (2002)
15. Walukiewicz, I.: Difficult Configurations—on the Complexity of LTrL. ICALP 1998 26(1), 27–43 (2005); In: Larsen, K.G., Skyum, S., Winskel, G. (eds.) ICALP 1998. LNCS, vol. 1443, pp. 27–43. Springer, Heidelberg (1998)

Deciding Bisimilarity of Full BPA
Processes Locally[*]

Lingyun Luo[1,2]

[1] Laboratory of Computer Science, Institute of Software, Chinese Academy of
Sciences, P.O.Box 8718, Beijing, China, 100190
[2] Graduate School of the Chinese Academy of Sciences
luoly@ios.ac.cn

Abstract. We propose a tableau algorithm to decide bisimilarity of
guarded normed and unnormed BPA processes, which is very intuitive
and direct. It also has the advantage of helping us to show that the equational theory proposed by Hüttel and Stirling for normed BPA systems
is also complete for arbitrary guarded BPA systems. As a result, the first
equational theory for full BPA processes is found.

1 Introduction

It has been well established that strong bisimilarity is not only decidable for
normed BPA processes[1,3,5,8], but also decidable for full BPA processes[4].
Consequently, many deciding algorithms have been brought out. In [8,9], Hans
Hüttel and Colin Stirling proved the decidability result of normed BPA by using
a tableau decision method. Furthermore, a fast algorithm was proposed in [7] and
later a polynomial algorithm for this problem was given in [6]. As for arbitrary
context-free processes corresponding to full BPA, [4] proved that bisimulation
equivalence is decidable and suggested an algorithm based on two semi-decision
procedures. Finally in [2], along the same lines of [6], Burkart, Caucal, and
Steffen introduced an elementary decision procedure to solve this problem. All
these results are recorded by J.Srba[13], and he keeps an updated online version
too. In the paper [12], Srba also showed that strong bisimilarity checking on full
BPA is PSPACE-hard.

The decision procedure comprises three steps in [2], just as that in [6]. At first,
an initial bisimulation-complete base is computed. Then it is refined by fixpoint
iteration, generating a bisimulation base, with the help of which a branching
algorithm can be run to decide the bisimilarity of any given processes. To ensure
the finiteness of the initial base, the existence of a separability bound must be
guaranteed, which is the key point throughout the whole procedure in [2]. Actually, we can view these algorithms in [2] and [6] as global, for the bisimulation
bases capture all the essential parts of the greatest bisimilarity $\sim$. As a contrary,
the tableau method in [8,9] provides a local algorithm since it is goal-directed
and only generates necessary bisimilar pairs specific to the relevant given pair.

---

[*] Supported by Chinese NSF grant 60496320.

Cha et al. (Eds.): ATVA 2008, LNCS 5311, pp. 347–360, 2008.
© Springer-Verlag Berlin Heidelberg 2008

Under the help of the tableau technique, Hans Hüttel and Colin Stirling also provided an equational theory for the bisimulation equivalence of normed BPA processes given in 3-GNF([8,9]).

Based on the idea in [2], we give a tableau method to decide bisimulation equivalence for full BPA processes, providing a counterpart of that in [8,9] for normed BPA processes. We prove that the depth of every tableau is bounded by a number involved with the *seminorm* of the root. That means, we do not have a general bound but only have a local bound for the specific pair to be decided. However, this is sufficient to guarantee the termination of our local algorithm. Not only does this tableau method give us a direct and intuitive algorithm, it also helps us to show that the equational theory in [8,9] is also complete for both normed and unnormed BPA processes. As there has not been any equational theory for full BPA processes so far, this result is interesting.

The rest of this paper is organized as follows: Section 2 gives some preliminaries on BPA processes and bisimulation relations. In Section 3 we describe the tableau method for deciding bisimulation equivalence relation of context-free languages, and provide proofs for its termination, soundness and completeness. In Section 4, we prove the completeness of the equational theory given by Hüttel and Stirling. Finally, a conclusion is made in Section 5.

2   Preliminaries

2.1   BPA Processes and Bisimulation

Let $\mathcal{V}$ be a set of variables, Act a set of actions, the set of BPA expressions are given by the following syntax:

$$E ::= a | X | E_1 + E_2 | E_1 \cdot E_2$$

such that a is an atomic action ranging over Act and X over $\mathcal{V}$. The operator $+$ is interpreted as nondeterministic choice while $\cdot$ is sequential. We usually omit the $\cdot$.

A BPA process is defined by a finite system of recursive process equations

$$\Delta = \{X_i \stackrel{def}{=} E_i | 1 \leq i \leq n\}$$

where the X_i are distinct and the E_i are BPA expressions, and free variables in each E_i range over set $\{X_1, \ldots, X_n\}$. In this paper, we concentrate on guarded BPA systems.

Definition 1. *A BPA expression is guarded if every variable X occurs within the scope of an atomic action, and a BPA system is guarded if each E_i is guarded for $1 \leq i \leq n$.*

We use $X, Y, \ldots$ to range over variables in $\mathcal{V}$ and Greek letters $\alpha, \beta, \ldots$ to range over elements in $\mathcal{V}^*$. The empty process is denoted by ϵ and for any α, $\epsilon\alpha = \alpha\epsilon = \alpha$.

It was shown in [1] that any guarded system can be effectively transformed into a 3-GNF normal form

$$\Delta = \{X_i \stackrel{def}{=} \Sigma_{j=1}^{m_i} a_{ij}\alpha_{ij} | 1 \leq i \leq n\},$$

where for all i, j such that $1 \leq i \leq n$, $1 \leq j \leq m_i$, $|\alpha_{ij}| < 3$. So we only consider BPA processes given in 3-GNF in this paper.

Example 1. Consider the system $\Delta = \{A \stackrel{def}{=} aD + a, B \stackrel{def}{=} aD, C \stackrel{def}{=} bC, D \stackrel{def}{=} b\}$, then Δ is in 3-GNF normal form.

Definition 2. *The operational semantics of a guarded BPA system can be described by a labelled transition system $(\mathcal{V}^*, Act, \rightarrow)$ where the transition relation $\rightarrow$ is generated by the rules in Table 1.*

Table 1. Transition rules

$$a \stackrel{a}{\rightarrow} \epsilon, a \in Act \qquad \frac{E \stackrel{a}{\rightarrow} E'}{X \stackrel{a}{\rightarrow} E'} \, X \stackrel{def}{=} E \in \Delta$$

$$\frac{E \stackrel{a}{\rightarrow} E'}{E + F \stackrel{a}{\rightarrow} E'} \qquad \frac{F \stackrel{a}{\rightarrow} F'}{E + F \stackrel{a}{\rightarrow} F'}$$

$$\frac{E \stackrel{a}{\rightarrow} E'}{EF \stackrel{a}{\rightarrow} E'F}$$

For guarded BPA systems, it can be easily seen that the corresponding transition graph is finite-branching, so it is also image-finite.

Definition 3 ([11]). *A binary relation $R \subseteq \mathcal{V}^* \times \mathcal{V}^*$ is a bisimulation if whenever $(\alpha, \beta) \in R$ then for each $a \in Act$,*

$$- \; \alpha \stackrel{a}{\longrightarrow} \alpha' \Rightarrow \exists\beta'.\beta \stackrel{a}{\longrightarrow} \beta' \text{ and } (\alpha', \beta') \in R.$$
$$- \; \beta \stackrel{a}{\longrightarrow} \beta' \Rightarrow \exists\alpha'.\alpha \stackrel{a}{\longrightarrow} \alpha' \text{ and } (\alpha', \beta') \in R.$$

Two processes α and β are said to be bisimulation equivalent, written as $\alpha \sim \beta$, if there is a bisimulation relation R such that $(\alpha, \beta) \in R$.

Definition 4. *A match for (α, β) is a set M s.t. for all $a \in Act$,*

$$- \; \alpha \stackrel{a}{\longrightarrow} \alpha' \Rightarrow \exists\beta'.\beta \stackrel{a}{\longrightarrow} \beta' \text{ and } (\alpha', \beta') \in M.$$
$$- \; \beta \stackrel{a}{\longrightarrow} \beta' \Rightarrow \exists\alpha'.\alpha \stackrel{a}{\longrightarrow} \alpha' \text{ and } (\alpha', \beta') \in M.$$
$$- \; (\alpha', \beta') \in M \Rightarrow \exists a \in Act \text{ s.t. } \alpha \stackrel{a}{\longrightarrow} \alpha' \& \beta \stackrel{a}{\longrightarrow} \beta'.$$

Since the transition graphs for α and β are finite-branching, there can only be finitely many matches for $\alpha = \beta$ and every match will be finite.

In [3], Caucal introduced the notion of self-bisimulation and showed that all pairs in a self-bisimulation are bisimulation equivalent.

Definition 5. *For any binary relation R on V^*, we denote the least precongruence w.r.t. sequential composition containing R by $\overrightarrow{R}$, the symmetric closure of $\overrightarrow{R}$ by $\overleftrightarrow{R}$, and the reflexive and transitive closure of $\overleftrightarrow{R}$ by $\overleftrightarrow{R}^*$.*

Definition 6. *A relation $B \subseteq V^* \times V^*$ is a self-bisimulation if $(\alpha, \beta) \in B$ implies that for each $a \in Act$*

- $\alpha \xrightarrow{a} \alpha' \Rightarrow \exists \beta'.\beta \xrightarrow{a} \beta'$ and $(\alpha', \beta') \in \overleftrightarrow{B}^*$.
- $\beta \xrightarrow{a} \beta' \Rightarrow \exists \alpha'.\alpha \xrightarrow{a} \alpha'$ and $(\alpha', \beta') \in \overleftrightarrow{B}^*$.

Lemma 1 ([3]). *If B is a self-bisimulation then $\overleftrightarrow{B}^* \subseteq \sim$.*

2.2   Norm, Decomposition and Seperability

The norm of a process α, written as $\|\alpha\|$, is the length of the shortest $\omega \in Act^+$ such that $\alpha \xrightarrow{\omega} \epsilon$. It is assumed that $\|\epsilon\| = 0$. If $\|\alpha\| < \infty$, we said α is *normed*, otherwise($\|\alpha\| = \infty$), α is said to be *unnormed*. The length of any action sequence ω is denoted by $|\omega|$. As a result, the set V can be divided into two disjoint sets $V_N = \{X \in V | X \text{ is normed }\}$ and $V_\infty = \{X \in V | X \text{ is unnormed }\}$.

After the division of normed and unnormed processes, it is not difficult to see that:

$$\text{If } X \in V_\infty, \text{ then } \alpha X \beta \sim \alpha X.$$

So in the remainder of this paper, it is reasonable to restrict our attention to processes in $V_N^* V_\infty \cup V_N^*$.

On the basis of norm, *seminorm* is also defined, which is always finite.

Definition 7. *The seminorm of every α , denoted by $\|.\|_s$, is defined as follows:*

$$\|\alpha X\|_s = \begin{cases} \|\alpha X\| & if \ X \in V_N \\ \|\alpha\| & otherwise \end{cases}$$

Moreover, we define a partial order on $(V_N^* V_\infty \cup V_N^*) \times (V_N^* V_\infty \cup V_N^*)$ as $\sqsubset$ given by $(\alpha_1, \alpha_2) \sqsubset (\beta_1, \beta_2)$ if $max\{\|\alpha_1\|_s, \|\alpha_2\|_s\} < max\{\|\beta_1\|_s, \|\beta_2\|_s\}$.

For the system in Example 1, $\|AC\|_s = \|A\| = 1$, $\|BC\|_s = \|B\| = 1$.

Definition 8. *$X\alpha \sim Y\beta$ is decomposable if $X, Y \in V_N$ and there is a γ such that*

- $X\gamma \sim Y$ and $\alpha \sim \gamma \beta$ if $\|X\| \leq \|Y\|$.
- $X \sim Y\gamma$ and $\gamma\alpha \sim \beta$ if $\|Y\| < \|X\|$.

In the case of normed processes, any bisimilar pair $X\alpha \sim Y\beta$ is decomposable.

Another definition of $\sim$ is via a sequence of approximations.

Definition 9. *The sequence of bisimulation approximations $\{\sim_n\}_{n=0}^{\infty}$ is defined inductively as follows.*

1. $\alpha \sim_0 \beta$ for all processes α and β,
2. $\alpha \sim_{n+1} \beta$ if for each $a \in Act$
   - $\alpha \xrightarrow{a} \alpha' \Rightarrow \exists \beta'.\beta \xrightarrow{a} \beta'$ and $\alpha' \sim_n \beta'$.
   - $\beta \xrightarrow{a} \beta' \Rightarrow \exists \alpha'.\alpha \xrightarrow{a} \alpha'$ and $\alpha' \sim_n \beta'$.

For any family Δ of guarded BPA processes, $\sim = \bigcap_{n=0}^{\infty} \sim_n$ since it is image-finite. It can also be checked that for any n, $\sim_n$ is an equivalence relation, moreover it is a congruence relation w.r.t. the sequential operator·.

Based on the above definition, if $\alpha \not\sim \beta$ there must exist some m s.t. $\alpha \not\sim_m \beta$. We define the minimal such m as separability.

Definition 10. *We define the separability of α and β as:*

$$Sep(\alpha, \beta) = max\{\alpha \sim_n \beta\} + 1.$$

If $Sep(\alpha, \beta) = m < \infty$, then α and β are called m-separable. Obviously, for all $\alpha \not\sim \beta$, $Sep(\alpha, \beta) > 0$. Moreover, if $Sep(\alpha, \beta) = \infty$ then $\alpha \sim \beta$.
For example, $Sep(A, B) = 3$ in the system defined in Example 1.

Lemma 2. *When $\alpha \not\sim_1 \beta$ and $\alpha\gamma \sim \beta\gamma$, then $\alpha = \epsilon$ or $\beta = \epsilon$.*

3 The Tableau Method

3.1 Expanding BPA System

To guarantee the termination of the tableau algorithm, some essential preparations must be made beforehand.

Definition 11. *Suppose that X is normed and Y is unnormed, define the distance of X, Y, denoted as $d_{X,Y}$:*

$$d_{X,Y} = max\{\|\gamma\|_s | X \xrightarrow{\omega} \epsilon, Y \xrightarrow{\omega} \gamma \text{ and } \|X\| = |\omega|\}.$$

Because the system is finite-branching and the norm of X is bounded, the number of the γ is bounded. So $d_{X,Y}$ is well defined.

Lemma 3. *All of the sets below are finite:*

- $U_1 = \{(X,Y) | X, Y \in \mathcal{V}\}$.
- $U_2 = \{(X\gamma, Y) | X\gamma, Y \in \mathcal{V_N}^*, Y \xrightarrow{\omega} \gamma \text{ such that } \|X\| = |\omega|\}$.
- $U_3 = \{(X\alpha, Y) | X \in \mathcal{V_N}, \alpha, Y \in \mathcal{V_N}^*\mathcal{V_\infty}, \|\alpha\|_s \leq d_{X,Y}\}$.

Proof. Since the number of variables in a BPA system is finite, it is easy to see that U_1 is finite; U_2 is also finite for the norm of every normed variable is bounded by the maximal one; U_3 is finite because the number of the α such that $\|\alpha\|_s \leq d_{X,Y}$ is bounded. □

Let $\mathbb{S} = max\{Sep(X\gamma, Y) \mid X\gamma \not\sim Y \text{ and } (X\gamma, Y) \in U_2\}$ and $\mathbb{N} = max\{\|\alpha\| \mid \exists \beta.s.t.(\alpha, \beta) \in U_2\}$. Because of the remarkable result shown in [2, Theorem 3.12] that when $\alpha \not\sim \beta$ and α, β are normed, then $Sep(\alpha, \beta)$ is bounded, this $\mathbb{S}$ we defined here can be calculated effectively. Define $\mathcal{S}$ as $\mathcal{S} = max(\mathbb{S}, \mathbb{N})$.

Definition 12. *When* $||X|| \leq ||Y|| < \infty$ *and the following conditions hold:*

- $X \xrightarrow{\omega} \epsilon$, $Y \xrightarrow{\omega} \gamma$ *such that* $||X|| = |\omega|$.
- $X\gamma \xrightarrow{\omega'} \epsilon$, $Y \xrightarrow{\omega'} \eta \neq \epsilon$ *or* $Y \xrightarrow{\omega'} \epsilon$, $X\gamma \xrightarrow{\omega'} \eta \neq \epsilon$ *such that* $|\omega'| \leq \mathcal{S}$.
- $Z_1 \overset{\Delta}{=} \eta Z_1$ *and* $Z_2 \overset{\Delta}{=} \gamma Z_1$ *where* Z_1, Z_2 *are fresh variables.*

After changing $Z_1 \overset{\Delta}{=} \eta Z_1$ and $Z_2 \overset{\Delta}{=} \gamma Z_1$ to 3-GNF form, we said that (Z_1, Z_2) is a generated pair of X, Y.

Because the number of the γ and the η is bounded, X, Y can only have finite generated pairs. Let $U_4 = \{(XZ_2, YZ_1)|(Z_1, Z_2)$ is a generated pair for (X, Y) such that $||X|| \leq ||Y|| < \infty\}$. U_4 must be finite.

The reason to add generated pairs will be explained in the proof for completeness. Note that adding new unnormed variables Z_1, Z_2 to $\mathcal{V}_\infty$ will not change the bisimulation relation of any old processes. As a result, we can add all fresh variables in those generated pairs to $\mathcal{V}_\infty$ and let $\mathcal{V}'$ be the resulting variable set. Note that $\mathcal{V}_\mathcal{N}$ remains unchanged. Besides, let Δ' be the new BPA system expanded by added equations like $Z_1 \overset{\Delta}{=} \eta Z_1$ and $Z_2 \overset{\Delta}{=} \gamma Z_1$. It is sufficient to check bisimulation relations on the new expanded system Δ'. As a result, in the next sections, we'll deal with the revised system Δ' but still use Δ to denote it.

Example 2. For the system Δ defined before, $||A|| < ||B|| < \infty$, and we have

- $A \xrightarrow{a} \epsilon$, $B \xrightarrow{a} D$.
- $B \xrightarrow{ab} \epsilon$, $AD \xrightarrow{ab} D \neq \epsilon$ such that $|ab| \leq 2$.

Let $Z_1 \overset{\Delta}{=} DZ_1$ and $Z_2 \overset{\Delta}{=} DZ_1$. We change the new definitions to 3-GNF form and get $Z_1 \overset{\Delta}{=} bZ_1, Z_2 \overset{\Delta}{=} bZ_1$. Then (Z_1, Z_2) is a generated pair for A and B. The new expanded system is $\Delta' = \{A \overset{def}{=} aD + a, B \overset{def}{=} aD, C \overset{def}{=} bC, D \overset{def}{=} b, Z_1 \overset{\Delta}{=} bZ_1, Z_2 \overset{\Delta}{=} bZ_1\}$

Again define the following sets on $\mathcal{V}'$ as follows:

- $U_1' = \{(X, Y)|X, Y \in \mathcal{V}'\}$.
- $U_2' = \{(X\gamma, Y)|X\gamma, Y \in \mathcal{V}_\mathcal{N}^*, Y \xrightarrow{\omega} \gamma$ such that $||X|| = |\omega|\}$.
- $U_3' = \{(X\alpha, Y)|X \in \mathcal{V}_\mathcal{N}, \alpha, Y \in \mathcal{V}_\mathcal{N}^* \mathcal{V}_\infty'$ and $||\alpha||_s \leq d_{X,Y}\}$.

It is not hard to see that $U_1 \subseteq U_1'$, $U_3 \subseteq U_3'$ and $U_2 = U_2'$. Define $U = U_1' \cup U_2' \cup U_3' \cup U_4$. Actually, this set U is the initial base constructed in [2].

3.2   The Tableau Rules

In [8,9], Hans Hüttel and Colin Stirling gave a tableau method to decide bisimilarity of normed BPA. In the following, we'll introduce a counterpart of it: A tableau system for all normed and unnormed BPA systems. The tableau method involves goal-directed rules, which means that the prefix of a rule is the goal to be achieved while the consequents are the subgoals. Those decision rules for our system are shown in Table 2. In the remainder, if we say a DSUB rule, we mean DSUBL or DSUBR. Similarly for ESUB and DEDUCE. A SUB rule stands for a DSUB or an ESUB.

The corresponding side conditions of the tableau rules in Table 2 are listed as follows:

1. X, Y normed and $\alpha, \beta \neq \epsilon$, $\|X\| \leq \|Y\|$, and $\exists \omega. X \xrightarrow{\omega} \epsilon, Y \xrightarrow{\omega} \gamma . s.t. |\omega| = \|X\|$ and $\|X\gamma\| = \|Y\|$.
2. X, Y normed and $\alpha, \beta \neq \epsilon$, $\|X\| > \|Y\|$, and $\exists \omega. Y \xrightarrow{\omega} \epsilon, X \xrightarrow{\omega} \gamma . s.t. |\omega| = \|Y\|$ and $\|X\| = \|Y\gamma\|$.
3. X, Y normed, α, β unnormed and $\|X\| \leq \|Y\|$, (Z_1, Z_2) is a generated pair for (X, Y).
4. X, Y normed, α, β unnormed and $\|X\| > \|Y\|$, (Z_1, Z_2) is a generated pair for (Y, X).
5. X normed, Y unnormed, $\|\alpha\|_s > d_{X,Y}$ and $\exists \omega. X \xrightarrow{\omega} \epsilon. Y \xrightarrow{\omega} \gamma . s.t. |\omega| = \|X\|$.
6. Y normed, X unnormed, $\|\beta\|_s > d_{Y,X}$ and $\exists \omega. Y \xrightarrow{\omega} \epsilon. X \xrightarrow{\omega} \gamma . s.t. |\omega| = \|Y\|$.
7. $(X\alpha, Y\beta) \in U \cup U^{-1}$, $\{(\alpha_i, \beta_i)\}_{i=0}^k$ is a finite match of $(X\alpha, Y\beta)$.

From those rules we can see that for $\alpha = \beta$, at most one rule can be applied except for the condition when $\alpha \equiv X\alpha'$, $\beta \equiv Y\beta'$, X, Y normed, and $\|\alpha'\| = \|\beta'\| = \infty$. In that case, both ESUB and DSUB are applicable. However, this will not be a problem. It is like adding a finite number of choices to generate children for $\alpha = \beta$, among which one will be successful if $\alpha \sim \beta$.

A tableau is successful if every leaf of it is a successful terminal, while a successful terminal has one of the following forms:

1. $\alpha = \alpha$;
2. $\alpha = \beta$ with $\alpha = \beta$ or $\beta = \alpha$ above it in the tableau, which is an UNFOLD node.

We also give the termination conditions for the unsuccessful leaves. An unsuccessful terminal $\alpha = \beta$ satisfies one of the conditions below:

1. $\|\alpha\| \neq \|\beta\|$;
2. no rule can be applied but not successful.

Example 3. A successful tableau for $AC = BC$ is as follows:

3.3   Termination, Soundness, and Completeness

Lemma 4. *The depth of any tableau rooted with $\alpha = \beta$ is bounded.*

Proof. As we know, along any path in a tableau, the number of UNFOLD nodes is bounded by $|U \cup U^{-1}|$. Define SN as $SN = max\{\|\alpha\|_s | \exists \beta. \alpha = \beta \text{ or } \beta = \alpha \text{ is the child of an UNFOLD node}\}$. Next we show that the number of non-UNFOLD nodes between any two successive UNFOLD nodes is bounded by SN.

It is sufficient to prove that any non-UNFOLD sequence is seminorm decreasing.

Table 2. Decision rules for BPA processes

$$\text{DSUBL} \qquad \frac{X\alpha = Y\beta}{X\gamma = Y \ \alpha = \gamma\beta} \qquad (1)$$

$$\text{DSUBR} \qquad \frac{X\alpha = Y\beta}{X = Y\gamma \ \gamma\alpha = \beta} \qquad (2)$$

$$\text{ESUBL} \qquad \frac{X\alpha = Y\beta}{XZ_2 = YZ_1 \ \alpha = Z_2 \ \beta = Z_1} \qquad (3)$$

$$\text{ESUBR} \qquad \frac{X\alpha = Y\beta}{XZ_1 = YZ_2 \ \alpha = Z_1 \ \beta = Z_2} \qquad (4)$$

$$\text{DEDUCEL} \qquad \frac{X\alpha = Y}{X\gamma = Y \ \alpha = \gamma} \qquad (5)$$

$$\text{DEDUCER} \qquad \frac{X = Y\beta}{X = Y\gamma \ \gamma = \beta} \qquad (6)$$

$$\text{UNFOLD} \qquad \frac{X\alpha = Y\beta}{\{\alpha_i = \beta_i\}_{i=0}^k} \qquad (7)$$

Table 3. A successful tableau

$$\cfrac{\text{AC=BC}}{\cfrac{AZ_2 = BZ_1}{\cfrac{Z_2 = DZ_1}{Z_1 = Z_1}(7) \quad \cfrac{DZ_2 = DZ_1}{D = D \ \cfrac{Z_2 = Z_1}{Z_1 = Z_1}(7)}(1)}(7) \quad \cfrac{C = Z_2}{C = Z_1}(7) \quad \cfrac{C = Z_1}{C = Z_1}(7)}(3)$$

– DSUB rule:

$$\frac{X\alpha' = Y\beta'}{X\gamma = Y \ \alpha' = \gamma\beta'}$$ Assume w.l.o.g. that DSUBL is used. $X\gamma = Y$ will be an UNFOLD node. Since $\|X\gamma\| = \|Y\|$, $\|\gamma\beta'\|_s < \|X\gamma\beta'\|_s = \|Y\beta'\|_s$, $\|\alpha'\|_s < \|X\alpha'\|_s$, $(\alpha', \gamma\beta') \sqsubset (X\alpha', Y\beta')$ holds.

– ESUB rule:

$$\frac{X\alpha' = Y\beta'}{XZ_2 = YZ_1 \ \alpha' = Z_2 \ \beta' = Z_1}$$ Assume ESUBL is used, $XZ_2 = YZ_1$ will be an UNFOLD node. Since $\|Z_1\|_s = \|Z_2\|_s = 0$, $(\alpha', Z_2) \sqsubset (X\alpha', Y\beta')$, $(\beta', Z_1) \sqsubset (X\alpha', Y\beta')$.

– DEDUCE rule:

$$\frac{X\alpha' = Y}{X\gamma = Y \ \alpha' = \gamma}$$ Assume DEDUCEL is used. $X\gamma = Y$ will be an UNFOLD node. Since $\|\alpha'\|_s > d_{X,Y} \geq \|\gamma\|_s$, $(\alpha', \gamma) \sqsubset (X\alpha', Y)$.

As a result, the depth is bounded by $|U \cup U^{-1}| \times max\{SN, \|\alpha\|_s, \|\beta\|_s\}$. $\qquad \square$

This theorem guarantees that once the root $\alpha = \beta$ is determined, the tableau depth is bounded. This bound is specific to the seminorm of the root. However, We can't get a bound for all the pairs. For example, let $A \stackrel{\Delta}{=} aA$, for any natural number n, the tableau for $a^n A = A$ will have depth n, which is not bounded. Fortunately, for this local tableau method, a bound specific to the root is sufficient.

Proposition 1

- Every tableau for $\alpha = \beta$ is finite.
- The number of tableaux for $\alpha = \beta$ is finite.

Proof. In a tableau, each node has only a finite number of children. So if there was an infinite tableau, then according to König's lemma, it would have an infinite path, which contradicts lemma 4. The latter part is guaranteed by the two facts that the depth is bounded and there are finitely many choices at each step. □

Proposition 2. If $\alpha = \beta$ has a successful tableau T, then $\alpha \sim \beta$.

Proof. Let $S = \{(\alpha, \beta) | \alpha = \beta$ is a node in the tableau $T\}$. It is easy to show that S is a self-bisimulation. □

Proposition 3. If $\alpha \sim \beta$, then it will have a successful tableau.

Proof. We build a tree for $\alpha = \beta$ in such a way that for each node labelled with $\alpha' = \beta'$ we have $\alpha' \sim \beta'$.

1. $\alpha \equiv \beta \equiv \epsilon$. then the root is a single leaf.
2. $\alpha \equiv X\alpha'$ and $\beta \equiv Y\beta'$, X, Y normed and $\alpha', \beta' \neq \epsilon$. $X\alpha' \sim Y\beta'$ is decomposable. Suppose w.l.o.g. that $\|X\| \leq \|Y\|$, then $\exists \gamma'.X\gamma' \sim Y$ and $\alpha' \sim \gamma'\beta'$. Let $|\omega| = \|X\|$, $X \stackrel{\omega}{\longrightarrow} \epsilon$, so $X\gamma' \stackrel{\omega}{\longrightarrow} \gamma'$, then $\exists \gamma.Y \stackrel{\omega}{\longrightarrow} \gamma$ and $\gamma' \sim \gamma$ since $X\gamma' \sim Y$. So here $\exists \omega.X \stackrel{\omega}{\longrightarrow} \epsilon, Y \stackrel{\omega}{\longrightarrow} \gamma, X\gamma \sim Y$ and $\alpha' \sim \gamma\beta'$.
3. $\alpha \equiv X\alpha'$ and $\beta \equiv Y\beta'$, X, Y normed and $\alpha', \beta' \neq \epsilon$. $X\alpha' \sim Y\beta'$ is not decomposable. Suppose $\|X\| \leq \|Y\|$, since $X\alpha' \sim Y\beta'$, then $\exists \gamma.X \stackrel{\omega}{\longrightarrow} \epsilon$, $Y \stackrel{\omega}{\longrightarrow} \gamma$ such that $|\omega| = \|X\|$, $\alpha' \sim \gamma\beta'$ and $X\gamma\beta' \sim Y\beta'$. So $X\gamma \not\sim Y$.

$$
\begin{array}{cc}
X\gamma \not\sim_m Y & \qquad X\gamma\beta' \sim Y\beta' \\
a_1 \downarrow \quad \downarrow a_1 & \qquad \downarrow \quad \downarrow \\
\delta_1 \not\sim_{m-1} \eta_1 & \qquad \delta_1\beta' \sim \eta_1\beta' \\
\vdots \quad \vdots & \qquad \vdots \quad \vdots \\
a_{m-1} \downarrow \quad \downarrow a_{m-1} & \\
\delta_{m-1} \not\sim_1 \eta_{m-1} & \quad \delta_{m-1}\beta' \sim \eta_{m-1}\beta'
\end{array}
$$

Let $Sep(X\gamma, Y) = m$, there must exist a sequence $\delta_i \not\sim_{m-i} \eta_i$ and $\delta_i\beta' \sim \eta_i\beta'$ ($1 \leq i \leq m - 1$) such that $X\gamma \stackrel{a_1}{\longrightarrow} \delta_1, Y \stackrel{a_1}{\longrightarrow} \eta_1$ and $\delta_i \stackrel{a_{i+1}}{\longrightarrow} \delta_{i+1}, \eta_i \stackrel{a_{i+1}}{\longrightarrow} \eta_{i+1}$ for $1 \leq i \leq m - 1$. As a result, we find $\delta_{m-1} \not\sim_1 \eta_{m-1}$ but $\delta_{m-1}\beta' \sim \eta_{m-1}\beta'$. Recall lemma 2, $\delta_{m-1} = \epsilon$ or $\eta_{m-1} = \epsilon$. If $\delta_{m-1} = \epsilon$, then $\eta_{m-1} \neq \epsilon$ and

$\beta' \sim \eta_{m-1}\beta'$, let $Z_1 \overset{\Delta}{=} \eta_{m-1}Z_1$; else if $\eta_{m-1} = \epsilon$, $\delta_{m-1} \neq \epsilon$ and $\beta' \sim \delta_{m-1}\beta'$, let $Z_1 \overset{\Delta}{=} \delta_{m-1}Z_1$. In both cases, $\beta' \sim Z_1$. Define $Z_2 \overset{\Delta}{=} \gamma Z_2$, so that $\alpha' \sim \gamma\beta' \sim \gamma Z_1 \sim Z_2$. What's more, since $|a_1a_2\ldots a_{m-1}| = m - 1$, if γ is unnormed, then $m - 1 < \|Y\| \leq \mathbb{N}$, else if γ is normed, $m - 1 \leq \mathbb{S}$. That is, $m - 1 < \mathbb{S}$. Change the equations for Z_1 and Z_2 to 3-GNF, then (Z_1, Z_2) is a generated pair for X, Y and $XZ_2 \sim YZ_1$.

4. $\alpha \equiv X\alpha'$ and $\beta \equiv Y$, X normed, Y unnormed, $\|\alpha'\|_s > d_{X,Y}$. Since $X\alpha' \sim Y$, then $\exists \gamma.X \overset{\omega}{\longrightarrow} \epsilon$, $Y \overset{\omega}{\longrightarrow} \gamma$ such that $|\omega| = \|X\|$ and $\alpha' \sim \gamma$, $X\gamma \sim Y$.

5. $\alpha \equiv X$ and $\beta \equiv Y\beta'$, Y normed, X unnormed. $\|\beta'\|_s > d_{Y,X}$. Similar to the case above.

6. The rest case is that $(\alpha, \beta) \in U \cup U^{-1}$. $\alpha = \beta$ will be applied to UNFOLD and it surely have a match in which all pairs are bisimilar.   □

Why do we introduce generated pairs here? That is in spark of [2]. Intuitively, we can find that for every unnormed α, there must exist some β and γ such that $\alpha \sim \beta\gamma^\omega$. Here new variables Z_1, Z_2 are introduced to represent sequences like γ^ω to make the proof neat and clear.

4   The Equational Theory

We will show that the equational theory proposed by Hüttel and Stirling in [8,9] for the bisimulation equivalence of normed BPA processes given in 3-GNF also work for any guarded BPA system. The inference rules in the theory are shown in Table 7, and the semantics are given as follows:

Definition 13. $\Gamma \models_\Delta E = F$ if $\{(X\alpha, Y\beta)|X\alpha = Y\beta \in \Gamma\} \cup \{(X_i, E_i)|X_i \overset{def}{=} E_i \in \Delta\} \subseteq \sim$ implies $E \sim F$.

As a result, $E \sim F$ will follow from the special case that $\emptyset \models_\Delta E = F$. The most difficult thing in the proof of completeness lies in UNFOLD nodes. Since derivatives of an UNFOLD node are generated according to the operational semantics of the processes, while rules of inference in the equational theory only rely on the syntax. However, for guarded BPA systems, it is not hard to develop the relationship between an UNFOLD node and the root of a *basic* step proposed in [8,9]. By using a basic step as a bridge, we can get the desired result.

Recalling a *basic* step introduced in [8,9] composed of REC, SUM and PREFIX rules shown in Table 4, we can investigate the relationship between an UNFLOD node and a basic step as follows:

Lemma 5. *In a successful tableau, if $\alpha_1\alpha = \beta_1\beta, \ldots, \alpha_k\alpha = \beta_k\beta$ are children of an UNFOLD node $X\alpha = Y\beta$, then $\alpha_1\alpha = \beta_1\beta, \ldots, \alpha_k\alpha = \beta_k\beta$ can be all the leaves of a subtree(named as T) generated by a basic step and rooted with $X\alpha = Y\beta$(See Table 5).*

Proof. Let $\dfrac{X\alpha = Y\beta}{E\alpha = F\beta}$ be an application of the REC rule.

Since $M = \{(\alpha_i\alpha, \beta_i\beta)|1 \leq i \leq k\}$ is a match for $(X\alpha, Y\beta)$ and $(E\alpha, F\beta)$, the following facts holds:

Table 4. Rules within a basic step

REC $\dfrac{X\alpha = Y\beta}{E\alpha = F\beta}$ $X \triangleq E, Y \triangleq F \in \Delta$
PREFIX $\dfrac{a\alpha = a\beta}{\alpha = \beta}$
SUM $\dfrac{(\sum_{i=1}^{m} a_i\alpha_i)\alpha = (\sum_{j=1}^{n} b_j\beta_j)\beta}{\{a_i\alpha_i\alpha = b_{f(i)}\beta_{f(i)}\beta\}_{i=1}^{m} \ \{a_{g(j)}\alpha_{g(j)}\alpha = b_j\beta_j\beta\}_{j=1}^{n}}$
where $f : \{1,\ldots,m\} \longrightarrow \{1,\ldots,n\}$, $g : \{1,\ldots,n\} \longrightarrow \{1,\ldots,m\}$ with $m, n \geq 1$

- $E\alpha \xrightarrow{a} \alpha' \Rightarrow \exists\beta'. F\beta \xrightarrow{a} \beta'$ and $(\alpha', \beta') \in M$
- $F\beta \xrightarrow{a} \beta' \Rightarrow \exists\alpha'. E\alpha \xrightarrow{a} \alpha'$ and $(\alpha', \beta') \in M$

So we can construct the subtree T as follows:

For any $E\alpha \xrightarrow{a_i} \alpha_i\alpha$ and $F\beta \xrightarrow{a_i} \beta_i\beta$ such that $(\alpha_i\alpha, \beta_i\beta) \in M$, choose $a_i\alpha_i\alpha = a_i\beta_i\beta$ as the children for the SUM node $E\alpha = F\beta$. And also for any $F\beta \xrightarrow{b_j} \beta_j\beta$ and $E\alpha \xrightarrow{b_j} \alpha_j\alpha$ such that $(\alpha_j\alpha, \beta_j\beta) \in M$, choose $b_j\alpha_j\alpha = b_j\beta_j\beta$ as the children for the SUM node $E\alpha = F\beta$.

As a result, every leaf is an element in M. Next we prove that every element in M is a piece of leaf in T: According to the definition of a match, for any $1 \leq i \leq k$, there exists $a_i \in Act$ s.t. $E\alpha \xrightarrow{a_i} \alpha_i\alpha$ and $F\beta \xrightarrow{a_i} \beta_i\beta$. From the construction of T above, $\alpha_i\alpha = \beta_i\beta$ will be a piece of leaf after PREFIX is applied. □

Table 5. A *basic* step

$$\dfrac{\dfrac{\dfrac{X\alpha = Y\beta}{(\sum_{i=1}^{m} a_i\alpha_i)\alpha = (\sum_{j=1}^{n} b_j\beta_j)\beta} \text{REC}}{\dfrac{a_1\alpha_1\alpha = a_1\beta_1\beta}{\alpha_1\alpha = \beta_1\beta} \quad \cdots \quad \dfrac{a_k\alpha_k\alpha = a_k\beta_k\beta}{\alpha_k\alpha = \beta_k\beta} \text{PREFIX}}}{} \text{SUM}$$

Lemma 6. *Let $X\alpha = Y\beta$ be an UNFOLD node with children $\alpha_1 = \beta_1,\ldots,\alpha_k = \beta_k$ in a successful tableau. If for some Γ we have $\Gamma \vdash_\Delta \alpha_i = \beta_i$ for $1 \leq i \leq k$. then $\Gamma\backslash\{X\alpha = Y\beta\} \vdash_\Delta X\alpha = Y\beta$.*

Proof. $\alpha_1 = \beta_1,\ldots,\alpha_k = \beta_k$ must be of the forms $\alpha_1'\alpha = \beta_1'\beta,\ldots,\alpha_k'\alpha = \beta_k'\beta$. From lemma 5, $\alpha_1'\alpha = \beta_1'\beta,\ldots,\alpha_k'\alpha = \beta_k'\beta$ are the leaves of a basic step shown in Table 5. Since $\Gamma \vdash_\Delta \alpha_i'\alpha = \beta_i'\beta$ for $1 \leq i \leq k$, it is not hard to get $\Gamma \vdash_\Delta (\sum_{i=1}^{m} a_i\alpha_i')\alpha = (\sum_{j=1}^{n} b_j\beta_j')\beta$, denoted as $\Gamma \vdash_\Delta E\alpha = F\beta$. So we have $\Gamma\backslash\{X\alpha = Y\beta\}, X\alpha = Y\beta \vdash_\Delta E\alpha = F\beta$. Then $\Gamma\backslash\{X\alpha = Y\beta\} \vdash_\Delta X\alpha = Y\beta$ follows by R12. □

Definition 14. *In a successful tableau T, we define $unf(X'\alpha' = Y'\beta')$ for the node $X'\alpha' = Y'\beta'$ as the set of UNFOLD nodes above $X'\alpha' = Y'\beta'$.*

Lemma 7. *Given a successful tableau T. For each node $X'\alpha' = Y'\beta'$ in T we have that $unf(X'\alpha' = Y'\beta') \vdash_\Delta X'\alpha' = Y'\beta'$.*

Proof. Induction in the structure of T.

- $X'\alpha' = Y'\beta'$ is a successful leaf. For condition i), R1 gives $unf(X'\alpha' = Y'\beta') \vdash_\Delta X'\alpha' = Y'\beta'$ immediately. For condition ii), if $X'\alpha' = Y'\beta' \in unf(X'\alpha' = Y'\beta')$ then the result holds by R11; If $Y'\beta' = X'\alpha' \in unf(X'\alpha' = Y'\beta')$, the result follows by R11 and R2.
- $X'\alpha' = Y'\beta'$ is a DSUB node, take DSUBL for example. IH gives that $unf(X'\gamma = Y') \vdash_\Delta X'\gamma = Y'$ and $unf(\alpha' = \gamma\beta') \vdash_\Delta \alpha' = \gamma\beta'$. Observe that $unf(X'\gamma = Y') = unf(\alpha' = \gamma\beta') = unf(X'\alpha' = Y'\beta')$, $unf(X'\alpha' = Y'\beta') \vdash_\Delta X'\alpha' = Y'\beta'$ follows by R5 and R3.
- $X'\alpha' = Y'\beta'$ is an ESUB node or a DEDUCE node. Similar with the case above.
- $X'\alpha' = Y'\beta'$ is an UNFOLD node. Let $\alpha_1 = \beta_1, \ldots \alpha_k = \beta_k$ be its children. We have that $unf(\alpha_1 = \beta_1) = unf(\alpha_2 = \beta_2) \ldots = unf(\alpha_k = \beta_k)$ and $unf(X'\alpha' = Y'\beta') = unf(\alpha_1 = \beta_1) \backslash \{X'\alpha' = Y'\beta'\}$. IH gives that $unf(\alpha_1 = \beta_1) \vdash_\Delta \alpha_i = \beta_i$ for $1 \leq i \leq k$. According to lemma 6, $unf(\alpha_1 = \beta_1) \backslash \{X'\alpha' = Y'\beta'\} \vdash_\Delta X'\alpha' = Y'\beta'$, which is exactly $unf(X'\alpha' = Y'\beta') \vdash_\Delta X'\alpha' = Y'\beta'$. $\square$

Theorem 1. *If $\Gamma \vdash_\Delta X\alpha = Y\beta$ then $\Gamma \models_\Delta X\alpha = Y\beta$.*

The proof for soundness can be found in [9].

Theorem 2. *If $X\alpha \sim Y\beta$ then $\emptyset \vdash_\Delta X\alpha = Y\beta$.*

Proof. Since $X\alpha \sim Y\beta$, $X\alpha = Y\beta$ will have a successful tableau. The desired result is given directly by lemma 7 and the fact that $unf(X\alpha = Y\beta) = \emptyset$. $\square$

It should be pointed out that the whole equational theory is still applied on the expanded BPA system because the completeness is achieved by referring to tableau and the tableau method is implemented on the expanded system.

Example 4. Abbreviate $\vdash_\Delta$ as $\vdash$ for simplicity. The main steps for deriving that $\vdash AC = BC$ is shown in Table 6.

Actually, there is a way to get rid of the use of a basic step, which can be achieved by changing R12 to

$$\text{R12'} \quad \frac{\Gamma, \alpha = \beta \vdash_\Delta \{\alpha_i = \beta_i\}_{i=0}^k}{\Gamma \vdash_\Delta \alpha = \beta} \quad \text{where } \{(\alpha_i, \beta_i)\}_{i=0}^k \text{ is a match of } (\alpha, \beta).$$

It is very easy to show the soundness and completeness of this new equational theory. But we chose to stick to Hüttel and Stirling's theory because R12' has been involved with the operational semantics somehow.

Table 6. The proof sequence for $\vdash AC = BC$

$$\cfrac{\cfrac{\vdash bZ_1 = bZ_1}{\vdash Z_2 = DZ_1}\text{(R12)}}{\vdash C = Z_1} \qquad \cfrac{\vdash D = D \quad \cfrac{\cfrac{\vdash bZ_1 = bZ_1}{\vdash Z_2 = Z_1}\text{(R12)}}{\vdash DZ_2 = DZ_1}}{\cfrac{\vdash Z_2 + DZ_2 = DZ_1}{\cfrac{\vdash (a + aD)Z_2 = aDZ_1}{\vdash AZ_2 = BZ_1}}} \qquad \cfrac{\cfrac{C = Z_1 \vdash bC = bZ_1}{\vdash C = Z_1}\text{(R12)}}{\cfrac{\vdash bC = bZ_1}{\vdash C = Z_2}\text{(R12)}}}{\vdash AC = BC}$$

Table 7. Rules in the equational theory

Equivalence

R1 $\quad \Gamma \vdash_\Delta E = E$

R2 $\quad \dfrac{\Gamma \vdash_\Delta E = F}{\Gamma \vdash_\Delta F = E}$

R3 $\quad \dfrac{\Gamma \vdash_\Delta E = F \quad \Gamma \vdash_\Delta F = G}{\Gamma \vdash_\Delta E = G}$

Congruence

R4 $\quad \dfrac{\Gamma \vdash_\Delta E_1 = F_1 \quad \Gamma \vdash_\Delta E_2 = F_2}{\Gamma \vdash_\Delta E_1 + E_2 = F_1 + F_2}$

R5 $\quad \dfrac{\Gamma \vdash_\Delta E_1 = F_1 \quad \Gamma \vdash_\Delta E_2 = F_2}{\Gamma \vdash_\Delta E_1 E_2 = F_1 F_2}$

BPA axioms

R6 $\quad \Gamma \vdash_\Delta E + F = F + E$

R7 $\quad \Gamma \vdash_\Delta (E + F) + G = E + (F + G)$

R8 $\quad \Gamma \vdash_\Delta E + E = E$

R9 $\quad \Gamma \vdash_\Delta (E + F)G = EG + FG$

R10 $\quad \Gamma \vdash_\Delta E(FG) = (EF)G$

Recursion

R11 $\quad \Gamma, X\alpha = Y\beta \vdash_\Delta X\alpha = Y\beta$

R12 $\quad \dfrac{\Gamma, X\alpha = Y\beta \vdash_\Delta E\alpha = F\beta}{\Gamma \vdash_\Delta X\alpha = Y\beta} \quad X \overset{def}{=} E, Y \overset{def}{=} F \in \Delta$

5   Conclusion

We have given a tableau algorithm to decide bisimulation equivalence relation of full BPA processes. The whole procedure is direct and easy to understand. It also helps us to show the completeness of Hüttel and Stirling's equational theory on all normed and unnormed BPA systems. As a result, the first equational theory for full BPA processes is found.

The study of bisimulation decision problems in the fields of BPA and BPP processes are rather sophisticated already.

All of the results, as well as open problems, are recorded and updated by J.Srba([13]). About algorithms, the remaining things need to be considered is how to lower complexity and improve efficiency.

Future works concerned, as the equational theory in this paper depends on assumptions, it is somewhat different from that of Milner's for regular processes ([10]). So one direction of interest is to construct a standard equational theory of $\sim$ as elegant as that in [10]. Another direction worth attention may be the construction of equational theory for weak bisimulation since many decision results for them are already given.

References

1. Baeten, J.C.M., Bergstra, J.A., Klop, J.W.: Decidability of bisimulation equivalence for process generating context-free languages. In: de Bakker, J.W., Nijman, A.J., Treleaven, P.C. (eds.) PARLE 1987. LNCS, vol. 259, pp. 94–113. Springer, Heidelberg (1987)
2. Burkart, O., Caucal, D., Steffen, B.: An elementary bisimulation decision procedure for arbitrary context-free processes. In: Hájek, P., Wiedermann, J. (eds.) MFCS 1995. LNCS, vol. 969. Springer, Heidelberg (1995)
3. Caucal, D.: Graphes canoniques de graphes algébriques. Informatique Théorique et Applications(RAIRO) 24(4), 339–352 (1990)
4. Christensen, S., Hüttel, H., Stirling, C.: Bisimulation equivalence is decidable for all context-free processes. In: Cleaveland, W.R. (ed.) CONCUR 1992. LNCS, vol. 630. Springer, Heidelberg (1992)
5. Groote, J.F.: A short proof of the decidability of bisimulation for normed bpa-processes. Inform. process. lett. 42, 167–171 (1991)
6. Hirshfeld, Y., Jerrum, M., Moller, F.: A polynomial algorithm for deciding bisimulation of normed context-free processes. Theoretical Computer Science 15, 143–159 (1996)
7. Hirshfeld, Y., Moller, F.: A Fast Algorithm for Deciding Bisimilarity of Normed Context-Free Processes. In: Jonsson, B., Parrow, J. (eds.) CONCUR 1994. LNCS, vol. 836, pp. 48–63. Springer, Heidelberg (1994)
8. Hüttel, H., Stirling, C.: Action speaks louder than words: Proving bisimilarity for context-free processes. In: Proceedings on Logic in Computer Science (1991)
9. Hüttel, H., Stirling, C.: Action speaks louder than words: Proving bisimilarity for context-free processes. Journal of Logic and Computation 8(4), 485–509 (1998)
10. Milner, R.: A complete inference system for a class of regular behaviours. Journal of Computer ans System Sciences 28, 439–466 (1984)
11. Milner, R.: Communication and Concurrency. International Series in Computer Science. Prentice Hall, Englewood Cliffs (1989)
12. Srba, J.: Strong Bisimilarity and Regularity of Basic Process Algebra is PSPACE-Hard. In: Widmayer, P., Triguero, F., Morales, R., Hennessy, M., Eidenbenz, S., Conejo, R. (eds.) ICALP 2002. LNCS, vol. 2380, pp. 716–727. Springer, Heidelberg (2002)
13. Srba, J.: Roadmap of Infinite Results. Bulletin of the European Association for Theoretical Computer Science, columns: Concurrency 78, 163–175 (2002)

Optimal Strategy Synthesis in Request-Response Games[*]

Florian Horn[1,2], Wolfgang Thomas[2], and Nico Wallmeier[2]

[1] LIAFA, Université Paris 7, Case 7014, 2 place Jussieu, F-75251 Paris 5, France
[2] Lehrstuhl für Informatik 7, RWTH Aachen University, 52056 Aachen, Germany
horn@liafa.jussieu.fr,
{thomas,wallmeier}@informatik.rwth-aachen.de

Abstract. We show the solvability of an optimization problem on infinite two-player games. The winning conditions are of the "request-response" format, *i.e.* conjunctions of conditions of the form "if a state with property Q is visited, then later a state with property P is visited". We ask for solutions that do not only guarantee the satisfaction of such conditions but also minimal wait times between visits to Q-states and subsequent visits to P-states. We present a natural class of valuations of infinite plays that captures this optimization problem, and with respect to this measure show the existence of an optimal winning strategy (if a winning strategy exists at all) and that it can be realized by a finite-state machine. For the latter claim we use a reduction to the solution of mean-payoff games due to Paterson and Zwick.

1 Introduction

Infinite two-player games are a natural model of reactive systems in which a controller interacts with moves of its environment and has to guarantee certain conditions on the infinite runs on the system (*i.e.*, infinite plays in the game theoretic view). A typical condition that arises in many contexts is the "request-response condition". It refers to state properties $Q_1, \ldots, Q_k$ which capture k different types of "requests", and other state properties $P_1, \ldots, P_k$ which represent the corresponding "responses". The associated request-response condition is the following requirement on an infinite state sequence (play of the game): *For each i, whenever a state in Q_i is visited, then now or later a state in P_i is visited.* In linear time temporal logic the condition is formalized as $G(Q_i \rightarrow FP_i)$. In practice, request-response conditions often occur in the presence of safety conditions. We assume here that the state space is restricted to states that satisfy the safety condition.

In this paper we analyze request-response games over finite arenas, taking in account not only the mere satisfaction of the winning condition but also the quantitative aspect of minimizing the delay between Q_i visits and the corresponding subsequent P_i-visits. A quantitative sharpening of liveness conditions

---

[*] Research partially supported by ANR AVERISS and by the Research Networking Programme AutoMathA of ESF (European Science Foundation).

has been studied by several authors. For instance, in their work on parameterized temporal logic, Alur et al. [1] supplement temporal operators by constants that give bounds in the semantics, *e.g.*, F_k meaning "eventually, within k steps". A more abstract view is to ask for the existence of an unspecified bound: Kupferman, Piterman, and Vardi [11] define the "prompt" operator F_p, meaning that there is a constant k that bounds the satisfaction of an eventuality formula over all runs of a system. Chatterjee and Henzinger [4] consider finitary games, where the wait time between a request and its satisfaction must be ultimately bounded. In the present paper we go a step further in the sense that we try to achieve "best bounds" rather than asking whether given bounds can be met or whether some bound exists. Thus we study an optimization problem rather than a decision problem. Moreover, we work in the context of open rather than closed systems.

In order to solve this optimization problem, we introduce valuations for infinite plays (by real numbers) that measure globally the delays in a play between visits to request- and subsequent response-states. The approach we take here is to associate with any position where a request is "open" a corresponding "penalty". In Section 2 we discuss possible conventions and then pursue a definition which stresses the requirement of avoiding long wait times, namely the case of strictly growing and diverging penalties. The penalties $v_1, v_2, v_3, \ldots$ for waiting $1, 2, 3, \ldots$ moments of time strictly increase and give a diverging sequence of real numbers. For a finite play prefix we take the sum of the occurring penalties divided by its length, and as value of a play we define the limsup of the prefix values. The corresponding notion of optimal winning strategy (of player "controller") is now obvious.

Our main result states that for a finite-state request-response game (with some given initial state) one can not only decide whether controller wins and provide a finite-state strategy (which was known), but that also – with respect to the mentioned valuation – an optimal winning strategy exists, is computable, and can be realized by a finite-state machine.

The paper is structured as follows: In the subsequent Section 2 we introduce the technical preliminaries on game arenas, request-response games, the valuation of plays, and optimality of strategies. In Section 3 we state the main result. Section 4 is devoted to the key lemma which states that an optimal strategy realizes a uniform bound on the delays. This allows to study the optimization problem over a finite game graph (resulting from the given one by attaching all possible tuples of delays up to the mentioned bound) and to invoke (in Section 5) known results on mean-payoff games for computing an optimal strategy. In Section 6, we conclude with a discussion and some open problems.

The paper extends (and gives a more streamlined exposition of) results of the third author's dissertation [12, Chapter 4].

2   Definitions

2.1   Games

We recall here some background on infinite games used in specification and verification. We refer the reader to [13,7] for more details.

Arenas. A *game arena* G consists of a directed finite graph (S,T), a partition (S_E, S_A) of S, and an initial state s_0. The states in S_E (resp. S_A) are *Eve's states, or Controller's states* (resp. *Adam's states, or Environment's states*), and are graphically represented as $\bigcirc$ (resp. $\square$) in figures.

Plays and Strategies. A *play* over G is a finite or infinite sequence $\rho = \rho_0 \rho_1 \ldots$ of states such that $\rho_0 = s_0$ and $(\rho_i, \rho_{i+1}) \in T$ for all $i <$ length of ρ. The set of *occurring states* is $\mathrm{Occ}(\rho) = \{s \in S \mid \exists i \in \mathbb{N}, \rho_i = s\}$.

A *strategy for Eve* is a function σ from $S^* S_E$ to S such that for any path w ending in state q, there is a transition in T between q and $\sigma(w)$. Intuitively, it is a "recipe" to extend a finite play ending in one of Eve's states.

A *strategy with memory M* for Eve is a function computed by a transducer (M, m_0, ν, μ) with initial memory m_0, where $\nu : S_E \times M \to S$ is the "next-move" function such that $(s, \nu(s, m)) \in T$, and $\mu : S \times M \to M$ is the "memory-update" function. A strategy is *finite-memory or finite-state, respectively memoryless* if it is computed by a finite-state transducer, respectively by a transducer with singleton memory.

For two given strategies σ and τ, the outcome of the game is an infinite play $\rho^{\sigma,\tau}$. A play ρ is *consistent with* σ (resp. τ) if there is a strategy τ (resp. σ) such that ρ is a prefix of, or equal to $\rho^{\sigma,\tau}$.

Winning Conditions. A *winning condition* $\mathcal{C}$ is a boolean function used to partition the plays between those *winning for Eve* and those *winning for Adam*. The main problem is then to find *winning strategies*: A strategy σ is winning for Eve if for every strategy τ of Adam, the play $\rho^{\sigma,\tau}$ is winning for Eve. When games are *determined* (as are request-response games), there is always a winning strategy for one of the players.

2.2   Request-Response Games

Request-Response games were introduced in [15]. They are a special case of ω-regular games. Let $G = (S, S_E, S_A, T)$ be an arena. A play is winning for Eve under the *request-response condition* $\mathcal{C} = (Q_j, P_j)_{j=1 \ldots k}$ (where $Q_j, P_j \subseteq S$) if

$$\bigwedge_{j=1}^{k} \forall n (\rho_n \in Q_j \Rightarrow \exists m \geq n \ \rho_m \in P_j)$$

Rather than the mere satisfaction of the request-response condition, we study the question *how well* the controller (Eve) can satisfy it. As a trivial example consider a game where controller has to operate traffic lights for a one-lane bottleneck of a road, in each round giving the green light to one direction. For each of the two directions there is one request-response condition: Whenever a car is waiting, it is (now or later) allowed to pass. A simple winning strategy would be to alternate giving green between the two directions. This may, however, result in unnecessary phases of waiting (when in the opposite direction no car is waiting). A "better" solution could be to give, at each moment, the green light to the side where the "oldest" car is waiting, or to the one with the majority of cars.

In order to capture the quality of strategies, we define the *value* of a play as a real number. This is done in two steps: to each position in a play, we associate a *penalty*, depending on the time since when the open requests are waiting for a response; and secondly we define the value of a play as the limsup over the averages for all finite play prefixes. The penalties (paid by Eve) count only steps for as yet unanswered requests. In particular, the value of a play without any request is zero, while a play winning for Adam has an infinite value.

There are many alternative versions of valuations. For example, rather than considering the proportion between sums of penalties and the length of a play prefix, one can consider sums of penalties divided by the number of "activations" of request-response conditions (i.e., first visits to Q_j without a matching P_j-visit) that occur in a play prefix. The present results carry over to this variant of valuation.

Formally, we use the following definitions in order to define the value. The wait time for the condition (Q_j, P_j) at the end of the (finite) play prefix w, denoted by $t_j(w)$, is the number moves since the earliest unanswered visit to Q_j in w. If all visits to Q_j have been answered, its value is 0. The value $t_j(w)$ is defined recursively. We set $t_j(\epsilon) = 0$ and let

- if $t_j(w) = 0$
  - $t_j(ws) := 1$ if $s \in Q_j \setminus P_j$
  - $t_j(ws) := 0$ otherwise
- if $t_j(w) > 0$
  - $t_j(ws) := 0$ if $s \in P_j$
  - $t_j(ws) := t_j(w) + 1$ otherwise.

By definition of the wait times, we can immediately derive the following remark about their evolution:

$$\forall v, w \in S^*, s \in S : t_j(v) < t_j(w) \Rightarrow t_j(vs) < t_j(ws) \tag{1}$$

Based on the wait time $t_j(w)$ for condition (Q_j, P_j) at play prefix w we can introduce different kinds of "penalties" (for Eve). A simple choice would be to count one unit of penalty for each time instance of waiting; this leads to a linear increase of the accumulated penalties while time elapses. In this measure, an extra moment of waiting costs the same regardless of the past. In realistic scenarios it seems more appropriate to let the penalties increase, reflecting the idea that longer wait times pose higher pressure for delivering response. A natural implementation of this idea is to associate penalty p for the p-th moment of (successive) waiting, which leads to a quadratic increase of accumulated penalties over time. In order to capture the different options, we introduce (for condition (Q_j, P_j)) a *penalty function* $f_j : \mathbb{N} \to \mathbb{R}_{\geq 0}$ where $f_j(n)$ is the penalty for the n-th moment of waiting after a visit to Q_j without a later visit to P_j. In the two scenarios above, we used the constant 1, respectively the identity on $\mathbb{N}$. Let *penalty $p_j(w)$ of play prefix w* be $f_j(t_j(w))$. The *global penalty* over all conditions (Q_j, P_j) is the sum $p(w)$ over all $p_j(w)$, and the *value of an infinite play ρ*, denoted $v(\rho)$, is the mean value of the costs $p(w)$ of its prefixes w. Accordingly, the *value of a strategy* σ, denoted $v(\sigma)$, is the limsup of the values of the plays consistent with this strategy. To sum up:

- $p_j(w) = f_j(t_j(w))$
- $p(w) = \sum_{j=1}^{k} p_j(w)$
- $v(\rho) = \limsup_{n \to \infty} \frac{1}{n} \cdot \sum_{i=1}^{n} p(\rho_0 \ldots \rho_{i-1})$
- $v(\sigma) = \limsup_\tau v(\rho^{\sigma,\tau})$

Our main result below is stated for the case of *strictly increasing and unbounded penalty functions* f_j. We have argued for this restriction from a pragmatic point of view. Let us also observe that – for example – for the case of constant penalties one cannot hope to construct optimal winning strategies.

Example 1. In the game of Figure 1, two requests are made each time the token reaches the central state. We indicate membership in Q_1, Q_2, P_2, P_1 by corresponding annotations. Eve can choose to satisfy either request, by going left or right. Consider the strategy σ_k which repeatedly does the P_1-loop k times and then the P_2-loop once. This gives a penalty sum of $3k + 7$ for the corresponding $2k + 4$ moves; hence (for constant penalties) we obtain $v(\sigma_k) = 3/2 + 1/(2k+4)$. Thus we can always improve the value of a strategy by increasing the portion of P_1-loops; hence there is no optimal winning strategy for Eve.

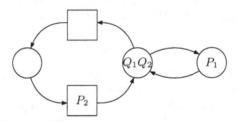

Fig. 1. No optimal solution for constant penalties

Our main result shows that for increasing and diverging penalty functions optimal strategies exist and can be computed.

3   Main Result

In the following, we consider request-response games with k conditions (Q_j, P_j) $(j = 1, \ldots, k)$, and we assume strictly increasing and unbounded penalty functions f_j for $j = 1, \ldots, k$. We state the main result:

Theorem 2. *If a request-response game is won by Eve, then Eve in fact has (with respect to strictly increasing and unbounded penalty functions) an optimal winning strategy, which moreover is finite-state and effectively computable.*

As a preparation we recall the solution given in [15] for classical ("Boolean") request-response games and deduce a bound for the value of a canonical winning strategy.

Proposition 3. *If Eve wins in a request-response game over G with n states and k conditions, she has a winning strategy of value $\leq M := \sum_{j=1}^{k} f_j(n \cdot k)$.*

Let us sketch the proof, which involves an easy reduction to Büchi games. Starting from a game arena $G = (S, S_E, S_A, T)$ and k conditions, an expanded graph is constructed over the vertex set $S' := S \times \{0,1\}^k \times [0, \ldots, k]$; the bit vector signals which of the k conditions have an open request, and the final component says which request is chosen to be served next (in cyclic order). The index 0 is assumed everytime after index k is reached, signalling a successful cycle of satisfaction of requests. (The Büchi condition then requires to visit vertices in S' with final component 0 again and again.) Using well-known fixed point computations (see [13,7]) one can decide whether Eve wins this Büchi game. Moreover, it is easy to see that the winning strategy σ_0 derived from the game reduction will guarantee uniformly bounded wait times for each condition. A "next response" is reached after $\leq n$ steps (where n is the size of the arena), and it can take k such responses until the currently considered request is served. Thus, the reduction to Büchi games yields a bound of $n \cdot k$ for the wait times, and the value of the corresponding strategy σ_0 is $v(\sigma_0) \leq M := \sum_{j=1}^{k} f_j(n \cdot k)$.

We often refer to the value $f_j^{-1}(M)$, i.e. the smallest number s of steps (of waiting) such that $f_j(s) \geq M$. We shall show that for any strategy with value $\leq M$, there exists a strategy with smaller or equal value that *uniformly* bounds the wait times for each pair (Q_j, P_j). Let us state the main technical lemma.

Lemma 4. *There is a function $d : \mathbb{N}^2 \to \mathbb{N}$ such that the following holds for request-response games over graphs with n vertices and with k conditions: from any winning strategy σ with value $v(\sigma) \leq M$, we can compute a winning strategy σ' that bounds, for $j = 1, \ldots, k$, all wait times for the pair (Q_j, P_j) to $b_j = f_j^{-1}(M) + d(n, k-1)$, and such that $v(\sigma') \leq v(\sigma)$.*

This result is the essential step in our analysis of request-response games. It says that in the domain of strategies of value at most M, we can achieve a uniform bound on the wait times and still keep or improve the value of the strategy. Intuitively this means that it is not possible to improve the value of a strategy by deferring the responses for some condition more and more while preferring to "serve" another condition. In other words, the effect of Example 1 is excluded.

To obtain the main result, we shall show how these "bounded" strategies can be interpreted as strategies in finite-state mean-payoff games.

4   Bounding Wait Times

This section gives the proof of Lemma 4.

The main problem in the construction of optimal strategies is that *a priori*, the wait times for the pairs can be unbounded if the long spells where a condition remains open occur rarely. The point of this section is to show that we can restrict our study to strategies where the wait times are bounded. Furthermore, the bounds can be computed beforehand, directly from the parameters of the game.

In order to prove Lemma 4, we modify a strategy σ_0 k times, thus constructing strategies $\sigma_1, \ldots, \sigma_k$. At step j, the strategy σ_{j-1} is "improved" into one respecting the desired wait time bound for condition (Q_j, P_j), with the following constraints:

- the value of σ_j is less or equal to the value of σ_{j-1};
- for any pair (Q_i, P_i), if σ_{j-1} ensures a bound B for the wait times w.r.t. (Q_i, P_i), then so does σ_j.

The function d occurring in Lemma 4 comes from a special version of Dickson's Lemma [5]. Recall that Dickson's Lemma is a statement about infinite sequences of vectors of natural numbers; it guarantees that in such a sequence of pairwise distinct vectors eventually a vector must occur that is strictly greater than some previous one (*i.e.*, all components are $\geq$ the previous vector, and some component is strictly larger).

We distinguish here play prefixes w by their last state *and* their wait time vector $t(w) := (t_1(w), \ldots, t_k(w))$. Let us call "non-Dickson sequence" a finite sequence over $S \times \mathbb{N}^k$ where there is no pair of elements such that the later is larger than the former ("larger" meaning larger vector *and* same state). Note that in a play the components $t_j(w)$ can only increase by 1 or be reset to 0.

This allows us to bound recursively the length of the longest non-Dickson sequence. It is clear that for n states and 0 pairs, this length is n, so $d(n, 0) = n + 1$. Let us consider now a non-Dickson sequence for n states and $k + 1$ pairs. The length between two positions such that $t_{k+1} = 0$ is at most $d(n, k) - 1$: as t_{k+1} is non-decreasing, removing it must yield a non-Dickson sequence for n states and k pairs. The wait times can only increase by 1, so their values cannot exceed $d(n, k) - 1$, and the number of possible configurations in a non-Dickson sequence is at most $n \cdot (k + 1)^{d(n,k)-1}$. We define the function d recursively as follows:

- $d(n, 0) = n + 1$
- $d(n, k + 1) = n \cdot (k + 1)^{d(n,k)-1} + 1$

Thus, we have shown the following lemma:

Lemma 5. *In a request-response game with n states and k conditions, in any play w of length at least $d(n, k)$, there are two prefixes x and y such that x is a prefix of y, x and y end in the same state of the game, and $t(x) \leq t(y)$.*

Let us turn to the improvement of a strategy $\sigma(= \sigma_{j-1})$, aiming at bounding the wait times for the condition (Q_j, P_j). A path segment v, prefixed by w, is considered undesirable and will be removed if the following holds:

1. $P_j \notin \mathrm{Occ}(v)$
2. $t_j(w) \geq f_j^{-1}(M+1)$
3. $t(w) \leq t(wv)$

The value of the final bound — $f_j^{-1}(M) + d(n, k-1)$ — is then clear from the conditions 2 and 3. In order to guarantee that we remove only costly factors, we wait until the price from condition (Q_j, P_j) alone is more than the worst average penalty of the original strategy. And, in order to get a better strategy, we remove factors only when everything is worse at the end of the factor: it is always the case for pair j because of condition 1, and it is the case somewhere for all the other pairs if the factor is longer than $d(n, k-1)$ by Lemma 5.

We describe now the improvement for pair (Q_j, P_j). To ease notation, we denote the initial strategy (σ_{j-1}) by σ, and the new one (σ_j) by τ. This strategy τ is defined as a strategy with memory: the memory states of τ are words over the vertices of S (more specifically, prefixes of plays consistent with σ). Let us explain the notation to avoid confusion between the four functions involved in the definition:

$\nu : S^* \times S_E \to S$, the "next-move" function: Here the first component of the argument is a memory state (*i.e.* a play consistent with σ), not the history of the play.

$\mu : S^* \times S_E \to S^*$, the "memory-update" function: Again, the first component of the argument is a memory state.

$\Omega : S^* \to S^*$, the extension of μ to words: $\Omega(\epsilon) = \epsilon$, and $\Omega(ws) = \mu(w, s)$. Here, the argument is the history of the play (thus consistent with τ).

$\tau : S^* \to S^*$, the resulting strategy: It can be defined from Ω: $\tau(ws) = \nu(\Omega(w), s)$. Again, the argument is the history of the play.

We define only the functions ν and μ, as the two others derive from them. Let y be the current memory and s the current vertex of S. We consider only the case where ys is a finite play of G consistent with σ, as the update guarantees that this holds during the whole play. There are two cases, depending on whether the immediate penalty for condition (Q_j, P_j) in ys is greater than M or not. If it is not so, the update is done by adding the current state at the end of the memory: $\mu(s, y) = ys$. If it is Eve's turn to play, her move mimics σ's move: $\nu(s, y) = \sigma(ys)$.

On the other hand, if $t_j(ys) > f_j^{-1}(M)$, we first check if there is an "undesirable factor" to remove. We consider the game tree G^σ, rooted in ys and limited to the path segments up to the next visit to P_j. This tree is finite, as an infinite branch would be a losing play – in the boolean sense. We consider the nodes of this tree such that the last visited state is s, and the wait times for *all* conditions (Q_i, P_i) are greater than the corresponding wait time in ys. Notice that ys itself is one of these nodes. Let zs be a path of maximal length to a node satisfying these conditions. Then, $\mu(y, s) := zs$. Likewise, if it is Eve's turn to play, she mimics the behavior of σ after the prefix zs and we set $\nu(y, s) := \sigma(zs)$.

Notice that in both cases, the contents of the memory remain to be plays consistent with σ. We claim that with such a definition, τ behaves as desired.

We prove separately the Propositions 7, 8, and 9 that describe the different attributes we want to ensure in τ. Proposition 6 is a useful step in the proofs of Properties 7 and 8:

Proposition 6. *For any finite play w consistent with τ, we have $t(w) \leq t$ $(\Omega(w))$.*

Proof. We prove by induction on the length of v that (2) holds for any finite play v consistent with τ:

$$t(v) \leq t(\Omega(v)) \tag{2}$$

By definition of Ω, we have $\Omega(\epsilon) = \epsilon$. Thus, (2) holds for ϵ. For the induction step, suppose that (2) holds for w; we show that (2) also holds for ws provided that ws is consistent with τ. From (2) applied to w and (1), we obtain

$$t(ws) \leq t(\Omega(w)s) \tag{3}$$

We need now to check the two possible cases:

- $t_j(\Omega(w)) \leq f_j^{-1}(M)$: By definition of μ, $\Omega(ws) = \Omega(w)s$. Thus, the fact that (2) holds for ws follows from (3).
- $t_j(\Omega(w)) > f_j^{-1}(M)$: In this case, the update of memory guarantees that $t(\Omega(ws)) \geq t(\Omega(w)s)$. From this and (3), we derive that (2) holds for ws.

Thus, (2) holds for any finite play v consistent with τ, and Proposition 6 holds.   □

We proceed now to the proof of Proposition 7.

Proposition 7. *If σ uniformly bounds the wait time for pair (Q_i, P_i) to B, then so does τ.*

Proof. Let us suppose that σ bounds uniformly the wait time for pair (Q_i, P_i) to B. Let w be a finite play consistent with τ. The corresponding memory state $\Omega(w)$ is a finite prefix consistent with σ. Thus, $t_i(\Omega(w)) \leq B$. By Proposition 6, $t_i(w) \leq t_i(\Omega(w))$. Thus, $t_i(w) \leq B$.   □

Proposition 8. *The value of τ is $\leq$ than the value of σ.*

Proof. In order to prove this proposition, we extend the function Ω to infinite plays consistent with τ: $\Omega(\rho)$ is the limit of the $(\Omega(w_i))_{i \in \mathbb{N}}$, for w_i the prefix of ρ of size i. This definition is sound, as $\Omega(w_{i+1})$ is always a strict suffix of $\Omega(w_i)$. Furthermore, as all the $\Omega(w_i)$ are consistent with σ, $\Omega(\rho)$ is an infinite play consistent with σ.

We show that for any play ρ consistent with τ, $v(\rho) \leq v(\Omega(\rho))$. We do so by considering separately two sets of prefixes of $\Omega(\rho)$: A prefix w of $\Omega(\rho)$ belongs to H if there is a prefix v of ρ such that $\Omega(v) = w$. Otherwise, the prefix w belongs to K.

We consider first the case of the prefixes in K. The corresponding conditions have been added to the memory during a "leap". By definition, all the positions in such a leap have a penalty for pair (Q_j, P_j) that is greater than $M + 1$. Thus, for all $w \in K, p(w) \geq M + 1$. As the mean value for all the positions is $v(\rho) \leq v(\sigma) \leq M$, it follows that the mean value for the prefixes in H is less than $v(\rho)$.

Let v be a prefix of ρ. By Proposition 6, we have for all $i \in 1 \ldots k$ that $t_i(v) \leq t_i(\Omega(v))$, and thus $p(v) \leq p(\Omega(v))$. Thus, the average penalty for the prefixes of ρ is less or equal than the average penalty for the prefixes in H. This yields $v(\rho) \leq v(\Omega(\rho))$, and Proposition 8 follows.   □

Proposition 9 expresses the essential property of strategy τ:

Proposition 9. *The strategy τ uniformly bounds the wait time for the pair (Q_j, P_j) to $f_j^{-1}(M) + d(n, k - 1)$.*

Proof. This proof is done by contradiction and derives directly from the definition of the strategy and Lemma 5. We suppose that there is a path w consistent with σ_j such that $t_j(w) > f_j^{-1}(M) + d(n, k - 1)$. Let $w = uv$, where $|v| = d(n, k - 1)$. Thus, for any word between u and w, the wait time for pair (Q_j, P_j) is greater than $f_j^{-1}(M + 1)$, and the memory is updated to a maximal branch in the tree. More formally, the definition of μ imposes that there cannot be two words x and y such that:

- $u < x < y < uv$
- $last(x) = last(y)$
- For $i = 1, \ldots, k : t_i(\Omega(x)) < t_i(\Omega(y))$

This contradicts Lemma 5, which states that there cannot be such a sequence of length $d(n, k - 1)$ (the second argument is $k - 1$ because we do not need to consider the pair j). Thus, Proposition 9 holds.   □

It is now easy to complete the proof of Lemma 4. From a strategy σ, one can derive strategies $\sigma_1, \sigma_2, \ldots, \sigma_k$ by successively applying the improvement scheme with respect to each pair (Q_j, P_j). Each time, a new pair is bounded (Proposition 9); the bounds hold through any improvement (Proposition 7); and the value of the strategy never increases (Proposition 8). Thus, the resulting strategy bounds each pair to the desired bound, and its value is less than the one of the original strategy. Lemma 4 follows.

5   From Request-Response Games to Mean-Payoff Games

By Lemma 4, we know that we can restrict our search for optimal strategies to strategies in which the wait times for each condition (Q_j, P_j) are bounded by

$$b_j := f_j^{-1}(M) + d(n, k - 1).$$

In this section, we show how to interpret such strategies in a reduced mean-payoff game, and derive from this interpretation optimal strategies with finite memory. We assume here familiarity with mean-payoff games ([6,17]).

From a real-valued request-response game over $G = (S, S_E, S_A, T)$ with conditions (Q_j, P_j) and increasing unbounded penalty functions f_j (where $j = 1, \ldots, k$) we derive the mean-payoff game over the arena $G^+ = (S^+, S_E^+, S_A^+, T^+)$ with a weight function w on the edges as follows:

- $S^+ = S \times \prod_{j \in 1 \ldots k} [0, b_j]$,
- S_E^+ and S_A^+ are defined accordingly,
- $(q, n_1, \ldots, n_k) \rightarrow (q', n_1', \ldots, n_k') \in T^+ \iff q \rightarrow q' \in T$, and for all $j = 1, \ldots, k$
  - if $n_j = 0$ then $n_j' = 1$ if $q' \in Q_j \setminus P_j$ and $n_j' = 0$ otherwise,
  - if $n_j > 0$ then $n_j' = 0$ if $q' \in P_j$ and $n_j' = n_j + 1$ otherwise,
- $w((q, n_1, \ldots, n_k), (q', n_1', \ldots, n_k')) = \sum_{j=1}^k f_j(n_j)$.

This construction consists essentially in adding wait times (and penalties) to the graph, as long as they keep to the bounds we defined. Notice that the evolution of the "wait times" part depends directly on the first component. Thus there is a natural bijection between the plays of the original game and the plays of the corresponding mean-payoff game.

We now apply a classical result on mean-payoff games:

Theorem 10 ([17]). *In a finite-state mean-payoff game (with designated initial vertex), there are (computable) optimal memoryless strategies for the two players.*

The counterpart of a memoryless strategy in the mean-payoff game is a finite-state strategy in the original request-response game:

- The set of memory states is $\prod_{j \in 1 \ldots k} [0, b_j]$.
- The strategy mimics the moves of the mean-payoff game:
  If $\sigma(q, m_1, \ldots, m_k) = (q', m_1', \ldots, m_k')$, then the next-move function μ and the memory update function ν are defined as follows:
  - $\mu(q, m_1, \ldots, m_k) = (m_1', \ldots, m_k')$
  - $\nu(q, (m_1, \ldots, m_k)) = q'$.

Theorem 2 follows.

6   Conclusion

We have studied request-response games in a setting where optimal strategies are to be constructed – in the present paper with respect to increasing and unbounded penalty functions. The main result says that if Eve (controller) wins a request-response game, then also an optimal winning strategy exists and can be effectively constructed as a finite-state strategy. This result fits into current research on valued games, such as studies on optimality of (mostly memoryless) strategies in stochastic and mean-payoff games [8,9,16]. In our case, however, we start from a discrete game, introduce a real-valued game, and after a reduction to mean-payoff games arrive again at a discrete entity (a finite-state controller) as optimal solution. Another methodological aspect is the necessity to find a balance between possibly conflicting aims when different request-response conditions (Q_j, P_j) have to be satisfied, a feature which often is only attached to multiplayer games.

Let us finally state some open problems:

1. The existence result of this paper involves very high complexity bounds (notably, in the present version of Dickson's Lemma). A more efficient synthesis procedure to optimal strategy synthesis should be found.
2. One may ask for more efficient solutions when the value of the constructed strategy only has to be an approximate of the optimal value.
3. The idea of approximation can also be invoked when bounded penalty functions are considered: The task of synthesis is then to find a strategy which realizes the limit of strategy values up to a certain factor.
4. Heuristic solutions should be developed, with an emphasis on games where the penalties of the request-response conditions are different.
5. It should be analyzed whether the framework of Bouyer, Brinksma, and Larsen [2], in which costs and rewards are distinguished as parameters for optimizing infinite runs of transition systems, can be lifted to the present game-theoretic context.
6. More general ω-regular winning conditions might be considered ([3]). For example, "eager strategies" where Adam and Eve complete their cycles as fast as possible (related to McNaughton's work [12]), or finitary games where requests must be answered in bounded time ([4,10]).

References

1. Alur, R., Etessami, K., La Torre, S., Peled, D.: Parametric temporal logic for model measuring. ACM Trans. Comput. Logic 2, 388–407 (2001)
2. Bouyer, P., Brinksma, E., Larsen, K.G.: Staying alive as cheaply as possible. In: Alur, R., Pappas, G.J. (eds.) HSCC 2004. LNCS, vol. 2993, pp. 203–218. Springer, Heidelberg (2004)
3. Büchi, J.R., Landweber, L.H.: Solving sequential conditions by finite-state strategies. Trans. Amer. Math. Soc. 138, 367–378 (1969)
4. Chatterjee, K., Henzinger, T.A.: Finitary Winning in omega-Regular Games. In: Hermanns, H., Palsberg, J. (eds.) TACAS 2006. LNCS, vol. 3920, pp. 257–271. Springer, Heidelberg (2006)
5. Dickson, L.E.: Finiteness of the odd perfect and primitive abundant numbers with n distinct prime factors. Amer. J. Math. 35, 413–422
6. Ehrenfeucht, A., Mycielski, J.: Positional strategies for mean payoff games. Int. J. of Game Theory 8, 109–113
7. Grädel, E., Thomas, W., Wilke, T. (eds.): Automata, Logics, and Infinite Games. LNCS, vol. 2500. Springer, Heidelberg (2002)
8. Gimbert, H., Zielonka, W.: Games Where You Can Play Optimally Without Any Memory. In: Abadi, M., de Alfaro, L. (eds.) CONCUR 2005. LNCS, vol. 3653, pp. 428–442. Springer, Heidelberg (2005)

9. Gimbert, H., Zielonka, W.: Deterministic Priority Mean-Payoff Games as Limits of Discounted Games. In: Bugliesi, M., Preneel, B., Sassone, V., Wegener, I. (eds.) ICALP 2006. LNCS, vol. 4052, pp. 312–323. Springer, Heidelberg (2006)
10. Horn, F.: Faster Algorithms for Finitary Games. In: Grumberg, O., Huth, M. (eds.) TACAS 2007. LNCS, vol. 4424, pp. 472–484. Springer, Heidelberg (2007)
11. Kupferman, O., Piterman, N., Vardi, M.Y.: From Liveness to Promptness. In: Damm, W., Hermanns, H. (eds.) CAV 2007. LNCS, vol. 4590, pp. 406–419. Springer, Heidelberg (2007)
12. McNaughton, R.: Playing infinite games in finite time. In: Salomaa, A., Wood, D., Yu, S. (eds.) A Half-Century of Automata Theory, pp. 73–91. World Scientific, Singapore (2000)
13. Thomas, W.: On the synthesis of strategies in infinite games. In: Mayr, E.W., Puech, C. (eds.) STACS 1995. LNCS, vol. 900, pp. 1–13. Springer, Heidelberg (1995)
14. Wallmeier, N.: Strategien in unendlichen Spielen mit Liveness-Gewinnbedingungen: Syntheseverfahren, Optimierung und Implementierung, Dissertation, RWTH Aachen (2007)
15. Wallmeier, N., Hütten, P., Thomas, W.: Symbolic synthesis of finite-state controllers for request-response specifications. In: Ibarra, O.H., Dang, Z. (eds.) CIAA 2003. LNCS, vol. 2759, pp. 11–22. Springer, Heidelberg (2003)
16. Zielonka, W.: An Invitation to Play. In: Jedrzejowicz, J., Szepietowski, A. (eds.) MFCS 2005. LNCS, vol. 3618, pp. 58–70. Springer, Heidelberg (2005)
17. Zwick, U., Paterson, M.: The complexity of mean payoff games on graphs. Theor. Comput. Sci. 158, 259–343 (1996)

Authentication Revisited: Flaw or Not, the Recursive Authentication Protocol

Guoqiang Li[1] and Mizuhito Ogawa[2]

[1] NCES, Graduate School of Information Science, Nagoya University
li.g@nces.is.nagoya-u.ac.jp
[2] Japan Advanced Institute of Science and Technology
mizuhito@jaist.ac.jp

Abstract. Authentication and secrecy have been widely investigated in security protocols. They are closely related to each other and variants of definitions have been proposed, which focus on the concepts of corresponding assertion and key distribution. This paper proposes an *on-the-fly model checking* method based on the pushdown system to verify the authentication of recursive protocols with an unbounded number of principals. By experiments of the Maude implementation, we find the recursive authentication protocol, which was verified in the sense of (weak) key distribution, has a flaw in the sense of correspondence assertion.

1 Introduction

Security protocols, although each of them only contains several flows, easily cause attacks even without breaking cryptography algorithms. Design and analysis of security protocols have been a challenging problem over 30 years.

Woo and Lam proposed two goals for security protocols, *authentication* and *key distribution* [1]. By authentication, we mean that after termination of the protocol execution, a principal should be assured that it is "talking" to the intended principal. Key distribution means that if a principal receives a session key, then only the principal who sent the key (and the server) knew the key. They also gave the formal definitions: authentication is defined as *correspondence assertion*, and key distribution is defined as *secrecy*. Note that this secrecy is stronger than the one widely used later [2,3]. Correspondence assertion is later widely used to define the authentication [2,3,4]. The intuitive meaning is, when B claims the message it accepted from A, then A exactly sent the same message.

These properties has various different points of view. For instance, Bellare et. al. stated that key distribution is "very different from" authentication [5]. Bella pointed out that two goals "are strictly related" and "might be equivalent" [4].

Paulson et al. formally defined the key distribution[1], which intuitively means, if a principal receives a session key, then only the principal who sent the key (and the server) *can know* the key [4,6]. Its difference from the key distribution Woo and Lam defined is quite subtle, since "can know" implies "may not know". In

---

[1] This "key distribution" is weaker than what Woo and Lam has defined in [1].

their sense of key distribution, Paulson proved the correctness of the *recursive authentication protocol* (referred to as the RA protocol) [6].

This paper proposes an *on-the-fly model checking* method [7,8,9] based on the pushdown system to verify the authentication property of recursive protocols with an unbounded number of principals. By experiments with the Maude implementation, we find out that the RA protocol has a flaw in the sense of correspondence assertion.

The model checking method tackles various sources of infinity in the verification of the RA protocol. Our main ideas are summarized as:

- Lazy instantiation on messages, i.e., message contents that do not affect protocol actions will be left unsubstantiated.
- Lazy instantiation on names, i.e., names, such as encryption keys, are extended from constants to terms, and left uninstantiated until actual principals are assigned during communications.
- Identification of fresh messages by contexts, i.e., since the RA protocol does not repeat the same context (i.e., once pop starts, never push again), each nonce in a session is identified by the stack content.

The first idea is realized by a *parametric semantics* and a *refinement step*. The second and the third ideas are realized by *binders* [7]. These ideas supply sound and compete model checking for verifying authentication of the RA protocol.

Note that this methodology covers only a restricted class of recursive protocols, which are described by *sequential recursive processes*. To the best of our knowledge, this is the first model checking applied to recursive protocols.

This paper is organized as follows. Section 2 presents an environment based process calculus for security protocol descriptions, and a trace equivalence to specify the authentication property. Section 3 shows how to describe and analyze the RA protocol in our setting. The encoding of the pushdown system and experimental results by Maude are reported in Section 4. Section 5 presents related work, and Section 6 concludes the paper.

Due to the lack of space, we omit detailed explanations, examples and theorems; these can be found in the extended version [10].

2   A Process Calculus for Security Protocol Descriptions

2.1   The Syntax of the Calculus

Assume three disjoint sets: $\mathcal{L}$ for *labels*, $\mathcal{B}$ for *binder names* and $\mathcal{V}$ for *variables*. Let $a, b, c, \ldots$ denote labels, let $\mathrm{m}, \mathrm{n}, \mathrm{k}, \ldots$ for binder names, and let $x, y, z, \ldots$ for variables.

Definition 1 (Messages). *Messages $M, N, L \ldots$ in a set $\mathcal{M}$ are defined iteratively as follows:*

$$pr ::= x \mid \mathrm{m}[pr, \ldots, pr]$$
$$M, N, L ::= pr \mid (M, N) \mid \{M\}_L \mid \mathcal{H}(M)$$

A message is ground, if it does not contain any variables.

- pr ranges over a set of undecomposable *primary messages*.
- A binder, $\mathtt{m}[pr_1,\ldots,pr_n]$ is an atomic message indexed by its parameters, $pr_1,\ldots,pr_n$. A binder with 0 arity is named a *name*, which ranges over a set $\mathcal{N}$ ($\mathcal{N} \subseteq \mathcal{B}$).
- (M, N) represents a *pair* of messages.
- $\{M\}_L$ is an *encrypted message* where M is its *plain message* and L is its *encryption key*.
- $\mathcal{H}(M)$ represents a one-way *hash function message*.

Definition 2 (Processes). *Let $\mathcal{P}$ be a countable set of processes which is indicated by $P, Q, R, \ldots$. The syntax of processes is defined as follows:*

$$P, Q, R ::= \mathbf{0} \mid \bar{a}M.P \mid a(x).P \mid [M = N]\,P \mid (\mathbf{new}\ x : \mathcal{A})P \mid (\nu n)P \mid$$
$$\mathbf{let}\ (x, y) = M\ \mathbf{in}\ P \mid \mathbf{case}\ M\ \mathbf{of}\ \{x\}_L\ \mathbf{in}\ P \mid$$
$$P\|Q \mid P + Q \mid P; Q \mid \mathbb{A}(\tilde{pr})$$

Variables x and y are bound in $a(x).P$, $(\mathbf{new}\,x : \mathcal{A})P$, $\mathbf{let}\ (x, y) = M\ \mathbf{in}\ P$, and $\mathbf{case}\ M\ \mathbf{of}\ \{x\}_L\ \mathbf{in}\ P$. The sets of free variables and bound variables in P are denoted by $f_v(P)$ and $b_v(P)$, respectively. A process P is closed if $f_v(P) = \emptyset$. A name is free in a process if it is not restricted by a restriction operator ν. The sets of free names and local names of P are denoted by $f_n(P)$ and $l_n(P)$, respectively.

Their intuition is,

- $\mathbf{0}$ is the *Nil* process that does nothing.
- $\bar{a}M.P$ and $a(x).P$ are *communication processes*. They are used to describe sending message M, and awaiting an input message via x, respectively.
- $(\mathbf{new}\ x : \mathcal{A})P$ and $(\nu n)P$ are *binding processes*. The former denotes that x ranges over $\mathcal{A}$ ($\subseteq \mathcal{N}$) in P; The latter denotes that the name n is local in P.
- $[M = N]\,P$, $\mathbf{let}\ (x, y) = M\ \mathbf{in}\ P$ and $\mathbf{case}\ M\ \mathbf{of}\ \{x\}_L\ \mathbf{in}\ P$ are *validation processes*. They validate whether the message M is equal to N, whether it is a pair, and whether it is an encrypted message, respectively.
- $P\|Q$, $P+Q$, and $P; Q$ are *structure processes*. $P\|Q$ means that two processes run concurrently; $P + Q$ means nondeterministic choices of a process; $P; Q$ means when P terminates, then Q runs.
- For each *identifier* $\mathbb{A}(pr_1,\ldots,pr_n)$, there is a unique definition, $\mathbb{A}(pr_1,\ldots,pr_n) \triangleq P$, where the $pr_1,\ldots,pr_n$ are free names and variables in P.

We assume a set of *identifier variables*, X will range over identifier variables. A *process expression* is like a process, but may contain identifier variables in the same way as identifers. E, F will range over process expressions.

Definition 3 (Recursive process). *A recursive process is defined as an identifier, with the format, $\mathbb{A}_i \triangleq E(\mathbb{A}_1,\ldots,\mathbb{A}_i,\ldots,\mathbb{A}_n)$.*

If a process is not a recursive process, we name it a *flat process*.

Definition 4 (Sequential). *Let E be any expression. We say that an identifier variable X is sequential in E, if X does not occur in any arguments of parallel compositions. An expression E is sequential if all variables in E are sequential. A sequential process is an identifier defined by an sequential expression.*

2.2   Characterizations and Restrictions on the Process Calculus

We use an environment-based process calculus [3], while traditional process calculi, such as π-calculus [11], use channel-based communications. There are several notable differences between two types of calculi.

- Communications.
  - In channel-based calculi, two processes communicate through a specific channel. For example, a communication in π-calculus [11] is,

$$((\nu\, z)\overline{x}\, z.P) \mid x(y).Q \mid R \longrightarrow^{+} ((\nu\, z)P \mid Q\{z/y\}) \mid R$$

  The first process sends a local name z through the channel x, while the second process awaits a name via y on the same channel x. Thus the name z will be communicated between two processes.
  - In the environment-based process calculus, all processes communicate through a public environment, which records all communicated messages. The calculus is thus natural to describe a hostile network.
- Freshness of names.
  - Channel-based calculi adopt scopes of local names for fresh names. In the example above, the scope of z enlarges after the transition. Although R is included in the system, it cannot "touch" the z during the transition. Due to α-conversation, z can be substituted to any fresh name.
  - All local names in the environment-based process calculus will be substituted to fresh public names during transitions. Since when two principals exchange a message through a hostile network, we assume that all other principals will know the message. Several techniques will be performed to guarantee that each public name is fresh to the whole system.
- Infinitely many messages that intruders and dishonest principals generate.
  - Channel-based calculi adopt recursive processes to generate these messages. Thus even describing a simple protocol, the system is complex [12].
  - The environment based process calculus adopt deductive systems to generate the messages generated by intruders and dishonest principals [3,8]. Security protocols can be described in a straightforward way.

For both types of calculi, there are two representations for infinite processes, *identifiers* and *replications*. Identifiers can represent recursive processes. Replications take the form $!P$, which intuitively means an unbounded number of concurrent copies of P. For fitness to model as a pushdown system, we choose identifiers with the sequential restriction.

2.3   Trace Semantics and Equivalence

An *environmental deductive system* (represented as $\vdash$, see [10]) generates messages that intruders can produce, starting from the the logged messages. It produces, encrypts/decrypts, composes/splits, and hashes messages.

An *action* is a term of form $\overline{a}M$ or $a(M)$. It is ground if its attached message is ground. A string of ground actions represents a possible run of the protocol, if each input message is deduced by messages in its prefix string. We named such a kind of string (concrete) *trace*, denoted by $s, s', s'', \ldots$. The messages in a concrete trace s, denoted by $msg(s)$, are those messages in output actions of the concrete trace s. We use $s \vdash M$ to abbreviate $msg(s) \vdash M$.

Definition 5 (Concrete trace and configuration). *A concrete trace s is a ground action string, satisfying each decomposition $s = s'.a(M).s''$ implies $s' \vdash M$. A concrete configuration is a pair $\langle s, P \rangle$, in which s is a concrete trace and P is a closed process.*

The extended version [10] presents the trace semantics, the parametric semantics and a refinement step as the lazy instantiation. We proved the sound and complete correspondence between two semantics [7,9].

Abadi and Gordon adopted *testing equivalence* to define security properties [2], in which the *implementation* and the *specification* of a security protocol are described by two processes. If they satisfy the equivalence for a security property, the protocol guarantees the property.

Testing equivalence is defined by quantifying the environment with which the processes interact. Intuitively, the two processes should exhibit the same traces under arbitrary *observers* (as intruders). In our calculus, capabilities of intruders are captured by the environmental deductive system. Thus, a *trace equivalence* is directly applied for the authentication property without quantifying observers.

For simplicity, we say a concrete configuration $\langle s, P \rangle$ *generates* a concrete trace s', if $\langle s, P \rangle \longrightarrow^* \langle s', P' \rangle$ for some P'.

Definition 6 (Trace equivalence). *P and Q are trace equivalent, written $P \sim_t Q$, if for all trace s, P generates s if and only if Q generates s.*

3   Analysis of the Recursive Authentication Protocol

3.1   The Recursive Authentication Protocol

The recursive authentication protocol is proposed in [13]. It operates over an arbitrarily long chain of principals, terminating with a key-generated server.

Assume an unbounded number of principals intending to generate session keys between each two adjacent principals by contacting a key-generated server once. Each principal either contacts the server, or forwards messages and its own information to the next principal. The protocol has three stages (see Fig. 1):

Communication stage. Each principal sends a request to its next principal, composing its message and the message accepted from the previous one. *Submission stage.* One principal submits the whole request to the server. *Distribution stage.* The server generates a group of session keys, and sends back to the last principal. Each principal distributes the session keys to its previous principal.

The RA protocol is given informally as follows. For simplicity, we use a convenient abbreviation of the hash message,

$$\mathcal{H}_K(X) = (\mathcal{H}(K, X), X)$$

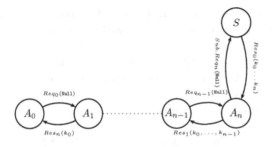

Fig. 1. The Recursive Authentication Protocol

Communication Stage

$$A_0 \longrightarrow A_1 : \qquad \mathcal{H}_{K_{A_0 S}}(A_0, A_1, N_{A_0}, \text{Null})$$
$$A_i \longrightarrow A_{i+1} : \qquad \mathcal{H}_{K_{A_i S}}(A_i, A_{i+1}, N_{A_i}, X_i)$$

Submission Stage

$$A_n \longrightarrow S : \qquad \mathcal{H}_{K_{A_n S}}(A_n, S, N_{A_n}, X_n)$$

Distribution Stage

$$S \longrightarrow A_n : \quad \{K_n, S, N_{A_n}\}_{K_{A_n S}}, \{K_{n-1}, A_{n-1}, N_{A_n}\}_{K_{A_n S}},$$
$$\{K_{n-1}, A_n, N_{A_{n-1}}\}_{K_{A_{n-1} S}}, \{K_{n-2}, A_{n-2}, N_{A_{n-1}}\}_{K_{A_{n-1} S}},$$
$$\ldots$$
$$\{K_1, A_2, N_{A_1}\}_{K_{A_1 S}}, \{K_0, A_0, N_{A_1}\}_{K_{A_1 S}},$$
$$\{K_0, A_1, N_{A_0}\}_{K_{A_0 S}}$$
$$A_i \longrightarrow A_{i-1} : \{K_{i-1}, A_i, N_{A_{i-1}}\}_{K_{A_{i-1} S}}, \{K_{i-2}, A_{i-2}, N_{A_{i-1}}\}_{K_{A_{i-1} S}}, \cdots$$
$$A_1 \longrightarrow A_0 : \quad \{K_0, A_1, N_{A_0}\}_{K_{A_0 S}}$$

where Null is a special name, and X_i is the message from A_{i-1} to A_i.

3.2 Authentication of the RA Protocol

To represent authentication, *declaration processes* will be inserted into a protocol description [2,9]. For instance, the implementation, SYS^{RA}_{imp}, of the RA protocol below contains a declaration process $\overline{acc}\,x.\mathbf{0}$ for authentication.

$$\mathbb{O}_a(x_1, x_2) \triangleq \overline{a1}\,\mathcal{H}_{1k[x_1, S]}(x_1, x_2, \text{N[Null]}, \text{Null}).a2(x).case\ x\ of\{y_1, y_2, y_3\}_{1k[x_1, S]}.$$
$$[y_3 = \text{N[Null]}]\,\overline{acc}\,x.\mathbf{0}$$

$$\mathbb{R}_a(x_1, x_2) \triangleq (b1(x).let\ (y_1, y_2, y_3, y_4, y_5) = x\ in\ [y_2 = x_1]$$
$$\overline{b2}\,\mathcal{H}_{1k[x_1, S]}(x_1, \text{A}[x_1], \text{N}[y_3], x).(\mathbb{R}(\text{A}[x_1], x_1)$$
$$+ \overline{b3}\,\mathcal{H}_{1k[x_1, S]}(x_1, S, \text{N}[y_3], x).\mathbf{0})); (b4(x).let\ (z_1, z_2, z_3) = x\ in$$
$$case\ z_1\ of\ \{z_4, z_5, z_6\}_{1k[x_1, S]}\ in\ [z_5 = \text{A}[x_1]]\,[z_6 = \text{N}[y_3]]$$
$$case\ z_2\ of\ \{z_7, z_8, z_9\}_{1k[x_1, S]}\ in\ [z_8 = x_2]\,[z_9 = \text{N}[y_3]]\,\overline{b5}z_3.\mathbf{0})$$

$$S \triangleq s1(x).\overline{s2}\,(\mathscr{F}(x)).\mathbf{0}$$

$$SYS^{RA}_{imp} \triangleq \mathbb{O}_a(\text{A[Null]}, \text{A[A[Null]]}) \| \mathbb{R}_a(\text{A[A[Null]]}, \text{A[Null]}) \| S$$

In the description, we use a group of nested binders to describe unbounded number of fresh names. For instances, by $N[Null], N[N[Null]], \ldots$ we describe fresh nonces $N_{A_0}, N_{A_1}, \ldots$.

$\mathscr{F} : \mathcal{M} \to \mathcal{M}$ is an iterative procedure that generates an arbitrarily long message. We name this kind of messages *recursive messages*.

$\mathscr{F}$ is defined as follows:

$$\mathscr{F}(x) = \texttt{let } (y_1, y_2, y_3, y_4, y_5) = x;$$
$$\texttt{let } t = \epsilon;$$
$$\texttt{while } (y_1 = \mathcal{H}(y_2, y_3, y_4, y_5, \texttt{lk}[y_2, S]) \ \&\& \ y_5! = \texttt{Null})$$
$$\texttt{let } (z_1, z_2, z_3, z_4, z_5) = y_5;$$
$$\texttt{if } (z_1 = \mathcal{H}(z_2, z_3, z_4, z_5, \texttt{lk}[z_2, S]) \&\& z_3 == y_2)$$
$$\texttt{then } t = (t, \{\texttt{k}[y_4], y_3, y_4\}, \{\texttt{k}[y_3], z_2, z_4\});$$
$$\texttt{else raise error}$$
$$\texttt{endif}$$
$$(y_1, y_2, y_3, y_4, y_5) := (z_1, z_2, z_3, z_4, z_5);$$
$$\texttt{endwhile}$$
$$t := (t, \{\texttt{k}[y_4], y_3, y_4\});$$
$$\texttt{return } t;$$

The specification for the authentication, SYS_{spe}^{RA}, is a process that replaces x in $\overline{acc}\,x.0$ with $\{\texttt{k}[Null], A[A[Null]], N[Null]\}_{\texttt{lk}[A[Null]], S]}$.

Authentication between the originator and its recipient is defined by

$$SYS_{imp}^{RA} \sim_t SYS_{spe}^{RA}$$

The implementation and the specification may fail to generate the same traces after certain message comparisons. The specification will guarantee that the message received and validated by one principal should be the same as the message sent by other principal, while these messages would be different in the implementation due to the ill-design of a protocol. Hence, we can explicitly check the equality of the two messages in traces generated by the implementation [7,9], which is another way to encode the correspondence assertion.

Definition 7 (Action terms[3]). *Let α and β be actions, with $f_v(\alpha) \subseteq f_v(\beta)$, and let s be a trace. We use $s \models \alpha \hookleftarrow \beta$ to represent that for each ground substitution ρ, if $\beta\rho$ occurs in s, then there exists one $\alpha\rho$ in s before $\beta\rho$. A configuration satisfies $\alpha \hookleftarrow \beta$, denoted by $\langle s, P \rangle \models \alpha \hookleftarrow \beta$, if each trace s' generated from $\langle s, P \rangle$ satisfies $s' \models \alpha \hookleftarrow \beta$.*

Characterization 1. *[Authentication for the RA protocol] Given the formal description of the RA protocol, the recipient is correctly authenticated to the originator, if $\langle \epsilon, SYS_{imp}^{RA} \rangle \models \overline{b5}\,x \hookleftarrow \overline{acc}\,x$.*

4   Model Checking by the Pushdown System

4.1   Encoding as Pushdown Model

To analyze recursive protocols with a pushdown system, the restrictions for a process are, (i) a system is restricted to contain at most one recursive process; (ii) the expression that defines the recursive process is sequential.

When analyzing protocols in bounded sessions, fresh messages that processes generate are bounded. We can fix a set of distinguished symbols to describe them [7]. However, for the analysis of recursive protocols, fresh messages can be unbounded. We represent an unbounded number of fresh messages by nested binders. With the restrictions of a single recursive process, the same context (stack content) will not be repeated; thus freshness will be guaranteed.

Definition 8 (Pushdown system). *A pushdown system* $\mathcal{P} = (Q, \Gamma, \Delta, c_0)$ *is a quadruple, where Q contains the control locations, and Γ is the stack alphabet. A configuration of $\mathcal{P}$ is a pair (q, ω) where $q \in Q$ and $\omega \in \Gamma^*$. The set of all configurations is denoted by* $\mathtt{conf}(\mathcal{P})$. *With $\mathcal{P}$ we associated the unique transition system* $\mathcal{I}_\mathcal{P} = (\mathtt{conf}(\mathcal{P}), \Rightarrow, c_0)$, *whose initial configuration is c_0.*

Δ is a finite subset of $(Q \times \Gamma) \times (Q \times \Gamma^*)$. If $((q, \gamma), (q', \omega)) \in \Delta$, we also write $\langle q, \gamma \rangle \hookrightarrow \langle q', \omega \rangle$. For each transition relation, if $\langle q, \gamma \rangle \hookrightarrow \langle q', \omega \rangle$, then $\langle q, \gamma\omega' \rangle \Rightarrow \langle q', \omega\omega' \rangle$ for all $\omega' \in \Gamma^*$.

We define a set of messages used for the pushdown system as follows,

Definition 9 (Messages in the pushdown system)

$$pr ::= x \mid \top \mid \mathtt{m}[\,] \mid \mathtt{m}[pr, \ldots, pr]$$
$$M, N, L ::= pr \mid (M, N) \mid \{M\}_L \mid \mathcal{H}(M)$$

Two new messages are introduced. $\top$ is a special name, substituting a variable that can be substituted to an unbounded number of names. $\mathtt{m}[\,]$ is a *binder marker*, representing nested binders, together with the stack depth. For instance, $\mathtt{A}[\mathtt{A}[\mathtt{Null}]]$ is represented by $\mathtt{A}[\,]$, with two stack elements in the stack.

Definition 10 (compaction). *Given a parametric trace $\hat{s}$, a compaction $\hat{tr}$ is a parametric trace by cutting off redundant actions with the same labels in $\hat{s}$.*

We represent the parametric model with at most one sequential recursive process by the pushdown system as follows,

- control locations are pairs $(R, \hat{tr})$, where R is a finite set of recursive messages, and $\hat{tr}$ is a compaction.
- stack alphabet only contains a symbol $\star$.
- initial configuration is $\langle (\emptyset, \epsilon), \varepsilon \rangle$, where ϵ represents an empty parametric trace, and ε represents an empty stack.
- Δ is defined by two sets of translations, the translations for the parametric rules, and the translations for the refinement step.

An occurrence of **0** in the last sequence process of a recursive process means a return point of the current process. We will replace it to a distinguished marker, **Nil**, when encoding a parametric system to the pushdown system.

The key encodings of the parametric transitions are as follows, in which $\hat{tr}$ and $\hat{tr}'$ are compactions of $\hat{s}$ and $\hat{s}'$, respectively.

1. For parametric transition rules except *PIND* rules, $\langle (R, \hat{tr}), \omega \rangle \hookrightarrow \langle (R, \hat{tr}'), \omega \rangle$ if $\langle \hat{s}, P \rangle \longrightarrow_p \langle \hat{s}', P' \rangle$.

```
Solution 1 (state 415)
states: 416  rewrites: 67367 in 7689676981ms cpu (824ms real) (0
    rewrites/second)
ML1 --> {{{(k[Mk],name(1)},px(32)}lk[px(31),name(1)],{{(Mk,px(33)},px(32)}lk[px(
    31),name(1)]},{(Mk,px(31)},px(34)}lk[px(33),name(1)]
TR1 --> < a(1),o,H(lk[MA,name(1)],{(MA,A[MA]),MN),null) > . < b(1),i,H(lk[MA,
    name(1)],{(MA,A[MA]),MN),null) > . < b(3),o,H(lk[A[MA],name(1)],{(A[MA],
    name(1)),N[MN]),H(lk[MA,name(1)],{(MA,A[MA]),MN),null) > . < s(1),i,H(lk[
    A[MA],name(1)],{(A[MA],name(1)),N[MN]),H(lk[MA,name(1)],{(MA,A[MA]),MN),
    null)} > . < s(2),o,{{(k[Mk],name(1)),N[MN])lk[A[MA],name(1)],{(Mk,MA),N[
    MN])lk[A[MA],name(1)]},{(Mk,A[MA]),MN)lk[MA,name(1)] > . < a(2),i,{(Mk,A[
    MA]),MN)lk[MA,name(1)] > . < acc,o,{(Mk,A[MA]),MN)lk[MA,name(1)] >
STACK --> empty
```

Fig. 2. Snapshot of Maude Result for the Recursive Authentication Protocol

2. For $PIND$ rule, when $\mathbb{R}$ is firstly met, $\langle(R,\hat{tr}),\omega\rangle \hookrightarrow \langle(R,\hat{tr}'),\omega\rangle$ if $\langle\hat{s},P\rangle \longrightarrow_p \langle\hat{s}',P'\rangle$, where $\mathbb{R}(\hat{pr}) \triangleq P$; Otherwise $\langle(R,\hat{tr}),\omega\rangle \hookrightarrow \langle(R,\hat{tr}),\star\omega\rangle$.
3. $\langle(R,\hat{tr}),\gamma\rangle \hookrightarrow \langle(R,\hat{tr}),\varepsilon\rangle$ if $\langle\hat{s},\mathbf{Nil}\rangle$ is met.

In the refinement step, we need to satisfy *rigid messages* by unifications [10,9]. A rigid message is the pattern of a requirement of an input action that can be satisfied by messages generated only by legitimate principals. We distinguish two kinds of rigid messages, *context-insensitive*, and *context-sensitive*.

Definition 11 (Context-sensitive/insensitive rigid messages). *Context-sensitive rigid messages are rigid messages that contain binder markers, while context-insensitive rigid messages do not contain any binder markers.*

Intuitively, a context-sensitive rigid message has an bounded number of candidate messages within the current context to unify with, while a context-insensitive one has an unbounded number of candidate messages to unify with.

The transition relations for the refinement step in Δ are defined as follows.

4. $\langle(R,\hat{tr}),\omega\rangle \hookrightarrow \langle(R,\hat{tr}\hat{\rho}),\omega\rangle$, if N is context-sensitive and $\hat{\rho}$-unifiable in $R \cup el(\hat{s}_1)$.
5. $\langle(R,\hat{tr}),\omega\rangle \hookrightarrow \langle(R \cup N',\hat{tr}\hat{\rho}'),\omega\rangle$, if N is context-insensitive and $\hat{\rho}$-unifiable to N' in $el(\hat{s}_1)$, and $\hat{\rho}'$ is the substitution that replaces different messages in N and N' with $\top$.

4.2 Implementing in Maude

We implemented the pushdown system above by Maude [14]. It describes model generating rules by rewriting, instead of constructing directly. The reachability problem can be checked at the same time while a model is being generated. We tested the RA protocol by our Maude implementation. A counterexample is automatically detected. The result snapshot is in Fig. 2, in which MA, MN, and Mk are binder markers. name(1) is the server name S. It describes attacks showed in Fig. 3, which actually represents infinitely many attacks. An intruder intercepts the message sent by S, splits it, and sends the parted message to A_0. The minimal one is,

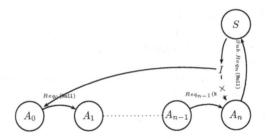

Fig. 3. The Attack of the RA Protocol

$$A_0 \longrightarrow A_1 : \quad \mathcal{H}_{K_{A_0S}}(A_0, A_1, N_{A_0}, \text{Null})$$
$$A_1 \longrightarrow S : \quad \mathcal{H}_{K_{A_1S}}(A_1, S, N_{A_1}, \mathcal{H}_{K_{A_0S}}(A_0, A_1, N_{A_0}, \text{Null}))$$
$$S \longrightarrow I(A_1) : \quad \{K_1, S, N_{A_1}\}_{K_{A_1S}}, \{K_0, A_0, N_{A_1}\}_{K_{A_1S}}, \{K_0, A_1, N_{A_0}\}_{K_{A_0S}}$$
$$I(A_1) \longrightarrow A_0 : \quad \{K_0, A_1, N_{A_0}\}_{K_{A_0S}}$$

This result obstructs that: (1) further update of the session key of A_0 is disabled, and (2) traceability of the session key of A_0 is violated, which are frequently required in the real-world security.

The implementation contains about 400 lines for the general structures and functions, and 32 lines for the protocol description. The test was performed on a Pentium M 1.4 GHz, 1.5 G memory PC. The flaw is detected at the last step.

protocols	states	times(ms)	flaws
recursive authentication protocol	416	824	detected

The reason of attacks is that S sends the message without any protections. One modification is that S protects the message it sends iteratively with long-term symmetric keys shared with principals. In the two-principal case,

$$A_0 \longrightarrow A_1 : \quad \mathcal{H}_{K_{A_0S}}(A_0, A_1, N_{A_0}, \text{Null})$$
$$A_1 \longrightarrow S : \quad \mathcal{H}_{K_{A_1S}}(A_1, S, N_{A_1}, \mathcal{H}_{K_{A_0S}}(A_0, A_1, N_{A_0}, \text{Null}))$$
$$S \longrightarrow A_1 : \quad \{\{K_1, A_2, N_{A_1}\}_{K_{A_1S}}, \{K_0, A_0, N_{A_1}\}_{K_{A_1S}},$$
$$\{K_0, A_1, N_{A_0}\}_{K_{A_0S}}\}_{K_{A_1S}}$$
$$A_1 \longrightarrow A_0 : \quad \{K_0, A_1, N_{A_0}\}_{K_{A_0S}}$$

The fixed protocol is checked secure by the same Maude implementation.

protocols	states	times(ms)	flaws
fixed recursive authentication protocol	416	1,068	secure

5   Related Work

G. Lowe proposed a taxonomy that elucidates four levels of authentication [15]. Let us suppose that in a session of a protocol, a sender A communicates with a receiver B.

- *Aliveness* of B guarantees that B attended the protocol.
- *Weak agreement* of B guarantees that B attended the protocol with A.
- *Non-injective agreement* of B guarantees that B attended the protocol with A, and two principals agreed on a set of messages $\mathcal{H}$.
- *Injective agreement* of B guarantees non-injective agreement of B, and that A corresponds to a unique run of B in the session.

Each level subsumes the previous one. This paper, together with other researches [12,3], took non-injective agreement as the standard authentication, which can be specified by the correspondence assertion.

Paulson took a weak form of key distribution property, and used Isabelle/HOL to prove that the correctness of the RA protocol with bounded number of principals [6]. Bella pointed out that non-injective agreement authentication and the weak form of key distribution "might be equivalent" [4]. However, we showed in this paper that the weak form of key distribution does not hold non-injective agreement, specified by the correspondence assertion.

Bryans and Schneider adopted CSP to describe behaviors of the RA protocol with the same assumption as Paulson's. They considered the correspondence assertion between the server and the last principal who submitted the request, and used PVS to prove the correctness of the authentication for the RA protocol [16].

Basin et al. proposed an on-the-fly model checking method (OFMC) [17] for security protocol analysis. In their work, an intruder's messages are instantiated only when necessary, known as *lazy intruder*. Their research is similar to our work in analyzing authentication in bounded sessions without binders.

A *tree transducer-based* model was proposed for recursive protocols by Küsters, et al. [18]. The rules in this model are assumed to have linear left-hand sides, so no equality tests can be performed. Truderung generalized the limitation, and proposed a *selecting theory* for recursive protocols [19]. Both of the two works focused on the secrecy property of the RA protocol. Recently, Küsters and Truderung considered the arithmetic encryption algorithm for the RA protocol, detected the known attack [20] automatically [21]. Since we assume a perfect cryptography, this attack is out of our methodology.

6   Conclusion

This paper presented the pushdown model checking of authentication of the RA protocol. It extended our previous work [7], allowing to analyze protocols with at most one recursive procedure. Our Maude implementation successfully detected a previously unreported attack that violates authentication in the sense of corresponding assertion of the RA protocol automatically. This result shows the effect of the subtle difference among security definitions.

Acknowledgements. The authors thank Prof. Kazuhiro Ogata for fruitful discussions. This research is supported by the 21st Century COE "Verifiable and Evolvable e-Society" of JAIST, funded by Japanese Ministry of Education, Culture, Sports, Science and Technology.

References

1. Woo, T.Y., Lam, S.S.: A Semantic Model for Authentication Protocols. In: Proceedings of the S&P 1993, pp. 178–194. IEEE Computer Society Press, Los Alamitos (1993)
2. Abadi, M., Gordon, A.D.: A Calculus for Cryptographic Protocols: The Spi Calculus. In: Proceedings of the CCS 1997, pp. 36–47. ACM Press, New York (1997)
3. Boreale, M.: Symbolic Trace Analysis of Cryptographic Protocols. In: Orejas, F., Spirakis, P.G., van Leeuwen, J. (eds.) ICALP 2001. LNCS, vol. 2076, pp. 667–681. Springer, Heidelberg (2001)
4. Bella, G.: Inductive Verification of Cryptographic Protocols. PhD thesis, University of Cambridge (2000)
5. Bellare, M., Rogaway, P.: Provably Secure Session Key Distribution: The Three Party Case. In: Proceedings of the STOC 1995, pp. 57–66. ACM Press, New York (1995)
6. Paulson, L.C.: Mechanized Proofs for a Recursive Authentication Protocol. In: Proceedings of the CSFW 1997, pp. 84–95. IEEE Computer Society Press, Los Alamitos (1997)
7. Li, G., Ogawa, M.: On-the-Fly Model Checking of Security Protocols and Its Implementation by Maude. IPSJ Transactions on Programming 48, 50–75 (2007)
8. Li, G., Ogawa, M.: On-the-Fly Model Checking of Fair Non-repudiation Protocols. In: Namjoshi, K.S., Yoneda, T., Higashino, T., Okamura, Y. (eds.) ATVA 2007. LNCS, vol. 4762, pp. 511–522. Springer, Heidelberg (2007)
9. Li, G.: On-the-Fly Model Checking of Security Protocols. PhD thesis, Japan Advanced Institute of Science and Technology (2008)
10. Li, G., Ogawa, M.: Authentication Revisited: Flaw or Not, the Recursive Authentication Protocol. Technical Report IS-RR-2008-002, Japan Advanced Institute of Science and Technology (2008)
11. Sangiorgi, D., Walker, D.: The Pi-Calculus: A Theory of Mobile Processes. Cambridge University Press, Cambridge (2003)
12. Lowe, G.: Breaking and Fixing the Needham-Schroeder Public-key Using FDR. In: Margaria, T., Steffen, B. (eds.) TACAS 1996. LNCS, vol. 1055, pp. 147–166. Springer, Heidelberg (1996)
13. Bull, J.A., Otway, D.J.: The Authentication Protocol. Technical report, Defence Research Agency, UK (1997)
14. Clavel, M., Durán, F., Eker, S., Lincolnand, P., Martí-Oliet, N., Meseguer, J., Talcott, C.: Maude Manual (Version 2.2) (2005)
15. Lowe, G.: A Hierarchy of Authentication Specifications. In: Proceedings of the CSFW 1997, pp. 31–43. IEEE Computer Society Press, Los Alamitos (1997)
16. Bryans, J., Schneider, S.: CSP, PVS and a Recursive Authentication Protocol. In: Proceedings of the DIMACS FVSP 1997 (1997)
17. Basin, D.A., Mödersheim, S., Viganò, L.: OFMC: A Symbolic Model Checker for Security Protocols. International Journal of Information Security 4(3), 181–208 (2005)
18. Küsters, R., Wilke, T.: Automata-based Analysis of Recursive Cryptographic Protocols. In: Diekert, V., Habib, M. (eds.) STACS 2004. LNCS, vol. 2996, pp. 382–393. Springer, Heidelberg (2004)
19. Truderung, T.: Selecting Theories and Recursive Protocols. In: Abadi, M., de Alfaro, L. (eds.) CONCUR 2005. LNCS, vol. 3653, pp. 217–232. Springer, Heidelberg (2005)
20. Ryan, P., Schneider, S.: An Attack on a Recursive Authentication Protocol: A Cautionary Tale. Information Processing Letters 65, 7–10 (1998)
21. Küsters, R., Truderung, T.: On the Automatic Analysis of Recursive Security Protocols with XOR. In: Thomas, W., Weil, P. (eds.) STACS 2007. LNCS, vol. 4393, pp. 646–657. Springer, Heidelberg (2007)

Impartial Anticipation in Runtime-Verification*

Wei Dong[1], Martin Leucker[2], and Christian Schallhart[3]

[1] School of Computer, National University of Defense Technology, P.R. China
[2] Institut für Informatik, Technische Universität München, Germany
[3] Formal Methods in Systems Engineering, FB Informatik, TU Darmstadt, Germany

Abstract. In this paper, a uniform approach for synthesizing monitors checking correctness properties specified in linear-time logics at runtime is provided. Therefore, a generic three-valued semantics is introduced reflecting the idea that *prefixes* of infinite computations are checked. Then a conceptual framework to synthesize monitors from a logical specification to check an execution incrementally is established, with special focus on resorting to the *automata-theoretic approach*. The merits of the presented framework are shown by providing monitor synthesis approaches for a variety of different logics such as **LTL**, the linear-time μ-calculus, **PLTL**^{mod}, **S1S**, and **RLTL**.

1 Introduction

Runtime verification (RV) is an emerging lightweight verification technique in which executions of systems under scrutiny are checked for satisfaction or violation of given correctness properties. While it complements verification techniques such as model checking and testing, it also paves the way for not-only detecting incorrect behavior of a software system but also for reacting and potentially *healing* the system when a correctness violation is encountered.

Typically, a *monitor* is employed in RV, checking whether the execution meets a certain correctness property. Such a monitor may on one hand be used to check the *current* execution of a system. In this setting, which is termed *online monitoring*, the monitor should be designed to consider executions in an *incremental fashion* and in an *efficient manner*. On the other hand, a monitor may work on a (finite set of) *recorded* execution(s), in which case we speak of *offline monitoring*. In this paper we focus on online monitoring.

In online monitoring, often an—at least ideally—non-terminating system is checked. In the very end, this asks for checking correctness of an infinite execution trace. Clearly, this cannot be done at runtime. In fact, we aim at deriving a verdict whether an infinite execution satisfies a correctness property by considering its *finite prefixes*. In [1], we formulated two maxims a monitor should ideally follow to capture implications of this idea:

---

* This work has been supported in part by National Natural Science Foundation of China (Grant No.60673118).

Cha et al. (Eds.): ATVA 2008, LNCS 5311, pp. 386–396, 2008.

- *Impartiality* requires that a finite trace is not evaluated to *true* or *false*, if there still exists an (infinite) continuation leading to another verdict.
- *Anticipation* requires that once every (infinite) continuation of a finite trace leads to the same verdict, then the finite trace evaluates to this verdict.

Intuitively, the first maxim postulates that a monitor only decides for *false*—meaning that a misbehavior has been observed—or *true*—meaning that the current behavior fulfills the correctness property, regardless of how it continues—only if this is indeed the case. Clearly, this maxim requires to have at least three different truth values: *true*, *false*, and *inconclusive*, but of course more than three truth values might give a more precise assessment of correctness. The second maxim requires a monitor to indeed report *true* or *false*, if the correctness property is indeed violated or satisfied.

Typically, monitors are generated automatically from some high-level specification. Runtime verification, which has its roots in model checking, often employs some variant of linear temporal logic, such as Pnueli's **LTL** [2]. However, typically these logics and corresponding verification algorithms are considered on infinite executions. To follow the ideas of impartiality and anticipation, we defined in [3] a three-valued semantics for **LTL** obtaining the logic **LTL$_3$**. Moreover, in [3,4], we presented a monitor synthesis algorithm for **LTL$_3$**. Using similar ideas, we also introduced a three-valued semantics for a real-time version of **LTL** and provided a corresponding monitor synthesis algorithm.

However, there is large variety of linear-time logics, for which monitor synthesis algorithms are of interest. In this paper, a uniform approach for synthesizing monitors checking correctness properties specified in linear-time logics at runtime is provided, which is based on our approach in [3]. To this end, we define *linear-time logics* as logics interpreted over infinite words, for example, **LTL**, **PLTL^{mod}** [5], linear μ-calculus, timed **LTL** etc. Uniformly, we give an impartial and anticipatory semantics for linear-time logics suitable for runtime verification. We identify key *decision* and *abstraction* functions from which a monitor for a formula of the respective logic is directly obtained.

Satisfiability and *model checking* are common problems addressed for logics. A pattern emerging for solutions of these problems is the so-called *automata-theoretic approach*: In satisfiability checking, it means to construct for a given formula ϕ the automaton $\mathcal{A}_\phi$ accepting (abstractions of) words satisfying ϕ, so that the language of $\mathcal{A}_\phi$ is non-empty iff ϕ is satisfiable. Model checking, though, is often reduced to constructing the automaton $\mathcal{A}_{\neg\phi}$ accepting the *counter examples* of ϕ and checking the intersection of a model and $\mathcal{A}_{\neg\phi}$ for emptiness. Also for the exemplifying linear-time logics the automata-theoretic approach for checking satisfiability has been studied and it seems beneficial to reuse such automata constructions when looking for monitors—provided this is possible. We define precisely the automata-theoretic approach and we elaborate certain criteria (*forgettable past* and *faithfulness of abstraction*) under which a monitor is directly obtained from automata accepting the models of a formula at hand. We show that automata constructions existing in the literature for several linear-time logics satisfy the introduced criteria such that we derive easily impartial and anticipating monitors, e.g., for the linear-time μ-calculus [6,7], monadic second-order logic (over words) [8], **RLTL** [9], and **PLTL**^{mod} [5] which is interpreted over sequences of integer valuations.

2   Anticipatory Monitors

Definition 1 (Linear-time Logic). *A linear-time logic L defines a set F_L of L-formulae and a two-valued semantics $\models_L$. Every L-formula $\phi \in F_L$ has an associated and possibly infinite alphabet Σ_ϕ. For every formula $\phi \in F_L$ and every word $\sigma \in \Sigma_\phi^\omega$, we require the semantics to be well-defined, i.e., either $\sigma \models_L \phi$ or $\sigma \not\models_L \phi$ must hold.*

Furthermore, we require a linear-time logic L to satisfy the following properties:

(L1) $\forall \phi \in F_L \ : \ \neg\phi \in F_L$. Note that this property does *not* require that negation is applicable to every *subformula* of ϕ.
(L2) $\forall \sigma \in \Sigma_\phi^\omega \ : \ (\sigma \models_L \phi \ \Leftrightarrow \ \sigma \not\models_L \neg\phi)$. Note that $\neg\phi \in F_L$ must hold because of property **(L1)**.

Definition 2 (Anticipation Semantics). *If L is a logic following Definition 1, then we define the* anticipation semantics *$[\pi \models \phi]_L$ of an L-formula $\phi \in F_L$ and a finite word $\pi \in \Sigma_\phi^*$ with*

$$[\pi \models \phi]_L = \begin{cases} \top & \text{if } \forall \sigma \in \Sigma_\phi^\omega \ : \ \pi\sigma \models_L \phi \\ \bot & \text{if } \forall \sigma \in \Sigma_\phi^\omega \ : \ \pi\sigma \not\models_L \phi \\ ? & \text{otherwise} \end{cases}$$

Note that the definition of anticipation semantics fulfills both, the *impartiality* and *anticipation* requirements stated in the introduction: It is impartial since for every prefix $\pi \in \Sigma^*$ with two continuations $\sigma, \sigma' \in \Sigma^\omega$ such that $\pi\sigma \models_L \phi$ and $\pi\sigma' \not\models_L \phi$ hold, the semantics $[\pi \models \phi]_L$ evaluates to the inconclusive verdict ?. On the other hand, once only satisfying or unsatisfying continuations exist, the semantics $[\pi \models \phi]_L$ evaluates to the corresponding verdict $\top$ or $\bot$.

Since we want to use the anticipation semantics in runtime verification, we have to develop a monitor procedure monitor$_\phi(a)$ which reads a trace incrementally: It takes a symbol a in each invocation and returns thereupon the valuation of the currently processed prefix. To this end, we evaluate the core question arising in the anticipation semantics $\forall \sigma \in \Sigma_\phi^\omega \ : \ \pi\sigma \models_L \phi$ using the equivalence

$$\forall \sigma \in \Sigma_\phi^\omega \ : \ \pi\sigma \models_L \phi \ \Leftrightarrow \ \nexists \sigma \in \Sigma_\phi^\omega \ : \ \pi\sigma \not\models_L \phi \ \Leftrightarrow \ \nexists \sigma \in \Sigma_\phi^\omega \ : \ \pi\sigma \models_L \neg\phi$$

which holds for every logic L which satisfies property **(L2)**. By handling the complemented case analogously, we obtain the following rule to evaluate the anticipation semantics:

$$[\pi \models \phi]_L = \begin{cases} \top & \text{if decide}_{\neg\phi}(\pi) = \bot \\ \bot & \text{if decide}_\phi(\pi) = \bot \\ ? & \text{otherwise} \end{cases}$$

where $\mathsf{decide}_\phi(\pi)$ is defined to return $\top$ for $\phi \in F_L$ and $\pi \in \Sigma_\phi$ if $\exists \sigma \in \Sigma_\phi^\omega$: $\pi\sigma \models_L \phi$ holds, and $\bot$ otherwise. Note that $\mathsf{decide}_\phi(\pi)$ is well-defined since ϕ and $\neg\phi$ are both in F_L. Observe that a computable anticipatory semantics requires the satisfiability problem of the underlying logic to be decidable.

Remark 1. A linear-time logic has a computable anticipatory semantics, only if the satisfiability problem for the logic is decidable.

In order to give an *incrementally* working monitor procedure, we have to avoid reevaluating the entire prefix π in $\mathsf{decide}_\phi(\pi)$ whenever a symbol is read. Instead, we want to use an *automaton construction* to compute $\mathsf{decide}_\phi(\pi a)$ for $\pi \in \Sigma_\phi^*$ and $a \in \Sigma_\phi$ after having already processed π. Hence, we introduce a procedure $\mathsf{step}_\phi(S, a)$ which takes a set $S \subseteq \mathcal{S}_\phi$ of states and a symbol $a \in \Sigma_\phi$ and returns a new set $S' \subseteq \mathcal{S}_\phi$. By executing step_ϕ stepwise on a finite prefix $\pi = a_1 \ldots a_n$ we obtain the *automaton abstraction* $\alpha_\phi(\pi)$ of π with

$$\alpha_\phi(\pi) = \mathsf{step}_\phi(\ldots (\mathsf{step}_\phi(\mathsf{step}_\phi(I_\phi, a_1), a_2), \ldots), a_n)$$

where I_ϕ is an initial set of states for ϕ. Then we apply a suitably defined procedure check_ϕ on the resulting set of states $\alpha_\phi(\pi)$ to obtain $\mathsf{check}_\phi(\alpha_\phi(\pi)) = \mathsf{decide}_\phi(\pi)$. We summarize these terms in the following definition:

Definition 3 (Automaton Construction with Emptiness Check). *A logic L has an* automaton construction with emptiness check *if we have for every formula $\phi \in F_L$, (a) a finite set $\mathcal{S}_\phi$ of states, (b) a set $I_\phi \subseteq \mathcal{S}_\phi$ of initial states, (c) a transition function $\mathsf{step}_\phi(S, a)$ which maps a set of states $S \subseteq \mathcal{S}$ and a symbol $a \in \Sigma_\phi$ to a new set $S' \subseteq \mathcal{S}$ of states, and (d) a function $\mathsf{check}_\phi(S)$ with $\mathsf{check}_\phi(\alpha_\phi(\pi)) = \mathsf{decide}_\phi(\pi)$ for all $\pi \in \Sigma_\phi^*$ where we define automaton abstraction α_ϕ with $\alpha_\phi(\epsilon) = I_\phi$ and recursively with $\alpha_\phi(\pi a) = \mathsf{step}_\phi(\alpha_\phi(\pi), a)$ for all $\pi \in \Sigma_\phi^*$ and $a \in \Sigma_\phi$.*

If a logic L has an automaton construction with emptiness check, we use the following rule to evaluate the anticipation semantics

$$[\pi \models \phi]_L = \begin{cases} \top & \text{if } \mathsf{check}_{\neg\phi}(\alpha_{\neg\phi}(\pi)) = \bot \\ \bot & \text{if } \mathsf{check}_\phi(\alpha_\phi(\pi)) = \bot \\ ? & \text{otherwise} \end{cases}$$

which leads to the procedure $\mathsf{monitor}_\phi(a)$ as shown in Figure 1.

As an example for a logic which directly yields an automaton abstraction with emptiness check, consider **LTL** [2]. The set of **LTL** formulae is inductively defined by the grammar $\phi ::= \mathit{true} \mid p \mid \neg\phi \mid \phi \vee \phi \mid \phi \, U \, \phi \mid X\phi$.

```
procedure monitor_φ(a)
init
    S_φ := I_φ;  S_¬φ := I_¬φ
begin
    S_φ := step_φ(S_φ, a);
    S_¬φ := step_¬φ(S_¬φ, a);
    if check_φ(S_φ) = ⊥
        then return ⊥;
    if check_¬φ(S_¬φ) = ⊥
        then return ⊤;
    return ?;
end
```

Fig. 1. Procedure $\mathsf{monitor}_\phi(a)$

Recall that a *(nondeterministic) Büchi automaton (NBA)* is a tuple $\mathcal{A} = (\Sigma, Q, Q_0, \delta, F)$, where Σ is a finite alphabet, Q is a finite, non-empty set of states, $Q_0 \subseteq Q$ is a set of initial states, $\delta : Q \times \Sigma \to 2^Q$ is the transition function, and $F \subseteq Q$ is a set of accepting states. For an NBA $\mathcal{A}$, we denote by $\mathcal{A}(q)$ the NBA that coincides with $\mathcal{A}$ except for the set of initial state Q_0, which is redefined in $\mathcal{A}(q)$ as $Q_0 = \{q\}$.

Let $\mathcal{A}^\phi = (\Sigma, Q^\phi, Q_0^\phi, \delta^\phi, F^\phi)$ denote the NBA which accepts all models of the **LTL**-formula ϕ, and let $\mathcal{A}^{\neg\phi} = (\Sigma, Q^{\neg\phi}, Q_0^{\neg\phi}, \delta^{\neg\phi}, F^{\neg\phi})$ denote the NBA which accepts all words falsifying ϕ. The corresponding construction is standard [10]. Now we define step and check for **LTL** as follows:

- step$_\phi$: $2^{Q^\phi} \times \Sigma \to 2^{Q^\phi}$ does the Büchi automaton steps of $\mathcal{A}^\phi$. That is, step$_\phi(S, a) = \bigcup_{q' \in S} \delta^\phi(q', a)$ for $S \subseteq Q^\phi$ and $a \in \Sigma$. Analogously, step$_{\neg\phi}$: $2^{Q^{\neg\phi}} \times \Sigma \to 2^{Q^{\neg\phi}}$ is defined based on $\mathcal{A}^{\neg\phi}$.
- check$_\phi$: $2^{Q^\phi} \to \{\top, \bot\}$ does the emptiness check for the states. That is, check$_\phi(S) = \top$ iff $\bigcup_{q' \in S} \mathcal{L}(\mathcal{A}^\phi(q')) \neq \emptyset$ for $S \subseteq Q^\phi$, otherwise check$_\phi(S) = \bot$. Analogously, check$_{\neg\phi}$: $2^{Q^{\neg\phi}} \to \{\top, \bot\}$ is defined in terms of $\mathcal{A}^{\neg\phi}$.

Note that we essentially get the monitor procedure established in [3].

3 Monitors Via the *Automata-Theoretic Approach*

So far, we have understood that there is a canonical anticipatory semantics well-suited in runtime verification for a wide range of linear-time logics, which is based on the function decide$_\phi$. Thus, for any linear-time logic, a (non-incremental) RV semantics can be computed, provided that for each formula ϕ of the logic a computable decide$_\phi$ can be constructed. Moreover, a monitor construction for checking an input sequence incrementally was developed for linear-time logics, provided an *automaton abstraction* is given.

In consequence, runtime verification support for a linear-time logic is reduced to providing the corresponding functions/abstractions. We have shown that this task is simple in the setting of Pnueli's **LTL**. However, for some relevant richer logics, like real-time logics [11] or logics interpreted over the integers [5], this task is considerably more involved [4]. Nevertheless, as the approach given for **LTL** suggests, there is a typical *pattern* for deriving those functions, which we describe in this section. In simple words, we show that whenever for the underlying logic the so-called (a) *automata-theoretic approach* to satisfiability checking is followed—as it is the case for many logics (see also Section 4)—and certain (b) *accuracy criteria* are fulfilled, a general pattern is applicable to derive monitors in a uniform manner.

We first give a generic definition of nondeterministic ω-automata which covers various well-known classes of ω-automata such as Büchi, Muller, Rabin, Street, Parity etc. Note that we decided against generalizing the concept to cover also event-clock or timed automata, mainly to keep the technical details simple.

Definition 4 (Nondeterministic ω-Automata). *A (non-deterministic) ω-automaton $\mathcal{A}$ is a tuple $\mathcal{A} = (\Sigma, Q, Q_0, \delta, Acc)$, where Σ is a (possibly infinite) alphabet, Q is a finite non-empty set of states, $Q_0 \subseteq Q$ is a set of initial states,*

$\delta : Q \times \Sigma \rightarrow 2^Q$ *is the* transition function, *and Acc is an* accepting component *(which varies for different automata types.)*

For example, we derive the notion of non-deterministic Büchi automata with a subset of the states $Acc \subseteq Q$ as accepting component.

A *run* of an ω-automaton $\mathcal{A} = (\Sigma, Q, Q_0, \delta, Acc)$ on a word $w = a_0 a_1 \cdots \in \Sigma^\omega$ is a sequence $q_0, q_1, \ldots$ with $q_0 \in Q_0$ and $q_{i+1} \in \delta(q_i, a_i)$ for $i \geq 0$. The run is called *accepting* if it meets the *acceptance condition*. For example in case of Büchi automata, the acceptance condition requires at least one of the states $q \in Acc$ to be visited infinitely often. The *accepted language* (or *language*, for short) $\mathcal{L}(\mathcal{A})$ of $\mathcal{A}$ is the set of words w for which an accepting run exists.

Yet dependent on the actual acceptance condition, emptiness of the accepted language of an automaton can usually be checked easily and is one of the standard problems extensively studied for various automata types. In the following, we silently assume that every automaton type comes with an emptiness procedure.

Definition 5 (Satisfiability Check by Automata Abstraction). *Given a linear-time logic L with its formulae F_L, the* satisfiability check by automata abstraction *proceeds as follows.*

1. *Define an* alphabet abstraction *which yields for each formula $\phi \in F_L$ with its possibly infinite alphabet Σ_ϕ an abstract alphabet $\bar{\Sigma}_\phi$, which is finite.*
2. *Define a* word abstraction *which yields an abstraction function $\beta_\phi : \Sigma_\phi^\omega \rightarrow \bar{\Sigma}_\phi^\omega$ for each $\phi \in F_L$.*
3. *Define an* automaton construction *(a computable function), which yields for all $\phi \in F_L$ an ω-automaton $\mathcal{A}_\phi$ reading words over $\bar{\Sigma}_\phi$, such that for all $\bar{\sigma} \in \bar{\Sigma}_\phi^\omega$ it holds $\bar{\sigma} \in \mathcal{L}(\mathcal{A}_\phi)$ iff $\exists \sigma \in \Sigma^\omega : \bar{\sigma} = \beta_\phi(\sigma)$ and $\sigma \models \phi$.*

The satisfiability check by automata abstraction then proceeds as follows: For a given formula $\phi \in F_L$ of the logic L construct the automaton $\mathcal{A}_\phi$ and check the language of $\mathcal{A}_\phi$ for emptiness. Clearly, ϕ is satisfiable iff $\mathcal{L}(\mathcal{A}_\phi) \neq \emptyset$.

To distinguish Σ_ϕ and $\bar{\Sigma}_\phi$ and corresponding words literally, we call $\bar{\Sigma}_\phi$ an *abstract* alphabet and elements of $\bar{\Sigma}_\phi^*$ or $\bar{\Sigma}_\phi^\omega$ *abstract* words or *symbolic abstractions*. To simplify notation, we often drop the subscript ϕ when ϕ is given by the context. For example, we write $\mathcal{A} = (\Sigma, Q, Q_0, \delta, Acc)$ for the automaton accepting symbolic abstractions $\bar{\sigma} \in \bar{\Sigma}^\omega$ of words $\sigma \in \Sigma^\omega$ (i.e. $\bar{\sigma} = \beta(\sigma)$) satisfying a fixed formula ϕ.

For a wide range of linear-time logics, the satisfiability check by automata abstraction is followed and corresponding automata constructions are provided in the literature. For example, for **LTL** as described in the previous section, the abstraction function β is simply the identity function and the automaton construction was first described in [10]. In the setting of the real-time logic **TLTL** [11], an *event-clock automaton* is constructed accepting precisely the models of the formula at hand. In the setting of Demri's **PLTL**^{mod} [5], words over an infinite alphabet (representing integer valuations) are abstracted to words of a finite alphabet and a suitable construction of a Büchi automaton accepting these symbolic evaluations is provided.

The goal is now to reuse such automata constructions for generating monitors. Reconsidering the example for **LTL** given the previous section, one is drawn to the following approach: Given an ω-automaton accepting symbolic abstractions of words satisfying the formula to check, reuse its transition function δ for defining the function step. Moreover, check may be defined as checking emptiness of the accepted language of the automaton when starting the automaton in the states reachable via step/δ. Recall that we assume the satisfiability check by automata abstraction to come with an emptiness check for the automaton at hand.

However, δ reads words $\bar{\pi}$ over the symbolic alphabet while, in runtime verification, we want to derive the semantics for words π over Σ. Hence, we would like to use the symbolic abstraction function β to abstract π to $\bar{\pi}$. However, β is defined for ω-words rather than for finite words. To deal with symbolic abstractions of finite prefixes of infinite words, we introduce extrapolate(π) as

$$\text{extrapolate}(\pi) = \left\{ \beta(\pi\sigma)^{0\cdots i} \mid i + 1 = |\pi|, \sigma \in \Sigma^\omega \right\} \tag{1}$$

as the set of possible abstractions of π where $\beta(\pi\sigma)^{0\cdots i}$ denotes the first $i + 1$ symbols of $\beta(\pi\sigma)$. We require that there is an algorithm that yields for each ϕ a computable function extrapolate : $\Sigma^* \rightarrow 2^{\bar{\Sigma}^*}$.

By means of extrapolate, we transfer a (finite) word π to a set of symbolic words extrapolate(π), which guide the automaton from its initial states Q_0 to a set of states $\bigcup_{q' \in Q_0} \delta(q', \text{extrapolate}(\pi))$, for which we check the emptiness with check(S) = $\top$, iff $\bigcup_{q' \in S} \mathcal{L}(\mathcal{A}(q')) \neq \emptyset$, and check($S$) = $\bot$ in all other cases, where S is a subset of state set Q of the automaton for ϕ.

Now we are tempted to assume that function decide is obtained as decide(π) = check $\left(\bigcup_{q' \in Q_0, \bar{\pi} \in \text{extrapolate}(\pi)} \delta(q', \bar{\pi}) \right)$. However, in general this might not be correct. In the real-time setting, for example, a prefix of a timed trace typically imposes a *post-condition* for the remainder of the string. Depending on the automaton construction employed, such post-conditions of prefixes are overlooked when solely checking emptiness for states. This may then result in incorrect results. See [4] for a detailed discussion of the real-time case.

If, however, the automaton abstraction satisfies a certain accuracy condition, our intuition meets the facts:

Definition 6 (Accuracy of Abstract Automata). *A satisfiability check by automata abstraction for a given linear-time logic L is said to satisfy the accuracy of abstract automata property, if, for all $\pi \in \Sigma^*$,*

- *if π has a satisfying continuation σ, then there must exist an accepting abstract continuation $\bar{\sigma}$ for some $\bar{\pi} \in$ extrapolate(π), i.e.: ($\exists \sigma : \pi\sigma \models_L \phi$) $\Rightarrow$ ($\exists \bar{\pi} \exists \bar{\sigma} : \bar{\pi}\bar{\sigma} \in \mathcal{L}(\mathcal{A}_\phi)$) with $\bar{\pi} \in$ extrapolate(π),*
- *and if an abstract prefix $\bar{\pi}$ has an accepting abstract continuation $\bar{\sigma}$ then there must exist a satisfying concretization σ for some π with $\bar{\pi} \in$ extrapolate(π), i.e.: ($\exists \bar{\sigma} : \bar{\pi}\bar{\sigma} \in \mathcal{L}(\mathcal{A}_\phi)$) $\Rightarrow$ ($\exists \pi \exists \sigma : \pi\sigma \models_L \phi$) with $\bar{\pi} \in$ extrapolate(π).*

Note that the accuracy of abstract automata property implies that the automaton only accepts valid symbolic abstractions, i.e., $\mathcal{A}$ only accepts words $\bar{\sigma}$ which are indeed images of some σ under β.

The discussion and notions introduced so far give now rise to the following theorem:

Theorem 1 (Correctness of decide). *Given a satisfiability check by automata abstraction for a linear-time logic L satisfying the* accuracy of automata *property, we have* $\mathsf{decide}(\pi) = \mathsf{check}\left(\bigcup_{q' \in Q_0, \bar{\pi} \in \mathsf{extrapolate}(\pi)} \delta(q', \bar{\pi})\right)$. *Moreover, if there is an algorithm yielding for each formula of L a computable function* extrapolate *satisfying Equation 1,* decide *is computable.*

However, as mentioned in the previous section, decide is mainly useful for obtaining non-incremental monitors, as π has to be stored for deriving abstractions of its extensions. Nevertheless, if the abstraction β satisfies further properties, we come up with an incremental monitor construction:

Definition 7 (Forgettable Past and Faithful Abstraction). *Given β of a satisfiability check by automata abstraction. We say that*

- *β satisfies the* forgettable past *property, iff $\beta(\pi a \sigma)^{i+1 \ldots i+1} = \beta(a\sigma)^{0 \ldots 0}$ for all $\pi \in \Sigma^*$, $|\pi| = i + 1$, $a \in \Sigma$, and $\sigma \in \Sigma^\omega$.*
- *β is called* faithful, *iff for all $\pi \in \Sigma^*$, $|\pi| = i + 1$, $a \in \Sigma$, $\sigma, \sigma' \in \Sigma^\omega$ for which there is some $\sigma'' \in \Sigma^\omega$ with $\beta(\pi\sigma)^{0 \ldots i}\beta(a\sigma')^{0 \ldots 0} = \beta(\sigma'')^{0 \ldots i+1}$ there also exists a $\sigma''' \in \Sigma^\omega$ with $\beta(\pi\sigma)^{0 \ldots i}\beta(a\sigma')^{0 \ldots 0} = \beta(\pi a\sigma''')^{0 \ldots i+1}$*

The intuition behind forgettable past is that a prefix of some infinite string has no effect on the abstraction of the suffix (while the suffix might influence the abstraction of the prefix). Moreover, for a faithful abstraction, we have the following: whenever the prefix of length $|\pi|$ of the abstraction of $\pi\sigma$, followed by the first letter of the abstraction of $a\sigma'$ can be written as the abstraction of some infinite word, then we obtain the same result for πa continued by a suitable suffix σ'''. Roughly speaking, this is a kind of a homomorphic property for prefixes of representatives. We then get, setting $\mathcal{L}_\beta = \{\beta(\sigma) \mid \sigma \in \Sigma^\omega\}$:

Lemma 1 (Incremental Extrapolation). *For $\pi \in \Sigma^*$, $|\pi| = i+1$, $a \in \Sigma$, we have* $\mathsf{extrapolate}(\pi)\mathsf{extrapolate}(a) \cap \mathcal{L}_\beta^{0 \ldots i+1} = \mathsf{extrapolate}(\pi a)$ *where β satisfies the forgettable past and faithful abstraction properties.*

Lemma 2 (Incremental Emptiness for Extrapolation). *Let $\mathcal{A}$ be a Büchi automaton obtained via a satisfiability check by automata abstraction satisfying the accuracy of automaton abstraction property with a faithful abstraction function having the forgettable past property. Then, for all $\pi \in \Sigma^*$ and $a \in \Sigma$, it holds $\mathcal{L}(\mathcal{A}(\mathsf{extrapolate}(\pi a))) = \mathcal{L}(\mathcal{A}(\mathsf{extrapolate}(\pi)\mathsf{extrapolate}(a)))$.*

We are now ready to define the essential procedure for an incremental monitor construction: Let step be defined by $\mathsf{step}(S, a) = \bigcup_{q' \in S, \bar{a} \in \mathsf{extrapolate}(a)} \delta(q', \bar{a})$.

Theorem 2 (Correctness of step and check). *Consider a satisfiability check by automata abstraction that has the accuracy automaton abstraction property and comes with a faithful abstraction function that moreover satisfies the forgettable past property. Then $\mathsf{check}(\alpha(\pi)) = \mathsf{decide}(\pi)$ for all $\pi \in \Sigma^*$. Moreover, if there is an algorithm yielding for each formula of L a computable function* extrapolate *satisfying Equation 1, α and check are computable.*

In other words, under the mentioned criteria, we have identified an automaton construction according to Definition 3, resulting in a monitor as depicted in Figure 1. In the next section, we illustrate the general scheme developed in this section for various linear-time logics.

4   Applications: Monitors for Various Linear-Time Logics

The anticipation semantics is suitable for various linear-time logics and a monitor synthesis by the automaton construction with emptiness check is directly obtained by establishing the functions step and check. Reusing the results of satisfiability check by automata abstraction, these functions are obtained easily. In the following, we present several linear-time logics as example applications including **LTL**, **PLTL**^{mod}, linear-time μ-calculus, **RLTL** and **S1S**.

Linear-time Temporal Logic (LTL) [2]: Because the alphabet of **LTL** is finite, the abstraction functions for **LTL** formulae are trivial, i.e. $\beta_\phi(\sigma) = \sigma$ and $\text{extrapolate}(\pi) = \{\pi\}$. The resulting functions step_ϕ and check_ϕ are exactly the ones that we get in Section 2. Furthermore, a monitor synthesis algorithm is also obtained for the **LTL** enriched by past operators or *forgettable past operators* [12] with a corresponding satisfiability check by automata abstraction.

PLTL^{mod} *[5]:* **PLTL**^{mod} is a decidable fragment of Presburger **LTL**, which extends **LTL** with first-order integer arithmetic constraints. The alphabet of a **PLTL**^{mod} formula is infinite because it includes all valuations of variables over $\mathbb{Z}$. [5] proposed an approach of mapping all valuations to the finite symbolic valuations which are equivalence classes. Let ϕ be a **PLTL**^{mod} formula with alphabet Σ. The symbolic alphabet $\bar{\Sigma}_\phi$, the symbolic abstraction function $\beta_\phi : \Sigma_\phi^\omega \to \bar{\Sigma}_\phi^\omega$ and the automaton construction can be obtained, which are three essential elements in satisfiability check by automata abstraction. A careful investigation shows that the abstraction function is faithful and satisfies the forgettable past property and that the automaton abstraction is accurate. Thus, functions step_ϕ and check_ϕ and an anticipatory monitor can easily be constructed along the lines of Theorem 2. Details can be found in an extended version of the paper.

Linear-time μ-calculus (νTL) [6,13]: νTL extends standard modal logic with maximal and minimal fixpoint quantifiers, and can express regular expressions. In [7], a first automata-theoretic approach to νTL is presented. Given a νTL formula ϕ, the Büchi automata of $\mathcal{A}$ that accepts precisely the pre-models of ϕ and $\bar{\mathcal{A}}$ that seeks an infinite regeneration sequence for least fixpoint formula in *closure* of ϕ can be generated. The Büchi automaton $\mathcal{A}_\phi$ that accepts precisely the models of ϕ is the intersection of $\mathcal{A}$ and $\bar{\mathcal{A}}$. Thus, the abstraction functions for νTL formulae are also trivial ones, and the functions step_ϕ and check_ϕ will be established just like for **LTL**. A more direct automaton construction was presented in [14], which makes use of *parity automata*. While emptiness of the accepted language for a set of states is computed differently due to the parity acceptance condition, it is easily verified that the requirements for applying Theorem 2 are fulfilled.

RLTL *and* **S1S**: Simlar as νTL, also regular linear temporal logic **RLTL** is a formalism that can express every ω-regular language [9]. For a **RLTL** formula ϕ, an alternating Büchi automaton accepting precisely the ω-words satisfying ϕ can be generated. This automaton can be translated into an equivalent Büchi automaton. A monadic second order (MSO) logic interpreted over words, also called **S1S**, consists of formulae having a single individual free variable, for which a Büchi automaton can be generated [8]. Again, it is easily verified that the requirements for applying Theorem 2 for **RLTL** and **S1S** are fulfilled.

5   Conclusion

In this paper, a uniform approach for synthesizing monitors checking correctness properties specified in a linear-time logic is provided. After making the notion of linear-time logics precise, a generic three-valued semantics has been introduced reflecting the idea that *prefixes* of infinite computations are checked for correctness. Then we established a conceptual framework to synthesize monitors from a logical specification to check an execution incrementally. Moreover, the main elements of the *automata-theoretic approach* for checking satisfiability of correctness properties are identified as starting point in reusing them as components for a general monitor generation procedure. We applied the presented framework and sketched monitor synthesis algorithms for a variety of logics such as **LTL**, the linear-time μ-calculus, **PLTL**^{mod}, **S1S**, and **RLTL**.

Besides the plain practical benefits of the developed framework, the results shed light on the similarities and differences of satisfiability checking, model checking, and runtime verification.

References

1. Bauer, A., Leucker, M., Schallhart, C.: The good, the bad, and the ugly—but how ugly is ugly? In: Sokolsky, O., Taşıran, S. (eds.) RV 2007. LNCS, vol. 4839, pp. 126–138. Springer, Heidelberg (2007)
2. Pnueli, A.: The temporal logic of programs. In: Proceedings of the 18th IEEE Symposium on the Foundations of Computer Science (FOCS), pp. 46–57 (1977)
3. Bauer, A., Leucker, M., Schallhart, C.: Monitoring of real-time properties. In: Arun-Kumar, S., Garg, N. (eds.) FSTTCS 2006. LNCS, vol. 4337. Springer, Heidelberg (2006)
4. Bauer, A., Leucker, M., Schallhart, C.: Runtime verification for LTL and TLTL. Technical Report TUM-I0724, TU München (2007)
5. Demri, S.: LTL over integer periodicity constraints. Theoretical Computer Science 360(1-3), 96–123 (2006)
6. Emerson, E.A., Clarke, E.M.: Characterizing correctness properties of parallel programs using fixpoints. In: de Bakker, J.W., van Leeuwen, J. (eds.) ICALP 1980. LNCS, vol. 85, pp. 169–181. Springer, Heidelberg (1980)
7. Vardi, M.Y.: A temporal fixpoint calculus. In: POPL, pp. 250–259 (1988)
8. Büchi, J.: Weak second order logic and finite automata. Z. Math. Logik, Grundlag. Math. 5, 62–66 (1960)

9. Leucker, M., Sánchez, C.: Regular linear temporal logic. In: Jones, C.B., Liu, Z., Woodcock, J. (eds.) ICTAC 2007. LNCS, vol. 4711, pp. 291–305. Springer, Heidelberg (2007)
10. Vardi, M.Y., Wolper, P.: An automata-theoretic approach to automatic program verification. In: Logic in Computer Science (LICS), pp. 332–345 (1986)
11. Raskin, J.F., Schobbens, P.Y.: State clock logic: A decidable real-time logic. In: Maler, O. (ed.) HART 1997. LNCS, vol. 1201, pp. 33–47. Springer, Heidelberg (1997)
12. Laroussinie, F., Markey, N., Schnoebelen, P.: Temporal logic with forgettable past. In: LICS (2002)
13. Barringer, H., Kuiper, R., Pnueli, A.: A really abstract concurrent model and its temporal logic. In: POPL, pp. 173–183 (1986)
14. Lange, M.: Weak automata for the linear time μ-calculus. In: Cousot, R. (ed.) VMCAI 2005. LNCS, vol. 3385, pp. 267–281. Springer, Heidelberg (2005)

Run-Time Monitoring of Electronic Contracts

Marcel Kyas*, Cristian Prisacariu**, and Gerardo Schneider**

Department of Informatics, University of Oslo,
P.O. Box 1080 Blindern, N-0316 Oslo, Norway
{kyas,cristi,gerardo}@ifi.uio.no

Abstract. Electronic inter-organizational relationships are governed by contracts regulating their interaction, therefore it is necessary to run-time monitor the contracts, as to guarantee their fulfillment. The present work shows how to obtain a run-time monitor for contracts written in $\mathcal{CL}$, a formal specification language which allows to write conditional obligations, permissions, and prohibitions over actions. The trace semantics of $\mathcal{CL}$ formalizes the notion of *a trace fulfills a contract*. We show how to obtain, for a given contract, an alternating Büchi automaton which accepts exactly the traces that fulfill the contract. This automaton is the basis for obtaining a finite state machine which acts as a run-time monitor for $\mathcal{CL}$ contracts.

1 Introduction

Internet inter-business collaborations, virtual organizations, and web services, usually communicate through service exchanges which respect an implicit or explicit *contract*. Such a contract must unambiguously determine correct interactions, and what are the exceptions allowed, or penalties imposed in case of incorrect behavior.

Legal contracts, as found in the usual judicial or commercial arena, may serve as basis for defining such machine-oriented *electronic contracts* (or e-contracts for short). Ideally, e-contracts should be shown to be contradiction-free both internally, and with respect to the governing policies under which the contract is enacted. Moreover, there must be a run-time system ensuring that the contract is respected. In other words, contracts should be amenable to formal analysis allowing both static and dynamic verification, and therefore written in a formal language. In this paper we are interested in the run-time monitoring of electronic contracts, and not in the static verification of their consistency or conformance with policies.

$\mathcal{CL}$, introduced in [12], is an action-based formal language tailored for writing e-contracts, with the following properties: (1) Avoids most of the common philosophical paradoxes of deontic logic [18]; (2) Has a formal semantics given

---

* Author supported by the EU-project IST-33826 *"CREDO: Modelling and analysis of evolutionary structures for distributed services"* (http://credo.cwi.nl).

** Authors supported by the Nordunet3 project *"COSoDIS – Contract-Oriented Software Development for Internet Services"* (http://www.ifi.uio.no/cosodis/).

Cha et al. (Eds.): ATVA 2008, LNCS 5311, pp. 397–407, 2008.

Table 1. Syntax of the $\mathcal{CL}$ language to use for specifying contracts

$$
\begin{aligned}
\mathcal{C} &:= \mathcal{C}_O \mid \mathcal{C}_P \mid \mathcal{C}_F \mid \mathcal{C} \wedge \mathcal{C} \mid [\beta]\mathcal{C} \mid \top \mid \bot \\
\mathcal{C}_O &:= O_{\mathcal{C}}(\alpha) \mid \mathcal{C}_O \oplus \mathcal{C}_O \\
\mathcal{C}_P &:= P(\alpha) \mid \mathcal{C}_P \oplus \mathcal{C}_P \\
\mathcal{C}_F &:= F_{\mathcal{C}}(\alpha) \mid \mathcal{C}_F \vee [\alpha]\mathcal{C}_F \\
\alpha &:= \mathbf{0} \mid \mathbf{1} \mid a \mid \alpha \& \alpha \mid \alpha \cdot \alpha \mid \alpha + \alpha \\
\beta &:= \mathbf{0} \mid \mathbf{1} \mid a \mid \beta \& \beta \mid \beta \cdot \beta \mid \beta + \beta \mid \beta^* \mid \mathcal{C}?
\end{aligned}
$$

in terms of Kripke structures [13]; (3) It can express (conditional) obligations, permissions, and prohibitions over concurrent actions; as well as (4) *contrary-to-duty obligations* (CTD) and *contrary-to-prohibitions* (CTP). CTDs/CTPs specify the obligation/prohibition to be fulfilled and which is the *reparation/penalty* to be applied in case of violation. The use of e-contracts, and in particular of $\mathcal{CL}$, goes beyond the application domain of service-exchanges, comprising component-based development systems, fault-tolerant and embedded systems.

The main contribution of this paper is an automatic procedure for obtaining a run-time monitor for contracts, directly extracted from the $\mathcal{CL}$ specification. The road-map of the paper starts by recalling main results on $\mathcal{CL}$ in first part of Section 2 and we give a trace semantics for the expressions of $\mathcal{CL}$ in the second part. This expresses the fact that a trace respects (does not violate) a contract clause (expression of $\mathcal{CL}$). In Section 3 we show how to construct for a contract an alternating Büchi automaton which recognizes exactly all the traces respecting the contract. The automaton is used in Section 4 for constructing the monitor as a Moore machine (for monitoring the contract). Though we concentrate on theoretical aspects, we use throughout the paper the following small example to exemplify some of the main concepts we define.

Example 1. "If the *Client* exceeds the bandwidth limit then (s)he must pay [*price*] immediately, or (s)he must delay the payment and notify the *Provider* by sending an e-mail. If in breach of the above (s)he must pay double."

2 $\mathcal{CL}$ – A Formal Language for Contracts

$\mathcal{CL}$ is an *action-based* language for writing contracts [12]. In this paper we are interested in monitoring the actions of a contract. Therefore, we give here a slightly different version of $\mathcal{CL}$ where we have dropped the assertions from the old $\mathcal{CL}$, keeping only the modalities over actions. Other differences are in the expressivity: we have incorporated the Kleene star operator over the actions in the dynamic box modality, and we have attached to the obligations/prohibitions the corresponding reparations (modelling the CTDs/CTPs directly).

Syntax: $\mathcal{CL}$ formulas are defined by the grammar in Table 1. In what follows we provide intuitions for the $\mathcal{CL}$ syntax and define our notation and terminology.

We call an expression $\mathcal{C}$ a (general) *contract clause*. $\mathcal{C}_O$, $\mathcal{C}_P$, and $\mathcal{C}_F$ are called respectively *obligation*, *permission*, and *prohibition* clauses. We call $O_{\mathcal{C}}(\alpha)$, $P(\alpha)$, and $F_{\mathcal{C}}(\alpha)$ the *deontic modalities*, and they represent the obligation, permission, or prohibition of performing a given *action* α. Intuitively $O_{\mathcal{C}}(\alpha)$ states the obligation to execute α, and the *reparation* $\mathcal{C}$ in case the obligation is *violated*, i.e. whenever α is not performed.[1] The reparation may be any contract clause. Obligations without reparations are written as $O_{\perp}(\alpha)$ where $\perp$ (and conversely $\top$) is the Boolean `false` (respectively `true`). We usually write $O(\alpha)$ instead of $O_{\perp}(\alpha)$. The prohibition modality $F_{\mathcal{C}}(\alpha)$ states the actual forbearing of the action $F(\alpha)$ together with the reparation $\mathcal{C}$ in case the prohibition is violated. Note that it is possible to express nested CTDs and CTPs.

Throughout the paper we denote by $a, b, c \in \mathcal{A}_B$ the *basic actions*, by indexed $\alpha \in \mathcal{A}$ *compound actions*, and by indexed β the actions found in propositional dynamic logic [4] with intersection [5]. Actions α are used inside the deontic modalities, whereas the (more general) actions β are used inside the dynamic modality. An *action* is an expression containing one or more of the following binary constructors: *choice* "$+$", *sequence* "$\cdot$", *concurrency* "$\&$" and are constructed from the basic actions $a \in \mathcal{A}_B$ and $\mathbf{0}$ and $\mathbf{1}$ (called the *violating* action and respectively *skip* action). Indepth reading and results related to the α actions can be found in [13]. Actions β have the extra operators Kleene star * and *test* $?$.[2] To avoid using parentheses we give a precedence over the constructors: $\& > \cdot > +$. *Concurrent actions*, denoted by $\alpha_{\&}$, are actions of $\mathcal{A}_B^{\&} \subset \mathcal{A}$ generated from basic actions using only the $\&$ constructor (e.g. $a, a\&a, a\&b \in \mathcal{A}_B^{\&}$ and $a+b, a\&b+c, a \cdot b \notin \mathcal{A}_B^{\&}$). Note that $\mathcal{A}_B^{\&}$ is finite because $\mathcal{A}_B$ is defined as finite and $\&$ is defined idempotent over basic actions. Therefore, we consider concurrent actions of $\mathcal{A}_B^{\&}$ as sets over basic actions of $\mathcal{A}_B$. We have now a natural way to compare concurrent actions using $\subseteq$ set inclusion. We say that an action, e.g. $a \& b \& c$ is *more demanding* than another action, e.g. $a \& b$ iff $\{a, b\} \subseteq \{a, b, c\}$. The *negation* $\overline{\alpha}$ of action α is a function $^{-} : \mathcal{A} \to \mathcal{A}$.

We use the propositional operators $\wedge$, $\vee$, and $\oplus$ (exclusive or). The dynamic logic modality $[\beta]\mathcal{C}$ states that after the action β is performed $\mathcal{C}$ must hold. The $[\cdot]$ modality allows having a *test* inside, and $[\mathcal{C}_1?]\mathcal{C}_2$ must be understood as $\mathcal{C}_1 \Rightarrow \mathcal{C}_2$. In $\mathcal{CL}$ we can write *conditional* obligations (permissions and prohibitions) of two kinds: $[\beta]O(\alpha)$ read as "after performing β, one is obliged to do α", and using the test operator $[\mathcal{C}?]O(\alpha)$ to simulate implication. Similarly for F and P.

Example 1 in $\mathcal{CL}$ syntax: The transition from the conventional contract of introduction to the $\mathcal{CL}$ expression below is manual,

$$[e]O_{O_{\perp}(p \cdot p)}(p + d\&n)$$

where the basic actions are $\mathcal{A}_B = \{e, p, n, d\}$ (standing for "extend bandwidth limit", "pay", "notify by email", and "delay"). In short the expression is read as: After executing the action e there is the obligation of choosing between either p or at the same time d and n. The $\mathcal{CL}$ expression also states the reparation $O_{\perp}(p \cdot p)$

---

[1] The modality $O_{\mathcal{C}}(\alpha)$ (resp. $F_{\mathcal{C}}(\alpha)$) represents what is called CTD (resp. CTP) in the deontic logic community.

[2] The investigation of the PDL actions β can be found in the literature related to dynamic and Kleene algebras [7].

Table 2. Trace semantics of $\mathcal{CL}$. Dynamic and propositional operators are omitted [6].

$$\sigma \models O_{\mathcal{C}}(\alpha_\&) \text{ if } \alpha_\& \subseteq \sigma(0), \text{ or if } \sigma(1..) \models \mathcal{C}.$$
$$\sigma \models O_{\mathcal{C}}(\alpha \cdot \alpha') \text{ if } \sigma \models O_{\mathcal{C}}(\alpha) \text{ and } \sigma \models [\alpha]O_{\mathcal{C}}(\alpha').$$
$$\sigma \models O_{\mathcal{C}}(\alpha + \alpha') \text{ if } \sigma \models O_\perp(\alpha) \text{ or } \sigma \models O_\perp(\alpha') \text{ or } \sigma \models \overline{[\alpha + \alpha']}\mathcal{C}.$$
$$\sigma \models F_{\mathcal{C}}(\alpha_\&) \text{ if } \alpha_\& \not\subseteq \sigma(0), \text{ or if } \alpha_\& \subseteq \sigma(0) \text{ and } \sigma(1..) \models \mathcal{C}.$$
$$\sigma \models F_{\mathcal{C}}(\alpha \cdot \alpha') \text{ if } \sigma \models F_\perp(\alpha) \text{ or } \sigma \models [\alpha]F_{\mathcal{C}}(\alpha').$$
$$\sigma \models F_{\mathcal{C}}(\alpha + \alpha') \text{ if } \sigma \models F_{\mathcal{C}}(\alpha) \text{ and } \sigma \models F_{\mathcal{C}}(\alpha').$$
$$\sigma \models \overline{[\alpha_\&]}\mathcal{C} \text{ if } \alpha_\& \not\subseteq \sigma(0) \text{ and } \sigma(1..) \models \mathcal{C}, \text{ or if } \alpha_\& \subseteq \sigma(0).$$
$$\sigma \models \overline{[\alpha \cdot \alpha']}\mathcal{C} \text{ if } \sigma \models \overline{[\alpha]}\mathcal{C} \text{ and } \sigma \models [\alpha]\overline{[\alpha']}\mathcal{C}.$$
$$\sigma \models \overline{[\alpha + \alpha']}\mathcal{C} \text{ if } \sigma \models \overline{[\alpha]}\mathcal{C} \text{ or } \sigma \models \overline{[\alpha']}\mathcal{C}.$$

in case the obligation above is violated which is an obligation of doing twice in a row the action of paying. Note that this second obligation has no reparation attached, therefore if it is violated then the whole contract is violated. Note also that we translate "pay double" into the $\mathcal{CL}$ sequential composition of the same action p of paying.

Semantics on Respecting Traces: The rest of this section is devoted to presenting a semantics for $\mathcal{CL}$ with the goal of monitoring electronic contracts. For this we are interested in identifying the traces of actions which are *respecting* or *violating* a contract clause. We follow the many works in the literature which have a presentation based on traces e.g. [11]. For a complete presentation of the theoretical notions (and proofs), as well as more explanations and examples see the extended version of this paper in [14].

Definition 1 (traces). *Consider a trace denoted $\sigma = a_0, a_1, \ldots$ as an ordered sequence of concurrent actions. Formally a trace is a map $\sigma : \mathbb{N} \to \mathcal{A}_B^\&$ from natural numbers (denoting positions) to concurrent actions from $\mathcal{A}_B^\&$. Take $m_\sigma \in \mathbb{N} \cup \infty$ to be the length of a trace. A (infinite) trace which from some position m_σ onwards has only action $\mathbf{1}$ is considered* finite. *We use ε to denote the* empty *trace. We denote by $\sigma(i)$ the element of a trace at position i, by $\sigma(i..j)$ a finite subtrace, and by $\sigma(i..)$ the infinite subtrace starting at position i in σ. The concatenation of two traces σ' and σ'' is denoted $\sigma'\sigma''$ and is defined iff the trace σ' is finite; $\sigma'\sigma''(i) = \sigma'(i)$ if $i < m_{\sigma'}$ and $\sigma'\sigma''(i) = \sigma''(i - m_{\sigma'})$ for $i \geq m_{\sigma'}$ (e.g. $\sigma(0)$ is the first action of a trace, $\sigma = \sigma(0..i)\sigma'$ where $\sigma' = \sigma(i+1..)$).*

Definition 2 (Semantics of $\mathcal{CL}$). *We give in Table 2 a recursive definition of the satisfaction relation $\models$ over pairs $(\sigma, \mathcal{C})$ of traces and contracts; it is usually written $\sigma \models \mathcal{C}$ and we read it as "trace σ respects the contract (clause) $\mathcal{C}$". We write $\sigma \not\models \mathcal{C}$ instead of $(\sigma, \mathcal{C}) \notin \models$ and read it as "σ violates $\mathcal{C}$."*

A trace σ respects an obligation $O_{\mathcal{C}}(\alpha_\&)$ if either of the two complementary conditions is satisfied. The first condition deals with the obligation itself: the trace σ respects the obligation $O(\alpha_\&)$ if the first action of the trace includes $\alpha_\&$. Otherwise, in case the obligation is violated,[3] the only way to fulfill the contract is by respecting the reparation $\mathcal{C}$; i.e. $\sigma(1..) \models \mathcal{C}$. Respecting an obligation of a choice action $O_\mathcal{C}(\alpha_1 + \alpha_2)$ means that it must be executed one of the actions α_1 or α_2 completely; i.e. obligation needs to consider only one of the choices. If none of these is entirely executed then a violation occurs (thus the negation of the action is needed) so the reparation $\mathcal{C}$ must be respected. An important requirement when modelling electronic contracts is that the obligation of a sequence of actions $O_\mathcal{C}(\alpha \cdot \alpha')$ must be equal to the obligation of the first action $O_\mathcal{C}(\alpha)$ and after the first obligation is respected the second obligation must hold $[\alpha]O_\mathcal{C}(\alpha')$. Note that if $O_\mathcal{C}(\alpha)$ is violated then it is required that the second obligation is discarded, and the reparation $\mathcal{C}$ must hold. Violating $O_\mathcal{C}(\alpha)$ means that α is not executed and thus, by the semantic definition, $[\alpha]O_\mathcal{C}(\alpha')$ holds regardless of $O_\mathcal{C}(\alpha')$.

From [6] we know how to encode LTL only with the dynamic $[\cdot]$ modality and the Kleene $*$; e.g. "*always* obliged to do α" is encoded as $[\mathbf{any}^*]O(\alpha)$ where $\mathbf{any} \overset{\Delta}{=} +_{\gamma \in \mathcal{A}_B^\&} \gamma$ is the choice between *any* concurrent action.

3   Satisfiability Checking Using Alternating Automata

Automata theoretic approach to satisfiability of temporal logics was introduced in [17] and has been extensively used and developed since. We recall first basic theory of automata on infinite objects. We follow the presentation and use the notation of Vardi [16]. Given an alphabet Σ, a *word over* Σ is a sequence $a_0, a_1 \ldots$ of symbols from Σ. The set of *infinite words* is denoted by Σ^ω.

We denote by $\mathcal{B}^+(X)$ the set of positive Boolean formulas θ (i.e. containing only $\wedge$ and $\vee$, and not the $\neg$) over the set X together with the formulas **true** and **false**. For example $\theta = (s_1 \vee s_2) \wedge (s_3 \vee s_4)$ where $s_i \in X$. A subset $Y \subseteq X$ is said to *satisfy* a formula θ iff the truth assignment which assigns *true* only to the elements of Y assigns *true* also to θ. In the example, the set $\{s_1, s_3\}$ satisfies θ; but this set is not unique.

An *alternating Büchi automaton* [2,10] is a tuple $A = (S, \Sigma, s_0, \rho, F)$, where S is a finite nonempty set of *states*, Σ is a finite nonempty *alphabet*, $s_0 \in S$ is the *initial* state, and $F \subseteq S$ is the set of *accepting* states. The automaton can move from one state when it reads a symbol from Σ according to the transition function $\rho : S \times \Sigma \to \mathcal{B}^+(S)$. For example $\rho(s_0, a) = (s_1 \vee s_2) \wedge (s_3 \vee s_4)$ means that the automaton moves from s_0 when reading a to state s_1 or s_2 and at the same time to state s_3 or s_4. Intuitively the automaton chooses for each transition $\rho(s, a) = \theta$ one set $S' \in S$ which satisfies θ and spawns a copy of itself for each state $s_i \in S'$ which should test the acceptance of the remaining word from that state s_i. Alternating automata combine existential choice of nondeterministic finite automata (i.e. disjunction) with the universal choice (i.e. conjunction) of $\forall$-automata [9] (where from a state the automaton must move to *all* the next states given by the transition function).

---

[3] Violation of an obligatory action is encoded by the action negation.

Table 3. Computing the Fischer-Ladner Closure (see [6] for the standard operators)

$$FL(\top) \triangleq \{\top\} \qquad FL(\bot) \triangleq \{\bot\} \qquad FL(P(\alpha)) \triangleq \{P(\alpha)\}$$

$$FL(O_{\mathcal{C}}(\alpha_\&)) \triangleq \{O_{\mathcal{C}}(\alpha_\&)\} \cup FL(\mathcal{C})$$

$$FL(O_{\mathcal{C}}(\alpha \cdot \alpha')) \triangleq \{O_{\mathcal{C}}(\alpha \cdot \alpha')\} \cup FL(O_{\mathcal{C}}(\alpha)) \cup FL([\alpha]O_{\mathcal{C}}(\alpha'))$$

$$FL(O_{\mathcal{C}}(\alpha + \alpha')) \triangleq \{O_{\mathcal{C}}(\alpha + \alpha')\} \cup FL(O_\bot(\alpha)) \cup FL(O_\bot(\alpha')) \cup FL(\mathcal{C})$$

$$FL(F_{\mathcal{C}}(\alpha_\&)) \triangleq \{F_{\mathcal{C}}(\alpha_\&)\} \cup FL(\mathcal{C})$$

$$FL(F_{\mathcal{C}}(\alpha \cdot \alpha')) \triangleq \{F_{\mathcal{C}}(\alpha \cdot \alpha')\} \cup FL(F_\bot(\alpha)) \cup FL(F_{\mathcal{C}}(\alpha'))$$

$$FL(F_{\mathcal{C}}(\alpha + \alpha')) \triangleq \{F_{\mathcal{C}}(\alpha + \alpha')\} \cup FL(F_{\mathcal{C}}(\alpha)) \cup FL(F_{\mathcal{C}}(\alpha'))$$

Because the alternating automaton moves to all the states of a (nondeterministically chosen) satisfying set of θ, a run of the automaton is a *tree* of states. Formally, a run of the alternating automaton on an input word $\alpha = a_0, a_1, \ldots$ is an S-labeled tree $(T, \mathcal{V})$ (i.e. the nodes of the tree are labeled by $\mathcal{V}$ with state names of the automaton) such that $\mathcal{V}(\varepsilon) = s_0$ and the following hold:

for a node x with $|x| = i$ s.t. $\mathcal{V}(x) = s$ and $\rho(s, a_i) = \theta$ then x has k children $\{x_1, \ldots, x_k\}$ which is the number of states in the chosen satisfying set of states of θ, say $\{s_1, \ldots, s_k\}$, and the children are labeled by the states in the satisfying set; i.e. $\{\mathcal{V}(x_1) = s_1, \ldots, \mathcal{V}(x_k) = s_k\}$.

For example, if $\rho(s_0, a) = (s_1 \vee s_2) \wedge (s_3 \vee s_4)$ then the nodes of the run tree at the first level have one label among s_1 or s_2 and one label among s_3 or s_4. When $\rho(\mathcal{V}(x), a) = \mathbf{true}$, then x need not have any children; i.e. the branch reaching x is finite and ends in x. A run tree of an alternating Büchi automaton is *accepting* if every infinite branch of the tree includes infinitely many nodes labeled by accepting states of F. Note that the run tree may also have finite branches in the cases when the transition function returns **true**.

Fischer-Ladner closure for $\mathcal{CL}$: For constructing the alternating automaton for a $\mathcal{CL}$ expression we need the Fischer-Ladner closure [4] for our $\mathcal{CL}$ logic. We follow the presentation in [6] and use similar terminology. We define a function $FL : \mathcal{CL} \to 2^{\mathcal{CL}}$ which for each expression $\mathcal{C}$ of the logic $\mathcal{CL}$ returns the set of its "subexpressions". The function FL is defined inductively in Table 3 (see also [14]).

Theorem 1 (automaton construction). *Given a $\mathcal{CL}$ expression $\mathcal{C}$, one can build an alternating Büchi automaton $A^{\mathcal{N}}(\mathcal{C})$ which will accept all and only the traces σ respecting the contract expression.*

Proof: Take an expression $\mathcal{C}$, we construct the alternating Büchi automaton $A^{\mathcal{N}}(\mathcal{C}) = (S, \Sigma, s_0, \rho, F)$ as follows. The alphabet $\Sigma = A_B^\&$ consists of the finite set of concurrent actions. Therefore the automaton accepts traces as in Definition 1. The set of states $S = FL(\mathcal{C}) \cup \overline{FL(\mathcal{C})}$ contains the subexpressions of the start expression $\mathcal{C}$ and their negations. Note that in $\mathcal{CL}$ the negation $\neg\mathcal{C}$ is $[\mathcal{C}?]\bot$, thus $\forall \mathcal{C} \in FL(\mathcal{C})$ then $[\mathcal{C}?]\bot \in \overline{FL(\mathcal{C})}$. The initial state s_0 is the expression $\mathcal{C}$ itself.

The transition function $\rho : S \times A_B^\& \to \mathcal{B}^+(S)$ is defined in Table 4 (the dynamic logic operators are omitted; see [14]) and is based on the following

Table 4. Transition Function of Alternating Büchi Automaton for $\mathcal{CL}$

$$\rho(\bot,\gamma) \triangleq \textbf{false} \qquad \rho(\top,\gamma) \triangleq \textbf{true} \qquad \rho(P(\alpha),\gamma) \triangleq \textbf{true}$$

$$\rho(O_C(\alpha_\&),\gamma) \triangleq \text{ if } \alpha_\& \subseteq \gamma \text{ then } \textbf{true} \text{ else } \mathcal{C}$$

$$\rho(O_C(\alpha \cdot \alpha'),\gamma) \triangleq \rho(O_C(\alpha),\gamma) \wedge \rho([\alpha]O_C(\alpha'),\gamma)$$

$$\rho(O_C(\alpha + \alpha'),\gamma) \triangleq \rho(O_\bot(\alpha),\gamma) \vee \rho(O_\bot(\alpha'),\gamma) \vee \mathcal{C}$$

$$\rho(F_C(\alpha_\&),\gamma) \triangleq \text{ if } \alpha_\& \not\subseteq \gamma \text{ then } \textbf{true} \text{ else } \mathcal{C}$$

$$\rho(F_C(\alpha \cdot \alpha'),\gamma) \triangleq \rho(F_\bot(\alpha),\gamma) \vee F_C(\alpha')$$

$$\rho(F_C(\alpha + \alpha'),\gamma) \triangleq \rho(F_C(\alpha),\gamma) \wedge \rho(F_C(\alpha'),\gamma)$$

$$\rho([\alpha_\&]\mathcal{C},\gamma) \triangleq \text{ if } \alpha_\& \subseteq \gamma \text{ then } \mathcal{C} \text{ else } \textbf{true}$$

$$\rho([\mathcal{C}_1?]\mathcal{C}_2,\gamma) \triangleq \overline{\rho(\mathcal{C}_1,\gamma)} \vee (\rho(\mathcal{C}_1,\gamma) \wedge \rho(\mathcal{C}_2,\gamma))$$

dualizing construction: for a Boolean formula $\theta \in \mathcal{B}^+(S)$ the dual $\overline{\theta}$ is obtained by switching $\vee$ and $\wedge$, **true** and **false**; and the dual of a state $\overline{\mathcal{C}}$ is the state $[\mathcal{C}?]\bot$ containing the negation of the expression. By looking at the definition of ρ we see that the expression $[\beta^*]\mathcal{C}$ is the only expression which requires repeated evaluation of itself at a later point (causing the infinite unwinding) in the run tree. It is easy to see that if a run tree has an infinite path then this path goes infinitely often through a state of the form $[\beta^*]\mathcal{C}$, therefore the set of final states F contains all the expressions of the type $[\beta^*]\mathcal{C}$.

The rest of the proof shows the correctness of the automaton construction.

Soundness: given an accepting run tree $(T,\mathcal{V})$ of $A^{\mathcal{N}}(\mathcal{C})$ over a trace σ we prove that $\forall x \in T$ a node of the run tree with depth $|x| = i$, labeled by $\mathcal{V}(x) = \mathcal{C}_x$ a state of the automaton (i.e. subexpression $\mathcal{C}_x \in FL(\mathcal{C})$), it is the case that $\sigma(i..) \models \mathcal{C}_x$. Thus we have as a special case that also $\sigma(0..) \models \mathcal{V}(\varepsilon) = \mathcal{C}$, which means that if the automaton $A^{\mathcal{N}}(\mathcal{C})$ accepts a trace σ then the trace respects the initial contract $\mathcal{C}$. We use induction on the structure of the expression $\mathcal{C}_x$.

Completeness: given a trace σ s.t. $\sigma \models \mathcal{C}$ we prove that the constructed automaton $A^{\mathcal{N}}(\mathcal{C})$ accepts σ (i.e. there exists an accepting run tree $(T,\mathcal{V})$ over the trace σ). $\qquad\qquad\qquad\qquad\qquad\qquad\qquad\qquad\qquad\qquad\qquad\qquad\qquad\quad$ $\square$

Example 1 as alternating automata: We shall now briefly show how for the $\mathcal{CL}$ expression $\mathcal{C} = [e]O_{O_\bot(p\cdot p)}(p + d\&n)$ of page 399 we construct an alternating automaton which accepts all the traces that satisfy $\mathcal{C}$ and none others. The Fischer-Ladner closure of $\mathcal{C}$ generates the following set of subexpressions:

$$FL(\mathcal{C}) = \{\mathcal{C}, O_{O_\bot(p\cdot p)}(p + d\&n), O_\bot(p), \bot, O_\bot(d\&n), O_\bot(p \cdot p), [p]O_\bot(p)\}$$

The set $\mathcal{A}_B^\&$ of concurrent actions is the set $\{e,p,n,d\}^\&$ of basic actions closed under the constructor $\&$. The alternating automaton is:

$$A^{\mathcal{N}}(\mathcal{C}) = (FL(\mathcal{C}) \cup \overline{FL(\mathcal{C})}, \{e,p,n,d\}^\&, \mathcal{C}, \rho, \emptyset)$$

Note that there is no expression of the form $[\beta^*]\mathcal{C}$ in $FL(\mathcal{C})$ because we have no recursion in our original contract clause from Example 1. This means that the automaton is accepting all run trees which end in a state where the transition function returns **true** on the input symbol.[4] The transition function ρ is defined in the table below where $C_1 = O_{O_\perp(p \cdot p)}(p + d\&n)$:

$\rho(state, action)$	e	p	d	$e\&d$	$e\&p$	$d\&n$	$e\&d\&n$
C	C_1	true	true	C_1	C_1	true	C_1
C_1	$O_\perp(p \cdot p)$	true	$O_\perp(p \cdot p)$	$O_\perp(p \cdot p)$	true	true	true
$O_\perp(p)$	$\perp$	true	$\perp$	$\perp$	true	$\perp$	$\perp$
$O_\perp(d\&n)$	$\perp$	$\perp$	$\perp$	$\perp$	$\perp$	true	true
$O_\perp(p \cdot p)$	$\perp$	$O_\perp(p)$	$\perp$	$\perp$	$O_\perp(p)$	$\perp$	$\perp$
$[p]O_\perp(p)$	true	$O_\perp(p)$	true	true	$O_\perp(p)$	true	true

Computing the values in the table above is routine; e.g.:

$$\rho(C_1, e) = \rho(O_\perp(p), e) \vee \rho(O_\perp(d\&n), e) \vee O_\perp(p \cdot p) = \perp \vee \perp \vee O_\perp(p \cdot p)$$

Because from the state $\perp$ nothing can be accepted (as it generates only **false**) we have written in the table only $O_\perp(p \cdot p)$. There are 2^4 labels in the alphabet of $A^N(C)$ but we show only some of the more interesting ones. Moreover, none of the states from $\overline{FL}$ (i.e. $[C_1?] \perp$, the complemented expressions) are reachable nor do they contribute to the computation of any transition to a reachable state (like e.g. $O_\perp(d\&n)$ contributes to the computation of $\rho(C_1, e)$), so we have not included them in the table. The line for state $\perp$ is omitted.

4   Monitoring CL Specifications of Contracts

We use the method of [1] and we consequently use a 3-valued semantics approach to run-time monitoring. The monitor will generate a sequence of observations, denoted $[\sigma \models C]$, for a finite trace σ defined as:

$$[\sigma \models C] = \begin{cases} \textbf{tt} & \text{if } \forall \sigma' \in \Sigma^\omega : \sigma\sigma' \models C \\ \textbf{ff} & \text{if } \forall \sigma' \in \Sigma^\omega : \sigma\sigma' \not\models C \\ ? & \text{otherwise} \end{cases}$$

We use a standard method [16] to construct an exponentially larger nondeterministic Büchi automaton $NBA(C)$ from our alternating automaton $A^N(C)$ s.t. both automata accept the same trace language. Therefore $NBA(C)$ is exponential in the size of the expression.

The method of [1] is the following: take the $NBA(C)$ constructed above for which we know that $[\sigma \models C] \neq \textbf{ff}$ if there exists a state reachable by reading σ and from where the language accepted by $NBA(C)$ is not empty. Similarly for $[\sigma \models C] \neq \textbf{tt}$ when taking the complement of $NBA(C)$ (or equivalently we can take the $NBA(\neg C)$ of the negated formula which is $[C?] \perp$). Construct a function $F : S \to \{\top, \perp\}$ which for each state s of the $NBA(C)$ returns $\top$ iff $\mathcal{L}(NBA(C), s) \neq \emptyset$ (i.e.

---

[4] Note that for this particular example we do not see the power of alternating automata. More, the alternating Büchi automata behaves like a NFA.

the language accepted by $NBA(\mathcal{C})$ from state s is not empty), and $\bot$ otherwise. Using F one can construct a nondeterministic finite automaton $NFA(\mathcal{C})$ accepting finite traces s.t. $\sigma \in \mathcal{L}(NFA(\mathcal{C}))$ iff $[\sigma \models \mathcal{C}] \neq \bot$. This is the same NBA only that the set of final states contains all the states mapped by F to $\top$. Similarly construct a $NFA(\neg\mathcal{C})$ from $NBA(\neg\mathcal{C})$. One uses classical techniques to determinize the two NFAs. Using the two obtained DFAs one constructs the monitor as a finite state Moore machine which at each state outputs $\{\mathbf{tt}, \mathbf{ff}, ?\}$ if the input read until that state respectively satisfies the contract clause $\mathcal{C}$, violates it, or it cannot be decided. The monitor is the product of the two $DFA(\mathcal{C})$ and $DFA(\neg\mathcal{C})$.

We need that the monitor can read (and move to a new state) each possible action from the input alphabet. When doing the product of the two DFAs, if one of them does not have a transition for one of the symbols then this is lost for the monitor too. Therefore we add to each DFA a dummy state which is not accepting and which collects all the missing transitions for all states.

Correctness of the method [1] states $\lambda(\rho(s_0, \sigma)) = [\sigma \models \mathcal{C}]$, i.e. the output function $\lambda : S \to \{\mathbf{tt}, \mathbf{ff}, ?\}$ of the Moore machine returns for the state reached by reading σ from the starting state s_0 the semantics of $\mathcal{C}$ on the finite trace σ. The monitor generated is proven to have size double-exponential in the size of the expression; one exponent coming from translation of $\mathcal{A}^\mathcal{N}$ into the NBA and the other from determinization.

5 Conclusion

The work reported here may be viewed from different angles. On one hand we use *alternating automata* which has recently gained popularity [8] in the temporal logics community. We apply these to our rather unconventional logic $\mathcal{CL}$ [12]; i.e. a process logic (PDL [4]) extended with deontic logic modalities [18]. On another hand we presented the formal language $\mathcal{CL}$ with a trace semantics, and showed how we specify electronic contracts using it. From a practical point of view we presented here a first fully automated method of extracting a run-time monitor for a contract formally specified using the $\mathcal{CL}$ logic.

Note that our main objective is not to enforce a contract, but only to monitor it, that is to observe that the contract is indeed satisfied. The trace semantics presented in this paper is intended for monitoring purposes, and not to explain the language $\mathcal{CL}$. Thus, from the trace semantics point of view $[\alpha_\&]\mathcal{C}$ is equivalent to $F_\mathcal{C}(\alpha_\&)$, but we need such a distinction since this is not the case in $\mathcal{CL}$ (see $\mathcal{CL}$ branching semantics [13]).

Related work: For run-time verification our use of alternating automata on infinite traces of actions is a rather new approach. This is combined with the method of [1] that uses a three value (i.e. *true, false, inconclusive*) semantics view for run-time monitoring of LTL specifications. We know of the following two works that use alternating automata for run-time monitoring: in [3] LTL on infinite traces is used for specifications and alternating Büchi automata are constructed for LTL to recognize *finite* traces. The paper presents several algorithms which work on alternating automata to check for word inclusion. In [15] LTL has semantics on *finite* traces and nondeterministic alternating finite automata are used to recognize these traces. A determinization algorithm for alternating automata is given which can be extended to our alternating Büchi automata.

We have taken the approach of giving semantics to $\mathcal{CL}$ on *infinite* traces of actions which is more close to [3] but we want a deterministic finite state machine which at each state checks the finite input trace and outputs an answer telling if the contract has been violated. For this reason we fount the method of [1] most appealing. On the other hand a close look at the semantics of $\mathcal{CL}$ from Section 2 reveals the nice feature of this semantics which behaves the same for finite traces as for infinite traces. This coupled with the definition of alternating automata from Section 3 which accepts both infinite and finite traces gives the opportunity to investigate the use of alternating finite automata from [15] on the finite trace semantics. This may generate a monitor which is only single-exponential in size.

References

1. Bauer, A., Leucker, M., Schallhart, C.: Monitoring of real-time properties. In: Arun-Kumar, S., Garg, N. (eds.) FSTTCS 2006. LNCS, vol. 4337, pp. 260–272. Springer, Heidelberg (2006)
2. Chandra, A.K., Kozen, D., Stockmeyer, L.J.: Alternation. J. ACM 28(1), 114–133 (1981)
3. Finkbeiner, B., Sipma, H.: Checking finite traces using alternating automata. Formal Methods in System Design 24(2), 101–127 (2004)
4. Fischer, M.J., Ladner, R.E.: Propositional modal logic of programs. In: STOC 1977, pp. 286–294. ACM, New York (1977)
5. Göller, S., Lohrey, M., Lutz, C.: PDL with Intersection and Converse Is 2 EXP-Complete. In: Seidl, H. (ed.) FOSSACS 2007. LNCS, vol. 4423, pp. 198–212. Springer, Heidelberg (2007)
6. Harel, D., Tiuryn, J., Kozen, D.: Dynamic Logic. MIT Press, Cambridge (2000)
7. Kozen, D.: A completeness theorem for kleene algebras and the algebra of regular events. Information and Computation 110(2), 366–390 (1994)
8. Kupferman, O., Vardi, M.Y., Wolper, P.: An automata-theoretic approach to branching-time model checking. J. ACM 47(2), 312–360 (2000)
9. Manna, Z., Pnueli, A.: Specification and verification of concurrent programs by ∀-automata. In: POPL 1987, pp. 1–12 (1987)
10. Muller, D.E., Saoudi, A., Schupp, P.E.: Weak alternating automata give a simple explanation of why most temporal and dynamic logics are decidable in exponential time. In: LICS 1988, pp. 422–427 (1988)
11. Pratt, V.R.: Process logic. In: POPL 1979, pp. 93–100. ACM Press, New York (1979)
12. Prisacariu, C., Schneider, G.: A formal language for electronic contracts. In: Bonsangue, M.M., Johnsen, E.B. (eds.) FMOODS 2007. LNCS, vol. 4468, pp. 174–189. Springer, Heidelberg (2007)
13. Prisacariu, C., Schneider, G.: CL: A Logic for Reasoning about Legal Contracts – Semantics. Technical Report 371, Univ. Oslo (2008)
14. Prisacariu, C., Schneider, G.: Run-time Monitoring of Electronic Contracts – theoretical results. Technical report, Univ. Oslo (2008)
15. Stolz, V., Bodden, E.: Temporal Assertions Using AspectJ. In: RV 2005. ENTCS, vol. 144, pp. 109–124. Elsevier, Amsterdam (2006)

16. Vardi, M.Y.: Alternating Automata: Unifying Truth and Validity Checking for Temporal Logics. In: McCune, W. (ed.) CADE 1997. LNCS, vol. 1249, pp. 191–206. Springer, Heidelberg (1997)
17. Vardi, M.Y., Wolper, P.: An automata-theoretic approach to automatic program verification (preliminary report). In: LICS 1986, pp. 332–344 (1986)
18. von Wright, G.H.: Deontic logic. Mind 60, 1–15 (1951)

Practical Efficient Modular Linear-Time Model-Checking

Carlo A. Furia[1] and Paola Spoletini[2]

[1] DEI, Politecnico di Milano, Milano, Italy
[2] DSCPI, Università degli Studi dell'Insubria, Como, Italy

Abstract. This paper shows how the modular structure of composite systems can guide the state-space exploration in explicit-state linear-time model-checking and make it more efficient in practice. Given a composite system where every module has input and output variables — and variables of different modules can be connected — a total ordering according to which variables are generated is determined, through heuristics based on graph-theoretical analysis of the modular structure. The technique is shown to outperform standard exploration techniques (that do not take the modular structure information into account) by several orders of magnitude in experiments with Spin models of MTL formulas.

1 Introduction

Systems are complex; as apparent as it sounds, *complexity* is the primal hurdle when it comes to describing and understanding them. Abstraction and *modularization* are widely-known powerful conceptual tools to tame this complexity. In extreme summary, a large system is described as the composition of simpler modules. Every module encapsulates a portion of the system; its internal behavior is abstracted away at its interface — the set of input/output variables that are connected to other modules [10]. Modularization is widely practiced in all of computer science and software engineering.

A class of systems that are especially difficult to analyze is given by *concurrent* systems. In such systems the various parts are often highly coupled, as a result of their ongoing complex synchronization mechanisms. Nonetheless, over the last decades the state of the art in specifying and verifying concurrent systems has made very conspicuous advancements. A significant part of them is centered around the formalisms of temporal logics [2] and finite-state automata [13], and the algorithmic verification technique of model-checking [1].

Although model-checking techniques target primarily closed monolithic systems, modularization has been considered for model-checking in the research trends that go by the names *module checking* [8] and *modular model-checking* [7]. Both extend model-checking techniques to *open* systems, i.e., systems with an explicit interaction with an external environment (that provides input) [5]. Then, in module checking properties of the system are checked with respect to *all* possible environments, whereas in modular model-checking properties are checked with respect to environments satisfying a temporal-logic specification (according to the *assume/guarantee* paradigm).

In this paper we take a different approach, which exploits the information that comes from the modular decomposition of systems to ameliorate model-checking performances

Cha et al. (Eds.): ATVA 2008, LNCS 5311, pp. 408–417, 2008.

in practice. We consider explicit-state model-checking techniques for linear-time temporal logic: the system and the property are represented as finite-state automata, and checking that all runs of the system satisfy the property amounts to performing an exploration of the state-space of the overall automaton — resulting from the composition of the various component automata — in order to detect cycles (which correspond to runs where the property is violated) [1]. This exploration is the more efficient the earlier we are able to detect "unproductive" paths that lead to no cycle. If the various components of a system are decomposed into communicating modules, the information about how these modules are connected is useful to guide such state-space exploration paths.

Our approach aims at being practical, in that we do not claim any asymptotic worst-case gain over traditional algorithms. In fact, our technique is essentially based on heuristics that may or may not be effective according to the particular structure of the system at hand, and that cannot escape the inherent worst-case complexity of automated verification. However, we demonstrate the significant practical impact of our technique by means of a verification examples where traditional "vanilla" techniques are compared against our optimized modular approach. Our technique clearly outperforms the unoptimized algorithm by several orders of magnitude. This abridged version of the paper omits several items, including a discussion of related work, a few details about the experiments of Section 4, and a more practical description of some implementation aspects. These missing points can be found in [3].

2 Definitions

Variables and Computations. A *variable* v is characterized by the finite domain D_v over which it ranges; if no domain is specified the variable is assumed to be Boolean with $D_v = \{0, 1\}$. For a set of variables $\mathcal{V}$, $\mathcal{V}'$ denotes the set of primed variables $\{v' \mid v \in \mathcal{V}\}$ with the same domains as the original variables.

The behavior of systems — and components thereof — is described by ω-sequences of variable values called computations. Formally, given a finite set of variables $\mathcal{V}$, a *computation* over $\mathcal{V}$ is an ω-sequence $w = w_0, w_1, w_2, \ldots \in D^{\omega}$, where D is the Cartesian product $\prod_{v \in \mathcal{V}} D_v$ of variable domains. Also, given a subset of variables $Q \subseteq \mathcal{V}$, the *projection* of w over Q is a computation $x = x_0, x_1, x_2, \ldots$ over Q obtained from w by dropping the components of variables in $\mathcal{V} \setminus Q$, that is $x_j = w_j|_Q$ for all $j \geq 0$. Projection is extended to sets of computations as obvious: for a set of computations C, its projection over Q is $C|_Q = \{w|_Q \mid w \in C\}$. The set of all computations over $\mathcal{V}$ is denoted by $\mathcal{C}(\mathcal{V})$.

Modules and Composition. A system is described by the composition of modules; $\mathcal{M}$ denotes the set of all modules.

The simplest component is the *primitive module*, defined as $M = \langle I, O, H, W \rangle$, where:

- I, O, and H are sets of input, output, and hidden (i.e., internal) variables, respectively. We assume that these sets are pairwise disjoint. $P = I \cup O \cup H$ denotes all variables of the module.

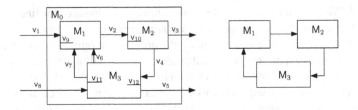

Fig. 1. Flat composite open module M_0 (left) and its connection graph (right)

- W is a set of computations over P, describing the module's semantics. In practice, the behavior of modules is specified as the language $L(F)$ of some finite-state automaton or temporal logic formula F.

  Usually, one assumes that the value of input variables is provided "from the outside", hence it should not be constrained in W; this can be stated formally by requiring that $W|_I \triangleq \{w|_I \mid w \in W\}$ equals $C(I)$. However, this assumption is not strictly required for the discussion of this paper, as it will be clear in the following.

We introduce a graphical representation for (the interface of) primitive modules: a module is represented by a box with inward arrows corresponding to variables in I, outward errors corresponding to variables in O, and internal lines corresponding to variables in H.

Example 1. Primitive module M_3, pictured in Figure 1, has input variables $I = \{v_4, v_8\}$, output variables $O = \{v_5, v_6, v_7\}$, and hidden variables $H = \{v_{11}, v_{12}\}$.

Primitive modules can be composed to build *composite modules*. A composite module is defined as $N = \langle I, O, n, \eta, C, X \rangle$, where:

- $n > 0$ is the number if internal modules;
- η is a finite set of module identifiers such that $|\eta| = n$;
- $C : \eta \to \mathcal{M}$ provides the module definition $C(i)$ of every internal module $i \in \eta$. We denote the components of every module $C(i)$ with superscripts as in I^i, O^i, H^i, etc. Also, we define the sets of all input, output, and hidden variables of internal modules as: $\mathcal{I} \triangleq \bigcup_{i \in \eta} I^i$, $\mathcal{O} \triangleq \bigcup_{i \in \eta} O^i$, and $\mathcal{H} \triangleq \bigcup_{i \in \eta} H^i$ respectively. Accordingly, $\mathcal{V} \triangleq \mathcal{I} \cup \mathcal{O} \cup \mathcal{H}$.
- $X \subseteq \mathcal{O} \times \mathcal{I}$ is a connection relation, which defines how the inputs and outputs of the various modules are connected: $(o, i) \in X$ iff output o is connected to input i.
- I, O have the same meaning as in primitive modules. Hence, input and output variables of composite modules are defined as those of internal modules that are not connected, namely: $I = \{i \in \mathcal{I} \mid \forall o \in \mathcal{O} : (o, i) \notin X\}$ and $O = \{o \in \mathcal{O} \mid \forall i \in \mathcal{I} : (o, i) \notin X\}$.

We extend the graphical notation to composite modules as obvious, by representing connections through connected arrows.

A module is *closed* iff $I = \emptyset$, otherwise it is *open*. A module is *flat* iff it is primitive or it is composite and all its internal modules are primitive; if a module is not flat it is *nesting.* A module is *non-hierarchical* iff it is flat or it is nesting and all its components are flat; otherwise it is *hierarchical.*

For a composite module $N = \langle I, O, n, \eta, C, X \rangle$, its *connection graph* is a directed graph $G = \langle V, E \rangle$ with $V = \eta$ and $(h, k) \in E$ iff there is a connection $(o, i) \in X$ with $o \in O^h$ and $i \in I^k$. We stretch the terminology by "lifting" attributes of the connection graph to the modules themselves. So, for instance, if the connection graph is acyclic (resp. connected), the modular system is called acyclic (resp. connected), etc.

Example 2. Figure 1 (left) pictures flat composite open module M_0 with $I = \{v_1, v_8\}$, $O = \{v_3, v_5\}$, $n = 3$, $\eta = \{M_1, M_2, M_3\}$. For graphical simplicity, variables that are connected are given a unique name. To the right, we have the connection graph of M_0.

Let us define the *semantics* of modules. For a primitive module M, the semantics is trivially given by $W = L(M)$, which is called the *language* of M.

Let us now consider a composite module N. The language $L(N)$ accepted by such a module is a set of computations over V defined as follows. A computation w is in $L(N)$ iff: (1) w is compatible with every component module, i.e., $w|_{P^i} \in L(M^i)$ for all component modules $i \in \eta$; and (2) connections between modules are respected, i.e., for all connections $(o, i) \in X$ we have $w|_{\{o\}} = w|_{\{i\}}$.

Notice that, for linear-time models, semantics of open modules is trivial, and implicit in our previous definitions. To make this apparent, we introduce the notion of maximal environment, which is a module generating all possible inputs to another (open) module. Given a set V of variables, a *maximal environment* $\mathcal{E}(V)$ is a primitive module such that $I = H = \emptyset$, $O = V$, and the language $L(\mathcal{E}(V))$ is exactly $\mathcal{C}(V)$. So, for an open module K (either primitive or composite), the language $L(K)$ can be defined as the language of the composite closed module K' obtained by composing K with a maximal environment. Hence, $K' = \langle \emptyset, O^K, 2, \{e, m\}, \langle \mathcal{E}(I^{K'}), K \rangle, X \rangle$ with $X = \{(x', x) \mid x \in I^K\}$. However, for any computation $x \in \mathcal{C}(V \cup I^{K'})$ it is $x \in L(K')$ iff $x|_{I^{K'}} \in L(\mathcal{E}(I^{K'})) = \mathcal{C}(I^{K'})$ and $x|_V \in L(K)$ and $x|_{I^{K'}} = x|_{I^K}$. Hence, $L(K')|_V = L(K)$.

3   Efficient Design of Generators

Practical Module Checking. Let us consider what happens in practice when performing explicit-state model-checking of a modular system using an automata-based approach. In this setting, the model-checking algorithm is basically an on-the-fly state-space search for cycles (or absence thereof). Correspondingly, the modular structure of the system can be exploited to greatly improve the performances of the check in practice. Essentially, structure can guide the state-space exploration in order to minimize the degree of unnecessary nondeterminism.[1]

We take advantage of these remarks in the following way. For every module M in a system we introduce a *generator* component $\mathcal{G}(M)$. The generator is responsible for

---

[1] In a sense, a model with shared-variable concurrency is transformed into one with message-passing concurrency, according to the functional dependencies among variables of different modules.

setting the value of all variables in M. It operates as an interface between M and the other modules in the system. Namely, it can receive input variables from the other modules, once they have generated them, and it is responsible for setting the value of hidden and output variables, according to the behavior of M. We also define a *total ordering* over all generators in a system. This induces a generation order for environment variables in the whole system. As we have shown in the previous example, this can influence the efficiency of the system state-space exploration.

Notice that generators are not additional modules of the system, but they are components that pertain to a lower level of abstraction, namely the system description in the model-checking environment. These components realize in practice the coordination among modules in an efficient way. This framing of the problem has been especially inspired by our experience with the Spin model-checker and its implementation of ProMeLa processes [6], in particular the one based on a translation from TRIO metric temporal logic formulas [12,9,11]. However, we present the results in a more general setting which is exploitable also with other linear-time explicit-state model-checkers (see [3] for more implementation details).

In the remainder, we show a strategy to design an ordered set of generator for any given modular system. The strategy aims at designing and ordering the generators so as to cut down the state-space exploration as soon as possible. It is based on a set of heuristics and built upon the analysis of the modular structure of the system.

Clearly, we can assume that the the connection graph of our system is connected. In fact, if it is not connected, we can partition it into a collection of connected components, such that every connected component can be treated in isolation as discussed below.

Acyclic Flat Modules. Let $M = \langle I, O, n, \eta, C, X \rangle$ be an acyclic flat connected module; without loss of generality we assume it is a composite module (otherwise, just consider a composite module with a single primitive component). For every $i \in \eta$ the generator $\mathcal{G}(i)$ of module $C(i)$ is responsible for generating the following variables: $H^i \cup O^i \cup (I^i \cap I)$. That is, $\mathcal{G}(i)$ generates all hidden and output variables, and all input variables that are not connected to any output variables of other modules.

Cyclic Flat Modules. Let $M = \langle I, O, n, \eta, C, X \rangle$ be a cyclic flat connected module; note that such a module is also necessarily composite. In order to design generators for such a module we recall the notion of *feedback arc set*. Let $G = \langle V, E \rangle$ be the cyclic connection graph of M. A feedback arc set (FAS) is a set of edges $F \subseteq V$ such that the graph $\langle V, E \setminus F \rangle$ is acyclic. In practice, we can consider M as an acyclic module with (self-)connections going from some of its output variables to some of its input variables; these connections correspond to edges F of the FAS. It is clear that a FAS always exists for a cyclic module; in general, however, the FAS is not unique.

Through the definition of FAS we can re-use the simple strategy for designing generators that we applied in the acyclic case. Namely, let $I^F \subseteq \mathcal{I} \setminus I$ and $O^F \subseteq \mathcal{O} \setminus O$ be the sets of input and output variables, respectively, corresponding to the edges in F. Then, for every $i \in \eta$ generator $\mathcal{G}(i)$ of module $C(i)$ is responsible for generating the following variables: $H^i \cup (O^i \cap (\mathcal{O} \setminus O^F)) \cup (I^i \cap I) \cup (I^i \cap I^F)$. That is, $\mathcal{G}(i)$ generates all hidden variables, all output variables that are not in the cycle (because these are the same as the input variables they are connected to, and these input variables are generated by the generator of the corresponding modules), all input variables that are not connected to any output variables of other modules (hence coming from the environment), and all input variables that belong to the FAS.

Example 3. Consider the connection graph of cyclic module M_0 in Figure 1. If we choose $F_1 = \{(M_3, M_1)\}$ as FAS, the generators would generate the following variables: $\mathcal{G}(M_1) = \{v_9, v_2, v_1, v_6, v_7\}$, $\mathcal{G}(M_2) = \{v_{10}, v_3, v_4\}$, $\mathcal{G}(M_3) = \{v_{11}, v_{12}, v_5, v_8\}$. If we choose instead $F_2 = \{(M_1, M_2)\}$ as FAS, we would generate: $\mathcal{G}(M_1) = \{v_9, v_1\}$, $\mathcal{G}(M_2) = \{v_{10}, v_3, v_4, v_2\}$, $\mathcal{G}(M_3) = \{v_{11}, v_{12}, v_5, v_6, v_7, v_8\}$.

In order for the generation to be correct all variables in the system must be generated, in some order, in such a way that all constraints imposed by the modules' semantics are satisfied. Any FAS guarantees a correct generation in this sense, because it simply induces a particular generation order on the set of all variables, such that no variable is ignored. While correctness is guaranteed regardless of which FAS is chosen, it is advisable to choose the arcs corresponding to the minimum number of variables, so that the minimum number of variables is generated first. Hence, we introduce the following minimization problem to select a suitable FAS.

Consider the *weighted connection graph*, a weighted enhancement of the connection graph defined as follows. Let $G = \langle V, E \rangle$ be the (unweighted) connection graph. The corresponding weighted version $G_\mathcal{W} = \langle V, E, \mathcal{W} \rangle$ introduces a weight function $\mathcal{W} : E \to \mathbb{N}_{>0}$ that associates with every edge $e = (M_1, M_2) \in E$ a weight $\mathcal{W}(e) = \prod_{v \in M_1 \succ M_2} |D_v|$ where $M_1 \succ M_2$ is the set of output variables of M_1 connected to input variables of M_2 (i.e., $M_1 \succ M_2 = \{o \in O^{M_1} \mid \exists i \in I^{M_2} : (o, i) \in X\}$).

Finding the optimal generator design amounts to solving the (weighted) minimum FAS problem over the weighted connection graph. This problem is well-known to be NP-complete [4], while it is solvable in polynomial time for planar graphs. However, the connection graph of a modular system is not likely to be significantly large, hence it is acceptable to use exact algorithms that have a worst-case exponential running time. Indeed, one can solve the problem with a brute-force algorithm which finds the minimum FAS MINFAS(G) for a weighted connection graph $G = \langle V, E, \mathcal{W} \rangle$ in time $O(2^{|E|}|V|^2)$.

Example 4. For module M_0 in Figure 1, the weighted minimum FAS problem suggests to choose (M_1, M_2) (or (M_2, M_3)) over (M_3, M_1) as FAS. Notice that, if arc (m, n) is chosen, one must start generating from module n, where the broken cycle is entered. In fact, in the previous example we have shown that choosing (M_3, M_1) involves generating variables for modules 5, then 3, then 4, whereas choosing (M_1, M_2) involves generating variables for modules 2, then 4, then 6.

Non-Hierarchical Nesting Modules. In increasing order of complexity, let us now consider nesting modules that are non-hierarchical. The connection graph of such modules must be first analyzed at the top level, in order to cluster its component flat modules into two classes. To this end, we have to identify the strongly connected components of the connection graph.

A *strongly connected component* (SCC) of a directed graph is a maximal sub-graph such that for every pair v_1, v_2 of its vertices there is a directed path from v_1 to v_2. The

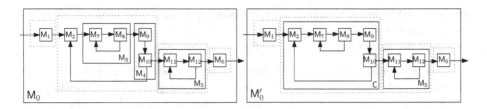

Fig. 2. Non-hierarchical nesting module M_0 and its 4 SCCs (dotted boxes)

collection of all strongly connected components of a directed graph form a partition such that the "higher-level" graph where each SCC is represented by a single node is acyclic. The collection of SCCs of a graph $G = \langle V, E \rangle$ can be computed in time $\Theta(|V| + |E|)$.

For a non-hierarchical nesting module $M = \langle I, O, n, \eta, C, X \rangle$ let $G = \langle V, E \rangle$ be its connection graph, and let $S = \{S_1, S_2, \ldots, S_{|S|}\}$ be a partition of V such that $\langle S_i, E_i \rangle$ with $E_i = \{(v_1, v_2) \in E \mid v_1, v_2 \in S_i\}$ is a SCC for all $1 \leq i \leq |S|$. Then, every SCC $\langle S_i, E_i \rangle$ belongs to exactly one of the following two categories: (1) $|S_i| = 1$, that is the SCC S_i represents a single flat module; and (2) $|S_i| > 1$, that is the SCC S_i represents a collection of (more than one) flat modules. We build the generators for every module in a SCC according to the following strategy:

1. If $|S_i| = 1$ we just apply the techniques for flat modules that we presented in the previous sections;
2. If $|S_i| > 1$ we "flatten" the collection of corresponding modules as follows.
   Let $S_i \subseteq \eta$ with $|S_i| > 1$, such that every $j \in S_i$ is a flat module. Let $C = \langle I^C, O^C, n^C, \eta^C, C^C, X^C \rangle$ be a new composite module defined as follows. For every composite module $C(j) = \langle I^j, O^j, n^j, C^j, X^j \rangle$ with $j \in S_i$, we introduce in C the set of primitive modules $\{C^j(k) \mid k \in \eta^j\}$ by adding: (1) $n^j = |\eta^j|$ to n^C, (2) η^j to η^C, (3) the mappings $\{k \mapsto C^j(k) \mid k \in \eta^j\}$ to C^C, and (4) the tuples $\{(o, i) \in X^j\}$ to X^C. Also, for every primitive $C(j)$ with $j \in S_i$ we simply increase n^j by one, add the new identifier j to η^C and the new mapping $\{j \mapsto C(j)\}$ to C^C. I^C and O^C are defined accordingly as $\bigcup_{j \in S_i} I^j$ and $\bigcup_{j \in S_i} O^j$ respectively. Finally, C replaces all modules $\{C(j) \mid j \in S_i\}$ in the system.

   In all, informally, we have removed the "wrapper" of every composite module in S_i by merging its components directly into the top level of C. Now, C is a flat (composite) module, which can be analyzed through the techniques presented in the previous sections.

Example 5. Consider non-hierarchical nesting module M_0 in Figure 2 (left). Its components M_2, M_3, M_4 form a SCC with more than one node, which can be flattened into module C in M_0' (right). The SCC of M_0' are the singletons $\{M_1\}, \{C\}, \{M_5\}$, hence they can be analyzed according to the discussions in the previous section.

Hierarchical Modules. For a hierarchical module M we can apply recursively the strategies discussed in the previous sections. First, we build the connection graph for M, which represents the structure of the system at the top level. By analyzing this graph as shown before, we identify, for every node in the graph, a set of variables that must be generated for its lower-level components. Then, we recur on every node in the graph: we consider the corresponding modules in isolation from the rest, we build the corresponding (lower-level) connection graph, and further partition the variables according to the discussed techniques. In the end, we will have introduced a generator for every component at the lowest level.

Choosing the Total Ordering of Generators. Let us now discuss how to choose a total ordering over the generators. Consider a directed acyclic weighted connection graph $G = \langle V, E, \mathcal{W} \rangle$ such that for every module $M \in V$ we have defined a generator $\mathcal{G}(M)$. This setting is without loss of generality, because if the graph is cyclic we choose a FAS F as described above in this section and consider the "cut" acyclic graph $\langle V, E \setminus F, \mathcal{W} \rangle$. Also, for composite modules M we may have one generator for every component of M; however, we first consider M as an aggregate component (so $\mathcal{G}(M)$ represents a collection of generators that we consider atomic) and then recursively apply the enumeration technique to M itself.

The acyclic graph G defines the partial order $E \subseteq V \times V$ on its nodes V. Through a standard technique, we select a total order $E \subseteq \preceq \subseteq V \times V$ by repeatedly selecting a pair $M_1, M_2 \in V$ of nodes such that M_1 and M_2 are not comparable in E and adding either (M_1, M_2) or (M_2, M_1) to $\preceq$. Pairs are selected according to the *generation domain dimension* (GDD) heuristic. For a module M_i we define:[2]

$$\text{gdd}(M_i) = \begin{cases} \prod_{\pi \in \Gamma^+} \mathcal{W}(\pi) + \prod_{\pi \in I^i \cap I} |D_\pi| & \text{if } M_i \text{ is a source node} \\ \prod_{\pi \in \Gamma^+} \mathcal{W}(\pi) - \prod_{\pi \in \Gamma^-} \mathcal{W}(\pi) & \text{otherwise} \end{cases}$$

with $\Gamma^+ = \{(M_i, v) \in E\}$ and $\Gamma^- = \{(v, M_i) \in E\}$ the sets of outgoing and ingoing edges, respectively, and $I^i \cap I$ the set of input variables of M_i that are generated. Then, we let $M_1 \preceq M_2$ iff $\text{gdd}(M_1) < \text{gdd}(M_2)$. This corresponds to putting first the generators corresponding to modules that "filter out" the most variables. Hence it hopefully cuts down as soon as possible several possible future states to be considered in the state-space exploration.

4   Examples and Experiments

Our experiments are based on a reservoir system example whose precise behavior is formalized in [3]. The reservoir system is made of four primitive modules: two reservoirs, a controller, and a pipe connecting the two reservoirs (see Figure 3, where the top "wrapper" module is not pictured for simplicity). We verify that, under suitable choices for the parameters, the following two properties hold for the modular system: (1) the level of both reservoirs is always in the range $[1..M - 1]$; and (2) if level_1 reaches a minimum threshold $\text{min}_{\text{thr}} = 5$ it grows back to the value $M/2$ in no more than $M/2 - \text{min}_{\text{thr}}$ time units.

In order to evaluate the effectiveness of our approach we verified the reservoir system using both the flat "vanilla" approach — as presented in [9] — and the modular

---

[2] A source node is a node without ingoing edges.

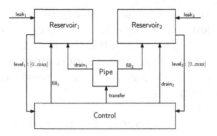

Fig. 3. The Reservoir System

approach of this paper. The model for the flat verification can be automatically generated using the TRIO2ProMeLa translator.[3] In a nutshell, TRIO2ProMeLa translates MTL (and TRIO) formulas in ProMeLa models, the input language of the Spin model-checker [6]. The generated ProMeLa models simulate alternating automata, which are finite-state automata over infinite computations, potentially exponentially more concise variants of Büchi automata [13]. The ProMeLa simulation accepts (or rejects) computations by analyzing the validity of the current value of variables at each step, also taking in account the current history of the computation. In the flat approach, the modular structure of the system is ignored, hence computations are generated by a unique global generator that proceeds exhaustively step by step, until acceptance or rejection can be decided. In the modular setting, we translated MTL formulas similarly as in the flat case but we associated different ProMeLa processes to each system module.

Table 1. Experiments with the Reservoir System

F/M	M	Prop.	Gen. order	MStates	MTrans.	Mem.	Time
F	12	(1)		34.00	36.92	∞	165
F	12	(2)		34.00	36.92	∞	166
M	12	(1)	PCR_1R_2	11.34	12.03	632	75
M	12	(2)	PCR_1R_2	11.34	12.03	632	75
M	12	(1)	PR_1R_2C	1.81	1.95	94	11
M	12	(2)	PR_1R_2C	1.81	1.95	94	11
M	12	(1)	R_1R_2CP	0.53	0.58	28	3
M	12	(2)	R_1R_2CP	0.53	0.58	28	3
M	12	(1)	CPR_1R_2	16.04	17.11	896	105
M	12	(2)	CPR_1R_2	16.04	17.11	896	103
M	20	(1)	PR_1R_2C	6.43	6.92	357	42
M	25	(1)	PR_1R_2C	13.31	14.33	773	90
M	31	(1)	PR_1R_2C	29.42	31.68	1667	193
M	32	(1)	PR_1R_2C	29.43	31.70	∞	194

Table 1 shows several test results obtained by running modified TRIO2ProMeLa models of the reservoir system described above with the Spin model-checker. For each test the table reports: whether a flat or modular model is used (F/M), the value of parameter M in the specification, the checked property, the total ordering of modules according to which variables are generated, the number of explored states and

---

[3] TRIO2ProMeLa is available at http://home.dei.polimi.it/spoleti/TRIO2ProMeLa.htm, together with the code used in the experiments.

transitions (in millions), the used memory (in MBytes, ∞ means "out of memory"), and the verification time (in seconds). The tests have been performed on a PC equipped with an AMD Athlon64 X2 Dual-Core Processor 4000+ and 2 GBytes of RAM. The experiments show clearly that the reservoir system cannot be analyzed with the flat approach, and taking into account the modular structure is needed.

In addition to the modular technique, in the experimentation we also tinkered with some *ad hoc* optimizations, that are reported in [3], together with several details about the example.

5   Conclusion

We showed how the information on the modular structure of composite systems can be availed to increase the efficiency of the state-space exploration in explicit-state linear-time model-checking. We introduced heuristic techniques that extract a total ordering among modules of a complex system according to its topology. Experiments have shown clearly very relevant performance enhancements when the state-space exploration is done according to the technique. In particular, the verification of the example system has been made possible with limited resources.

Acknowledgements. We thank the anonymous reviewers for their useful remarks.

References

1. Clarke, E.M., Grumberg, O., Peled, D.A.: Model Checking. MIT Press, Cambridge (2000)
2. Emerson, E.A.: Temporal and modal logic. In: van Leeuwen, J. (ed.) Handbook of Theoretical Computer Science, vol. B, pp. 996–1072. Elsevier Science, Amsterdam (1990)
3. Furia, C.A., Spoletini, P.: Practical efficient modular linear-time model-checking (July 2008); (extended version), http://home.dei.polimi.it/furia/
4. Garey, M.R., Johnson, D.S.: Computers and Intractability: A Guide to the Theory of NP-Completeness. W.H. Freeman, New York (1979)
5. Harel, D., Pnueli, A.: On the development of reactive systems. In: Logics and Models of Concurrent Systems, pp. 477–498 (1985)
6. Holzmann, G.J.: The SPIN Model Checker: Primer and Reference Manual (2003)
7. Kupferman, O., Vardi, M.Y.: An automata-theortetic approach to modular model checking. ACM TOPLAS 22(1), 87–128 (2000)
8. Kupferman, O., Vardi, M.Y., Wolper, P.: Module checking. Information and Computation 164(2), 322–344 (2001)
9. Morzenti, A., Pradella, M., San Pietro, P., Spoletini, P.: Model-checking TRIO specifications in SPIN. In: Araki, K., Gnesi, S., Mandrioli, D. (eds.) FME 2003. LNCS, vol. 2805, pp. 542–561. Springer, Heidelberg (2003)
10. Parnas, D.L.: On the criteria to be used in decomposing systems into modules. Communications of the ACM 15(12), 1053–1058 (1972)
11. Pradella, M., San Pietro, P., Spoletini, P., Morzenti, A.: Practical model checking of LTL with past. In: ATVA 2003, pp. 135–146 (2003)
12. Spoletini, P.: Verification of Temporal Logic Specification via Model Checking. PhD thesis, DEI, Politecnico di Milano (May 2005)
13. Thomas, W.: Automata on infinite objects. In: van Leeuwen, J. (ed.) Handbook of Theoretical Computer Science, vol. B, pp. 133–164. Elsevier Science, Amsterdam (1990)

Passive Testing of Timed Systems*

César Andrés, Mercedes G. Merayo, and Manuel Núñez

Dept. Sistemas Informáticos y Computación
Universidad Complutense de Madrid, 28040 Madrid, Spain
{c.andres,mgmerayo}@fdi.ucm.es, mn@sip.ucm.es

Abstract. This paper presents a methodology to perform passive testing based on invariants for systems that present temporal restrictions. Invariants represent the most relevant expected properties of the implementation under test. Intuitively, an invariant expresses the fact that each time the implementation under test performs a given sequence of actions, then it must exhibit a behavior in a lapse of time reflected in the invariant. In particular, the algorithm presented in this paper are fully implemented.

1 Introduction

Testing consists in checking the conformance of an implementation by performing experiments on it. In order to perform this task, several techniques, algorithms, and semantic frameworks have been introduced in the literature. The application of formal testing techniques to check the correctness of a system requires to identify the *critical* aspects of the system, that is, those aspects that will make the difference between correct and incorrect behavior. In this line, the time consumed by each operation should be considered critical in a real-time system.

Most testing approaches consist in the generation of a set of tests that are applied to the implementation in order to check its correctness with respect to a specification. Thus, testing is based on the ability of a tester to stimulate the implementation under test (IUT) and check the correction of the answers provided by the implementation. However, in some situations this activity becomes difficult and even impossible to perform. For example, this is the case if the tester is not provided with a direct interface to interact with the IUT or the implementation is built from components that are running in their environment and cannot be shutdown or interrupted for a long period of time. The activity of testing could be specially difficult if the tester must check temporal restrictions. In these situations, the instruments of measurement could be not so precise as required or the results could be distorted due to mistakes during the observation. As a result, undiscovered faults may result in failures at runtime, where the system may perform untested traces. In these situations, there is a particular interest in using other types of testing techniques such as *passive testing*. In

---

* Research partially supported by the Spanish MEC project WEST/FAST (TIN2006-15578-C02-01) and the Marie Curie project TAROT (MRTN-CT-2003-505121).

Cha et al. (Eds.): ATVA 2008, LNCS 5311, pp. 418–427, 2008.

passive testing the tester does not need to interact with the IUT. On the contrary, execution traces are observed and analyzed without interfering with the behavior of the IUT. Passive testing has very large domains of application. For instance, it can be used as a monitoring technique to detect and report errors (this is the use that we consider in this paper). Another area of application is in network management to detect configuration problems, fault identification, or resource provisioning. It can be also used to study the feasibility of new features as classes of services, network security, and congestion control. Usually, execution traces of the implementation are compared with the specification to detect faults in the implementation. In most of these works the specification has the form of a finite state machine (FSM) and the studies consist in verifying that the executed trace is accepted by the FSM specification. A drawback of these first approaches is the low performance of the proposed algorithms (in terms of complexity in the worst case) if non-deterministic specifications are considered. A new approach was proposed in [1]. There, a set of properties called *invariants* were extracted from the specification and checked on the traces observed from the implementation to test their correctness. One of the drawbacks of this work was the limitation on the grammar used to express invariants. A new formalism that overcomes this restriction for expressing invariants was presented in [2]. It allows to specify wildcard characters in invariants and to include a set of outputs as termination of the invariant. In addition, a new kind of invariants was introduced: Obligation invariants.

In this paper we extend [2] in order to deal with timed restrictions. We will use a simple extension of the classical concept of *Finite State Machines* that allows a specifier to explicitly denote temporal requirements for each action of a system. Intuitively, transitions in timed finite state machines indicate that if the machine is in a state s and receives and input i then after t time units it will produce and output o and it will change its state to s'. Next, we informally introduce the formalism to express temporal conditions in the invariants: Timed invariants. We distinguish between timed restrictions related to each action in the trace represented in the invariant and the one corresponding to the whole trace. For example we could represent properties as *"Each time that a user applies "a" and observes "y" the amount of time the system spends to perform the action is between 3 and 5 time units, if after performing some operations the user applies "b" then he observes "z" in 2 time units and the performance of all these actions does not exceed 10 time units"*.

In our approach, we perform two types of property verification: One on the specification and another one on the traces generated by the implementation. Due to the fact that we assume that the timed invariants can be supplied by the tester, the first step must be to check that the invariant is in fact correct with respect to the specification. An extension of the algorithm proposed in [2] to check this correctness is provided, taking into account the timed conditions that appear in the timed invariants. The next step is to check whether the trace produced by the IUT respects timed invariants. In this case, we propose an algorithm that is an adaption of the classical algorithms for string matching.

It works, in the worst case, in time $O(m \cdot n)$ where m and n are the length of the trace and the invariant, respectively. Let us remark that we cannot achieve complexities as good as the ones in classical algorithms because we have to find all the occurrences of the pattern. Due to the last of space we could not include this part of our research in this paper. A longer version of this paper, including all the previously mentioned algorithms, can be found at [3].

The rest of the paper is organized as follows. In Section 2 we present the notation we apply along the paper. We also introduce our timed extension of the classical finite state machine model. In Section 3 notions of timed invariant and passive testing are presented, as well as the algorithms to check the correctness of invariants with respect to the specification. Finally, Section 4 presents the conclusions of the paper and some lines for future work.

2   Preliminaries

First we introduce notation regarding the definition of time intervals. In this paper we consider that these intervals are contained in $\mathbb{R}_+$, that is, they contain real values greater than or equal to zero.

Definition 1. *We say that* $\hat{a} = [a_1, a_2]$ *is a time interval if* $a_1 \in \mathbb{R}_+$, $a_2 \in \mathbb{R}_+ \cup \{\infty\}$, *and* $a_1 \leq a_2$. *We assume that for all* $t \in \mathbb{R}_+$ *we have* $t < \infty$ *and* $t + \infty = \infty$. *We consider that* $\mathcal{I}_{\mathbb{R}_+}$ *denotes the set of time intervals. Let* $\hat{a} = [a_1, a_2]$ *and* $\hat{b} = [b_1, b_2]$ *be time intervals. We consider the following functions:*

- $\oplus : \mathcal{I}_{\mathbb{R}_+} \times \mathbb{R}_+ \to \mathcal{I}_{\mathbb{R}_+}$ *defined as* $\oplus(\hat{a}, t) = [a_1 + t, a_2 + t]$.
- $\boxminus : \mathcal{I}_{\mathbb{R}_+} \times \mathcal{I}_{\mathbb{R}_+} \to \mathcal{I}_{\mathbb{R}_+}$ *defined as* $\boxminus(\hat{a}, \hat{b}) = [\min(a_1, b_1), \max(a_2, b_2)]$ *where* $\min$ *and* $\max$ *denote the minimum and maximum value respectively.*
- $+ : \mathcal{I}_{\mathbb{R}_+} \times \mathcal{I}_{\mathbb{R}_+} \to \mathcal{I}_{\mathbb{R}_+}$ *defined as* $[a_1, a_2] + [b_1, b_2] = [a_1 + b_1, a_2 + b_2]$. □

Time intervals will be used to express time constraints associated with the performance of actions. The idea is that if we associate a time interval $[t_1, t_2] \in \mathcal{I}_{\mathbb{R}_+}$ with a task we indicate that this task should take at least t_1 time units and at most t_2 time units to be performed. Intervals like $[0, t]$, $[t, \infty]$, or $[0, \infty]$ denote the absence of a temporal lower/upper bound and the absence of any bound, respectively. Let us note that in the case of $[t, \infty]$ we are abusing the notation since this interval represents, in fact, the interval $[t, \infty)$.

Next we introduce our timed extension of the classical finite state machine model. The main difference with respect to usual FSMs consists in the addition of *time* to indicate the lapse between offering an input and receiving an output.

Definition 2. *A Timed Finite State Machine, in the following* TFSM, *is a tuple* $M = (S, \mathcal{I}, \mathcal{O}, Tr, s_{in})$ *where* S *is a finite set of states,* $\mathcal{I}$ *is the set of input actions,* $\mathcal{O}$ *is the set of output actions,* Tr *is the set of transitions, and* s_{in} *is the initial state.*

A transition belonging to Tr *is a tuple* (s, s', i, o, t) *where* $s, s' \in S$ *are the initial and final states of the transition,* $i \in \mathcal{I}$ *and* $o \in \mathcal{O}$ *are the input and output*

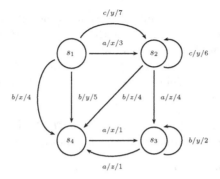

Fig. 1. Example of TFSM

actions, respectively, and $t \in \mathbb{R}_+$ denotes the time that the transition needs to be completed. We say that M is *input-enabled* if for all state $s \in S$ and input $i \in I$, there exist $s' \in S$, $o \in O$, and $t \in \mathbb{R}_+$ such that $(s, s', i, o, t) \in Tr$.   □

Intuitively, a transition (s, s', i, o, t) indicates that if the machine is in state s and receives the input i then, after t time units, the machine emits the output o and moves to s'. We denote this transition by $s \xrightarrow{i/o,t} s'$. In Figure 1 we give a graphical representation of a TFSM where s_1 is the initial state. In this paper we assume that all the machines are input enabled. Next, we introduce the notion of *trace* of a TFSM. As usual, a trace is a sequence of input/output pairs. In addition, we have to record the time that the trace needs to be performed.

Definition 3. Let $M = (S, I, O, Tr, s_{in})$ be a TFSM. We say that a tuple such as $(s, s', (i_1/o_1, \ldots, i_r/o_r), t)$ is a *timed trace*, or simply *trace*, of M if there exist $(s, s_1, i_1, o_1, t_1) \ldots (s_{r-1}, s', i_r, o_r, t_r) \in Tr$ such that $t = \sum t_i$. We will sometimes denote a trace $(s, s', (i_1/o_1, \ldots, i_r/o_r), t)$ by (s, σ, s'), where $\sigma = ((i_1/o_1, \ldots, i_r/o_r), t)$.   □

3   Timed Invariants

In this section we introduce the notion of timed invariant. These invariants allow us to express temporal properties that must be fulfilled by the implementation. For example, we can express that the time the system takes to perform a transition always belongs to a specific interval. Thus, timed invariants are used to express the temporal restrictions of a trace. In our formalism we assume that timed invariants are given by the tester and are derived from the original requirements. Alternatively, we could consider that invariants are extracted from the specification. In fact, we can do this easily by adapting the method given in [1] to our timed framework. However, this leads to a huge set of invariants, where not all of them are relevant. In our approach we need to check that the timed invariants proposed by the tester are correct with respect to the specification. Once we have a collection of correct timed invariants, we will have to check if these invariants are satisfied by the traces produced by the implementation. In the extended version of the paper [3] we provide an algorithm to check the correctness of the log, recorded from the implementation, with respect to an invariant.

In order to express traces in a concise way, we will use the wildcard characters ? and $\star$. The wildcard ? represents any value in the sets I and O, while $\star$ represents a sequence of input/output pairs.

Definition 4. *Let $M = (S, \mathcal{I}, \mathcal{O}, Tr, s_{in})$ be a TFSM. We say that the sequence I is a (simple) timed invariant for M if the following two conditions hold:*

1. *I is defined according to the following EBNF:*

$$I ::= a/z/\hat{p}, I \mid \star/\hat{p}, I' \mid i \mapsto O/\hat{p} \triangleright \hat{t}$$
$$I' ::= i/z/\hat{p}, I \mid i \mapsto O/\hat{p} \triangleright \hat{t}$$

In this expression we consider $\hat{p}, \hat{t} \in \mathcal{I}_{\mathbf{R}_+}$, $i \in \mathcal{I}$, $a \in \mathcal{I} \cup \{?\}$, $z \in \mathcal{O} \cup \{?\}$, and $O \subseteq \mathcal{O}$.

2. *I is correct with respect to M.*
3. *We denote the set of simple timed invariants by* SIMPLETINV.   □

Let us remark that time conditions established in invariants are given by intervals. However, machines in our formalism present time information expressed as fix amounts of time. This fact is due to consider that it can be admissible that the execution of a task sometimes lasts more than expected: If most of the times the task is performed on time, a small number of delays can be tolerated. Moreover, another reason for the tester to allow imprecisions is that the artifacts measuring time while testing a system might not be as precise as desirable. In this case, an apparent wrong behavior due to bad timing can be in fact correct since it may happen that the *watches* are not working properly. A longer explanation on the use of time intervals to deal with imprecisions can be found in [4].

Intuitively, the previous EBNF expresses that an invariant is either a sequence of symbols where each component, but the last one, is either an expression $a/z/\hat{p}$, with a being an input action or the wildcard character ?, z being an output action or the wildcard character ?, and $\hat{p}$ being a timed interval, or an expression $\star/\hat{p}$. There are two restrictions to this rule. First, an invariant cannot contain two consecutive expressions $\star/\hat{p}_1$ and $\star/\hat{p}_2$. In the case that such a situation was needed to represent a property, the tester could simulate it by means of the expression $\star, (\hat{p}_1 + \hat{p}_2)$. The second restriction is that an invariant cannot present a component of the form $\star/\hat{p}$ followed by an expression beginning with the wildcard character ?, that is, the input of the next component must be a *real* input action $i \in \mathcal{I}$. In fact, $\star$ represents any sequence of inputs/outputs pairs such that the input is not equal to i.

The last component, corresponding to the expression $i \mapsto O/\hat{p} \triangleright \hat{t}$ is an input action followed by a set of output actions and two timed restrictions, denoted by means of two intervals $\hat{p}$ and $\hat{t}$. The first one is associated to the last expression of the sequence. The last one is related to the sum of time values associated to all input/output pairs performed before. For example, the meaning of an invariant as $i/o/\hat{p}, \star/\hat{p_\star}, i' \mapsto O/\hat{p'} \rhd \hat{t}$ is that if we observe the transition i/o in a time belonging to the interval $\hat{p}$, then the first occurrence of the input symbol i' after a lapse of time belonging to the interval $\hat{p_\star}$, must be followed by an output belonging to the set O. The interval $\hat{t}$ makes reference to the total time that the system must spend to perform the whole trace. This notion of invariant allows us to express several properties of the system under study. Next we introduce some examples in order to present how invariants work.

Example 1. The simplest invariant we can define with our framework for expressing a property of the system follows the scheme $i \mapsto \{o\}/[2,3] \rhd [2,3]$. The idea is that each occurrence of the input i is followed by the output o and this transition is performed between 2 and 3 time units.

We can specify a more complex property by taking into account that we are interested in observing the output o after the input i only if the input i_0 was previously observed. In addition, we include intervals corresponding to the amount of time the system takes for each of the transitions and the total time it spends in the whole trace. We could express this property by means of the invariant $i_0/?/[1,4], \star/[2,5], i \mapsto \{o\}/[2,3] \rhd [2,12]$. An observed trace will be correct with respect to this invariant if each time that we find a (sub)sequence starting with the input i_0 and any output symbol which has been performed in an amount of time belonging to the interval $[1,4]$, then if there is an occurrence of the input symbol i before 5 time units pass then the input i must be paired with the output symbol o and the lapse between i and o must be in the interval $[2,3]$. In addition, the whole sequence must take a time belonging to the interval $[2,12]$. Let us remind that the notion of *correctness* that we just discussed concerns traces observed from the IUT and invariants. A different correctness concept, that we analyze in this paper, relates invariants and specifications.

We can refine the previous invariant if we consider only the cases where the pair i_0/o_0 was observed. The invariant for denoting this property is the following $i_0/o_0/[1,4], \star/[0,5], i \mapsto \{o\}/[2,3] \rhd [2,12]$. Let us remark that we could not deduce that we have found an error if the pair i_0/o_0 appears in the observed trace but the input i is not detected afterwards in the corresponding trace. In such a situation we cannot conclude that the implementation fails. Similarly, if we find the pair i_0/o_1 we cannot conclude anything since the premise of the invariant, that is, the whole sequence but the last pair was not found. Again, the situation is different when analyzing the correctness of an invariant with respect to a specification. For instance, if the specification cannot perform the trace induced by the invariant then we will consider that the invariant is not correct with respect to the specification.

Finally, an invariant such as $i \mapsto \{o_1, o_2\}/[1,4] \rhd [1,4]$ indicates that after input i we observe either the output o_1 or o_2 in a time belonging to [1,4].   □

Since we assume that invariants can be defined by a tester, we must ensure that they are correct with respect to the specification. Next we explain the most relevant aspects of our algorithm to decide whether an invariant is correct with respect to a specification. We separate the algorithm into three different parts.

in : $M = (S, \mathcal{I}, \mathcal{O}, Tr, s_{in})$.

$I = \{a_1/\hat{p_1}, \ldots, a_{n-1}/\hat{p_{n-1}}, i_n \mapsto O/\hat{p_n} \triangleright \hat{p}\}$ where for all $1 \leq k \leq n-1$ we have that $\hat{p_k} \in \mathcal{I}_{\mathbb{R}_+}$, and either $a_k = i_k/o_k$, with $i_k \in \mathcal{I} \cup \{?\}$ and $o_k \in \mathcal{O} \cup \{?\}$, or $a_k = \star$; $i_n \in \mathcal{I}$, $O \subseteq \mathcal{O}$, and $\hat{p_n}, \hat{p} \in \mathcal{I}_{\mathbb{R}_+}$.

out: *Bool*.

$b :: $ array of $\mathcal{I}_{\mathbb{R}_+}[|S|]$;
// *an array containing time intervals, having size* $|S|$,
//*and being* $\perp$ *the initial value of all positions*
$I' = I$; $S' \leftarrow S$; $j \leftarrow 1$; $S'' \leftarrow \emptyset$;
while $(j < n)$ **do**
$\quad$ $b' :: $ array of $\mathcal{I}_{\mathbb{R}_+}[|S|]$;
$\quad$ **if** $(\mathbf{head}(I') = (\star/\hat{t}))$ **then**
$\quad\quad$ **while** $(S' \neq \emptyset)$ **do**
$\quad\quad\quad$ **Choose** $s_\alpha \in S'$;
$\quad\quad\quad$ $S' \leftarrow S' \setminus \{s_\alpha\}$;
$\quad\quad\quad$ $S_{aux} \leftarrow \mathbf{afterInt}(s_\alpha, \hat{t}, i_{j+1})$;
$\quad\quad\quad$ **while** $(S_{aux} \neq \emptyset)$ **do**
$\quad\quad\quad\quad$ **Choose** $(s_p, t) \in S_{aux}$;
$\quad\quad\quad\quad$ $S_{aux} \leftarrow S_{aux} \setminus \{(s_p, t)\}$;
$\quad\quad\quad\quad$ $S'' \leftarrow S'' \cup \{s_p\}$;
$\quad\quad\quad\quad$ **if** $(b'_p = \perp)$ **then**
$\quad\quad\quad\quad\quad$ $b'_p \leftarrow \oplus(b_\alpha, t)$;
$\quad\quad\quad\quad$ **else**
$\quad\quad\quad\quad\quad$ $b'_p \leftarrow \boxminus(\oplus(b_\alpha, t), b_p')$;

$\quad$ **else**
$\quad\quad$ **while** $(S' \neq \emptyset)$ **do**
$\quad\quad\quad$ **Choose** $s_a \in S'$;
$\quad\quad\quad$ $S' \leftarrow S' \setminus \{s_a\}$;
$\quad\quad\quad$ $Tr' \leftarrow \mathbf{afterCond}(s_a, i_j, o_j, \hat{p_j})$;
$\quad\quad\quad$ **while** $(Tr' \neq \emptyset)$ **do**
$\quad\quad\quad\quad$ **Choose** $(s_a, s_b, i_j, o_j, t) \in Tr'$;
$\quad\quad\quad\quad$ $Tr' \leftarrow Tr' - \{(s_a, s_b, i_j, o_j, t)\}$;
$\quad\quad\quad\quad$ **if** $(b'_b = \perp)$ **then**
$\quad\quad\quad\quad\quad$ $b'_b \leftarrow \oplus(b_a, t)$;
$\quad\quad\quad\quad$ **else**
$\quad\quad\quad\quad\quad$ $b'_b \leftarrow \boxminus(\oplus(b_a, t), b_b')$;
$\quad\quad\quad\quad$ $S'' \leftarrow S'' \cup \{s_b\}$;

$\quad$ $I' = \mathbf{tail}(I')$;
$\quad$ $b \leftarrow b'$; $S' \leftarrow S''$; $S'' \leftarrow \emptyset$; $j \leftarrow j + 1$;

Fig. 2. Correctness of an invariant with respect to a specification (1/3)

The first part of the algorithm (see Figure 2) is responsible for treating the *preface* of the invariant, that is, to determine the states that can be reached in the specification after the first $n - 1$ input/output/time tuples have been traversed. The second phase (see Figure 3, left) is used to check that the last pair of the invariant is correct for the specification. In other words, to detect that for all the states computed in the previous step, if the last input of the invariant can be performed then the obtained output belongs to the set of outputs appearing in this last expression of the invariant. In addition we also check that these transitions are performed in the time interval appearing in the invariant. Finally, the third part of the algorithm (see Figure 3, right) verifies the last part of the invariant: The sequence is always performed in a time belonging to the corresponding interval. Next we introduce additional notation.

Definition 5. Let $M = (S, \mathcal{I}, \mathcal{O}, Tr, s_{in})$ be a TFSM, $s \in S$, $a \in \mathcal{I} \cup \{?\}$, $z \in \mathcal{O} \cup \{?\}$, and $\hat{t} \in \mathcal{I}_{\mathbb{R}_+}$. We define the set $\texttt{afterCond}(s, a, z, \hat{t})$ as the set of transitions belonging to Tr having as initial state s, as input a, as output z, and such that its time belongs to the interval $\hat{t}$.

$$\texttt{afterCond}(s, i, o, \hat{t}) = \{(s, s', i, o, t) | \exists s' \in S, t \in \mathbb{R}_+(s, s', i, o, t) \in Tr \wedge t \in \hat{t}\}$$

$$\texttt{afterCond}(s, ?, o, \hat{t}) = \bigcup_{i \in \mathcal{I}} \texttt{afterCond}(s, i, o, \hat{t})$$

$$\texttt{afterCond}(s, i, ?, \hat{t}) = \bigcup_{o \in \mathcal{O}} \texttt{afterCond}(s, i, o, \hat{t})$$

$$\texttt{afterCond}(s, ?, ?, \hat{t}) = \bigcup_{i \in \mathcal{I}, o \in \mathcal{O}} \texttt{afterCond}(s, i, o, \hat{t})$$

We define the function $\texttt{afterInt}(s, \hat{t}, i)$ as the function that computes the set of pairs (s', t) of states $s' \in S$ that can be reached from state s after t time units, belonging t to the interval $\hat{t}$, and such that the input i is not performed. We will use an auxiliary function so that $\texttt{afterIntAux}(s, \hat{t}, i) = \texttt{afterIntAux}(s, \hat{t}, i, 0)$, being this function defined as follows:

$$\texttt{afterIntAux}(s, \hat{t}, i, tot) = \{(s, tot) | tot \in \hat{t}\}$$

$$\bigcup$$

$$\bigcup_{\substack{(s, s'', i', o, t) \in Tr \\ \hat{t} \odot (tot + t) \\ i \neq i'}} \texttt{afterIntAux}(s'', \hat{t}, i, tot + t)$$

where $\odot : \mathcal{I}_{\mathbb{R}_+} \times \mathbb{R}_+ \rightarrow \{true, false\}$ is defined as $[t_1, t_2] \odot t = (t \leq t_2)$.   □

In the first phase of the algorithm we have to initially obtain the set of states that can perform the first input/output of the invariant. We compute the states that can be reached from that initial set after performing that transition and such that the time value associated with the transition falls within the range marked by the invariant. We iterate this process until we reach the last expression of the invariant. We consider two auxiliary functions: **head()** returns the first element of the invariant and **tail()** removes this first element from the invariant. Let us remark that we distinguish between input/output pairs, possibly including the wildcard ?, and occurrences of $\star$. In the latter case we will use the previously defined $\texttt{afterInt}()$ function to compute the corresponding reached states.

```
error ← false;
if (S' = ∅) then
    error ← true;
end
b' :: array of I_{ℝ_+}[|S|];
while (S' ≠ ∅) do
    Choose s_a ∈ S';                          if (S'' = ∅) then
    S' ← S' \ {s_a};                              error ← true;
    Tr' ← afterCond(s_a, i_n, ?, [0, ∞]);     end
    while (Tr' ≠ ∅) do                        while (S'' ≠ ∅) do
        Choose (s_a, s_b, i_n, o, t) ∈ Tr';       Choose s_i ∈ S'';
        Tr' ← Tr' \ {(s_a, s_b, i_n, o, t)};      S'' ← S'' \ {s_i};
        if ((o ∈ O) ∧ (t ∈ p̂_n)) then            if (¬(b'_i ⊆ p̂)) then
            if (b'_b = ⊥) then                        error ← true;
                b'_b ← ⊕(b_a, t);
            else                                  return (¬error);
                b'_b ← ⊟(⊕(b_a, t), b'_b);
            S'' ← S'' ∪ {s_b};
        else
            error ← true
```

Fig. 3. Correctness of an invariant with respect to a specification (2/3) and (3/3)

The *input* of the second phase of the algorithm (see Figure 3, left) is the set of states that can be reached after the preface of the invariant is performed. In addition, we also record the time that it took to reach each of these states. If this set is empty then the invariant is not correct. The idea is that we should not use an invariant such that its sequence of input/output/interval cannot be performed in the specification. If this set is not empty, we will check that for all reached states if they can perform the last input of the invariant then the obtained output must belong to the set of outputs appearing in this last expression of the invariant. In addition, time values have to belong to the time interval of the invariant.

The third step of the algorithm (Figure 3, right) will be devoted to check that the time behavior of the whole invariant is correct with respect to the specification. In order to do this, in the previous stages we recorded all the time values associated with the performance of input/output pairs. We use the functions ⊕ and ⊟ to operate with the recorded time values and construct an interval. Thus, in the position k of the array b we store an interval that has as bounds the minimal/ maximal times that are needed to reach the state k after performing the whole invariant. If a state is not reachable after the sequence associated with the invariant then $b[k] = ⊥$. Next, we concentrate only in states of the specification that can be reached, that is, $b[k] ≠ ⊥$ and check that all those intervals are contained in the interval appearing at the very last position of the invariant.

Lemma 1. *Let $M = (S, \mathcal{I}, \mathcal{O}, Tr, s_{in})$ be a TFSM. The worst case of the algorithm given in Figures 2 and 3 checks the correctness of the invariant $I = i_1/o_1/\hat{p}_1, \ldots, i_{n-1}/o_{n-1}/\hat{p}_{n-1}, i_n \mapsto O/\hat{p}_n \triangleright \hat{t}$ with respect to M:*

- *in time $\mathcal{O}(n \cdot |Tr|)$ and space $\mathcal{O}(|Tr|)$ if I does not present occurrences of $\star$.*
- *in time $\mathcal{O}(k \cdot |Tr|^2 + (n-k) \cdot |Tr|)$ and space $\mathcal{O}(|Tr|)$ if I presents occurrences of $\star$, being k the number of $\star$'s in I.*   □

4   Conclusions and Future Work

In this paper we have introduced a new methodology for passive testing systems that present timed constraints over the duration of the actions. We introduced an extension of the classical Finite State Machine model in order to deal with this kind of systems. This methodology extends the definition of an invariant, allowing to express properties regarding temporal conditions that the IUT must fulfill. We presented an algorithm which allows to establish the correctness of the proposed invariants with respect to a given specification. In a longer version of this paper [3] we also deal with the correctness of an observed trace with respect to an invariant.

Regarding future work, we plan to extend the family of invariants. In fact, we have already developed a timed version of *obligation invariants* [2]. The second line of future work consists in performing *real* experiments. The experience gained with the WAP protocol during the preparation of [2] makes this a good candidate to study time properties in our passive testing framework.

References

1. Cavalli, A., Gervy, C., Prokopenko, S.: New approaches for passive testing using an extended finite state machine specification. Journal of Information and Software Technology 45, 837–852 (2003)
2. Bayse, E., Cavalli, A., Núñez, M., Zaïdi, F.: A passive testing approach based on invariants: Application to the WAP. Computer Networks 48(2), 247–266 (2005)
3. Andrés, C., Merayo, M., Núñez, M.: Passive testing of timed systems (2008), http://kimba.mat.ucm.es/~manolo/papers/atva08-passive-extended.pdf
4. Merayo, M., Núñez, M., Rodríguez, I.: Formal testing of systems presenting soft and hard deadlines. In: Arbab, F., Sirjani, M. (eds.) FSEN 2007. LNCS, vol. 4767, pp. 160–174. Springer, Heidelberg (2007)

Author Index

Lecture Notes in Computer Science

Sublibrary 2: Programming and Software Engineering

For information about Vols. 1– 4634
please contact your bookseller or Springer